OXFORD

UNIVERSITY PRESS

Great Clarendon Street, Oxford, OX2 6DP,
United Kingdom

Oxford University Press is a department of the University of Oxford.
It furthers the University's objective of excellence in research, scholarship,
and education by publishing worldwide. Oxford is a registered trade mark of
Oxford University Press in the UK and in certain other countries

© Early English Text Society 2022

The moral rights of the author have been asserted

First edition published in 2022

Impression: 1

British Library Cataloguing in Publication Data

Data available

ISBN 978–0–19–287189–3

Typeset by John Waś, Oxford
Printed in Great Britain
on acid-free paper by
TJ Books Ltd, Padstow, Cornwall

Links to third party websites are provided by Oxford in good faith and
for information only. Oxford disclaims any responsibility for the materials
contained in any third party website referenced in this work

End of the life of St Audrey and beginning of the life of John the Baptist. Edinburgh, Advocates Library, Abbotsford MS, f. 120[rb]

Reproduced by permission of the Faculty of Advocates, Edinburgh

OSBERN BOKENHAM
LIVES OF SAINTS

EDITED BY

SIMON HOROBIN

VOLUME II

Published for
THE EARLY ENGLISH TEXT SOCIETY
by the
OXFORD UNIVERSITY PRESS
2022

PREFACE

This edition of Osbern Bokenham's *Lives of Saints* will be published in three volumes, comprising text, explanatory notes, glossary, and an index of proper names. A fuller list of acknowledgements will appear in volume III, but at this stage I would like to express my thanks to the Faculty of Advocates, Edinburgh for permission to reproduce the text of the Abbotsford manuscript, and to the officers of the Early English Text Society for overseeing its publication.

CONTENTS

LIST OF ILLUSTRATIONS

ABBREVIATIONS

ERRATA FOR VOLUME I

LIVES OF SAINTS
(cont.)

[66. SECUNDUS]

The life of Seynt Secundus knyght

Secundus, first a worthy knyght in the worlde and aftir a noble cheventeyn of Cristis feith, was martired in the citee of Ast, thurgh whos glorious
presence the seid citee is gretely adorned and ioyeth in hym as in their singuler patrone. This worthy knyght Secundus was conuertid and instruct in 5
the feith by an hooly man whos name was clepid Calocerus, which was for
Cristis sake enprisoned in the same citee of Ast by the prefect that tyme of
the cuntre, clepid Sapricius. In which meantyme blissid Marcianus for the
seid cause was by the same prefect putte in holde in the citee Cerdonence.
And not longe aftir, whan the prefect Sapricius went to the citee Cerdo- 10
nence to compellen blissid Marcian to the sacrifise of ydols, seid Secundus,
desiryng to seen blissid Marcian, went with hym, pretendyng to goon oute
for his and the prefectis solace.

And as sone as they were riden oute of the citee of Ast, vnwarly a dowe
cam doun and sett hym even on Secundys hede. The which seeyng, the 15
prefect Sapricius seid thus to the knyght Secundus: 'See, Secunde, see
how our goddis loven the that thei maken hevenly foulis to commen doun
to visiten the.' Aftir which tyme whan they come to a flode clepid Tana-
grus, Secundus sawe an angel goyng on the watir and seyeng to hym thus:
'Secund, loke thou haue ful perfite feith and, liche as I goo vpon the watir, 20
so shalt thou surmounten and goon abouen al the worshippers of ydols.'
Quoth Sapricius: 'Brothir Secunde, me thynkith that I here goddis spekyng to the.' 'Yea sir, no fors', quoth Secundus, 'late vs goon forth whider
your hert desireth.' And aftir this, whan they commen to a flode callid
Buruna an angel appierid there ageyn vnto hym and seid: 'Secund, levist 25
in God or els doutist.' | 'Syker', quoth Secundus, 'I bileve the truthe of
his passion.' Aftir this, whan they entrid the citee of Tridona, Marcianus,
at the commaundement of an angel, came oute of the pryson and appierid
to Secunde and seid to hym thus: 'Secund, entre into the wey of truthe and
goo so that thou may take the palme of martirdam.' 'What is he this that 30
thus dremyng spekith to the?' quoth Sapricius. 'Siker', quoth Secundus
ageyn, 'though it be a dreme to the, to me it is a wakir and a comfortable
ammonicion.'

Aftir which tyme Secundus went toward Melan where Faustinus and
Iouita weren in prison, whom the angel of God brought oute withoute the 35
citee to Secundus, whom they baptised there, a cloude mynistryng hem
watir. Which doon, sodeynly came a dowe from heven and brought to

Faustyn and Iouyte Cristis body and his blode, the which thei deliverid
to Secunde, chargyng hym to beren it to Marcian there he was in pry-
40 son. With which present Secundus, turnyng ageyn, by than he came to the
ryver Pade, it wex nyght and anoon an angel toke his hors by the bridel and
led hym ovir the poole and forth to Cerdona and brought hym to Marcian
in the pryson. To whom he deliverid Faustyns present, and he it received
with grete reuerence on this wise: 'The body and the blode of my lorde
45 God, Ihesu Criste, mote conducten me into evirlastyng life.' Which doon,
at the angels commaundement which was his guyde, Secundus avoided the
prison and went to his inne.

Aftir this the next day, Marcian, by the prefectis decree, was hefdid and
Secundus hent his body and honestly buried it. Of which dede Sapricius
50 enfourmed, anoon sent for Secundus and seid to hym thus: 'Secund, as
fer as I kan perceive, thou shewist the to ben a cristen man.' 'That, to ben
soth, I professe me.' 'Verreily than, as me semyth, thou desirest an evil
deth', quoth Sapricius. 'Nay, that is more due to the', quoth to hym ageyn
Secundus. But whan he wolde nat doon sacrifise at his commaundement,
55 the prefect chargid hym to ben spoyled oute of his clothis. To whom an
angel of God anoon was present and araied hym with anothir garnement.
Whom, eftesones spoiled, the prefect chargid to ben hangen vpon a iebett
and so longe to be tormentid and beten til the ioyntes of his armes were
dissoulued. But anoon, thurgh the mercy of God, he was made perfitely
60 hool, and forthwith to the prison sent by the prefect, where an angel came
to hym seyeng on this wise: 'Rise vp, Secund, and folow me, and I shal
lede the to thy creatour.' And anoon the angel led hym hoom ageyn to the
citee of Ast and into the pryson where Calocerus was, and our saluatour
Ihesu with hym. Whom whan Secundus saw, he devoutely and mekely fel
65 doun at his fete. To whom our saluatour seid: 'Be nat aferde, Secund, for
I am thy lorde God which shal deliveren the from al evels.' Which wordis
seid, he blissid hym and stey vp ageyn into heven.

On the next morowe, whan Sapricius sent for Secunde, his apparitours
founden the prison fast shett but Secund therin they fonde not. Whan
70 Sapricius the prefect herd this, in grete hast he lefte Cerdone and returned ageyn to Ast to vengen his angir at the lest vpon Callocere, whom
f. 86ᵛᵃ   anoon | he chargid to be presentid to hym. And whan he was enfourmed
that Secundus was there with hym, he was right glad, and chargid hem
bothe to be brought to hym. And whan thei were commen he seid thus
75 to hem: 'For as moche as our goddis knowen you bothen her rebel con-
temptours and despisers, thei willen that ye bothen deyen togider.' And
whan he saw that in no wise thei wolden doo sacrifise, he made picche and

rosyn to be molt togider and to be throwen vpon her heedis and porid
into her mouthis. The which thei drunken in as gladly as it had ben swete
watir, seyeng with a clere voice: '*Quam dulcia faucibus meis eloquia tua &* 80
cetera: ful swete be to my chekys, lorde, thy wordis, and swetter to my
mouth than ony hony.' This heryng, Sapricius anoon yafe this sentence:
that Secundus shuld ben hefdid there in his owen cite, and Calocerus
shuld be ledde to a citee clepid Albigan and punysshid there. This sentence youen, anoon Secundus was hefdid there, whos body angels buryed 85
with ympnes & armonye and manyfolde preysyng, whos martirdam was
the thrid kalend of April & cetera.

[67. MARY EGYPTIAN]

The prologe of Marie Egipcian
    Writen I wil, liche as I kan,
    The life of Marie the Egipcian,
    Euen as Ianuence me doth teche.
    But here at the begynnyng, I biseche
    Al them which it redyn or here   5
    Shul in tyme commyng, that thei nyl here
    Loken that I shuld first descrie
    Of this womman the genealogie,
    Of the pedegre, that is to seyn.
    That I shuld tellyn in wordis pleyn,   10
    Hir fadris name and modris, & so forth procede
    In the descent of hir kynrede,
    From the progenitours hir biforn,
    And the placis name where she was born,
    Whethir it citee were or toun,   15
    Of al which matiers I aske pardoun.
    And whoso aske the cause why
    I pardoun aske, I sey sikerly:
    For I yit nevir coude aspy
    Writyng of hir that gan so hy.   20
    Wherfore to myn auctour ageyn
    I wil returne, and in wordis pleyn,
    Aftir his doctryne forth procede,
    As grace my witte and penne wil lede;

25   Which me to senden thurgh his mercy,
            For me to God be mean, O Mary, amen.

The life of Marie Egipcian
            This blissid Mary, as seith Ianuence,
            Seventen yere in grete abstinence,
            Both of mete and drynk and clothe also,
30   And of al that longith the bodies ease to, |
f. 86vb   Lived in desert, vnto euery man
            Al that tyme vnknowe, but not forthan,
            Whan it plesid God hir knowe to be,
            On this wise folowyng founde was she.
35   It happid an abbot, an holy man,
            Zozimas by name, to passe Iordan,
            The famous flode, into wildernesse,
            For this entent specially, as I gesse,
            There to seekyn yf he myght fynde
40   Some blissid fadir in ony kynde,
            There seruyng God solitarily.
            And whan he had wandrid a grete party
            Of the waste wildernesse, biforn his y,
            Nat fer hym fro, he gan to aspy
45   How oon, al nakid, not fast went,
            Whos skynne al blak was and sunne brent.
            And this was, as myn auctour doth expresse,
            Marie the Egipcian in sothnesse.
            Which, whan she sawe hir folowen a man,
50   A ful gode paas awey she ran.
            The abbot, Zozimas, hir seeyng flee,
            As fast as he myght, aftir ran he.
            And whan she perceived that he drow ny,
            Thus to hym she seid ful benygnely:
55   'Abbot Zozimas, in this degree,
            Why is it that thou folowist thus me?
            Pardon me, fadir, of thy grace,
            I may nat turne to the my face,
            For as moche as a nakid womman
60   I am, fadir; but not forthan,
            Yf ye your mantel wold take me
            To cure my nakidnesse, than myght we

Come togider and talke more ny,
Withoute shame or vilany,
Whatevir vs lest.' And whan Zozimas   65
Thus herd hir spekyn, amarvailed was
He therof sore, and specially
That she hym clepid so verreyly
By his propir name, and not oonly so,
But by his name of office also.   70
Wherfore, withouten ony more taryeng,
His mantel he hir kest and, doun fallyng
Platt to grounde, with gode deuocion
Hir mekely preyed of hir benyson,
And that she vouchesafe wolde hym to blis.   75
'Nay, fadir, more reson me semyth it is,
That thou, of prestehode whom the dignyte
Adorneth, shuldist rather blissen me,
Than I the.' Whan he this herd,
More amarvailed he was, and more aferd,   80
And specially sith that she,
Not oonly his name and his dignyte
Of office knew, but eke verreyly
His ordre of prestehode; he devoutely,
Eftesones, to grounde fel plat doun,   85
And bisought hir ageyn of hir benysoun, |
From the place he lay willyng no wise,   f. 87ra
Til hym she had blissid ageyn vprise.
Whan she sawe this, with a sad chere,
She bigan to seyen on this manere: 90
'That blissid lorde which is creatour
Of our soulis, and the redemptour,
Mote evir be blissid, and eke blissen ws.'
And whan compendiously she had thus
Blissid and seid, both handis on hy   95
She vplifted, and preyed devoutely.
And in the meantyme that she did prey,
Sodeynly vplyfted he hir sey,
Aboue the erthe a cubite or more.
Which, whan he saw, he doutid therfore   100
In his hert, wenyng it a spirite had be,
And, feynyng preyer, had begunne to fle.

And, as sone as he thus did ymagine,
Hir hede dounward to hym she did incline,
105   And, as though she had knowen his thought withyn,
Thus hym to snybben she did begyn:
'God foryiue the, fadir, the mysdemyng,
Which in thyn hert thou hast of me, wenyng
That I an vnclene spirite were,
110   Which am a womman and a synnere,
And haue the shap and the figure
In body, of mankyndis nature,
Albeit that synne me hath disfigured.
Yet, thurgh Goddis mercy, I shal be pured,
115   Whan it plesith hym; wherfore thy thought
Amende, and evil spirite deme me nought.'
And whan Zozimas perceived thus, that she
Of his inward thought knew the privete,
And hym this wise rebukid therfore,
120   He wex amarvailed, evir more and more.
Nevirtheles, sone aftir, armed in feith,
Thus, with a bolde spirite, to hir he seith:
'I coniure the, O Goddis creature,
By vertue of hym, which of a virgyn pure,
125   For mankyndis sake in erthe born wasse,
And bitwixen an oxe leid, and an asse,
In a pore cribbe, and wrappid in hey,
That thou pleynly telle me, or thou parte awey,
What thy name is, and of what cuntre
130   Thou born were, and in this degree,
Why thou thus wandrist here in wildernesse
Nakid, and suffrist such grete duresse.'
To whom ageyn, thus seid she:
'Spare me, fadir, for charite,
135   For yf I tolde you what I am,
What I was, and fro whens I cam,
I trowe verreily that ye fro me,
Than from a serpent, wold faster flee,
For shame of myn abhomynabilnesse.
140   Your eeris shuld eke, as I gesse,
Abhorren to heren the tellyng,
Of the wrecchidnesse of my livyng, |

And the eyre also shuld enfectid be f. 87rb
With the filthe of the iniquite,
Which I haue vsid here byfore. 145
Spare me, I you biseche therfore,
More in this mater, fadir to seyn.'
But nat forthan, he hir ageyn
Required and chargid, as he first dede,
That she ne remevyn shuld fro the stede 150
Which she was in, til solucion
She made had to his question.
'Than, fadir', quoth she, 'sith it is so,
That I nedis must obey you to,
And telle you al my grete offence, 155
I biseche your fadirly reuerence,
That ye me wil heryn paciently,
And I shal you tellen, even by and by,
Al the cours of my livyng.
Wherfore, fadir, at the begynnyng, 160
I wil ye wete that in Egipt bore
I was, and whan but litle more
Than twelue yere I was of age,
Of foule lust stired with the corage,
To Alisaundre I went, the grete cite, 165
Where to the plesaunce I offrid me,
Of euery wight which me wold han,
My body denyeng to no man,
Which with me wolde his foule lust vse;
This was my life, I it ne may excuse, 170
Ful yeris seventene, and my name,
Marie, men callid, which lost had shame.
Aftir which tyme, the soth to telle,
Men of that cuntre, as it bifelle,
To Ierusalem tookyn her viage 175
To the holy crosse, on pilgrymage,
With whom I was stired eke to goon.
Wherfore to the shypmen I went anoon,
Bisechyng hem that it myght so be.
And for the ship hyre I offrid me 180
And my body, therof to haue
Her lust, as ofte as thei it lyst craue,

Both outeward and homeward ageyn.
What in this mater shuld I more seyn?
185   Forth we went, and as I had hight,
Redy I was, bothe day and nyght,
Her wille to folowen ful synfully,
And thus to Ierusalem forth cam y.
Where whan I came with othir mo,
190   And into the temple wolde haue go,
And to the dore cam, er I was ware,
I ne wote who me awey bare,
Inuisibly, and fro the dore fer sett,
And that I ne shuld entren me did lett;
195   Natwithstandyng that me fast by,
Al othir folke entrid in frely.
Thus twyes or thries to the dore ageyn
I went, but entren I ne myght, certeyn, |
f. 87ᵛᵃ   Alwey born thens, as I first was.
200   And whan I sawe this mys[t]erious caas,
And that I myght no grace fynde,
To entren in, vnto my mynde
Anoon it came that, thus shamefully,
For my myslivyng, reiect was y
205   Fro the fre entre into Goddis hous.
And anoon compunct, my life vicious
I bigan to detestyn within myn hert,
And teeris oute shedde, bitter and smert,
And myghtely to wryngen myn handis two,
210   And with hem my brest to knocken also,
And to sobben and sighen as I shul dye.
And sone aftir, as I kest vp myn ye
To the temple-ward, fast me by,
An ymage I perceived, of our lady.
215   Biforn which, with hert entere,
I knelid doun, preyeng on this manere:
"O lady, which art the sool refute
Of synners, desolat and destitute,
The founteyn of grace and of mercy,
220   Vouchesafe to be mean to thi sone, that y
Of my synful life mow haue pardoun,

200 mysterious] myserious

Thurgh his mercy, and remissioun.
And that he vouchesafe of his grace,
To suffre me entren into this place,
And worship the crosse, on which the raunsoun   225
He paide, for al mankyndis transgressioun.
And with al myn hert promitte y,
That, thurgh the help of his mercy,
My forlife wickid I wil forsake,
And of that mys i[t] amendis make,   230
Nevir willyng therto to turnen ageyn."
Which preyer thus endid, I roos, certeyn,
And in our lady puttyng my confidence,
The temple dore, withoute resistence,
I entrid, and forth to the crosse in went,   235
And worshippid it, with as devoute entent
As God for the tyme wolde yiue me grace.
And whan I there had ben a certeyn space,
And outeward ageyn bigan to goon,
Thre pens of almesse me yafe oon.   240
And forth a vois thus seid to me:
"Womman, yf thou wilt savid be,
Passe ovir the flode of Iurdon."
And with my thre pens, thre loves anoon
I bought and, as I boden was,   245
Ovir Iurdon I me spedde a paas,
Hider into this waste wildernesse,
Where I haue lived now, as I gesse,
Othir seventen yere, and nevir me
Saw man this tyme but now ye,   250
Whom God now, of his special grace,
Hider hath sent for my solace.
The loves which I brought with me,
As ony stoones hard waxen be, |
And yit fode, thurgh help of Goddis mercy,   f. 87ᵛᵇ
Thoo haue me founden sufficiently,   256
Al the tyme that I here haue ben.
Clothis haue I noon, as ye seen,
For tho with me which I hider brought,
Ben werid and rooten, and brought to nought.   260

230 it] is

And so my nakid body with to cure,
Safe myn heer, I ne haue othir vesture.
Blissid be the lorde which me hath sent,
Therwith a wryeng sufficient,
265   As for the felauship that I with mete,
In wynter from colde and in somer from hete,
It me defendith competently,
That me it sent, lorde, gramercy,
Which in nede thi seruauntis nevir doost faile.
270   In this meantyme, eke grete bataile
With my flessh I had, and right grete fight.
But now, thurgh help of Goddis myght,
Of this I haue gett the victorye.
And also of eche of myn othir enemye,
275   As devil and worlde, and now al thre,
With help of grace, thus venquysshid be.
Loo, fadir, now hasthou herd how y,
At thy commaundement, even by and by,
The lamentable processe of my livyng
280   Haue tolde the, from the begynnyng,
Even to the ende, liche as it was.
Now, blissid fadir, in this hevy caas,
Be myn helper and my comfortour,
And for me prey Ihesu, our saluatour,
285   That he vouchesafe of his pytee,
Of my myslivyng to pardon me,
And receive me to his grace and his mercy.'
And whan Zozimas had herd this story,
Doun platte he felle vnto the grounde,
290   And blissid God and thankid the same stounde
In his seruaunt, and aftir did prey.
Which doon, to hym she ageyn did sey:
'Now finally, fadir, I biseche the,
That on Shryfthursday ageyn to me
295   Thou wilt commen, to Iordan flode.
And with the bryng the moste souereyn gode,
That evir in erthe was lefte with vs,
I mene the body of my lorde Ihesus,
Which on the cros for me was dede,
300   And here in erthe remayneth in forme of brede.

Bryng with the this fode so swete,
To the seid flum where I the mete
Shal redily, and thereof the,
With the seid body, I commoned wil be,
Of body and soule, to my singuler solas,   305
For sith I here came, nevir houselid I was.'
This seid, whider she wolde, certeyn,
She went, and he to his monastery ageyn
Returned, ful glad that he had see
Goddis seruaunt. And whan the tyme that she | 310
Assigned hym had, he diligently   f. 88ra
Toward his iourney hym made redy,
Nothyng forgetyng that she hym bad.
And forth he went, ful mery and glad,
Sore hir desiryng ageyn to see.   315
And whan he came where assigned had she,
And ovir Iordan as he kest his y,
On that othir side stondyng, he hir did aspy.
And whan she hym saw ageyns hir stonde,
She anoon hir blissid with hir right honde,   320
And ovir the watir she swyftely did glide,
And to hym came on the same side
Where he stode, nothyng wetyng
Hir feet with the watir, to his semyng.
Whan he saw this, ammaruailed gretely,   325
Doun bifore hir feet he fel mekely,
Hir worshippyng; but anoon she
Hym blamed therfore, and bad that he
Shuld vprisen, and not so do
To hir no wyse, for causis two: 330
'First', quoth she, 'for thou art a preste.
The secund is for, biforn thy breste,
Of my lordis body the sacrament,
Thou berist, for which either entent
I aught moche rather to worship the,   335
In moste meke wise, than thou me.
Wherfore, fadir, sith it is so,
That assemblid togider be now we two,
And with the is commen my soulis leche,
Delay me no lenger, I the byseche,   340

But yiue me that I haue desired so sore.'
Which wordis seid, withoute more,
He hir communed with Cristis body,
Which she received ful devoutely,

345 With many a teer ful sore wepyng.
Whan she had doon, thus concludyng,
And seyeng to hym: 'O my fadir dere,
I you biseche with hert entere
That ye vouchesafe the next yere,

350 On Estern day, to mete me here.'
Which seid, she hir blissid ageyn,
And ovir Iordan anoon, certeyn,
She glood as swyftely as she cam,
And forth in wildernesse hir wey she nam;

355 But whider she went, he nyst sikerly.
Wherfore hoom ageyn to his monastery
Zozimas went, aftir his vsage,
His obseruaunce kepyng, with devoute corage,
Aftir the rule he professid was by.

360 And whan Estern the next aftir cam ny,
With devoute entent he hym avised
To goon ageyn, thider he had promysed,
And so he did. And whan he came thider,
Where first of al they mett togider,

365 Er he was ware, aside lokyng,
He sawe where dede she was lyeng. |

f. 88rb Where whan he saw hir so lyen dede,
He pullid the heeris of hi[s] hoor hede,
And knockid his brest, ful sore wepyng.

370 But hir touche he darst for nothyng,
Seyeng in his hert thus inwardly:
'To touche this wommans bare body
I am vnable, for my wrecchidnesse,
Ne hap that I hir holynesse

375 Shuld offende, for my presumpcion.'
And while he was in this ymaginacion,
Not doryng hir putten to sepulture,
At hir hede he aspied this scripture,
Writen in the erthe even openly:

368 his] hir

'Zozima, drede not to buryen the body   380
Of Marie, and erthe to erthe ageyn
To yelden, for it is hir wil, certeyn,
That thou so doo, and that thou for hir prey
That lorde, which hir from the valey
Of wrecchidnesse toke, even the thrid day   385
Of April.' And w[han] this olde man say
This scripture, and it had red avisily,
Anoon he knew right wele therby
That she there on erthe dede had leyn,
Sith he hir communed, this is certeyn.   390
Wherfore, sith he knew that hir entent
Was that hir body to erthe were sent,
As from erthe it came, he did his cure,
Ful busily it to sepulture
To bryng, aftir his power and his myght,   395
The grave to make he hym anoon dyght.
But the erthe so hard was that he
Myght therin entren in no degree.
For which cause, as he stode sory,
An huge lyon he sawe come forby,   400
To whom Zozimas thus seid, with bolde chere:
'O thou creature of God, I the prey come nere,
And help to buryen this holy womman,'
At whos commaundement the lyon anoon bigan,
With his forme fete the erthe to scrape,   405
Ful hastily, as though he had had rape
In his iourney, and anoon depe ynough,
And brode also, it was, albeit right tough
The erthe were, and for the body,
Whan depe and brode it was sufficiently,   410
He halp the body in for to ley.
Which doon, the lyon toke forth his wey,
And went whider hym list to goo,
And Zozimas of hym saw aftir no moo.
And whan thus perfourmed was this dede,   415
Hoom to his monastorie hym did spede,
This holy abbot, God thankyng,
And in his seruaunt hym magnyfyeng,

386 whan] with

Al his life aftir til he did dye.
420   Now blissid Egipcian, O Marye,
Which of thy synne, thurgh Goddis grace
And penaunce doyng, didest purchace |
f. 88ᵛᵃ   Not oonly indulgence and remission,
But also atteyneddest to perfeccion
425   Of holy life, and of contemplacion.
Help, lady, thurgh the mediacion
Of thy grace and of thy socoure,
That of thy life the translatoure
Into Englissh may of his synne
430   Foryifnesse han, and no more therinne
Fallen ageyn, as he often hath doo.
Now, gode lady, help it may be soo.
And finally, whan endid is the fate
Of his temperal life, within the gate
435   Of endeles blisse he may duelle with the,
Sey eche man 'amen', for charitee.

[68. AMBROSE]

The prologe into Seynt Ambrosis life

As myn auctour Ianuence techith vs,
Four wise may this worde Ambrosius
Ben dirivied, and first, aftir his entent,
Of *Ambra*, which is a spice redolent,
5   Right delectable and right precious.
So was Ambrose to Goddis hous,
Ful precious in forme of livyng,
Redolent in doctryne and in techyng,
As in his bookis, whoso hem rede diligently,
10   He shal mow fynden evidently.
The secund wise to the same purpoos,
Ambrosius of *Ambra* and of *Syos*
Dirivied is, which is to seyn
The aumbre of God, in wordis pleyn.
15   Aumbre is redolent, as biforn seid is,
And so was Ambrose in his werkis,
Ful wele savourid and in his wordis therto,

Wherby diffoundid was also
Cristis gode odour, in many a cuntre.
The thrid wise eke this name, quoth he,   20
May be dirivied of *Ambor*,
Which fadir of light tokeneth, and of *Syor*,
That litle signifieth; and to our purpose,
These thre wele longen to Seynt Ambrose.
For first fadir he was, as we see moun,   25
Of many sonnes by gostely generacioun.
Light he was eke, both bright and pure,
By the exposicion of holy scripture.
Litle of mekenesse by the vertue,
Which from youthe evir with hym grue.   30
Or as it is seid in the glosarie,
This name hath significacions varie.
For Ambrosius, as seith this auctour,
Is hevenly odour, or hevenly savour.
Ambrosia signyfieth also, quoth he,   35
Angels fode, by gode congruyte.
But *Ambrosium* is flowyng hony hevenly,
And al these four thyngis congruently, |
Of blissid Ambrose mow be verified.   f. 88vb
And first it may nat be denyed,   40
That Ambrose was an hevenly odour,
By his redolent fame an hevenly savour.
He was eke by inward contemplacioun,
An hevenly hony flode, by exposicioun
Of holy Scripture, in which marveilously   45
He haboundid, and fynally
Angels fode he clepid may be,
By eternal fruicion of the trinite,
In which he glorified is, withouten ende.
Now, blissid Ambrose, on hem haue mende,   50
Which here in erthe the serven and loue,
And purchace hem grace in heven aboue,
Aftir this outelawrie with the to duelle,
Where ioye is which no tung can telle,
Ner hert thynke, ner ey see,   55
Sey eche man 'amen', pur charite.

The life of Seynt Ambrose

[W]hilome, as olde writyngis tellen vs
Of Rome a prefect, it happid to be,
Whos name was clepid Ambrosius,
60   A man of grete worship and dignyte,
Which of his wife, bothe faire and free,
A sone bigate, whom his owen name
He yafe, that contynue myght his fame.

This childe was fostrid ful tendirly,
65   By a norice at home, in his owen hous.
And on a day, as he in the norcery
Swathid lay in a cradel precious,
His norice stondyng by, a thyng marveilous
Byfelle, for sodeynly of bees a swarme,
70   Light on his face, hym doyng noon harme.

And whan al this swarme doun was light,
Wondirful it was to seen her werkyng.
For in at his mouth, and oute ful right,
Liche as in an hyve thei went crepyng.
75   His norice anoon, this perceivyng,
Ran to his fadir and hym did telle
This grete marvaile, liche as it felle.

And whan the fadir thider came, and sey
This wondirful sight, and marveilous,
80   Aftir avisement he did sey,
As man both prudent and vertuous,
To driven hem awey it were perilous.
Wherfore he chargid nought to be doon hem too,
Til men seyen what thei wolde doo.

85   And whan thei longe had to and fro,
Cropen in and oute, thus marveilously,
Yunge Ambrosis mouth, withoute mo,
Al at oones they risen vp sodeynly,
And oute at the wyndowe, by and by,

---

57 Whilome] hilome; *initial W has been cut out*   60 A man] man *due to removal of initial W in line 57*

So high into the eyre thei toke her flight,   90
That where thei become, no man see myght. |

And whan, how these bees on this manere   f. 90ra
Departid were, and in this degree,
Saw Ambrose the fadir, with a sad chere,
Gretely amarvailed of that noueltee,   95
The childe nat hurt, thus concludid he:
'Yf this childe live, and to age atteyn,
Some grete thyng he shal be, this is certeyn.'

Aftir this, whan yung Ambrose gan growe,
And sawe his modir, and his sustir also,   100
Kyssen prestis handis, stoupyng lowe,
His hand, his sustris mouth he to
Put, merily seyeng that she must doo
The same wise to hym, anothir day,
And she ageyn disdeynously seid to hym 'nay'.   105

Moreovir, whan in the sciencis liberal,
As in gramer, logik, and in philosophie,
And in rethorike and eloquencie moste special,
He instruct was, he hym did hye
To the pretorie, where so marveilouslye   110
He causis pletid, and on so crafty wise,
That singuler laude he had amonge the wise.

And whan Probus, which iuge was of the pretorie,
Of Ambrose perceived the grete excellence,
And eloquence eke in his plees dayly,   115
And that he nevir wolde mayntene fals sentence,
Markyng in hym truthe and prudence,
His witte and his kunnyng the bettir to preve,
He hym singulerly chees, counseil to yive.

In which office, so true diligence   120
He did, that themperour Valentinian
Putt in hym so grete a confidence,
That he hym sent as his right trusty man,
Of two grete provincis the rule to han,

125   As Emylie and Ligurie, and them to guye,
        Aftir the discrecion of his policye.

        Which doon, he streight went to Melan,
        Where whan he came bisshop Auxence
        Dede was, an heretik, an Arrian,
130   Which to blissid Dyonisie did such offence
        That he drofe hym awey, with grete violence,
        And by intrusion occupied Melan cherche,
        Which to the cite moche sorowe did werche.

        For by his cursid ambiciousnesse,
135   Divided was the cite myschevously,
        Into Arrians and of true bilevenesse
        The feithful peple, and eche party
        Labourid with al that thei coude busily,
        A bisshop to han of her opinyon,
140   And this in the citee made grete diuision.

        Wherfore, whan the parties both two
        Were in the chirche, assemblid in fere,
        Ambrose thought that it was to do
        To goon thider, and their mater to here,
145   And hem in pees and vnyte to stere,
        As man sage, prudent and wise,
        Theffect t'accomplisshen of his offise. |

f. 90ʳᵇ   And whan he to the chirche was cum,
        And exorten hem bigan to vnyte,
150   Sodeynly hem amonge, with a shirle soun,
        An infauntis vois cried in this degree:
        'Ambrose bisshop, noon othir wil we.'
        Of which vois, to theffectuel entent,
        Both parties hoolly youen her assent.

155   And anoon, forthwith, withouten more,
        Thei al gun crien concordely:
        'Ambrose bisshop', wherof ful sore
        He amarvailed was, and seid: 'Sirs, why
        Crie ye thus? Knowe ye nat that y

Am nat of your sect, ner of your bileve?　　　　　　　160
Wherfore your cryeng may nat you releve.'

But nat forthan they no wise wolde cese,
Evir 'Ambrose bisshop' to cryen and to seyn.
But rather more to crien thei did encrese,
'Ambrose bisshop', even, in wordis pleyn.　　　　　165
'Yit', quoth he lowde, 'I counseil you, certeyn,
Of your desire to cese, which no wise be may.'
But lowde cryeng, with oo vois, al seiden 'Nay!'

And whan he saw that othir wise it nolde be,
But that hym bisshop thei wolde han alle,　　　　　170
Oute of the chirche anoon went he,
And sett hym vpon his tribunal stalle,
And moche peple biforn hym he did calle,
And with grevous peyn hem did distresse,
Ageyns his vse, and with grete duresse.　　　　　175

But not forthan the peple nolde blynne,
Evir vpon hym thus to calle and crye:
'Syr, vpon ws mote falle thy synne,
Be so thou to be bisshop wil nat denye.'
But he nolde consent, but philosophye　　　　　180
He professid, and also of myslyvyng:
He made men wommen into his hous bryng.

And al this he did for that entent,
To revoke the peple from his eleccion.
For he, in no wise, to hem synne ment.　　　　　185
But this natwithstondyng, their entencion
They nolde change, ner her opinyon.
But eftesones thei cried loude and thus:
'Sir, thy synne mote fallen on vs.'

And whan he saw, as to his conclusion,　　　　　190
That al that he did availe ne myght,
He purposid in his privy entencion,
The nyght folowyng to ascape by lyght.
And whan he wende to haue goon to Pauye, right

195   On the morowe, whan gan spryngen Aurora,
        At the gate of Melan he was, clepid Romana.

        Whom the peple kept stille, while relacion
        Was made to themperour Valentinian,
        Plenerly and truly of his eleccion,
200   And how therto assentid euery man.
        Wherof themperour to ioye bigan,
        And laude and thankyng to God yafe he,
        That his iuges were chosen bisshops to be. |

f. 90ᵛᵃ   Probus Iudex was right glad also,
205   Whan he herd seyn of this tidyng,
        For as moche as the worde was doo,
        That he had seid in his partyng
        To Ambrose, aftir his charge yivyng,
        Whan he seid: 'Goo and doo, I the devise,
210   Rather as a bysshop than as a iustise.'

        Yit, in the meanwhyle, eftesones ageyn,
        While suspens henge the relacion,
        Ambrose fledde and darkid, certeyn,
        For a short tyme in the possessioun
215   Of a worthy man of Melan toun,
        Whos name, as the story techith ws
        Of the legende, was clepid Leoncius.

        And whan fro themperour was commen aunswere,
        That to her eleccion he yafe assent,
220   And the viker was chargid, which was there,
        To perfourmen diligently her entent,
        Anoon he proclamed a commaundement
        Of life and goodis vp peyn and forfeiture,
        Whoso knew where he was, shul hym discure.

225   This precept youen, Leoncius anoon
        Bothe hym bywreyed and to Melan did bryng.
        And whan Ambrose saw the mater thus goon,
        And vndirstode that it was Goddis werkyng
        That was doon, withoute taryeng

He hym disposid paynymrie to forsake,   230
And the feith of cristen men to take.

But thus, fynally, he was avised,
Sith he algatis cristen shuld be,
That of noon Arrian to be baptised
He wolde assentyn in no degre.   235
For with that sect accorden no wise myght he,
Wherfore to be cristenyd he hym offrid redy
Of a bisshop, clepid cristen vniuersally.

Loo, how sone grace bigan to growe
Within the brest of this blissid man,   240
Thurgh which, enspired he was to knowe
The maliciousnesse of the sect Arrian.
For which cause he nolde tan
Cristis marc of tho in his begynnyng,
Whom he impugne shuld aftir in his techyng.   245

Whan baptised was this blissid Ambrose,
And Cristis feith received had into his breste,
So grace, as it is seid, hym did dispose,
That the chirchis offices, both most and leste,
He anoon parfourmed, and was made preste   250
And sacred bisshop the eight day folowyng,
Al the peple glad, and god thankyng.

Four yere aftir his consecracion,
Whan blissid Ambrose to Rome went,
His sustir, a womman of religion,   255
An holy maiden, his right hand hent,
And kissid it with devoute entent.
'Sustir', quoth he, smylyng to hir ageyn,
'Loo, now kissist thou a prestis hand, certeyn, |

As who seith, sustir, haue remembraunce   f. 90ᵛᵇ
How whilom, whan I was but ying,   261
And sawe my modir and the, with devoute obseruaunce,
Kissen prestis handis, lowly stoupyng,
I offrid the myn hand, this wise seyeng:

265   "Haue kisse it, sustir", and thou seidest "nay",
        And I seid thou shuldest anothir day.'

        Sone aftir this, whan hoom ageyn
        To Melan was commen blissid Ambrose,
        To a certeyn cite he clepid was, not veyn,
270   To hem of a bisshop for to dispose,
        Contrarie to Iustyn thempressis purpose.
        For there to han an Arrian was hir entent,
        Wherto blissid Ambrose wolde nevir consent.

        For which cause, malapertly a nyce damysel
275   Of the Arrians sect, and irreuerently,
        Styrte vp and hent hym by the mantel,
        And wolde haue drawen hym to the wommans party,
        That he so blyndid myght shamefully
        As effemynat be cast oute of the chirche,
280   And so ageyns her emperesse no more to werche.

        And whan this blissid man perceived had,
        Of this damysel the grete presumptuousnesse,
        To hir he seid thus, with chere sad:
        'Damysel, though I for my sympilnesse,
285   To his high presthode haue no worthynesse,
        Yit aughtist nat thou, the sooth to seyn,
        On a preste thus violently thyn handis to leyn.

        The fereful doom of God thou aughtist to drede,
        Which whan on the shal falle thou knowist nought.
290   For thynke noon othir, but that this dede
        Shal in short while to iugement be brought,
        And this thy presumpcion shal dere be bought.'
        And so it was, for on the next day,
        Withoute more respite, on bere she lay.

295   And yit, forto shewen his high charite
        Ageyns the contumely which she hym had do,
        With hir cors on the morowe to chirche went he,
        And there for hir devoutely preyed also.
        And whan knouleche of this thyng cam to

The peplis eeris, eche man aferde   300
Was of that vengeaunce, whan he it herde.

For this cause, and for many anothir mo,
Of Iustina, the moste cruel emperesse,
Many weyes were sought to doon hym woo.
For bihestis of worship and of richesse   305
She sent aboute, to more and lesse,
With which she blyndid ful many a man,
And made hem her bisshop in hate to han.

Amonge which al, oon moste singulerly
Fulfilled with the spirite of iniquite,   310
To perfourmen his entent the more oportunely,
Ioyned to the chirch, a place made he,
And a chare, al redy yf it myght be
Brought abouten, by ony crafte or wile,
Ambrose to ledyn therwith into exile. | 315

But of doctoures, aftir the commoun sentence,   f. 91ra
Al their werkis ben frustrat and veyn,
Which of Goddis eternal prouidence,
Theffectuel entent labouren ageyn,
This conclusion may no man withseyn: 320
Whatsoevir to doo ony wight purpose,
God aftir his wille shal the werkis dispose.

And that in this wicked man was seen,
Which for Ambrosis exile had ordeyned a chare.
For the day which it to performe he did wene,   325
Oute of his hous, er than he was ware,
Hym into exile the same quadrige bare.
And for Ambrose geyns malice wold shew charitee,
His necessarie expensis hym prouided he.

Songe and seruise in the chirch of Melan,   330
Aftir the vse which there yet kept is,
To be sungen and seid first Ambrose bigan,
Both respounes, antimes and ympnes.
In which tyme many vexid with devils,

335　In Melan, with grete voice did cry
　　　That of Ambrose tormentid thei were grevously.

　　　This heryng, Iustina and many oon mo
　　　Of the Arrians, which togider did duelle
　　　In Melan, weren in her hertis ful woo,
340　And falsly compassyng with her wittis felle,
　　　Amonge the peple did puplisshe and telle
　　　That Ambrose had hyred men to seyn and lye,
　　　That spiritis of hym suffrid grete tormentrye.

　　　And whan thei, busy to make sedicioun
345　Monge the peple, thus clamoureddyn importunely,
　　　In fortefyeng of her fals opynyon,
　　　Oon of her felawys, even sodeynly
　　　With a spirite vexid, lowde gan to cry.
　　　Thus mote them alle spiritis vex and greve,
350　Which on Ambrosis lore wil nat bileve.

　　　And whan his othir felaus stondyng by there
　　　Seyen hym with a spirite vexid thus sore,
　　　And so lowde cryeng, al they were
　　　In her inward hertis confuse therfore.
355　But that he the peple shuld stire no more,
　　　In a wattryng place, there fast beside,
　　　They hym dryncled and slough, the same tide.

　　　Whan oones an heretik, which in disputacioun
　　　Subtile was and curious, and eke right witty
360　But froward to the feith, in a sermoun
　　　While Ambrose prechid, stood right ny
　　　And saw an angel hym teche that he seid, pleynly
　　　In his eer, conuertid to the feith therfore.
　　　Which first he pursued, he defendid aftir evirmore.

365　Oo tyme devils a nygromancere
　　　Vpreised, and to noyen Ambrose hem sent.
　　　Which comen ageyn, seid that they not nere
　　　Myght commen ageyn, aftir his entent.
　　　For envirounyng his place so a grete fyre brent,

And so fervently, that fer awey therfro 370
It tormentid hem, so thei myght no ferther go. |

A demonyac, oones the citee entryng   f. 91rb
Of Melan, the devil from hym went,
And eftesones in his oute-goyng,
As he did biforn, he ageyn hym hent. 375
Wherof whan he was askid the entent,
He aunswerid and seid that cause why he fledde,
Was for bisshop Ambrose he so sore dredde.

Whilome at the instaunce of Iustyne themperesse,
Oon with a swerde, by nyght prively 380
Entrid his chambir, ful of cruelnesse,
Hym to haue slayn, withoute mercy.
And whan he his swerd lyfted had on hy,
Redy to smyten, even the same tide
His hand wex seer, and myght the swerd nat guyde. 385

Whan Thessalonica oones gretely agrevid
With the citezeyns, as the story tellith ws,
Was themperour Theodosie, and his angir remevid
With mean of his preyer had blissid Ambrosius,
Yit thurgh the werkyng of the curials malicius, 390
Ambrose nat knowyng, by themperours assent,
Thritty of her knyghtis had her life forlent.

Wherof whan Ambrose had the knoulecchyng,
And of themperours assent true certificacion,
Themperour into the temple he forbad entryng, 395
Denouncyng hym that he vndir excommunicacion
Stode, and so shulde til due satisfaccion
He doon had of that horrible cryme,
And fro the chirche absteyn so must he for the tyme.

And whan themperour for his excusacion, 400
Of Dauid alleggid the avoutery
And manslaughtir eke, so, withoute delacion,
Quoth Ambrose: 'As thou folowdist the folye
Of Dauid, folowe eke the remedye!'

405   Whos counseil themperour applied hym to,
       And offrid hym gladly open penaunce to do.

       Whan oo tyme, of Ambrose tormentid to be,
       A demonyac lowde bigan to crye,
       'Pees devil!' quoth Ambrose, 'For nat Ambrose the
410   Tormentith thus, but thi propre envie,
       For as moche as thou seest men thider vp stye
       Fro whens thou felle so shamefully.'
       Which seid, he helde his pees redily.

       Whan to Macedonyes paleys, maister of the offise,
415   Oones Ambrose went for oon to prey,
       And fonde the gatys sperid on such wise
       That he entre in haue myght by no wey,
       'Wele, Macedony', quoth he, 'to the I sey:
       In breef tyme to chirche thou shalt goon,
420   The dooris wide open, and entree fynde noon.'

       And liche as he seid, so siker it was.
       For nat longe aftir, in the seid citee,
       Macedonyes enemyes, so stode the caas,
       Pursued hym so sore that he did flee,
425   And to the chirche he ran, for moste suretee.
       Where whan he came, the dooris open stode wide,
       But entre fynde he coude on no side. |

f. 91va   Anothir tyme eke, whan blissid Ambrose
       To the citee-ward of Rome toke his viage,
430   His herbergeour for hym willyng dispose,
       At a riche mannes hous toke his hostage,
       Of Tuskayn, in a litle village,
       There to be logged as for a nyght,
       For othir place was there noon that myght.

435   This place ful roially was araied,
       And had stuffe of housholde ful grete plentee,
       Which Ambrose seeyng, he was afraied,
       Marueilyng of so grete solempnyte.
       And forthwith aftir his hoost sent he,

And, openly stondyng in the halle,   440
To hym thus he seid, biforn hem alle:

'Thou hast here, gode man, a stately place,
Wele stuffid with good and plentevously.
Telle me, therfore, what is thy grace,
And how fortune the favourid hath, pleynly.'   445
'Syr', quoth he ageyn, 'my wife and y
Han lived here togider in prosperite,
Sith we were weddid withoute aduersite.

Of richesse and tresour we ben copious,
Of children and seruauntis we han plente.   450
Was yit nevir thyng to ws contrarious,
Ner losse of catel, in no degree,
What sikenesse is yet nevir felt we.
And, withoute debate, angir or strife,
We thus hidertoward han led our life.'   455

Whan Ambrose had herd on this wise,
Of the riche man the pompous avauntyng,
Ful sore his hert it did agrise.
Wherfore to his meyne, withoute taryeng,
He seid: 'Sirs, anoon from this loggyng   460
Lete ws fast fleen while we haue space,
For, certeynly, God is nat in this place.

Fleeth fast, fleeth, o my sonnes dere,
From this place ful of wrecchidnesse,
Ne hap that the vengeaunce of God here   465
Inuolue ws in the duellers synfulnesse,
And ws destroie for her cursidnesse,
As it shal hem, for lacke of grace,
For, sikerly, God is nat in this place.'

As he commaundid was doon anoon,   470
And al men remevid were fro that inne.
And whan but litle thens thei were goon,
The erthe openyd sodeynly, and swelowed ynne
Place, man, wife and childe, and al the kynne

475 With which he duellid, in her company,
That no man where it was coude aftir aspy,

Safe as the duellers ny seyn,
A depe diche is now where was the place.
And whan Ambrose saw this, with wepyng eyn,
480 'Loo sirs', he seid, 'how grete a grace
God doth to a man, in this worldis space,
Whom he chastiseth with sikenesse and aduersite,
And how perilous it is to han contynuel prosperite.' |

f. 91vb Of this blissid mannys vertues, what shuld I more seyn?
485 But that of abstinence, in especial,
A singuler prerogatife he had, certeyn.
For eche day he fastid, bothe grete and smal,
Safe Satirday, Sunday and festis principal.
Large to pore men he was, al yivyng
490 To hem, to hymself nothyng kepyng.

So gretely he haboundid in compassion
Of synful men that, yf ony hym to
Confessid were, with due contricion,
So sore for hym wepyn he wolde, loo,
495 And so tendirly, that the synner also,
Yf ony grace in his herte were,
For his synnes of hym to wepe myght lere.

In mekenesse eke, and in laboure,
This blissid man so hym did delyte,
500 That tho bookis, which thurgh fervour
Of meditacion he did endyte,
With his owen handis he wolde wryte,
Lesse than sikenesse and inualitude,
Hym fro that busynesse did seclude.

505 Of pite to God-ward and of swetnesse,
So replenysshid was his cherite,
That whan to hym the deth men did expresse,
Of ony holy prest or bisshop, anoon wept he,
And so sore, that vnnethe be

Styntid he myght of his wepyng,   510
Al men abouten hym counceilyng.

And whan he was askid why he wept so sore,
For hem fro hens which went to blis,
'Nay, nay', quoth he, 'I wepe nat therfore
That thei goon hens, but my sorow is   515
That biforn me thei goon forth, ywis.
Or els ful hard it shal be to fynden a man,
Aftir hym worthy his place to han.'

But for to speken of his stedfastnesse,
And strength of zeel in Goddis lawe,   520
There was nevir noon with more boldenesse,
Which emperours and princis putt vndir awe,
Than did he ner with more fre sawe
Vndirnam openly her vice and synne,
Ne nevir wolde cessyn, til thei did blynne.   525

And whan he the rote sawe of al wickidnesse,
Auarice, more and more growen daily,
And moste in hem which in hygh worthynesse
Stodyn, both spiritual and temperal, where vniuersally
Al thyngis were venal, he wex wery,   530
And with a sorowful hert preyd God this grace:
Hym hens to deliveren, within short space.

Which boone, whan he by reuelacion
Knew grauntid hym, ful glad was he.
And sone aftir in a communicacion,   535
His brethern he tolde, how he shuld be
With hem, here in this mortalite,
Til Estern aftir, and no lengere;
Wherof thei al ful sory were. |

Aftir which tyme, [as] he seke lay,   f. 92ra
Doun in his bed, of his last seknesse,   541
To hym he clepid, vpon a day,
A notarie, his conceitis to expresse,

540 as] or

Of the four and fourty psalme which, as I gesse,
545   Is this, aftir true computacioun:
Eructauit cor meum verbum bonum.

And while of this psalme the exposicioun
As he yafe, the notarie did write,
Hym biholdyng from heven came doun
550   A shelde, liche fyre shynyng ful bright,
And, envirounyng his hede, on his mouth did light.
Entryng therin by a maner marveilous,
As a dueller entrith into his hous.

Which doon, his face gan waxen as white
555   As ony snowe, the sooth to seyn.
And anoon aftir, to the notaries sight,
Into the first liknesse it turned ageyn.
On which same day, this is certeyn,
Of writyng, Ambrose his leve did take;
560   For of the psalme bigunne, he noon ende did make.

And aftir the tyme not daies longe,
That the notarie had seen this visioun,
Ambrose was takyn with sikenesse stronge,
And vpon his dede bedde he leid was doun.
565   For whom was made grete lamentacioun,
Not oonly of Melan in the cytee,
But also abouten in al the cuntre.

And singulerly the Counte of Itayle,
Which that tyme was in Melan citee,
570   Made grete moone, dredyng that faile,
Yf Ambrose deyed, shuld al that cuntre.
Wherfore togider, anoon callid he,
Al the noble men and worthy of Melan,
Which, commen togider, thus he to seyen bigan:

575   'Syrs, me semyth that it is likly, iwys,
Al Ytaile to perisshe yf Ambrose dey.
Wherfore my counseil, as now, is thys:
That ye al togider to hym goo and prey,

At your instaunce, that he wil fynde a wey,
By mean of preyer, here lenger to be,   580
For your citees saluacion, and of the cuntree.'

And aftir his counceil, whan thei had doo,
He thus ageyn aunswerid ful demurely:
'Syrs, I hope amonges you I haue nat lived so,
That I lenger to liven shuld ben asshamed, sothly.   585
Ner also to deyen, nothyng drede I.
For our lorde is ful of mercy and pite,
Whos wille in al thyngis fulfilled mote be.'

The tyme of his sikenesse, vpon a day,
Four of his dekons, men of grete prudence,   590
In a corner of the chambir where he lay,
Talkid softely togider of good prouidence,
Who myght succedyn, whan her maister were hens.
And amonge her talkyng, in her mynde it ran,
To ablen an heremyte clepid Symplician. | 595

And, natwithstandyng that they spoke so softe   f. 92ʳᵇ
That vnnethe myght eche what othir seid here,
And from hem Ambrose lay fer alofte,
Yit to hem thries he seid on this manere:
'Though he be olde he is gode, my brothir dere.'   600
This seid, for feer to fleen thei bigan,
And, aftir his deth, bisshop they chosen Symplician.

And whan the tyme came of goyng hens,
Of blissid Ambrose to Goddis mercy,
Honoratus, the bisshop Vercellens,   605
As he to slepe was leid, even sodeynly
Herd a voice, thus thries seyeng on hy:
'Rise vp fast, bisshop, and tary no mo.
For sone anoon he shal hens goo.'

At which voice, Honoratus anoon   610
Rose vp, withoute more taryeng,
And to the citee of Melan bigan to goon,
And visited Ambrose, ful sore wepyng.
And anoon aftir, withoute lettyng,

615 Of Cristis body he hym mynistred the sacrament,
And he it received with devoute entent.

Which doon, Ambrose his handis anoon,
In forme of a crosse abrode did sprede.
And, a preyer made, his soule did goon
620 Oute of the body, withouten drede.
Which to heven blisse our lorde did lede,
Aboute the yeris of grace, to counte truly,
Thre hundrid, yf therto be sett nynty.

And whan thus was passid, this blissid man,
625 Oute of this worlde, to Goddis mercy,
The houre bifore nyght clepid Antilacan,
He to the high chirche born was sothly,
There to abiden ful solempnely.
His funeral office were complete and doo,
630 With exequyes, and al that longith therto.

And while the body in the chirche lay,
And vigilies were kept for Estern nyght,
Many yung infauntis baptised that day,
Of hym had many a wondirful sight.
635 For some seyen hym as he vpright
Had setten in his chayer tribunal,
Araied in his habite pontifical,

Somme as vpward, vnto heven blys,
Gloriously bihelde hym forth do stey,
640 And to her fadris and modris with her fyngrys
Made tokenys forto see that they sey;
But thei, that to see, had noon ey.
And somme seid that on the body stondyng,
A sterre they seyen, bright shynyng.

645 And whan al the funeral seruise was doo,
And the day brode bigan to spryng,
And men were busy, his owen chirche to,
Where it shuld be buryed, the body to bryng,
Devels in the eyre were herd cryeng,

That they of Ambrose were tormentid so sore,   650
That thei of torment myght suffre no more. |

Lo, by these examplis and many oon moo,   f. 92va
Euidently appierith the grete holynesse
Of blissid Ambrose, which, thus partid fro
The vale of this worldis wrecchidnesse,   655
Devels putt in so peynful distresse.
And nat oonly them, but eke the same
He did to men which detractid his fame.

For oones a preest, at a feste sittyng
With many othir folke, in a companye,   660
And of blissid Ambrose evil seyeng,
The plage of vengeaunce smett sodeynly.
Whom fro the feste to his bedde hastily
His felaus born, and whan he came there
He deyed, and went God wote where.   665

Aftir this, whan thre bisshops in Cartage
Togider were gadrid in a communicacion,
Oon of hem his tunge to detract gan swage
Seynt Ambrose, to whom was made relacion
Of the prestis vengeaunce for his detraccion,   670
Which at nought he sett; wherefore, the same day,
He sodeynly deyed, and on the bere lay.

[69. GEORGE]

The life of Seynt George

Seynt George, born of the noble blode of Capadocie, was nat oonly a
knyght but also a tribune of knyghtis; that is to seyn havyng vndir hym
and at his rule and retenue a thousand soudiours. This worthy tribune
George came oones into a cite of Lybie clepid Silena. Beside which citee   5
was a grete stagne liche an arme of the see, in which darkid a grete venemous dragon, the which had often putt grete multitude of armed peple to
flight, and commyng to the wallis of the citee had also with his pestilent
breeth ner infectid al the peple of the citee. For which cause they were fayn
eche day to yiuen hym twoo shepe to swage with his wodenesse, the which   10

yf ony day were withdrawen, anoon the dragon came fersly to the walles
and so venemously enfectid the eyr that moche peple deyed therof. And
whan shepe bigunne to failen, for as moche as that cuntree haboundith nat
moche in shepe, the kyng and the citezeyns a counseil had, by a commoun
15 assent ordeyned that eche day shuld be youen but oo shepe, ioyned therto
a man or a womman, such as the lottis youen, withoute ony excepcion of
grete or smale.

And whan so longe these lottis had procedid that nere al the sonnes and
the doughtri[s] of the citezeyns and al the peple were consumed and des-
20 troyed, it happid the kyngis doughtir to fallen in the lotte and so iuged to be
devoured of the dragon. The which whan the kyng herd, hevy and sory he
seid to the peple on this wise: 'Sirs, I biseche you takith alle my gold and al
my siluer, yea, and half my kyngdam therto and savith my doughtir that she
dey not.' To whom the peple aunswerid ageyn with grete angyr and wreth
f. 92ᵛᵇ on this wise: 'Sir kyng, thou thyself madist this decree | and now al our
26 children ben dede woldisthou saven thy doughtir. Certeyn, sir, but thou
fulfille thyn owen decree, we shul brennen the and thyn hous.' And whan
the kyng herd this he bigan to wepyn and to beweylen his doughtir, seyeng on this wise: 'Allas, allas myn owen swete doughtir, what shal I doo for
30 the or what shal I seyn of the?' And, turnyng hym to the peple, he preyed
hem to yiuen hym eight daies of respite to mournen and to lamentyn his
doughtir. The which grauntid of the peple, and the tyme complete and
perfourmed, they commen ageyn to hym in a grete angir and seid: 'Wilt
thou lesyn and destroyen al the peple for thy doughtir? Seesthou nat how
35 we al arn like to perisshen with the venemous breeth of the dragon?' And
whan the kyng sawe that he myght no lenger saven his doughtir, he did hir
ben araied in hir moste roial aray and kissid hir, wepyng, and seid: 'Woo
me, my swete doughtir, I hopid sometyme to haue norisshed in my lappe
thi children and now thou goost bareyn to be devourid of a dragoun! Woo
40 me and allas! I trustid and hopid to han clepid to thy mariage princis and
princesses and han araied my paleys with gemmys and precious stoones,
and to han herd tympans and organs, and now thou goost to be devourid of a dragoun.' And kyssyng hir he dymised hir thus, seyeng: 'Wolde
God, my doughtir, that I were dede biforn the rather than I shulde on this
45 wise lese the.' Which wordis seid, she fel doun on hir knees and toke hir
fadris blissyng and went forth to the lake, there to abiden the dragons commyng. Whom blissid George, by the ordenaunce of God that same tyme
commyng ridyng there forby and seeyng wepyng, askyd hir what she eyled.
'Gode yung man', quoth she, 'ageyn fast take thyn hors with thy spores and

19 doughtris] doughtrid

flee, ne hap that thou also deye here with me.' 'Be nought aferde, doughtir', 50
quoth George, 'but telle me what thou abidest here and why al the peple
stondith yundir afer and waiteth aftir the.' 'A, gode yung man', quoth she
ageyn, 'I see wele that thou hast a gode hert, but why desirest to deyen
with me?' 'Truly', quoth he ageyn, 'and I wil nat goon hens til thou haue
tolde me the cause why thou wepist.' And she than anoon tolde hym al the 55
caas. Which herd, he seid ageyn thus to hir: 'Doughtir, drede the not, for
in Cristis name I shal helpe the!' 'Gode yung knyght', quoth she, 'perisshe
nat here with me. It is ynough that I perisshe alone. For siker, though thou
woldist abide here with me, thou myghtist nat deliver me.'

And while she seid these wordis, the dragon bigan to lyften vp his hede 60
oute of his lake. This seeyng, the maide, [gretely] astoyned and abasshid,
seid to George: 'Flee, gode sir, flee swyftely!' And whan he sawe the dragoun bygynne to commen, he markid hymself with a token of the crosse
& reyned his hors, and went boldely ageyns hym. And, myghtely shakyng
his spere, he hurt the dragon grevously and myghtely bare hym doun to 65
grounde. Which doon, he turned hym to the maide and seid: 'Doughtir,
doute the nat, but boldely take thy girdil and cast it aboute his necke.' And
whan she had doon as he badde | hir, the dragoun anoon folowed as mekely f. 93ra
as a tame whelp. This seeyng the peple, and how she came toward the
citee and the dragon folowyng hir, anoon thei begunne to fleen vnto the 70
hilles and into the caves and cavernes, cryeng and seyeng: 'Woo vs, for now
shul we al perisshen!' To whom blissid George seid on this wise: 'Beth not
aferde, for our Lorde God hath for that entent sent me to you that I shulde
deliveren you from the vexacion and the perile of this dragon. Dooth oonly
aftir my counceil and bilevith into Criste, and euerich of you be baptised 75
in his name, and I shal sleen this dragon.' Att whos counceil, anoon the
kyng and al his peple were baptized.

Which doon, blissid George drowe oute his swerde and slow this lothly
dragon, and commaundid it to be borne oute of the citee. The which, four
peyr oxen vnneth myght drawen oute into a grete felde withouten the citee. 80
And that day were baptised in that citee twenty thousand peple, beside
wommen and smale children. And for this dede the kyng anoon did maken
a chirche in the name of God and of our Lady and of blissid George, of
grete quantite and largenesse, vndir the autier wherof sprang a welle of
which the watir drunken curid and made hole alle maner sikenesse. Which 85
doon, blissid George instruct and infourmed the kyng briefly of four thyngis. That is to seyn that he shuld han diligent cure of Goddis chirches, that
he shuld worshippen preestis, that he shuld devoutely and diligently heren

61 gretely] and gretely

Goddis seruise, and that he shuld alwey haue mynde of pore men. Which
90   doon, he kyssid the kyngis doughtir and went his wey thens into anothir
cuntree clepid Persida, and into a cite therof clepid Diospolis.

Aboute which tyme holdyng thempire Dioclisian and Maximian vndir
the lieftenaunt of hem, clepid Dacian, so grete a persecucion of cristen
men was reised, that within a moneth were martired seventen thousend or
95   mo. In which persecucion, for drede of torment, many cristen men failed
and didden sacrifise to ydoles. And whan blissid George saw that, touchid
with sorowe of his hert inwardly, therfore anoon he dispercled alle that
he had, and yafe it to pore men; kest awey his knyghtis habite and clad
hym in the habite of cristen men, and stirte forth in myddis of the perse-
100 cutours cryeng and seyeng: 'Al goddis of hethen folk ben devils! But the
lorde of cristen men allone made hevyns!' Whom whan Dacian herd seyn
thus, he angrely askid hym by what presumpcion he durst clepyn her goddis devyls. 'But first', quoth he, 'telle me of whens thou art, and what is
thy name.' 'George', quoth he, 'I am clepid, borne of the noble blode of
105 Capadocie. Palestyne, by Cristis favour I haue ovircommen, and al thyngis
I haue forsaken for to seruen God in heven.' And whan Dacyan saw that he
myght in no wise enclynen his hert to ydolatrie, he commaundid hym to
ben hangyn vpon a iebett, and to[r]ent with nailes al his body, membre by
membre, and brennyng brondis to ben putt to his sides til men myght seen
110 his entrailes. And, aftir al these, he made his tormentours myghtely with
f. 93rb   salt | to rubben his woundis and, that doon, to be shette in a derke pri-
soun. And the same nyght our lorde Ihesus appierid vnto hym with grete
light, and swetely comfortid hym. Where-thurgh he was so gretely comfortid and refresshid that he sett right nought by al the peynes that he had
115 and myght haue suffrid.

And whan Dacian saw that he myght nat ovircommen hym with peynes,
he clepid vnto hym a wicche and seid vnto hym on this wise: 'What mow we
doo? These cristen men with her wycchecrafte ludifien and scornen al our
tormentis, and setten at nought al our goddis sacrifises.' 'Sir', quoth this
120 wicche ageyn, 'yf I ovircome nat al Georgis craftis I wil lese myn hede therfore.' And anoon, with werkyng of his craftis and by clepyng of his goddis
names, he made a drynke with wyne and venym medlid togider, and toke
it George to drynken. Wherupon he made a token of the crosse and dranke
it vp, withoute either hurt or blemysshement in ony partie. Eftesones the
125 wicche medelid a myghtyer venym, the which George also, a token of a cros
made therovir, dranke of harmeles. And whan the wicche saw this, anoon
he fel doun at Georgis feet and lamentably askid foryifnesse of his offence,

108 torent] tobrent

and preyed hym entierly to makyn hym a cristen man, whom forthwith the
iuge made for to ben hefdid. And on the next day Dacian made hym to
be sett on a whele, the which was on euery side besett with double eggid 130
swerdis, so that what wey that evir it turned it shul al tohewen hym. But, by
Goddis werkyng the whele sodeynly brast, and George ascapyd harmeles.
Aftir this Dacian in his wodenesse commaundid hym to be cast in a grete
fryeng panne ful of molt lede, wherin, aftir a token of the crosse made, he
was as wele at ease as he had ben in a bath. 135

And whan Dacian saw al this, he bithought hym that he wolde assayen
to souplen hym with fair glosyng wordis, whom he myght nat ovircome
with thretis ner with tormentis. Whervpon he seid to George on this wise:
'George, sonne, see now and biholde the mansuetude and the buxomnesse
of our goddis, the which han so longe suffrid the to blasphemyn hem and 140
to scornen hem. And yet not forthan thei ben redy to foryiven the al her
offence, yf thou wilt be conuertid. Wherfore, my swete sonne, doo now
aftir my counseil. Leve al the supersticion of cristen men and doo sacrifise vnto our goddis, and thou shalt getyn bothen of hem and of me grete
thank and worships.' Quoth George ageyn smylyng: 'Why, sir, ne haddis- 145
thou made me these suasions at the begynnyng with fair wordis, and not
assailed me with so sharp tormentis? Loo, sir, now for thy fair speche I am
redy to perfourmen thy counceil.' Whan Dacian had this biheste of blissid George he was passyngly glad, and anoon he sent a bedel thurghoute
the citee to make a crye that al men shuld commen to seen how George, 150
which longe had wrestlid ageyns hym, was conquerid for to doon sacrifise
to her goddis. And forthwith al the citee was araied for ioye of these tidyngis. And whan George was entrid into the ydols temple forto sacrifise,
as Dacian wende, and al the peple stode ioyeng to see the ende, anoon he
knelid doun on bothen his knees, | and liftyng vp bothen his handis he f. 93ᵛᵃ
preyed God entierly that he wolde, to the laude and preisyng of his name 156
and for the conuersion of the peple, so vttirly to destroien that temple that
no thyng therof shuld remayne and abyde. Which preyer endid, there came
sodeynly a fire from heven and brent the temple with al the prestis which
mynistred the sacrifise, and with that the erthe openyd and devourid and 160
swellid in the residue and relevis of bothen.

Whan Dacian herd this, he callid vnto hym blissid George and seid vnto
hym on this wise: 'What maner thyng ben these thi wicchecraftis by which
thou hast doon so grete a synne?' 'Nay, nay, O Kyng, trowe', quoth he,
'nat so, but come now and goo with me and thou shalt see thyself how that 165
I shal sacrifisen.' 'Siker', quoth Dacian, 'I perceive wele thy fraudulent
menyng. Thou woldist maken the erthe to swellyn in me as it hath doon

the temple of our goddis and her prestis.' 'Sey me than, wrecche', quoth
blissid George, 'sith thy goddis myght nat saven hemself, how shuld they
170 than helpen the? A symple god is he than, as me semyth, the which neither
may hymself saven ner othir men helpen.' And whan Dacian herd this he
wex wrothe ageyn and, in his ire, seid thus to Alexandria his wife: 'Iwys,
wife, I trowe that I shal deyen for sorowe that I see me thus to be ovircommen of a man.' To whom she aunswerid ageyn on this wise: 'Thou cruel
175 tiraunt and manqueller, haue I nat often seid to the that thou shuldist nat
be thus boistous and thus comerous with cristen men? For as I seid, siker
her God fighteth for hem. Wherfore I wil that thou knowe that now, at the
leste, I wil ben a cristen womman.' Att which worde Dacian, gretely astoyned, with a lowde voice cryed: 'Art thou', quoth he, 'deceived? Woo me!'
180 And whan he saw hir stedfast and constaunt he made hir to ben hangen
vp by the heer, and a longe tyme to be betyn with whippis and scourgis.
And, while she was in scourgyng, she seid to George thus: 'O George, the
light of truthe, where trowyst I shal be commen, stondyng that I am nat
baptised?' 'Doute nothyng, doughtir', quoth George ageyn, 'for the she-
185 dyng of thi blode shal stonde the for baptesme and for thy corowne.' With
which wordis she, gretely comfortid, made a preyer and therwith yald vp
hir spirite into Cristis handis.

    And whan Dacian saw that neither with thretyng ner with bihetyng,
ner neither with exortacion, ner with peynful examynacion, he ne myght
190 chaungen blissid Georgis entent, on the next day folowyng he yafe this
decree: that he shuld be drawen thurghoute the citee by the feet and aftir
that hefdid. And whan he went to his iewesse he made a preyer, and
bisought God þat whosoevir preyed to hym for helpe in ony nede, that he
myght be spedde. To whom anoon came a vois from heven and seid that his
195 boone was grauntid. And forthwith, withoute more, he was hefdid, aboute
the yeris of oure Lorde two hundrid, four score and seven. And as Dacyan
returned hoom ageyn to his paleys aftir blissid Georgis decollacyoun, a
fyre fel doun from heven and devourid hym with his mynistres et cetera. |

[70. MARK]

f. 93vb The life of Seynt Marc the evangelist
    Marc, the evangelist of the kynrede of Leui and a preste, Petris sone
in baptesme and his disciple in Goddis worde, went with hym to Rome.
Where, whan Petir prechid the gospel, the feithful men whiche weren there

---

197 Georgis decollacyoun] Georgis; cf. LgA in quo decollatus est

preiden Marc that he wolde writen hys maistris gospel to the instruccion 5
and comforte of hem & of al feithful in tyme that was to come. At which
request he wrote as he had herd of his maisters mouthe. The which, examyned by his maister Petir and founden true, was approued to be red as
for sufficient and autentik amonge al Cristen peple. Aftir which tyme Petir,
seeyng Marc constaunt and stedfast in the feith, sent hym into Aquiley 10
where, prechyng the worde of God, he conuertid innumerable multitude
of peple to the feith of Criste, and wrote ageyn to hem the gospel which is
yit kept in Aquiley chirche, and had there in grete reuerence and worship.

At which tyme he conuertid there a citezeyn of Aquiley clepid Hermogeras and led hym to Rome to Seynt Petir, for to han hym sacrid of hym 15
bisshop of Aquileia. The which Hermogeras, sacrid bisshop of Aquiley
and returned hoom ageyn, whan he a longe tyme had governed his chirche
worshipfully and graciously, he was taken there of paynyms and sent to
heven by martirdam.

Aftir this Marc was sent to Alisaundre by Seynt Petir, where he was the 20
first that prechid the worde of God. Where at his first entre, as seith *Philo
Disertissimus Iudeorum*, a grete multitude was gadrid togider anoon in feith
and deuocion and in obseruaunce of continence and clennesse. Whos preconye and laude *Papias Ieropolitanus Episcopus* writeth with an high stile,
Piers Damyan writeth of hym also, seyeng on this wise: 'So grete grace', 25
quoth he, 'grauntid God to Seynt Marc at Alixaundre, that as many as
come by his techyng to the rudymentis and the first principles of the feith,
anoon thei atteyned and flowen to the height of monastial perfeccion, and
to the stedfastnesse of hevenly conuersacion. To which high perfeccion',
quoth he, 'nat oonly he prouokid hym with wondirful werkis of myraclis 30
and gracious and marueilous eloquence of prechyng, but also moste singulerly by excellent examplis of livyng.' And anoon aftir, he seith thus:
'Resonably it was doon that aftir his deth he shuld returnen ageyn to Ytaile,
that the londe in which was youen hym grace to writen in the gospel shuld
han and kepyn the hooly reliques of his body. Blissid be thou therfore, O 35
Alexandria', quoth he, 'the which were purpurat and made rody with the
triumphal and victorious blood of blissid Marc, and nat lesse blissid and
happy art thou, O Itaile, the which art adorned and made riche with the
tresore of his precious body.' *Hec ille*.

It is seid that Seynt Marc was so profoundid in mekenesse that he 40
cutte of his thombe, that thurgh mannys doom he shuld nat ben holden
worthy the ordre of prestehode. But nat forthan the disposicion of God
and the auctorite of Seynt Petir preuayled, the which sent hym bisshop
to Alixaundre. And as | sone as he came to Alixandre, the speryng of his f. 94ra

45 shoo brak and was vndoon, the misterie wherof he knowyng in spirite seid:
'Truly, God hath grauntid me a spedy iourney, ner Sathanas myght nat
lettyn me whom God hath now assoyled from dedely werkys.' And whan
he came into the cytee and sey oon sitten and refresshen olde shoon, he
toke his shoo to amenden, the which in his werkyng grevously hurte his
50 lefte hande. Wherfore he cried anoon and seid: 'Oo God.' And whan Marc
herd this, he seid: 'Now wote I wele that God hath sped my iournee.' And
anoon he made a plastor of spatyl and cley and anoyntid his hande, and
forthwith it was hool. This man hurt, seeyng this sodeyn cure, led Marc
into his hous and enquerid of hym what he was and fro whens he came.
55 'Forsothe', quoth Marc, 'I knouleche me to be the seruaunt of our lorde
Ihesu Criste.' Quoth this shoomaker ageyn: 'And hym wolde I fayn seen.'
'Iwys', quod Marc, 'and even here I shal shew the hym.' And anoon he
bigan to prechyn hym our lorde Ihesu Criste.

And whan men of the citee herdyn that there was comen a Galilee, the
60 which despised the sacrifise of goddis, thei begunne to setten waites and
wecchis vpon hym. And whan Marc aspyed this he made the man whom he
had cured, whos name was Anianus, bisshop of that citee, and he hymself
went *ad Pentapolim*. And whan he had ben there two yere, he returned to
Alixaundre and multiplied such feithful men as he fonde there, and con-
65 fermed hem in her new grace. This perceivyng, the bisshops of the templys
busied hem for to taken hym. And whan blissid Marc in the solempte of
Estern was at his messe, thei come togider and threwen a rope abouten his
necke and drowen hym al abouten the citee, seyeng on this wise: 'Loo, we
drawen a wilde oxe vnto a wilde bestis stalle!' And as he went, with the vio-
70 lence his blode ran oute so fast þat the stoones in the wey were made rede
therwith. And anoon thei putt hym in a derk prison, wherin not oonly he
was comfortid by visitacion of an angel, but also our lorde Ihesu Criste
hymself visited hym and comfortid hym, and seid to hym on this wise:
'Pees to the, Marc, myn evangeliste. Fere the nat, for I am with the and shal
75 deliver the.' And on the next morowe thei tokyn hym ageyn oute of prison
and putten a rope aboute his necke and drowen hym to and fro, hiderward
and thiderwarde, boistously and cruelly seyeng and cryeng: 'Drawith the
wilde oxe or the bugle to the place of bugles deen!' And while thei thus
drowen hym, he thankid hertly God and seid: 'Into thyn handis, Lorde, I
80 commende my spirite.' And with tho wordis he yalde vp the goost, aboute
the yeris of our lorde fifty and seven, vndir Nero themperour. Whos body
whan the paynyms wolde haue brent, sodeynly the eyre wex troubelous and
bigan to hailen, thundren and lighten so sore that eche man was busy to
ascapyn and to saven hemself, and leften there the blissid body vntouchid

and harmlees. The which cristen men tokyn and buried in a chirche with 85
grete reuerence.

The descripcion of this blissid Markis fame & forme was this: he had a
longe nose, hangyng browes and | bent, fair, ferballid, longeberdid, mean f. 94rb
aged, sprencled with horenesse, of menable stature, in affeccion contynent
and ful of the grace of God. *Hec Ianuensis.* 90

The yere from Cristis incarnacion four hundrid sixty and seven, the
Venicians with stronge hand broughten awey the body of Seynt Marc from
Alixandre and maden for hym a roial chirche in Venyse, and buried the
body therin with grete solempnyte. And how thei come by the body it is to
ben vndirstonden that certeyn marchauntis of Venyse, the which wenten 95
to Alixandre, what with preyers and promysses and with yiftis, brought
abouten that the two prestis which weren kepers of Markis body, that thei
suffrid hem to stelyn awey the body prively and to caryen it vnto Venyse.
But whan the body was lifted oute of the tombe, so grete and so swete a
savour came oute with al and fulfilled al the citee of Alixaundre, that al 100
wondrid wherof it myght ben. And whan thei were forth into the see and
tolden to othir shippes which wentyn with hem that thei hadden Seynt
Markis body, oon of hem seid ageyn that perauenture thei had somme
Egipcians body and wenden han had Seynt Markis body. And anoon the
shippe wherin Seynt Markis body was swyftely turned by the self, and 105
with a grete cours ran ageyns the shippes side in the which he was that
seid the worde, and brak a part therof, ner nevir wolde awey therfro til al
tho which were therin knoulecchid verreily that thei bilevid that there was
truly Seynt Markis body. Which doon, it depertid from their shippe and
did it no more harme. 110

Vpon a nyght, as they seyled a grete cours, sodeynly grue a grete tempest and so grete a thirkenesse with al, that they wist nevir where thei were
ne whider they went. And anoon Seynt Marc appierid to a muncke which
was keper of the body and bad hym seyn to the shypmen that they shuld
striken her saile, for thei were nat fer fro londe. And anoon thei did so. 115
And on the morowe thei founden hemself besiden an ylelonde, the duellers wherof, natwithstondyng that no man tolde hem, come to hem and
seiden: 'Blissid be ye, the which bryngen with you Seynt Markis body,
suffrith ws that we mow worshippen it.'

Anothir shipman also wolde nat bilevyn that there was Seynt Mar- 120
kis body, and anoon he was vexid with a devil vnto the tyme þat he was
brought to the body and knoulecchid that he bylevid that it was Seynt
Markis body, and yafe thankyng to God and to Seynt Marc for his deli-
veraunce, the which evir aftir had Seynt Marc in grete reuerence and in

125 singuler affeccion. Anothir reuelacion of Seynt Marc made to a frere of his
owen ordre in the covent of Pauye, aboute the yere of our lorde a thousand,
two hundrid and oon & fourty, tellith here Ianuence, the which I passe ovir
at this tyme.

[71. MARCELLINUS POPE]

The life of Seynt Marcellyn the pope.

Marcellinus, a Romayn born, whos fadris name was Proiectus, gouernyd
f. 94ᵛᵃ the chirch of Rome nyne yere and four monethis, the tyme of | Dyocli-
sian and Maximian themperours. In whos tyme the persecucion of Cristis
5 feith was so grete that within a moneth in diuers prouinces were martired
aboute seventene thousand or mo, as it is remembrid biforn in Seynt Georgis life. This Marcellinus, at the seid emperours commaundement, was
taken with othir and led to doo sacrifise. But whan he sawe the grete and
many tormentys the which were ordeyned for hym, he failed hert and so
10 kest two greynes of frankencense in the fire, and therby ascapid. The which
dede to the paynyms was cause of ioye and gladnesse, and to the true cristen
it was mater of grete sorowe and hevynesse. But nat longe aftir he repen-
tid hym ful sore and was so penitent that, amonge many othir thyngis, he
deposid hymself from the worship of papal dignyte, whom al the multitude
15 of cristen peple chees ageyn to the same dignite and wolden hym livyng it
no wise chese noon othir.

Of this Marcellyn and of his penaunce, thus seith Martinus in *Cronica
sua* and also *Policronica*, what tyme that blissid Marcellyn had for drede
of peyn doon sacrifise to ydols, as it is seid biforn, anoon aftir, repentant,
20 he went into Champanye and gadrid togider a sean of an hundrid and four
score bisshops. In whos presence, clad in hayre and dust cast vpon his hede,
he knoulecchid mekely his defaute, bysechyng hem that thei wolde iugen
hym and assignen hym helthful penaunce. To whom, al with oo voice aunswerid ageyn and seide: 'Forbode be it of God that the hyest bisshop, that
25 is the pope, shuld be iuged of ws or of ony man. The maister Petir denyed
and forsoke God, and so hasthou. And who of al th'appostlis durst presumen to iugen hym, as whoso seith noon, ner we neither durn ner wiln
presume to iugen the. But we yiue this counceil to the: Petyr went oute
and wept bitterly, and thou gadre thy cause within thyself and with thyn
30 owen mouthe iuge and deme thiself.' At which counceil he anoon, soore
wepyng, yafe briefly this sentence vpon hymselfe: 'For as moche as I falsly
and vnkyndely forsoke my lorde, I iuge and condempne me vnworthy to

occupien the papal dignyte, and moreovir I curse hym whosoevir it be, the which puttith my body aftir my deeth vnto cristen sepulture.'

Which doon, he anoon went to Dioclisian and reuokid that he had doon 35 and resumyd ageyn the confession of Cristis feith. From which, for in no wyse he wolde declynen, he was commaundid to ben hefdid. And as he went forth to his iewesse-warde, he chargid Marcelle his preste, which was pope aftir hym, that he nevir shuld obeyen Dioclisians commaundementis. And whan he was hefdid, his body lay five and thritty daies vnburyed. 40 Aftir which tyme Seynt Petir appierid to Marcel the pope and Marcellyns successour, seyeng on this wise: 'Marcelle, brothir, slepysthou?' 'Who art thou that spekist to me?' quoth Marcelle. 'I am', quoth he ageyn, 'Prince of th'appostlis. Why latist my body so longe lyen vnburyed?' 'Sir', quoth Marcel ageyn, 'it is nat longe agoon sith thou were buryed.' 'Siker', quoth 45 Petir, 'so longe I holde myself vnburyed as I see Marcellyn vnburied.' 'Knowesthou not | wele, sir, that he cursid hym that buried his body aftir f. 94vb his deeth?' 'Hasthou nat red', quoth Petir, 'that whoso meke hymself, he shal ben exalted and enhaunced? Trowysthou nat that he mekely behad hym whan he iuged hymself vnworthy cristen buryels? This aughtisthou 50 to han considred. Wherfore I wil that thou rise fast and goo and burye hym even beside me, that, liche as oo grace hath vned and ioyned our soulis, right so oo grave mote coveren and kepyn our bodies.' And as Petir bad, Marcel did. Be laude and preysyng to God therfore, now and evir, amen.

[72. VITALIS]

The life of Seynt Vital knyght

Vitalis, a knyght of Melan, the which of his wife Valeria bigate two blissid men Geruasie and Prothasie, went to the cite of Ravenna with Paulyn the iuge. And whan, amonge many othir martirs, vpon a day he saw oon clepid Vrciscinus, a leche, led to the palme for to ben hefdid, and he bigan to 5 waveren and wexen aferde to the deth-ward, anoon he bigan to cryen vnto hym and seyn: 'Beware Vrciscine, leche, the which were wone to curen and to maken hole othir men from temperal deth, wyl not now slee thiself with the wounde of the darte of evirlastyng deeth. And sith thou by many passions and tormentis art commen to the palme, wil in no wise lesyn 10 the victorious coroun.' At which wordys Vrciscinus gretely was comfortid, and so, repentaunt of his feer, he gladly toke martirdam. Whom seid Vitalis buried worshipfully beside the citee of Rauen, and aftir that wolde no more goon ageyn to the iuge.

15 And whan Paulinus the iuge herd this, he had therof grete indignacion
what for he contempnyd hym and wolde nat commen to hym, what for he
withdrowe Vrciscine from sacrifise and comfortid hym to martirdam, and
also for that he openly shewid hymself a cristen man. And anoon he commaundid hym to be brought to his presence and there to be lyfted vpon a
20 iebett. Where whan Vitalis was, he seid to Paulyn on this wise: 'Thou art
a verrey fool, O Iuge, yf thou trowe and wene that I wolde for ony peyn
deceive myself, which haue alwey be busy for to deliveren other. Siker
thou labourist al in veyn.' And whan Paulinus herd this, anoon he com-
maundi[d] his mynistres to ledyn hym to the palme, for that was the name
25 of the place where cristen men were hefdid. Where whan he were, yf he
wolde nat doon sacrifise, he chargid hem to maken a depe pitte til thei come
to the watir and therin to buryen hym quycke, and casten vpon hym erthe
and stoones. And so thei diden, aboute the yere of grace seven and fyfty,
vndir themperour Nero. Which doon, anoon the preste of the temple, the
30 which yafe counceil of this maner of deth of Vital, was accept and takyn
of a devil and wex wode in the same place, six daies cryeng thus: 'Thou
brennyst me, Seynt Vital, thou brennyst me.' And on the seventh day the
f. 95ʳᵃ devyl threw hym in a flode, and so myserably and wrecchidly | he deid.

Aftir the passion of blissid Vital, his wife Valeria, goyng home-ward
35 ageyn to Melan, fonde certeyn men which were clepid Siluani makyng a
sacrifise to ydols, the which wolden haue made hir to sytten doun and to
han etyn with hem of such mete as they had offrid vp to her ydols. And
she aunswerid ageyn to hem and seid that neither she wolde ne myght, for
she was a cristen womman. And whan thei herd that, thei pullid hir doun
40 of hir hors and so cruelly betyn hir þat ner half dede hir men broughten
hir to Melan. Whider whan she was commen, within thre daies she deyed
and passid forth to Goddis mercy. The which he also mote grauntyn ws
which, mevid by mercy, deyed for vs. Amen.

[73. PETER OF MILAN]

The life of Seynt Petir of Melan

Petir, the new martir of the prechours ordre, born in the citee of Verone,
the noble cheventeyn of the feith, as a bright light oute of smoke & as
a white lilie amonge brusshalye and bremblis, and as a fair rede rose of
5 thornes, sprang of his progenitours a doctour, a maiden and a martir. For
his fadir and his modir weren vnfeithful and heretikis, but he kept hymself

pure and clene from her erroures and her vices. And whan this Petir was
but seven yere of age and came oo tyme fro scole, an eem of his, which
savourid heresie, mett with hym and askid hym what he lernyd in scole.
'My lesson, eem', quoth he ageyn, 'is this: *Credo in deum patrem omnipo-* 10
tentem & cetera: I bileve into God, fadir almyghty, maker of nought of
heven and of erthe.'

'Nay, neve', quoth his eem ageyn, 'sey nat maker of heven and of erthe.
For erthe, and al that is visible, God made nevir, but the devil made it.'
'Yea, eem', quoth Petir, 'I haue lever seyn as I haye lernyd, and bilevyn 15
as it is writen, than ony othir wise.' Than anoon he bigan to maken suasions to the childe by auctoritees, to makyn hym to seyn aftir his entent.
The which he, fulfilled with the holi goste, turned directly ageyns hym,
and so woundid hym with his owen swerd that vnnethe he wist which wey
he myght turnen hym. Wherof he, havyng indignacion and in maner con- 20
foundid in hymself to ben ovircommen of a childe, went to his brothir, the
childis fadir, and tolde hym al togider, counseilyng that algatis he shuld
removen hym from scole and no more letten hym lernen. 'For siker, I drede
gretely', quoth he, 'þat whan Petir is wele instruct and lerned, he wil flee
to that strumpett which is clepid *Ecclesiastica Catholica* and destroien and 25
confounden our feith and our bileve.' And, so as Caiphas prophecied of
Cristis deth and wist nat what he seid, right so he this ignorant seid truthe
whan he prophecyed that Petir, his neve, shuld confounden and destroyen
heretikes mysbileve. But, for as moche as this mater was guyded by Goddis
privey werkyng, the fadir of the childe toke noon heed to his brothirs coun- 30
sel, but rather he hopid that, whan his sone were instruct in his gramer,
he shuld moun by somme heresiarc, that is | to seyn by somme princi- f. 95rb
pal maister or doctour of heresye, be brought into her sect, and so ben a
meyntenour and a defender of the same.

But whan Petir bigan to growen and saw how his fadir and his moder 35
and his othir ny kyn weren infect with heresie, consideryng that it was nat
helthful ner siker to duellyn with scorpions, he forsoke the worlde and al
his worldly frendis and entrid into the frere prechours ordre. In which
ordre how laudably and how vertuously he lived Pope Innocent shewith
in a pistle, where he seith on this wise: 'Whan blissid Petir turned hym 40
awey from the fals deceites of the worlde in the tyme of his adolescencie,
he went into the ordre of the frere prechours. In which ordre the space
nere of thritty wynter he withsett with the grete felauship of vertues, as
with feith, hope and charite, so prevailed and profited in defence of the
feith, with the zeel wherof he was al enflaumed, that ageyns the cruel 45
enemyes therof with an vnfereful hert and a feruent spirite he exercised a

contynuel bataile, the which at the last he blissidly endid with a glorious
and victorious martirdam. And so Petir, stedfast in the stoon of the feith,
at the last hurt and bore doun with the stoon of peynful passion, rubrified
50 in his owen blood, stey vp to the cornerstoon Criste Ihesu, of hym worthily
to be laureat with the croun of endeles remuneracion.' *Hec Innocencius.*

The virgynyte bothen of body and of soule he kept evir vndefoulid,
ner he nevir of al his life was entecchid with spotte of dedely synne, as
it was proved by the feithful testymonye of hem which weren his con-
55 fessours. And for as moche as a seruaunt delicatly norisshed often tyme
rebellith ageyns his lorde, he refreyned his flessh with dayly scarsnesse of
mete and drynke and constreyned it to serven vnto the spirite. And that
by slouth and ydilnesse shuld noon entre appieren to his gostely enemyes,
he contynuelly was exercised in the studie of Goddis lawe and of his com-
60 maundementis. And in tho also he occupied the nyghtis silence ordeyned
to mannes rest, aftir a litle slepe, and in hooly meditacions and in devoute
preyers. The dayes eke he spent to the profite of mennys soulis, as in busynesse of prechyng and the solicitude of confessions heryng, or with myghty
resons the heretikis pestilencial doctrine confoundyng, wherin he had a
65 singuler and a special grace. Devoute he was also and meke, plesaunt in
obedyence, softe in benygnite, pitous, pacient and compacient, constaunt
and stedfast, charitable and abidyng, and in al thyngis adorned & araied
with maturite of maners. Wherby, as by an odour of swete oynementis, he
drowe many men to vertue and to gode livyng. He was also a fervent lover
70 and a synguler tylier of the feith, into the obsequye and seruise wherof he
had so bounden hymself that al his wordis and his werkis savourid alwey
the vertue of the feith with a fervent desire to deyen for the feith often, and
with many devoute supplicacions, bysechyng God that he wold nat suffren
hym to passen oute of this worlde til he had drunkyn the chalys of passion
75 and of bodily deth for the feith. And he was nat defraudid of his desire.

f. 95va   This blissid man was nat oonly | thus adorned with the grace of ver-
tuous livyng, but also God clarified hym with manyfolde and marveilous
myraclis werkyng. Oo tyme at Melan, whan blissid Petir stode openly and
examyned a bisshop of the heretikys whom feithful men had taken, and
80 many bisshops and religious men and the moste part of the peple of the
citee were commen thider to heryn h[y]m, and the day, what in prechyng
what in examynyng, was driven ferforth, and the fervour of hete gretely
vexid hem al, the heresiarc thus seid to Petir openly and lowde, heryng
hem alle: 'O peruers Petir, yf thou art so holy a man as this fonned peple
85 affermyth the to ben, why suffristhou hem thus to be grevid with hete, and

81 hym] hem

preyest nat God to putten a cloude bitwix the sunne and this fonned peple
to refreshe hem, that they dey nat?' To whom Petir boldely and feithfully
aunswerid ageyn on this wise: 'Yf thou wilt promytte me to forsaken thyn
heresie and to receiven cristen vniuersel feith, I shal prey God and he shal,
I vndirtake, doon that thou seyest.' And whan blissid Petir had seid thus, 90
anoon the fauctours of the heretikis criedden to the heresiarc and seiden:
'Bihete hym, bihete hym!' For thei trowid verreily that it myght nat be doon
that Petir had promysed biforn hem alle, in as moche as in the eyre appierid
nat so moche as a litle cloude. And than anoon the vniuersal feithful peple
bigan to be sory for blissid Petris biheste, dredyng that cristen vniuersel 95
feith myght therby be confoundid.

And whan this blissid man sawe that this heretike wolde in no wise be
bounde, with a grete trust in God he seid on this wyse: 'To that ende that
God may be shewid the verrey creatour of al thyngis, visible and invisible,
and to the comforte of feithful cristen men, and to the confusion of hereti- 100
kis, I prey God that a cloude may commen bitwix the sunne and the peple,
to relevyn hem and to comforten hem ageyns this grete hete.' Which seid,
and a tokne of a crosse made, there came a cloude and in maner of a tente
henge ovir the peple and shadowid hem a large houre aftir.

Oon also clepid Acerbus, the which five yere had be so contract that he 105
myght nat goon but by drawyng of his body on the erthe, was brought to
Melan to blissid Petir. Whom as sone as he had markid with a crosse, he
roos vp hool and heil.

Also Pope Innocent in the forseid epistle rehersith certeyn myraclis
doon by blissyd Petir, wherof oon is this. A certeyn worthy mannys sone 110
so sore was grevid with a bolnyng throte that he neither myght spekyn, ner
drawen his breeth. And as sone as blissid Petir had lifted vp his handis to
God and made a tokne of a cros, and taken his fadir his cope to leyen vndir
hym, and he had so doon, anoon the childe was heil and hole. This seid
worthy ientilman was aftirward so grevously tormentid with a gnawyng in 115
his body that he wende verreily and dred to han deyed therof. And anoon
he did bryng forth reuerently the seid cope, wherwith his sone was cured,
for he had kept it stille with hym. The which as sone as he had devoutely
leid to his breste, he vomyted and kest oute a werme, the which had two
heedis and was al ruggid & ful of heer. | And forthwith he was al hool f. 95vb
withoute ony othir medicyne.   121

A yunge man also, which was dom and myght nat speken, brought to
hym, he putte his fyngir into his mouth and anoon the strengis of his
tunge were laxed, and he had perfitely his speche. These and many moo

125 myraclis while he lived our lorde vouchidsafe to shewe by his seruaunt.
Hec Innocencius ut supra.

Aftir this, whan the pestilence of heresie sprange fast in Lombardie
and had infectid many citees with his contagious poyson, the pope sent
and assigned in many placis diuers inquisitours of the prechours ordre to
130 enserchen and to distroien that perilous infeccion brought in by the devil.
But for as moche as at Melan heretikes, nat oonly many in nombre but also
grete in seculer power, sharp in fraudelent eloquencie and ful of the devels
kunnyng, kepten her residence and her moste abidyng, the pope knowyng
and wele vndirstondyng þat Petir in Goddis cause was manly and grete
135 hertid and dred not the multitude of Goddis enemyes, consideryng also
wele Petris grete facundie and eloquencie wherby he shuld soon and lightly
detecten heretikis fallacies, aduertisyng also how fully he was instruct in
the wisdam of Goddis lawe and holy chirchis doctryne, by which he resonably shuld kun dissoluen heretikis veyn argumentis, he putt hym there and
140 in al that countee his inquisitour and al his ful power grauntid vnto hym.

Which doon, he anoon diligently exercised the office enioyned vnto
hym, and oviral sought oute heretikis and nowhere wolde laten hem han
rest, marveilously inpugnyng hem and confoundyng hem, myghtely expel-
lyng hem and wisely convictyng hem, so that noon of hem myght ne coude
145 resisten the spirite that spak within hym. And whan the heretikis sey this,
they wex right sory and right hevy. And anoon with her fauctours thei
begunne to tretyn of his deeth, trowyng and wenyng verreily that thei
shuld pesibly liven yf he, which was so myghty a persecutour of hem, by
deeth were oones sett aside. Whan than this worshipful prechour went oo
150 tyme fro Cume to Melan to exercisen his office in inquisicion of heretikis, in the wey thiderward he received the palme of martirdam, as Pope
Innocent declarith vsyng these wordis: 'Whan Petir', quoth he, 'went fro
Cumys, where he was priour, to Melan-ward forto executen the inquisicion ageyns heretikes committed vnto hym by the auctoritee of the chirche
155 of Rome, as he had puplisshid biforne openly in his sermoun, oon of the
heretikes seruauntis, at her preyer and request and for a rewarde grauntid hym amongis hem, came vpon hym as he was pursuyng the iournee of
his hooly purpose and cruelly assailed hym as a wulf a lambe, a cruel man
a meke man, an vnpitous man a pitous, a wode man a buxom man, and
160 as a lawles man an hooly man, cruelly assawtid hym and did his diligent
busynesse to sleen hym. And with his swerd he woundid his hooly hede
with cruel woundis, hym not turnyng awey from his oost but in pacience
suffryng his mortal strokis, offryng hymself to God, an hooly ooste, he
sente to heven his spirite in the same place of his passyoun. Nevirtheles,

er than he deyed, whan the cruel lyctour | had youen hym two strokis in   f. 96ra
the hede, he, as I seid, nat turnyng awey, ne compleynyng ner grucchyng,   166
but paciently al thyngis suffryng, commendid to God his spirite and seid:
In manus tuas, domine & cetera, and aftir that the crede of the feith, wherof
in the article of his deth he cessid nat to ben a bedel or a cryer, as bare
wittenesse the cruel tortour the which was taken aftirward of feithful men   170
and also frater Dominicus, blissid Petris felawe, the which, also mortally
woundid of the cursid tormentour, deyed within few daies aftir his maister. But whan this new martir was throwen doun to the grounde with the
cruelle woundis which he had taken in his hede, and his bodye lay tremelyng and waueryng on the grounde, the cruel lictour toke his dagger or his   175
knyfe, and shofe it in atte his side.'
  See now how this blissid man, the same day of his martirdam, deserued
the worship of a confessour, of a martir, of a prophete and of a doctour.
A confessour he was in as moche as he amonge his tormentis constauntly
confessid the feith of Criste. And also, for as moche as he confession made   180
aftir the consuetude of the chirche, the same day offrid to God the sacrifise
of laude and preysyng. A martir he was in as moche as for defence of the
feith he shed his blode the same day. A prophete he was in as moche as he
tolde biforne bothen his passion and where he shuld loggen the same nyght
at even. For, in as moche as he hadde the quartan fevir, his brethern seid   185
vnto hym that he shuld nat mown that nyght atteyn to the citee of Melan.
To whom he aunswerid and seid: 'Yf we mow nat atteyn to commen to the
freris place, we shul mown be logged at Seynt Symplicians.' And so he
was. For aftir his passion, whan the freris caried forth his body, the prees
of the peple was so grete that they myght nat the same day bryngen hym   190
hoom to her hous, but setten hym doun at Seynt Symplicians. And there
he abode al that nyght. A doctour he was in as moche as in the tyme of his
passion he taught the verrey feith, whan he with a clere vois pronouncid
pleynly the crede of the feith.
  The passion of this blissid and holy man Petir semyth in many thyngis   195
to be like to our lordis passion. Crist suffrid for the truthe that he prechid,
and Petir for the truthe of the feith which he defendid. Crist suffrid by pro-
curacie of fals Iewys, and Petir by the mean of fals and vnfeithful heretikis.
Criste was crucified in Esterntyme, and Petir was martired the same tyme.
Crist, whan he shulde deyen, seid *In manus tuas, domine,* and Petir likewise   200
seid the same. Crist for thritty pens was bitraied for to be crucified, Petir
was solde for fourty Pauye poundis for to be slayn. Crist, by his passion,
brought many men to the feith, and Petir, by his deth, conuertid many heretikes. For albeit that, while he lived he myghtely pullid vp the pestilencial

205 rote of heresie and gretely confoundid heretikis, yet, nevirtheles, aftir his
deth his meritis and his myraclis were brode and shynyng, so vttirly he
destroied the rote of pernicious heresye that many of the heretikis forsoo-
ken her heresie and turned ageyn into the lappe of her modir, holi chirche.

f. 96ʳᵇ In so moche that the citee of Melan and al | the countee therof, where
210 so many conuenticles were resident and abidyng of heretikis, was so clene
purgid that somme expulsid and driven awey, and somme conuertid to the
feith, nevir oon durst appiere there more. Many also of hem grettest and
moste famous entrid the prechours ordre, the which with grete feruour
and diligent solicitude and busynesse pursued the residue of her forme
215 sect and vttirly destroied hem and her opynyon. Thus our Sampson slow
moo Philistens deyeng than he had doon livyng. Thus our whete greyn,
throw doun to the erthe with vnfeithful mennys handis, grue ageyn and
multeplyed into plentevous hervest corne. Thus eke our clustir of grapys,
troden in the presse of passion, redoundid into plentevousnesse of helth-
220 ful licoure. Thus our swete oynement, stampid in the morter of peyne,
diffoundid fer aboute the delectable redolence of right plesaunt odoure.
And thus also our mustard seed, groundyn with persecucion, manyfolde
wise shewid thencrees of the vertue.

For, as it is seid, God, aftir this holy mannys glorious tryumphe, glori-
225 fied and clarified hym with many grete myraclis, wherof summe the pope
touchith in his epistle, seyng on this wyse: 'Aftir the deth of this blissid
martir', quoth he, 'the lampes hangyng at his sepulcre were often tyme
founde light withouten ony helpe or mynisterie of mannys handis. For it
was convenyent', quoth he, 'which so excellently shoon with the fyre and
230 the light of feith shuld be claryfied by the myracle of fyre and light. Oon
also', quoth he, 'sittyng at mete with othir folke and depravyng the holynesse of this seynt and his myraclis, and puttyng a morsel into his mouth
with an obtestacion that yf he seid wronge he shuld nat mow swelowen,
it fel anoon it so sore fastenyd to his throte that he myght neither drawen
235 it in ner casten it oute. And whan he felt this and, his coloure chaungid,
was at the poynte of deth, he made a vowe within hymself to God and to
this blissid martir that he shuld no more vsen such maner of detraccion.
And sodeynly he vomyted oute that morsel and was perfitely hool.' Five
or six moo myraclis he compendiously tellith there, which, forto eschew
240 prolixite, stepdame of favour, I passe ovir at thys tyme.

What tyme that Pope Innocent the fourth had canonized this blissid
martir and ascrived hym to the nombre and the worship of seyntis in heven,
freris come to her chapitre at Melan and willyng, as they were licencid,
lyften vp his body and transferren it to an hyer and a worshipfuller place,

whan it had leyn vndir the erthe more than a yere, it was founden as hool 245
and as heyl, withouten any exalacion of stynke, as it had be buried even the
same day. And whan the freris seyn this, thei leid the body reuerently on
a fair feretre beside the strete, to be seen and worshipped of al the peple.
And aftirward, with grete solempnyte, thei borne it to the shryne ordeyned
therfore, there to restyn in worship of men in erthe til the day come of the 250
grete assise, whan the soule, vnyd and knytte ageyn therto bothe togider,
shul be translatid vp to the blisse of heven.

    Beside the myraclis putte, as it is seid byforne, in the popis lettris, many
othir be founden writen, bothe | doon in his life and eke aftir his deth. f. 96va
The which al, for her innumerable multitude it were [to longe] to write. 255
Wherfore somme of the moste notable, aftir my conceite, I purpose compendyously forto touchen, to the worship and laude of the blissid martir
and to comforte of them which han singuler deuocion vnto hym; and first
tho which were doon in his live. Oo tyme whan an heretik, a subtile arguer
and a man of singuler eloquencie, disputid with blissid Petir, and craftely 260
and colourably had purposid his errourys, and importunely cried on Petir
to aunsweren therto, he askid deliberacion and avisement while he went
into a chirche there beside and come ageyn. Where whan he came, he knelid doun devoutely and wepyng preyed God to defenden the cause of his
feith, and to reducen that proude iangeler to the truthe of the feith, or els to 265
punysshe hym by priuacion of his language, that he shulde no more therby
be bolne and proude ageyn the truthe of the feith. Which preyer endid, he
went ageyn to the heretik and, biforn al the peple, required hym to rehersen ageyn his resons. But he vttirly was so dom that he neither coude, ner
myght, rehersen oo worde of alle. For which cause the heretikis wenten 270
confuse awey and true feithful peple youe laude and thankyng to God.

    A matrone eke, Girolda by name, wife of Iamys de Vallesana, whan she
had fourtene yere ben vexid with vnclene spiritis, she came to a preste and
seid: 'I am a demonyac and evil spiritis vexen me.' And whan the preste
herd this, anoon he went from hir into the vestiarie and fett forth a boke, 275
wherin weren coniuracions for spiritis, and toke with hym a stoole prively
vndir his cloke, and with a gode felauship came ageyn to the womman.
Whom as sone as she sawe, she cried and seid: 'A thefe, whider wentist-
hou? What hasthou broughte there, prively vndir thi cloke?' And whan the
preste had redde the coniuracions which weren in the boke and it availed 280
not, she, by counseil of hir frendis, went to blissyd Petir, preyeng hym for
to helpen hir. To whom he, with a prophetical voice, aunswerid and seid:
'Womman, be of hope and dispeyr nat! Though I mow nat now perfourme

    255 to longe] om.

that thou askist, there shal commen a tyme heraftir whan þat thou desirest
285 shal plenerly and perfitely be grauntid the.' And so it was. For aftir his passion, whan the seid womman came to his grave, she was perfitely deliverid
from al evil spiritis vexacion from that day evir aftir.

Also, whan on the Palme Sonday biforne his passion he prechid at
Melan, and there was gadrid a grete multitude bothen of men and of wom-
290 men, he seid thus openly and with an high vois even biforn hem al: 'I wote
wele', quoth he, 'for sikernesse that heretikes tretyn my deeth in so moche
that the mony is in depose for my deth. But late hem doon whatsoevir they
willen and mown, yet not forthan I shal pursuen more dede than I doo now
quycke and alive.' And as he prophecied it bifelle, as it is declarid biforn.

295   At Florence also in the monasterie *De Ripulis*, a nunne, beyng in hir
preyere the same day that blissid Petir suffrid deth, sawe our lady sitten in
an high trone in blisse, and two frere prechours styen vp to heven and sett
f. 96vb that oon on that oo side and the | tothir on the tothir side of our lady. And
whan she askyd what thei weren, it was aunswerid hir thus: 'That oon is
300 frere Piers, the which this day appierith in the sight of God, glorious and
precious as a redolent fume of swet smellyng oynementis.' And aftirward
it knowen was for siker soth that he deyed the same day that the nunne had
the seid reuelacion. For which reuelacion, whan the same nunne which
longe had langured in right grevous sikenesse turned hir hert to preyen
305 to hym for helpe, anoon she was restorid vnto perfite helthe. These and
many mo he wrought in his life and in his deyeng, but these suffisen as
now. Infinite nombre of myraclis also he wrought aftir his deth, wherof
these ben somme.

A yung man of the citee of Cumys, Gunfred by name, shewid an here-
310 tik that he talkid with oo tyme a pece of the cloth of Seynt Petris cote, the
which he kept for a relik. The heretic scorned hym ageyn and seid: 'Yf
thou bileve hym to ben a seynt, throw that cloth into the fyre. And yf it
brenne nat, withoute doute he is a seynt, and I shal turne to his feith.' Atte
which worde, with a grete confidence, the yung man kest the cloth into
315 the fyre. And anoon it sprange oute fer awey fro the fyre. And forthwith it
stirte ageyn into the fyre and quenchid al the coolys even sodeynly. Quoth
the heretik ageyn: 'A pece of my cote shal doo the same.' And forthwith
a pece of the heretikis clothe was leid on oo parte of the coolis, and the
pece of Seynt Petris cloth on that othir. The pece of the heretikis cloth, as
320 sone as it touchid the fyre, it was sodeynly brent and wastid. But that othir
so clene quenchid the fyre that nothyng abode therof, ner oon threde was
hurt of the clooth. At which myracle the heretik was conuertid.

In Florence, a yung man corupt with heresie, as he with othir stode in

the freris chirche, lokyng on a table whereon was depeynted Seynt Petris
martirdam, and seeyng the lictour with his swerde yiven hym a wounde,   325
seyde on this wise: 'Wolde God I had ben there, for than I shuld haue youen
hym a more myghty wounde.' And, as sone as he had seid that worde, he
wex dom and myght nat speke oo worde more. And whan his felaws askid
hym what hym eyled, and he myght no worde aunswern hem, thei ledden hym hoom to his hous. And, as he went, he sawe a chirche of Seynt   330
Mychael and vnwarly he braid oute of his felaus handis and went into the
chirche. And, knelyng, preyed Seynt Petir to sparen hym & bonde hymself in herte with a vowe that, yf he were deliverid, he shuld be shriven and
forsaken al heresye. Which a vowe made, sodeynly he recoverid his speche
and forthwith went ageyn to the prechours and, knoulecchyng his defaute, 335
he abiured his heresie and aftir stode vp amonge al the peple at a freris and
tolde hem al the processe. A womman in Flaundris, whan she had brought
forth thre children and al dede, for which cause hir husbonde hated hir, she
preyed Seynt Petir of Melan to ben hir helpe. And whan she had brought
forth the fourth child it was dede also, which whan she sawe dede, with   340
al her wittis and myght she gadrid hirself into hirself and | preid Seynt   f. 97ra
Petir entierly that hir childe myght lyven. Which preyer vnneth endid,
the childe appierid quyk which was born dede. The which childe born to
the baptesme and was ordeyned for to haue be clepid Iohannes, whan the
preste shuld haue seid 'Iohannes' he vnwarly seid 'Petyr', the which name 345
he held stille for the modris deuocion to Seynt Petir.

In Duchelonde, in a cite clepid Traiect or Tryit, certeyn wommen, stondyng in the strete and spynnyng and seeyng moche multitude of peple
goyng to the frere prechours chirche in worship of Seynt Petris fest, thus
bigunnen to seyn amongis hem: 'Bihold how these freris haue founden al   350
the crafte of lucre and wynnyng. For to that entent to makyn hoordis of
money and to bielden hem grete new and stately paleys, they han founden hem a new martir!' And while thei busily occupied hem in this maner
of talkyng, sodeynly al the thredis which thei spunne were rubrified with
blode, and her fyngris also that they spunne with. And, whan thei aspied   355
these thyngis, grete amaruailed they busied hem for to wypen her fyngris,
wenyng that thei had be cutte. And whan thei perceived that her fyngris
were nat hurt but hool and heil, and seyn her threde so rede as it had be
wasshen in blode, thei begunne to tremelyn for fere and, repentaunt of her
forme wordis, seiden: 'Verreily, for as moche as we han detractid this blis- 360
sid martirs blode, this wondirful myracle of blode is fallen vnto ws.' And
anoone forthwith they runne al togider to the freris and tolde the priour al
the processe and shewid hym her blody thredis. And anoon the seid priour,

at the instaunce of hem and of many othir worthy folke, made a sermoun
365 and clepid the peple togider. And the wommen, beyng present, tolde hem
the processe and shewid hem the blody thredis. At which sermoun, a maister of gramer stondyng present bigan to scornen the prechoure, seyeng on
this wise to hem which stoden besyden hem: 'See how craftely these freris
deceiven the symple peplis hertis. For perauenture they han hyred somme
370 of her seruauntis wives for to dippen her threde in somme bestis blode,
and forto seyn that it came myraculouse.' And forthwith as he had seid
these wordis, anoon he felt the plage of Goddis vengeaunce. For sodeynly
he was smette with so myghty a fevir and, al men seeyng, so vexid that
from the sermoun he was born hoom in mennys armes. And whan he sawe
375 the fevir alwey growen, and therwith the perile of deth neighen, he sent
for the priour of the seid place and, mekely knoulecchyng biforn hym his
defaute, made a vowe to God and to Seynt Petir that, yf he myght recuren
helth, he shuld han Seynt Petir in singuler deuocion evir aftir, and nevir
vsen his tunge to such language more. A wundir thyng! This vowe was nat
380 sonner made than perfite helth was had.

A scoler eke, of a toun in Lombardie clepid Magalona, as he went oones
to Mount Pessulan, happid of a skippyng vnwarly to be brosten and brosid in the liendis, that he myght neither goon, stonden ner sitten. And
therwith his peyn was so grevous and so intollerable that, withoute redy
f. 97rb relef, he myght nat longe liven. And as he lay ful of sorowe | and hevy-
386 nesse, came to his mynde sodeynly how he had oones herd prechid that a
womman, which had a legge nere frett thurgh with a cancre, toke of the
erthe which was sprencled with the blode of this blissid martir Seynt Petir
of Melan, and anoon she was deliverid of the cancre and perfitely heelid.
390 And anoon he seid on this wise: 'Allas, I haue here noon of that erthe. Not
forthan, lorde God', quoth he, 'I knowe wele and fully bileve that thou
maist yiuen the erthe here as moche vertue in his name as hath the erthe
there in his blode.' Which wordis, with a grete confidence and trust in God
and of Seynt Petir, he toke of the erthe besiden hym and blissid and clepid
395 Seynt Petris helpe, and leid it to the place of his hurt. And anoon he was
nat oonly deliverid of his peyne, but also he was ful curid and made hool
of his hurt and of his disease.

There was also a nunne in Almayne of a monasterie clepid Occunbath
in the diocese of Constaunce, the which twelue monethis and more suffrid
400 a grevous gowte in hir knee so that she myght nat goon ne stiren, ne by
no medicyne remedyed ner relevid. And for as moche as she was a religious and vndir obedience, and also for she was so sore oppressid with

386 oones herd] oones

grief of hir sikenesse, she myght nat visiten the grave of Seynt Petir as she had herd seyn that many seke folke didden and hadden remedy. For which causis she thought in hir hert that she wolde visiten his tombe gostely and with diligent deuocion. Wherupon, hauyng lernyd that in fourten daies a man myght goon from hir monasterie into Melan, she disposid hir for eche daies iournee to seyn an hundrid *Pater Noster* in worship of God and of Seynt Petir. And so she bigan and procedid. And as she succes- sifly bigan to seyn these daies iournees in hir soule, so alwey by litle and by litle she bigan to amendyn in hir body. And whan she came to the last daies iournee, and with the paas of hir mynde came to the tombe, she kne- lid doun reuerently, as though she had in body ben there present, and with right grete deuocion seid an hoole sawtiere. The which doon, she felt hir of hir sikenesse so gretely relevid that vnnethe it grevid hir ought. And turnyng hoomward ageyn by the dyettis, bi than she had perfourmed the last daies iournee she was perfitely hool and felt right nought of al hir grete sikenesse.

The yere of our lorde a thousand, two hundrid and nyne and fyfty, ther was a man in Compostella whos name was Benedictus. This man had leggis bolned as tankardis or botels, a wombe as a womman with childe, his face and al his body so horribly blowen that he sempt rather to ben a monstre than a man. And oo tyme as he, vnnethe havyng power and myght to sustene hymself with a staffe, askid almesse of a matrone, she aunswerid ageyn and seid that he had more nede of a grave than of mete. 'Nevirtheles, man', quoth she, 'by my counseil goo to the frere prechours & be shriven, and prey Seynt Petir of Melan to help the.' At whos counceil, on the next morow erely he went thider, or than the gate was opened, and he sett hym doun beside the gate and fel aslepe. And as hym thought there cam to hym a worshipful man in a frere prechours | habite and curid hym with his cope, and ledde hym into the chirche. And whan he woke he fonde hymself within the chirche and perfitely curid and hool of al his sikenesse. To God and to Seynt Petir be laude and thankyng for this and al such othir. Amen.

[74. PHILIP]

The life of Seynt Philip

Whan th'appostles of our lorde and saluatour Ihesu Crist, and othir disciplis, were diuided by diuers provincis of the worlde for to prechyn the

worde of God, the holy appostle of the seid lorde, Philip, twenty wynter
5   continuelly prechid in Syrie. Aftir which tyme the paynyms tooken hym
and leddyn hym to the statue of Mart, for to compellyn hym to doon sacrifise. Where sodeynly, from vndir the baas, came oute a grete dragoun and
slowe the bisshops sone, the which mynistred the fyre in the sacrifise, and
two tribunes, also the officers of whom helden Philip in pryson, and with
10 his breeth so infectid the eyre that al tho which were there present wex seke
therof. To whom Philip seid on this wise: 'Sirs, yiueth credence to that I
shal seyn. Bilevith on my lorde Ihesu Criste and brekith this statue of Mart
and throwith it oute, and settith in stede therof the crosse of my lorde and
worshippith it, and nat oonly your seke men shul be made heil and hoole,
15 but also thei that ben dede shul be reised ageyn to life!' And anoon, they
which were tormentid with sikenesse bigunne to cryen and seyn: 'Sir, do
so moche that we be made hool and we anoon shul breke this Mart.' And
forthwith Philip commaundid the dragon to goo thens into a desert place
where no man duellith, and that in his passage he shuld no man hurten.
20 And so he did, ner nevir was seyn thereaftir. Which doon, he heelid the
sike men and reised ageyn to life them the which were dede. And thus al
the peple conuertid to Cristis feith.

Philip an hole yere abode there with hem, and prechid and taught hem
and ordeyned prestis and dekones amonge hem, and fro thens went into
25 Asie and into a cite therof clepid Ieropolis, and there distroied the heresie of the Hebionytis, the which prechidden and taughten that Criste toke
a fantasticalle body and not verrey flessh and blode of his modir blissid
Marie. And there were with hym his two doughtris, right holy maidens,
by whom our lorde turned moche peple to his feith.

30   This blissid apostle Philip, seven dayes biforn his deth, clepid vnto hym
al the bisshops & prestis and seid to hem on this wise: 'These seven daies
hath my lorde grauntid me for to amonessh you in. Wherfore I exorte
you that ye haue mynde of our lorde Ihesu Criste and stondith stifly and
manly in his feith, and our lorde mote fulfillen his biheste in you and mote
35 strengthen his chirche.' These and many othir thyngis the blissid appostle
prechyng and techyng, paynyms commen and tokyn hym and crucified
hym liche his maister whom he prechid, whan he was four score yere and
seven of age. And aftir thei stooned hym and so blissidly he deid and wente
to our lorde, and in the same citee was buried his holy body.

f. 97ᵛᵇ   And aftir certeyn yeris his two hooly doughtris deid | and were buried
41 by her fadir, that oon on the right hand, that othir on the lefte hande. Of
this Philip thus seith Isid[o]re in his boke *De Vita et obitu & ortu sancto-*

42 Isidore] Isidre

rum patrum: 'Philip th'appostle prechid Criste to a peple which were clepid
Galli, and the wilde bestial peple [in] thirkenesse and ioyned to the bolnyng
occian, he ledd to the porte or the haven of feith, and to the light of perfite 45
kunnyng.' *Hec Isiderus.*

There was also anothir Philip, the which was oon of the seven decones,
the which the Actis of th'appostelis spekith of, and Seynt Ierome also in his
Martiloge, *Octauo ydus Iulij*, where he seith thus: 'Philip, oon of the seven
dekones, clarified with many signes and wondirful tokenys, deyed at Cesa- 50
rie and there he restith, and beside hym his thre doughtris, prophetisses,
and his fourth doughtir at Ephesum.' 'The difference bitwix these two Phi-
lips', quoth Ianuence, 'is this: that the first Philip was apostle, this was but a
dekon. The first lyeth at Ieropolym, this at Cesaree. Philip th'appostle had
but twoo doughtris, prophetisses, the dekon had four.' And this suffiseth 55
att this tyme.

[75. JAMES THE LESS]

The life of Seynt Iames the lesse.

This Iamys, whos feste holy chirche this day solempnizeth with his co-
apostle Philip, is clepid and named four sundry wises. For he is clepid
Iamys Alphei, that is to seyn the sonne of Alphei, Iamys our lordis brothir,
Iames the lesse and Iames the rightful. The first nominacion pertenyth to 5
hym nat oonly aftir his flesshly birthe but also aftir the interpretacion of his
fadris name. Alpheus by interpretacion is as moche to seyn as taught, doctrine, fugitif or a knyght low. Iamys than is clepid Iamys Alphei for he was
taught by inspiracion of kunnyng and that he taught othir by his doctrinal
prechyng, he was a fugitif from the worlde that vttirly despisyng, and a 10
lowe knyght by meke reputacion of hymself in his owen felyng. Iamys our
lordis brothir he was callid, for aftir the face, as it is seid, he was moste
like hym, in so moche that many were often deceived in knouleche of her
persones. Wherfore whan the Iewys wentyn to taken Criste, that thei shuld
nat erren in Iamys persone they tokyn of Iudas, the which of grete famu- 15
liarite knew wele inough that oon from that oothir. Of this similitude and
likenesse bodily spekith Seynt Ignase in an epistle to his maister Iohannes
the Evangelist, seyeng on this wise: 'Yf it be leeful to me, by thi counseil I
wil goon vp to Ierusalem that I mow seen that worshipful Iamys which is
clepid rightful, the which men tellyn to be moste like to our lorde Ihesu, 20
bothen in face in life and in maner of conuersacion, as though he had be

born with hym of the same wombe. Whom thei seyn, yf I see I shal seen
Ihesu hymself aftir al the lyneamentis of the body.' *Hec Ignasius.*
    Or els he is clepid Cristis brothir. For as moch as Criste and he com-
25 men of two sustris, and the consuetude of scripture is to clepen sustris
children and bretherns children, brethern and sustren, so Abraham clepid
f. 98ra Looth, his | brothirs sone, his brothir gentilis. Or els Iamys was clepid
Frater domini, our lordis brothir, for the grete prerogatife and excellence
of holynesse for which biforn al that othir appostles he was ordeyned for
30 to ben bisshop of Ierusalem. This Iamys is also clepid the lesse for a difference fro Iamys, Zebedees sonne, which is clepid Iamys the more. For
albeit that this Iamys were of birthe first and borne bifore that othir, yet
Iamys Zebedee was biforn hym in vocacion and in callyng to the dignite
of appostle. And therfore to hym is ascried the primacie and the maiorite.
35 By occasion wherof it is yet obserued and kept in sundry religions that he
that first entrith is alwey clepid the elder, and he that foloweth the yunger,
albeit that he be elder of yeris by his byrthe, more of kunnyng and holyer in
livyng. Iamys the rightful is this Iamys clepid also for the excellent merite
of his holynesse. For as Seynt Ierome seith, he was of so grete reuerence
40 and opynyon of holynesse in the peple, that wheresoevir he went thei desired by and by, eche aftir other, to touche the hemme of his garnement.
Of whos holynesse thus writeth Egesippus, the which was nye the apostlis
tyme, as it is redde in *Historia Scolastica:* 'Iamys, our lordis brothir, toke
the chirche of Ierusalem to gouernen, the which of al men was clepid right-
45 ful, the which endurid in Ierusalem from our lordis tyme vnto vs.' Quoth
he: 'This Iamys was holy from his modris wombe. He drank nevir neither
wyne ne sither, he eet nevir flessh, ther came nevir rasour ner sheris vpon
his hede, he was nevir anoynted with oile, he vsid nevir no bath, he was
al clad in lynen and werid no wullen. And so often he was accustumed
50 to knelyn that the skynne on his knees was as hard as on his heelis. And
for this incessable and high souereyn perfite rightwisnesse he was clepid
singulerly rightful. This Iamys oonly, for his grete holynesse, amonge al
th'appostlis was suffrid to entren in *Sancta Sanctorum* within the temple',
hec Egesippus, 'nat for to offren but forto preyen.'
55   It is also seid and openyd that he amonge al th'appostlis seid first messe
aftir [the] ascencion of Criste in Ierusalem, and er than he was made a bisshop. And for whan it is seid in *Actibus Apostolorum* that Cristis disciplis
were perseuerant in doctrine and in communyon of the brekyng of brede,
it is vndirstonden of messe seyeng. Or els happely it is seid that he seid
60 first messe in Antioche and Marc in Alixandre.

56 the] his

This Iames eke on Gode Friday whan Crist deid, as Iosephus and Seynt Ierome *De Viris Illustribus* seyen, made a vou that he shuld nevir eetyn mete til he sey our lorde risen from deth to life. And in the day of Cristis resurreccion, er than Iamys touchid ony brede, our lorde appierid vnto hym and to hem which weren with hym and seid 'Puttith or settith a table and brede 65 theron'. Which doon he toke brede and yafe it to Iamys the rightfull and seid: 'Rise vp, brothir myn Iamys, and ete! For sikerly the sonne of man is risen from deth.'

The seventh yere of his bisshopriche, whan th'appostlis were commen togider to Ierusalem to the pascal fest, he askid hem how many thyngis 70 God had doo by hem biforn the peple; thei tolden hym by and by. And whan he with that othir | apostlis had seven daies togider prechid in the f. 98ʳᵇ temple biforn Caiphas and othir mo Iewys and thei were nere in wille for to be baptised, vnwarely came oon into the temple and bigan to cryen on this wise: 'O ye men of Israel, what do ye? Why suffre ye you to ben deceived of 75 these wicchis?' And in so moche with his wordis he stired and mevid that thei wolden haue stooned th'appostlis. And forthwith that same man went vp vnto the gree where Iames prechid and threw hym doun bakward, and evir aftir that Iames somwhat haltid. And this was the sevynth yere aftir Cristis ascencion. 80

In the thrittenth yere of his bisshopriche, the Iewys seeyng that they myght nat sleen Poule in as moche as he had appelid to themperour and was sent forth to Rome, they turned al the tyrannye of her persecucion into Iamys, sekyng occasion ageyns hym. And as Egesippus seith, as we fynden in *Ecclesiastica Historijs*, thei come togider to Iamys and seiden: 'We prey 85 the that thou wil reuokyn and clepyn ageyn the peple, for thei erren in Ihesu, wenyng that he were Crist. We biseche the that thou make suasion to al that come togider on pask day of Ihesu. To the we al shul obeyen, for of the bothe we and the peple bere testymonye and wittenesse þat thou art rightful and exceptist ner acceptist no mannes persone.' Which doon, 90 they anoon lifted hym vpon the pynnacle of the temple and with a grete vois thus diden crye: 'O moste rightful of al men, to whom we al owen and willen obtempren and obeyen, for as moche as this peple errith aftir Ihesu which was crucified, shewe ws and here openly declare what the semyth in this mater.' To whom Iamys with a myghty spirite thus aunswerid ageyn 95 and seid: 'Wherfore and what aske ye me of the sonne of man? Takith hede and seeth that he sitteth on the right side of the moste souereyn vertue and shal commen ageyn to iugen and denyen the quycke and the dede.' This heryng, the cristen peple were glad and mury and with right gode wyl herden hym. But the Phariseus and the scribes were sory and hevy and seiden 100

eche to othir: 'We diden evil to asken such a wittenesse to be youen. But
goo we vp and throwe we hym doun hedelyngis that othir mow ben aferde
and presume nat to bileven hym.' And anoon thei cryed al with a lowde
voice and seiden: 'Oo the rightful man errith.' Which seid they wenten
105 vp and diden as they seyden. And whan thei had hedlyngis throwen hym
doun, thei kest at hym stoones and seiden: 'Stoone we now Iamys the rightful.' But, notwithstondyng the cruel and boistous throwyng doun, yit he
myght nat deyen, but with grete laboure and peyne he turned hymself vp
on his knees and liftid vp his handis and seid: 'Foryive hem lorde, I bi-
110 seche the, for thei wote nat what thei doon.' And than oon of the prestis
of the sonnes of Recab cried and seid: 'Sparith, sirs, I prey you. What doo
ye? This rightful man whom ye stoonen preyeth for you.' Than oon of
hem hent a fullers batte in his hande, and with a grete stroke hitte hym on
the hede and smett oute his braynes. *Hec Egesippus*. And with this martir-
115 dame he went to our lorde, whos body thei buried beside the temple. And
f. 98va whan the peple wold han vengid his deth | and taken and punysshed the
malefactours, thei priuely fledden awey.

Aftir Iosephus opynyon, for the synne of this Iamys deth wax the
destruccion of Ierusalem and the dispersion of the Iewys. But our doc-
120 tours seyn that not oonly for his deth, but principally for Cristis iniurious
deth, was the destruccion of Ierusalem, aftir that our lorde seid therof in
the gospel: 'They shul nat thyn enemyes levyn in the or [oo] stoon vpon
anothir, for as moche as thou hast nat knowen the tyme of thy visitacion.'

But, for as moche that God wil nat synful mannes deth, and that thei
125 shuld noon excusacion han, he abode here penaunce fourty wynter and
clepid hem to penaunce by his apostlis, and moste by Iamys which contynuelly and dayly prechid amongis hem. And whan our lorde saugh that he
myght nat reuokyn hem ageyn by ammonicion and prechyng, he wolde han
ferid hem at the lest by wondirfull tokenes shewyng. For, in these fourty
130 wynter grauntid hem to doon in penaunce, many wondirful and marveilous tokenys were shewid amonge hem, as seith Iosephus. For a bright
shynyng sterre, in al thyngis like a swerd, was seen hangen ovir the citee
an hole yere togider byfore the excidion brennyng as a flame of fyre. Also
at a certeyn fest clepid *Festum Azimorum*, at nyne of the clok at even, such
135 a brightnesse of a lightenyng environed the temple and the autier that al
men wende that it had ben light day. In the same fest also a yung hekfere,
that is to seyn a yung cowe, the which was brought to ben offrid amonge
the mynistres handis, brought forthe a lambe. Also a few daies aftir, ner
at the sunnes goyng doun, there were seyn by al that region chariettis and

122 oo] *om.*

charis born abouten in the eyre, and hoostis of armed men medlid amonge   140
the cloudis and vnwarly to bysiegen the citees. In anothir feste also clepid Pentecost, whan the prestis were goon into the temple for to doon
the custumable cerimonyes of her sacrifises, thei herdyn certeyn noyses
and voises seyeng on this wise: 'Go we hens fro this place.' Four yere also
biforn the bataile, a man whos name was Ihesus the sonne of Ananye, at   145
[the fest of] the tabernaclis bigan to cryen and seyen: 'A vois from the est,
a vois from the west, a vois from the four wyndis, a vois vpon Ierusalem
and vpon the temple, a vois vpon husbondis and wives, and a vois vpon
al the peple.' This man was takyn and betyn for his cryeng, but he myght
noon othir seyn, and the more that he was betyn the more myghtily he did   150
cryen. He was also brought to a iuge, examyned with cruel tormentis and
his flessh rent even vnto the boones. But he neither preyed ner wept, but
with a moornyng and an howlyng vois euery othir worde rehersid ageyn
the same wordis, addyng this therto: 'Wo, wo vnto the men of Ierusalem.'
Hec Iosephus.   155
      And whan the Iewys than, neither by ammonicions and prechyng wold
be conuertid and turned, ner by wondirful signes and prodigious tokenys
wolde be ferid, aftir the fourtith yere God brought Vaspasian and Tite,
themperours, the which vttirly destroied the citee of Ierusalem. Of whom
commyng thider this was the occasion as it is writen | in *quadam historia*   f. 98vb
licet apocripha. Pilat, seeyng that he wrongefully had condempned inno-   161
cent Ihesu, and dredyng the offence of Tiberye themperour, for to excusen
hym he sent to Rome oon clepid Albinus. The which same tyme Vaspasianus held in Galacia the monarchia vndir Tiberie. And so the massager of
Pilate, driven in the see with contrarie wyndis, was brought to Galacie and   165
ledde to Vaspasian. For the custoume was in that cuntree that whosoevir
were shypbroken and come vp there, he shuld ben bondeman & seruaunt
to the prynce. And whan this Albinus was brought to Vaspasians presence
he freyned of hym what he was, fro whens he came, and whider he wolde
haue goon. 'Of Ierusalem', quoth he, 'I am, and fro thens I entendid to han   170
goon to Rome.' 'Thou commest', quoth Vaspasian ageyn, 'fro the londe of
wise men. I trowe thou art a leche and knowist the crafte of medicyne, and
therfore thou must cure me.' This Vaspasian had a grevous disease, for of
youth he bare in his nosethrilles a certeyn kynde of wormes clepid waspis,
whereof his name was clepid Vaspasian, and nevir no leche coude coveryn   175
hym therof. 'Siker sir', quoth Albyn, 'leche am I noon, ner I can no skille
of medicynes and therfore I may nat cure the.' 'Certeyn', quoth Vaspasian
ageyn, 'and but thou cure me thou shalt dey therfore'. 'Now truly, sir',

146 the fest of] the fest of the fest of

quoth Albinus, 'he that made blynde men to seen, made clene lepris, drofe
180 oute devils fro mennys bodies and reised vp men from deth to life, knoweth wele that I kan no skille of lechecrafte.' 'Who is he that thou spekist
of?' quoth Vaspasian ageyn. 'Forsothe', quoth he, 'this was Ihesus of Nazareth, whom the Iewys for envie han crucified. In whom yf thou bileve thou
shalt sone aftir han helth.' 'This I bileve verreily' quoth Vaspasian, 'that
185 he which reised vp dede myght lightly curen me of my sikenesse.' And as
sone as he had seid this the wormes fellen oute of his nosethril and he was
perfitely hool. Wherof Vaspasian, fulfilled with grete ioye and gladnesse for
his sodeyn helth, seid thus: 'I am right siker that he which thus hath curid
me and made me hool was Goddis sone. Wherfore sikerly I wil taken leve
190 of themperour and goon to Ierusalem with stronge hand and vengyn his
deth vpon tho fals treitours which slowen hym'. And with that he turned
hym to Albyne and seid: 'I graunte the life and thy goodis, and licence to
turnen hoom ageyn to thyn owen cuntree bicause of thy gode tidyngis.'

And anoon he hymself went to Rome and toke licence of themperoure
195 to goon vnto Ierusalem and to destroien that and the Iewys. Which licence
had he went hoom ageyn and prouidence made for his iournee. And certeyn yeris aftir the tyme of Nero, whan the Iewys rebellid ageyns thempyre,
Vaspasianus gadrid a grete peple and went to Ierusalem. And on Pasch day
he leid a siege therto stronge and myghty and closid therin grete multi-
200 tude the was commen to the solempnyte of the feste. And a certeyn tyme
biforn that Vaspasian cam to the feithful peple the which weren in Ierusalem were monestid by the holi goste to goon oute of Ierusalem and that
f. 99ra thei shuld goon ovir Iordan into | a strength clepid Pellam, that, whan thei
were oute, the vengeaunce of God myght fallen vpon the cursid citee and
205 on the synful peple.

But yit first, or than Vaspasianus cam to Ierusalem, he assautid a citee
of Iuerie clepid Ionaperam, wherin Iosephus was prince and duke and souereyn ruler. But Iosephus with his soudiours myghtely resistid hem at the
begynnyng. But aftirward, whan he saw that the citee must nedis be dis-
210 troied, he, with elleven othir Iewys, wenten into a cave vndir the erthe and
there hidde hem. Where whan thei had ben four daies ovircommen with
hungir, the Iewys, withoute assent of Iosephus, had levir deyen there than
to yelden hem to Vaspasianus seruise. And the advise of hem was that eche
of hem shuld sleen othir and offren vp her blode to God in a sacrifise. And
215 for as moche that Iosephus was the worthiest of hem alle, thei wolden haue
slayn hym first, that thurgh shedyng of his blode God myght be quemyd.
Or as anothir cronicle seith, the cause why thei wolden haue slayn hemself
was that thei shuld nat yelden hem into Romayns handis. But Iosephus, as

a prudent man and nat willyng to deyen, made hymself bothe iuge of the
deth and of the sacrifise, and made lottis to be youen bitwix two and two   220
which shul dyen first. And thus thurgh lottis al slayne safe oon and hymself, Iosephus as a man swyfte and deliver hent the swerd oute of his felaus
hande and bad hym chesyn withoute more delay whethir he had lever liven
or deyen. 'Siker', quoth he, tremelyng for feer, 'I recuse nat to liven, yf I
mow fynde grace of the.'   225

And anoon aftir Iosephus spak prively with a seruaunt of Vaspasian with
whom he had ben famuliar biforn, and preyed hym to getyn hym. And so
he did. And whan Iospehus was brought to Vaspasians presence he seid to
hym thus: 'Siker thou haddist deserued deth ne had this mannys preyer
deliverid the.' 'Sir', quoth Iosephus ageyn, 'whatsoevir is mysdoon it may   230
be changid into bettir.' 'Why,' quoth Vaspasian, 'what may he doon the
which is bounden?' 'Somwhat, sir', quoth Iosephus, 'shal I doon, yf thou
wilt enclynen thyn eeris to my wordis.' 'I graunte the', quoth Vaspasian,
'to spekyn. And what gode thyng thou wilt seyn I shal pesibly heren it.'
Quoth Iosephus ageyn: 'Syr, themperour of Rome is dede and the senat   235
hath chosen the in his place.' 'Yf thou be a prophete', quoth Vaspasian,
'why ne warneddist thou this that thei shuld be subiect vnto my power?'
'Siker', quod Iosephus, 'fourty daies togider I tolde hem so.'

In this meantyme come the legatis of the Romayns and tolde hym how
he was chosen emperour and ledden hym forthe with hem to Rome. And   240
he lefte Titus his sone in the siege of Ierusalem, and Titus, as it is in *eadem
historia Ypocrifa*, heryng that his fadir was enhauncid to thempyre, fel in
a sodeyn ioye thurgh which there toke hym a palesye, by drawyng togider of his synews, and tormentid hym grevously in that oo thye. Iosephus,
heryng that Titus was seke, diligently enquerid the sekenesse, the cause   245
and the tyme. The cause and the sore was nat knowen. But Iosephus of
the tyme, as a man prudent and wise, coniectid bothe cause and sore, kno-
wyng wele that of a sodeyn | superexcellent ioye he was made thus feble. f. 99rb
Wherfore, consideryng that contraries ben curid with contraries: as colde
with hete, and ioye with sorowe, and gladnesse with angir, he bigan anoon 250
to enqueren yf there were ony man which that he did gretely haten. And
anoon he was enfourmed that there was oon in the hoost whom withoute
grete trouble and angir he myght neither seen ner heryn hys name spoken
of. This knowen, he went to Tite and seid to hym on this wise: 'Sir, yf
thou desire to ben curid, graunte me that whomsoevir I bryng to thi pre- 255
sence he shal goon awey harmelees.' Which grauntid, he made a table to
be sett even ageyns Titis table, where he sett hymself to mete, and on his

right hand hym whom Titus so sore hatid. And whan Titus saw hym sitten
so nere hym and putt to so grete worship, anoon he grucchid in hymself
260 and wex angry and troublyd that he myght nat vengen hym. And sodeynly
enflamed with wretth, his senewys slakid ageyn with hete, the which were
contract with colde, and brought ageyn to temperaunce and so curid. For
which cause Titus toke Iosephum into singuler frendship, and hym that
he hatid biforn to grace and foryivenesse. Aftir which tyme Titus two yere
265 bisiegid the citee of Ierusalem.

In which tyme, amonge many myschievis that fellen vnto the Iewys,
this was a grete: that such an hungir and famyn was amongis hem that
the children from her fadris and modris, and fadris and modris from her
children, husbondis from her wives, and wyves from her husbondis, nat
270 oonly oute of her handis but eke henten awey her mete from her mouthis.
Yung men, stronge by wey of age, goyng as ymages fel doun dede by the
wey for hungir. Such as buried dede men, ful often for verrey febilnesse
and hungir fel doun dede vpon hem. The stynke of the caraynes of dede
folke was so intollerable that they myght nat suffren it within the citee,
275 wherfore they kesten tho that they myght not buryen ovir the wallis. And
whan walkyng aboute the wallis he sawe the valis lyen ful of dede bodies,
and al the ny cuntre corrupt with the stynke therof, he lifted vp his handis
to heven and with wepyng eyne seid: 'Lorde God, thou seest wele that I
doo nat this.' And so grete was the famyn that they eten her shoes and her
280 girdels and dowys dung was solde by the weight.

A worthy matrone also bothe of nature and eke of fortune, as it is redde
in *Ecclesiastica Historia*, there was in that cuntre. Whom on a tyme bri-
gauntis and thevis robbid and spoiled so bare that thei lefte hir right nought
to eetyn. This noble matrone had but oo childe, a yung sone whom she had
285 hidde fro the thevis, and whan thei were past and goon she toke hym in
hir armes and, constreyned by hungir, seid on this wise: 'Of an infortunat
and vnhappy modir, o more vnhappy sone, in this bataile tyme and tyme of
direpcion and hungir, to whom shal I reseruen and kepyn the? Come hider
to me now, o swet sone, and to thi modir be mete, to thevis and raveynours
290 wodenesse, and to worldis which arn to commen fable and talkyng.' Which
f. 99ᵛᵃ wordis seid, anoon she slough hir sone & | seeth hym and ete the haluen-
dele and hid that othir part. And whan the soudiours and ravenours felt
the odour of flessh, anoon thei brosten into the hous and thretid hir to dyen
lesse than she wolde deliveren hem the flessh wherof thei felt the savour.
295 At which thretis she brought forth the delicate membris of hir tendir sonne
and seid: 'Loo, sirs, the best part I haue reserued and kept to you.' Which,
whan thei seyn, such an horrour came vpon hem of the sight that thei coude

nat spekyn oo worde. 'Fere ye nat', quoth she, 'this is my sonne. The synne of the deth is myn. Wherfore etith sikerly, for I haue bigunne to eten first the childe that I bare. Yf pitee and horrour so ovircome you that ye wil nat 300 eetyn, I shal eten vp that othirdele as I haue bigunne.' And whan thei herd this, tremelyng for feer eche of hem wenten awey, oon aftir anothir, and leten hir allone with al togider.

Aftir this the secund yere of Vaspasians empyre, Titus toke Ierusalem and destroied vttirly the temple and subuertid the citee. And liche as Iudas 305 solde the Iewys Criste for thritty pens, so he for oo peny solde thritty Iewys. And, as Iosephus tellith, nynty and seven thousand were sold, and elleven vndir thousand perisshed with swerd and hungir. It is red also, quoth Ianuence, that whan Titus entrid Ierusalem he fonde a grete thicke wal therin, the which he made anoon to be bored thurgh, wherin he fonde an olde com- 310 mely man. Which whan he askid who he was he aunswerid and seid that he was Ioseph of Arimathie, whom the Iewys mured for he buried Criste. 'Not forthan', quoth he, 'fro the tyme that I was mured vnto this, I haue be fedde with hevenly fode and refresshid with Godly light.' Nevirtheles Nichodemus in his gospel seith that, whan the Iewys had shett vp Ioseph 315 of Arimathie, Crist in his vprist deliverid hym and ledde hym hoom. But forto accorden hem bothen it may be seid that whan he was ledde oute by Criste, for as moche as he wold nat cessyn to prechen Criste, taken by the Iewys he was shett vp ageyn.

Whan Vaspasianus was dede Titus his sone was emperour aftir hym, 320 the which was a man of grete pitee and of grete liberalite. And so gode he was, as seith Eusebie Cesarience in his cronicle, and Seynt Ierome wittenessith the same, that what day he remembrid hym that he had noo gode dede doon, he wolde sey to hem that weren abouten hym on this wise: 'O frendis, frendis, this day haue I loste.' Longe aftir this tyme, certeyn 325 Iewys wolden han reedified and renewid the citee of Ierusalem. And whan thei commen erely on a morowe thei founden many crossis in the place congelid of the dewe, the which whan they seyn thei fledde awey, gretely aferde. And whan thei commen ageyn on the next morowe, as seith Miletus in his cronicle, they founden eche man sowed to his garnementis blody 330 crossis, wherof thei ageyn, grete aflemyd, turned ageyn to flight. But the thrid tyme whan thei commen ageyn, thei were enflamed with the grete hete which cam oute of the erthe, and weren vttirly brent and consumed.

333 and weren] weren

[76. INVENTION OF THE CROSS]

The feste of the Inuencion of the holy crosse |

f. 99vb   The Inuencion or the fyndyng of the holy cros was aftir two hundrid
yere from the resurreccion of our lorde Ihesu Criste. In the gospel of
Nichodeme is red that whan Adam was seke, Seeth his sone went to the
5   gatis of paradise and askid of our lorde the oile of mercy, with which he
myght anoynten his fadris hert and so recuren his helth. To whom Michael
th'archangel appierid and seid: 'Neither laboure ner wepe forto optenyn
and geten the oile of the tree of mercy. For pleynly it may nat be gett til
five thousand and five hundrid yere be fulfilled', albeit that from Adam to
10   the passion of Criste aftir somme computacion runne but five thousand
yere and thre and thritty.

In anothir place, quoth Ianuence, it is red that the angel toke Seeth of
the tree that Adam synned in, and seid that whan it brought forth frute
his fadir shuld be made hool. And whan Seeth came ageyn to his fadir and
15   fonde hym dede, he plantid the braunche vpon his fadris grave, the which
grew into a fair tree and endurid vnto Salamons tyme.

Salamon, consideryng the beautevousnesse of the tree, commaundid it
to ben hewen doun and to be leid in the hous where the trees leyn which
were ordeyned for the bieldyng of Salamons temple. And, as Iohannes
20   Belett seith, it myght nevir be founden apt ner even to no werk which it
was applied to. For it was evir to short or to longe, natwithstondyng the
rightful mesure takyng therof. Wherfore the werkmen in her indignacion
reprovyd it, and, as a tree vnworthy to ony othir occupacion or mynisterie,
thei kest it ovir a lake there beside and made therof a fote pety brigge.

25   And whan the queen of Saba cam to heryn of the wisdam of Kyng
Salamon, and wolde haue passid the seid lake, she saw in spirite that the
saluatour of the worlde shuld ben hangen on the same tree, she wold nat
passen ovir but knelid doun and worshippid it. Nevirtheles in *Historijs*
Ecclesiasticis it is redde that the quene of Saba sawe the seid tree in *Domo*
30   *Saltus*, that is to seyn in the hous wher al the tymbre which longid to the
bieldyng of the temple was leid. And whan she came hoom ageyn to hir
hous, she sent worde to Salamon that on that tree shuld oon ben hangyn
by whos deth the kyngdam of the Iewys shuld be distroyed. This heryng,
Salamon made it to be take thens and depe to be buried in the inwardly
35   depthe of the erthe.

Longe aftir which tyme where it lay was made a wattryng wayre in
which the peplis clepid Nathanei wesshen in the hoostis which shuld ben

offrid in the temple. And this was the watir the which an aungel came
doun to at certeyn tymes and mevid it. Aftir which mevyng, what seke
man entrid first was cured and made hool whatsoevir his sikenesse were, 40
as seith the gospel. And this cure was nat oonly causid of the commyng
doun of the angel but also of the vertue of the tree which lay therin, as
it is commounly opyned of doctours. But whan the tyme of Cristis passion bigan to neighen the seid tree bigan to houen aboue the watir and to
swymmen. Which whan the Iewys seyn, thei tooken it and made therof a 45
crosse with othir thre divers trees. For, as it is commounly seid and hol-
den, Cristis crosse was made of four sundry kyndis of trees: as of palme, |
cipresse, olive and cedyr. The foote bynethen in which was the morteys f. 100ra
was of a cedre tree, the stocke stondyng right vp wheron the body lenyd
was of cipresse, the ovirthwerte tree whereto his handis were nailed were 50
of palme, and the table abouen his hede wherin his title was writen: 'Ihesus
Nazarenus Rex Iudeorum' was of an olive tree. These four maner differen-
cis and distinccions of trees semyth mystily to touchen Poule th'appostle in
his Epistle *ad Colocenses*, where he seith thus: 'Be ye groundid and foundid
in charite, so that ye mow comprehendyn and vndirstonden what is the 55
brede, the length, the height and depthe.' The which wordis Seynt Austyn expowneth on this wise: 'This is vndirstonden of the crosse of Crist:
the brede wherof is seid the tree lyeng ovirthwert whereto Cristis handis
were nailed. The leng[th] is from the erthe to the brede in which al the
body henge. The height is fro the brede vpward, in which the hede lenyd. 60
The depth is that which was hyd in the erthe.' *Hec Augustinus*.

This holi crosse two hundrid yere and more was hyd in the erthe and
of blissid Helene, Constantyns modir, founden on this wise. Vpon a tyme
whan Constantyne was emperour, a grete multitude rebellyng ageyns
thempire assemblid at the grettest flode of Europe, clepid Danubius, pur- 65
posyng to passen ovir and to subiugaten, or to putten vndir her empire, al
the regions from thens into the east. Ageyns whom Constanty[n]e themperour came with al his powere and leid his hoste beside the seid flode.
And whan he sawe the multitude of the wilde peple daily growen and
encresen, and proudely begynnen to passyn ovir the flode, he wex right 70
sore aferd, consideryng wele and wenyng that the next day aftir thei were
like to make a bataile. And on the next nyght an angel woke themperour
and bad hym loken vp to hevenward, where he sawe a tokne of a crosse of
a grete light, wherin was writen with lettris of golde: 'Constantyne, thou
shalt ovircommen in this signe and haue the victorie.' Thurg[h] which 75
vision themperour gretely comfortid anoon did maken a signe of a crosse

59 length] lenght   67 Constantyne] Constantyme   75 Thurgh] thurg

and made it to be borne bifore his hoost, and, a sawte made vpon his enemyes, he putt hem to flight and slough of hem a grete multitude. Which
doon, themperour anoon gadrid togider al the bisshops of the templis and
80 diligently enquerid of hem what goddis signe it was in which he had the
victorye. And al them aunsweryng that they wist nevir, certeyn cristen
men putten hem in prees and declarid vnto themperour the misterie of
the crosse and the feith of the trinite. And anoon he bilevid perfitely into
Criste, and received the holy baptesme of Eusebie the bisshop Cesarience.
85 But somme seyn that this Constantyn was nat he whom we redyn baptised
of the Pope Siluestir, but it was his fadir as somme cronicles seyn.

    And whan this olde Constantyne was dede, his sonne Constantyn, reig-
nyng for hym aftir that he was baptised of Seynt Siluestir, remembryng of
his fadris victorie, sent his modir to Ierusalem forto fynde the crosse as it
90 shal be seid aftir. Nevirtheles *Historia Ecclesiastica* tellith this victorie to
haue ben had of anothir persone and in othir wise. For there it is seid that
when Maxencius the tiraunt vsurpid the Romayn empire ageyns the sena-
f. 100rb tis decree, Constantyne | came to fighten with hym besiden the brigge of
Malbin. And whan he often had liftid vp his eyen to heven and askid help,
95 he, by nyght in his slepe, saugh in the east a tokne of the crosse as bright
as fire and angels stondyng by, which seiden to hym thus: 'Constantyne,
in this signe thou shalt haue victorie.' And as Constantyn, as seith *Historia tripartita*, stode marueilyng what this myght meanen, Criste the next
nyght appierid vnto hym with the same signe of the crosse, and bad this
100 signe shuld ben enprentid in al parties of his oost and it shuld helpen hem.
By this reuelacion Constantyn made glad, conceived ful hope of victorie
and anoon he enprentid the signe of the crosse in his forhede and chargid that in euery knyghtis baner shuld be sett the same. And in his right
hand beryng a crosse of golde, preyed God that he wolde nat suffre that
105 right hande which was adorned with the signe of the crosse to be defoulid
with the rede moisture of Romayns blode, but that he wold graunten hym
victorie of the tiraunt withoute shedyng of blode.

    And Maxence, as it is seid, there had ordeyned for a deceit that ship-
pis cheyned togider shuld stonden from that oo side of the flode to that
110 othir, al of oon height and so cured with erthe and flackis as it had ben
a pleyn wey, þat whan Constantyn and his peple came therupon shuld so
toltren and waueryn that thei shuld nat mow stonden forto fighten. And
whan Constantyn cam ny to the flode, Maxence, with a grete brunt of spirite, with a few peple went hastily ageyns hym, chargyng al his peple to
115 folowen anoon aftir hym. And, not remembryng of his brigge, or he was
ware he, with his few, was even theron. And so with that he wolde haue

deceived Constantyn he was deceivid hymself, and so fel into the flode and was drynkelid. Which doon, anoon al the oost of Maxence receivid Constantyn gladly and concordely for her lorde and for her emperoure, and so victorie was had withoute blode-shedyng. And, as it is red in an autentik cronicle, Constantyne at that tyme bylevid nat perfitely ner was nat baptised til longe aftir whan he had seyn vision of Petir and Poule, and was made clene from his lepre by Seynt Siluestir, as it is seid biforn in his life. Aftir which tyme he bilevid fully.

And aftir that he sent his modir to Ierusalem to seke the holi crosse in whos signe he had biforn of Maxence the victorie. This Helene was Kyng Colkyns doughtir of Colchestir, as the cronicle seith, whom Constantyn the elder, commyng into Ingelonde, weddid both for hir beaute and also for she was hir fadris oonly childe and his eyre. And whan this blissid womman came to Ierusalem, she chargid al the wise men thurghoute al that region to ben gadrid togider and to ben brought byforn hyr. This heryng the Iewys, thei wex sore aferd and seid thus amonge hem: 'What trowe ye is cause that the quene makith vs to ben gadrid togider?' And anoon oon clepid aunswerid ageyn and seid: 'I wote wele', quoth he, 'she wil enqueryn of ws where the crosse bicame wheron Ihesu was crucified. But beth al right ware that noon of you be it aknowe. For this I warn you sikerly, yf ye doo, our lawe shal be sett aside and voided and al our fadris tradicions shul vttirly be destroied. Zacheus my grauntfadir | tolde to Symon my fadir and he, whan he shuld deyen, tolde me that the crosse of Crist shuld be sought. "Wherefore, sone", quoth he, "whan it is sought, shew where it is or than thou suffre torment therfore. For aftir the tyme that it is founden shal nevir kynrede of the Iewys reignen. But thei which worshippen hym that was crucified shul reignen, for he is Criste the sone of God". And I', quoth he, 'seid ageyn to hym on this wise: "Fadir, sith our fadris knowen hym verreily to ben the sone of God, why crucified thei hym?" "God knoweth", quoth he sone ageyn, "that I nevir was in the counceil of hem. But often and many sithes I geynseid hem. But, sonne, this is the verrey truthe. For as moche as he vndirnam the Pharisens vices and synnes, they made hym to ben crucified. Nevirtheles he rose ageyn the thridde day and the fourtyth day aftir, hys disciplis seeyng, he thirled heven. Into whom Stevyn thi brothir bilevid, whom also the Iewis wodenesse stooned. Wherfor, sonne", quoth he, "beware that thou neither blaspheme hym ner his disciplis".' 'Iudas', quoth the Iewys ageyn to hym, 'we nevir herdyn ner knewen such thyngis. Wherfore, yf the quene aske the ony thyng herof, beware thou tel hir no thyng therof.'

And whan thei were brought bifore the quene and she askid hem of the

f. 100va

place where Criste was crucified and they wolde nat tellen it hir, she commaundid hem alle anoon to be brent. Of which sentence they sore aferde
deliverid to hir Iudas, seyeng on this wise: 'This man, lady, which was the
160 sonne of a rightful man and of a prophete, knoweth the lawe best of ws
alle. And therfore he shal telle the al that evir thou wilt asken of hym.' At
which worde she anoon lete goon al that othir, callid Iudas to hir and seid:
'Deth and life arn sett bifore the; chese which thou wilt. Shew me the place
clepid Golgatha where Crist was crucyfied that I may fynden his crosse.'
165 'How myght I', quoth Iudas, 'knowen that place, sith two hundrid yere ben
past sith this was doon and I was nat borne that tyme?' 'By hym that was
crucified', quoth she ageyn, 'but yf thou telle me truthe I shal make the
to deyen for hungir.' And forthwith she made hym to be cast into a grete
depe dyche and there to ben enfamyned.

170 And whan he had ben there six daies withoute mete, he preyed that
he myght be taken oute and he shuld telle the quene al that she askid.
Takyn vp than and led to the place where he assigned and a preyer made of
hym in the same place, sodeynly the erthe bigan to styren and meven and
therewith came vp oute of the grounde an odour of marveilous swetenesse,
175 and so refresshid Iudas that he knelid doun and clappid bothen his handis and seid on this wise: 'In truthe, Criste, thou art the saluatour of the
worlde!' And in that same place, as it is red in *Ecclesiastica Historia*, was
Venus temple, the which themperour Adrianus had doo made there for
that entent that whatsoevir cristen man wolde doo worship in that place
180 he shulde semyn to worshippen Venus. For which cause the place was litle
f. 100vb vsid and nere foryeten. Which temple | anoon the quene made vttirly to be
distroied and the place to be made clene and purified. Which doon, Iudas
tuckid vp his lappis and manly bigan to delven and twenty fote within the
grounde he fonde thre crossis, the which anoon he toke vp and brought
185 hem to the quene. But whan thei coude nat discernen and knowen Cristis
crosse from the thevis crossis, anoon they born al thre and leyden hem in
the myddis of the citee, preyeng God there to shewen his glorie and worship, thurgh which they myght knowen his crosse from that othir. And
anoon, aboute nyne of the clocke, a yung man was brought forby for to
190 be buried, whom Iudas made forto be sett doun there vpon his bere. And
first he leid oo crosse vpon hym and sithen anothir, and he rose nat. But
as sone as the thridde crosse was leid vpon hym, even forthwith he rose
vp ageyn from deth to life. In *Historijs Scolasticis* it is seid that this experi-
ment of the crossis shuld haue be doon vpon oon of the worthy wommen
195 of the citee which lay on deyeng. Seynt Ambrose seith that Cristis crosse
was discerned and knowen from that othir by the title which Pilat had sett

vpon the crosse and was founden therwith. And whan this was doon, the
devil cried in the eyre alofte and seid: 'O Iuda, Iuda, what hasthou doon?
Thou hast doon contrary to anothir Iudas. For he, by my suasion, betraied
his maister and thou, Ihesu restreynyng me, hast founden his crosse. By   200
hym I wan many soulis, by the me semyth I shal lesyn thoo which I had
wunnen. By hym I reigned in the peple, by the I am throwen oute of my
reigne. Nevirtheles I shal quyte the thi while for I shal reisen ageyns the a
kyng which shal forsaken the feith of crucified Criste, and make the with
tormentis for to doo the same or els cruelly to deyen.' And this the devil   205
ment by Iulian the Apostata, the which aftirward, whan Iudas was bisshop
of Ierusalem, examyned hym with many tormentys and made hym Cristis
martir, as it shal be seid anoon aftir. And whan Iudas herd the devil cryen
on this wise, he was nothyng aferd, but boldely and constauntly he cursid
the devil and seid: 'Criste mote dampne the, o wicked, in the botomeles   210
depthe of evirlestyng fyre.'

Aftir which tyme Iudas was baptised and named Quiriacus. And whan
the bisshop of Ierusalem deyd, he was ordeyned bisshop aftir. And whan
blissid Helene had thus gete the holy crosse, she aftir desired to han the
nailes which weren in his handis and in his fete. Wherfore she went to the   215
bisshop Quiriac and preyed hym to goon ageyn to the seid place and to see-
kyn hem. Whider whan he came and had made his preyer to God, anoon
the nailes appierid in the erthe, shynyng as bright as golde, the which he
anoon bare vnto the quene. And she, knelyng and bowyng doun, worshippid hem and receivid hem with grete reuerence. Which had, she departid   220
the holy crosse into two partis and left that oon al closid in a caps of siluer,
and that othir she bare vnto hir sone with the nailes. Wherof, as Eusebius Cesariensis, she made hym bridels to riden with to bataile and araied
the helme for his hede. Somme othir seyen, as Gregorius Turonensis, that
of the four nailes which weren | in Cristis handis and fete, twoo Helene   f. 101ra
putte in themperours bridel, oon vpon his ymage at Rome and the fourth   226
she did throwe in a swelow in Mari Adriatico, where bifore that dede no
shippe mygiht passen vnperisshed, and aftir the passage was pesible. And al
these thyngis doon, she ordeyned this feste of the Inuencion of the crosse
solempnely to ben halowyd. Seynt Quiriac was slayn aftirward by Iulyan   230
the Apostata for bicause that he fonde the holy crosse.

Whan this Iulyan oo tyme went to bataile ageyns the Persys, he wold
haue compellid the blissid bysshop Quiriac to the sacrifise of ydols. And
whan he sawe that he in no wise wold doon sacrifise, he did smyten of his
right hande, for as moche as with that hand he had writen many epistles by   235
which he reuokid many oon from the sacrifise of ydols. To whom Quiriacus

seid on this wise: 'Oo, wode hounde, moche hasthou now doon for me. For,
er than I bilevid in Criste, I wrote many a lettre to the synagogys of the
Iewys, makyng grete suasions that noon of hem shuld bileven in Criste.
240 And now thou hast cutte awey the membre that sclaundrid my body.'
Whan Iulian herd this, he commaundid boilyng lede to be porid in his
mouth & aftir to be streyned vpon a bedde of iron, and hote coolys thervn-
dir and grees and salt to be cast therin. But Quiriacus nothyng mevid
therwith, Iulian thus seid to hym: 'At the leste, yf thou wilt nat sacrifisen
245 to our goddis, knouleche and sey the to be no cristen man, and I shal be
content.' And whan he in no wise wolde consent therto, Iulian did makyn
a depe pitte and filled it with venemous serpentis and made Quiriac to be
cast in even amongis hem for to han be stungen to the deth of hem. But
sodeynly al thei deiden and noon of oonys touchid hym. Aftir this Iulian
250 chargid hym to be plounchid in a cawdron ful of boilyng oile, wherein,
aftir he had signed hym with a tokne of the crosse, he went in frely and
gladly, preyeng that therin he myght ben baptised with the baptesme of
martirdam. Where Iulian made hym to be shoven thurgh the breste with a
swerde, and so he made an ende and slept in our lorde.

255   And how grete myght and vertu is it may ben evidently knowen by a
feithful notarie, whom, as we redyn, a wicche deceived and led hym into
a certeyn place where he gadrid togider a grete multitude of devels, bihe-
tyng hym that he shuld han habundaunce inough of richesse and worldly
goodis. And anoon he sawe a grete Ethyop sett vpon an high trone, and
260 rounde abouten hym other Ethiops stondyng with speris and battys in her
handis. And the grete Ethiope askid the wicche what he was whom he
had brought with hym. 'Sir,' quoth the wicche, 'it is your owen seruaunt.'
'Yf thou wilt than', quoth the Ethiope to the notarie, 'worshippen me
and be my seruaunt and forsaken Criste, I shal make the to sitten on my
265 right hand.' And whan the notarie herd this, anoon as he had blissid hym
and knoulecchid hym to be Cristis seruaunt, sodeynly al that multitude
of devels vanysshid awey. Not longe aftir which tyme, whan this notarie
went with his lorde into the temple of Seynt Sophie and both stoden |
f. 101rb bifore the ymage of the saluatour, his lorde sawe how the forseid ymage
270 sett his eyen fix vpon his notarie and diligently bihelden hym. And anoon
he made his seruaunt to stonden on the right hand of hym. Which doon,
he saw how the ymage turned his eyen and sett hem fixe ageyn vpon his
notarie. And yit efte ageyn he sett hym on his lefte hand and the ymage
chaungid his eyen. Whan the lorde perceived this, he chargid his notarie
275 to tellen hym of what merite he was anempst God, that his ymage in thys
wise fixed his eyen vpon hym. To whom he aunswerid ageyn and seid he

wist nat why it was, but it were for that oones biforn the devil he wold nat
forsakyn hym.

[77. JOHN BEFORE THE LATIN GATE]

The fest of Seynt Iohannes ante portam latinam

 Whan Seynt Iohannes th'appostle and euaungelist prechid in the citee
clepid Ephesus, the proconsul of the citee toke hym and wolde haue doon
hym sacrifis[e] to her goddis. And for he wolde nat he was putte in prison
and relacion was made to Domician themperour ageyns hym. In which 5
writyng he was clepid a cursid wycche, a contemptour of goddis and a
worshipper of hym that was crucified, wherfore anoon Domician chargid
hym to be brou3t to Rome. Whider whan he was commen, anoon for a despite his hede was shaven and he at the gate clepid *Porta Latina* was throwen
into a tunne ful of boilyng oyle, oute of which he came withoute ony hurt or 10
harme. In which place aftirwarde, of cristen men was made a chirche and
the day ordeyned to ben halowid as the day of his martirdam. And for as
moche as he wolde for nothyng cessen of prechyng of Cristis name, themperour Domician banysshid hym and exiled hym into the yle of Pathmos,
where by Goddis reuelacion he wrote the visions of the Apocalips. 15

 And nat oonly the Romayn emperours pursued th'appostles for thei
prechid Criste, but also and principally for they, withoute licence and auctorite of the senate, youen hym the name and the worship of a god, the
which they had defendid for to be doon. For, as it is seid in *Historia Ecclesiastica*, oo tyme whan Pilat had writen to Tibery themperour of Criste 20
many wundirful thyngis, and Tibery had assentid that his feith shuld be
received of the Romaynes, the senate geynseid and wolde nat admitten it,
for as moche as he was received and named a god withouten her auctorite.

 Anothir cause assigneth maister Iohannes Belett why themperour and
the senate pursued Criste and his disciplis. 'For as it to hem semyd', quoth 25
he, 'Criste was both proude and envious, for as moche as he wolde haue
no felawe with hym in godhede.' Orosius tellith anothir cause of her persecucion and is this: 'For as moche as Pilat wrote to Tiberie of Cristis
marveilous werkyng lettris and nat to the senate, thei had indignacion
therof and wold not suffren Crist to ben admitted amonge her goddis. 30
Wherfore Tiberie was wroth, and in his angir slow many of the senatours,
and many he banysshid and exiled.'

 Salome eke, Iohannes modir, heryng seyn that hir sonne was at Rome in

4 sacrifise] sacrifised

f. 101va prison, mevid by modirly compunccion | and pitee came to Rome to visi-
35 ten hym. And whan she came thider and herd seyn that he was banysshid
into the Ile of Pathmos, she wex ful hevy and sory. But in the returnyng
homeward ageyn she deied in Campanye, besiden a citee clepid Verulana,
and was buried in a cave of a cragge, where many a day it lay vnknowen
to cristen men, but aftirward it was knowen by the reuelacion of Iamys,
40 hir sonne. The which taken vp, was ful of marveilous redolence and so,
clarified with many and grete myraclis, was translatid into the seid citee
of Verulana and there buried with grete solempnyte; whos fest fallith the
eleventh kalend of Nouembre.

[78. MONICA]

The life of Seynt Monica Seynt Austyns modir
The blissid and holy matrone Seynt Monica, the modir of that glorious
and moste excellent doctour Seynt Austyn, as it may be founden in hir
sonnes writyng, sprange of hethen men liche as a rose doth of a thorne,
5 and in hir childehode was so educat & brought forth in the drede of God
in a feithful hous and in a gode membre of holi chirche and vndir Cristis yerde, that she forsoke such fode of metys as that age askith and moste
desireth, and in hir drynkyng was so demenyd that she dranke not watir to
ful seeth of hir threst. And so modestly was she brought forth, quoth he,
10 that rather by God she was made subiect to hir fadir and modir, than by
hir fadir and modir to God. 'And whan she came to ful yeris of age mari-
able she was youen by hir frendis to a paynym whos name was Patricius,
to whom she servid with al humbilnesse and busyed hir', quoth Austyn
spekyng to God of hir, 'to wynnen hym to the, lorde, spekyng of the to
15 hym by hir maners and condicions thurgh which thou madist hir faire and
reuerently marveilous, and marveilously amyable to hir husbonde.'
This Patricius, whan he was in gode mode was right curteys, ientle
and beniuolent. And in contrarious wise, yf he were in ony wise mevid
or grevid he was passyngly hasty, angry and malencolious. Which condi-
20 cion knowen of hir, she nevir wolde contrarien ner geynseyn hym in worde
ner in dede. Wherfore whan many othir matrones, whos husbondis were
not so fers ner so cruel, wolde in her communicacion, for the woundis
thei hadden in her face and elliswhere, vndirnymen her husbondis vices
and grucchen ageyns her condicions, she wolde benygnely blamen hem
25 and sadly ammonestyn hem to remembraunce how, sith thei had herd the
matrimonyal tablis rehercid as instrumentis by which thei were ordeyned

to ben subiectis and as handmaydens, thei aught not to grucchen ageyns
her husbondis. And whan thei marveiled how she demenyd hir, knowyng
wele that hir husbonde was a passyng hasty and fers man, that he nevir
bete her that ony body coude seyn, ne that nevir dissencion ner debate was   30
bitwix hem day ner nyght, and askid of hir the cause, she mekely aunswerid
h[e]m ageyn and tolde hem hir rule. The | which thei that obserued and   f. 101ᵛᵇ
kept it founden grete ease therin, and thankid hir for hir doctryne. And
thei that kept it nat were vexid as thei weren byforn.

And oo grete singuler yifte of grace amonge many othir had this blissid   35
Monica: for to setten rest and pees bitwix womman and womman, yf there
fel ony dissencion. For evir so pesibly she had hir and so prudently bitwix
hem, that whatsoevir either partie seid to hir of othir in hir absence, were it
nevir so cruelly vttrid and seid as commounly rancour and discorde vsith,
she nevir wolde tellen the absent partie more therof than ony thyng myght   40
availen to her reconciliacion and to setten pees and rest bitwix hem. And
for as moche as Seynt Poule seith that an vnfeithful man shal be savid by
a feithful womman, she wan hir husbonde to Cristis feith in his last daies.

And with how many teeris and with how gret labours she gat hir sonnes
conuersion, bothen in his legend it appierith and also he tellith it hym-   45
self in his Confessions. And whan, thurgh the merite of hir preyers and
the prechyng and the hooly exortacions of Seynt Symplician, hir sone
was conuertid and made a perfite cristen man and bigan to seruen God,
in felauship with many othir she anoon bicam the seruaunt of Goddis
seruauntis and had cure of alle, as though she had born hem alle, and so   50
serued hem al as thogh she had ben doughtir of hem al. Whosoevir knew
hir preysid, honoured and lovid God in hir chere outeward and the frutes
of hir conuersacion testifyeng, felt the presence of God in hir soule inward.
She was nevir but oo mannes wife, she quytte hir to hir fadir and to hir
modir as she aught by Goddis lawe. She governed hir hous to Goddys   55
worship, she had testymony in gode werkis, and as often she thought she
lost hir children as often as she sawe hem goon wille fro God.

And so, aftir the descripcion of Seynt Poule, she was a verrey perfite,
true widue. Moreovir, so perfitely the loue of God had woundid hir hert
that, as she had be fastenyd and nailed on the crosse with Criste, she bare   60
contynuelly the passion of Criste in hir mynde. Wherthurgh, vpon a day,
prevent of God in the blissyngis of swetnesse as she with hole deuocion
ententifly considerid the benefettis of our lorde Ihesu Criste, the which
of his benygnyte he shewid vnto ws in our nature, anoon she was profoundid with so grete grace of compassion and of compunccion that there   65

32 hem] hym

folowid aftir such and so plentevous dew of teerys wrongyn oute thurgh
the presse of the crosse, that a man myght seen the steppis therof in the
chirche on the pavyment. And the more busy she was to stoppen hem, the
more plentevously they diffoundid hem.

70   Also, ful often tyme the soule of hir was ravasshid with so grete a
drunkeship of the holy goste that, while she lay and restid somtyme al a
day togider and the kyng of blisse was in the reclinatorie of hir hert, neither voice was herd of hir ner sence, ner felyng was perceived in hir. For
that pees of God which passith al witte and kunnyng had so ovirleid and
75   buryed al hir bodyly felyngis and wittes that vnnethe the matrones and hir
next neighbours pluckyng and prickyng hir myght exciten hir and awaken
f. 102ra   hir from that | pricke of deuocion.

Anothir tyme also, whan the seid handmaiden of Criste shuld receiven
the sacrament of Cristis precious body, she was so rapt with the spirite of
80   compunccion and deuocion that she was seen lyfted vp a cubite from the
erthe. And notwithstondyng that she was wone to be moste quyete, cried
moste swetely and seid: 'Flye we to heven, flye we to heven!' With which
crie she replevisshid and fulfilled Austyn hir sone, and al the meynee of hir
housholde, with an inestimable ioye and gladnesse, seeyng the grete grace
85   of compunccyon and of deuocion that God had shewid in hir.

This blissyd womman loued excellently wele the holy bysshop Seynt
Ambrose, for as moche as he was cause of the gostely helthe of Austyn hir
sonne. And he therageyn lovid hir singulerly for hir hooly and religious
conuersacion, and for she was feruent in spirite in gode werkis, and for
90   noon houre she lefte withoute preyer and preysyng of God, gretely rei-
oyssyng that he sawe such a modir of such a sonne. And of hir natural
witte, enflamed with natural wisdam thurgh the special grace of God, spekyng hir sone in sentence seith on this wise: 'In disputacion of a not litle
thyng, but of a right grete thyng, the which I remembrid me and putt it
95   into a boke, so grete and so excellent hir reson and hyr witte appierid vnto
me, that aftir my felyng and myn vndirstondyng nothyng myght more ably
and more conueniently ben alludid and ascried to verrey and true philosophie. Wherfore', quoth he, 'fro thensforward I provided and ordeyned that
whan leyser and oportunyte haboundid that ony thyng of diuinite shuld be
100   communed and disputid, that she shuld nat ben absent, so grete excellence
of witte and reson I fonde in hir communyng.'

And whan that Austyn hir sone was conuertid and baptised and made
a perfite cristen man, and he and she with many othir returnyng ageyn to
Affric weren at Hostye abidyng shippyng, it happid hem tweyn to stonden
105   togider allone at a wyndowe, commonyng and talkyng of the evirlastyng

life of seyntis in heven, the which neither eigh hath seyn, ner eer herd, ner hert fully thought. In which communicacion the worlde, with alle the delectacions therof, was so litle apprised and sette by in hir affeccion and so lothesumme and so tedious to hir, that at the last she brak oute with these wordis and seid: 'Siker sone, what I shuld lenger doon here or why 110
I am here now I wote not, for fully al the hope of this worlde is to me in contempte and in despite. Oo thyng oonly, certeyn, there was for which I desired to taryen and abiden here a while, that is to seyn that I myght, er than I passid hens, seen the, sonne, a perfite cristen man. And God of his mercyful grace hath perfourmed my desire more plentevously than I askid 115
it, sith I see the, al erthely felicite had in contempt, the feithful seruaunt of Criste.'

'Aftir whiche tyme five daies she langured in the accesse, so grevously laboured that she sempt to ben alienat somwhat from her wittis. But sone aftir, whan she came ageyn to hirself and bihelde me and my brethern ston- 120
dyng abouten hir astoyned with moornyng and hevynesse, she seyde thus to me and to my brothir: "Puttith here to sepulture your modir, the which sone shal deyen." And at that | worde', quoth Austyn, 'whan I gan moor- f. 102rb
nen and wepyn, my brothir seid that he wolde nat that she shuld deyen there in her pilgrymage, but rather goon hoom and be buryed in hir owen 125
cuntre. Which worde she heryng, turned hir eyen with an hevy chier to hymward first and aftirward to me, and seid: "See what he seith." And aftir that she spake to ws both togider and seid: "Puttith this body where-soevir you list. Latith nobody be troublid with busynesse therfore. But this oonly I prey you: that wheresoevir ye ben, whan ye stonde at Goddis awtier, 130
than hath mynde vpon me." And whan she had expletid this sentence with such wordis as she myght, she seid no more. But the sekenesse evirmore encresyng, she was exercised therwith vnto hir last endyng.'

The nynthe day than of hir sikenesse, the fyftith yere of hir life and the thrittith of Austyn hir sonnes life, the holy and religious soule of hir 135
was vnbounden and deliverid from the prison of hir body and went to the ioye and blisse which endurith endelesly. Whos body was buryed even there liche as she had commaundid, many religious men and wommen hir exequyes halowyng, and God with many grete myraclis hir glorify-eng, in the citee of Hostie, twelue myle beyunde Rome, where she restid a 140
thousand yere and more. But as it plesid our lordis mercy, the yere of grace a thousand foure hundrid and thritty, vpon Palme sunday that yere fallyng on the nynth day of April, by Pope Martyn the fyfte, at the instaunce of his confessour and sexteyn of his chapel frere Petir, bysshop Electence, a frere

111 wote not] wote

145 Austyn and of frere Austyn of Rome, that tyme Priour General of the same
ordre, she was translatid to Rome solempnly and leid in the chirche which
Magister Egidius de Roma made in the honour and worship of hir sone
Seynt Austyn, beside Seynt Triphones, vndir attestacion and testificacion
of many and grete myraclis shewid there that tyme, the which were now
150 to longe to writen. Prey we now than fynally al to our lorde God that, for
the merites and preyers of blissid Monic, he vouchesafe to senden ws nat
richessis, ner worshippis, ner no such fluxible thyngis that commen and
goon withoute stabilnesse, which she despised of al hir hert, but that such
thyngis mote fallen vnto ws that mow makyn ws souereyn gode and soue-
155 reyn blissid. And that the wille of God may be so parfourmed in this world
in ws, that in the tothir worlde we mow duellyn with hir and hir sone in
evirlastyng blisse. Amen.

[79. JOHN OF BEVERLEY]

The life of Seynt Iohannes of Beuirlee
    Seynt Iohannes of Bevirlee, born in the marchys of Ingelonde, while he
was yung was sent to the Archebisshop of Caunterbury, that tyme clepid
Theodore, for to ben educat in livyng and in kunnyng. And he instruct hym
5 in al maner of manhode and godenesse, and taught hym the vndirstondyng
of holy Scripture, the which had perfitely he went abouten in diuers cuntrees and sew abrode the sede of Goddis word, and made many decones
f. 102ᵛᵃ and prestis by th'archebisshops | auctorite. Of whos educacion and colle-
gie was worshipful Bede, the which wrote many profitable thyngis to the
10 sustenaunce of the vniuersal feith of the chirche of Ingelond.
    And whan this seid Iohannes came to ful perfite age, by the disposi-
cion of God and the assent of the nobil Kyng of Northumbirlond, Elfrid,
he was made bisshop of the chirche of Hangustaldence. But longe aftir,
whan blissid Wilfrid, which longe had ben caste oute of his bisshopriche
15 and duellid in the courte of Rome, came hoom ageyn into his cuntre with
the popis lettris, and by al the synodal counceil received ageyn the chirche
of Hangustaldence, than Iohannes was made Bisshop of Yorc; the which
he gouerned nobly thre and twenty yere, and holily lived and perfitely.
    In which meantyme, oones as this holy man was in his preyer in a chapel
20 of Seynt Michael, the Holy Goost sat biforn hym on the awtier in likenesse of a light brighter than the sunne beem. And, whan many stondyng
withouten hugely marveilid of the light that was within, a decon of his ran
to the dore and at a cravas he lokid in and saw the bysshop stondyn de-

voutely in his preyer, and the grete brightenesse which stode byforn hym,
the which semp to han sette al the hous on a fyre. And anoon his face was 25
so scorcled that al the skynne of his chekis ferde as it had be rymplid liche
an olde brent purce. But whan this holy man was taught therof in spirite,
anoon he callid hym to hym and with his hooly hand touchid al hys face
and made hym ful hool ageyn, and chargid hym that he shuld telle this
myracle to no man while he were livyng.   30
     This blissid man lived a bisshop and an archebisshop thre and thritty
wynter, eight monethis and thritten daies. And whan he myght no lenger
labouren for to goon aboute and prechyn, he, by al the peplis assent, com-
mittid his bisshopriche to his preste Wilfrid, and went hymself to Beuyrlee,
to Bruthune, whom he had made there in his monasterie, and lived there 35
with hym, longe seruyng God in holynesse and rightwisnesse al the dayes
of his life aftir. And, on the seventh day of May, passid to God and was
buryed in a chapel of seynt Iohannes the Evangelist where, clarified with
many grete myraclis, he lay to the tyme of Bysshop Alfric, the which was
the sevententh Archebisshop of Yorc and the seventh aftir Seynt Iohan-   40
nes. This seid Alfric, the thrid yere of his consecracion, went to Rome
and of Pope Iohannes received a palle. And whan he came hoom ageyn,
th'archebisshop of Caunterbury and he nere with al the bisshops of the
prouince crowned at Wynchester on Estern day Kyng Edward the confessour, Kyng of Ingelonde. Aftir which tyme he did maken at Bevirlee a caps 45
of golde and siluer and precious stoones, and putt Seynt Iohannes boones
therin, with many othir reliquyes, and with grete ioye and gladnesse bothe
of the clergie and of the peple, solempnely translatid it from there it lay
biforn into the quere, and sett it aboue the high autier the eight kalend
of Nouembre, the thrid hundrid yere and sixten aftir his deth, the yere of 50
grace a thousand and seven and | thritty. In which place habounden many f. 102vb
grete myraclis unto this day, to laude and preisyng of the name of God and
of his glorious confessoure.

[80. LITANIES]

The Letanyes
     Letanyes ben kept in holy chirche twyes in the yere, as on Seynt Mar-
kis day, and that is clepid *Letania Maior*, and also the thre daies imme-
diat biforn the ascencion of our lorde, and tho ar clepid *Letanie Minores*.
And letanye is as moche to seyn as 'supplicacion' or a 'rogacion', and 5

therfore commounly in our vulgar [thei] convenyently ben clepid the rogacion dayes.

The first letanye on Seynt Markis day is clepid on thre maner wises.
First it is clepid, as is seid byforn, the More Letanye. The secund is the
10 Sevenfold Procession, and the thrid name is the Blake Crossis. The first
name, that is to seyn the More Letanye, it hath for thre causis. First for
cause of hym that it was ordeyned of, that is to seyn of grete Gregory the
pope of Rome. The secund for cause of the place that it was ordeyned in,
that was Rome. The thrid for the cause that it was ordeyned fore, as for a
15 right grete and a right grevous soor. For as moche as the Romayns, whan
thei had lived in lenton [contynently] and at Estern received the sacrament
of Cristis body, aftirward anoon youen to festis and ryotte, to drunkeship
and leccherie, our lorde, prouokid to vengeaunce, sent amonge hem a
pestilence clepid *Pestis inguinaria*, that was a posteme or a bolnyng aboute
20 the shore. The which pestilence was so violent that often tyme in the wey,
at mete, at pley and in commoun talkyng, men deyed sodeynly. Also whan
men nesid sodeynly and often mennys spirite passid. Wherfore, whan ony
man saw anothir nesyn, anoon he ran to hym and seid 'God help the!' And
fro thensforward in euery place commounly this customme is kept that,
25 yf oo man here anothir nesyn, he seith 'Sir, God help the!' Also in that
pestilence ofte, whan a man yaned or gasped, he sodeynly deied. Wherof,
as ofte as a man so gaspid, anoon he made a crosse vpon his mouth. And
this same custome is also kept yet and obserued. But how and wherof this
pestilence was occasioned it is tolde biforn in the life of Seynt Gregorie.
30 The secund name of this letanye is *Processio Septiformis*, for as moche as
the processions which Seynt Gregory made ageyns this pestilence was disposid by seven ordres. For in the first ordre was the clergie. In the secund
al munkis and religious men. In the thrid al nunnes. In the fourth al yung
children. In the fyfte al the lay men, al widdowes and continentis, and in
35 the seventh al wives and maried wommen. And that we now mow nat perfourmen in the nombre of persones, we representyn & perfourmen in the
nombir of letanyes.

The thrid name of this letanye is the Blake Crossis. For on this day
shuld blak crossis be borne in signe of moornyng for the grete mordre of
40 peple in that pestilence. That othir letanye which is ordeyned to be kept
the thre daies |

---

6 thei] thei and   16 contynently] incontynently   41 *Ends defective.*

[81. ASCENSION OF OUR LORD]

[. . .] it was convenient that there shuld ben moo dayes of that oon than   f. 104ra
of that othir. The thrid reson is for mysty significacion, that therby shuld
be youen an vndirstondyng that the comfortis of God arn comparid to
tribulacions as dayes arn to an houre and as yeris to a day. And that the
comparison be as a yere to a day it semyth by that is seid Ysaie 61°: *Predi-* 5
cate annum placabilem deo & cetera: 'Prechith', quoth he, 'a placable yere
to our lorde and a day of vengeaunce to our God.' Lo, here by a day the
tyme of tribulacion and by a yere the tyme of consolacion. And that the
comparison be as a day to an houre, it semyth by that oure lorde lay fourty
houris dede, the which was the tyme of tribulacion, and that he appierid 10
fourty daies to his disciplis, the which was the tyme of consolacion. And
this is the sentence of the glose vpon the same place.

    As touchyng the thrid principal notabilite, that is to seyn how he went
vp, it is to be knowen that he went vp myghtily, openly, gladly and swyftely.
First I sey that he went vp myghtely, for he went vp by his owen myght and 15
strength, as it is seid Ysaie 6[3]°: *'Quis est iste qui et cetera?* Who is he this
which commeth from Edom, goyng in the multitude of his vertue?' And
also by the evangelist he seith, Iohn 3°: *'Nemo ascendit ad celum et cetera*: No
man styeth into heven, that is to seyn aftir the glose by his propre vertue,
but he which cam doun from heven, the sonne of man that is in heven.' 20
And albeit that he went vp to semyng in a maner of a cloude, yit did he
nat that for he nedid the seruise of a clowde, but for therby he wold shewen that euery creature is redy to seruen the creatour therof. For no doute
therof he stey vp by the myght of his godhede, and in that appierith the
grete difference bitwix his goyng vp and Ennok and Helyes. For Ennok 25
was translatid vp, Hely was lifted vp, but Ihesus by his propir myght stey
vp. And, aftir Seynt Gregory, Ennok was gendrid and ge[n]drid. Helye
was gendrid but he gendrid not. Criste neither gendrid ner was gendrid.

    The secund wise he stey vp openly, al his disciplis seeyng, and therfore
he seid Iohn 16: *'Vado ad eum qui misit me & cetera*: I goo', quoth he, 'to hym 30
which sent me, and noon of you askith me ner seith whider goosthou.' As
whoso seith, aftir the glose, 'so openly I goo that it nedith nat you to asken,
that ye mow seen with your eyne'. 'And therfore', quoth Austyn, 'he stey
vp, his disciplis seeyng, for he wolde han hem wittenessis of hys vpgoyng,
and also that thei shuld ioyen and be glad to seen mannys nature borne vp 35
into heven and also desiren for to folowen hym thider aftir.' The thrid wise

---

    1 *Begins defective.*   16 63] 66   27 gendrid] gedrid

he went vp gladly and meryly. For, as seith Dauid in a psalme, our lorde
went vp in iubilacion with angels songe. And, as seith Seynt Austyn, whan
Criste went vp al heven was astoyned, al sterris wondrid, al the felauships
40 of angels ioyed and gladid, the trumpe of heven soundid, and al the queris
of heven sungen and madyn armonyous melodie. *Hec Augustinus.*

The fourth wise he stey vp swyftely. For, as Dauid seith, he ioyed as
a geaunt to ren the wey. His goyng oute was from high heven, and his |
f. 104rb goyng ageyn was to the height of heven. And nedys he must goon swyftely
45 that shuld passen so grete a space in so litle tyme. For Raby Moyses, the
grete philisophre, seith that euery cercle of eche planete hath in thycke-
nesse the wey of five hundrid yere, that is to seyn it occupyeth as moche
space as a man shuld mow goon of pleyn wey in five hundrid yere, yf he
myght live so longe. And moreovir, the distaunce from cercle to cercle is
50 also the wey of five hundrid yere. Wherfore, sith there be seven hevens,
aftir hym there shuld ben from the centre of the erthe vnto the concavi-
tee of Saturne, which is the seventh planete, [the] space of seven thousand
yere. And to the concavetee of the eight spere shuld ben seven thousand
and seven hundryd yere, that is to seyn as moche space as a man shulde
55 goon in that tyme, yf he myght liven so longe, so that eche yere shuld conteyn thre hundrid dayes and sixty, and euery daies iournee fourty myle, and
euery myle to conteyn two thousand paas or cubitis. *Hec Raby Moyses.* But
whethir this be true or nat God allone knowith, the which made al thyngis in nombre, weight and in mesure. This was than a grete skyppe, the
60 which Crist made from erthe to heven. Of which skippe, and of othir the
which Criste made, seith Seynt Ambrose on this wise: 'With a maner of
skyppe Crist cam into this worlde. He was at his fadir and skipped doun
into the maide. From the maide he sailed into the cribbe, from the cribbe
he descendid into Iordan. From Iordan he went vp into the crosse, from
65 the crosse he skippid into the grave, from the grave he roos and skippid vp
ageyn vnto his fadir and there he sittith on his right hand.' *Hec Ambrosius.*

As touchyng the fourth principalle, that is to seyn with what felauship
he went vp, it is to be knowen that he stey vp with grete pray of men and
grete felauship of angels. That he went vp with grete pray of men semyth
70 by that is seid in the psalme *Ascendisti in altum & cetera*: 'Thou wentist
vp, lorde, into high heven and leddist with the thi pray, the pore captiues',
quod Hugo de Vienna, 'the which thou haddist brought oute of helle.' And
that he went vp with copious multitude of angels it semyth wele by tho
questions which the lesser angels purposid and mevid to the higher angels
75 in the tyme of his ascencion, whan thei seiden, as it is writen Ysaie 6[3]:

52 the] shuld ben the   75 63] 66

Quis est iste qui venit de Edom & cetera? 'Vpon which place', seith the glose, 'that summe angels, nat fully knowyng the misterie of Cristis incarnacion, passion and resurreccion and seeyng hym commen vp to hevenward by his propir vertue and myght, and with hym grete multitude of angels and of othir hooly seyntis, gretely amaruailed therof mevid to the angels which 80 commen with hym this question: "Who is this, the which commeth from Edom?"' Dyonisius, in his boke *De Angelica Ierarchia* capitulo 7 seith that thre questions were mevid of aungels the tyme of Cristis ascension. The first, quoth he, was mevid of the gretter and the higher angels amonge hemself. The secund mevid the seid angels to Crist, and the thrid mevid 85 the lower angels | to the higher, as is seid bifore. The first question mevid f. 104va of the higher angels within hemself was the forseid question: 'Who is he this which is commen from Edom & cetera?' Edom, by interpretacion, is forto seyn 'blody'. Bosra is as moche as 'defencid' or 'strengthid'; as who seith: 'Who is this which commyth from the world blody by synne and 90 strengthid or defencid ageyns God by malice, or els fro the synful worlde and fro the myghtily defencid helle?' To which question Crist aunswerid to hem, quoth he, by the wordis which folowen and seid: '*Ego qui loquor iusticiam*: I am he which speke rightwisnesse and am a fornfighter for mennys saluacion.' In the redempcion of mankynde, quoth Denys, was rightwis- 95 nesse, in as moche as the creatour brought his creature from the captiuite of a wrongeful lorde. But here mevith Denys a question and is this: 'Sith the higher angels ben ner to God and immediatly ben illumyned of hym, why meven thei this question as though eche of hem wolde lernen of othir?' To this question he aunswerith, as the comentatour expowneth, on this wise: 100 'In that', quoth he, 'that they asken, they shewen that thei desire kunnyng. In that thei commownen amonge hemself they shewen that thei durn nat preventyn Goddis illumynacion. Wherfore', quoth he, 'they first makyn deliberacion within hemself or than they aske, ne hap that they prevent nat the illumynacion which is made to hem of God. But this maner of ques- 105 tion', quoth he, 'is not inquisicion, but it is a knowleche of ignoraunce.' *Hec ille*.

The secund question is made of the seid hyer angels to Crist on this wise: *Quare rubrum est indumentum tuum & cetera*: 'Why is thi clothyng rede and thy garnementis as the garnementis of hem which tredyn grapes 110 in a presse?' Our lorde was seid to han his clothyng, that is to seyn his body, rede and sprenclid with blode, for as moche as in his ascencion he reserued and kept in hym the steppis and the markis of his woundis. And tho he kept in his body stille for five causis: first to affermen the feith of his resurreccion. The secund to representyn hem to the fadir of heven, 115

preyeng for mankynde. The thrid is that at the day of doom gode men mow seen how mercyfully they be redempt. The fourth that shrewis mow knowen how rightfully thei be dampned. The fifte to shewen the perpetuel tryumphe of his victorye. To this question Crist [seid] '*Torcular calcaui so-*
120 *lus & cetera*: I haue trode the presse allone and of the folke was no man with me.' And conveniently may the crosse be clepid a presse. For liche as in a presse the grapis ben brosid and pressid til the wyne come oute, so was Criste on the crosse til al his blode was runnen oute. Or els by this presse may ben vndirstonden the devil. For, liche as in a presse the grapis ben
125 pressid til al the wyne be runne oute and nothyng remayneth and abideth but the bare husk, so mankynde was bounden and involued in the ropes of synne by the cruel force of the devil, til al spiritual grace was driven oute therfro and nat oonly the huske of synne and wrecchidnesse abode with al. Thus our noble cheventeyn myghtily trode vndir fote the malicious presse,
f. 104vb the devil, til he had broken al his boondis & relessid | mankyndis synne in
131 his passion, and now stey vp a glorious conquerour to heven. And ten daies aftir he sett open his tavern and plentevously poored oute new must of the hooly goostis grace to his disciplis, and by hem to al tho he mynistrid it forth: to al mankynde generally, but to hem moste specially which mekely
135 disposid hem to receiven it.

The iij^{de} question mevid by angels to angels, that is to seyn by the lower aungels to the hyer, was this: '*Quis est iste rex glorie?*: Who is he, this kyng of blisse?' To which question that othir angels aunswerid ageyn and seiden: 'The lorde of vertues is kyng of blisse.' Of this question and the convenient
140 aunswere seith Seynt Austyn in a sermon on this wise: 'In Goddis ascencion with his holy felauship al the huge eyre was sanctificat and halowid, and al the foule flocke of devels flickeryng aboute the same was chacid awey and fledde.' And anoon gode angels metyng Crist mevid this question and seid: 'Who is this, the kyng of blisse?' To whom othir angels aunswerid:
145 'This is he which is white and rede. This is he which whilom had neither fairnesse ner beaute, which was feble in the crosse and stronge in helle, foule in body and armed in his soule, foule in deth, fair in his resurreccion, white fro the maide, rede on the crosse, swart and pale in the despite of his passion, clere and bright in the glorie of his ascencion and in his hevenly
150 mansion.' *Hec Augustinus.*

As for the fyfte principal notabilite, that is to seyn by what merite he ascendid, it is to be notid and vndirstonden that he ascendid vp by threfolde merite, that is to seyn for truthe, for buxomnesse and for right-wisnesse. And this affermyth Seynt Ierome, seyeng thus: 'For truthe',

quoth he, 'lorde, thou stey vp which truly fulfilliddest tho thyngys which 155
thou haddist promysed and behight by the prophetis. For buxomnesse, for
liche a shepe thou were offrid for the peplis helth. For rightwisnesse, in as
moche as not by myght but by right thou deliveriddest man oute of the
devels danger. Wherfore marveilously thy right hand, thy myght that is to
seyn, and thy vertue, now ledith the vp to heven.' *Hec Ieromus in summa.* 160

And for the sixt principalle, whider he ascendid, it is to knowen that
he ascendid aboue al hevens. There is heven material, racional, intellectual and supersubstancial. Material heven is sevenfolde as the nethir mysty
eyre, the ovir-clere eyre, the space abouen that is clepid Olimpus, that is
to seyn al bright, the fyry heven, the sterrid heven, the cristallyn heven 165
and the last and the seventh is clepid *Celum Empirum.* Racional heven is
a rightful mannys soule for thre skilles. First for cause of Goddis duellyng, for liche as heven is Goddis sete and his duellyng place, as seith the
prophete Ysaie, right so is a rightful mannys soule, as seith Salamon. The
secunde cause why a rightful mannys soule is clepid heven is for holy conu- 170
ersacion. For gode rightful men, by hooly desires and affeccions, ben alwey
conuersant in heven as, seyth Seynt Poule. The thrid cause is for contynuel werkyng. For liche as heven nevir restith but evir is in mevyng, right
so a rightful man evir contynueth in gode werkyng.

Intellectual heven is angel also for thre causis. First for thei ben high 175
by dignyte and excellence, wherof spekith |

[82. PENTECOST]

[. . .] secund, that is to seyn how many wises the holi goste is sent, that is to f. 106ʳᵃ
seyn visibly and invisibly. Invisibly as whan he infoundith grace in mennys soulis; visibly as whan he appierith in ony visibl[e] signe. Of the first
maner is seid Iohn 3°: 'The spirite inspirite where he wil and thou wust nat
fro whens he commeth or whider he gooth.' And no wondir, for as seith 5
Seynt Bernard *De Verbo Inuisibili*, he seith: 'Nat in by the eyen for he is
nat colourid, ner by the eeris for he soundith nat, ner by the nosethrilles
for he is nat medlid with the eyr, ner by palett of the mouth for he is neither eetyn ner drunken, ner by no felyng of the body for he is nat palpable.
Than perauenture thou askist', quoth he, 'sith his weyes ben inuisible, how 10
I know his presence. Siker', quoth he ageyn, 'I vndirstond his presence by
the mevyng of myn hert, and by the flight of vices I perceive the myght of
his vertue, and by discussion and vndirnymyng of my privey thoughtis I

175 *Ends defective.*   1 *Begins defective.*   3 visible] visibly

marveil the depthe of his wisdam. And of the sum emendyng of my maners
15 I fele by experience the godenesse of his buxomnesse. And of reformacion
and renouacion of the spirite of my soule I perceived somwhat a likenesse
of his beaute. And in byholdyng of al these togider I abasshid to see the
multitude of his gretenesse.' *Hec Bernard.*

And as touchyng the visible sendyng of the holi goste in a sensible signe,
20 it is to ben vndirstonden that in five maner likenessis he hath be shewid.
First in likenesse of a dowe vpon Criste in his baptesme. Luc 3°. The
secund in likenesse of a bright skye vpon Crist in his transfiguracion. Matt
17°, where the glose seith thus: 'Liche as whan Crist was baptised, so whan
he was clarified the misterie of the holy trinite was shewyd there in a dowe
25 and here in a bright skye.' The thrid was in a breeth of wynde. Iohannis
20°. The fourth in liknesse of fyre, and the fyfte in liknesse of tungis; and
in these two likenessis he appierid this day.

And in these five maner of likenessis the holi goste appierid specially
for to yiuen ws vndirstondyng that he werkith the propirtees of tho in
30 the hertis of hem which he commeth in. The dowe hath moornyng for
hir songe, she wantith galle, she abideth in the hoolis of a stoon. The holi
goste, whom he fulfilleth he makith to moornen for her synnes. Ysaie 59° is
seid *Quasi columbe & cetera*: 'As dowes, thynkyng on our synnes, we shul
moornen'. Ad Rom. seith Poule capitulo 8°, *in texti & in glossam*: 'The
35 holi goste makith ws to asken remission of God with inenarrable teeris.'
The holi goste makith also his to be withoute the galle of bittirnesse'. Sap.
12°. 'O how softe and easy and swete is thi spirite, lorde, in ws' & capitulo 7°: 'He is clepid the softe, the benygne and the manly spirite. For
as moche as he makith hise softe in worde, benygne in hert and manly in
40 werkyng, he makith hem also to abiden and to duellyn in the hoolis of the
stoon, that is to seyn in the woundys of Crist, the cornerstoon.' Cantic. 2°:
'Rise vp my dowe, my spouse, and come, my dowe.' 'In the hoolis of the
stoon norisshyng to me', quoth the glose, 'yunge pigeons, by infusion of
the grace of the holy goste in the woundis of Crist.' *Tren ult.*: 'The spirite
45 of our mouth, Crist our lorde, is takyn in our synnes, to whom we han seid:
f. 106rb "In thy shadowe we shul liven | amonge folke", as who seith: "The spirite
of our mouth, the which mouth of ws is Crist Ihesus, makith vs to seyen to
Criste: 'In thy shadowe, that is to seyn in thy passion in which thou were
derk and despised, we shul liven by contynuel mynde therof'."'

50 The secund thyng that the holi goste was shewid in was a bright skye.
A skye is lifted vp from the erthe, it yiueth refresshyng geyns hete and it
causith reyn. So the holi goste whom he fulfilleth he lifteth vp by contempt
of erthely thyngis. Ezek. 8°: 'The spirite liftid me bitwix heven and erthe

and led me into Ierusalem in the vision of God.' Also the same prophete
seith: 'Whersoevir the spirite went the whelis weren also lifted vp folo- 55
wyng hym, for the spirite of life was in the whelis.' And Seynt Gregory
seith that, as sone as the savour of the [spirite] is tastid, anoon the flesh
waxith vnsauory.

The holi goste yiueth also refresshyng and shadowyng ageyns the
ardour and the hete of vices. Wherfore it was seid to our lady, Luc 2°, 60
'The holy goste shal commen vnto the, and the vertue of hym that is hyest
shal shadowe the from the hete of al synnes.' Also the holi goste is clepid
for it is strength to refresshen in hete. Iohn 7°: 'Floodis of quyk watir shul
flowen oute of his wombe that bilevith in me', quoth Criste. And this he
seid of the holi goste, the which they shuld receiven which that bilevid in 65
hym. A skye also gendrith reyn and the grace of the holi gost the dew of
teeris.

The thrid thyng that the holy goste was shewid in was a breeth of Cristis
mouth. A brethe is light and hote, so the holi goste is light and swyfte to dif-
founden hys grace. For as the glose seith vpon this worde, 'Acta: *Factus est* 70
repente de celo sonus & cetera: The grace of the holy gost can make no longe
taryengis. Brethe is also hote.' Luc 12°: 'I cam', quoth Crist, 'to sende fyre
into erthe and I wil that it brenne.' Wherfore the holi goste is likenyd to the
southwynde which is hote. Cantus 4°: 'Rise vp, thou colde northwynde,
and goo hens! And thou, warm southe wynde, come and blowe in my gar- 75
dyn, and the swete odoramentis therof shul flowen.' Breth is also softe to
souplyn with hard thyng; so the holi goste for his softenesse in souplyng is
likened to an oynement. Iohn 2°: 'The oynement of hym shal techyn you.'
And by due, and therfore holy chirch preyeth in the orison of the holi goste
that he wil makyn our hertis plentevous with the inward sprenclyng of his 80
dewe. Brethe is also necessarie for inspiryng and respiryng and so necessarie that, yf it were but a litle while withsett or stoppid in, a man shulde be
dede anoon. And so it farith gostely. For liche as with breth no man may
liven bodily, so withoute grace of the holi goste no man may liven gostely.
Dauid seith: 'Lorde, yf thou take awey her spirite, thei shul failen and tur- 85
nen ageyn into her powdir. And therfore send thy spirite and thei shul ben
create & cetera.'

The fourth wise he was shewid in the liknesse of fyre and the fyfte in
the liknesse of tungis, of which it shal be seid | aftirward. As touchyng f. 106va
the thrid principal, that is to seyn what tyme the holi goste was sent, it is 90
to ben vndirstonden that he was sent the fyftith day from Estern. Wherin

---

57 spirite] spirite went, the whelis weren also lyftid vp folowyng hym, for the spyrite of
life was in the whelis. And Seynt Gregory seith that, as sone as the savour of the

was signyfied that of the holi goste is the lawes perfeccion, eternal remuneracion and of synnes the remissyon. The perfeccion of the lawe is in the
nombre of fyfty. For, aftir the glose, the fiftyth day aftir the immolacion of
95 the paschal lambe was the lawe youen in fyre. And also the fifty day aftir
Cristis immolacion was the holy goste sent doun to th'appostlis in likenesse of fyre. The lawe was youen in the Mount Synay, the holy goste in
the Mount Syon, the lawe in feer, the holi goste in lowe. The which, as
seith Seynt Poule, is fulnesse and the perfeccion of the lawe.

100 Eternal reward or remuneracion is representid also in nombre of fifty.
For, as seith the glose, liche as the fourty dayes in the which Crist aftir
his resurreccion was conuersaunt with his disciplis signifieth this present chirche, right so the fyftith day in which the holi goste was youen
signifieth the peny of endeles remuneracion. Remission of synnes is also
105 shewid in the nombre of fyfty. For liche as in fyfty yere, aftir the glose,
was indulgence of bodily seruage, so by the holi goste youen the fyfty day
in indulgence of gostely seruage, the which is synne. And anoon it folowith in the glose thus: 'In spiritual iubile the gilty of deth ben vnbounden,
dettis ben foryouen, banysshid men ben callid ageyn into her cuntre. Heri-
110 tage lost is restorid, bonde men ben bought ageyn and deliuerid from the
yocke of seruage.' *Hec glossa*. First the glose seith that thei which be gilty
of deth ben assoiled and deliverid, as seith Poule ad Rom . 8°: 'Thus the
lawe of spirite of life hath deliuerid from the lawe of synne and of deth.'
Also the dettis of synne ar foryouen, seith the glose. For charite curith and
115 wrieth the multitude of synnes, as seith th'appostle Petir. Also it clepith
ageyn flemyd and banysshid men into her cuntre. Thus seyeng Dauid: 'Thi
gode spirite shal reducen me into the right wey. Also heritage loste is gote
ageyn', thus seyeng Poule ad Rom. 8°: 'The spirite of God yiueth wittenesse to our spirite that we be the sonnes of God. And yf we be sonnes,
120 we ben heires. Also seruauntis be deliverid fro synne. For as seith Seynt
Poule ad Cor. 3°: 'Where the spirite of God is, there is liberte.'

As touchyng the fourth principal, that is to seyn how often the holi goste
was sent or youen to the disciplis, it is to be notid, aftir the glose, that thries
the holi goste was youen to his disciplis: oones biforn his passion, oones
125 biforn his ascencion, and oones aftir. The first yifthe was power to make
myraclis. The secund to relaxen synne and the thrid was to confermyn men
in grace.

First whan he, that is to seyn Crist, sent hem to prechen and yaf hem
power vpon al devils and for to curen langours, al was doon by the holi
130 goste, as it is seid Matt 12°. But yit folowith it not hereof that euery man
which hath the holi goste shulde doo myraclis. For, as seith Seynt Gregory,

myraclis makyn nat a man hooly, but shewen. Ner, on that othir side, |
it folowith nat that euery man which werkith myraclis hath the holi goste.   f. 106vb
For reproued of God shul seyn at the day of dome that thei diden myraclis,
prophecied, and kestyn oute devils in Goddis name. And yit God shal seyn   135
to hem: 'Sothly, sirs, I knowe you not, that is to seyn I approue you not.'
For in truth God allone werkith myraclis by his propir auctorite. Angels by
abilnesse of the mater, devils by natural vertues sett in thyngis, wycchis by
privy contractis and convenauntis with devels, gode cristen men by open
and true rightwisnesse, and wickid cristen men by signes feyned of true   140
rightwisnesse.

The secund tyme that Crist yafe the holi goste to his disciplis was whan
he blew vpon hem and seid: 'Takith the holi goste. Who[s]oevir synnes
ye shul foryiuen shul be foryouen & cetera.' Not forthan no man may
foryiuen the spotte of vnclennesse made in mannys soule by synne, ner   145
the gilt by which he is bounden to evirlestyng peyn, ner th'offence of God,
the whiche ben oonly foryouen of God by the infusion of grace and the
vertue of contricion. Nevirtheles the prest is seid to assoilen, for he shewith hym assoiled of his synne, or for he chaungith the peyn of purgatorie
into temporal peyne, or for he relaxith a parte of his temperal peyn.   150

The thrid tyme that Crist the holi goste sent to his disciplis was this
day, wherby her hertis were made so sad in grace that thei aftir dred no
peyn. For, as seith Seynt Austyn, 'such is the grace of the holi goste that,
yf it fynde hevynesse in a soule it dissolueth it, consumyth wickid desire
and castith awey ferfulnesse'. *Hec Augustinus.*   155

As for the fifte principal, that is how the holi goste was sent, it is to be
knowen that he was sent in sounde and in tungis of fyre and the t[ung]is
apperid sittyng. The sounde was sodeyn, hevenly, huge or grete, and fillyng. Sodeyn, for, as it is seid biforn, the grace of the holi goste can make no
taryeng. Hevenly, for it made hem hevenly into whom it came. Vehement   160
or huge, for it brought in sone drede, or for it toke awey evirlastyng woo.
For vehemens in oo wise is forto seyn 'takyng awey woo', or it was vehement for it lyftid her soulis from al fleshly loue. For vehemens in anothir
wise is forto seyn '*vehens mentem*'. Liftyng the soule it was also fillyng,
for it fulfilled hem al. And therfore it is seid, Acta 2°: '*Repleti sunt omnes*   165
spiritu sancto & cetera: Thei weren al fulfilled with the holi goste.' And
of fulnesse ben thre tokenys, the which weren excellently in th'appostlis.
The first token of fulnesse of a vessel that, though a man knocke theron,
it soundith nat. Io[b] 7°: '*Numquid mugiet bos & cetera*: Shal the oxe roren
whan he is biforn a ful cribbe?' As who seith, whan the cribbe of the hert   170

143 Whosoevir] whos soevir   157 tungis] tinctis   169 Iob] Iohannis

of Goddis oxe is ful of grace, the rore of murmour and impacience hath therin no place. This tokne hadden th'appostlis which were Goddis oxen, whan in tribulacions thei made no sounde of murmour, ner impacience, but rather wenten glad and mury from the counseil, in as moche as thei
175 were had worthy to suffre reprofe for the name of Ihesu.

f. 107ra The secund signe of fulnesse is no | more to receiven but to be saciat. For whan a vessel is ful of licour it may no more receiven. Also a man whan he is ful he desireth no more. In liche wise whan holy men han the fulnesse of grace thei mow receive no foreyn licour of erthely delectacion.
180 And thei that oones han tastyd hevenly swetnesse han no savour in flesshly lust. Seynt Austyn seith, accordyng herto, that 'he the which hath drun-kyn of the flode of paradyse, whos oo drope is more than the occean see, it nedis must be that the thrust of this worlde is quenchid in hym'. This fulnesse had th'appostlis, the which wolde noon erthely thyng han propre,
185 but diuided al thyng commounly.

  The thrid signe of fulnesse is ovirflowyng, as whan a river ovirflowyth the brynkis it is a tokne that it is ful. Eccl. 24°: 'Implet quasi Phison sa-pientiem: Phison is oon of the four floodis of paradys', the whiche hath his propirtee to ovirflowen and to wattren al the cuntree thereabouten. So
190 th'appostlis ovirflowid. For, whan thei were fulfilled with the holi goste, they bigunne to speke with diuers tungis. Where the glose seith thus: 'See a tokne of fulnesse. A ful vessel lightly ovirrennyth and fyre in a mannys bosomme may nat ben hydde.' Wherfore thei anoon bigunne to ovirflowen and to wattren the cuntre abouten. For anoon Petir bigan to prechyn and
195 he conuertid thre thousand men.

  The holi goste also this day was sent in tungis of fyre, and here mow be mevid as touchyng this part thre questions. The first is why he was sent in these two ioyned togider: tungis and fyre. The secund why more in fyre than in ony othir element. The thrid why rather in tungis than in ony othir
200 membre.

  The first, it may be seid, that for thre causis he appierid in tungis of fyre. The first cause is that thei shuld spekyn fyry wordis. The secund is þat thei shuld prechyn and spekyn the firy lawe, that is to seyn the lawe of loue. Of these tweyn spekith Seynt Bernard on this wise: 'The holi goste
205 came in fyry tungis that thei with al folkis tungis shuld spekyn fyry wordis, and that fyry tungis shuld prechyn fyry lawe.' Hec Ille. The thrid skille is that by hem men shuld knowen the holy goste spekyn, the which is fyre, and that for they shulde no diffidence han, and that they shuld nat ascryen to hemself othir mennys conuersion.

210 As touchyng the secund question it may ben seid that for many skilles.

The first skille is taken anempst the sevenfolde grace of the holy goste. The holi goste in maner of fyre makith low hy thyngis by the yifte of feer, makith softe hard thyngis by the yifte of pite, illumyneth derk thyngis by the yifte of kunnyng, restreyneth fluxible thyngis by the yifte of counseil, makith sadde nesshe thyngis by the yifte of strength, clarifieth metals, put- 215 tyng awey rust by the yifte of vndirstondyng, and goth vpward by the yifte of wysdam.

The secund skille is taken anempst the dignyte and excellence of that element. For fyre excellith al othir elementis in beaute, ordre and in ver- tue. In beaute bicause of the fairenesse therof in light. In ordre bicause of 220 the height in sight. In vertue bicause of the myght therof in werkyng. So in these the holi goste excedith al othir | thyngis. For the first he is seid f. 107rb vndefoulid, for the secund he is seid incomprehensible, for the thrid he is seid inuincible.

The thrid cause why youen was the holi goste in the liknesse of fyre is 225 for his effectuel werkyng. This reson assigneth Rabanus, seyeng on this wyse: 'Fyre hath four natures: it brennyth, it purgith, it hetith and it illu- myneth. So the holi goste', quoth he, 'brennyth and consumeth synnes, purgith hertis, he warmeth and chasith our sluggidnesse and illumyneth our ignoraunce.' *Hec Rabanus*. First I sey the holi goste brennyth and con- 230 sumeth synnes. Zacariah seith, or the holi goste by hym: 'By fyre I shal brennen hem as siluer is brent.' Siluer is brent to consumen the storie or the filthe therof. With this fyre desired the prophet to be touchid whan he seid: 'Lorde, brenne my reynes, that is to seyn my flesshly synnes, and myn hert, that is my spiritual synnes.' He also purgith hertis. The prophete 235 seith, Ysaie 4°: 'I putte awey the blode, that is the synne of Ierusalem, from the myddis therof, that is from the hert in the spirite of doom and in the spirite of brennyng.' He warmyth our slouthe and dulnesse. And therfore seith Seynt Poule of hem whom the holi goste fulfilleth, ad Rom. 12°, that thei ben fervent and hote in spirite. And therfore the holi goste appierid in 240 fyre. For, from euery hert which he fulfilleth, he puttith awey the leuke- nesse of slouth and makith it hote in desire of his eternyte. He illumyneth also ignorauntis. Sap. 9°: 'Who shal kunne thy witte, but thou yiue wisdam, and but thou sende thyn hooly spirite from abouen.'

The fourth skille why the holi goste was youen in fyre is taken anempst 245 the nature of loue, the which may be signfied by fire for thre causis. Fyrst for fyre is evir in mevyng, so the loue of the holi goste, tho whom he filleth, makith alwey to ben in the mevyng of gode werkis. For, as seith Seynt Gre- gory: 'The loue of God is nevir ydil. For yf it be verrey loue, it werkith, and yf it wil nat werkyn, pleynly it is no charite.' *Hec Greg*. The secund 250

skille is for fyre amonge al othir elementis is moste formal and leste material. So whom the loue of the holi goste fulfilleth makith to han but litle
of erthely loue and moche of gostely loue, and makith hem nat to louen
erthly thyngis erthely, but rather spritually. Seynt Bernard makith a dis-
255　tinccion of loue and seith that four maner of loves there ben: as to louen
flesh flesshly, to loue the spirite flesshly, the spirit to loue the flessh spiritually, and the spirite spiritually. The thrid skil why by fyre is signified
loue, for the propirtee of fyre is to enclynen high thyngis, the self to goon
vpward, and to gadren togider fluxible thyngis. And by these thre is vndir-
260　stonde threfolde strength of loue. For loue, as it may ben had of Denys
wordis *de Diuinis nominibus*, hath threfolde strength, as inclinatif, eleuatif
and coordinatif. Inclinatif for it bowith doun the hyer thyngis to the lower.
Eleuatif for it liftith vp the lower thyngis to the higher, coordinatif for it
settith in ordre egal to egal. These thre myghtis of loue causith the holi
265　goste in them whom he fulfilleth. For he bowith hem by mekenesse and
contempt of hemself, he lifteth hem vp into desire of hevenly thyngis, and
coordeyneth hem togider by vniformyte of maners.

f. 107ᵛᵃ　　As | touchyng the thrid, that is to seyn why the holi goste appierid
rather in tungis than in ony othir membre, it may be seid that for thre
270　skilles. 'The tung is a membre', as seith Iamys, 'enflamed with the fyre of
helle, hard to governe and profitable wele gouerned.' For as moche than as
tungis weren enflaumed with the fyre of helle, it nedid the fyre of the holi
goste forto quenchyn it. And for as moche as it is harder to gouerne than
ony othir membre, therfor it nedid the grace of the holi goste to rulyn it
275　and to govern it. For as Iamys seith Cᵒ 3ᵒ: 'Al nature of bestis & foulis and
of al othir thyngis is chastised and taught of the nature of man, but the
tunge may no man chastise but the holi gostis grace.' And for as moche as
it is a profitable membre yf it be wele governyd, therfore it nedid to han
the holi goste the ruler and the governour therof.

280　　He also appierid in tungis, signifyeng that he is ful necessarie to hem
that shul vsyn prechyng. For he makith hem to spekyn feruently and
withouten feer, and therfore he was sent in liknesse of fyre. 'The holi
goste', quoth Seynt Bernard, 'came vpon the disciplis in brennyng tungis, that they shuld spekyn brennyng wordis and feithfully prechyn the
285　brennyng lawe with brennyng tungis withoute pusillanimite or feyntnesse
of hert.' *Hec Bernard*. But that these fyry tungis appierid sittyng, it
signifieth that the holi goste is necessarie to presidentis and iuges. For it
yiueth hem auctorite to foryiven synne in the forme bifornseid. He yiueth
also wisdam to yiuen rightful doomes Ysaie 14ᵒ: '*Ponam spiritum meum &*

cetera. He yiueth hem also buxomnesse to supporten', *Num* 1[1]°: '*Dabo* 290
eis de spiritu qui est in te & cetera: I shal yiuen hem of the spirite that is in
the & cetera.' That was mansuetude or buxomnesse, for as it is seid, Num
12°: '*Erat Moyses mitissimus & cetera*: Moyses was the moste meke man
vpon erthe.' He yiueth also the ornament of holynesse to enformen, Iob
26: '*Spiritus domini ornauit celos & cetera*. The ornamentis', quoth Seynt 295
Gregory, 'ben the vertues of hem that prechyn.'

   As for the sixt principal, that is to seyn into whom the holi goste was
sent, it is to be knowen that he was sent into the disciplis, the which were
clene vessels of receite and able to conteynen the grace of the holy goste
for seven thyngis which weren within hem. First thei were quyete in soule 300
and that is notid in the first clause of the epistle of thi feste: *Dum com-
plerentur dies Pentecostes*: that is to seyn the daies of rest. Ysaie 66: '*Super
quem & cetera*: vpon whom shal my spirite resten but on the meke and the
quyete?' The secund is that thei were vned and knytte in loue and that
is notid there: '*Et erant omnes pariter & cetera*: they weren al togider for 305
there was to hem oon hert and oo soule.' And liche as the spirite of a man
quyketh nat the membris of his body but thei ben vnyd and knytte togider,
no more doth the holi goste the spiritual membris. And as fyre by diuision
of stickes is quenchid, so by discorde and diuision is the grace of the holi
goste amonge men. Wherfore it is sungen in the seruise of the holi goste 310
that he fonde hem concorde and so illumyned hem. The thrid thyng was
congruence of place: *In eodem loco*. That was in the | place where Crist f. 107vb
made his maundee, a clene place and a solitarie. [*Hos.*]: '*Ducam eos in so-
litudinem & cetera*: I shal', quoth the holi goste by prophete, 'ledyn hem
into a solitarie place and there shal I spekyn to her hert.' The fourth is þat 315
thei were occupied busily in preyer: '*Erant perseuerantes*: thei were perseuerant togider in preyer.' Wherof syngith the chirch: '*Orantibus apostolis
& cetera*: while th'appostlis preyed the holy goste came.' And that preyer
be necessarie to receiuen the holi goste it semyth Sap. 7°: '*Inuocaui & venit
& cetera*: I haue clepid inward and the spirite of wisdam came into me.' 320
   The fifte thyng was that thei weren endewid with mekenesse, notid in
this worde '*sedentes*': sittyng. For he that sittith semeth lower than he is.
Dauid seith: '*Qui emittit fontes & cetera*: he sendith oute wellys in valis',
that is to seyn habundaunce of grace in meke men. The sixt thyng is that
thei were conioyned in pees. For thei weren in Ierusalem, that is to seyn 325
the sig[ht] of pees. And in tokne that pees is necessarie to the receiuyng of
the holi goost, our lorde first offrid hem pees or than he yafe hem the holi
goost, seyeng: 'Pees be to you.' And anoon aftir he blew vpon hem and

seid: 'Takith the holi goste.' The seventh thyng is that thei weren erect
330 and liftid vp in contemplacion. And this is notid in þat thei received the
holi goste in the ovir lofte of the cenacle, aftir the glose which seith that
whoso desireth the holy goste, he styeth vp and tredith vndir the fete of
the affeccion of his soule, the duellyng hous of his flessh.

For the sevynth principal, that is wherfore the holi goste was sent, it is
335 to be vndirstonden that he was sent for six causis which mow be markid
in this auctorite of the gospel: '*Paraclitus autem spiritus sanctus quem mittet
pater & cetera.*' First he was sent to comforten hem which were sory, notid
in the first worde '*Paraclitus*', which is to seyn a comfortour. 'A comfortour', quoth Seynt Gregory, 'is the holi goste seid for as moche as while he
340 makith redy hope of foryifnesse to hem the which moornen for her wickidnesse, he lifteth vp her soulis from the affliccion of hevynesse.' The secund
cause of his sonde is for to quyken dede men, notid in this worde '*spiritus*'
. And that the spirite yiveth life appierith wele Ezel. 37, where it is seid
thus: '*Ossa arida & cetera*: o ye drie boones, herith the worde of God &
345 cetera.' And anoon aftir he concludith this: 'anoon the spirite of life entrid into the bodies and thei livedden and stooden vpon her fete'. The thrid
cause was to makyn holy hem that weren vnclene, notid in this worde '*sanctus*' . And liche as the holi goste is clepid '*spiritus*' for he quyketh, so is he
clepid '*sanctus*' for he halowith and purifyeth. The fourth cause is to refor-
350 men and to confermen bitwixen hem that weren at discorde, markid in this
worde '*pater*' . The fadir naturally lovith his children: '*Ipse pater amat vos*',
seith Crist. Yf we be this fadris sonnes we be brethern, and bitwix brethern
aught to ben perfite loue. The fifte cause it to saven the rightful, and this
is vndirstonden in that he seith: '*In nomine meo*'; his name is Ihesus, which
355 is as moche to seyn as saluacion. In the name of Ihesu than the fadir sent
f. 108ʳᵃ the holi goste to shew that he came to save folkis. The sixt cause | was
to teche the ignorant notid there: '*Ille vos docebit omnia & cetera*: he shal
techyn you al thyngis.'

As touchyng the eight principal and the last, that is to seyn wherby or by
360 what thyng the holi goste was youen, it may be seid that principally by thre
thyngis he was youen in the first chirche. First to the disciplis by preyer:
Orantibus apostolis & cetera. In confirmacion wherof, while Ihesu preyed
the holi goste light vpon hym, Luc [3]°. The secund thyng that he was
youen by devoute and attent deuocion in heryng of Goddis worde, Acta
365 1[o]°: '*Adhuc loquente Petro & cetera*: even while Petir spak in prechyng,
the holi goste fel vpon al tho which herd the worde.' The thrid thyng is
by busy good werkyng, and that is signified by puttyng to of handis, Acta

363 3] 12   365 10] 12

7°: '*Tunc inponebant manus super illos & cetera*: thei putten her handis vpon the peple & thei received the holi goste.' Or els by puttyng to of handis is vndirstonden the absolucion which is made in confession, wherby is often 370 received the grace of the holi goste & cetera.

[83. GORDIANUS AND EPIMACHUS]

The life of Gordian and Epymachus

Gordianus whilom was a vicarie of Iulyan themperour and apostata. This Gordianus, by the prechyng and techyng of a cristen man clepid Ianu-arius, whom he had in his kepyng, was conuertid to the feithe, and his wife also. And whan cursid Iulian herd this, anoon he sent Ianuarie into exile 5 and to be banysshid, and Gordian, yf he wolde nat sacrifisen, he sentencid to ben hefdyd. And as he chargid anoon was doon. And his body lay thro-wen into the felde seven daies aftir, for to haue ben devourid of doggis or wuluys. But whan aftir seven daies it was founden vntouchid, his meynee stoolen it and buried it in a place nat past a myle from the cite, in the same 10 graue that oon Epimachus was nat longe toforn buryed in, whom the seid Iulyan had slayne for Cristis sake.

[84. NEREUS AND ACHILLEUS]

The life of Nereus and Achilleus

Nereus and Achilleus, whos passion writen Eutices, Victorinus and Macro, seruauntis of Ihesu Criste, whom also Seynt Petir baptised, weren the eunukys and the cubiculers of a grete lady, the which was nyfte vnto Domician themperour, whos name was Flauia. This damicelle Flauia was 5 despousid but nat ful maried to a consuls sone clepid Aurelian. And oo tyme whan she was araied with purpil garnementis sett ful of precious gemmys, Nereus and Achilleus prechid hir the feith of Criste and gretely commendid vnto hir the dignyte and the worthynesse of virginite, shewyng that to be ny to God as spouse to husbonde and nye also to angels as sustren 10 to brethern. Also thei declarid hir wyves worldely must nedis ben subiec-tis to her husbondys and obeyen hem, wil thei or nyl, and often beten with her fystis and spurned with her heelis, and han moch peyn and travaile with bryngyng forth of children and somtyme perauenture bryng forth monstruous and disfigured children. And fynally, tho that vnnethe kan 15 beren | the softe and swete ammonicion of her modir must nedis suffren f. 108rb

grete rebukis and reprovis of her husbondis. And whan she sadly had herd
al that other, she seid ageyn: 'This wote I wele', quoth she, 'that my fadir
was ielous of my modir and many a rebuke she suffrid of hym. Whethir
20 my husbonde shul be such oon?' 'Siker', quoth thei ageyn, 'al men in tyme
of spousail arn benygne and ientle, but ful many, whan thei ben a while
marites, thei cruelly behan hem to her wyves and ful often preferren and
cherisshen her handmaidens byforn hir. Wherfore, lady, to excluden al
these myseries and myschevis, we counceil you to kepe stille your virgi-
25 nyte while ye han it. For yf it be oones lost, it is impossible evir to be had
ageyn. Euery gilt may be putte awey by penaunce, but virginyte lost may
nevir be callid ageyn by no penaunce.' At whos exortacion Flauia bilevid
and avowed virginyte, and of Seynt Clement was baptized and veiled.

And whan Aurelian hir spouse herd thys, anoon he toke leve of Domi-
30 cian themperour and banysshid hir with hir two eunukys, Nerey and Achil-
ley, to the yle clepid Pontus, a place of grete miserie and wrecchidnesse,
hopyng therby to changen the tendir and delicatly norisshid maidens hert.
And aftir a certeyn tyme thei had ben there, he went thider hymself and
promised many grete yiftes to hir chambirleyns, be so they wolde changen
35 hir hert and hir purpose. But thei forsoken al his yiftes and his profres, and
counceilid hir to constaunce and stedfastnesse in hir hooly entent. Whan
Aurelyan knew this, he wolde han compellid hem to sacrifise, but thei seid
pleynly that, sith thei were baptised of Seynt Petir, thei in no wise wold doo
sacrifise but to God in heven. Wherfore thei were bothe hefdid, aftir many
40 grete tormentis, of oon clepid *Monimus Rufus consularis*, to whos exami-
nacion Aurelianus committed hem. Whos bodies Auspicius, her disciple
and the norissher of the holy ladye Flauye, stale prively and put hem in a
shyppe and ledde hem to Rome and buried hem there, *Via Ardeatina*, in a
cripte of a gravel place besiden a manoir of the seid lady.

45 Which martirs slayn, as it is seid, this consularye Monimius toke Euticen, Victorin and Macron, the counselours and the comfortours of the
blissid maiden, & made hem daily to labouren as seruauntis in his manours,
and at even yafe hem brynne to eetyn. And whan thei longe had belabourid
and vexid thus, at the last he made Euticen to be betyn til he deid. Victo-
50 ryne he did be stranglid in stynkyng watir, and Macron he made to ben
oppressid and born doun to the grounde with a passyng grete and hevy
stoon, the which vnnethe seventy men myght remevyn or stiren. And natwithstondyng that grete weight of the stoon, he lifted hit vp and on his
shuldris bare it two myle thens. For which cause whan many men weren
55 conuertid, the consularie made hym to be slayn.

And aftir this Aurelianus clepid hoom ageyn Flauie from hir exile to

Rome and sent vnto hir two maidens, the which weren somtyme hir pley-
feres, Aufrodisiam and Theodoram, that thei shuld stiren hir to consentyn
vnto hym, whom she conuertid to the feith. Aftir whiche tyme | Aurelia- f. 108va
nus, with the spousis of tho maidens and thre dysours, came to Flauies 60
hous forto wedden hir and, yf she wolde nat assenten, violently to oppres-
sen hir. But she anoon conuertid the two yung men to the feith. And whan
Aurelian sawe that, anoon he led hir into the chambir and bad the disours
syngen and al othir besiden to daunsen, purposyng aftir that to defoulyn
hir. And whan the disours of syngyng and al the othir failed and cessid of 65
daunsyng for werynesse, he cessid nat. But two dayes aftir he evir dauncid
til at the last he fel doun and deyed, wherby al that othir were conuertid.
Luxurius, Aurelians brothir, heryng this, leve takyn of themperour, slough
al tho which bilevid and sett fyre vpon the chambyr wherin Flauie duellid with the two maidens. The which anoon maden a preyer and deiden in 70
our lorde, whos bodies on the morowe founden, vntouchid with the fyre,
blissid Cesarius buryed devoutely.

[85. PANCRAS]

The life of Seynt Pancrace

   Pancracius, born of worthy and noble kynrede in Friselonde, his fadir
and his modir dede, was lefte vndir the cure and tuicion of his eeme,
his fadris brothir, Dionisius clepid, which bothen turned ageyn to Rome,
where seid Pancracius had a large patrimonye in the same strete where Cor- 5
nelius the pope darkid with othir true and feithful peple. And whan by the
seid pope Dionisius and Pancracius were conuertid, Dionisius deid sone
aftir, but Pancracius was taken and presentid to themperour whan he was
aboute fourten yere of age. To whom themperour seid on thys wise: 'Yung
sone, I counceil the not to wille deyen on evil deth. For as moche as thou 10
art but a childe, thou art easy to be deceived. And for as moche as thou art
the sonne of hym that was my welbiloued frende, I byseche the leve this
maddenesse and I wil haue the as my sone.' To whom Pancracius sadly seid
ageyn thus: 'Sir, though I be yung and a childe in body, yit I bere within
me an aged hert. And, by the vertue of our lord Ihesu Criste, your terrour 15
and your feer to vs is no more than the picture which I see biforn me. Thi
goddys which thou monestist me to worshippen be deceivours; for somme
defoulid her owen sustris and sparid neither fader ner modir. And yf thou
knew thy seruauntis such at this day, anoon thou woldist maken hem to
be slayne. Wherfore I marvaile that thou art nat asshamed to worshippen 20

such goddis.' Themperour, felyng hymself to ben ovircommen of a childe,
commaundid hym to ben hefdid in *Via Aureliana*, whos body diligently
buried a worthy senatrice, Octouilla by name. Wheraftir, by processe of
tyme, was made in honour of hym a chirche. At whos grave, as seith Gre-
25 gorius Turonensis, whoso presume to sweren fals or than he come at the
chauncel dore of the quere, or he shal be rapt of a devil, or he shal fallen
doun dede sodeynly.

Oones fel a grete contencion and strife bitwix two men biforn a iuge,
f. 108ᵛᵇ and eche of hem had so apparent resons that | the iuge coude no wey ver-
30 reily knowen the gilty. Wherfore he, mevid with the zele of rightwisnesse
and desiryng to knowe the truthe, led hem bothe to Seynt Petris autier
and constreyned hym whom he supposid gilty to purgen hym and proven
his innocence with an ooth. And therwith he preyed Seynt Petir that, with
signe or token, he wold shewen the truthe. And whan this man had made
35 his ooth and noon harm cam to hym, the iuge, havyng ful suspicion that
he shuld be gilty, inflaumed with the zeel of rightwisnesse, cried lowde
and seid: 'This elder fadir Petir, or he is ovir mercyful or he differrith
this mater to his yunger. Goo we to yung Pancrace and enquere the truthe
of hym.' Whider whan thei come and the gilty had leid his hand presump-
40 tuously vpon the autier and sworne, he myght nat pullen awey his hand
from the autier. But whan he had abiden there a litle while he fel doun and
deyed. Wherfore vnto this day it is obserued in Rome that in such strange
and douteful causys men tryen the truthe by an ooth made vpon Seynt
Pancracis reliquyes & cetera.

[86. BONIFACE]

The life of Seynt Bonyface

Whilom in Rome duellid a worthy matrone clepid Aglaes, whos stiward, hight Bonifacius, a certeyn tyme medlid with hir vnleeffully. But at
the last, by Goddis inspiracion, thei were bothe compunct and repentaunt
5 with ful purpose of amendement and for to synne so no more. Whervpon,
by her bothyns assent, Boniface went for to sekyn martirs and to doon hem
obsequye, that thurgh mean of her meritis and the suffrage of her preyers
thei shuld mow be savid.

And whan he came to a citee clepid Thars, where in tho daies were made
10 many martires, he seid to the men which wenten with hym: 'Sirs, goth and
getith ws an in and I shal seen hem whom to seen I gretely desire: martirs
in her conflict.' And in grete haste he cam to the place where he sawe oon

hangen vp by the fete and fyre made vndir, anothir spred abrode on foure
trees, somme rent with nailes of iron, somme the handis smett of, and so
by diuers and many sundry tormentis examyned as the cruel iuge had dis-   15
posid. And whan he afer seigh al this, enflaumed with the loue of Criste,
he bigan to cryen and seyen: 'O grete is the God of these martires!' Which
seid, anoon he ran to hem and sat at her fete and seid: 'Fightith myghtily, ye
martirs of Cryste, tredith doun the devil vndir your fete! Beth perseuerant
a while, for your labour is but litle and your rest aftir grete, and evirlas-   20
tyng your ioye and blisse. These tormentis which ye suffren for Goddis
loue ben but temporal and passen awey in a moment. Beth glad therfore
and myry, o ye blissid martirs! For aftir short tyme space ye shul goon vp
to evirlestyng ioyes, where ye shul endelesly see your kyng and, clad with
the stoole of immortalite, shul syngen amonge angels, and vndir you seen   25
in the botomme of helle your cruel persecutours | perpetuelly peyned and   f. 109ra
tormentid.'

And whan the iuge, S[impl]icius by name, herd this and sawe, anoon
he commaundid hym to be presentid to his benche. To whom he seid on
this wise: 'Who art thou?' 'A cristen man', quoth he ageyn, 'and am clepid   30
Boniface.' With which aunswere the iuge angry commaundid hym anoon
to ben hangyn vp and to be scrapid with nailes til his bare boones appierid,
and forth with sharp reed spires to be shoven vndir his nailes. And whan
he saw that the martir of Crist, lokyng to heven, suffrid al this gladly, he
commaundid boilyng leed to ben poured in his mouth. But he yafe laude   35
and preysyng vnto our lorde Ihesu Criste. Wherfore the iuge chargid hym
to be putt doun hedelyngis into a bras potte ful of boilyng picche. But whan
the cruel iuge saw that he was nothyng hurt therby, he commaundid his
hede to be smett of. Which doon, anoon came a grete and sodeyn erthe-
quave wherby many, perceivyng the vertue of Criste in his martir, bilevid   40
on hym.

In this meantyme the conseruauntis of the martir wenten aboute the
citee sekyng hym. And whan thei founden hym nought, thei seiden amongis hem eche of hem to othir: 'Siker, whersoevir he be now, or he is in the
bordel hous or he is in the taverne.' And as thei talkid thus togider it happid   45
oon of the clerkis of the commoun place to mete with hem, whom thei askid
yf he sey ony strange pilgryme of Rome ony where. 'Yisterday', quoth he
ageyn, 'a stranger and a pilgryme was hefdid in the commoun place. But
what maner man was he whom ye sekyn?' 'Siker', quoth thei ageyn, 'he
whom we sekyn is a square fatte man, grete heerid and is clad in a slaveyn   50
of silke.' 'That man, douteles', quoth he, 'yisterday with vs endid his life

28 Simplicius] Sulpicius

thurgh martirdam.' That is nat sothe', quoth they, 'for he whom we sekyn
is an advoutour and a drinklew man.' 'Sirs', quoth he, 'than commeth and
seeth hym and therby shul ye weten.' And whan he had shewid hem the
55 body of this blissid martir and the hede, thei knew hym wele, and preyed
hym that he wolde leten hem han it. 'Certeyn, sirs', quoth he, 'I may nat
yiuen you this for nought.' And anoon they youen hym five hundrid shil-
lyng and born awey the body and anoynted it with precious oynementis
and, swete smellyng, they wounden it in lynen clothis and leiden it in an
60 hors bere and turned ageyne homeward, glorifyeng God and preysyng.

In which meantyme an angel of God appierid to Aglaes, his lady, and
tolde hir al that was doon. And she anoon, with right grete deuocion, went
ageyn to the holy body and reuerently received it and worshipfully buried
it in a chirch which she did make therfore, litle more than five furlonge
65 oute of Rome. Martired was this blissid martir Boniface the fourtenth day
of May at Thars, the hede cite of Cicile, and buried it at Rome the fifte
day of Iune. Which doon, blissid Aglaes renouncid the worlde and al the
pompis therof, yiuyng al that she had to pore men and to monasteries,
relessyng al hys seruauntis from the yocke of seruage and exercisyng hir in
f. 109rb gode werkis, lived evir aftir in the seruise of oure | lorde Ihesu Criste so
71 forferth that many myraclis were shewid in hir name. And whan she had
lived aftir in holy habite twelue yere, she deyed and was buryed beside the
seid martir Seynt Boniface.

[87. DUNSTAN]

The life of Seynt Dunstan

The holy and blissid man Seynt Dunstan was brought forth of such
fadir and modir in this worlde which aftirward he shuld mow seen for her
meritis amonge the queres of angels in that othir worlde. And, for God
5 wolde shewen biforn what he shuld ben both in this worlde and in that
othir, it happid vpon the fest of the presentacion of Ihesu in the temple,
while he was in his modris wombe, whan al men stoden in the chirche eche
man light with a tapre in his hand, al the tapris sodeynly to ben quenchid
at oones. And sone aftir, vnwarly his modris tapir was light ageyn, wherof
10 al men which weren in the chirche commen and light her tapris: wherin
was signyfied what grete habundance of light of grace shuld procedyn of
hym of whom she bare in hir wombe at that tyme. Whan this childe was
born and baptised in the name of the trinite and clepid Dunstan, wenyd,

63 ageyn to] ageyn   66 it at] at

educat and norisshid, he was sent to Glastynbury there to ben enformed
in goddis seruise.   15

   And whan he was instruct and wele growen in knouleche and exercise of Goddis seruise, he drowe to his eem, his fadris brothir, that tyme
archebisshop of Caunterbury, blissyd A[th]elm. In whos conuersacion and
maners whan the seid archebisshop had founden a plesaunce, he benygnely
presentid hym to Kyng Athelstan, the which received hym gladly and tre- 20
tid hym worshipfully, aftir whos deth also he was singulerly cherisshid of
his brothir Kyng Edmunde. By whom, for singuler trust of his conuersacion and his gode livyng, he toke the rule and the gouernaunce of the place
where he was educate and brought forthe in, that is to seyn Glastynbury.
Where, as sone as he was made abbote, he ordeyned a scole of monasterial 25
disciplyne so that, liche as of his modris tapir while he was in hir wombe al
othirs tapris toke light in the chirche, so now hym beyng Abbote of Glastynbury of his scole from that place the ordre of reguler was diffoundid
and spred abrode thurghoute al the chirche of Ingelonde. In which tyme
to the seid kyng was born a sone and in his baptesme named Edgar. And in 30
the houre of his byrthe Dunstan, beyng in his celle occupied in contemplacion and meditacion of godly thyngis, herd aungels hye alofte syngyng and
seyeng on this wise: 'Pees to the chirche of Ingelonde in oure Dunstans
and this childis new born tyme.'

   Vpon a tyme while the chirch was in makyng, a grete beem was drawen 35
vp to the height of the chirche, Dunstan beyng there present. And whan it
was even at the place where it shuld lyen, sodeynly the cabyl brak and the
beem bigan to fallen dounward, for which cause the peple pitously bigan to
crie. And Dunstan, hert and eyen fixed in heven, | preyed and, liftyng vp   f. 109va
his right arme, made a tokne of a crosse therageyns. Where anoon myght 40
be seyn the myghty hand of God in saluacion of moche peple which the
seid beem shuld haue slayne yf it had fallen. For, as sone as Dunstan had
putt therageyns a signe of the crosse, the beem styrte vp ageyn and restid in the place where it was ordeyned to ben, to laude and worship of the
blissid Trynite.   45

   Vpon a nyght, as this blissid man was in his preyer, the devil cam vpon
hym in likenesse of a bere and wolde haue pullyd awey fro hym the crokid
staffe which he leenyd vpon. But the seruaunt of God, nothyng aferde of
hym, liftid vp his crokid staffe and boldely drofe hym awey, seyeng this
psalme of the Sawter: '*Exurgat deus & dissipentur inimici eius et fugiant et* 50
cetera.'

   Aftir this, whan Kyng Edgarus had optenyd and gete the monarchie

18 Athelm] Aldelm

of al Britagne, he made Dunstan bisshop of Worcestre. In whos consecracion th'archebisshop the title of Worcestre suppressid expressely entitled
55 hym to the chirch of Caunterbury, al men heryng and marveilyng wherof.
Whan of them which stoden abouten he was modestly vndirnomyn, he
sadly and sobirly aunswerid ageyn and seid: 'I wote wele, brethern, I wote
wele what our lorde God spekith in me.' Aftir this the chirche of Londoun
was addid vnto hym, and so he occupied and exercised for a tyme two bis-
60 shopryches. And aftirwarde, whan Odo th'archebisshop of Caunterbury,
which first sacrid hym, was past forth to his fadris by the commoun high
wey of al mankynde, Dunstan, by the eleccion of al the clergie, succedid in his chayer liche as the Holy Goost had entitled hym in his first
consecracion.

65   Ner it oweth nat to be passid vndir silence how twyes while he lived he
sawe the Holi Goste in likenesse of a dove. Vpon a nyght also, whan he was
leid to rest, he was ravasshid vp to heven where he gretely was comfortid
and refresshid with the armonyous melodie of aungels songe, the which in
worship of the Trinyte coriously sungyn: 'Kyriel Christel kyriel'. Another
70 tyme also, as he was in his celle in contemplacyon of hevenly thyngis, the
glorie of God appierid vnto hym and anoon his harp hangyng on the walle,
the which was sanctificat with the touchyng of his hooly fyngrys, withouten ony erthely creaturis werkyng resouned curiously and marveilously the
antiphone of martirs: 'Gaudent in celis et cetera'. But he, the which often
75 knewe hevenly secretis, sawe and vndirstode an angel that tyme occupyen
his harpe.

It is also writen amonge the myraclis of our lady that oones she appierid to Seynt Dunstan in a vision, in a moste glorious liknesse and with
hir a grete multitude of maidens. And anoon she toke the bisshop by the
80 hande and seid that he must daunce with hir, and forthwith oon of the maidens the tothir hande, and so eche maiden othirs hand til they al were sett
ordynelly on a rowe. Which doon, our lady bigan to dauncen, syngyng
on the moste delectable wise and seyeng thus: 'Cantemus socie domino,
cantemus honorem. Dulcis amor Christi personet ore pio.' And whan our lady
f. 109vb had sungen these two vers, as for the refret of the | songe the two mai-
86 dens goyng next on that othir hand of the bisshop bigunne to syngen othir
two vers, seyeng on this wise: 'Primus ad ima ruit magna de luce superbus.
Sic homo qui tumuit, primus ad ima ruit.' Which sungen, our lady bigan
ageyn the refreit: 'Cantemus socie et cetera.' And than the next couple bigan
90 thus: 'Vnius ob meritum cuncti periere minores. Cun[c]ti saluantur vnius ob
meritum.' And thus couple aftir couple sungen til thei had fully complete.

90 Cuncti] Cunti

Sedulius songe in the ende of his paschal metre our lady alwey rehersyng
the refreit *'Cantemus socie et cetera.'* And whan the daunce was doon and
al the songe sungen, our lady with hir maidens went ageyn to heven, and
Dunstan awoke of his sweuen.

95

This blissid and hooly bisshop duri[d] seven kyngis tymes seruyng God
in gode werkys. And whan the tyme of his clepyng hens cam nere, as it was
shewid by reuelacion, not oonly by hymselfe but also to many othir, anoon
he commendid his chirch to God, instruct it with hooly exortacion and,
by the auctorite of the hooly apostoile, he assoiled it from al synnes. And,   100
pees and charitee commendid to al men, he made hys last farewele. And on
ascencion day he bigan by litle and litle to be destitute of his bodily streng-
this and, langour encrecyng, he was leid in his bedde where, restyng al the
friday and the nyght folowyng, on the satirday erely, whan matyns were
doon, he sent aftir al the congregacion. Which stondyng abouten hym,   105
he received the sacrament of Cristis body and, amonge wordis of preyer,
he yalde vp his spirite into Goddis handis, and restid in pees and went to
blisse; whider bryng vs Crist Ihesus for his mercy. Amen.

Here endith the thrid part of Legende Aurea and begynneth the fourth &
the last   110

Now that is seid in this parte past of the festes which falle within the
tyme of reconciliacion, the which tyme representith ws holi chirch from
the resurreccion of Criste vnto the vtaas of Pentecoste, now it is convenyent
for to speken of the festis which fallen within the tyme of Peregrinacion,
or of pilgrimage goyng, the which tyme the chirche representith vnto vs   115
from the Octaue of Pentecost vnto aduent. The begynnyng of this tyme
fallith nat alwey here, but it varieth and chaungith aftir the pascal nombre.
And this part aftir myn auctour is clepid the fourth parte of the hole werk
and the laste. |

[88. URBAN]

The life of Seynt Vrban   f. 110ra

[V]rbanus, a Romayn borne of the most worthi kynrede of the citee,
whos fadir hight Poncianus, was the eightenth pope aftir Seynt Petir, and
in grete age toke the pontifical chayer of Rome, aftir that blyssid [Ca]lixt
was with the palme of martirdam sent to the [bl]isse of heven. This Vrban,   5

---

96 durid] duris   2 Vrbanus] rbanus; *letter missing owing to removal of initial, which
has also led to the loss of the opening letters of* 4 [Ca]lixt *and* 5 [bl]isse

er than that he was pope, was a worthy confessour and, aftir tyme that
he toke the papal dignyte, he was seven sithes examyned for Cristys sake
and suffrid moche tribulacion and aduersite for Cristis sake. Nevirtheles,
with his prechyng and his holy conuersacion in livyng, he conuertid to the
10　feith moche peple and many worthy men, as Valerian, the spouse of Seynt
Cicile, and Tiburcie, his brothir, and many othir.

In this meantyme Almachius, the prefect of Rome, the which slowe
Seynt Cicile, exercised grete and cruel persecucion of cristen men. And
aftir the deth of Seynt Cicile and many othir, he did diligently seeken Seynt
15　Vrban, whom oon Carpasius, a cruel viker, fonde darkyng in a cave and
preisyng God with five clerkys, and led hym oute and brought hem to the
prefect, and he anoon sent hem into prison. And on the next morowen,
whan they were brought biforn hym, he seid to Vrban on this wise: 'Thou',
quoth he, 'hast deceived five thousand men with that wicche Cicile, and the
20　worthy men Valerian and Tiburce. But now telle me where Cicilies tresour
is bicome.' 'I see wele', quoth Vrban ageyn, 'that covetise rather stireth the
to pursuen cristen men, than doth the worship of your goddis. Wherfore
I wil thou wete that Cicilies tresour is born vp to heven by poore mennys
handis.' For which aunswere he bad hym and his felaus to be betyn with
25　whippes of leed. And while thei weren in betyng amonge al othir, Seynt
Vrban callid the grete name of God 'Elyon'. The which heryng, the prefect smyled and seid: 'This olde felawe wil ben holden wise and therfore
he spekith straunge language.' And whan he sawe that they myght nat ben
f. 110ʳᵇ　ovircommen with betyng . . . | [conuer]tid and cristenyd thre tribunes
30　which commen to hym, and the keper of the prison whos name was Anolinus. And whan the prefect herd that Anolinus was bicome a cristen man
he sent for hym and, for he wolde nat doon sacrifyse, anoon he was hefdid.

Which doon, blissid Vrban, with his felawes, was ledde to the symulacre for to doon sacrifise with frankencense in fyre. And as sone as he
35　had made a preyer, the symulacre fel doun and slow two and twenty prestis which mynistred the fyre. For which thyng thei were tormentid ageyn
grevously, and aftir that ledde eftesones to sacrifisen to Diane. And yf thei
wolde nat, withoute ony more lettyng, to ben hefdid.

Than Carpasius seid to the prefect on this wise: 'By thi buxomnesse, O
40　Iuge, I sey that, but yf these be sone extinct, thei shul alyenen and turnen
many mennys hertis. For we, which stonden here byforn your presence,
how we ben chaungid in hert we wete nevir, but wele I wote our wittis arn
vacillant and waueryng, and half alienat in our self, and in maner doutyng

---

16 to the] to　　29 *Text is missing owing to the removal of the border.* LgA: *iterum in*
carcerem recluduntur.　conuertid] tid

what we mow doon.' 'Late no taryeng be, therfore', quoth the prefect, 'that
yf they wil nat sacrifisen, anoon doo smyten of her heedis. For truly, that 45
ye seyen is sothe.' And anoon the devils mynistris tookyn hym in a grete
rage and drowen hem to the phane of Dyane, stondyng beside the markett
place. And they wenten glad and mury from the presence of the counceile,
thankyng God entierly that thei were founden worthy to suffren despite
and reprofe for the name of Ihesu. And than blissid Vrban strengthid hem 50
in our lorde, and seid: 'Brethern, hidertoward we han foughten, but now
we shul commen to the crowne or the reward! Hidertoward we han seyn
God in a myrour and in a redels, and now anoon we shul seen hym face to
face!'

Thus and many othir wises this blissid man admonestid hem that they 55
shuld not dredyn to deyen. To whom thei gladly aunswerid ageyn, and
seid: 'It is bettir to ws, and lever, to deyen with the, than lenger to liven
in this wickid and wrecchid worlde.' Aftir this blissid Vrban knelid doun
and his handis spred abrode, and, his eyen lifted vp to heven-ward, seid
on this wise: 'Lorde God, kyng of aungels and the ioye of al seyntis, take 60
in this houre our soulis to the, and lete ws nat be confoundid sith we come
to the, but nombre vs amonge thyn holy seyntis, aftir thy plesaunce into
evirlastyng life.' And whan eche of hem had kissid othir and markid her
forhefdis with a crosse, knelyng doun and yivyng thanke and preisyng to
God, they al with oo vois seiden to the tormentours: 'What doo ye, sirs? 65
Tarieth no lenger, but perfourmeth that ye be commaundid to doon!' And
anoon they were hefdid the thrittenth kalend of Iune, whos bodyes leyen
five dayes biforn Dyanes temple.

Aftir which tyme thre worthy men, Fabianus, Kalixtus and Amonius,
come by nyght and buryed hem in the place which is clepid *Cimiterium* 70
Praetaxati & cetera.

[89. ALDHELM]

The life of Seynt Aldelme |
Seynt Aldelme was born of the roial blode of Ingelonde, whos fadir f. 110ᵛᵃ
hight Reuter, brothre vnto Kyng Ine, a man right devoute vnto God-ward
and in admynistracion of worldely occupacions right prudent, manly and
wise outeward. This Aldelme, whan he came past childehode, by his fadir 5
and his eem was putt to lerne liberal sciencis. In which, within short tyme
he profited so that nat oonly he was comparable to his maistris which he
had bothe in Grue and in Latyne, but eke to al mennys estymacion he

superexcellid hem, so apt was his witte in lernyng, and his mynde in kepyng
10 of that he lernyd.

And notwithstondyng this, he worshippid evir benygnely and lowly his
maistris as his bettris, ner nevir was proude ne bosteful of his kunnyng,
but in that evir he did or seid he mekely and prudently bihad hym to al
maner peple.

15   And whan he was past his adolescencye and atteyned to the age which
is clepid '*iuuentus*', youth, he anoon forsoke al the worlde and al the vanitee
therof, and was made a muncke in *monasterio Meduliensi*, and sith a preste,
and aftir, by processe of tyme, abbot in the same monastery, where his
conuersacion was such that al his werkys savoured hevenly. For whatso-
20 evir he did, charite bigan his werk and mekenesse endid it. Wherfore the
fame of his demenyng and of his holy livyng diffoundid was. For abouten
not oonly in Ingelonde, but also beyonde the see and vnto the courte of
Rome, whider also he went hymself, where he was worshipfully received
by the pope, which that tyme was clepid Sergius, for the opinyon of his
25 hooly livyng. And God also clarified hym by myraclis werkys.

The vse and custome of this hooly abbot was that, whidersoevir he went
on pilgrimage, he had alwey caryed with hym al the ornamentis the which
longen to a preste to seyn with a messe. And oo tyme whan he had seid
messe at Seynt Iohannes Lateranence in Rome and kest of his chesible, it
30 happid by the providence of God that noon of his men was redy to takyn
it of his hand. And whan he lete it goon oute of his hande, wenyng that
somme man had taken it of hym, sodeynly a beem of the sunne came in at
an hole of a glasse wyndowe, helde vp the chesible a gode while til summe
man come and toke it therof. The which chesible was aftirward kept pre-
35 ciously as for a relike in *monasterio Meduliensis* in remembraunce of the seid
myracle.

It happid also aboute the same tyme, the popis fame to ben hurt in
Rome by the birthe of a childe whos modir was nat cured by an husbonde
and was famuliar in the popis court. This heryng, blissid Aldelme adiured
40 the childe, but nyne dayes of age, that he shuld tellen who bigat hym.
And anoon the childe excusid the pope and seid that he was nat his fadir,
wherthurgh anoon the infamye cessid.

This mannys holynesse was so grete and so exceptable in the syght of
God that oo tyme a beem which was ordeyned to ben in the chirche of his
f. 110vb monasterie and was to shorte . . . | ynough.

46   Thus, and many othir wises, the life of this blissid man was so redolent

---

45 *Here a complete line has been cut away along with the border on the preceding recto.*

in vertues that al the hous of God was fulfilled with the odour of the opinyon of the fame of his gode name. And so diligently he was exercised in
spiritual occupacions that bothe with worde & werk he excited his subiectis
to the same forme of livyng. Of mete and drynke he was right abstynent,   50
and to slepe he was ful loth more than nature askid. In redyng and preyeng
he was moste occupied, evir folowyng pees and fleeyng strives, a lover of
pacyence and a folower of mansuetude and of buxomnesse. And for to seyn
al compendiously, there was no thyng in hym, neither worde ner werk, but
it savoured gostely and godly.   55

And whan he longe had contynued thus, abouten the yere of our lorde
seven hundrid and five, whan Hedda the bisshop was, and his diocise diuided into two, blissid Aldelme was chosen to govern oon . . . of the which
whan he had kept . . . enfourmyng his peple nat fer . . . In which a while,
exercised by . . . myght be plenerly purgid he . . . ta]bernacle and by angels 60
handis . . . the hevenly habitacle and his . . . procession of his brethern
fecch . . . fully buried in his monasterie.

[90. ELEUTHERIUS]

The life of Eleutherie pope & ma[rtir]

Eleutherius, a grec born, whos fadris name was Habundius of a toun
clepid Nychopolim, was pope of Rome oon and twenty yere, six monethis
and five dayes. This pope received of the Kyng of Britons an epistle that at
his commaundement he myght be made a cristen man. And as it is foun-   5
den in the legende of the apostle of Ingelonde, the yere of our lorde an
hundrid and six and fifty, the Britons received first Cristis feith by the
forseid pope. For he sent thider two religious men, Stiganum and Damia-
num, the which baptised the kyng and al his peple. And in that tyme were
eight and twenty bisshops of ydols which were clepid Flamines, wherof   10
thre were clepid Archiflamines. And these men, at the popis commaundement and by his auctorite, ordeyned that tho which were clepid Flamines
shuld be clepid *Episcopi*, and tho which were clepid Archiflamines shuld
be clepid *Archiepiscopi*.

This same pope also ordeyned that noon vsual mete shuld be refusid of   15
cristen men, namely yf the mete were resonable and convenient to ben etyn
of man. This Pope Eleutherius ordeyned also that no man of dignyte shuld
be prived or putt doun, but he first were accusid and the cause provid. 'For

58 *Part of the text of these lines is missing owing to the removal of an initial on the preceding*
recto.   1 martir] ma; *letters missing owing to the removal of an initial*   5 it is] it
6 of the] the

notwithstondyng', quoth he, 'that our lorde Ihesu Criste knew that Iudas
20 was a thefe, in as moche as he was nat accusid', quoth he, 'our[e] lorde suffrid hym to be stille with hym and in the me[an]while what he did amonge
f. 111ʳᵃ th'appostlis for the dig[nyte]. . . . | This seid pope defendid that, in the
absence of hym whos cause was ventiled, no doome shuld be youen ageyns
hym. This pope was buried beside Seynt Petir in Vaticano þe sixt kalend
25 of Iune, and five daies aftir the papal see was voide and empty.

[91. AUGUSTINE OF ENGLAND]

The life of Seynt Austyn of Inglond
   This blissid and holy pope, Seynt Gregory, in the fifte yere of his
papal dignyte sent the seruaunt of God, Austyn, and many othir munkys with hym, dredyng God, to preche the worde of life to the Englissh
5 peple. Which tyme in Caunterbury was a myghty kyng clepid Ethelbertus.
And whan Seynt Austyn, strengthid with the auctorite of the holy apostoile, came to Britaigne with his felauship, aboute the nombre of fourty
persones, thei arrived in an yle clepid Tenedos and brought with hem,
at the commaundement of Seynt Gregory, interpretours of the peple of
10 Fraunce. Whider whan thei were applied, Austyn sent worde to Kyng
Ethelbert in Caunterbury that they were commen fro Rome and brought
with hem right gode tidyngis. To which, whoso obtempren and obeyen, he
behight hem evirlastyng ioyes in heven and reigne with verrey livyng God
duryng douteles withouten ende. And whan that Kyng Ethelbert had herd
15 her massage, he commaundid that thei shuld abiden in the same yle, and
ordeyned for her necessaries vnto the tyme that he had takyn his counseil
and were avised what aunswere he wolde yiven hem.
   And aftir a few certeyn dayes the kyng went to the seid yle, the which is
nat fer oute of Caunterbury at the east plage, and, sittyng in an open place
20 vndir a tent, sent for Austyn and his felauship to appieren in his presence.
Atte whos commaundmen[t] they, enspired with the grace of God, commen anoon, havyng a crosse born biforn hem in stede of a baner, and an
ymage of our saluatour depeyntid on a tablett, syngyng devoutely letanyes
for hemself and for the helth and the welefare of hem that they come to.
25 And whan Austyn, at the kyngis commaundement had doon his ambassiat,
that is to seyn had prechid the wordis of life, the kyng aunswerid ageyn and

      20 oure] our; *letter missing owing to the removal of the initial*   21 meanwhile] me-
while; *two letters are missing owing to the removal of the initial*   22 dignyte] dign.; *part
of this word and the following line have been lost owing to the removal of an initial on the reverse
of the leaf*   91. 21 commaundment] commaundmen

seid: 'Your promisses', quoth he, 'which ye bryngen, ben right faire. But
for as moche as thei ben nouel and vncerteyn, we wil not yet, withoute
more avisement, yiuen assent therto. Nevirtheles, for as moche as ye ben
pilgrymes commen fro fer and desiren to commownen to ws, such thyngis 30
as ye trowen and bileven to ben true and right gode and holsomme to ws,
we wil nat be grevous ner hevy to you, but benygnely we wil receive you
to herborowe and mynistren you such thyngis as ben necessarie to your
livyng, ner we wil nat defendyn you to associen to your sect and to your
felauship as many as ye kun getyn.' And anoon he assigned hem a place 35
to duellyn in in Caunterbury, the hede citee of his reigne. Whidertoward
as they commen, with the crosse biforn hym and the tablett with the |
ymage of the saluatour processionally, thei devoutely sungen this letanye: f. 111rb
'We biseche the, lorde, for thy grete mercy, that thyn angir and thy wratthe
mote be putte awey fro this citee and from thyn holy hous. For we haue 40
synned.'

    And anoon whan thei were entrid into the place youen hem by the kyng,
they bigunne th'appostlis life of the first chirche, that is to seyn in fastyng, wakyng, preyeng, and prechyng and conformely aftir her doctrine
livyng. The kyng than, seeyng her clene life and her holy conuersacion, 45
gretely delityng hym in her promisses, was conuertid and baptised. At
whos example al the peple forsoke her paynym rites and were conuertid to
the feith of Criste and cristenyd. This doon, the seruaunt of God, Austyn,
went ovir the see into Fraunce, to the citee of Arelas, and of the archebisshop of the same citee, Etherie, at the commaundement of Seynt Gregorie 50
the pope, was sacrid archebisshop of Ingelonde and came hoom ageyn to
the olde chirche in the seid citee of Caunterbury and halowed it in the
name of the saluatour, that is our lorde Ihesu Crist, and ordeyned there to
ben the duellyng place of hym and of his successours. At whos exortacion
and counseil the Kyng Ethelbert made vp anothir chirche fro the founde- 55
ment, withoute the wallis esteward, nat fer fro the citee, in honour of the
hooly appostlis Petir and Poule, to ben the sepulture and the buryeng place
of hym and of the bisshops, and also of al the kyngis of the seid citee. And
whan Austyn had fulfilled and complet the daies of his temporal livyng, he
passid hens to the life evirlastyngly duryng, whos body was buryed in the 60
seid chirche the seventh kalend of Iuyl, reignyng our lorde Ihesu Crist, to
whom be honour and glorie now and endelesly. Amen.

    And yf ony bodie desire to knowen more of this blissid Austyns life, and
how he demaundid Seynt Gregorie many questions, and Seynt Gregories
aunswers ageyn, also how this blissid man demenyd hym in execucion of 65

his cure and his grete solicitude theraboute, I remitte hym to Bede *de Gestis Anglorum*, where in the last ende of the first boke and in the thre first chapitres [of the second boke], he shal fynden al this clerely and diffusely tretid. The which, for the prolixite, I passe ovir at this tyme.

[92. JOHN POPE AND MARTYR]

The life of Iohannes, pope and martir

Iohannes, a Tuskayn borne, whos fadir hight Constantyne, was pope two yere nyne monethis and sixten daies in the tyme of Iustyne the cristen emperour and of Kyng Theodoric the heretik and of cristen peple a cruel
5 tormentour. The which Theodoric sent for the pope to commen to hym to [R]auenne, whom he preyed, whan he came, to goon to Constantynople to themperour Iustin. The which emperour, for the grete fervent zeel that he had to cristen religion, busied hym that tyme to han exiled oute of his empyre al heretikis. For which cause, al the heretikis chirchis he made to
10 ben halowid vnto cristen feithful vse. This heryng, Kyng Theodoric the
f. 111va heretik wolde han destroied al Itaile | by swerde, which he had not founden conforme and accordyng to his heresye. And for this skille he sent the pope to themperour in legacie. Which cause knowen, Iohannes the pope, vexid with grevous sikenessis, went wepyng and morenyng forth on his iourneye,
15 and senatours and consuls with hym. Theodorus Inportunus, Agapitus and anothir Agapitus Patricius havyng this in commaundement for her legacie that the chirchis in the east shuld be yolden ayen to the heretikes or els he wolde destroien al Itaile with swerde. And whan thei weren twelue myle from Constantynople, al the citee went oute in procession ageyns hym
20 with crossis and tapris in worship of the blissid apostlis Petir and Poule. For as the olde men of the Grekys testified and seid fro the tyme of Constantyne themperour and Siluestir the pope, to this tyme now of Iustyn themperour, the cuntre of Grece was nevir worthy to receiven Cristis viker and Seynt Petris successour with ioye and with worship. Wherfore, at the
25 first metyng, Iustinus themperour, yivyng honour to God, fel doun platte to the grounde and worshippid the pope Iohannes. And anoon blissid Iohannes the pope and the senatours, sore wepyng, besoughten themperour Iustyn that her legacie at that tyme myght ben acceptable in his sight. To whom for her reuerence and for ioye of her presence, Iustyn themperour
30 grauntid al her askyng, and so was Ytaile savid and deliverid from Theodorkis tyrannye. And for the ioye which Iustyn had, in as moche as

68 of the second boke] *om.*   6 Rauenne] Pauenne   19 oute in] oute

in his daies he was worthy to seen Goddis viker in his teritorye, with grete
glorie and solempnyte he made hymself to be crowned of Pope Iohannes
handis. In which meantyme, while Pope Iohannes and the thre senatours
Theodorus, Importunus and Agapitus the elder, for Agapitus Patricius 35
deid at Thessalonica, weren at Constantynople with themperour Iustyn,
Kyng Theodoric the heretik toke two worthy senatours, Simacum and Boi-
cium, whom toforn he had baunysshid oute of Rome, and cruelly put hem
to deth. And whan al thyngis were perfourmed and sped for which thei
wenten, the pope and the senatours commen hoom ageyn. Theodoricus 40
the kyng received with grete symulacion and deceite and hate of hert, and
wolde haue slayn hym anoon forthwith but for drede of indignacion of
Iustyn themperour. But not forthan he putt hem in prison and so tormentid hem there that blissid Iohannes the pope deyed therin a martir and
was buried in Ravenne, the twelf kalend of Iune. But by the werkyng of 45
God, the nynty day and eight aftir that Pope Iohannes deyed in prison,
Kyng Theodoric deid sodeynly and went to Goddis evirlastyng prison.
This Iohannes performed the cimitery of Nerei and Achillei, Via Ardeatina and renewid the cimitery of Felic and Adauncti and the cimitery also of
blissid Priscille. In his tyme also Iustinus Imperator offrid a patene of pure 50
golde araied with gemmys and precious stoones weyeng twenty pounde,
a chalys of golde with gemmys weyeng five pounde, two coopis of siluer,
five pallys of golde wouen werk. The which yiftis alle blissid Pope Iohannes
brought hoom with hym from Constantynople to the blissid apostlis Petir
and Poule, to Seynt Marie and to Seynt | Laurence. In his tyme also was f. 111ᵛᵇ
putt an ornament vpon the confession of Seynt Poule de gemmis Prassinis 56
& Iacinctinis. This blissid man eke in his daies ordeyned and made fiften
bisshops in diuers placis, whos body was translatid fro Ravenne to Rome
and buried in Seynt Petris chirche the sixt kalend of Iune, and aftir his
deth the see papal stode voide eight and fourty dayes & cetera. 60

[93. PETRONILLA]

The life of Petronilla

Seynt Petronilla, as the stories seyn, was Seynt Petris doughtir, and at
the wil of hir fadir she lay longe benomyn and bedlaure. And on a tyme, as
it happid many of Petris disciplis to be with hym at mete, amonge othir oon
Titus seid to Petir on this wise: 'Sith al sike folke here-aboute ben curid by 5
the and made hole, why lettist thou lyen nomen with a pallesie in hir?' 'For
it is expedient for hir to ben so', quod Petir ageyn. 'But the impossibilite

of hir helth shul haue noon excusacion. Pernel', he seith, 'rise vp and go
serue vs!' And withoute ony moo wordis she rose vp heyl & hole, and went
10 busily and servid hem al the mete. Aftir which doon, Petir bad hir goon
ageyn to hir bedde and anoon she was nounpowred as she was biforn. But
aftirward, whan she wex ful perfite in the drede of God and in his loue,
nat oonly she was made hool hirself, but also she to many othir by hir holy
preyers gate both bodily and gostely helth.

15   And, for as moche as she was excellently fair and beautevous, a worthy
man clepid Comes Flaccus came to hir with many soudiours for to taken
hir to his wife. To whom Pernel seid on this wise: 'Why commesthou, sir,
to a maiden vnarmed with so many armed men? Yf thou algatis desirest
to han me to thy wife, goo hoom with thy men of armes and, aftir thre
20 daies, send vnto me honest matrones and clenely maidens, that with hem
worshipfully I may commen hoom to thyn hous.' And whan he was goon,
in these three daies of respite askid, this blissid maide Pernel occupied hir
diligently in vigilies, fastyngis and preyers, havyng with hir hir collecta-
nee, the blissid maiden Felicula, the which was also perfite in the loue and
25 drede of God.

       And on the thrid day came to hir an holy and blissid preste Nichome-
des and celebrat there the misterie of Cristis body. Of whos handis, as sone
as she had received the sacrament of Cristis precious body, she leenyd hir
doun in hir bedde and yalde vp hir spirite into our lordis handys. Whos
30 body was first buried Via Ardiatina and aftirward, by processe of tyme,
she was translatid fro thens into hir fadris chirche Seynt Petir, where in
a chapel on the south side she lyeth in a fair tombe of white marbyl. To
whom is grete sekyng there for the hedeache and for many othir diseasis,
to the laude of God and of Seynt Petir hir fadir, to whom be worship and
35 preysyng withouten ende. Amen.

       Moreovir, whan Flaccus sey that he was thus deludid of Pernel, he
turnyd hym to Felicula, Pernels felawe, and bad that either she shuld con-
f. 112ra senten | to be weddid to hym, or to doon sacrifise to his ydols. And, for she
neither wold doo, he made hir to be shett in a prison seven daies withou-
40 ten mete or drynke. Aftir which tyme she was brought oute and longe
tormentid on a iebett, and than slayne and hir body throwen into a gonge.
The which the holy preste Nichomedes pullid vp and buryed it; for which
cause, clepid of Flaccus Comes and examyned, for he wolde nat sacrifisen
he was betyn to deth with leden whippes and his body cast into Tybre,
45 whos clerk Iustus by name lifted it vp and worshipfully buried it.

[94. PETER EXORCIST AND MARTYR]

The life of Petir exorcist & martir

The tyme of Dioclisians empire an holy exorcist clepid Petir was shett in a derk prysoun, myghtily bounden with cheynes of iron in oones hous which was clepid Arthemius, the which had a doughtir whom he loued tendirly, grevously vexid with a devil. And whan often hir fadir lamentid 5 and sorowid for hir, Petir the exorciste seid to hym on this wise: 'Arche-mye, here my counseil and bileve Ihesu Criste to ben the oonly sone of God, and that he is the helper and the deliverer of al them which bilevyn in hym, and thi doughtir shal be deliverid and made hoole.' 'I marvaile', quoth Archemy ageyn, 'thyn vnprudence, Petir. Thy God may nat deli- 10 veren, on whom thou levist, notwithstondyng that euery day thou suffrist grevous peynes for his sake. How shuld he than mowe save my doughtir?' 'Yis truly', quoth Petir, 'my lorde God may deliver me yf he wil, but his wille is rather that by these temporal peynes I and al his seruauntis mow come to eternal ioye.' 'Wele, Petir', quoth Archemye, 'yf thou wilt that I 15 bileve to thi God, loo, I shal doublen or treblen al thy bondys and putte the in the lowest and derkest pitte of the prison and myghtely shette al the doores. And yf he deliver the from al these I shal bileven in hym.' To al these Petir assentid and promysed Archemye that he shuld into his hous to hym. 'But this shal I nat doon to fulfillen the plesaunce of thy temptacion, 20 but for the declaracion of the godly myght of our lorde Ihesu Criste.' And whan Archemius herd these wordis, he waggid his hede and seid: 'This man is so weryed and altred with passion and peyn that he spekith and wote nat what.'

Which seid he went into his hous and tolde al that was doon and seid 25 vnto hys wife which hight Candida. And while thei setten and talkid of this mater and othir in the begynnyng of the nyght, sodeynly the seruaunt of God, Petir, appierid in hir presence, clad in a white stole and hol-dyng a tokne of a cros in his hande. At whos fete Archemius and his wif Candida fel doun prostrate, cryeng and seyeng: 'Oo God and ver- 30 rey God is our lorde Ihesu Criste whom thou, Petir, seruest.' And anoon hir doughtir Paulina, a maiden, was made hool and clerely deliuerid from the vexacion of a devil. For which cause al that weren in Archemyes hous bylevid; and nat oonly thei but also a grete multitude of neighbours moo than two hundrid. But of wommen was | the more part commen in and f. 112rb cryed: 'Beside Crist there is noo God almyghty.' And whan with oo vois 36

thei desired to be cristen men, Petyr fett thider a blissid preste clepid
Marcellinus and he baptised hem euerichoon.

Also Archemius lete lose al thoo which weren in prison and they also
40 bilevid and weren baptised. And whan Serenus iudex herd this, anoon he
chargid that al the prisoners shulde ben brought to his presence. Whom
Archemius gadrid al togider and kissid her handis and seid: 'Whoso wyl
goon to martirdam, lete hym withouten drede or feer. And who so wil not,
lete hym goo whider hym best liketh'. And whan thei come to the iuges
45 presence and he fonde that Petir had conuertid hem and Marcellyn had
baptised hem, anoon he examyned hem two by hemself. And her constance
provid, he made Marcellyn to ben buffettid on bothe chekys with mennys
fystis til the beters failed for werynesse. Which doon and Petir disseuerid
from hym, he commaundid hym to be ledde to prison and there nakid to be
50 leid vpon the syndris of glasse withoute light or mete. This seeyng, Petir
turned hym to the iuge and seid: 'Albeit that by thy name thou art clepid
bright, yit by thi werkis thou shewist to be right derk.' For which wordis
the iuge chargid hym anoon to ben myghtily stockid in anothir streite and
hard prison. And anoon an angel of God deliverid bothe Marcellyn & Petir
55 oute of prison and led hem bothen to Archemyes hous where thei weren
seven daies and comfortid the peple.

And whan the iuge Serenus had sent to the prisons and fonde hem nat
there, he sent for Archemye. And, for he wolde nat sacrifisen, he chargid
hym and his wife and hir doughtir to be shett in a cave and there to be
60 slayne. And whan blissid Marcellyn and Petir herden this, they commen
thider and in the same cave, cristen men defendyng hem, blissid Marcellyn
seid there a messe. Which doon the cristen men seiden to the paynymes:
'Loo, sires, yf we had wolde we myght haue deliverid Archemye and han
hid ws fro you, but we wold nat letten his passion ner oure.' And at this
65 worde, the paynyms in grete angyr smett of Archemyes hede and stooned
to the deth his wife and his doughtir. And aftir that thei toke Marcellyn and
Petir and bounden her backis behynden hem to a tree, and senten worde to
the iuge to knowen what was his wille to be doon with hem. And he anoon
commaundid hem to be ledde to a wode, that tym clepid *Silua nigra* and
70 now into this day in honoure of these is clepid *Silua candida*, and in the
same wode to ben hefdid. And whan thei weren in the myddis of the wode,
with her owen handis thei made clene the place, knelid doun and preyed
and eche of hem kissid and there were hefdid. Whos soulis he that hefdid
hem, Dorotheus by name, sawe, royally araied, born vp with angels into
75 heven. Wherfore aftir he did penaunce and was baptised vndir pope Iulius
in a gode age. And these martirs bodyes, by her owen reuelacion, two right

gode wommen, Lucilla and Firmina, token vp and buried beside Seynt
Tiburce in the inner part of the cave, the v^{te} kalende of Septembre. |

[95. ERASMUS]

The life of Seynt Herasme   f. 112va

Seynt Herasme in Campania vndir Dyoclisian and Maximian suffrid
grete and cruel martirdam. For first he was cruelly betyn with leden whippes, and aftir that with grete battis, syth he was plounchid in a vessel ful
of rosyn, brimstoun, lede, picche, waxe and oyle boyled togider. Oute of   5
which, not withouten a grete myracle, he came heil, hool & harmlees; for
which myracle many sad mynded men forsoken her ydolatrie and turned
to Cristis feith and were baptised. But he, forthwith as he came oute of
that vessel, bounden with myghty cheynes and grete weight of yron trus-
sid vpon hym, was shett in a derk prison. Where, by an angels visitacion,   10
he was both comfortid and deliverid oute of prison.

And aftir that, whan the rumour of his grete and many myraclis divul-
gid and spred abrode by the commoun fame cam to Maximians eeris, and
anoon he putte hym ageyn to many diuers tormentys, in so moche that
he did putte vpon hym a cote of iren brennyng hote, and eftesones putte   15
hym in a potte ful of boilyng lede, picche, wax, rosyn and oyle, which al
he ovircame and ascapid awey withouten ony hurt thurgh the vertue of
God, which reserued hym to confermen othir, alwey sekyng the plesaunce
of Ihesu Criste and not his privat or personal profite, aftir the sentence of
Seynte Poule which seid thus: '*Cupio dissolui & cetera*: I coveite to be dis-   20
solued and to be with Criste, but to abiden a while in this flesshly life is
necessarie for you.' Ad Philippenses primo.

Wherfore this blissid Erasmus, armed in charite and in zeel of lucre
of mannys soule, turned ageyn into Campanye and cristenyd ful many
there which were nat cristenyd, and confermyd and stablisshid many which   25
weren vacillaunt and titubant & nat perfitely of them which were cristenyd.
Which doon, at the clepyng of our lorde Ihesu Criste, he restid in pees and
went to that blisse which with grete martirdam he worthily had deserued.

[96. PRIMUS AND FELICIANUS]

The life of Primus and Felicianus

Primus and Felicianus were two citezeyns of Rome duellyng in Monte

Celio and Cristis true seruauntis, whom the bisshops of the templis accusid
to themperours Dioclisian and Maximian seyeng that, but yf thei sacrifi-
5 sed, her goddis wolde yiven hem no moo aunswers. And therfore anoon
they were brought to themperours presence and at her commaundement
weren fast bounden and put hem in prysoun, where thei were comforted
by an aungel and vnbounden of her bondis, and sone aftir presentid ageyn
to themperours. Whom thei commaundid to be led to the statue of Hercu-
10 les where, yf thei wolde nat sacrifisen, he chargid that thei shuld myghtily
f. 112vb be tormentid. | And whan, sore tormentid, they in no wise wold consen-
tyn to sacrifisen, themperours committed hem to the meyre of the citee
of Numance, Promotus by name, that he shuld compellen hem to sacrifisen or els maken an ende of hem with diuers peynes. And whan thei were
15 brought thritten myle oute of Rome to Numance, myghtily bounden with
iron, they were putte there in pryson beside the markett of the citee, where
they also were confortid by angels visitacion.

A longe tyme aftir this thei weren presentid to the meyr, sittyng protri-
bunally in the open market place, whom he commaundid to be disseuerid
20 and departid asundir. Which doon, anoon he clepid biforn hym blissid
Felician and seid to hym on this wise: 'Why puttist nat awey the obstinat madnesse of thyn hert? Counseil bettir thyn age and rather chese to
han gode dayes and mury than to suffre thy body to be slayne with diuers
peynes.' 'Siker', quoth Felician ageyn, 'I haue lived fourscore yere, and
25 these thritty wynter I haue knowe the truthe and chose to seruen my lorde
God which may, yf he wolde, deliveren me oute of thyn handis.' This
heryng, the meyr commaundid hym to be bounden to a stocke, and sharp
nailes to be driven into his handis and into his fete, seyeng to hym that
thus he shuld abiden til he wolde be consentid vnto hym. And thre daies
30 he abode thus, withoute mete or drynke. And aftir the thrid day he did
hym be taken from the stok and to be shett ageyn in prison, aftir that he to
be cruelly scourgid.

Which doon, he sent aftir Primus and seid to hym on this wise: 'Loo,
thi brothir hath consentid to themperours decree, and therfore is he now
35 gretly worshippid in the court. Wherfor, do thou now as he hath doon,
and thou shal han as he hath.' 'Albeit', quod Primus ageyn, 'th[ou] art the
devils sonne, which is fadir of lesyngis, yit in party thou seist true. For my
brothir hath consentid to the decree of themperour of heven.' With which
aunswere the meyr wroth, commaundid hym anoon first to be betyn and
40 sith hangen vpon a iebett, his sides to ben brent with flamyng fyre brondis. And aftir, taken doun from the iebett, Felician brought forth to ben

29 wolde be] wolde   36 thou] that

present, he did poren boilyng lede in his mouthe, the which he drank in as
softely as it had ben but colde water. And whan this cruel meyr saugh hem
invincible, he made hem to be led to the commoun pleyeng place and there
two lyons to be letten vnto hem, the which anoon fel doun at her fete and   45
weren as meke as it had ben two lambren. Aftir that two beres were slakid
vnto hem, the which anoon by the martirs vertue losten al her sauagen-
esse and wexen tame and mylde. Wherfore a thousand and fyve hundrid of
hem which stooden there aboute were conuertid. The meyr, seeyng that,
anoon did hem ben hefdid and her bodyes to be throwen into the felde,   50
there to ben devouri[d] of foulis and of bestis. But cristen men stolen hem
and buried hem in a gravel place the nynte day of Iune and the xiiijth myle
oute of Rome.

[97. BARNABAS]

The life of Seynt Barnabe |

Barnabas, the which also was clepid Ioseph, a dekon born in Cipre, was   f. 113ra
oon first of the seventy and two disciplis. And aftirward, by clepyng of
the holi goste, the thrid yere aftir the passion of Crist, was chosen to the
dignite of apostoile to prechyn with Poule to paynyms and othir hethen   5
peple. And how wele and how perfitely he labourid in the mynistery and
office assigned vnto hym, Seynt Luc sufficiently declarith in his boke which
he wrote of th'appostlis actys. But how he came to the coroun of blisse by
the palme of martirdam, Iohannes his disciple, whos surname was Marc,
clerely declarith forseid Luc, abidyng contynuelly with Poule, myght not   10
seen Barnabees ende.

Whan Poule and Barnabe had longe prechid in Antioche and weren in a
citee clepid Iconium, our lord Ihesu Criste appierid to Barnabe by a vision
and seid to hym on this wise: 'Be stedfast and constaunt, Barnabe, & ver-
eily bileve that for thyn holy deuocion, thurgh which thou hast forsaken   15
thi kynrede for my name, thou shalt receiven therfore evirlestyng ioye.'
Aftir this, whan Poule and Barnabe were goon ageyn fro Icony to Antioche, an angel appierid to Poule by nyght & seid: 'Hastily goo to Ierusalem
and make no taryeng, for thy brethern there ful gretely desiren thi commyng.' And whan Poule had tolde this vision to Barnabe, he seid ageyn on   20
this wise: 'For as moche as it is nat expedient to geynseyn the wil of God,
our lordis wil mote be fulfilled. Wherfore oonly I biseche the, Poule, prey
for me to our lorde, that my iournee may ben acceptable and plesaunt in

his sight. For now I goo to Cipre and sone aftir I shal fulfillen the ende
25 of my life and no more see the.' And with that he fel doun at Poulis fete
and bygan bittirly to wepe. On whos hevynesse, Poule, havyng compassion, seid thus: 'Wepe nat, brothir Barnabe, for that is doon is nat doon
withoute mistery of God. For thys nyght our lorde Ihesu appierid vnto me
and seid on this wise: "Lette not Barnabe to goon to Cipre, for my grace
30 is ordeyned to hym to illumynen many folkis and to perfourmen holy martirdam. Goo thou to Ierusalem to visiten holy placis".' Which wordis seid,
thei bothe knelid doun and, aftir a preyer made, eche of hem kissid othir
and departid.

And there Barnabas toke with hym his disciple Iohannes and by watir
35 went to Laodicie and fro thens to Cipre, where he fonde two seruauntis of
God: Timon and Aristion. Timon was vexid with an agu. Vpon whom, as
sone as Barnabe had putte his hande and red ovir hym the holi gospel, by
the inuocacion of Goddis name anoon the accesse left hym. And so perfitely he was made hole and myghty that forthwith he folowed Barnabe
40 with grete ioye and gladnesse.

This Barnabe, by the doctrine of th'appostlis, bare with hym the gospel
of Seynt Mathu, and wheresoevir he fonde ony seke men he leid it vpon
hem and anoon thei were hole, whatsoevir sikenesse it were. And whan
Barnabe had ben at Cipre and visited his frendis and confermyd hem in the
f. 113rb feith, he went fro Cipre toward a citee clepyd | P[a]phum by name, where
46 he mette with a Iew clepid Elimas, whom Poule for a tyme had prived of
his sight, and at the request of Sergius, the proconsul whom Poule conuertid, was restorid therto ageyn, but aftirward as Symon Magus was ageyn
apostata. This Elimas, this apostata, knowyng wele Barnabe, defendid hym
50 the entree of the citee of Paphum. Wherfore th'appostle, turnyng ageyn,
went into a citee clepid Salamina and fonde there a synagoge of Iewys into
which he entrid and prechid hem an exortacion to the feith of Ihesu Criste.
And whan this Elimas or Barien, which al is oon, he movid there anoon a
sedicion ageyns Barnabe and made hym to be takyn and troublid gretely,
55 thei wolde han deliuerid hym to the iuge of the citee. But whan thei perceived that oon clepid Euseby, a grete man of Neroes kyn, was come thider,
dredyng that by hym he shuld haue ben lett goon and restorid to his libertee, they putten a rope abouten his necke by nyght tyme and drowen hym
from the synagoge oute at the gate of the citee, and maden a grete fyre and
60 brentyn hym to the deth.

And, her malice not so saciat, they tookyn his body and shett it in a
webbe of lede, and purposid hem to han cast hym into the see. But Iohan-

nes his disciple, with othir cristen men, stoolyn awey by nyght and buried
it in a cript, where whilom was the habitacion or the duellyng place of the
Iebuseis, the eleventh day of Iune, where tho leyn hid and vnknowen, as 65
seith Sigisbert, to the tyme of themperour Zenon and Golasie the pope. In
whos tyme, the yere of our lorde five hundrid, by his owen reuelacion tho
were founden and worshipfully buryed.

[98. ANTHONY OF PADUA]

The life of Seynt Antony the Menour

[I]n Spayne, at the west ende of Portyngale, stant a royal citee clepid
Lussheboon, in thextremal marchis of al the londe. In which citee is a
solempne chirche of our lady wherin is worshipfully buryed the body of
the glorious dekon and martir Seynt Vincent. And at the west ende of 5
the seid chirche was born blissid Antony, whom in his baptesme his fadir
and his modir made to be clepid Fernandus, whom aftirward, in the same
chirch, they putt to ben educat and taught bothe in kunnyng and in maners.
This Fernand, whan he came to age, al worldly and fleshly thyngis despised, went to a monsterie of Seynt Austyns chanons withoute the citee 10
and devoutely received here holy habite. And, for as moche as he wolde
han the quyete of his soule as he desired, for ovirmoche hauntyng and
commyng to hym of his carnal frendys, whan he had ben there ny two yere,
with grete difficulte licence had, he went to anothir monastery of the same
ordre clepid the chirch of Seynt Cros de Columbria, more fer somwhat fro 15
his kynrede.

Whider whan he came, he so profited in religious obseruaunce that his
translacion myght in no wise ben ascrived to vnstedfastnesse | ner to dis- f. 113va
solucion. And there by the stiryng of the holi goste he yafe hym busily to
the study of holy scripture, contynuelly labouryng nat oonly how by tilthe 20
of his owen felde he shuld kun drawen vp the wedys of synne and planten
vertues in the felde of othir mennys, but also he stuffid hym plentevously
with the sentence of holy fadris and true doctours, where he myghtily
myght confermen the tru feith of holy chirche and confounden and destroien errours and heresies. And so, by inspiracion of hym which in techyng 25
nedith no longe tyme, he was replevisshid with kunnyng and fulfilled with
grete wisdam.

In this meantyme, at Maroche, a cruel kyng, an heretik, in his wodenesse shedde moche innocent blode of the frere menours for thei geynseid

2 In]; *initial I has been cut out of the manuscript*

30 and resisted his heresyes. And to shewen that he was her reward, for whom
    thei deiden, manye grete myraclis were shewid for hem. Whos relikes
    a famous man of gode livyng commyng fro Marroche into that cuntre
    brought with hym, declaryng openly the cause and the articles of her pas-
    syon. And whan the rumour of this new conflict came to the eerys of seid
35 Fernand, liche as an elefaunt seeyng fressh shed blode is the more feruent
    to bataile, so he, woundid with the swerd of compassion and armed with
    the zeel and feruour of Cristis feith, thought anoon that he myght lesse
    doon than to goon thider and, withsettyng the kyngis pertynacie, takyn
    with hem for Cristis feith the same palme of martirdam. And whan in his
40 inward feruour he ymagyned and diuised how this purpos myght moste
    redily be brought abouten, hym thought it best to take the habite of the
    same ordre of hem which thus were slayn for Cristis sake and folowen her
    livyng. For so shuld he sonnest mow atteyn to the fyn and theffect of his
    feruent purpos.
45   And on a day whan freris of the same ordre, which duellid besiden the
    citee of Colimbria, commen as they often were wone to his monasterye
    to askyn for charitee, as sone as he sawe hem he mi[ght no lon]ger con-
    teynen hym, but anoon he toke hem aside and tolde hem al thentent of his
    hert. Wherof the seid freris weren ioyeful and glad and anoon they setten a
50 day bitwixen hem whan her bothyns desire and ioye shuld be perfourmed.
    Ageyns whiche tyme blissid Fernand, with grete difficulte, gat leve of his
    souereyn there and at the tyme prefixid, the freris bryngyng an habite for
    hym, he gladly put it on and went forth with hem. At which tyme oon of
    the chanons, sory of his goyng awey, in the bitternesse of his soule seid
55 thus vnto hym: 'Goo Fernand, goo! For happely thou shalt ben a seynt.'
    To whom he symply aunswerid ageyn on this wise: 'Whan thou herist me
    to ben a seynte, tha[n] sothly shalt thou preysen God.' And whan this blis-
    sid man came to the place where the freris duellid, the which was clepid
    Seynt Antonyes, he preyed al hys brethern that fro thensforward he myght
60 be clepid Antonye and not Fernand, for that entent that, thogh ony of his
    kyn or ony othir came thider to seekyn hym, the chaunge of the name shuld
f. 113ᵛᵇ deludyn her solicitude, | and vndir a strange name he shuld eschewen her
    importune familiaritee.
        And whan he herd how the kyng of erthe wodyd ageyns the kyng of
65 heven, the feruent desire of martirdam wold nat suffren hym to resten, til
    aftir his first purpos leve taken, he went toward the londe of the Sarasyns.
    But not forthan, for al the busynesse he coude doon, he myght nevir atteyn

    47 might no longer] mi ger; *text missing owing to the removal of the initial on the other side
    of the leaf.*   57 than] that

to his desire. For anoon as he came there he was taken with so grevous a
sikenesse, and so longe a langure, that he was compellid to turnen ageyn
to the cristen marchis.   70

And as he came saylyng homward ageyn to Spayne-ward, it happid
that they were wynd-driven into Cicile, aboute such tyme as the general
chapitre of his ordre shuld ben holden in Ytaile at Assise. Wherof whan
Antony was enfourmed there by freris of that cuntre, feble as he was and
seke with grete laboure, he came thider. And whan the chapitre was endyd 75
and al doon, and euery dimised and sent hoom to his dwellyng place, Antonye, as vnknowen and as it sempt vnprofitable, was there askid of no man.
Wherupon he went to oon which was Gracianus clepid and wardeyn of the
couent at Romaginolo and lowly bisought hym that he wolde asken hym of
her mynistir general, and taken hym and instructen hym in reguler disci-   80
plyne of the ordre, whom he benygnely received and led hym with hym to
Romaginolo.

And, for as moche as he desired to ben in a solitary place, he sent hym
to a place clepid *Heremus Montis Pauli.* Where whan he came he fonde a
celle in a cave wele awey from othir convenyently for his desire the which, 85
by mean of preyer, he gat of a frere, the which had ordeyned it for his
owen vse. Where he lived as solitarily as it plesid hym in holy meditacions and strengthyng his spirite ageyns temptacions and stablisshyng in
the loue of God in vigilies and hooly preyers, commendyng hym hoolly to
the disposicion of Goddys ordenaunce. There also he chastised his flessh 90
with so grete abstynence of mete and drynk that often tyme, as they boren
wittenesse which weren present, the houre of collacion, whan he came to
his brethern, his fete faltrid so that he myght nat supporten and beren vp
hymself.

Thus the blissid man of God, Antonye, beyng ful of the spirite of wis- 95
dam and of excellent kunnyng, longe lived symply amonge symple freris.
And thus also thurgh mekenesse of hert, declynyng the vice of veyn arro-
gaunce vndir the face of an vntaught ydiot, he longe hyd the light of grete
grace. And albeit that he was evir a right fervent zelatour of Goddis hous,
as it semyth by þat is seid biforn, yit, for as moche as he oones by Goddis 100
werkyng frustrat of his desire, he wolde nat of hymself temerarily presumen to taken vpon hym the burthen and the charge til it plesid hym to whos
disposicion he had commyttid hym to, to lat his fame spryngen amonges
his brethern, which, by Goddys wille daily growyng and encresyng, the
rumour therof | came to her mynistre generals eer. And he anoon lifte vp f. 114ra
the lantarn from vndir the busshel and sett it vpon a candelstick; that is to 106
seyn he assigned Antonye th'office of prechyng, willyng that al the hous of

holy chirche shuld ben illumyned with the light of his gracious doctrine
and techyng. In which this seid Antony was so copious and so marveilously
110 affluent, and so egally departid to al men the doctryne of rightwisnesse,
that whethir he spak to grete or to smal, to high or to lowe, he evir kept
hym in the wey of truthe. And with so grete seuerite and rigour he vndirnam and blamed certeyn persones gilty and reprehensible diuers tymes,
that diuers othir famous doctours, whan thei herden it, weren abasshid
115 of his vnfereful constaunce, and, desiryng for to haue ben absent, smette
with the shamefastnesse of pusillanymyte, hidden her facis and her forhefdis with her slevis and wenten her wey. And no wondir though he had so
grete constaunce in prechyng that, for no drede of deth, he sparid, ne for
gretnesse of no man, to seyn the truthe but boldely resisted, and stedfastly,
120 grete mennys tyrannye, sith he long tyme biforn in his flouryng daies, with
so grete feruent desire had thristid to haue drunk the chalice of deth by
suffraunce of martirdam and passion.

Thus this blissid man, whos euery worde was so made savory with the
salt of discrecion thurgh grace that he was both gracious and rigorous,
125 wherby in his prechyng he drowe moche peple to louen God and to dredyn.
And whan he longe tym had contynued in this occupacion of doctryne and
techyng, goyng abouten busily by citees, castels and townes, moch peple
clepyng fro synne and confermyng in vertue and grace, at the last our lorde
clepid hym to his blisse and shewid to the world the high perfeccion of his
130 holy livyng aftir his deth by the habundaunce of many wondirful werkis
for his sake werkyng. To whom be ioye and laude withoute endyng. Amen.

[99. VITUS AND MODESTUS]

The lives of Vitus, Modestus & Crescencia

Vitus, a noble childe of byrth but nobler in maners, born in Cicile, whan
he was but twelue yere of age suffrid martirdam for Cristis sake. This childe
Vitus was nat oonly blamed but also beten of his fadir, clepid Yla, for he
5 despised her ydolis and wold nat worshippen hem.

And whan Valerian the prefect herd this, he clepid hym to hym, whom
for he wold nat sacrifisen he made to be betyn with battis. And anoon the
armes of hem that betyn, and the handys of Valerian, wexen drye and seer
and of nounpower. And anoon the prefect cried and seid: 'Allas and woo
10 me, for I haue lost myn handis!' To whom Vitus seid on this wise: 'Now
late thi goddis come and make the hool, yf they mow.' 'Maisthou nat make
me hole?' quoth the prefect. 'In the nam of my lorde Ihesu Crist', quoth

Vitus, 'I may.' And forthwith he preyed and gate hym helth. Which doon, the prefect seid to Yla: 'Take hoom thy sone with the, and correcte hym and chastise hym that he dey not evil.' Than Yla | led hym hoom into his f. 114rb hous and busied hym to changen his hert with myrth and mynstralcie, and 16 with dauncyng and iapyng of wommen, and with many othir meanys of delices. And whan he had shett hym in a chambir for þat entent, anoon a marveilous swete odour came oute of the chambir, the which replevisshid nat oonly Yla, his fadir, but also al his householde. Wherof Yla, desiryng 20 to knowe the cause, ran and lokid in at an hole beside the dore and he sawe seven angels stonden aboute his sone, and anoon bigan to cryen and seyen: 'Goddis ben commen into myn hous.' And with that he wex blynde and myght not seen. But nat forthan he cessid nat of cryeng til al the cytee of Lucan with the prefect Valerian came thider, and askid hym what hym 25 eyled to crie so on that wise. 'I sawe', quoth he, 'goddis brennyng as bright as fyre, and I myght nat sustene the sight of hem.'

And anoon he was ledde to Iupiters temple where, for to getyn ageyn his sight, he promysid to offren a bole with golden hoornes. And, whan he sawe that it profited hym not, he preyed his sone to prey for hym; and so 30 he did. And he was cured and sawe ageyn. But, notwitstondyng al this, he, obstynat in his opynyon, not oonly wolde nat bileven but eke in his hert he purposid to sleen his sone. Wherfore an angel appierid to oon clepid Modestus and bad hym taken his wife Crescencia and yung Vite and goon into anothir cuntree. And anoon he toke a shyp and went ovir the see and 35 comen to a place clepid *Territorium Tonogritanum* and there thei thre abiden besid a flode clepid Siler and serued God, whom an egle brought her mete. These Modestus and Crescencia weren Vitis norices. And, whan thei had ben there a while, the peple of al the cuntre aboute, heryng devils knoulec-chyn her holynesse, come thider to hem and herden of hem the wordis of 40 life, and so weren conuertid to the feith of oure lorde Ihesu Crist. In this meantyme themperours sonne Dioclisian wax vexid of an vnclene spirite, the which cried by his mouth and seid: 'But yf Vitus come hider I shal nat goon oute'. 'And where shul we fynden hym?' quoth Dioclisian. 'In *Ter-ritorio Tonogritano*', quoth the devil ageyn. And anoon Dioclisianus sent 45 for hym. And whan he was brought to his presence he seid to hym thus: 'Childe, maisthou maken hole my childe?' 'Nay sir', quoth Vitus, 'but my lorde may and shal!' And forthwith he leid his hande vpon themperours sone, and anoon the devil fled oute of hym. Which doon, themperour with fair spechis and byhest of grete yiftes, addyng therto yf he wold nat doon 50 aftir his counseil dedely thretis, labourid to doon hym and his felaus sacri-fisen to his goddis. And whan in no wise he myght meven her hertis, he

sent hem first into a depe prisoun myghtily bounden. Where whan thei
come, Vitus seid to Modest: 'Be of gode hert, fadir, for now begynneth
55 our corowne to come nere.' At which worde the myghty bondys with which
thei were bounden brosten asundyr and the prison was ful of light. And
whan this was tolde to Dioclisian, anoon he sent for hem and eftesones
bad hem sacrifisen. 'We sacrifisen', quoth Vitus, 'to our lorde Ihesu Crist
f. 114ᵛᵃ and to noon ydols.' Wherfore anoon he did | hem ben putte in a potte ful
60 of picche and of roseyn, and hote boilyng lede to ben throwen vpon hem.
Wherin they, in maner of thre children, sungen an ympne and a laude to
God, and, that doon, they commen oute harmeles. Aftyr this was letten
loos to hem a cruel lyon, and he anoon fel doun and licked her fete. And
whan the cursid tyrant sawe grete multitude of peple conuertid to Crist,
65 seeyng this grete myracle, anoon he commaundid a grete bedde of iron to
be brought forth, and the seruauntis of God cruelly to be streyned abrode
theron. And whan thei were beten therin til her boones were broken oute
of the flesh, blissid Vitus cried to God and seid: 'Lorde God, deliver vs.'
And anoon the eyr bigan to be troublid, lightenyngis to fleen aboute, and
70 thundryng to roren, the erthe to shaken and the templis to tumblen doun
and to sleen many men in her fallyng.

      This seeyng, themperour faste bigan to fleen, and in fleyng he bete
hymself with his fistis and seid: 'Woo me, for of a childe I am ovircommen.' In which meantyme came doun an angel from heven and vnbounde
75 hym. And sodeynly thei appierid beside the flode Siler, where thei were
first, and restid hem vndir a tree and preyed God to receiven her soulis
in pees. And anoon they deiden and wenten to the blisse of heven, whos
bodies kept by an egle from al bestis and foulis a worthy matrone clepid
Florencia, by reuelacion of blissid Vite fonde and, araied and anoyntid with
80 many swete smellyng oynementis, buried worshipfully in a place clepid
Marianus, about the yere of our lorde two hundrid four score and seven.

[100. BOTOLPH]

The life of Seynt Botolfe
      Whan Saxones with myghty hand had conquerid Britaigne and had
enhabited it with folk of her nacion, by processe of tyme and by diuers
doctours thei received the feith of cristen religion. In which meantyme
5   the blissid man Seynt Botolf was borne of the blode of the same Saxones,
from his youthe evir wele disposid and stedfastly purposid to ben Goddis
seruaunt. Wherfore, whan he came to the age of discrecion, seeyng that the

perfeccion of hevenly conuersacion and the doctryne of streyte religious
livyng was nat yet knowen ner exercised in his natal sool, enspired with
grace he went into Saxonye, the first norye of nacion, that he myght lern   10
there more plenerly that he desired: the obseruaunce of reguler disciplyne
and the institucions of the streytenesse of holy fadris livyng. For which
entente he forsoke worldely habite and toke the habite of religion, and so
encrecid bothe in lernyng and in werkyng of holy religious obseruaunce
that he ascendid to the ordre of presthode.   15

Aftir which tyme he disposid hym, thurgh the grace of God, to returnen ageyn hoom to his owen cuntree, bothe to perfourmen there that he
had bygunne oute, and to enfourmen and to techyn other to doo the same.
And in the same monastery where Botulph duellid weren also two yung
maidens, sustirs of Edelmund | which that tyme was kyng of the south   f. 114vb
Englissh men, the which weren also sent thider to lerne the disciplyne of   21
hevenly philosophie. And thei louedden singulerly wele seid Botulph as a
souereyn techer of holynesse and of chastite, and for the zele that they hadden to bryng the perfeccion of religious livyng into his cuntree and hers.
And whan these yung ladies knewen that he wolde turnen hoom ageyn   25
into the cuntre of his byrthe, thei sent hoom tidyngis by hym to the kyng,
her brothir, and to the queen, Sumare by name, her modir, the which for
the tendyrnesse of the kyngis nounage bare the charge and the burthen
of the remys rule. And specially thei writen to hem for to ben fauorable
to his hooly entent and that thei wolde, for the reuerence of God and for   30
the reward of evirlastyng mede, graunten hym a place to founden on a
monasterie, wherin he myght hymself liven and ben exercised in the rule
of monasterial disciplyne, and techen othir the same.

And whan this blissid man came hoom into Ingelonde he was received of the kyng and of the queen worshipfully, bothe for reuerence of his   35
religiousnesse and his hooly conuersacion, wherof thei had received biforn
sufficient informacion, and also for loue of the kyngis sustris, which writen moste special wyse for hym. And anoon, by inspiracion of the grace of
God, the kyngis hert was yolden beniuolent vnto hym, and fully enclyned
to perfourmen his hooly entencion; the queen effectuelly labouryng to the 40
same conclusion.

It happid also þat, the same tyme of this fadris commyng, ther were present othir two Englissh kyngis, Adellerus and Adelwoldus, ny kynnesmen
of the seid kyng Edelmund, the which bothen stired the kyng diligently
to perfourmen this holy mannys peticion. And they hemself ellys profrid   45
hym, with a devoute hert, somme of her manoirs to the obsequye and

seruise of hevenly conuersacion. But this holy and blissid man, willyng
no man to ben hurt ner damagid for his cause, thankid hem of her profres.
And, for as moche as his cosyns and ny kynnesmen hadden grete rule vndyr
50 the seid Kyng Edelmund, vndir the same kyng he desired his entent to be
perfourmed. And of oo thyng he bisought the kyng mekely: that no man
shuld, by the kyngis wille, be putte oute and excludid from his heritage for
his cause, but that of his owen grounde vntilled, wast wilde and vnoccu-
pied, he wolde graunten hym as moche as he myght bilden a chirche or a
55 monasterie. Wherein he, with othir which wolde drawen to hym, myght
seruen God religiously, thurgh whos devoute preyers his kyngdam myght
ben stablisshid temperally, and he aftirward rewardid in the blisse of heven
endelesly. To whos peticion the kyng assenting, grauntid hym that wheresoevir the grace of God enspired hym to chesyn a place congruent to his
60 purpos, and accordyng to his desire, withoute ony more delay he shuld
han it. This graunt had of the kyng, anoon this blissid fadir Botulph went
abouten by many wilde wast placis and forsaken of men, and at the last,
as Goddis wille was, a place clepid Ykano fel in his affeccion, and there he
f. 115ʳᵃ chees to abiden. And anoon in the | same place he knelid doun and made a
65 preyer and areryd vp a signe of the crosse, with which he drofe awey thens
al the noyous felauship of devils. And by the myghty vertue of his wordis
he enterdited hem and defendid hem, al that region, by goddis grace and
the kyngis grauntid vnto hym. Which doon, as a noble shepherd he gadrid
vnto hym hevenly knyghtis ful of shepely innocence and sympilnesse and, a
70 monasterie by the kyngis help made, he led hem by the helthful pasture of
reguler obseruauncis and taught hem to eschewen and to fleen the discri-
mynous periles of the horrible and detestable pitte of helle, and to chesen
and holden the solacious pathis and weyes which fynally ledyn and bryngen the folowers to the pesible and delectable paleys of florisshyng paradys
75 withouten ende.

In which place, aftir longe exercise in vertuous livyng, the cours of
his temporal life consummat and fulfilled, in grete age he passid hens to
eternal life, the fiftenth kalend of Iule, and was buried in the same place.
The whiche monasterie, not longe aftir whan Seynt Edmunde the kyng
80 martired was, was vttirly destroied by the seid kyngis persecutours, the
Daanes. Aftir which tyme reignyng the glorious and noble Kyng Edgar,
a religious and a worshipful man, Adelwoldus the bisshop of Wynchestir
gat leve of the kyng to gadre the holy seyntis bodies which leyen neclect
in diuers destroied monasteries and to translaten hem into othir monas-

teries which the seid kyng had bilded. And whan he came to Ikano and 85
disposid hym to translaten Seynt Botulphis body, he lete the kyng haue
knouleche therof. And he, devoutely entendyng into this blissid abbottis
meritis, ordeyned his body to be diuided into thre partis: his hede he sent
to Ely, half his body to Tornence chirch, and the residue he reserued to
be kept amonge the regal reliques. The which, longe aftir, Seynt Edward, 90
kyng and confessour, yafe to the monastery of Westmynster.

[IOI. MARINA]

The life of Seynt Maryne

Whilome there was a gode blissid man the which, excited and stired
with the spirite of deuocyon, purposid and disposid hymself to goon into
a monasterie and to ben a religious. This man had but oo childe, a doughtir, and hir name was Marina. And whan he shuld goon to religion, he 5
chaungid his doughtris clothyng that she shuld nat be knowen for a womman & led hir forth with hym to the monastery, preyeng the abbot and al
his brethern that thei wolde receiven his sone also to her holy ordre. And
they, at his request, diden so. And he of al men was clepid Marinus, the
whiche anoon bigan to liven religiously and to ben obedyent to hir soue- 10
reyns and benygne and meke amonge al the brethern. And whan she was
seven and twenty yere olde, and hir fadir bigan to drawen fast to deth-ward
and felt wele that he shuld nat longe liven, he clepid hir to hym and yafe
hir an holy exortacion to perseuerance and confermyd hir in hir religious
purpos, fynally hir | chargyng that nevir while she lived she, in no wise, f. 115rb
for no cause, shuld ben aknowe that she was a womman.   16

And whan hir fadir was dede she went often with a carre and tweyn oxen
to caryen home wode to the monastery, and often was wone to ben hostid
at a mannys hous duellyng in the wey. Whos doughtir, whan she had conceived of a soudyour and wex grete with childe, examyned of hir fadyr and 20
hir frendis, seid boldely and affermyd it that frere Marinus had oppressid hir and defoulid hir. And whan the pleynt was made to the abbot, and
askid why he had doon so grete a synne and brought vp so foule a sclaundir vpon the monasterie, he aunswerid ageyn and seid: 'Yf I haue synned, I
aske foryifnesse and must doo penaunce for my defaute.' Wherfore anoon 25
she was cast oute of the monastery and abode withoute the gate, and thre
yere abidyng there was susteyned with brede and watir. And as sone as the
childe was wenyd, it was sent hoom to the abbot and he deliverid it to frer
Maryne to educaten it, and to norisshen it and to bryngen it forth. And

30 two yere aftir it duellid there with hir. And she suffrid al thyng paciently
and thankid alwey God hertely of that was doon to hir. And at the last
the abbot and his brethern had ruthe vpon hir, seeyng hir mekenesse and
hir grete pacience, and toke hir ageyn into the monasterie, and putten hir
to the foulest occupacions which were vsid within: as wasshyng of disshis
35 and swepyng of housis and such othir. And al these she evir did gladly and
paciently withoute murmour or grucchyng.

And aftir longe exercise in many gode dedys, she endid hir life and passid to our lorde. And whan she was despoiled aftir the guyse of religious,
and hir body shuld be wasshen nakid, she was founden a womman. Which
40 perceived, al the munkys weren astoyned and gretely abasshid and sory that
thei had so offendid and trespacid ageyns Goddis seruaunt. And anoon al
the munkis runne to this marveilous spectacle, and al they askid foryifnesse
of her ignoraunce and of her trespas. Which doon and the body clad ageyn
and born into chirch, anoon she that had diffamed hir was arrept with a
45 devil and cruelly vexid. The which, openly knoulecchyng hir defaute, came
to Marynes graue and askid foryifnesse and was deliuerid. At whos toumbe
dayly wer wrou3t many myraclis. This blissid and holy womman Marina
deid and went to blisse the fourtenth kalend of Iule, vpon which day also
fallith the fest of the two glorious brethern Marc and Marcellian, whos
50 passion declaryd biforn in the life of Seynt Sebastian in Ianuarie & cetera.

[102. GERVASE AND PROTHASE]

The life of Geruase and Prothase

Geruasius and Prothasius weren two brethern born at oones, and
soones of Seynte Vital and his wife blissid Valeria. And whan her fadir and
modir were dede and they succedid in her bothyns enheritaunce, with oon
5 assent thei solden the hous that thei were born in and the smale housis |
f. 115ᵛᵃ longyng therto, and al thyngis that weren her fadris and her modris, and
youen the price therof to pore men and to her bonde men whom they had
made free. And this doon they shetten vp hemself in a litle hous, where
ten yere togider they youen hem to redyng and to preyer. And the xvth
10 yere of her conuersion thei atteyned to the palme of martirdame by this
occasion.

The counte Astasie commyng to Melan to the batail-ward, the which
was reised a Marcommannys, the bisshops of the templis commen vnto
hym and seid on this wise: 'Yf thou wilt glad and victour turnen hoome
15 ageyn to our emperours, compelle Geruasie and Prothasie to doon sacri-

fise to our goddis. For thei ben so offendid and grevid with her contempt
that they willen noon aunswere yiuen vs'. Whan Comes Astasius herd this,
anoon he chargid hem to ben brought to his presence. Which doon he seid
to hem on this wyse: 'I exorte you, sirs, and monest that ye leve the contempt of our goddis and dispose you to doon hem sacrifise, that my spede   20
in this iourney may be the bettir and that I may han victorie of hem ageyns
whom I goo.' To whom blissid Geruasius thus seid ageyn: 'Thou aughtist
to sekyn victory of almyghty God in heven and nat of these symulacres, the
which han eyen withoute sight, eerys withoute heryng, mouth withouten
worde, handis withouten touchyng and fete withoute goyng, bely withoute   25
entrails and brest withouten breeth or wynde.' At which wordis Astasius
havyng indignacion, anoon commaundid hym so longe to be betyn with
leden whippis til he yolde vp his spirite. Which doon he did brynge forth
Prothasie, to whom he seid thus: 'Thou wrecche, at the leste studie thou for
to liven and wil nat deyen an evil deth with thy brothir!' Quoth Prothasius 30
ageyn: 'Lete vs wete who is a wrecche, whethir I which drede the not or
thou which semyst to drede [m]e.' 'How shuld I drede the, wrecchid man?'
quoth Astasie ageyn. 'In that thou dredist me', quoth Prothasie, 'for thou
wenyst to ben hurt yf I sacrifise nat to thi goddis. For yf thou dreddist the
nat to ben hurt, thou woldist nat compelle me to doon sacrifise to ydols.   35
But I, nothyng dredyng the, despise thy thretis and al thyn ydols countyng
dung and filthe, worshippe God that is in heven.' At which worde Astasius wrothe commaundid hym to ben betyn with battys and aftir to ben
hangen vpon a iebett, seyeng to hym thus: 'Wherfore, Prothasie, art thou
so proude and rebel as thou seest that thi brothir Geruase hath perisshed?' 40
'I wil nat be wroth with the', quoth he ageyn, 'for I see how blynde the
eyen of thyn hert ben, but I rather rue vpon the for thou wotist nat what
thou maist doon. Nevirtheles perfourme that thou hast bigunne, that the
benygnyte of my saluatour may this day mete with me with my brothir.'
And anoon aftir these wordis he made do smyten of his hede. Which doon   45
a seruaunt of Crist, clepid Philip, with his sonne stoolen the bodies and
buried hem prively in his hous in an arch of stoon, and a libel conteynyng
the birthe of hem and the processe of her lyfe he leid at her heedis. The
passion of hem was aboute the yeris of our lorde seven and fyfty, whos
bodies | Seynt Ambrose fonde by reuelacion on this wise.   f. 115vb

In a lenton tyme whan Seynt Ambrose was in his preyer in the chirch of   51
Naboris and Felicis and was nat ful slepyng ner ful wakyng, there appierid
beside hym two comely yung men araied al in white bothe cote and mantel, hosid and shodde in the same sute, with her armes spredde abrode and

55 preyeng. Ambrose also preyed God that yf it were ony illusion it myght
vanysshen awey and no more appieren, and yf it were a true reuelacion
that it myght appieren ageyn anothir tyme. The thrid nyght aftir, Ambrosis body wery of feyntise of fastyng which he toke vpon hym for that
cause, while he was in his preyer thei appierid ageyn vnto hym not slepyng
60 but marvailyng with a thrid persone, the which was liche to th'appostle
Poule as he had lernyd by picture. And he, the tothir nat spekyng, seid to
Ambrose on this wise: 'These two', quoth he, 'ben tho persones which,
al erthely thyngis contempt and despysed, folowid my counseil and my
doctrine and here in this cite durid ten yere devoutely in Goddis seruise
65 and aftir, by the palme of martirdam, wenten to the blisse of heven. Whos
bodies thou shalt fynden in the same place where thou stondist, twelue fete
depe within the grounde in an arche, and at her hede a boke in which thou
shalt fynden her byrthe and the ende of her life.'

   And anoon aftyr Seynt Ambrose clepid vnto Melan to hym the bys-
70 shops of al the ny citees and tolde hem al his reuelacion. And he hymself
was the first that bigan to delven and than al that othir bisshops holpen to
delven with hym, til thei commen to the chest and founden al that Poule
had seid. And albeit that thre hundrid yere and more were bitwix her martirdam and this tyme, yit her bodies were founden as hole as thei had ben
75 buryed the same houre, and moreovir oute of the bodyes came a marueilous
redolent odour. At which tyme a blynde man touchid the bere whereon the
bodies were leid and anoon he had sight ageyn. And many othir seke folke
thurgh her meritis were curid and made hole.

   In the day also of her solempnyte was pees reformed bitwix the Longo-
80 bardis and the Romayn empire. And therfore thei put the introite of her
messe *Loquetur Dominus pacem in plebem suam*. Seynt Austyn also *de Ciuitate libro* 22° tellith that hym beyng there present, themperour and moche
othir peple, a blynde man at the bodies of Geruasie and Prothasie was restorid ageyn to sight. But whethir it was the same blynde man whos cure
85 is tolde of biforn it is doute. Also Seynt Austyn in the same boke tellith
that a yung man in a toun clepid Victoriana, the which is thritty myle from
Ypon, as he wessh an hors in a flode, sodeynly he was vexid with a devil
the which threw hym in the flode as dede, fro whens with difficulte he was
takyn alive. And whan in a chirch but litle thens the evensong of Geruase
90 and Prothase bigan to be sungen by note, he anoon smett with that noise
with a grete boistous pace he ran into the chirche and helde hym myghtily
f. 116ra by the awtier and myght no wise be mevid ner stired therfro, | as though he
had be bounden or nailed therto. And whan the devil was coniured to goon
oute of hym, he thretid that whan he were oute he shuld cutten awey his

membris. And whan algatis he was compellid to goon oute, anoon his eigh 95
fel oute and by a litle veyn henge on his cheke. The which as men myghten was putte vp ageyn into his hole. And within few daies aftir by meritis
of these blissid martires, Geruase and Prothase, he was marveilously and
perfitely made hole.

[103. SILVERIUS POPE]

The life of Seynt Siluery the pope

Siluerius of Champayne born, whos fadir hight Ormisda, was pope of
Rome but nyne monethis and elleven daies. In that tyme thempresse, sory
for Anthemye the patriarc whom pope Agapitus had deposid for he fonde
hym an heretik, by the counseil of themperour and of Vigilie, a dekon, sent 5
an epistle to Rome to Siluerie the pope, in which she desired that he shuld
callen in and restoren Anthemye to his dignyte or els, withoute ony taryeng, that he hymself shuld commen to Constantinople to themperour and
to hir. And whan blissid Siluerie had red the epistle, he sorowed and seid:
'Now wote I wele that this cause shal sone bryngen þe ende of my life.' 10
Wherfore, puttyng his trust in God & in Seynt Petir, he wrote ageyn and
seid: 'Lady empresse, siker I shal nevir doon this, that is to seyn that I
shuld reuoken and restoren ageyn to the dignyte of holy chirch such a man
as is dampned for his heresye and convicte in his wickidnesse.'

Of which aunswere themperesse havyng indignacion, anoon wrote let- 15
tris to Bellisarie *patricium* by hir dekon Vigilie conteynyng this sentence:
'Seke somme occasions ageyns Siluerie the pope and depose hym from his
bisshopriche, or els in hasty wise sende hym hider to ws. I sende vnto thyn
help Vigilium, an archedekon, and our welebiloued chapeleyn, the which
hath bihestid vs to reuokyn Anthemium the patriarc.' And whan Belisarius 20
had red thempressis lettris, he seid on this wise: 'I shal al redy receiven hir
commaundement, but siker, whosoevir is cause of Silueries deth, he shal
yiuen a rekenyng to our lorde Ihesu Crist of his dedis.' And anoon aftir
thentent of the commaundement there commen fals wittenessis, the which
affermyd and seid that at diuers tyme thei aspied Pope Siluerie to haue sent 25
to the kyng of Gothis in this sentence: 'Come vnto the gate clepid Asmaria
and I shal deliveren vnto the the citee of Rome and *Belizarium Patrium*.'

This accusacion heryng, Belizarius bilevid it not, first wetyng wele that
by envie this was feyned vpon hym. But aftirward, seeyng that many stoden constauntly and styfly in the same accusacion, than he bigan to dredyn. 30
For which cause he sent aftir the Pope Siluery to commen vnto hym into

a paleys clepid *Palacium Principis*, and at the first and the secund draught
chambyr he made al the clergie to stonden withouten. And Siluerius went
f. 116rb into the chief chambyr, and Vigilius | Diaconus oonly with hym, where
35 he fonde *Antoninam Patriciam* sittyng in a bedde and Belisarie at hir fete.
And whan she saw hym, anoon she seid to hym on this wise: 'Sey me, Sir
Siluery pope, what haue we and the Romayns doon to the that thou woldist
betrayen ws al into the Gothis handis?' And this seid, anoon withoute ony
aunswer came in the regionarie dekon of the first region and toke the palle
40 from aboute the popis necke and spoiled hym oute of his clothis, and putt
vpon hym munkys clothis and hid hym.

Which doon, oon clepid Sextus, the subdekoun of the sixte region,
seeyng this doon, went oute anoon and tolde vnto the clergie how sikerly
the pope was deposid and made a muncke. This heryng, thei fledden awey
45 anoon and durst no lenger abiden there. And a dekon clepid Iulius toke
hym into his rule and exiled hym *ad Aquas Poncianas* and there sustenyd
hym with brede and watir of tribulacion and anguyssh, where sone aftir
he deid and was buryed in the same place. Whider grete multitude of seke
folke commen and were made hoole. The day of his deyeng was the twelfth
50 kalend of Iule.

[104. ALBAN]

The life of Seynt Alban

The yere of our lordis incarnacion two hundrid and six, vndir the persecucion of Dioclisian and Maximian, it plesid the seid lordis grace to
enbelshen and enhauncen the yle of Britaigne with the confession of holy
5 martirs. Aboute which tyme, as seith Bede *De Gestis Anglorum* libro primo
capitulo 7, Maximyan reignyng in Britaigne, was martired the glorious
martir Seynt Alban. The which Alban, yet beyng a paynym and an ydo-
latre, received to hostel a clerc, Amphibolus by name, the which fledde
Maximians persecucion. Whom whan Alban sawe contynuelly nyght and
10 day occupied in preyers, vigilies and fastis, sodeynly, peruert with Goddis grace, bigan by example of hym to turne to Cristis feith. And by his
holy and helthful ammonicions al his ydols forsaken and destroied, he of
al his hole hert bycame a cristen man, with pure affeccion disposid as nede
required, to deyen for cristis sake.

15 And whan this clerc, this Amphibolus, had a certeyn tyme soiourned,
tidyngis were brought to the tyrauntis eer that þe clerc whom he so busily
toforn had pursued darkid in Albones hous. And he anoon chargid his

soudyour to goon thider and diligently to enquyren yf he were there. Whider, anoon as they were commen, Alban, enflamed with zele of martirdam,
araied in the clerkis pilgryme clothis, as hatte, tabbard and slaveyn in   20
which he came fro Rome, offrid hymself for his gest and his maister in
Cristis feith, and so bounden was brought biforn the iuge. And the same
houre that he came it happid the cruel iuge to stonden byforn an autier
and makyn an abhomynable sacrifise to his detestable ydols. And whan he
sawe Alban this wise offren hymself for his gest and thus putten hymself to 25
grete discryme, he wex wode wroth and forthwith made hym | to be dra-   f. 116va
wen to the autier of devils, where he stode seyeng to hym on this wise: 'For
as moche as thou haddyst lever counceilen and hiden in thyn hous than to
delyveren hym to my soudiours as a contemptour and a despiser of goddis, thou shalt worthily suffren the peyn of blasphemye. And yf thou wilt   30
algatis goon fro the worship of our goddis, [al the tormentis] and peynes
due to hym thou shalt beren and suffren.'

   But blissid Alban, which vttirly had offrid hymself for Cristis feith and
openly shewid hymself a cristen man, dred nothyng the tirauntis thretis,
defensid with the armes of spiritual chyualrie boldely and withouten feer,   35
seid that he nevir wolde obeyen his commaundementis. 'Sey me than',
quoth the iuge, 'of what progeny and kynrede art thou born.' 'What longith it to the to weten of what kynrede or lyneal progenye by succession I
am borne? Yf thou desire to knowen the truthe of my religion, knowe me
to ben a cristen man and to cristen offices oonly to intendyn.' 'Syth thou   40
wilt nat tellen me anoon, than what is thy name?' 'Albanus', quoth he, 'I
was clepid of my perentele, but I worship oonly and serue verrey quyk
God in heven which made of nought al thyngis.' With which aunswere the
iuge wroth seid: 'Yf thou wilt han the felicite of evirlestyng life, differre no
lenger to doon sacrifise to our goddis.' 'The sacrifices', quoth Alban ageyn,   45
'which be doon to your goddis mown neither help her subiectis, ner performen the desires and the vowys of hem that bisechyn to hem. But even
contrarywise, whoso sacrifise or prey to hem, he shal han evirlastyng peyn
and endeles dampnacion for his labour to his guerdon.'

   This heryng, the tyrant anoon commaundid hym myghtily to be betyn,   50
wenyng to brekyn his constant stedfastnesse with betyng; the which he
myght nat supplen with wordis ner with thretyng. And while he myghtily was betyn, not oonly constauntly but also gladly and ioyfully he stode
stille and suffrid it. And whan the iuge sawe that he neither myght ben
ovircome with torment and peyne, ner by no mean allectid and drawen   55
from the tilthe of cristen feithe, he fynally sentencid hym to ben hefdid.

31 al the tormentis] al the tormentis al the tormentis

And anoon whan he was led forth to his iewesse, he cam to a flode, the
which ran with a passyng stronge streem bitwix hym and the place where
he shuld ben hefdid. Moreovir he sawe a grete multitude of peple, bothe
60   men and wommen, the which by the wil and the werkyng of God were
clepid to the obsequy and the seruise of his blissid confessour and martir.
The which peple so occupied the passage of the brigge, that as by likly-
nesse vnnneth by evensonge ⟨. . .⟩ he shuld moun han commen ovir. For
so moche peple was commen oute off the citee that the iuge was ner left
65   therin allone withoute ony seruaunt.

f. 116vb   This seeyng blissid Alban, whos desire was feruent | to commen to
his passion, went nere to the riverside and, liftyng vp his eyen to heven,
preyed in his hert. And anoon the flode, which was impetous of cours and
wondir swyfte in rennyng, departid on two and yafe hym a drye wey in
70   the botome therof for to passen ovir. This seeyng, al the peple was gretely
astoyned and amarveiled of that wondir sight. Amonge which al specially
the bocher, which was ordeyned and deputat to smyten of his hede, stired
with the spirite of God hastid hym fast to the place iewyse, to mete with
Goddis holi ost. Where whan he came, anoon he threw doun his swerde
75   and fel doun at blissid Albanes fete, rather desyryng for to ben hefdid for
hym or with hym than for to hefdyn hym. And thus, while he of a perse-
cutoure was made a confessour and a felawe of feith and truthe, and the
swerde hynge stille, grew a pitous contencion amonge the bochers who
shuld doo this dede.

80   The holy confessour, with al the peple, went vp vnto an hille there
beside, nere five hundrid paas from the gravel where he was ordeyned
for to haue ben hefdid. This hil was an oportunely plesant place, peyn-
tid and clad with verdour and with many diuersitees of flouris, pleyn as
the see withouten stoones or craggis, a convenyent and worthy place for
85   the plesant beaute therof to ben dewid and enbawmed with this holy martirs blode. And whan this blissid Alban was commen vp vnto the toppe of
the hille, he desired of God to ben youen hym watir. And anoon at his fete
sprange vp a perpetuel welle, nevir to waxen drye aftir, that al men myght
knowen therby that broke in the vale had also doon the martir seruise. And
90   douteles it myght nat ben that this blissid man shuld nat han desired in the
height of the hille watir, the which he had nat left in the depthe of the
vale, yf it had not sempt vnto hym oportune and expedyent. For this welle
sprungen, and the mynisterie of the flode performed and doon, the river
turned ageyn vnto his and obserued his cours in rennyng as it did byforn.
95   Which doon, this blissid cheventeyn even there was hefdid, and went to the

63   *A single word is unreadable.*

blisse which is ordeyned to hem that louen God as he did. But he that executid this cruel werk was nat suffrid to reioyssen his vnpitous dede. For
with the martirs hede fel doun to the grounde bothen his [ey]en oute of
his hede. There was also hefdid with hym that same soudiour, the whiche
recusid biforn in the vale and refusid to doon that synful dede. Of whos   100
saluacion, though he were nat baptised in watir, no man owith to douten.
For sikerly, by the river of his blode he was purified and maad clene and
worthy to entren the kyngdam of heven.

Thus martirid was this blissid confessour of Criste, Seynt Alban, the
tenth kalend of Iule, the yere of grace seid biforn in the begynnyng of the   105
legende.

[105. PAULINUS]

The life of seynt Paulyn |

Seynt Gregorie in the thrid boke of his dialogis tellith that in the tyme   f. 117ra
that Ytaile in the parties of Champayn was gretely hurt and ovirriden with
Wandals and Gothis and many were ledde into Affric captives and prisoners, in a cite clepid Nola there was a blissid man bisshop clepid Paulinus,   5
the which al that evir he myght geten of his bysshopriche he delte to captiues and prisoners and to such as weren in myschief and in nede. And
whan he had youen al that he had, it happid that a pore widowe came to
hym preyeng hym of grace and comfort for hir sonne whom the Wandals
kyngis sonne-in-lawe helde in captiuite, and she had nat wherwith to rede-   10
myn hym. And whan this blissid bisshop had longe bithought hym whatt he
myght yiven hir and coude fynde right nought but hymselfe, he seid to this
careful widowe on this wise: 'Womman, I haue nothyng that I may yiue the
but myselfe. Wherfore take and lede me thider and sey that I am thi bonde
man and putte me in seruage for thy sonne.' And whan this sely womman   15
herd this worde of such a mannys mouth as he was, she wende rather it
had ben a worde of scorne than of comfort or compassion. But he, which
was an eloquent man and in outeward thyngis instruct of youthe, made
hir such suasions that she, avoidyng al diffidence, shuld yiue credence to
that he seide and nothyng douten to putten hym raunsomme for hir sonne.   20
Which doon thei wenten bothe togider to Affric vnto the kyngis court. And
whan she sawe the kyngis sonne in lawe come oute abrode she fel doun on
knees to hym, bisechyng hym for Goddis sake that he wolde vouchesafe
to yiuen hir frely hir sone. But he, as an hethen man, yung, ioly and ful

98 eyen] owen

25 of pride, list nat to loken on hir ner to heren hir. Wherfore she addid to
hir first peticion and seid: 'Lo sir, this man I brynge to ben plegge for my
sone. I biseche you haue pitee vpon me and acceptith hym & latith me
han hym, for I am a widowe and haue noon othir comforte but hym.' And
whan the kyngis sonne byhelde Paulyn and seigh that he was comely per-
30 sone & a wele favourid, he askid hym what craft he cowde: 'Sir', quoth he
ageyn, 'crafte kan I noon, safe I kan wele tylien a gardyn and planten herbys and norisshen hem.' Herof this hethen man right wele plesid received
hym right gladly to that seruise, and deliuerid ageyn the pore widowe hir
sonne. And so she which cam thider hevy and sory returned hoom ageyn
35 glad and myry. And whan Paulinus had take the charge of the kyngis sonnes
gardyn kepyng, he came often to hym and bihelde his maner of werkyng,
and, perceivyng in hym grete wisdam by his maner of talkyng, he bigan to
leven his famuliar frendis and goo to hym and talke with hym, and gretely
delyted hym in his communyng.
40   The vse commounly and the custom of this Paulyn was to bryng to his
lorde at the table herbis such as he perceived and knew wele that he loued,
and taken brede of hym and returnen ageyn to hys werk. And whan he had
longe vsid this maner of rule and bigan to wax familiar with his lorde, on |
f. 117ʳᵇ a day as thei talkid togider he seid to hym on this wise: 'Be wele ware and
45 avised, sir, what thou shalt doon, and how the kyngdam of Wandals shal be
disposid and rulid. For siker the kyng shal deyen and that in hasty wise.'
And whan he herd this, forasmoche as the kyng lovid hym past al othir
men, he wolde nat concelyn this matier fro hym but anoon he went and
tolde hym what his gardener whom he knew for right a wise man had seid
50 vnto hym. And whan the kyng had herd this processe, he seid that he wolde
also seen that man and han knouleche of hym. 'Forsothe', quoth the kyngis
sone ageyn, 'it is the same man which is wone to bryng me grene herbis to
the table, and today I shal doon hym commen the souner that thou maist
verreily knowen hym.' And as sone as the kyng sawe hym, anoon he cle-
55 pid his sonne-in-lawe to hym and tolde hym a thyng which til than he had
kept cloos fro hym, seyeng on this wise: 'Siker sone, now wote I wele that
it is soth that thou hast herd. For this nyght I sawe iuges sittyng on her
benche ageyns me. Amonge which oon was liche this man, and they youen
a doome and a decree that the scorge which I had received shuld be takyn
60 awey fro me.'
      And whan he herd this, anoon he toke Paulyn priuatly aside and enque-
rid of hym what maner man he was. 'I am, sir,' quoth Paulyn, 'thy seruaunt
whom thou receiveddest plegge for the widowes sone.' 'Nay', quoth he, 'I
aske nat what thou art now here, but what maner man thou were in thyn

owen cuntree er thou come.' And whan instauntly and importunely he 65
askid ageyn the same, and by many meanes adiured hym to tellen hym the
truthe, Paulinus myght no lenger concelyn ner hiden hymself fro hym, but
tolde hym pleynly that he was a bisshop. And whan he herd this he wex
sore aferde, and offrid hym cheys to aske what he wolde that he myght
returnen home ageyn bothe with richesse and with worship. To whom 70
Goddis seruaunt Paulinus seid ageyn on this wyse: 'Oo thyng I desire
the which thou maist doon, and it is that thou relesse and make free al
them whom thou hast here prisoners of my citee.' Which peticion gladly
grauntid and inquisicion made thurgh al Affric, al tho which were founden of Nola, Paulyns cite, were relaxid to her liberte. And anoon shippes 75
ordeyned and stuffid ful of whete for recompence and satisfaccion of Paulyns iniurie, he & his wenten home ageyn into her owen cuntre with gret
ioye and gladnesse, which commen oute with grete sorowe and hevynesse.

And not many daies aftir, as Paulinus had prophecied, the kyng of the
Wandals deyed. And so the scourge which by Goddis dispensacion he had 80
taken for his peplis castigacion and to thencrece of his owen dampnacion
was taken from hym. And thus thurgh the grace of God blissid Paulyn, his
seruaunt, prophecied truly the tyme of the kyng of Wandals deyeng, and
prophecid gretely to othir there in captiuite and in myserie abidyng. For he
which frely had yolden hymself allone for oon into captiuitee & thraldam | 85
with many was restorid to libertee and fredam, in this dede folowyng our f. 117va
lorde Criste Ihesu, the which wilfully and charitably came from heven to
erthe and toke the forme of a seruaunt here of men, that men no lenger
ben the seruauntis of synne.

[106. AUDREY]

The life of Seynt Audre
    Whilome in est [Y]nglonde there was,
    As in his gestis writith worshipful Bede,
    A noble kyng which hight Annas.
    A worthy man bothe of worde and dede,
    Whos famous name fer aboute did sprede, 5
    Not oonly of temporal and worldely habundaunce,
    But also of cristen and religious gouernaunce.

2 est Ynglonde] Estlynglonde

This worthy Annas, this noble knyght,
A wife had accordyng to his degree,
Bothe of byrthe and condicions a ful fair wight,
And Heriswitha clepid was she;
Which sustir was to blissid Hilde.
An hooly abbesse, the story seith thus,
Whos fadris name was Henricus.

This noble kyng and this worthy quene,
Ioyned togider in perfite charite,
As the lawe of mariage wolde it shuld bene,
Bitwix hem of issue had fair plentee,
The pedegrue of whom, whoso list to see,
At Ely in the munkys, bothe in picture
He it fynde mow shal, and in scripture.

Of which noble issue, for I may not al
Declaren at this tyme, the high worthynesse,
For litle is my kunnyng and my witte smal,
Oonly of oon the life forto expresse,
Chosen I haue aftir my rudenesse.
I mean of that gemme of virginytee,
Twyes wife and evir maide, blissid Audree.

This blissid virgyne, this hooly Etheldrede,
In hir nooneage fostrid in hir fadris hous
From hir norices brestis God to loue and drede,
Was tendirly taught, and al thyngis vicious
To fleen and eschue, and in werkis vertuous
Hir to exercise, and so in litle space
She passid hir techers helpyng hir grace.

Pride in hir myght kecche no place,
Flemyd awey by verrey mekenesse.
Ire and envie from hir hert did chace
Perfite cherite, and slouth, gode busynesse.
Coueitise repressid dame largesse,
Abstinence drofe awey gredy gloteny,
Contynence and chastite flemyd lecchery.

In hir demeanyng she was amyable,
In contenaunce and port sad and demure.
In communycacion benygne and affable,   45
In hir array honest and in hir vesture,
Noyeng ner hurtyng noon erthely creature;
But glad she was evir to helpen eche wight,
As fer as hir kunnyng strecchid, and hir myght. |

And whan to the yeris she did atteyn,   f. 117vb
That she was able maryed to be,   51
Ageyns hir plesaunce, the soth to seyn,
Maried she was with grete solempnyte
To the prince of Girueys, in the south cuntre,
Combert by name, and she assentid therto,   55
For hir fadir and hir modir wolde han it so.

Nevirtheles, that she hir holy entent
The more oportunely shuld mow fulfille,
God by his commoun messager deth sent
Aftir hir yung husbonde, as it was his wille,   60
Sone aftir hir mariage, she beyng stille
A maiden pure, bothe in wille and dede;
The same life purposyng evir aftir to lede.

Not forthan hir holy purpos
Of contynence, and of virginyte,   65
Hid in hir breste she kept so cloos
That no man privey therto myght be.
Neither her modir, but God and she,
Hopyng the lesse it were knowe to man,
Nempst God the more merite and mede to han.   70

And for she yung was and faire of face,
And issued oute from so royal blode,
And by mariage eke, within shorte space,
Leste to possedyn moche temporal gode,
And in grete opynyon also of godenesse stode,   75
Desired she was in mariage of many oon,
But in truthe she hirself desired noon.

But first of al, of Northumbirlonde
Kyng Edfrid, a right manly man,
80   Sent to the kyng of Est Ingelonde,
Forseid Annas, desiryng to taan
His doughtir to spouse, and hir to han
Past al othir, as for his queen,
Yf it hym liked that it myght been.

85   And whan that brought was the tidyng
To Kyng Annas, and to his queen also,
Of this mater, withoute lettyng
Thei bothe gladly assentid therto,
Thynkyng wisely that it was to doo
90   With so worthy a kyng to han allyaunce,
And that hir kynrede it moch myght avaunce.

And anoon, forthwith, thei did charge
Vpon hir blissyng her doughtir Audree,
That yf she yit stode at hir large,
95   And myght reioyssen hir libertee,
That to noon othir make shulde she
Promysse, ner biheste, but to hym oonly;
For that was best them thought pleynly.

Whan Audree had herd the massage
100   That, vpon hir fadris and modris blissyng,
She assentyn shuld to make mariage
With Edfrid of Northumbirlond kyng,
Gretely astoyned of that tidyng
She was, for which vpon this wise,
105   In hir privey thought she gan to silogise: |

f. 118ra   'Allas,' quoth she, 'how shuld I my purpoos
And myn entent kepyn of virginyte,
Which in myn hert hid and cloos
From al men, I haue kept secree?
110   Now must nedis disclosid be
My privey counseil and myn inward entent,
Or els to my frendis I must assent.

Yf I sey "nay" thei displesid wil be,
For my wille to hers I ne wil applye.
Yf I sey "yea" than my virginyte   115
Putten I shal in grete iupartye.'
But fynally in this contrauersye
She committed al thyng to Goddis wille,
And hir frendis counseil she assentid tille.

Which doon, in moste hasty wise   120
Solempnized was this high mariage,
As roially and as wele as coude devise
Both kyngis, with al her counseil sage,
Beyng present al the baronage
Of both kyngdams in her best aray,   125
In worship of that festful day.

In which meantyme she preyed inwardly
God of his grace hir so to spede,
And so to gouern thurgh his mercy,
That vndefoulid she hir maidenhede   130
Myght stille kepe, and so oute drede,
God of his grace did for hir provide,
That a maide stil she lived, and a maid dide.

But what maner meanys she vsid, certeyn,
To preserue with maidenly integrite,   135
Withoute the kyngis maugre, I ne can seyn,
But that the lover of pure chastite,
Criste Ihesu, wolde that it so shuld be.
For nevir fleshly the kyng cam hir nere,
While she abode with hym, ful twelue yere.   140

In which meantyme in hir demeanyng,
And in hir gouernaunce, she bihad hir so
That in as hole affeccion toward the kyng,
She stode as the day she first came hym to,
And as gode loue was bitwix hem twoo,   145
In speche and in talkyng, and eche othir wise,
As it is ony man possible to devise.

For wele he perceived and did aspye,
That she womman was of gode livyng.
150　　　And he eche day sawe with his eye,
By vigilies, preyers and by fastyng,
And of almesse by hir large yivyng,
Not disdeynous amonge pore to walke,
And with hem famuliarly for to talke.

155　　　Pitous she was, and ful of mercifulnesse,
To them geyns hir which did trespace,
Was noon so redy to aske foryivenesse
As she was redy to offren hem grace.
In etyng and drynkyng was hir solace:
160　　　Yf she ony sey which she thought had nede,
More busily them than hirself to fede. |

f. 118rb　　For which maner causis the kyng hymselue,
And for many othir moo which hym did meve,
In al the tyme of the yeris twelue,
165　　　For nothyng he hir did repreve,
Ner doon, ner seyn, that hir myght greve.
Ner nought of hir desired he, safe oonly
Aftir mariages licence, knoulech flesshly.

Nevirtheles, withouten hir propre assent,
170　　　Hir he therto wolde nevir constreyn,
Albeit he nevir so sore brent,
And in his sensual felyng suffrid grete peyn.
Yet lever he had his passions to refreyn,
Than ought of hir his flessh with to pese
175　　　Desire, or aske that hir shuld displese.

Wherfore ful often whan titillacion
Of flesshly lust hym ought did greve,
To hir confessour he made supplicacion
That he vouchesafe wolde hir to meve
180　　　T'assentyn therto, and to yiuen hym leve.
And he hym promysed, withoute faile,
Many grete yiftis for his travaile.

But whethir hir confessour bihight hym ought,
His mater to labouren effectuelly,
Or nay, siker that wote I nought.   185
But this dar I seyn certeynly,
That whatevir to the kyng he seid priuatly,
He nevir to hir wolde make suasion,
To inclynen hir hert to flessly corrupcion.

But this dare I presumen, to seyen pleynly,   190
That whan he came with hir to han dalyaunce,
He hir stired and exortid ful feithfully,
In hir holy purpoos to han constaunce.
For douteles, withoute perseueraunce,
Though a man begynne nevir so gode a dede,   195
Frustrat fynally shal ben his mede.

For aftir the philisophres determynacion,
As in his Phisikes writen fynde we,
Euery werk takith denomynacion
Of his ende, whedir either it be   200
Gode or ille, thus pleynly seith he.
Wherof it concludid may be, certeyn,
That, withoute perseuerance, gode dede is veyn.

I sey thus that but veyn is
Eche gode dede, whosoevir it doo,   205
As for to purchace with eternal blis,
And to encresyn with merite also,
But fynal perseueraunce be ioyned therto.
For not to the begynnyng of a gode dede,
But to the ende, God takith hede.   210

Example herof may be Iudas,
Which wele bigan whan that he
Folowid Crist, yit dampned he was
For lack of perseueraunce, Lottys wife for she
Lookid abak, and nolde perseuerant be,   215
Lost hir first shappe, and even anoon
She turned was into a salt stoon. |

In figure herof eke boden fynde we,
That of bestis in eche sacrifise,
220   That taile with the hede shuld offrid be.
Wherby is ment, as doctours devise,
That noo gode dede God doth apprise
Lesse than be knytte, withoute variaunce,
The ende to the begynnyng, withoute tariaunce.

225   What makith now in blisse so glorious to be,
Cristis appostlis and holy martirs also,
Confessours and virgynes in her degree,
But that no tyraunt myght makyn hem to doo
Whatsoevir peyn were put hem to,
230   Contrarie to that thei wele had bigunne,
By which perseueraunce heven thei wunne.

Thus to perseueraunce this worthy confessour,
And othir wise, moche bettir than I telle kan,
Exortid and stired eche day and hour
235   This noble quene, this blissid womman.
Assurance hir makyng that she shuld han,
For hir reward, whan she hens shuld wende,
That ioye and blisse that nevir shal ende.

By this, and many anothir exortacion,
240   Goddis chosen doughtir, blissid Audree,
Toke perfite and constaunt confirmacion
Of perseueraunce in virginyte.
Wherfore the kyngis wil, as in that degree
As he desired withouten doute,
245   Myght in no wise be brought aboute.

A man was this confessour of hy reuerence,
Of Yorc the bisshopriche was his dignyte.
Blissid Wilfride, to whom credence
Must for holynesse nedis yoven be,
250   Of this seid mater witnesse berith he.
Pleynly affermyng that it was doo,
For he knew the counseil of hem both twoo.

And whan thus twelue yere contynued had,
This blissid gemme of virginyte
In chast mariage with chere sad,   255
Of this grace the kyng preyed she,
That, withouten his offence, hir liberte
He wolde hir graunten, God forto serve
In anothir habite, til she did sterve.

That is to seyn that hir desire was   260
To ben a nunne in some religious place,
For he ne myght hir doon more solas.
And aftir many grete instance he yafe hir grace
Aftir hir wil, and within short space,
To abbesse Ebbe his aunte, he hir sent,   265
There to perfourmen hir holy entent.

Where, whan she came with grete deuocion,
The abbesse she preyed, mekely knelyng,
That she hir commyng and hir entencion,
Wolde acceptyn at reuerence of the kyng.   270
And anoon Bisshop Wilfrid, thurgh his blissyng,
Sacrid hir a nunne aftir hir entent,
Which doon, eche man, whider hym list went. |

But blissid Etheldrede there abode stille,   f. 118ᵛᵇ
The holy obedience of hir new abbesse   275
At al tymes hir offryng to fulfille
Of body and soule, with al the mekenesse.
What of hir gouernaunce shuld I more expresse,
But that aftir religion, whatevir was to doo,
Was noon of hir sustris more redy therto?   280

Now sith this precious gemme is shett,
Within the cloos of this hooly abbey,
And for a while must abiden there yett,
In the meantyme my muse may pley,
Where hir best list, for the soth to sey.   285
To this gemme ageyn she must sone returne,
For in this abbey it shal nat longe soiourne.

For, certeynly, it nedis must be,
Translatid vnto anothir place.
290   Not oonly but eke to anothir cuntree,
And that within a right short space.
There to shewen thurgh Goddis grace,
The brightenesse therof, and the grete light,
To comfort and help of many a wight.

295   Now farewele, lady, and do thy part,
For the litle while thou shalt here be,
So to ben exercised in religious art,
That whan thou commest hoom into thy cuntre,
Al folk there, which the shul here and see,
300   For such grace in the as they shul aspy,
Mow God preysen, and his name magnify.

Within the perordi[n]al circuyte of a yere,
That this noble gemme closid ben had,
The bright bemys therof shyne so clere,
305   That fer rounde aboute the bemys is sprad,
And not oonly Northumbirlonde is made glad,
But thurghoute al Ingelond, in length and brede,
The fame therof did sprynge and sprede.

And no wondir, for aftir the Gospel:
310   A citee on an hille may not hid be,
Ner no man puttith vndir a busshel
A lantarn, quoth Criste, but vp settith it he
On a candelsticke, that men mow it see.
Right so Criste wold nat this gemme hide,
315   But made it to shyne aboute on eche side.

For which cause, within a short space,
Bildid was in hir owen cuntre
A nunnery, a ful religious place,
Where abbesse to ben provided was she.
320   In thilk region which clepid was Elge,
In tho daies, but as now sothely,
It in our vulgár is clepid Ely.

302 perordinal] perordial

In which place, whan made abbesse
Was blissid Audree, ful diligently
She did hir cure and hir busynesse, 325
Hir sustris to fostren religiously
In al vertues, but principally,
She evir to hem commendid charite,
Mekenesse, obedience and chastitee. |

And nat oonly hir sustris thus vertuous to be, f. 119ra
She exortid aftir religious institucion, 331
But eke hirself so exercised she
In the seid vertues, that to perfeccion
She atteyned of high contemplacion.
For lich as al metals golde doth appalle, 335
So she, in holynesse, surmountid hem alle.

And as touchyng hir outeward demenyng,
First in mete and drynk, this is no nay,
Right seldom she wolde for ony thyng
More than oo mele takyn on the day. 340
And next hir skynne, stamyn or say,
Or wullen cloth, she evir did vse,
And al lynen to were she did refuse.

Bathid or wasshen at the mooste,
Past thries in the yere she nolde be, 345
Ageyns twelft Pasc or Pentecoste,
But at othir tymes, in no degree.
And yit last of al evir shuld she,
Both of sustris and seruauntis, goo therto,
And whan to hem al she seruise had doo. 350

Aftir matyns eke for the moste party
She accustumed was, nyght by nyght,
In the chirch to abiden, and devoutely
Knelyng to preyen, or stondyng vp right,
Lesse than sikenesse byrefte hir myght, 355
Or els such cause as must nedis be doo
For the comoun profite, and hir sustris also.

But in the tyme of hir seid preyer,
How many an holy meditacion
360   This blissid lady had of hert entier,
And how many a devoute and high contemplacion.
How many teerys eke of inward compunccion,
No man but God hymself doth knowe,
Which in his chosen hertis can such grace sowe.

365   And fynally the spirite of prophecie
She had, by which thurgh Goddis grace
How many persones she tolde shuld die,
And which by pestilence in hir place,
And how hirself amonge hem shuld pace,
370   Neither first ner last, but in such degree,
That myd hem alle hir passage shuld be.

And within short while aftir, so it byfelle,
Liche as she had seid, certeynly.
For in hir necke a pestilence swelle
375   Grete grue and rede even vpon hy,
Which whan she felt ful devoutely
Vp to heven-ward liftyng both her eyne,
Al folk hir heryng, thus did seyne:

'Gramercy, lorde, which of thy grete grace
380   Vouchistsafe mercyfully me to visite
With a pestilence soore, and on such place
Where I was wone me to delite,
In my youthe to beren grete wyte
Of golde and siluer, wherfor now there
385   Where I than synned, I peyne bere.' |

But not forthan, though she glad were
To be dissolued, and with Crist to goon,
Yit hir sustris, looth to forbere
Hir blissid presence, sentyn anoon
390   Aftir a leche, hym bisechyng eche oon
That he wolde doon his diligent cure,
Aftir his kunnyng, hir soore to cure.

And Kenefrid was this lechis name,
A ful famous man in his facultee,
Which anoon the sore to attame   395
With his launce bigan, and oute lete he
Of attir and mattir right grete plente,
Vndir the cheke the chynne fast by,
And she it suffrid right paciently.

Which doon, anoon she wex more light   400
Than she was biforn in sundry degre,
Wherof comfortid gretely was eche wight
Which hir sawe, hopyng that she
Myght of that sikenesse recurid be,
And youe laude to God and grete thankyng,   405
Hir stille to han sore desiryng.

But the souereyn leche which sittith aboue
Al thyng disposyng aftir his plesaunce,
Ordeyned had that no lenger his loue
Shuld here abiden in this worldis variaunce.   410
Wherfore ageyn hir first grevaunce,
The thrid day aftir, to hir he sent,
And in that agonye she forth hens went.

That is to seyn she chaungid hir hous
Which corruptible was, mortal and variable,   415
For anothir which right glorious
And incorruptible is, stedfast and stable,
Enduryng evir and incommutable.
O how gracious was this permutacion,
For erthe, in heven to han an habitacion!   420

And whan thus from this wrecchid valey,
The nynthe kalend of Iule, was went
This noble gemme vnto the place hy
Of heven, aboue the sterrid firmament,
Hir body they buried with humble entent   425
Myddis hir sustris, in a cophir of tree,
In the ordre she deied, as chargid had she.

O noble gemme, wele in the vertu
Groundid thou were of humylite,
430   Which of hym to be lerned commaundid Ihesu.
And Salamon seith yf men prince make the,
In no wise therof thou proude ne be,
But hem amonge as oon of them the bere,
These lessons to the weren not new to lere.

435   For albeit that thou were an abbesse,
And of royal blode right worthy bore,
A glorious queen eke aftir a pryncesse,
Yit in no wise woldisthou therfore,
Of worship vpon the takyn the more,
440   Quycke ner dede, but the lowest place
Evir thou chese, so gouernyd the grace. |

f. 119ᵛᵃ   Wherfore, though thou a while doo rest,
O noble examplarie of al humbilnesse,
Here lowly bigraved in a treen chest,
445   Not longe lyen here thou shalt in sothfastnesse.
For in the Gospel, as Crist doth wittenesse:
Who hymself exaltith, fallen shal he,
And who hymself mekith, enhauncid shal be.

And whan thus in hir fate was forth procedid
450   This worthy abbesse, this blissid Audre,
Hir sustir Sexburga aftir hir succedid,
The which of Caunterbury the kyngis wife had be,
Ercombert; and whan that dede was he
Al vanyte forsakyn to hir sustir she went,
455   And a nunne was sacrid with an holy entent.

But yit, for as moche as biforn seid ys,
That light vndir a busshel may nat hyd be,
Right so this gemme hir bright bemys
Wide spred abrode in many a cuntree,
460   Of myraclis werkyng by grete plentee.
For which moche peple came hir to seke,
In place where she lay lowly and meke.

And whan the abbesse Sexburgh such habundaunce
Of myraclis encresyn sawe there dayly,
She hir purposid to translate and enhauncen   465
Oute of that place, hir sustris body,
Where it lay first, and more reuerently
It leyn, that pilgrymes thider commyng shul moun,
The more therby to be stired to deuocioun.

For which entent, of hir monastery   470
To diuers brethern she yafe in charge,
In as moche as in the yle therby,
Ner nere aboute grew no stoones large,
That they anoon shuld taken hir barge
And ferther of goon into the cuntree,   475
Such a stoon to sekyn as convenyent myght be.

That is to seyn she desired to haue,
Aftir hir entent, so large a stoon
That therof a thorugh, or els a graue
Myght be made with a coveryng theron.   480
Of whos commaundement thei forth went anoon,
But where to spedyn or in what place
They wist nevir, but vpon Goddis grace.

And whan thei had sailed a litle stounde,
And not fully the iourney of oo day,   485
Vndir an olde citee wallis they founde,
Of white marbyl a thorugh where it lay,
Coueryd of the same, which whan thei say,
To her purpos them thought it convenyent,
Yf they myght geten the owners assent.   490

And Grauntcestre this olde citee hight,
Into which these massangers entrid anoon,
Diligently enquyryng of euery wight
Who myght ben owner of that fair stoon.
But it to chalangen pleynly wolde noon,   495
Of whom al siker this was the aunswere:
Biforn that day they it nevir seyn ere. |

And whan these men this aunswere had,
That chalange of the stoon wold no man make,
500   In her hertis they weren right glad,
And in her barge thei didden it take,
And from the teyeng anoon thei did it slake.
And rowyng hoom ageyn with grete gladnesse,
How they had spedde thei tolde the abbesse.

505   And whan she had herd al the processe,
And how graciously sped was her iournee,
She hertely thankyd Goddis godenesse,
Withoute which it myght nat haue be
So sone sped, as fully trustid she,
510   Where she it received, with as devoute entent
As though from heven God it hir had sent.

Not longe aftir 'this', this worthy abbesse,
Purposyng to perfourmen hir holy entent,
Aboute fourtenyght aftir Myghelmasse
515   Vnto hir sustris grave she went,
And did it ovircuren with a tent,
That no man shuld see that blissid body,
Til the boones were wasshen and made redy.

And rounde aboute the tent al the company
520   Of hi[r] sustris stooden, and prestis also,
Syngyng and preyeng ful devoutely,
While the abbesse with a fewe clepid hir to
Went in and did the grave vndoo.
Which doon, the body truly thei founde
525   As it was buried, al hole and sounde.

That is to seyn that no corrupcioun
Was therupon, ner feculencie,
From the hede abouen to the foot doun,
As fer as the abbesse coude aspye.
530   For forhede and cheke, mouth and iye,
And al the face eke, was as fresh to see
As she not dede but aslepe had be.

520 hir] his

And not oonly hir body but the clothis also,
In which it wrappid was and wounde,
With al othir thyngis longyng therto,   535
Withoute putrefaccion heyl were and sounde,
As though tho nevir had leyn on grounde.
And therto of odour as redolent, certeyn,
As tho amonge flouris or spices had leyn.

And whan the abbesse perceivid al this thyng,   540
With a lowde voice she thus gan cry:
'To the name of God, laude and preysyng
Mote be now and evirmore endelesly,
Which vs hath shewid here his mercy.'
And forthwith she the pavillioun dore vnshett,   545
And to see this wondir othir folk in lett.

Amonge which, of moste auctorite
And right sufficient witnesse forto bere,
Was blissid Wilfrid, which had be
Hi[r] confessour biforn ful many a yere.   550
Kenefrid the leche was also there,
Which biforn hir deth hir soore did stynge,
And was eke there with hem at hir buryeng. |

And oo thyng in special this leche Kenefride,   f. 120ra
Evir aftir while he lived did testifye: 555
That the wounde in hir neck moist and wide,
Which hymself made, was curid and drye,
So fair that vnnethe he coude aspye
Where it was, which, aftir his faculte,
Semyd impossible evir curid to haue be.   560

Hir clothis had also such vertu
That who hem touchid with ony sikenesse,
Thurgh grace of our lorde Crist Ihesu,
He curid was anoon, were it more or lesse.
And as al there present born wittenesse   565
The cophir eke, which was first hir grave,
From sekenesse of eyn many oon did save.

550 Hir] his

But of al the circumstauncis to make declaracion,
Of the myraclis which there weren wrought
570   At this blissid and hooly virgynes translacion,
And how fer and for what causis folke hir sought,
My witte is to litle and suffiseth nought.
Wherfore I biseche no wight me blame,
Though I presume nat the mater to attame,

575   But in my processe forth to procede.
Whan wasshen was this blissid body
And new araied in more precious wede,
Into the chirch it born was ful reuerently.
And in the fair thorugh which myraculously
580   God of his grace thider had sent,
Thei it to dressyn diden her entent.

And that al men ther present myght wele wete
That by grace al oonly it thider was brought,
It for the body was even as mete
585   As though it therfore had be special wrought.
And so it was sikerly, I doute it nought,
By angels handis, for no man coude truly,
Withoute a mesure, han made it so accordyngly.

For al abouen for the hede a place
590   Graven was of conuenyent quantite,
As bynethen eke was anothir space,
Where leggis and feet shuld leyed be.
And for the body in the myddis in conform degree,
Neither more ne lesse than it nedis be must,
595   Withoute pressure to lyen pleyn and iust.

The couertour abouen was conformely
Graven in aftir the nethir stoon,
So that it not touchyn shuld the body,
And so iustely ioyned that in myght goon
600   Wynde ner eyre, ner othir thyngis noon.
Wherin as cloos as in a chest,
This blissid body yet doth rest,

And so shal it stille I hope, certeyn,
Til the day come of the grete assise,
Whan the soule therto shal be knytte ageyn,   605
And glorified it makyn vp to rise,
And so both togider, in ful solempne wise,
Entren shullen into the court celestyal,
Where ioye and blisse is eternal. |

[Now] Seynt Audree, for the grete grace   f. 120rb
Which thou receiveddest of God in this life mortal,   611
Purchace thi seruauntis in this worldis space,
Pardon of her synnes both grete and smal,
And to the translatour gete in especial,
Of thy life into Englissh aftir his kunnyng,   615
Aftir this outelawry, in heven a wonnyng.

[107. JOHN THE BAPTIST]

The prologe of Seynt Iohan baptyst

Seynt Iohan baptist, as seith myn auctour Ianuence, is clepid nyne
diuers names, which shewen in hym nyne sundry prerogatives or priuilegis. For he is clepid a prophete, the frende of the husbonde, a lantarn,
an angel, a vois, Hely, the baptist of the saluatour, the iugis bedel and the   5
kyngis precessour or forngoer. In that he is clepid a prophete is signyfied
his prerogatife in knowyng. In that he is seid the spousis frende is markyd
his prerogatyf in loue. In the light lantarn, holynesse of livyng. In that he
is clepid an angel is tokenyd his clennesse of chastite. In the vois is markid his mekenesse or humylitee; in Helye the prerogatif of feruent zeel.   10
In that he is clepid the baptist of our saluatour is expressid his marveilous
worships and honour. In that he is clepid the iugis bedel is notid his priuilege in prechyng. In the kyngis forgoer is vndirstonden the priuilege of
redy makyng. And al these shul be shewid consequently in his legende &
cetera.   15

The natiuite of Seynt Iohan Baptist

The holy evangelist of our lorde Ihesu Crist Seynt Luc in the first chapitre of his boke compendyously declarith the birthe of the prophete Seynt
Iohan Baptist, seyeng on this wise: In the dayes of Heroude, kyng of Iuery,

610 Now *missing owing to the removal of a border decoration.*

20 there was a preste whos name was Zacharie of the while of Abie, which had
a wife of the doughtris of Aaron, Elizabeth by name. And bothe were rightful biforn God, goyng in his commaundementis withoute mater of offence.
But thei had no sonne, for as moche as Elizabeth was bareyn and bothen
were fer runne forth in her dayes. And as it happid on a day whan Zachary
25 executid his office in the ordre of his while, aftir the consuetude and custome of the presthode entryng into the temple of our lorde for to encensen
and al the peple abode withoute in the porche preyeng the houre of encen-
syng, an angel of God appierid vnto hym, stondyng on the right hand of
the autier of the encense. Whom Zachary seeyng wex abasshid and feer ran
30 vpon hym. To whom the angel seid on this wise: 'Drede the not, for thy
preyer is herd and thy wife shal bryng the forth a sonne. And thou shalt
clepyn his name Iohan and it shal ben to the ioye and gladnesse, and many
men shul ioyen in his birth. He shal be grete biforn our lorde, he shal no
wyne drynken ne syder. He shal be fulfilled with the holi goste from his
35 modris wombe. And he many hertis of the children of Israel shal conuer-
f. 120ᵛᵃ tyn to | her lorde God. And he shal goon biforn hym . . . and in the vertue
of Hely to conuertyn the hertis of the fadris into the sonnes and mysbile-
vyng men vnto the prudence of rightful men and to makyn redy a perfite
peple to our lorde.' Quoth Zacharie ageyn to the angel: 'How shal I knowe
40 this thyng that thou seyest, sith I am aged and olde and my wife is fer passid forth into age?' To whom the angel seid ageyn thus: 'I am Gabriel, the
which stonde biforn God, and am sent to speke to the and to telle the this
thyng. Lo this shal be thy tokne: thou shalt holde thy pees and not spekyn
vnto the day that these thyngis be doon, for as moche as thou woldist nat
45 bilevyn and yiuen credence to my wordis, the which shul ben fulfilled in
her tyme.' And in this meanwhile the peple was abidyng Zacharie withouten, and they marveiled that he taryed so longe in the temple. And whan
he came oute and myght nat speken to hem, thei knew wele that he had had
a vision in the temple. And whan he had perfourmed his cours he turned
50 hoom ageyn to his hous.

Aftir these dayes Elizabeth conceived and hid hir five monethis, thankyng God that he had so doon to hir and takyn awey hir obropbrie amonge
men. And whan the tyme of childyng was fulfilled she brought forth a
sonne. Which doon, whan hir neighbours and hir cosyns herd seyn that
55 God had magnyfied his mercy with hir, they comme and maden a rei-
oyssyng therof vnto hir. And the eight day aftir, whan men commen to
circumciden the childe, thei clepid hym by his fadris name Zacharie. To
whom the modir aunswerid and seid: 'Nay, that is to seyn he shal nat be

36 *Text missing owing to removal of border decoration.*

clepid Zacharie, but Iohan shal be clepid his name.' Quoth thei ageyn:
'There is no man in thy cognacion or in thy kynrede the which is clepid by   60
that name.' Wherfore they maden a signe to his fadir to weten what name
he wolde han hym clepid. And he askid an augryme stoon and wrote thus
and seid: 'Iohan is his name.' And al which were there marvailed gretely
therof. And anoon forthwith Zacharies mouth was openyd and his tunge
losenyd, and he spak preysyng God and blissyng. For which causis drede   65
and fere was made vpon al hir neighbours, and forthwith it was dyvulgid
and puplisshid vpon al the mountaynes of Iu[d]y. And al tho which herden these wordis put hem in her hertis, seyeng thus eche to othir: 'What
maner man hopist thou this childe shal been; sothely the hand of God is
with hym.' And anoon Zachary his fadir, fulfilled with the holi goste, pro-   70
phecied, seyeng on this wise: 'Blissid be the lorde God of Israel, for he
hath visited and made the redempcion of his peple', and so made vp al
that psalme. *Hec Lucus primo capitulo.*

For the more clere vndirstondyng of this forseid processe, Ianuence
notith the processe of the maister of storyes vpon the gospels, where he   75
seith that Dauid the kyng of Israel, willyng amplyfien and encresyn the
seruise of God, ordeyned four and twenty prestis to seruen in the temple.
Amonge which oon that was grettest was clepid the prince of prestis and |
of these xxiiij^{ti} sixten were of Eleazar and eight of Ithamar, Aarones sonnes,   f. 120vb
and ordeyned that eche of hem shuld han the woke of his while aftir lootis.   80
And Abia, of whom came Zacharie, had the eight woke. And this diuision
of wokis was thus ordeyned by lottis, that there shuld no dissencion ner
stryf ben amonge hem, though oo woke were bettir than anothir. And thus
the eight woke longid to Zacharie and to his succession. And convenyently,
quoth Bede, the bedel or the cryer of the new testament was conceivid in   85
the while of the eight lotte. For, right as in the nombre of seven bicause of
the Sabat is often signified the olde testament, so somtyme in the nombre of
eight for the sacrament of our lordis resurreccion or of our is vndirstonde
the new testament.

Than while Zacharie executid this office of presthode by ordre of his   90
lotte, entryng into the temple to castyn encence, an angel, as it is seid
byforn, appierid vnto hym & cetera. And this was as it verreily and coniec-
turabily supposid, quoth a notable postille vpon Luc, the tenth day of
Septembre. In which day were ioyned togider in tho daies thre solempne
festis: as the fest of affliccion, the fest of expiacion and the fest of propici-   95
acion. It was clepid the fest of affliccion for that day the Iewys moste and
leste peyned hemself, fastyng til even aftir the commaundement of God.

Leuiticus 22°. Where it is seid thus: 'The tenth day of the seventh moneth
shal be the right holy day of expiacion, and ye shul peynen or tormentyn
100 your soulis therin & cetera.'

And this day was clepid the day of expiacion, for þat day the prest entryng into *sancta sanctorum* sprenclid the wallis and al the ornamentis of the
temple with the blode of a rede hekfere. The which sprenclyng or aspersion
was a figuratif expiacion.

105 This day also were made of the rede hekfere asshys, wherwith al the
yere aftir was made the watir of expiacion. This day was also clepid the
day of propiciacion, for this day our lorde had mercy on his peple. For as
Raby Moyses seith on this same day: 'Moyses came doun from the hille
with the secund tablys and brought the peple tidyngis of foryifnesse and
110 propiciacion of her grete synne of the golden calf makyng; and therfore
this day was eternal to doon penaunce in and to seruen God.' For whiche
cause al bodily delectacion was inhibited that day, & al laborious werkis
which longen to the profite of the body. So that this day was nothyng leeful to be doon but confession and penaunce. Of which processe somme
115 men concludyn that Zacharie was the high preste of the lawe, that is to
seyn bisshop, for as moche as into the secunde tabernacle entrid no man
but the high preste oones in the yere with blode. This semyth to ben Seynt
Ambrosis opynyon. *Hec postilla praedictus.*

And whan Zacharie wex aferd of the angels sight, he confortid hym
120 ageyn and seid: 'Be nat aferde, Zacharie, for thi preyer is herd.' Where the
glose seith thus: 'It is the propirtee of gode angels, yf men ben aferde in her
f. 121ra apparicion, anoon to comfortyn hem ageyn with benygne ... | ... siden a
chirche of Seynt Iohan baptist. And not longe aftir oon, for couetise of the
gode, brak the grave and bare awey the tresoure that was therin. To whom
125 Seynt Iohan appierid and seid: 'Why were thou so hardy to beren awey
such thyngis as were commyttid to my kepyng? I warne the therfore that
fro hensforward thou shalt nat entren into my chirche.' And as he seid so
it felle. For whansoevir he wolde haue goon in, he was shoven oute ageyn
with as grete a violence as though a myghty champyon had takyn hym by
130 the throte and cast hym oute bakwarde.

[108. JOHN AND PAUL]

The story of Iohan and Poule
Such tyme as a peple clepid Gens Scitica violently occupied the

122 *Text is missing here owing to the loss of 3 leaves.*

cuntrees clepid Dacia & Tracia, a prince of the Romayn hoost clepyd
Gallicanus was ordeyned for to goon ageyns that peple, either for to
destroyen that peple or els for to bryngen hem ageyn to subieccion, and he 5
askid ageyn instantly for his rewarde to han to his wife Dame Constaunce
themperours doughtir. For which conclusion al the othir Romayn princys
maden to themperour contynuelly supplicacyon. This heryng, hir fadir
themperour was hevy and sory, for wele he wist that, sith she was made
hole of hyr sikenesse by Seynt Agnes and had made a vowe of chastitee, she 10
rather shuld willen deyen than changen hir purpoos. Nevirtheles, whan
Constance was enfourmed of this mater, she, trusting in God, counseiled
hir fadir that he shuld promytten hir to hym whan he come home victour
from his iournee, vp condicion that seid Gallicanus shuld levyn with
hir while he went his two doughtris, the which he had by his othir wife 15
biforne, that by hem she myght lernyn the maners and the wil of hym.
And she into ful sikernesse of hir fadris byhest shuld senden forth with
hym two brethern, Iohan and Poule, the which weren the chief men of hir
counseil and the stiwardis and the sool rulers of hir household and of al
hir goodis, preyeng entierly that she hys doughtris and they hym shuld 20
mown haue grace to conuertyn from paynymrie to the feith.

This graunt with the condicions gladly acceptid, Gallican toke with
hym Iohan and Poule with a grete hoost and went forth on his viage. Whider whan they commen, anoon the Romayn hoost brokyn and Gallicanus
bysiegid in a citee of Trace, and anoon Iohan and Poule seiden to hym 25
on this wise: 'Make a vowe to God of heven that thou shalt bycommen
his seruaunt, and thou shalt han a gretter victorie than evir thou haddist
bifore.' And whan Gallican had doon aftir hir counseil, anoon appierid
vnto hym a yunge man havyng a crosse vpon his shuldris, seyeng to hym
on this wise: 'Gallican, take thy swerd and folowe me', whom he ledde 30
thurghoute al the hoost and brought hym even to the kyng. And, no man
hurt, he subiugat the kyng and al his hoost and made hem tributaries to
the Romaynes. And as hym thought two men appierid | vnto hym and f. 121ʳᵇ
kepten hym on bothe sides of hym. Which myracle shewid, anoon Gallicanus bicame a cristen man. And whan he came hoom ageyn to Rome, 35
received with grete worship, he preyed themperour to han hym excusid of
weddyng of his doughtir, for he purposid hym fully to be Goddis seruaunt
and evir aftir to liven contynently. The which desire, whan it had gretely
pleasid themperour and Gallicans two doughtris were conuertid by Dame
Constance, forthwith Gallican renouncid al his worldly dignyte and al his 40
goodis solde and disposid in almesse, he in pouerte serued God with othir
seruauntis of God. And so holily and so perfitely he lived that he did many

grete myraclis, and oonly with his commaundement he droof devils oute of
mennys bodyes. And so the fame of his hooly opynyon grew rounde aboute
45　in the worlde that men fro the east and fro the west came to seen hym, the
which somtyme was of the dignyte of a consul, wasshen pore mennys feet,
pooren watir to her handys and busily mynistren to languryng seke men
and to exercisen th'offices of meke seruyse.

Aftir this, whan by processe of tyme Iulianus apostata, sonne of Con-
50　stancius which was brothir to Constantyn, the sonne of grete Constantyn,
and enfect with the Arrians heresye, by helpe of the devils crafte aspired
to thempire and was made emperour. He chargid Gallican either to doon
sacrifise to goddis or els to voiden oute of Rome, for he durst nat putten
hym to deeth for his dignyte. And whan Gallicanus came to the citee of
55　Alisaundir, at the privey commaundement of Iulyan as it is supposid, he
was smett thurgh the body with vnfeithful men and so martired.

Iulyan than, anoon as he was confermyd into thempyre, he colourid his
auarice and his cursid coueytise vndir coloure of the gospel. For whan he
spoiled cristen men of her goodys, he wolde seyn to hem on this wise:
60　'Your Criste seith in the gospel: "Whoso renounce nat al thyngis that he
hath and forsake hem, he may nat ben my disciple".' And whan he herd
seyn that Iohan and Poule sustenyd and kept moche pore cristen peple with
the tresour and richesse which the holy maiden Constancia in hir deyeng
lefte with hem, anoon he chargid hem that they shuld drawen to hym and
65　waiten vpon hym as they diden to Constantyn. To whom they aunswerid
ageyn and seiden: 'While the glorious emperours Constantinus and Constancius his sonne were Goddis seruauntis in heven, we drowe to hem and
serued hem. But for as moche as thou hast forsaken the religion of cristen
feith, ful of vertues, we forsakyn the and wil nat obeyen vnto the.' To whom
70　Iulyan seid ageyn on this wise: 'I was in the cristen chirche a munke and
had the degree of a clerk. And yf I had wolde I myght han atteyned to the
highest degree and dignyte therin. But, consideryng that it was but a veyn
thyng to folowen slouthe and ydilnesse, I yafe myn hert to chyualrie and
to manhode. And, offryng sacrifises to goddis, I am thurgh her help and
75　suffrage commen vnto thempyre. Wherfore ye, the which were brought vp
f. 121ᵛᵃ　and norisshed in the | emperial halle, owen nat to withdrawe you fro my
presence, whom I wolde han principal in my paleys. And yf it be so that I
fele me to be contempned of you, I shal so doon that I shal nat mow be contempned or despised of you.' To whom with sad avisement thei aunswerid
80　ageyn and seyd: 'We doon not to the that iniurie or wronge to preferren
biforn the, for whos sake we drede nothynge thy thretis. Wherfore fynally
we wil that thou knowe that, while thou art vnkynde to thy lorde God and

rebel vnto his grace, we wil nevir saluse the, ner worshyp the, ner entren
within thy paleys.' 'Iwys', quoth Iulyan ageyn, 'yit shal I graunte the ten
dayes of respyte to ben bettir avised in. Aftir which ten dayes, yf ye wil 85
commen and submytten you to me, I shal receiven you as my frendis. And
yf ye commen not I shal punysh you as myn open enemyes.'

This graunte of avisement had, thei, ful avised on the first day as they
purposyd for to be on the last, anoon bygunne diligently to ordeyn for such
goodys as they must leven behynde hem and al tho dispendid in almesse 90
and in preyers. And the tenth day past, oon clepid Terencianus was sent
vnto hem aboute the houre of soper, where thei weren shett within her
hous. And fyndyng hem in her preyer he seid to hem thus: 'Our lorde
Iulyan hath sent hider vnto you a litle golden ymage of Iupiter, for that
entente that ye shuld offren therto frankencense. The which yf ye wil nat 95
doo, bothe ye shul deyen with my swerd. For it is nat semely that ye which
were norisshid in themperial paleys shulden be slayne openly.' To whom
they thus aunswerid ageyn ful demurely: 'Terencian, yf Iulyan be thi lorde,
haue thou pees with hym. And as for ws, we wil thou knowe that we han
noon othir lorde but our lorde Ihesu Criste, whom he was nat aferd to 100
forsaken. And for as moche as he is throwen oute from Goddis face, he
wolde ledyn with hym al othir men into endeles dampnacion.' Aftir this,
the thrid houre of the nyght, thei weren hefdid and prively buryed in a
pitt within her hous, and an open fame proclamed that at themperours
commaundement they weren outelawyd and banysshid. 105

And nat longe aftir this, whan Iulyan was slayne in the bataile of Per-
cys and Iouinian, a ful cristen prince, was made emperour, anoon chirchis
were openyd and cristen feith bigan to encresyn, and cristen peple to gla-
den and to reioyssen. In which tyme devels weren cast oute of bodyes which
thei vexid within the place of Iohan and Poule, knoulecchyng openly her 110
hooly passion. Amonge which many, the oonly sonne of Terencian was
vexid with a devil. And, as he came into the place of Iohan and Poule, the
devil cried by his mouth that Iohan and Poule brentyn hym. This heryng
the fadir of hym, Terencian, came thider anoon and fel doun vpon his face,
weylyng and wepyng, cryeng and knoulecchyng that he as a paynym igno- 115
raunt and not knowyng God had fulfillid themperours commaundement
and biddyng. And anoon he yafe vp his name and at the next Estern day
folowyng | he was cristenyd, contynuelly abidyng in the same mornyng, f. 121vb
wepyng til thurgh the holy martires meritis his sonne was delyuerid of the
devils vexacion. Of which Terencian was descrived and writen these holy 120
martirs passion, the which weren martired the sixt kalend of Iule, aboute
the yere of our lorde CCC sixty and foure Seynt Gregory, in the omelie

of this lesson of the gospel *Si quis vult venire post me & cetera*, tellith that
a worthy matrone of Rome, often tyme of singuler deuocion was wone to
125 visiten these holy martirs chirche. And on a day it happid, as she came
fro thens, she fonde stondyng beside the wey two munkys in a pilgrymes
habite, to whom she commaundid to be youen hir almesse. But, or than
the dispensatour came fully at hem, they stoden even ny by hir and thus
seiden vnto hir: 'Thou now visytest vs. Wherfore at the day of doome we
130 shul visiten the and, as moche as we moun, we shal doon for the.' Which
seid they sodeynly vanysshid awey from hir sight.

[109. LEO POPE]

The life of Seynt Leo the pope
      Leo the yunger, born in Cicile, whos fadris name was Poule, occupied
the papal see but ten monethis and seventen dayes. This Leo was a right
eloquent man, wele instruct in holy scripture, perfite in two tungis, that is
5 to seyn in Gru and Latyn, in syngyng and psalmodyeng crafty and curious,
in his tunge scolely and capcious; and with al these he was also vertuous.
For he was an exorter and a styrer of al gode werkys, vttryng his sentence to
the peple on the moste florisshyng wises, a singuler louer of pouerte. And
anempst pore men he was diligent, not oonly by compassion and pitee of
10 soule inward, but also by prouision of help with the solicitude and studie of laboure outeward. This same Leo toke the sixt holy sean or counceil
writen in Grec and in Latyn, the which by the prouidence of God was celebrat in the regal citee beyng present & president therat the noble excellent
and grete prince Constantyn within his regal paleys, the which is clepid
15 Trullus. In which sean were also the legatis of th'appostlis see, two patriar-
kys Constantynople and Antiochene, with an hundrid and fyfty bisshops.
In this sean were condempnyd Cirus, Sergius, Honorius, Pirrus, Paulus,
Petrus and also Macharius with his disciple Steven and al othir, the whiche
seiden, prechid and defencid but oo wil to ben in our lorde Ihesu Criste
20 but how in hym ben seid to ben two willys aftir the two natures in hym.
This seid Leo diligently and with grete studie translatid oute of Gru into
Latyn. These and many othir notable thyngis, the which it nedith nat to
be seid on Englissh, were doon in this blissid Leons tyme as his legende
makith mencyon.
f. 122ra   This seid Leo made also a chirche in Rome beside Seynt | Vinyans
26 wherin he closid the bodyes of the blissid martirs Simplicij and Faustini
and beattis and also of othir martires, and dedicat that chirche in the name

of Seynt Poule the xxij^{ti} day of Februarie. In this popis tyme also the
sixtenth day of April, the xjth indiccion, the mone was eclipsid and labourid ny al nyght in the likenesse and colour of blode, and til it was past the   30
cok crowe it gan nevir for to cleryn.

   This Leo, as it is writen in the boke of our ladies myraclis, on an Estern
day seid messe at Seynt Marie Maior and communed the peple. Amonge
which was a womman which for deuocion kissid his hande, and forthwith
ros in hym an huge temptacion of the flessh. And anoon the same day,   35
ovircarnelly vndirstondyng the gospel, the which seith that yf thyn hande
sclaundir the cutte it aweye and throwe it fro the, he cutte of his hande and
threw it from hym. Aftir which tyme there grew grete murmour in the
peple why the pope seid not messe as he was wone to doon. This heryng,
he anoon turned hym fully with hole hert vnto our lady and preyed hir   40
to prouide for hym, as it plesid hir, mercy and hir grace in that caas. To
whom the next nyght folowyng our lady did appiere and restorid ageyn his
hande hole, and bad hym goon forth on the next morowen and offren to hir
sone a placable sacrifise. And whan he woke and felt his hande ful hole, he
thankid our lady entierly and went forth and did as she had commaundid   45
hym. Which doon, he made a sermon vnto the peple and tolde hem al the
processe as it was, and shewid hem his hande which our lady thurgh hir
mercy had so marveilously restorid vnto hym ageyn. To whom be laude
and preisyng withouten ende. Amen. This Leo ordeyned first that mayde
Marie shuld be clepid the modir of God.   50

   In this tyme Attila the kyng did grete wast and destruccion in Ytaile.
Wherfore this holy fadir Leo lay thre dayes and thre nyght in Seynt Petris
chirche in hys preyer. Aftir which tyme he seid thus to his meyne: 'Whoso
wil folowe me, folowe me.' And forthwith he toke his iourney toward the
kyng Attila, whom as sone as the kyng sawe commyng to hym-warde, anoon   55
he light doun of his hors and fel doun platt at his fete and preyed hym to
askyn whatsoevir he wolde and it shuld be perfourmed. 'I aske nat elles',
quoth he ageyn, 'but two thyngis. Oon is that thou goo oute of Ytaile
withoute more harme. That othir is that thou relesse al the captives and
prisoners which thou hast takyn and distressid in Ytaile frely withoute   60
raunsomme.' Which peticion gladly grauntid, he with his meyne went
mery hoom ageyn. And whan they which weren aboute the kyng as thei
dursten, whan the pope was past, vndirnomyn hym and seiden that they
marvailed that he, which was triumphatoure of the worlde, was so cowardly
ovircommen of a preste. He aunswerid ageyn and seid: 'I provide wisely   65
for me and for myne. For I sawe on his right hande | stonden a glorious   f. 122rb

knyght with a bright blody swerde in his hand drawen; the which seid to me
on this wise: "But thou conforme the to this mannys wille, with this swerd
thou shalt deyen and so shullen al thyn".' And thus was Ytaile delyuerid.

70   Oones whan this blissid man had writen an epistle to Fabian, the bysshop of Constantynople, ageyns Eutice and Nestorie, heretikis, he leid
it vpon Seynt Petris autier and fastid and preyed, seyeng on this wise:
'Whatsoevir in this pystil I haue errid as man, thou, holy Seynt Petir to
whom is committed the cure and the charge of holy chirche, take and
75   amende it.' And whan it had leyn there fourty dayes, Seynt Petir appierid vnto hym as he lay in his preyer and seid: 'I haue redde thy pistil and
amendyd it.' And whan he toke awey the pistyl he fonde it correctid with
Seynt Petris hande and amendyd.

      This same pope Leo fourty othir dayes fastid and preyed at Seynt Petris
80 tombe, bysechyng hym and preyeng to getyn hym foryifnesse of his synnes.
To whom Seynt Petir appierid and seid: 'I haue bysought God for the and
he hath foryoue the al thy synnes, safe oonly thou shalt ben examyned *De
Imposicione manuum & cetera*, that is whethir thou hast wele or evil putt
thyn handis on ony man yivyng hym power of holy ammynistracion' &
85 cetera.

[110. PETER APOSTLE]

The life of Seynt Petir th'appostle
      Seynt Petir had thre names, for he was clepid Symon Bariona, Cephas
and Petrus. And congruently was he clepid by these thre names, for the
propirtees therof weren wele accordyng vnto hym. As for the first name,
5   that is Symon Bariona, it is to be notid that Symon is as moche to seyn by
interpretacion as 'obedient' or 'takyng hevynessis'. Bariona is to seyn 'the
sonne of a dowe'. For 'bar' in Syre tunge is a sone and 'Ione' in Hebru tunge
is a dowe. Petir than was worthily clepid Symon for the first significacion
therof, that is obedient. For Petir was obedient whan at the callyng of Ihesu
10 Crist withoute more he obeyed and folowid hym, takyng or puttyng hevynessis, the which is the secund interpretacion of this worde. Symon was
Petir the tyme of Cristis passion whan he was hevy for Cristis tradicion and
therto putte the hevynesse of the offence of hys threfolde negacion, addyng
therto the hevynesse of dooleful lamentacion whan by the inward respect
15 or biholdyng of Cristis mercy he went oute and wept bittirly. The sonne
of a dowe was Petir by sympilnesse of conuersacion in his owen livyng,
plentevous in propagacion by conuersyon of moche peple thurgh his doc-

tryne and prechyng and Galilees by pite and compassion of synful livers
hem to penaunce benygnely exortyng.

   The secund name of Petir was Cephas, the which by interpretacion as   20
caput, petra vel increpans ore, an hede or a stoone or blamyng by mouthe. |
An hede was Petir by the principal dignyte of primacie, in that Criste   f. 122va
principally commyttid to hym the charge of his folde and the cure of his
chirche, and specially deliverid hym the keyes of heven. A stoon was Petir
by stedfast tolleraunce of passion or the stoon vpon which Crist bilded   25
his chirche, blamyng by mouth them that maliciously rebellid ayenst the
doctryne of Cristis feith hem feruently and boldely vndirnymyng. This
name Petrus, the which by interpretacion is for to seyn *agnoscens, discalcians* or *dissoluens*: knoulecchyng, vnshoyng or vnbyndyng. *Agnoscens*, knowyng, was Petyr the godhede of Criste whan he in persone and name of al   30
th'appostlis aunswerid to Cristis question mevid to hem al and seid: '*Tu es
Christus & cetera*: Thou art Crist, the sonne of quycke God.' *Discalcians*,
vnshoyng, he was whan he disseuerid from the feet of his affeccion al dede
and flesshly werkis and appetitis, as whan in the transfyguracion of Crist
he seid: '*Domine bonum est nos hic esse*: Lorde it is gode vs to ben here,   35
yf thou wilt we may maken here thre tabernaclis.' And also whan he seid:
'*Ecce nos relinquimus omnia & cetera*: Lorde, we han forsaken al thyngis and
folowen the.' Vpon which gospel seith Seynt Gregory on this wise: 'Petir',
quoth he, 'was a fyssher, riche was he nought. He gat his livyng with his
hande and with his crafte and yit', quoth he, 'not forthan he spekyth feith-   40
fully and boldely: "Lo lorde, we han forsaken alle thyngis." What', quoth
Seynt Gregory, 'lefte he the which litle had and nere right nought left he
ony more than a fewe nettis. But in this mater', quoth he, 'vs must attendyn more th'affeccion than theffect. For he forsakith moche which levith
hymself right nought. He levith moche that, be it nevir so litle, he forsakith   45
alle. He levith moche the which with the possession of a thyng renouncith
the covetise or the desire of the thyng.' *Hec Gregorius*.

   Dissoluens, vnlosenyng and vnbyndyng, is Petyr dissoluyng and vnbyndyng the boondys of mennys synnes by vertue of the keyes and the power
grauntid hym of God, whan he seid to hym on this wise: '*Quodcumque*   50
ligaueris & cetera: Whatsoevir thou bynde vpon erthe shal be bounden
in heven, and whatsoevir thou vnbynde shal ben vnbounden.' This name
Petrus was first promysed or byhest hym, aftir youen vnto hym and the
thrid tyme confermyd vnto hym. Crist promysid and behight hi[m] this
name, *Iohan primo*, whan he seid to hym thus: 'Thou shalt ben clepid   55
Cephas, that is interpretid *Petrus*.' The secund tyme he perfourmed his

54 him] his

promys. For as it is seid, Marc 3°, *Imposuit Symoni & cetera*: 'Crist putte
to Symon this name Petrus.' And the thrid tyme he confermyd and stablisshid this name to hym, Matt 16°, seyeng on this wise: 'I sey to the that
60　thou art Petir and on the stoon, not which thou art but which thou hast
knoulecchid, I shal bilden my chirche and the gatis of helle shul not pre-
vailen ageyns it.' The martirdam of this blissid appostle was writen and
auctorized by foure famous and notable men, the whiche weren these:
Marcellus, Linus papa, Egesippus and papa Leo & cetera. |

f. 122vb　The life of Seynt Petyr

66　Petir, amonge al th'appostlis and abouen hem alle moste feruent was in
the loue of his maister, for whan he tolde hem that oon of the twelue shuld
betrayen hym he wolde fayn haue knowen who it was. But Crist, wele knowyng Petris hert, wolde nat openly namen hym for, as Seynt Austyn and
70　Crisus seyn, yf Crist had named hym Petir wolde haue risen vp and with
his teeth al torent hym, or with his swerd haue slayne hym. *Hec illi.*

This Petir went to our lorde vpon the see. This Petir was chosen to
ben with hym in his transfiguracion and in the resuscitacion of the maide,
the pryncis doughtir. He this fonde the money in the fisshis mouth to pay
75　with her shypfraught. He this toke of our lorde the keyes of the kyngdam
of heven and the cure of his sheep fedyng, bothe with worde of doctryne
and techyng with example of gode livyng, and with temperal subsidie in
her nede. For which thre maners of Goddis sheep pasturyng Crist bad hym
thries fedyn his sheep. Iohn.

80　This same Petir, at the fest of Pentecoste, by his prechyng conuertid
thre thousand men. He also with Iohan, at the houre of noon goyng into
the temple, heelid the halte begger at the specious gate of the temple. At
whiche tyme he conuertid also five thousand men. He condempnyd the
proprietaries Ananiam and Saphiram for her fraude and her lesyng ageyns
85　the holi goste. He made hole the palitik man and bedlaure, Eneam by name,
and conuertid Cornelie and baptized hym, and reysed vp ageyn from deth
to life a womman clepid Thabita; and with the shadeu of his body he made
hole many seke men.

This seid Petyr, for plesaunce of the Iewys to whom he was odious, was
90　prisoned by kyng Heroude and deliverid oute of prison by an angel. He
also, as it is seid, bare alwey a sudarie or a mokadoure in his hande to wipe
with the teeris the which ful often copiously flowed oute of his eyen. For
whan he remembrid hym on that oo perte of our lordis presence and the
swetnesse of his speche in talkyng, and on that othir part of his ingratitude

and vnkyndenesse in his lordis negacion or denyeng, he myght in no wise 95
conteynen hym fro wepyng.

What mete & clothyng he vsid, in Clementis boke he tellith to oon
w[hic]h askid hym that question, this wise seyeng: 'Brede with oyle, and
flessh with wortis is myn vsual diete. My clothyng is liche as thou seest:
a cote with a mantel.' Clement tellith of Petir also, as it is founden in *Hi-* 100
storiis Ecclesiastice, that whan his wife was led to martirdam he ioyed with
grete gladnesse and, clepyng hir by hir name, cried aftir hir and seid: 'O
wife, I biseche the haue mynde of our lorde.' In Clementis Itinerarie also it
is seid that oo tyme Seynt Petir sent forth two of his disciplis into a cuntree
forto prechyn. And whan they had goon twenty daies iourney, oon of hem 105
deyed and that othir turned ageyn to Petir to tellyn hym what was fallen.
There it is seid that the disciple which turned ageyn was | blissid Marcia- f. 123ra
lis, but in anothir place it is seid that it was blissid Fronto, the felawe of
hym which deyed presbiter Georgius. And anoon Petir toke hym his staffe
and bad hym goon and leyen it vpon his dede felawe. Which doon, he that 110
had leyn fourty dayes dede rose vp ageyn quycke.

Aboute this tyme was in Ierusalem a wicche the which was clepid
Symon, the which seid that he was the first vertue, and that he shuld
maken hem that levid vpon hym to liven perpetuelly. And moreovir he
seid that no thyngis weren impossible vnto hym. And, as it is seid in 115
Clementis boke, he vsid often this maner of talkyng. 'I shal', quoth he,
'be worshippid as God openly & I shal mow doon whatsoevir I wil. For
somtyme', quod he, 'whan my modir Rachel bad me goon into the felde
and repyn corne, I, seeyng a sythe lyeng beside me, bad it rysen vp and
goo repyn or mowen for me. And so it did, by the tenth part more than 120
ony othir sythe did.' And more yit he seid, as Seynt Ierome tellith. 'I am',
quod he, 'the worde of God; I am specious and fayre of shappe afore al
the sonnes of men. I am the holy comfortour. I almyghty am that longith
to God.' This wicche Symon made serpentis of brasse to meven and
stiren, and statues of bras and of stoon to laughen, and dogges to syngen. 125

This same Symon, willyng disputen with Petir and shewyng that he
was a god, at a day sette and assigned, Petir came to the place where thei
shuld meten. Whider whan he was commen, Petir seid to the peple which
stode therabouten: 'Pees be to you, brethern the which louen truthe.'
To whom Symon thus aunswerid ageyn: 'We willen nat thy pees. For yf 130
pees and concorde be amonge vs we shul not mow profyten forto fynden
the truthe. Thevis han peas amonge hem. Wherfore clepe nat aftir pees
but aftir werre. For yf two striven or fighten togider, whan that oon is

ovircommen than shal there ben pees.' 'Why', quoth Petir ageyn, 'art thou
135　aferde to heryn pees? Of synne grew batails. Where no synne is, there is
pees. In disputacions truthe, and in werkis is founden rightfulnesse.' 'It is
nought that thou seyest', quoth Symon, 'but I shal shewe the power of my
godhede and thou anoon shalt worshippen me. For I am the first vertue.
I may flyen by the eyre, make newe trees, chaungen stoones into looves,
140　duren in the fyre withoute hurt, and al that evir I wil doon I may doon.'
Ageyns whom Petir bigan to disputen, and bywreyed and openly shewid
al his fals craftys. And whan Symon sawe that he myght nat resisten
ageyns Petir, anoon he threw al his bookis of wicchecraft into the see,
that his wicchecraftis shal nat ben aspyed, and wente to Rome forto ben
145　worshippid there as a god.

This aspyeng, Seynt Petir anoon folowid hym and came thider the yere
of Claudius themperour and there was abidyng and prechyng five and
twenty yere. And Iohan Belet seith he ordeyned there two bisshops, Lyne
& Clete, to helpen hym. Where with his prechyng he conuertid moche
f. 123rb　peple and made hole many seke | men, and evir in his prechyng he preised
151　and magnyfied chastite. Wherby he conuertid four concubynes of Agrippa
the prefect, and was cause that thei forsoken hym and wolde no more commen at hym. Wherfore he was wroth and bigan to sekyn occasions ageyns
Petir. Aftir which tyme our lorde appierid to Petir and tolde hym that
155　Symon and Nero thoughten evil ageyn hym. 'But drede the not, Petir',
quoth Criste, 'for I am with the and shal deliveren the. And I shal yiuen the
solace & comforte by my seruaunt Poule, the which shal tomorow entren
into this citee.' Petir, as seith Linus, seeyng in spirite and knowyng that the
dissoluyng of the tabernacle of his body cam fast nere, he in covent of al
160　the congregacion toke Clement by the hande and ordeyned hym a bisshop,
and made hym to sitten in his see and in his chayer in his stede. And aftir
thys, as our lorde seid, Poule came to Rome and bigan to prechyn Crist
with Petir.

In this tyme Symon Magus stode in so grete opynyon and affeccion of
165　themperour Nero that douteles he helde hym the keper & the saver of his
life, and of his helth, and eke of al the cite. And on a day, as seith Leo papa,
while Symon stode bifore Nero, sodeynly the effigie and the likenesse of
his face chaungid. For now he sempt olde and eftesones ageyn yung, and
thus it chaunged dyuers tymes. Wherfore Nero wenyd verreily that he had
170　ben the sonne of God and anoon forthwith, as seith the seid Leo, Symon
seid to Nero: 'That thou mowe knowen, o worthy emperour, that I am
the sonne of God, commaunde me to ben hefdid and the thrid day I shal
risen vp ageyn.' And anoon Nero commaundid a manqueller to smyten of

Symones hede. The which, wenyng to smyten of Symones hede, smett of
a wedris hede and he by wicchecrafte ascapid awey harmeles and hyd the 175
wedris body, but the blode he lete lyen stille where the wedir was slayne.
And on the thrid day he appierid ageyn visible to Nero and bad hym do
gadren vp the blode which he shad in his hefdyng. 'For I which was hefdid
am commen ageyn to the liche as I promysed the.' Whom Nero seeyng
wex sore astoyned and than fully he bilevid that he had ben Goddis sonne. 180
Hec Leo.

And often tyme whan Symon was with Nero within his paleys, the devil
in his likenesse appierid withouten spekyng to the peple. Wherfore the
Romayns hadden hym in such reuerence and worship that they did makyn
in honour of hym an ymage, and writen this title therupon: 'To Symon, the 185
holy God'. Petir and Poule heryng this, as seith Leo, wenten into Nero and
openly detectyd and bywreyed al his fals wicchecrafte. Which doon Petyr
seid that, liche as in Criste ben two substauncys, as of God and man, so
in this wicche ben two substaunces, as of man and devil. Att which worde
Symon angrid, as testifien Marcellus and Leo, seid on this wise: 'I wil 190
no lenger suffren this man, myn enemye. Wherfore I shal chargen myn
angels that they shul vengen | me of hem.' Quoth Petir ageyn: 'I drede f. 123va
nothyng thyn angels, but wele I wote that thyn angels dredyn me.' 'What,
dredisthou not Symon', quoth Nero to Petir, 'the which hath affermed
his godhede with werkys?' 'Yf godhede be in hym', quoth Petir, 'lete hym 195
telle me what I thynke or what I doo. And that he shul not lyen and feynen
that I thought othir wise than I doo, I wille tellen the, sir emperour, aforn
what I thynke.' 'Come hider to me', quoth Nero than to Petir, 'and telle
me what thou thynkist.' To whom Petir came nere & seid to hym that he
shuld getyn hym a barly loof prively. The which had, Petir blissid it and 200
hyd it in his sleve and seid: 'Lete now Symon, the which makyth hymself
a god, tellen vs what I haue thought, seid and doon.' 'Nay', quoth Symon,
'lete rather Petyr tellyn what I thynke.' 'And that I knowe what Symon
thynkyth', quoth Petir, 'I shal shewen whan I perfourme þat I thynke.' At
which worde Symon, havyng indignacion, bigan to cryen and seyen: 'Blake 205
doggis commeth forth and devourith Petyr.' At which worde there come
forth huge grete doggis and fast gunne to renne toward Petir forto devou-
ren hym. To whom Petir profrid the blissid brede and thei sodeynly anoon
bygunne to fleen. And Petir turned hym to themperour Nero and seid:
'Loo, sir, now haue I shewid here byforn you not by worde but by werk 210
that I wist and knew what Symon mente and thought. For he that thretid
me that he shuld haue sent his angels for to han vengid hym on me hath
brought forth doggis. In which dede hath he shewid evidently that he hath

no godly angels but dogly.' 'Wele, wele', quoth Symon than to Petir and
215 to Poule, 'sirs, herith what I sey! Yf I mowe nat hurten you here, ye shul
commen thyder where I must demyn you. But at this tyme I spare you.'

Egesippus and Linus seyen that Symon was so elate & proude in hymself that he bostid that he myght reysen vp ageyn dede men. And so it
happid that amonge othir a man deyed, and anoon were clepid to Petir and
220 Symon to weten which of hem shuld reysen vp ageyn this yunge man.
And this sentence was confermyd bitwix hem with the assent of al the
peple, that which of hem failed and myght nat doon it shuld be slayne.
This doon, anoon Symon made his incantacions aboute the bedde wherin
this dede yung man lay. And anoon it sempt to al them that stoden there
225 abouten that this dede man shoke his hede. And anoon al the peple bigan
to cryen and wolde haue stooned Petyr. But with grete difficulte he made
silence and seide: 'Yf thys dede man verreily live, lete hym be made to
rysen vp to goon and to spekyn. And els wetith wele that it is but a fan-
tesme and a wicchecrafte that makyth the hede to meven.' And whan he
230 rose nat, Petir seide, al the peple heryng: 'Takith awey Symon fro the bed,
that al his feyned werkis mow be shewid and made openly!' Which doon
the dede body lay stille withoute stiryng. And Petir, stondyng arowme,
f. 123ᵛᵇ aftir a short | preyer made, cried lowde and seid: 'Yung man, in the name
of Ihesu Criste of Nazareth crucified, rise!'. And anoon, withoute more,
235 the yung man rose vp fro deth to life, went and spake.

And whan the peple wolde haue slayn Symon, Petir seid: 'Sirs, nay,
for it is peyne to hym ynough þat he seeth and knowith hymself ovircommen in his owen craftys. For our maister taught vs that we shuld doon gode
for evil.' 'Ywis', quoth Symon than, 'O Petir and Poule, I wil ye weten that
240 ye shul nat han that ye coveiten that I wolde vouchesafe to make you martirs.' To whom thei thus aunswerid ageyn: 'Mote it happen to ws that we
coveyten. To the mote it nevir be wele, for whan thou spekist thou lyest!'
Aftir this, as seith Seynt Marcel, Symon went to his disciplis hous, Marcel, and teyed a grete dogge at his dore and seid: 'Now shalt thou seen
245 yf Petir, the which is often wone to comen to the dore, may entren in at
thy dore.' And anoon aftir this Petir came and made a token of the crosse
& vnteyed the dogge, the which fawned and cherid al men safe Symon
allone, for he ran aftir hym and pursued hym felly and cruelly and pullid
hym doun to the grounde vndir his feet and wolde haue stranglid hym. But
250 Petir cried aftir and bad that he shuld nat hurten hym. At whos commaundement the dogge left hym, but his clothis he al torent and lete hym lyen
nakid, shamefastly and wrecchidly. This seeyng the peple, and specially

226 he made] made

children, runnen aftir hym with the dogge til thei had driven hym oute of
the citee as thei wolde haue doon a wolfe. The which shame and despite,
for he myght nat wele beren it, he durst nat appieren in Rome a yere aftir. 255
    Marcellus, which biforn was Symons disciple, seeyng these grete mar-
vails, aftir this drowe vnto Petir. But aftir this Symon came ageyn to Rome
and was newly received into Neroes frendship. And, as Leo seith, anoon
in his commyng he gadrid the peple togider and seid that he grevously
was offendid with the Galilees and therfore the citee which he was wone to 260
mayntene and defenden he wolde forsaken, and assigned hem a day whan
he wolde styen vp ageyn to heven. For he vouchid no lenger saaf to abiden
and duellyn in erthe. And whan the day assigned came, as seith Linus, he
stey vp vnto an hy toure of the Capitolie. Petir and Poule, with an infynyte
nombre of peple stondyng and biholdyng, he crowned with laurer, passid 265
fro the toure and bigan to styen. This seeyng Nero seid to Petir and Poule:
'This is a true man and ye arn but deceivers.' Quoth Petir than to Poule:
'Commaunde hym to come doun.' 'Nay', quoth Poule, 'to me it longith
to preyen and the to commaunden.' And whan Poule stoupid doun and
preyed, Petir seid ageyn vnto hym: 'Lyfte vp thyn hede, Poule, and see.' 270
And whan Poule seigh Symon flyen hye, he seid: 'Why tariesthou lenger,
Petir? Perfourme that thou hast bygunne, for now our lorde clepith vs.'
Quoth Petir than: 'I coniure angels of Sathanas which beren vp Symon
in the eyre, by the vertue of our lorde Ihesu Crist, that ye bere hym noon
higher but suffrith hym to fallen doun!' | At which worde, anoon the devils f. 124ʳᵃ
leetyn of and he felle doun and brake his necke. This heryng, Nero was 276
sory that he had lost such a man and anoon he seid to th'appostlis: 'Ye han
made me suspense in myself and therfore I shal destroie you with an evil
example.' *Hec Leo.*
    And anoon he commyttid hem to a worthy man clepid Paulinus and 280
he delyuerid hem to the kepyng of Mamortin, vndir the warde and the
cure of the knyghtis Processus and Martinianus, the which two knyghtis
th'appostlis conuertid while thei were in prison. And forthwith they
openyd the prison and losened the prisoners and yafe hem liberte to
goon whider thei wolden. For which cause Paulinus, aftir the passion of 285
th'appostlis, callid these knyghtis to examynacion. And whan he fonde
that they were cristen, at the commaundement of Nero they weren bothe
hefdid. And wha[n] the prison was openyd, as it is seid, the brethern
preyed Petir to goon awey but he wolde nat. Nevirtheles, at her grete
instaunce, at the last he went his wey. And whan he was oute at the gate 290
clepid *Porta Appia* and came, as seith Leo, to a place clepid now *Sancta*

288 whan] what

Maria ad passus, Petir sawe Crist commyng ageyns hym. And Petir seid
thus to hym: 'Lorde, whider goosthou?' 'I goo', quoth Crist, 'to Rome
forto ben crucified ageyn.' And Petir, vndirstondyng that Crist ment
295 by his suffraunce of passion, wherfore withoute more he turned hym
forward to Rome ageyn. And as he turned ageyn and tolde the disciplis
his reuelacion, anoon he was taken of Neroes mynistris and presentid to
the prefect of Rome, clepid Agrippa. And, as seith Linus, his face shoone
as bright as the sunne. To whom the prefect seid on this wise: 'Art thou
300 nat he the which art myry and glad amonge the peples and the wommen,
which thou makist to forsaken her husbondis?' Whom th'appostle blamed
and seid: 'Nay.' For he seid that he ioyed nevir but in the cros of lorde
Ihesu Criste. Than, at the commaundement of Nero, the prefect Agrippa
yafe sentence that Petir, as a foreyn and a stranger, shul be crucified and
305 Poule, for he was *ciuis Romanus*, shuld ben hefdid.

Of this sentence youen vpon hem spekith Seynt Denys in a pistil *ad
Timotheum de morte Pauli*, seyeng on this wise: 'O my brothir Tymothee,
yf thou haddist seyn her bataile, thou shuldist haue ben ovircommen and
failed in thiself for hevynesse and sorowe. Who shuld nat haue wept in
310 that houre that the precept of the sentence wente oute ageyns hem that
Petir shuld be crucified and Poule hefdid? The which sentence puplisshid,
thou shuldist haue seen a grete peple of Iewys and of paynyms cruelly smytyng hem and spittyng in her face. And whan the tyme came of her ende,
that they shulde departyn asundir, the cruel and vnmercyful men bounden
315 the columpnes or the pilers of the worlde, nat withouten grete lamentable
wepyng of the brethern stondyng there beside. Which doon, Poule seid
to Petir: "Pees be with the, o foundement of the chyrche and pasture and
f. 124rb   feder of Cristis shepe and his lambren." | And Petir to Poule aunswerid
ageyn: "Goo in pees, o prechoure of blissid men and mediatour and leder
320 of the helth of rightful men." And whan the[y] weren departid asundir',
quoth Denys, 'I folowid my maister, for thei were nat slayn bothe in oo
strete.' *Hec Dyonisius.*

And whan Petir, as seyn Leo and Marcellus, was commen to the crosse,
he seid on this wise: 'For as moche as my lorde Ihesu came doun from
325 heven to erthe, he was lifted vpon the cros with his hede vpwarde and his
fete dounwarde. But me whom by the crosse our lorde vouchithsafe to clepyn vp to heuen, it owith to setten on the reuers wise. Wherfore, sith I
am nat worthy forto ben on the cros such wise as my maister was, turneth
the cros, sirs, vpsodoun and crucifieth me on that wyse.' And anoon thei
330 turned the crosse and fastenyd his hede and hys handis dounwarde, and

320 they] the

his fete vpward. Which cruelte the peple seeyng wolde in her angir haue slayn themperour Nero and the prefect Agrippa also and haue deliverid hym, but he preyed hem that they wolde not letten his passion.

Egesippus seith that our lorde openyd the eyen of hem which stooden there and weptyn, and they seyn angels stondyng with crownes of roo- 335 sys and lylies and Petir stondyng on the crosse with hem and receivyng of Crist a boke, wherin were writen al the wordis that he seid to the peple, the which weren these: 'Lorde, I haue desired to folowen the, but I haue nat vsurpid to be crucified right vp liche as thou were. For thou art alwey, and evir hast ben, right and high. But we, the sonnes of the first man, the which 340 plounchid his hede doun into the erthe, whos falle the lyne of mankyndis generacion sewith, ben so born that we ben evir prone and bowyng to the erthe-warde. But now, lorde, is the condicion chaungid, for that the worlde wenyth to be right is lift and that, in contrary wise, the worlde demyth lyfte is right. Lorde, thou art to me euery thyng and noon othir thyng is so but 345 thou allone. Gramercy, lorde, to the with al the hole spirite, thurgh which I live, thurgh which I vndirstonde the, and thurgh which I clepe onto the.' *Hec Egesippus*, where also ben othir two causis assigned why Petir wolde nat ben crucyfied right.

And whan Petir perceived that the feithful men had seyn his glorie and 350 his ioye, he yafe laude and thankyng to God and yalde vp his spirite into his handis. This seeyng, two brethern, Marcellus and Appuleus, the which weren his disciplis, thei anoon token hym doun of the cros and, with diuers odoramentys and redolent oynementis, anoyntid his body and buried hit.

Of this blissid appostle Seynt Petir spekyng, Isidore in his boke *De* 355 *ortu vita et obitu sanctorum* seith on this wyse: 'Petir, aftir that he had foundid and bilded the chirche of Antioche vndir thempyre of Claudius, went to Rome ageyns Symon Magus and there, prechyng the gospel five and twenty yere, he helde the pontifical dignyte of the same citee. And the thrittyth yere from our lordis passion, of Nero, as he wolde, he was | 360 crucified.' *Hec Ysidore*.

On the same day of Petir and Poulys passion thei bothe appierid to Denys as he tellith in the forseid pistil vndir these wordis: 'Take hede, my brothir Tymothee, to the myracle and considre the wundir that byfel the day of her victimacion. For I was present the tyme of her departyng. 365 And aftir her deth I sawe hem bothe togider, hand to hand entryng into the citee, clad in garnementis of light and arayed with corownes of grete brightnesse.' *Hec Dyonisius*.

Aftir th'appostlis deth Nero abode nat longe vnpunysshid but, for her deth and othir abhomynable cursidnessis which he dyd, he slowe hymself 370

with his owen handys. Of which cursidnessis somme shul shortely here
ben touchid. It is red in *Historia Apocripha* that whan Seneca hys maister hoped and trustid to haue received condigne reward and mede for his
laboure, Nero bad hym chese what tree he wolde ben hangen on the braun-
375 chys of, seyeng that there he shuld receiven the reward of his labour. And
whan Seneca askid why he had deserued that maner of rewarde, Nero did
shakyn a bright nakid swerde ovir his hede. Wherfore Seneca, aferd, mevid
his hede aside and stoupid to eschewen the dynte of the swerde. 'Maister',
quoth Nero, 'why withdrawist thou so thyn hede from the thretyng of the
380 swerde?' 'For I am a man', quoth Seneca, 'I drede deth and wil nat deyen
gladly.' 'So on the same wise', quoth Nero, 'I drede the yit as I was wone to
doon whan I was a childe. Wherfore, as longe as thou livest, I kan nat liven
quyetly and in ease and rest.' 'Yf I nedys must dey than', quoth Seneca,
'sir, I biseche the at the leste graunte me leve to chesyn what maner kynde
385 of deth that I wil deyen.' 'Differre not thy deth ovir longe', quoth Nero,
'but dey and I graunte the thyn askyng.' And anoon Seneca did make a
grete fatte to be filled with hote watyr, and went and made hym to be letten blode on bothe armes and so bledyng, insensibly he deyed. And so he
fulfilled the ethymologie of his name. For Seneca is as moche forto seyn
390 as '*se necans*', a man sleeyng hymself. This Seneca, as it is seid, had two
brethern, of which that oon hight Iulius Gallio, an excellent declamatour,
the which also slowe hymself with his owen hande. His othir brothirs name
was Mela, fadir of Lucan the historial poete. The which Lucan deyed, as
it is red, at the commaundement of Nero, by incision and cuttyng of his
395 veynes, as Seneca his eem dyd. Anothir cursid cruelnesse, as it is red in the
forseid boke, did this execrable tyraunt Nero, for he made his modir to be
slayne and hir wombe to be cutte, for to seen where he lay therin and was
fodemyd. For which dede phisiciens, as they dursten, blamyd hym and seiden that the lawe of kynde defendid, and al reson abhorred, that the sonne
400 shuld sleen his modir, the which brought hym forth with so moche sorowe,
and fostrid and norisshid hym with so grete labour and busynesse. 'Wele',
f. 124vb quoth Nero to hem ageyn, 'sirs, I charge you that ye make me to be | with
childe, that I may brynge forth a childe and so proven by experience what
peyne my modir suffrid in childyng of me.' And this vnresonable wil forto
405 be with childe was nat oonly causid of the phisiciens wordis, but also for
oo tyme as he went by the citee he herd a womman in hir childyng lowde
cryen. 'Syr', quoth thei ageyn to hym, 'your desire is impossible and contrarye to nature and therfore it may nat be perfourmed.' 'Siker', quoth he
ageyn to hem, 'but ye make me with childe I shal make you al to deyen on
410 a cruel deeth.'

This heryng, they tokyn her counceil togider and youen hym prively
to drynken a yung frossh and with crafte of dyete maden it to growen in
his bely. And anoon his wombe, not mowyng suffren within that thyng
that was so contrary to nature, bigan gretely to bolnen, wherby Nero supposid and wenyd forto haue ben with childe. And than the lechys maden 415
hym to obseruen and kepen such diete as was convenyent to norisshen it.
Not longe aftir he bigan to be vexid with so grete peyn that he myght no
lenger suffren it. Wherfore he did clepen forth his lechys and seid to hem
thus: 'Sirs, fast hastith the tyme of childyng, for my peyn growith so grete
that vnnethe I may drawe my breeth. Wherfore fast, spede you fast!' And 420
they anoon madyn hym a drynke forto vomyten with, and forthwith he kest
oute a frosshe horrible to seen, and terrible infect with corrupt humours
al to wrappid in blode. And whan Nero sawe that he labourid it and gretly
marvayled that it is so monstruous. 'No wundir it is', quoth they, 'for ye
wolde nat abide the tyme of growyng.' And than he askid the phisiciens 425
yf he were such oon whan he was in his modris wombe and they seiden:
'Syker, yea', 'I wil than', quoth he, 'that my childe be kept and norisshid',
for which he did makyn a voute of lyme & stoon and made it to be kept
therin. *Hec in historia prefata.*

This devils lymme oo tyme marvailed of the gretenesse of the fyre that 430
brent Troye the grete citee, & desiryng an example he sett a fyre in Rome
and made it to brennen seven daies and seven nyghtis. And he hymself
biholdyng it, delited hym in the fayrnesse of the flaume and sange for ioye
of the sight, as the cronycle seith. He also vsid to fisshen with nettis of
golde. He delited eke so moche in musyk and in syngyng that he excellid 435
abouen al syngers and menstrals and al maner crafty musiciens. And diuers
othir abhomynable thyngis he did, as seith Orosius, the which I abhorre to
writen. For which causis and many othir the Romayns neither myghten,
ner wolden, lenger beren but hole risen vpon hym and pursued hym oute
of the citee. And whan he sawe that he in no wise myght ascapen hem, 440
not willyng be slayn of hem, he slowe hymself, somme seyn with his swerd
rennyng theron or with his baselard, somme seyn that wulfes devourid
hym as he fled the Romayns. And whan he was thus dede, shamefully the
Romayns turned home ageyn and tookyn his frosshe darkyng in his voute |
and brenten it withoute the citee. Aftir which tyme that part of the citee f. 125ra
where the frossh darkid in his voute was clepid Lateranys. 446

The tyme that Seynt Cornelie was pope, the cristen Grekis stoolen
the appostlis bodies and wolden haue borne hem awey into Grece. And
anoon the devils which duellid in the ydols, constreyned by Goddis vertue, cryedden and seid: 'Helpith, o Romayns, helpith, for your goddis 450

be stolen awey!' Wherfore anoon the cristen peple, vndirstondyng this of
th'appostlis bodyes and the hethen of her goddis, anoon a grete multitude
of bothe parties gadrid togider pursued hem. For which cause the Grekis
aferd, threwen the bodies in a depe pitte at a place clepid Cathacumbas.

455 Fro whens nat longe aftir by the feithful peple it weren pullid oute ageyn.
And whan they weren in doute which boones were Petris and which Poulis, as they fastid and preyed that God wolde senden hem somme token of
knouleche, an answere from heven was youen that the morer boones weren
the prechers, and the lessers the fysshers. Which aunswere had, they anoon

460 departid hem and leyden eithers body in his owen hucch, the which weren
made specially for hem. Other seyn that the holy pope Siluestir, purposyng
to consecraten her chirchis with grete reuerence, did powderen & weyen
al her boones grete and smale and by weight departid hem in two, and putt
that oo parte in that oo chirche and that othir parte in that othir & cetera.

465 It is doutid of many folkis whethir they weren bothe martired on oo day
or nat. Somme seyn that the same twelf moneth aftir that Petir was martired by crucifyeng, Poule was martired by hefdyng. But Seynt Ierome,
and nere al the seyntis which tretyn of this mater, concordely affermyn
that they bothe were martired vpon oo day, as it may evidently be shewid

470 by Seynt Denyse epistle sent to Tymothee. Seynt Leo also in a sermon of
the same appostlis, affermyng the same mater seith thus: 'Lete vs nat sup-
posen, ner trowen, that withoute grete cause they on oo day, in oo place,
and vndir oo tyraunt, suffrid the sentence of deeth. On oo day they suffrid
that togider at oones they shuld commen to Criste in oo place, that neither

475 of hem shuld ben absente fro Rome; vndir oo persecutour that egal cruelte
shuld constreynen bothen. The day', quoth he, 'was sette for her meryte,
the place for her glorie and the persecutour for her vertue.' *Hec Leo*.

But here it is to be notid that whan it is seid that they were martired
in oo place it is ment Rome, but not in oo part or in oo strete in Rome.

480 For Petir was crucified on the northwest plage of Rome, not fer fro thens
where now is Seynt Petris chirche, and Poule was hefdid on the southwest
plage of Rome, a litle beyonde where now is his chirche, in a place which is
clepid Seynt Anastasies, where somtyme was a fair monasterie of monkys
of Seynt Bernardys ordre til the kyng of Naplis destroied it that tyme he

485 bysegid Rome. In which monastery was somtyme abbote Pope Eugenye,
f. 125ʳᵇ to whom Seynt Bernard wrote his five | bookys *de Consideracione*. In the
chirch-yerde of which standith an olde rofeles chapel and a desolate, the
which Englissh men and no moo nacions clepid *Scala Celi*. I kan nat fynde
no cause why but that it be for that Seynt Bernard had oones in the same

490 chapel a reuelacioun liche Iacobs reuelacion, which he had whan at his

fadris commaundement he went toward Mesopotanye in Syria to Laban
his kynnesman. This Iacob, as he slept by nyght on his iournee, he leid
stoones vndir his hede and as he slepte hym thought that he sawe a ladder
stonden on the grounde, whos toppe raught and our lorde lenyd on the
ladder and angels wenten vp and doun on the same. Genesis 28°.   495

A liche vision had Seynt Bernard in the seid chapel, of which vision
that chapel is yit into this day of English men clepid *Scala celi*, but whethir there in that chapel ben such remyssions and delyuerauncys of soulis
oute of purgatory peynes as it is hopid of moche English men, I reporte me
to hem which ben wiser than I, for I kan no skille of such maner maters. 500
But this wote I wele that at the south gate of Seynt Anastace toward Seynt
Marie Annunciat ben thre fair wellys the which, as it is reportid there,
spri[n]gen vp at the thre sawtys or skippis which Seynt Poulis hede made
whan it was smett of, at ech skyppe soundyng this holy name 'Ihesus'. And
albeit that these two blissid apostlys weren bothe martired vpon oo day, as 505
it is seid bifore, yet not forthan Seynt Gregory ordeyned that the solempnyte of Seynt Petir as touchyng the office and the seruyse, and on the next
day shuld be solempnyzed the commemoracion of Seynt Poule, and that
for foure causis. First for that day was Seynt Petris chirche halowid, also
for Petris dignyte was more than Poulis. The thrid for Petir was conuer- 510
tid or than Poule, and the fourth is that Petir had the primacye in Rome
and first occupied the pontifical see and auctorite. Of these hooly appostlys
martirdame, place and tyme and prince vndir whom ben compendyously
made these vers folowyng:

Ense coronatur Paulus, cruce Petrus, eodem   515
Sub duce, luce, loco, dux Nero, Roma locus

Item alius:
Ense sacrat Paulum, dux par lux, vrbs, cruce Petrum.

Poule with a swerd crowned was,
And Petir on a cros was hangen ful hye.   520
Bothe two in Rome, but in diuers plaas,
By the cruel decree of Neroes tyrannye,
The penultyme of Iune, as bokys testifye.
Now, blissid appostlis, for your charite,
There ye be now, hereaftir bryngith me.   525

503 springen] sprinigen

[III. COMMEMORATION OF PAUL]

The commemoracion of Seynt Poule

    Paulus, aftir the interpretacion, is as moche to seyn as the mouthe of a trumpe or the mouth of hem, or a chosen marvaile, or a myracle of
f. 125ᵛᵃ eleccion. Or els Paulus is seid of *Pausa* Gru, the whiche | signifieth rest,
5 or of *Paulon* Greke, that is *modicus* in Latyn and litle in Englissh. By these six diuers signyficacions of this name Paulus mow ben vndirstonden six special priuilegis, the which the glorious appostle Seynt Poule had singulerly amonge al othir appostlis. The first priuilege was a fructuous tunge. For fro the see clepid *Illiricum mare* vnto Ierusalem he fulfillid the cuntrees
10 with the doctryne of Cristis gospel. And therof he hath the first propirte aftir the interpretacion of this name Paulus, the which is *os tube*, the mouth of a trumpe. The secund priuylege is his entiere and viscerous charitee, by which euery mannys disease and passion he made his by compassion. And that he shewid wele whan he seyde 'Who is seke and I am not seke, and
15 who is sclaundrid and I am nat brent?' As who seith no man. Also ad Phil. primo he seith, mevid of affectuel charite, on this wyse: 'Our lorde God is to me wittenesse how I desire and coveite you in the bowails, that is to seyn in theffectuel charite of Ihesu Crist. And this is my preyer: that your charite mote habounden and encresyn more.'
20   And to thys priuylege pertenyth the secund interpretacion of this name Paulus, the which is *os eorum*, the mouth of hem. This is the mouth of his hert wherof he spekith ad Cor., seyeng on this wise: '*Os nostrum ad vos patet o Corinthij*: The mouth of our soule, o ye of the citee of Corinthe, is open and patent to you by charitee. Our hert is dilatid abrode by compas-
25 sion and pytee.' The thrid priuylege is his marveilous conuersyon. For of a persecutour he was chosen to ben a prechour, of a wulfe to ben a shepe, and of a proude pursuer of Goddis name in Ierusalem and in Damasc he was singulerly chosen to ben a berer aboute of the same byforn kyngis and pryncis and peplis, as it is plenerly declarid biforn in the fest of his con-
30 uersyoun. The fourth priuilege of this glorious appostle was the busynesse of his handwerk, wherby he gat lyvyng that he shuld not ben onerous ner ovirchargeous to hem where that he prechid, as he seith hymself, primus ad Cor. iiᵒ & 2 ad Thessalonicenses 3ᵒ, whos sentence is there that he labourid day and nyght werkyng with hys handis for his livyng and frely
35 prechid Cristis gospel, where he spekith ageyns hem which wil nat labou-

14 seyde who is seke] seke

ren, seyeng thus: '*Quis non laborat & cetera*: he that not labourith oweth nat to eetyn.' And many liche sentence ben in diuers placis of his epistles.

The fifte priuilege was delicious contemplacion, for he was rapt vp to the thrid heven where he sawe many mysteries and her[d] secrete and pri- vey wordis, the which it is not leeful a man to spekyn, and in that he had 40 pausacion and rest of soule, the which ben necessarie to contemplacion. The sixt priuilege was mekenesse vertuous, in which he gretely haboundid, as it semyth by many wordys which he vsith in his writyngis. For primus ad Cor. 15°, where he, spekyng of Cristis apparicions to his disciplis, con- cludith on this wyse: | '*Nouissime tanquam abortiuo & cetera*: Last of al   f. 125ᵛᵇ our lorde to me as to a mysborne man and not in his tyme appierid of his 46 grace. I am sothely', quoth he, 'the leste of th'appostlis, the which am not worthy to be clepid apostle for bicause I pursued the chirche of God.' And *ad Ephes. 3°* he clepith hymself not oonly leste of th'appostlys, but also leste of al seyntis.   50

Of this name Paulus ben of diuers doctours diuers opynyons. Orige- nes seith that he was *binomius*, that is to seyn that he had two names alwey and was bothe clepid Saulus and Paulus. Wherto semyth to accorden the chirch, the which seith thus in an antiphone of his on this wise: *Saulus qui & Paulus magnus predicator & cetera*. Rabanus wil that he was clepid 55 Saulus biforn his conuersion of Saule the proude kyng, and aftir his con- uersion he was Paulus, that is litle, of his litle and meke spirite in his owen felyng, as it is seid biforn. Bedys opynyon is that he was clepyd Paulus of that worthy man Paulus Sergius, whom he conuertid to the feith of Crist, as the Actys of the appostlis tellith. *Actus*. The life of this blissid appostle 60 wrote *Linus papa & cetera*.

The commemoracyoun of Seynt Poule

Poule th'appostle aftir his conuersyon suffrid many persecucions, the which Seynt Hillary shortly completith, seyeng on this wise: 'Poule th'appostle', quoth he, 'in Philipp[i] was beten with yerdys, shett in 65 pryson and fastenyd by the feet in stockys. In Listrys he was stooned, in Iconio and Thessalonica he was grevously pursued of wickid men. In Epheso he was youen to wilde bestys. In Damasco he was lete doun in a skeppe by the citee walle. In Ierusalem he was presentid to the iuge, beten and bounden and waited in euery side. In Cesarea he was shett vp streytely 70 and cruelly accusid, as he sayled into Ytaile-ward he was shypbrokyn, and at Rome vndir Nero he was dempt to deyen and hefdyd.' *Hec Hillarius*.

This Poule, quod Ianuence, toke the dignyte longyng to a postyl amonge

39 herd] hert   65 quoth he] he   Philippi] Philippis

paynyms, as Petir did amonge Iewys. A yunge man also, the which fel doun
75 oute of a wyndow and was dede, he reysed ageyn fro deth to lyfe and many
othir myraclis he did. Oo tyme whan he came to an yle clepid Miletum, a
snake henge vpon his hand and hurt hym not, the which he anoon shoke
of his hande and threw it into the fyre. And, as it is seid, fro that tyme
forth al tho whiche be born of the kynrede of that man which that tyme
80 received Poule to herborowe shul nevir ben hurt of no venemous beste.
And therfore they that ben of that lynage, whan her children be born putten snakis in her lappys or in her bosoms to proven whethir thei ben her
children or not. Haymo seyth that fro the first crowyng of cockys to the
f. 126ra fyfte houre Poule exercised hym in werkyng with his | handis, and aftir
85 that tyme he occupied hym in prechyng, wherin ofte sithes he contynued
til it was nyght. And the residue of tyme he spent in preyeng, etyng and
slepyng. *Hec ille.*

Poule came to Rome er than Nero was ful confermed in thempyre. And
whan he herde seyn that the question of contrauersie bitwix Poule and the
90 Iewys was but of the Iewys lawe and of cristen feith which was the bettir,
he yafe noo force therof, ner toke noon hede therto; and so Poule frely went
and prechid where he wolde. Seynt Ierome in his boke *De Viris Illustribus*
seith that the xxvj^th yere aftir the ascencion of our lorde, the which was
the secunde yere of thempyre of Nero, Poule was sent bounden to Rome,
95 where two yere duellyng in fre holde he disputid ageyns the Iewys. Aftir
which, dymised by Nero, he went and prechid the gospel in the west parties, and in the fourtenth yere of the seid Nero, he was hefdid at Rome the
same day that Petir was crucified. *Hec Ieromus.*

In which meantyme his wysdam & his religion was fer and wyde dy-
100 vulged and spred abrode. Wherby he ioyned vnto his frendship many of
Neroes householde and conuertid hem vnto the feith of Criste. Many also
of his writyngis were rehersid byforn themperour and marveilously preysid of al men. And not oonly themperours hous, but also al the senat had
hym in singuler reputacion. It happid sone aftir, vpon a day, that Poule
105 prechid in a celer and a yonge man clepid Patroclus, the which was Neroes
boteler and syngulerly biloued of hym, willyng gladly heryn hym, went vp
into a wyndowe, where as he fel aslepe vnwarly he fel doun and deyde. The
which caas anoon was tolde to Nero and he was right sory of his deth and
anoon he ordeyned anothir in his stede. Poule, knowyng in spirite of this
110 yunge mannes deth, seid on this wise to hem which stoden besiden hym.
'Gooth', quoth he, 'and bryngith hider to me themperours boteler Patroclum, the which is dede.' Whom brought to hym he reysid ageyn from
dethe to lyfe, and sent hym ageyn to themperour with his felaus. And as

themperour was mornyng for hym, oon came and tolde hym that Patroclus
stode at the gate redy to commen in. Themperour heryng that he whom a 115
litle biforn he was enformed verreily to ben dede was alive, he wex gretly
abasshid and wolde nat suffren hym to come to his presence. But not forthan, sone aftir, at the suasion and preyer of his frendis, he was brought
in. To whom themperoure seid on this wise: 'Livesthou Patrocle?' 'Yea,
sir emperour', quoth he ageyn, 'live I.' 'And who, Patrocle, made the to 120
liven?' quoth Nero. 'Our lorde Ihesu Crist, kyng of al worldis, made me to
liven', quoth Patroclus. At which aunswere, Nero, wroth, seid ageyn thus:
'Yf he be kyng of al worldis, it folowith that he shuld reigne by al worldis and resoluen al the kyngdams of this worlde.' 'Yea, siker, that is sooth',
quoth Patroclus, whom Nero anoon yafe a buffett vndir the cheke & | seid: f. 126rb
'Than semyth it thou wilt ben his soudyour and seruen hym.' 'Gode skylle 126
it is, sir', quoth he, 'that I serue hym which reised me from deth to life.' At
whiche worde five mynistris and seruauntis of themperour which weren
alwey assistent to hym seiden to hym on this wise: 'Why, sir emperour,
smytisthou this prudent yung man, the which truly hath aunswerid the? 130
For sikerly, to that invincible kyng we also ben mynistris and seruauntis.'

And whan Nero herd this, anoon he chargid hem al six to be shett vp
in a streyt pryson, purposyng hym to punysshen hem the more grevously
that he had louyd hem byforn the more syngulerly. And anoon forthwith
Nero in his wodenesse chargid al cristen men to be sought vp and to be 135
brought to his presence and, withouten ony aunswere, horribly to be punysshid. And sone aftir, amonge many othir, Poule was brought biforn hym
bounden. To whom he seid on this wise: 'O thou grete kyngis seruaunt,
as thou wenyst, bounden bifore me. Why withdrawist my sowdiours and
my knyghtis fro me and makist hem subiectis to the?' 'Not oonly', quoth 140
Poule ageyn, 'oute of thy litle corner here I haue gadrid to my lorde and
my kyng soudyours and seruauntis, but also oute of al the worlde to whom
he shal yiuen reward and sowde which nevir shal faile, and also excluden al
indigence and nede. To whom also yf thou woldist submytten the and ben
subiect, thou shuldist ben savid. The which is so grete power and myght 145
that he shal commen and be iuge of al men and resoluen the figure of this
worlde by fyre.'

And whan Nero herd this, and specially that the figure of this worlde
shuld ben dissolued with fyre, he wex wode and in his wodenesse he commaundid al Cristis knyghtis to be brent. But Poule, as gilty of hurtyng of his 150
maieste, he chargid to ben hefdid. And anoon were slayn so grete multitude of cristen folke that the Romayn peple, reysid into sedicion, brast

150–1 his maieste] his

vp themperours paleys, cryeng and seyeng: 'Set a mesure and a maner of slaughter, o sir emperour, and tempre thy commaundement. For they
155 whom thou lesist ben our cuntre men, and defenden the Romayn empyre.'

Of which sedicious clamour themperour, aferd, changid his decree, chargyng that no man shuld putten noo cristen man to torment and peyne til he hymself had youen sentence vpon hym. Wherfore Poule was reduct ageyn and eftesones presentid to themperours sight. Whom as sone as
160 Nero sawe, with a grete voyce he cryed and seid: 'Takith awey this wicche, hefdyth this deceiver, suffrith no lenger this synful man, the which alienyth wittis and chaungith myndis!' To whom Poule seid boldely ageyn: 'Iwys, Nero, I shal suffren a lytle tyme, but aftir that I shal liven eternally with my lorde Ihesu Crist!' 'Smyte of his hede fro the body', quoth Nero, 'that
165 he may therby knowe me to be more myghty than his kyng whan I haue ovircommen hym, and so lete vs seen yf he shul liven endelesly.' 'And that
f. 126ᵛᵃ maist knowe verreily, o Nero', quoth Poule, 'me to liuen endelesly. | Whan myn hede is smett of I shal appieren ageyn to the quycke, and therby shalt thou mowe knowen evidently þat Crist Ihesu is bothe lorde of deth and
170 of life.'

Which wordis seid, he was ledde forth to the place of his iewesse. And as he went the thre knyghtis which ledden hym seyden to hym on this wise: 'Sey ws feithfully, Poule, what he is your kyng whom ye cristen men louen so moche that ye chesyn rather for his sake to deyen than to liven, and what
175 reward ye shul han therfore.' And anoon Poule bigan to prechyn so of the kyngdam of heven and of the peynes of helle that he conuertid hem to the feith of Crist. Which doon, they preyed hym forto goo freely whider he wolde. 'God forbede, brethern', quoth Poule, 'that I shuld fleen. I am, ner wil been, noo fugitife. But I am, and wil ben, a true soudyour of Crist. For
180 I knowe wele that by this transitorie lyfe I shal goon forth to evirlestyng life. And, as sone as I am hefdyd, feithful men shul stelyn awey my body and buryen it. Markith, therfore, ye wele the place and tomorowen erly commeth ageyn therto and ye shul fynde beside my graue two men prey-eng, Titum and Lucam. To whom whan ye haue tolde the cause why I sent
185 you, they shul crysten you and make you heyres of the kyngdam of heven.'

And while they were thus talkyng, Nero sent othir two soudyours to seen whethir Poule were slayn or not. And whan Poule wolde also haue conuertyd hem, they aunswerid ageyn and seyden: 'Whan thou art dede and risen vp ageyn, than shul we bileven that thou seyest. But now come
190 on fast and receive that thou hast deserued.' And as thei ledden hym forth, at the gate which ledith to Hostie he mett with a matrone the which was his

161 the which] the

disciplesse, Plantilla by name, the which aftir Denys seyeng hight Lemobia
(perauenture she had two names), and she anoon sore wepyng commendid hir vnto his preyers. To whom Poule seid thus: 'Goo, Plantilla, the
doughtir of the evirlestyng kyng, & lende me the kerche with which thou   195
curyst with thyn hede, that I may curen therwith myn eyen and aftir I shal
restoren it to the ageyn.' And whan the tormentours which ledden hym
seyen hir deliveren it to hym, they scorned hir and seiden that she toke
this precious cloth to a deceivour and to a wicche; and therfore she lost it.

And whan they come to the place where Poule shuld takyn his passion,   200
he turned hym to the este-ward and lyftid vp his handis to heven-ward, and
longe tyme he preied in his modris vois with plente of teerys, and yafe laude
and preysyng to God. Which doon he bad his brethren stondyng aboute
farewele. And with Plantilles kerchief curid his eyen and, knelyng on bothe
knees, he was hefdyd. And anoon as the hede fel fro the body it soundyd   205
with a clere vois this name, 'Ihesu', in Ebreu, the which was so swete to
hym in his life. For, as it is seid, he namyd in his pistlys the seid blissid
name 'Ihesu' five hundrid sythes. And, as it is shewid at Rome at Seynt
Anastasies in a chapel at the gate which goth toward Seynt Mary | Annun-   f. 126ᵛᵇ
ciat, the hede fallyng fro the body made thre skyppis, thries soundyng   210
the name of Ihesus, where sprungen thre fair wellys, as pilgrymes which
goon the stacions of Rome knowen by experience. Moreovir, that wondir
is to wetyn, oute of the wounde of his neck first cam a streem of mylke
and ran vnto the knyghtis clothis that hefdid hym, and aftir came blode. In
the eyre also there abouten wex a grete light, and oute of hys body came a   215
passyng swete savoure.

Of this blissid Poulis deth Denys in a pistil *ad Tymotheum* writith on
this wise: 'In that houre of sorowe and hevynesse, my welbyloued brothir
Tymothee, the tormentoure bad Poule make redy his necke. And anoon
blissid Poule lokid vpward to heven, markyng his forhede with a signe of   220
the crosse and seid on this wyse: "My lorde Ihesu Criste, into thyn handis I offre my spirite." Which seid, withouten ony sorowe or hevynesse, he
putt forth his necke and toke his crowne. And whan his hede was smette
of, and in the smytyng the blissid appostle leid abrode Plantilles kerchief
and gadri[d] with his owen handis his owen blode and falt it therin and   225
forthwith deliverid it hir ageyn.

And as the lictour came ageyn into the cite-ward, Lemobia askid hym
where he had lefte hir maister Poule. "In the felde", quoth he ageyn, "I
lefte hym with his felaus and his face curid with thy kerchief." "Nay forsothe", quoth she, "he is nat there. For right now Petir and Poule entrid   230

225 gadrid] gadris

the citee in a royal aray, havyng bright shynyng crownes vpon her heedys, and Poule deliverid me my kerchief ful of blode." And anoon she shewid it to hym and to al men that wolde seen it. For which cause many men bilevid to God and were cristenyd.' *Hec Dyonisius.*

235 Whan Nero herd seyn al these thyngis and al thyng as it was doon was tolde hym, he wex gretly abasshid and bigan to talkyn with his frendis and his philosophres of tho maters. And while they stonden thus talkyng togider, shett in a chambyr by hemself, sodeynly Poule come in, no doore openyd, and stode biforn Nero and seid to hym on this wise: 'Lo, Nero! I

240 am here, Poule, a knyght and a soudyour of the eternal and invisible kyng. Loo! I am nat dede but quycke. Wherfore now at the leste bileve! And yf thou wilt nat, thou wrecche shalt deyen evirlestyng, for as moche as thou hast vnrightfully slayn Goddys seruauntis.' Which wordis seid, Poule vanysshid awey and Nero, nere wode for feer, wist nat what he myght doon.

245 Nevirtheles, at the suggestyon and the counseil of his frendys, he deliverid oute of prison Patroclum and Barnabam and lete hem goon frely whider they wolden.

Aftir this, on the next morowe erely, the forseid knyghtis Longinus and Acestus commen to Poulis grave and there they perceived two men prey-

250 eng, Titum and Lucam, and Poule stondyng in the myddis. And whan Titus and Lucas perceived the two knyghtis commyng, for drede thei bigunne fast to fleen and Poule vanysshid awey. Aftir whom the knygh-

f. 127ʳᵃ tis cried and seid: 'Fleeth not, | sirs, for we come nat to pursuen you, as ye wenyn, but we wiln be cristenyd of you, as Poule whom right now we

255 seyn preyeng with you seid onto vs'. This heryng, they turned ageyn and baptised hem with grete gladnesse.

Seynt Poulis hede was cast in a grete vale where grete multitude of othir which were slayne and were cast, wherfore, whan it was sought, it myght nat be founden. And, as it is seid in the forseid pystil of Denys, longe

260 aftir, on a tyme whan a dyche in the same vale was purgid and made clene, amonge othir fith Poulis hede was cast oute of the same dyche. The which a shepherd fyndyng, he sett it on a stake of his folde. And thre nyght aftir, contynuelly the seid shepherde and his maister also seyen vpon the same hede a grete marveilous light shynen, wherof thei weren gretly astoyned.

265 And whan this was tolde vnto the bysshop and vnto othir feithful peple, anoon thei thoughten sikerly that it was Poulis hede. Wherfore the bys- shop, with a grete company of cristen peple, went oute and brought in this hede and on a table of golde they assaied to setten it to the body. To whom the patriarc seid on this wise: 'Sirs, we knowe wele that many feithful men

270 were slayn and her bodyes dispercled in the same place. And therfore I

doute to ioyne this hede to Poulys body. Wherfore I counseil that we doo thus: Lete vs leyen this hede at Poulys fete and preyen to God that, yf it be Poulis hede, that it may turnen vp to the body and be ioyned ageyn therto.' And, al men plesid with this counseil, they anoon perfourmed it. And as they weren in her preyer, al men seeyng and marveilyng, the body of Poule 275 turned aboute and ioyned the self vnto his hede. For which cause al men youen laude and preysyng to God and knewen wele thereby that it was Poulys hede.

Gregorius Turonensis tellith how that there was a man which was fal-lyn in dyspeyr and temptid forto hangen hymselfe. And as he was busy 280 to makyn redy the snare to hangen hym with, he cryed alwey and seid: 'Seynt Poule, helpe me!' And forthwith a derk and an horrible shadowe came to hym and seid: 'Ioye to the, gode man, and that thou doost, doo and tary not.' At which worde he sped hym fast, cryeng and seyeng as he did biforn: 'Blissid Seynt Poule, help me!' And as the snare was al redy to 285 be putte aboute his necke, anothir shadew as of a man appierid and seid to the horrible shadew on this wyse: 'Flee hens fast, thou wooful wrecche, for Poule, this mannys aduocat, commeth.' At which worde the horrible shadewe vanysshid awey, and the man came ageyn to hymself and thankid God and Seynt Poule that he was delyuerid of his temptacion. 290

Al that Ianuence in his legende seith more of this glorious and blis-sid appostle, Seynt Poule, stant for to seyn compendyously oonly in two thyngis. For first he rehersith a dolorous and a pitous lamentacion, dilatid with many a curyous exclamacion, the which Denys in a pistle to Tymothe, his condisciple of Poule, writith for sorowe | and hevynesse of her mais- f. 127rb tris deth. Aftir this he puttith a notable and excellent commendacion of 296 Poulis vertues, takyng oute of Iohan Crisus in his boke which he made *De Laudibus Pauli*. In which commendacion he comparith Poule to the moste part of the fadris of the Olde Testament, begynnyng at Abel and forth by Noe, Abraham, Ysaac and Iacob, and so forth to Seynt Iohan Baptist. And, 300 yivyng hym in maner a precellence abouen hem al, he comparith hym to angels in heven and to al thyngis precious in heven and in erthe.

And for as moch as bothe these origynals ben right prolix and han aftir my symple felyng more curyous dilatacion for lettrid men and clerkis tha[n] moral edificacion for symple men and vnlernyd, I translate hem not into 305 English. But fynally this entierly I byseche that blissid and holy appostil, that thurgh his preyer and merite we mow so obseruen and folowen his doctryne here in this worlde livyng that fynally we mow atteyn and come to the blisse where he is in evirlastyng. Amen. Mercy Ihesu and gramercy.

304 than] that

[112. PROCESSUS AND MARTINIAN]

The lives of Processus and Martinianus

The tyme that Symon Magus felle and brast, the cursid tyraunt Nero
deliverid the blissid appostlis Petyr and Poule to a man clepid Paulinus
which was maister potestat. And anoon he sett hem fast in the warde and
5 kepyng of Mamortyn, to whom came many cristen men which were seke
and they were curyd and made hole of her sekenessis. And many also that
were vexid with devils were delyuerid by the preyers of th'appostlis. Waytyng vpon th'appostlis there were assigned many soudiours, amonge which
there were two of the worthyest clepid Processus and Martinianus. These
10 two, consideryng the grete maruails which our lorde Ihesu Crist wrought
by his appostlis, were gretly ammarvailed therof. Wherfore vpon a day with
oon assent they come to hem and seiden on this wise: 'Worshipful sirs,
knoweth wele that Nero hath foryeten you and is oute of remembraunce
of your persones. For it is ful nyne monethis that ye haue ben here kept in
15 warde. Wherfore we biseche you oonly baptiseth ws in the name of hym by
whom we knowen that ye werkyn many wondirful thyngis and gooth your
wey whan and whider ye willen.' To whom the blissid appostlis aunswerid
ageyn and seiden: 'Yf it be so that ye lieven of al your hert and of al your
soule in the name of the trynyte, such thyngis as ye knowen that we doon
20 ye shul mow doon yourself.' And whan al the othir which were there in
prison herden this, thei cryed concordely seyeng on this wise: 'Getith ws
f. 127ᵛᵃ   watir, for we al perisshe for thurst.' 'Bilevith', | quoth Petir, 'in the fadir
omnipotent and almyghty and in Ihesu Crist his oonly bigoten and into
the holi goste, the vnyon and knotte of hem bothe, and al thyngis shul be
25 mynistred which be nedeful to you.'

Aftir which worde al that weren in prisoun fel doun at th'appostlys feet,
bysechyng hem for charite that they myght receiven the baptesme of hem.
And anoon the blissid appostlys turned hem to preyer.

Aftir which worde Petir made a tokne of the cros in the Mount Tarpeye
30 in Mamortynes warde. And anoon sprange a welle in the myddis of the
pryson wherin Processus and Martinianus were baptised. And not oonly
they, but also al that weren in the prison, fel doun to th'appostlis fete and
bysought hem of the same and were baptised, what of men and of wommen
the nombre of seven and fourty. Which doon, th'appostle Petir offred for
35 hem the holy sacrifise of Cristis body and his blode, with which they weren
al communed. Which doon Processus and Martinianus seid to the blissid
appostlis: 'Goth where ye wil, for Nero themperour hath foryeten you.'

Wherupon they wenten forth in the wey which is clepid *Via Appia*. And,
for as moche as Petrys leg was hurt with the fettris of iron which weren
theron while he was in pryson, it was bounden with clowtys. Wherof oon 40
fel awey from hym in a strete clepid *Via Noua* biforn a place callid *Sep-
tem Solia*. And whan Petir was a litle forth withoute the gate clepid *Porta
Appia*, he mett with our lorde Ihesu Crist. To whom Petir seid on this
wyse: 'Lorde, whider goost thou?' 'To Rome', quoth he, 'I goo to be crucified ageyn, and thou also turne ageyn to Rome.' A[nd] as sone as Petir 45
was returned to Rome, the soudiours *Ma[g]istriani Mello Principis* token
hym and ledden hym ageyn to pryson. In which meantyme relacion was
made to Paulyn that Processus and Martinianus weren bycommen cristen
men, and he anoon chargid hem to be shett vp in pryson and on the next
morowe to be brought to his presence. To whom he seid on this wise: 'Be 50
ye waxe such foolys to forsaken the goddis and the goddessys which our invincible pryncis worshippen and al our antiquyte hath hidertoward serued
and honoured, and in your foolhardynesse to folowen veyn thyngis and no-
uelries which no man knowith and so shamefully to lesyn the sacramentis
and the dignytees of your chyualrie?' To whom Martinianus, with a bolde 55
vois and a clere, aunswerid and seid: 'Now at the first we begynne to taken
the sacramentis of hevenly and incorruptible chyualrie which hidertoward
han veynly and wrecchidly ben exercised in the cursydnesse of erthely and
corruptible chyualrie.' Quoth Paulyn the maister of the office: 'Yit, sirs,
I counceil you puttith awey your madnesse and worshippith the goddis 60
the which ye han worshippid from your cradyl.' To whom they aunswerid
thus brefly with oo vois | withoute many wordis: 'We wil thou wete that f. 127vb
we be made cristen men and therfore we wil worshippen noo ydols ner
noo fals goddis.' 'Takith hede to me', quoth Paulyn ageyn, 'and lestenyth
what I sey, myn owen felaus knyghtis. Beth my frendis and exerciseth your 65
knyghthode and your chyualrie and ye shul ben right derworthy and right
acceptable to the princis and doth sacrifise to our almyghty goddis.' To
whom yet with oo mouth they aunswerid ageyn and seid: 'It is ynough to
vs that we han declarid to the that we ben verreily cristen men and seruauntis of our lord Ihesu Criste, whom the blissid appostlis of hym, Petir and 70
Poule, prechyn and techyn.' 'I haue seid you', quoth Paulyn maister of the
office, 'here byforn and ye haue herd me. Yet I sey ageyn to you: heryth
my counseil and liveth.' To whom they wolde yiven noon answere and he
efte and efte ageyn askid hem, but they stode stille as they had nat herde
hem. Wherfore Paulyn commaundid hem to be beten aboute the mouth 75
with stoones.

45 And] As   46 *Magistriani*] *Magristriani*

And whan they longe had be beten, thus with oo voice thei cried and
seid: 'Ioye and worship be to God, hye abouen in heven.' Quoth Paulyn
than to his soudyours: 'Bryngith forth the trefd, that they mow thuryfien
80 and offren frankencense to the maistris.' And they aunswerid ageyn and
seid: 'We han offrid vp ourself to our lorde God almyghty for a sacrifise.'
And whan the trefd was commen, quoth Paulyn to hem: 'Dooth as I haue
seid you.' And forthwyth they broughten forth also the brasen god Iupiter,
the which whan Processus and Martinianus seyen, thei spitte on bothen of
85 hem. Wherfore Paulyn commaundid hem to ben hangen vpon a iebett and
to be drawen with senewys and to be beten with battys. And they with a
glad chier, ioyeng, seiden: 'We thanke the hertely our lorde Ihesu Crist!'
Paulyn, ful of wodenesse, commaundid flawmes of fyre to ben applyed to
her sydes. And they anoon gun cryen and seyen: 'Blissid be the name of
90 our lorde Ihesu Crist whom his blissid appostlis han prechid and taught!'
  In the meantyme while this was doon there was a noble matrone and
a worthy womman clepid Lucina which stode byforn hem and comfortid
hem, seyeng on this wise: 'Beth constant and stedfast, Cristis knyghtis,
and feryth not these peynes the which lestyn but for a litle tyme.' Quoth
95 Paulyn to his knyghtis: 'Scourgith hem with scorpyons and doth a bedelle
cryen and seyen: "Wil ye not despysen the preceptis of the pryncis".' And
forthwith the same houre the maister of the office, Paulinus, lost his lefte
eigh. Wherfore as a mad man he bigan to cryen oute vpon the charmes of
wicchecraft. And anoon he bad hem to be takyn doun of the iebett and to be
100 shet in the warde of Mamortyn, where the nobil and worshiful matrone,
forseid Lucina, mynistred hem al her necessaries habundantly and plente-
f. 128ʳᵃ vously. And within thre dayes that they weren in prison | Paulinus was
taken and shaken with a devil and deied. This seeyng, Pompinus his sone
ran to the paleys cryeng and weilyng and seyeng on this wise: 'Ye that arn
105 rulers and gouernours of the commoun profite, helpith that tho maner of
men which ben instruct and lernyd in wicchecraft mow ben extinct and
destroyed.'
  [Whan the prefect of the citee clepid Cesarius herd this], he went and
tolde to themperour Nero the caas as it was byfallen, and he commaundid
110 that anoon, withoute taryeng, thei shuld be destroied. Wherupon, at the
grete importune callyng of Pompyne, Paulyns sone, the prefect Cesarie
yafe the sentence that they shuld be ledde withoute the wallys of the citee
in the wey which is clepid *Via Aurelia* and there ben hefdid. And as he
commaundid it was doon. Whider came the worthy and blissid matrone,

108 Whan the prefect of the citee clepid Cesarius herd this] Whan the prefect of the citee
herd this Whan the prefect of the citee clepid Cesarius herd this

forseid Lucina, and buryed her bodyes with many swete oynementis in a 115
manoir of hers in the same wey in a gravel pitte beside the conducte where
thei were hefdyd, where, thurgh her meritis, ben shewid grete benefice
into this daye.

[113. TRANSLATION OF THOMAS OF CANTERBURY]

The translacion of Seynt Thomas of Caunterbury

The yere aftir the passion of the glorious martir Seynt Thomas of Caunterbury even fyfty, his fourth successour aftir hym, Stephanus Langtone,
and the covent of the munkys purposyng to translaten the seid martirs body
into a more worshipful place than it was buryed in, procurid diligently 5
al maner thyngis which hem semyd necessarie to so grete a solempnyte.
Which doon and redy had, aftir certeyn tyme of fastyng and preyers, the
seid Archbisshop Steven and Richard the Bysshop of Salysbury and al
the covent of Caunterbury, the fifte kalend of Iule in the begynnyng of
the nyght, come togider devoutely into the place where was buried this 10
hooly martirs body. And whan thei hadden a litle whyle made her preyer
they did the stoon be remevid from the grave and there, al men present
seeyng, they fonde that holy and precious body, somtyme the instrument
and the organ of the holy goste, lyeng araied in prestys garnementis and
al othir thyngis which conuenyently longid to so high a fadris sepulture, 15
albeit that the vestymentis for the longe lyeng in the moiste erthe weren in
party consumed and wastid.

Al men this seeyng & for verrey ioye and gladnesse wepyng, certeyn
munkis which weren assigned therto tokyn vp this precious body in her
handis and deliverid it vnto the archbisshop to leyn it in a capse made and 20
ordeyned for the noones. The which holy body, while al the residue of
peple ther gadrid sange and preyed, th'archebisshop toke of tho munkys
handis and dressid it convenyently in the seid capse vpon a ferretre, safe
certeyn smale boones which he reserued oute for to yiuen to grete men
and chirchys to honour and worship of that blissid martir. | Which per- f. 128rb
formed and doon and the capse myghtily nayled vp, the seid capse with this 26
precious tresore was born vp by munkys handis into a secrete place, there
reuerently to be kept vnto the tyme ordeyned and prefixed whan this royal
translacion shuld be solempnyzed. And whan the day prefixed and puplisshid was commen, there resortid to Caunterbury innumerable peple, both 30
for to doon due reuerence and worship vnto this blissyd martir and also

to felen the suffrage and the benefice of Goddis grace by mediacion of his
preyer in the tyme of her nede.

At the solempnyte of this translacyon were present the worthy fadir
35 Pandulphus, the popis legat, Stephanus Cantuar and Williamus Remensis
archebisshops, Henricus kyng of Ingelonde with his baronage, bisshops,
abbottis and priours and othir men of the chirche of diuers statis and regions, which al to rehersyn in synguler and special wolde askyn grete tyme
and so myght causyn vrkesommenesse, wherfore we passen ovir that at this
40 tyme. And of the residue of peple the multitude was so grete that the citee
of Cauntirbury with al the villagis a grete viron aboute vnnethe myght conteynen hem. The tenth day aftir this was doon, that is to seyn the seventh
day of Iule, the which that tyme fel on the tuesday, aboute nyne of the clok,
whan the kyng, the legat, the archebisshop, the bysshops, erlis, barons and
45 lordis weren al gadrid togider they wentyn with al the othir peple to the
place where this holy tresour was hyd and openly broughten it forth to
the place which was prouyded therfore, and there sikerly shetten it vp and
myghtily the residue of the day ledyng forth and occupyeng in laude and
preysyng of God, reuerence and worship of hys holy martir blissid Seynt
50 Thomas.

And for as moche as the kyng and the archebisshop and the covent
and othir feithful peple, and specially the Londoners, porid oute bothe
her richesses and her busynessis habundantly and copiously that nothyng
shuld faile or wanten that myght ben to the blessid martirs honoure and
55 worship, he, willyng rewardyn hem for her bodily tresoure & quyten hem
the while of her devoute busynesse, refoundid ageyn plentevously his
gostely tresour al the tyme of his translacion bothe byforn and aftir many
grete and wondirful myraclis shewyng. Of which grete multitude oonly
thre or foure at this tyme, for to excluden prolixite, I wil briefly rehersyn
60 here in honoure and louyng of this blissid martir.

A knyght of the Countesse of Angeoy clepid Robert, with his yunge
sonne Robertulus by name, toke his iourney toward Cauntirbury to visiten the relikes of this blissid martir, the which entryng the see at Wytsand
half the wey seylid pesibly. Aftir which tyme his litle sonne awakyng of his
65 slepe, or for to maken watir or I note what ellis to doon, went to the ship-
pis syde, and as he stode vnwarly sodeynly he felle into the see. And whan
his fadir saw that, anoon he bigan to cryen and seyn on this wise: 'Seynt
f. 128va Thomas, haue mercy vpon me | and kepe me my sonne!' The childe also,
as sone as he was fallen doun into the see, he sodeynly sprange vp ageyn
70 to the brynke of the watir, seyeng thus: 'Seynt Thomas, yf thou wilt, thou

maist helpen me.' An[d] in this meanwhile the shyppe by the myght of the
wynde was driven awey from where the childe fel in more than two or thre
bowe shote. And than, at the grete importune instaunce of the knyght, the
shypmen striken seyle and returned ageyn the shyp for to sekyn the childe.
And aftir the space of an houre, as the seid knyght wittenessid, or aftir   75
his estymacion by the tyme that a man with a mevable paas myght haue
riden tweyn or thre frensh lenkis, they commen ageyn to the place where
the childe felle oute and founden hym sittyng on the watir withouten ony
harme, safe oonly that in the fallyng he toke in a litle of the salte watir. But
whan the childe sawe shippe goon aweye from hym, first for verrey sorowe   80
and dispeyr of his life, he diuers tymes for to makyn an ende of his life
and therby of his hertis sorowe he dipped doun his hede into the watir for
to haue drenklid hymself, as he knoulecchyd openly to his fadir whan he
was takyn vp. 'And moreovir', quoth he, 'at eche tyme that I wolde haue
drenklid myself, me thought that a bisshop helpe vp myn hede and lettid   85
me that I myght nat drenclyn.'

    Not longe biforn the tyme of this blissid martirs translacion there
was a womman of a towne clepid Keneballa which had but oo doughtir
livyng right yung, of foure which she had had of hir husbonde. This yung
doughtir, grevously sikenyng, vpon a day deyde vnwarely in his modrys   90
lappe. Wherfore the modir wept and sorowyd withoute ony mesure. To
whom amonge othir came in to comforten hir a ientle womman, a widowe
and a lady. And whan she sawe this womman in so grete hevynesse,
havyng compassion and pitee vpon hir, anoon she toke a threde and with
a grete deuocion she mett the childis body to Seynt Thomas, and anoon   95
the damysel rose vp heil and hool. And whan the modir of the maiden had
made a candel of her mesure, purposyng to sendyn it to Caunterburye,
anoon the damysel wex seke ageyn and, as the modir testified aftirward,
deyed ageyn. The modir anoon remembrid hir of hir ingratitude and litle
deucion to the blissid martir and forthwith she knelid doun and made   100
a vow that, yf hir doughtir myght han grace to liven ageyn, not oonly
she shuld sende to Seynt Thomas the candele, but also she shuld ledyn
thider hir doughtir in hir propre persone. Which vowe made, the maide
revived and hyr modir led hir to Caunterbury liche as by hir vowe she had
promysed.   105

    A man of the west cuntree, the tyme of Seynt Thomas translacion, com-
myng to Caunterburye-warde with many othir bicause of deuocion vnto
the blissyd martyr, in the myddis of Braundeforthbrigge metyng with a
charyett, vnwarly was throwen into the watyr. The which, in his fallyng,

110 devoutely preyed Seynt Thomas that he wolde nat suffren his pilgryme to
perysshen. And whan he four sithes had be drawe doun to the botomme of
f. 128vb the streme and as of[t] sithes returned vnto | the brymme of the watir, the
fyfte tyme he was caste vnto the drye londe. And as he with grete oothis
testified, he neither in his mouth, ner in his nosethrilles, ner in his eeris
115 felt no drope of watir which myghte diseasyn hym. And in the same tyme
that he felle in oon of his felauship loste his cloke in the same place, the
which nevir aftir mygt be ony craft be founden.

Moreovir there was a knyght in Northamptonshire which had weddid
a widowe whos [sonne was] aboute thre yere age, the which she had by hir
120 othir husbonde. As he toke of the seid knyghtis handis a morsel of mete
and wolde gredily han swelowid it, [he] was strangelid with the same morsel and deyed. Whos modyr seeyng the childe dede and havyng suspicion
to hir husbonde of his deth, bigan anoon to roren and cryen importunely
and often clepid hym homicide and manqueller.
125 The knyght heryng this, natwithstondyng that his conscience stode
clere as for the childis deth, yit for the importune clamour of his wife he
wexe verrey confuse in hymself. And aftir a short avisement he rose vp and
toke a peny, and with a goode deuocion bowed it ovir the childe, makyng
a byheste to God and to Seynt Thomas of Caunterbury that yf it plesid
130 her grace that the childe myght liven ageyn, he shuld ledyn hym to Caunterbury to Seynt Thomas. Which vowe made, anoon the morsel of flesh
which had shett the wey of life from the childe styrte oute of the childis
throte into his mouth, and he revived and by litle and by litle wex ful hool
by meritis and mediacion of the blissid martir Seynt Thomas. To whom
135 be laude and preysyng withouten ende. Amen.

[114. THEODORA]

The life of blissid Theodora
The tyme that Zenon was emperoure, in the citee of Alisaundre duellid
a noble womman and a fayre whos name was Theodora, the which had an
husbonde, a gode man and a riche, and dredyng God. The devil, hauyng
5 envie with Theodoraes holynesse, stired anothir riche man in the citee to
vnleeful and synful concupiscence of hir. For which cause he, bothe with
wordys and with yiftys, labourid hir for to consentyn to his entent and sent
to hir sundry massagers. But she sett at nought al his yiftis, and wolde in
no wise heeryn his mediatours ner his massagers. And at the last he sent

112 oft] of   119 sonne was] sonne   121 he] in

vnto hir an olde wicche, which sore labourid hir to perfourmen this mannys 10
desire for saluacion of his life. The blissid womman Theodora aunswerid
alwey ageyn to hir, and seid that she in no wise wolde doon so grete a synne
in the presence and sight of hym which biholdith and seeth al maner thyng.
'Nay, lady', quoth the wycche, 'nat so. But whatsoevir is doon, from the
tyme the sunne ryseth vnto the tyme that it goo downe, God seeth and 15
knowith. But whatsoevir | be doon from the sunne goo doun til it rise f. 129ra
ageyn, God neither seeth ner knowith.' 'Is this sooth that ye seyn?', quoth
Theodora. 'Yea, lady', quoth the wycche, 'withoute ony faile.' And thus
this blissid womman, deceiued, yafe ferme credence to the forseid wycche.
And so whan the sunne was doun he came and fulfillid his synful and wrec- 20
chid desire and went his wey. Which doon, Theodora, remembryng hir
fooly and hir mysdede, anoon bigan bittirly to wepe and, betyng hirself
vpon hir face, seid on this wise: 'Allas, allas, I haue destroyed and lost my
soule and al the plesaunce of my beautee!'

Aftir this, whan hir husbonde came hoom and fonde his wife thus 25
soroweful and moornyng and nat knowyng the cause, he did his gode
solicitude and busynesse to comforten hir; but it wolde nat ben, for she
wolde receiuen no comforte. On the next morowe she went to an abbesse
of nunnes in the same citee, enqueryng of hir whethir yf a grevous synne
were doon vpon the nyght tyme God knewe it or nought. 'Iwys', quoth 30
the abbesse, 'doughtyr, there is no thyng so priuily doon, neither by nyght
ner by day, but that God knowith it clerely.' And anoon blissid Theodora
bigan to wepen sore ageyn and, a gosspel boke askid, she casuelly openyd
it and fonde writen this worde: '*Quod scripsi, scripsi*': That I haue writen
is writen.' And anoon she turned hoom ageyn. And sone aftir, vpon a day 35
while hir husbonde was oute, she roundid hir hede and changid hir garnementis and wente to a monasterie of munkys eighten myle thens, mekely
bisechyng that she myght be received there to her holy ordre, and with
grete difficulte so she was. And whan they askid what was hir name, she
mekely aunswerid and seid that hir name was Theodorus. And anoon as 40
she was admyttid and received she mekely perfourmed al the lowly offices
of the place, busyeng hir to doon plesaunce and obsequye to al the brethern
of the place.

Aftir this a yere or two or moo the abbote clepid to hym Theodorum and
bad hym setten oxen in the wayn and fecchen hoom oyle from the citee. In 45
which meantyme an angel of God appierid vnto hir husbonde, the whiche
was alwey in sorowe and hevynesse, dredyng that she had be goon awey
with somme othir man, and seid to hym on this wise: 'Rise vp erely and
stonde in the wey of the martirdam of Petir th'appostle, and the womman

50 which thou shalt mete with is thy wife.' Which doon, Theodora came with
hyr wayne. And whan she knewe hir husbonde, albeit he knew not hir, she
knockid hir breste and seid within hirselfe: 'Woo me, my good husbonde,
how grete is the labour which I suffre for to be deliverid from the synne
which I haue doon ageyns the!' And whan she came forby hym she salusid
55 hym curteysly and seid: 'Ioye be to the, myn owen lorde.' But he in no wise
knewe who she was. And whan he longe had abiden and sey no womman
to his estymacyon, and helde hymself deceived and begiled, a vois came
to hym seyeng thus: 'That persone which yisterday in the morowe salusid
the so curteysly was thy wyfe sykerly.'
60   This blissid Theodora was of so high perfeccion and holynesse that
while she lived here in erthe she wrought many myraclis. Of which many
f. 129ʳᵇ this was oon. There | was a man rent to deeth of a wilde beest and not
oonly she thurgh hir meritis gate hym life ageyn, but also at hyr cursyng
the same wilde beste deyed. The devil, wrooth with hir holynesse and with
65 hir perfeccion, appierid oo tyme to hir, seyeng on this wise: 'Thou strumpett and advouteresse! Hasthou forsaken thyn husbonde and art commen
hider in contempt and despite of me? By my grete and dredeful vertues I
shal areryn a bataile ageyns the and make the to forsaken Crist crucified,
and so teche the who I am and what is my grete power.' At which worde
70 she markid hir with a token of Cristis cros and anoon the devil with al his
boste vanysshid. It happid oones as she came fro the cyte-warde with hir
chamailes to be logged in a place where the doughtir of the hous came to hir
at even, wenyng that she had ben a man, and wolde haue leyn with hir. And
whan she in no wise wolde assenten to hir desire, she went to anothir which
75 lay in the same inne and lay with hym and conceyved of hym. And whan hir
wombe bigan to ryse and she was examyned of whom she had conceived,
she boldely and pleynly seid that of the munke Theodorus. Wherfore, as
sone as the childe was borne, the frendys of the damysel sentyn it hoom
to the abbote. And anoon he clepid Theodorus and areyned hym of that
80 dede and blamed hym therfore. But he neither denyed it ner excusid it,
but oonly preyed to han foryifnesse of the offence. And therfore the abbot
anoon leyed the childe vpon his shuldir and drofe hem bothe from the
monasterie and oute at the gate, where she abode seven yere and fostrid
the childe and brought it forth with bestis mylke. Where the devil, havyng
85 envie with hir grete pacience, transfigured hymself into the liknesse of hir
husbonde and appierid to hir, seyeng on this wise: 'O myn owen spouse,
my lady, what doosthou here? Take hede and see how I langure for the
and kan no comforte receiven. Wherfore come now with me, my light and
my ioye, and albeit that thou hast leyn with anothir man, here and afore

God I foryive it the.' She, wenyng that it had ben hir husbonde the which 90
spake to hir, aunswerid ageyn and seid: 'How shuld I duellen ageyn with
the, forasmoche as the sonne of Iohan knight hath defoulid me and ley by
me? Therfore here I wil abyden and doon penaunce, for that I haue synned ageyns the.' And this seid she bigan to preyen and he vanysshid awey,
wherby she knewe wele that he was a devil. Anothir tyme the devil, willyng 95
makyn hir aferde, made many devils to appieren vnto hir in the symilitude
and liknesse of diuers wilde bestis. Amonge which oon in the liknesse of
a man excited hem and seid: 'Etith anoon and devourith this strompett,
this advouteresse', But, as sone as she bygan to preyen, her power cessid
and they vanysshid awey. Anothir tyme hir thought there came by hir a 100
grete multitude of knyghtis, byforn whom went oon whiche semyd to ben
a prynce whom al that multitude reuerencid and worshippid. Quoth oon
of hem to Theodore: 'Rise vp, thou, and worship our prince.' 'Nay siker',
quoth she, 'I worship my lorde God and noon othir.' And whan thys aunswere was tolde vnto the prince, he chargid hir to be brought to his presence 105
and so longe to be tormentyd til | she was lefte for dede, and than al that   f. 129va
companye vanysshid. And anoon aftir there came oon to hir with a skeppe
ful of al maner of mete and seid to hir on this wise: 'The prynce that made
the to be beten sent the this and bad that thou shuldist ben of gode chere
and eten, for that he did to the was of ignorance and nat of malice.' And 110
anoon as she made a token of the crosse al was goon.

And whan she had fulfilled seven yere of penaunce, the abbote, consideryng hir pacience, reconciled hir and toke hir ageyn into the monasterie,
and the childe with hir. Where, aftir that she had complete two yere worshipfully and religiously, she toke the childe with hir into hir celle and 115
shette the dore to hem. And anoon as that was tolde to the abbote, he sent
certeyn munkys to lystene what she shuld seyn to the childe. And whan
they were togider within allone, she halsed the childe in hir armes and kyssid hym, and seid to hym on this wyse: 'My welebiloued and swete sonne,
the tyme of my rest by deeth is commen. Wherfore I commytte the to God, 120
preyeng hym that he wil be thy fadyr and thyn helper. Swete sonne, yiue
the diligently to fastyngis and to preyers, and lowly and devoutely serue
thy brethern.' And with these wordis and liche she yalde vp the spirite and
slepte in our lorde. The which whan the child sey, he bigan sore to wepe.

And in that same nyght this maner vision was shewid vnto the abbot: 125
hym thought that he sawe a royal and stately mariage ordeyned & made
redy in a precious and glorious paleys. Wherto come doun the ordres of
angels and of prophetis, patriarkis, martirs and of al seyntis. And in the
myddis of hem alle he sawe a womman allone brought to the maryage,

130 environed and arayed with more ioye and blisse than may be spoken. And
she sette hir doun vpon the bedde of astate and al tho which stoden abouten
hir worshippid hir. Which doon, a vois was herd seyn on this wyse: 'This
is abbote Theodre which falsly was accusid of begettyng of a childe and
seven tymes ben chaungid vpon hym. She hath be chastised sufficiently

135 for the offence that she did to hir husbonde, defoulyng his bedde.' With
this vision the abbote sodeynly awoke and anoon clepid vp his brethern,
and went to hir celle and fonde hir dede. And whan they had despoyled
hir of hir clothis they founden hir a womman.

Wherfore the abbote forthwith sent for the fadir of the damysel which
140 had defamyd hir, and seid to hym thus: 'Thy doughtris husbonde is dede,
come and see.' And whan he had discoueryd the cors and sawe how it was
a womman, he wex sore aferde, and also al that seyen it. Which doon, an
angel appierid to the abbote and seyde: 'Anoon, take thyn hors and ryde
vnto the citee and that man whom thou first metist with, take hym with the

145 and brynge hym hyder!' The abbote anoon did as the aungel commaundyd
and, entryng into the cyte, he mette with a man fast rennyng. Whom whan
the abbote askyd whider he ran, 'Ywys', quoth he, 'my wife is dede and
I goo for to seen hir.' Whan the abbot herd this, he toke hym vpon horsbak and brought hym hoom with hym &, sore wepyng, they buryed hir

150 with grete solempnyte. Aftir which tyme hir husbonde entryd hys wifes
f. 129ᵛᵇ celle | and there contynue[d] an holy life, til that he deyed and was buryed
with his wife. The childe also, wele educate in his youthe, folowid his
noryces steppis in alle honeste maners and so grewe in perfeccion of religious obserua[n]cye that, whan the abbote deyed, he succedyd and was

155 made abbote aftir hym.

[115. MARGARET]

The prologe of Seynt Margaretis lyf
    Of Seynt Margarete, the virgyne pure,
    Which likenyd is to a precious margarite,
    And that worthily, as in olde scripture
    I fynde writen, I me delyte
5   The life to translate, yf me wil respyte
    Attropos a while, and nat to hastily

151 contynued] contynuel   154 obseruancye] obseruacye   1 *The opening*
rubric is in the hand of Scribe B.   4 I fynde] It is Ar   me] me now Ar

My fatal threde asundry smyte,
Which Lachesis hath twyned ful yeris fyfty.

And convenyently this virgyne glorious
May to a margarite comparyd be,   10
Which is white, litle, and eke vertuous,
As seyn auctours, of his propyrtee.
White was Margarite by virgynytee,
By mekenesse litle, and moste syngulerly
Vertuous by hir excellent charitee,   15
In myraclis werkyng shewid excellently.

Loovid she not wele virgynyte
And of body and soule to kepe clennesse,
Whan Olibrius hir profred his wyfe to be,
And that she shuld be clepyd a pryncesse,   20
And grete tresoure shuld haue and rychesse,
Lust, welth and worship excellently,
And for clennesse sake, as I doo gesse,
Al his grete profrys she sette not by.

Grete mekenesse she had for Cristis sake,   25
Whan the title of hir natal dignyte
In hir yunge age she dyd forsake,
And his handemaide she chees to be,
Not settyng by hir fadris enemyte,
And with hir norice duellid wilfully   30
In poore astate and in lowe degree,
Kepyng hir shepe ful diligently.

And yf we wil speken of charitee,
Therof she had grete habundaunce,
As in hir passyon wele shewyd she.   35
For, as hir legende makith remembraunce,
She stired evir the peple to repentaunce,
And to wynnen hem to God was ful busy;
And whan she shuld dye, with grete constaunce
She made a preyer moste charitably.   40

7 asundry] asundyr Ar   12 his] thylk Ar   16 excellently] plenteuously Ar
34 Therof] Iwys Ar   37 evir the peple] the pepyl euere Ar

Moreovir, as I do writen fynde,
In the boke clepid the golden legende,
And it is taken of the auctours of kynde,
The margarite, yf of blode descende
45   Grete flux, is gode it to amende;
And the cardyacle passion marvelously
From hurt of the hert it wil defende;
And mannys spirtis it comfortith souereynly. |

And for this threfolde propirtee
50   Of the margarite may Seynt Margarete
Vnto that gemme wele comparyd be.
For al th[r]e propirtees to hir were mete,
And as for the first, I you byhete,
Whan hir blode oute ran ful copyously,
55   She was so enflamyd with hevenly hete
That she it suffrid ful paciently.

As for the cardiacle which temptacioun
Bytokenyth, as clerkis doo declare,
Of our gostely enemye which is evir boun
60   Mankynde to trappe, and wil not spare
Hem to brynge into sorowe and care.
Yit hurt he hir nevir, though he were sly,
Ner hir no wise myght kecche in his snare,
But evir of hym she had the victory.

65   In that the margarite is a confortatife
Of mannys spiritis, it was wele seen
In our Margarete, which al hir lyfe
Was in hir spiritis bothe pure and cleen,
Thurgh whos clennesse many oon bydeen
70   Were in her spiritis comfortid inwardly,
And thurgh hir doctryne, as I doo ween,
Styred to leve synne and eke fooly.

---

42 the] a Ar   49 threfolde] threfolde manere of Ar   52 thre] the Ab
56 it] it al Ar   paciently] stedefastly Ar   57 which] that Ar   63 hir no wise
myght kecche] no wyse hyr kecche myht Ar   65 is a] is Ab

Thus for this sixefold propyrte
Of the margarite, which duly doo longe
To Seynt Margarete by congruyte   75
Of symilitude, I may vndirfonge
That in six vertues she was stronge,
As in chastitee, mekenesse, and singulerly
In charite, constaunce and suffryng of wronge,
In gostely comforte and in victory.   80

These six vertues ben figurid mystily
By the sixe wyngis which that Ysaie
Of the cherubyns in his vision sy
On the troone, with his gostely ie,
Stondyng, and to our purpoos now signyfy   85
That this maide Margarete worthely
By these six vertues to heven did sty,
In ioye there to duellyn perpetuelly.

Now, blissid virgyne, which in heven aboue
Art crowned in blisse ful gloriously,   90
To them in erthe which the serue and loue
Be evir propicious, and specially,
Vouchesafe of thy singuler grace, lady,
My witte and my penne so to illumyne
With kunnyng and eloquence that sufficiently,   95
Thy legende bygunne, I may termyne.

Here endyth the prologe & folwyth the lyf |

Whilome as the storye techith ws,   f. 130rb
In Antioche, that grete citee,
A man there was, clepid Theodosius,
Which in grete state stode and in dignytee.   100
For of paynymrie patriarc was he,

74 doo] *om.* Ar   76 I] we Ar   78 singulerly] suyngly Ar   79 constaunce]
in constaunce Ar   and] of Ar   of wronge] wronge Ar   82 By] In Ar   84 On]
Vpon Ar   troone] hy throne Ar   86 maide] blyssyd mayde Ar   88 In ioye there]
Ther in ioye Ar   91 which] that Ar   96.1 *The rubric is in the hand of Scribe B.*
100 in] *om.* Ar   101 patriarc] the patryark Ar

And had the rule and the gouernaunce,
To whom al prestis didden obeysaunce.

This Theodosius had a wife ful mete
105   To his astate, of whom was borne
A doughtir ful faire, and clepid Margarete,
As it was provided of God biforne.
But right as a ful sharp thorne
Growith a rose bothe faire and gode,
110   So sprange this Margarete of hethen blode.

For though hir fadir and modir in ydolatrie
Were borne and fostrid, and eke did fyne
Her life in the same, and myserablie
Aftir her deeth wenten to helle pyne,
115   Yit her doughtir did grace so illumyne
That she bothe cristenyd and martired was,
And went to heven, that glorious plaas.

Hir fadir ful glad was of hir byrthe,
Hopyng she shuld haue ben his comforte
120   In his olde age, and made grete myrthe.
To whom moche peple dyd resorte,
Bothe men and wommen, and made disporte,
Thankyng her goddis with hert glad
That her patriarc so faire yssue had.

125   I kan in no wise remembre me
That evir I redde in the hethen guyse
What rytes weren vsid, and what royaltee
In [nam]ys yivyng, but, as I devise,
It was doon in ful solempne wise
130   And with many a cerymonye, and specially
In childres birthe of statys hy.

Aftir this, as it was the guyse
In tho dayes, and yit it is so

102 the²] al the Ar   106 ful] *om.* Ar   107 As it] As Ar   was provided]
prouyded was Ar   108 as] as of Ar   110 sprange this] sprange Ar   of] of the
Ar   115 doughtir] *om.* Ar   120 age] dayes Ar   128 namys] mannys Ab
131 In] in the Ar

Amonge astatis, in ful godely wyse
A norice her doughtir they purveyed to, 135
Not fer from hoom, which shuld doo
Al hir diligence and eke busynesse
Their childe to fostren in al tendyrnesse.

This norice duellid from the cytee
Of Antioche furlongis but fyftene, 140
And prively a cristen womman was she
And in al hir conuersacion bothe pure & clene,
As in that which folowith it was wele sene;
For Margarete she fostrid in al vertu,
And taught hir the feith of Crist Ihesu. 145

But whan hir modir was from hens past,
Which deyde while she was tendir of age,
Margarete hir affeccion sett so fast
Vpon hir norice, bothe wyse and sage,
That she forsoke al hir high lynage, 150
And purposid hir fully there to soiourne,
For to hir fadir she nolde hoom retourne. |

And for she did Criste worshippen and loue, f. 130ᵛᵃ
And wolde not turnen ageyn to paynymrie,
Hir fadir hir hated and did reproue, 155
And yafe no force what vilenye
She had; but the souereyn lorde on hye
There ageyns hir filled with so grete graas,
That within fewe yeris she perfite waas.

And not oonly this excellence she had in grace, 160
But eke, to spekyn of hir nature,
Of al that cuntre of the rounde compace
Was nowhere so faire a creature;
For forme and shappe and eche feture

135 purveyed] prouydyd Ar
Ar 143 that which] that Ar 136 which] the wych Ar 138 Their] The
154 turnen ageyn] ageyn turne Ar 153 Criste worshippen] dede wurshepe Ar
159 within] in Ar waas] greu Ar 157 had] had had Ar 158 graas] vertu Ar
and shappe] shap & colour Ar 162 Of al] al Ab Of] in Ar 164 forme

165　Were conproporcyoned in such equalitee
　　That she myght be myrrour of al beautee.

　　Wherfore, yf the crafte of descripcion
　　I coude as wele bothe forge and fyle
　　As coude Boicius in his phisical consolacyon,
170　Or Omere, Ovide, or els Virgile,
　　Or Galfride of Ingelonde, I wolde compyle
　　A clere descripcion ful expressely
　　Of al hir fetures even by and by.

　　But siker I lacke bothe eloquence
175　And kunnyng such matiers to dilate,
　　For I nevir duellid with the fressh rethorience,
　　Gower, Chauncers, ner wyth Lydgate,
　　Which al be runnen to her fate.
　　Wherfore I prey eche man hertely,
180　Haue me excusid though I speke rudely.

　　Not oonly this virgyne had syngulerly
　　Of the yiftis of kynde grete plente,
　　But also with vertues ful excellently
　　In hir soule eke endewyd was she.
185　For she had feith, hope and cheryte,
　　The divyne vertues, and therwithal
　　The four grete vertues clepid Cardinal.

　　And whan she to fyften yere of age
　　Was commen, and herd how cruelly
190　Cristen blode thurgh the fiers rage
　　Of tyrauntis was shedde, even by and by,
　　For Crist to dey she hir made redy,
　　And in the meanwhile she did keep
　　Eche day in the felde hir norices sheep.

195　This same tyme vnto Antioche
　　A tyraunt, the prefect of that cuntre,

170 Or] Or as Ar　　176 nevir duellid] dwellyd neuere Ar　　178 Which al be run-
nen to her fate] Wych lyuyth yet lest he deyed late Ar　　180 speke] do Ar　　181 Not]
And not Ar　　184 eke] inward Ar　　194 Eche day in the felde] In the feld eche day
Ar

From Asya-ward did approche,
And Olibrius by name clepid was he.
And as he went, where he myght see
Ony cristen men, ful cruelly   200
He hem destroyed withoute mercy.

And casuelly as by the same wey
He rode where Margarete did pasture
Hir norice shepe, sodeynly his ey
On hir he kest, of countenaunce demure,   205
And anoon hir beaute so sore dyd lure
His her[te], that therwith he stent,
And toke of hir he more avisement. |

And whan he sawe hir forhede lyly white,   f. 130vb
Hir blake browes bent, and hir grey eyne,   210
Hir chery chekis, hir nose streyte and ryte,
Hir rody lippes, hir chyn, which as pleyne
Pulshid marbil shoon, and cloven on tweyne,
He was so astoyned in that caas
That vnnethe he wist where he waas.   215

He lokid no ferther than in hir face,
Where of natures yiftis was plente inow;
Hym thought that nevir in so litle space,
He had seen more which hym drow
As the magnete doth iron; and of his swow   220
Whan half amasyd he did abreyde,
Thus with sad chere to his men he seyde:

'Goth forth faste yundyr, where ye see
A ful fayr mayde here sheep kepynge,
And wetyth veryly whether bonde or free   225
She ys, and bryngyth me sykyr tydyng.

197 did] proudly dede Ar   199 And] But Ar   207 herte] her Ab   therwith]
euene stylle Ar   208 toke of hir] of hyr he took Ar   210 blake browes bent] bent
browys blake Ar   212 rody lippes] lyppys rody Ar   214 in that caas] of that
sodeyn caas Ar   215 where] wher that Ar   217 natures] natural Ar   was plente]
plente was Ar   219 seen more] more seyn Ar   hym] his herte Ar   220 and]
but whan Ar   221 Whan half] As a man Ar   he] he sodeynly Ar   222 chere]
contenaunce Ar

Yf she be fre, I wyl wyth a rynge
Here weddyn, and bryngyn to gret honour,
And here endewyn in many a castel and tour.

230   Yf she be bonde and vndyr seruage,
For noon othyr man I wyl doo wronge,
Hyre lord wyl I yiuyn ryght good wage,
And to my paramour hyre vndyrfonge.
Ha[styth] yow forth and taryith not longe,
235   For from this [p]lace I nyl passe, certeyn,
Tyl y[e] an answere me brynge ageyn'.

Whan this seyid was, ful hastyly
Hys men hem hyid tyl were she was
They come, to whom ful manerly
240   Of here comynge dede telle the caas;
And therwith al the blood of hyre face,
For sodeyn feer was stert awaye,
And deuouhtly to God she thus dede preye:

'Haue mercy, lord Ihesu, vpon me,
245   And lese not my soule with vnpitous men!
Make me, lord, euere to ioyin in the,
And with thy seruauntys the to preyse, amen.
And sende thyn aungel me with to ken,
And wysdam, how that withoute fere
250   I may this wykkyd prefect answere.

I see me, lord, as an innocent sheep
With rauenous wuluys enueyrond to be.
Help now, good lord, and from hem me keep,
Yf yt plese [thy] souereyn maieste.'
255   Whan they thys herd, they gunne to [f]le
As from a wycche, and wythin a breyid
To here lord thei come, and to hym thus seyid:

229 here endewyn] endewe hyr Ar   231 noon othyr man I wyl] I wyl noon othyr man Ar   234 Hastyth] Ha feyth Ab   235 place] Iolace Ab   passe] parte Ar 236 ye] ys Ab   237 seyid was] was seyd Ar   240 dede telle] they told Ar 241 therwith] anon Ar   of] owt of Ar   248 thyn] an Ar   252 to be] be Ar 254 thy] thys Ab   255 fle] sle Ab

'Lord, whom enhauncyd hath fortune,
And set in the staat of gret [dig]nyte,
I[n] no wyse thy power may comune   260
Ben to here to whom sent were we.
For Crist as hyre [God], lord, wourshypyth she,
And to oure goddys she nyl do seruyse,
But hem she blasphemth in voundyr wyse.' |

Whan Olibrius these wourdys herd,   f. 131ra
He chaungyd bothe colour and cher   266
And as a [man mad] anoon he ferd,
And what he myht don he was in dwer.
And aftir auysement he bad that ner
They shuld hyre fecche, and whan she come was,   270
He hyre thus arynyd with a pale faas:

'Sey me, damysel, of what ken thow art,
And whethir thow be bonde or ellys fre?'
'Seruage in me had neuere no part,
For cristene I am sykyr, syre', quod she.   275
'I haske of what byrthe thow art', quod he.
'I serue', she seyth, 'the souereyn godhede
Whiche hedyrto hath kept my maydynhede.'

'Thanne folwith yt thus, ful consequentlye,
That thow clepist Crist thi god', quod he,   280
'Whom that my fadris dede crucifye'.
'May no thyng be sothere seyid', quod she;
'Thy fadris naylyd Crist vpon a tre,
Whom I do wurshipe with hol herte,
And thei in helle sufferyn smerte.'   285

Whan Olibrius herde this conclusioun
Of mayde Margarete, he wex ner wood,
And to ben shet in a ful strong presoun
He hyre comaundyd, wych fast by stood,

259 dignyte] augnyte Ab   260 In] I Ab   261 whom] whom that Ar
262 God] God in Ab   267 man mad] mad man Ab   268 was] stood Ar
270 shuld hyre] hyr shuld Ar   276 byrthe] kynrede Ar   277 the] that Ar
278 Whiche] That Ar   282 sothere seyid] seyd sothere Ar   285 smerte] peynys
smerte Ar

290   Euere musynge in his marrid mood,
         How and by what maner of subtilite,
         He here mygh byreuyn hyre virginyte.

         Aftyr this, [in ful] pompous wyse,
         He entryd into Antioche cyte,
295   And to hys goddys mad a sacrifise,
         As yt was the custum of that cuntre.
         And on the nexte day comaundyd he
         Margarete be brouht to hys precense,
         And thus he here seyde hys sentence:

300   'What ys the skyl and the cause whi,
         Margarete, of thy gret cruelte,
         That of thyself thow ne hast mercy,
         And wylt thus spillyn thy gret bewte?
         Leue al this foly and consente to me,
305   I the counsele, and I the wyl auaunce
         Off gold and syluyr with gret habundaunce.

         Quod Margarete, 'Yf thou, o wykkyd man,
         Knew how lytyl that I sette by
         Alle thy profyrs, thou woldyst nat han
310   This besynesse abowte me, sothly.
         For from the weyis of trewthe neuere wyl I,
         But hym I wurshipe whom euer[y] creature
         Dredith, whos regne shal euere endure.'

         'Margarete', quod he, 'lystne what I seye.
315   Yf thow my goddys no wurshipe wylt do,
         With myn swerd, sekyr, thou shalt deye.
         Truste me veryly, for yt shal be so.
         And yf thou wilt mekely obeye me to,
         Yt xal be gretly for thy byhoue,
320   For thy body singulerly I wil loue.' |

         292 here mygh byreuyn hyre] myht bereuyr hyre hyr Ar   293 in ful] in a ful Ab
         298 be] to Ar   299 seyde hys] seyd hyr Ar   302 ne hast] ne Ar   303 wylt
         thus] thus wylt Ar   305 I the counsele] Be my councel Ar   308 Knew] Wystyst
         Ar   310 sothly] trewly Ar   312 euery] euere Ab   317 for yt] yt Ar
         320 singulerly I wil] I wyl syngulerly Ar

'My body', quod she, 'whan euere thow leste   f. 131rb
To excercysyn in me thy tiranny,
With holy virgyns that I may reste,
To Goddys sacrifice I offere redy;
For this I wyl thou knowe pleynly,   325
I nothyng dowte, for Cristis sake
Wiche for alle men deyid, 'deth' to take.'

Wan he thys herde, of gret cruelte
He bad hyre byn hangyn in the eyr ful hye,
And be betyn with battys, were whan shee   330
Tormentyd was, to heuene here yie
Deuo[uh]thly she lyfth, and thus dede seye:
'In the, lord, I truste, and in thy mercy.
Lete me not be confoundyd, lord, vttyrly.'

And wyl she thus ocupeyid was in preere,   335
The tormentours here shorgyd so cruelly
That lych as watir in a ryuere
So ran hyre blood owt plenteuously.
And whyl they betyn, a bedel dede crye:
'Byleue, Margarete, I counsele the,   340
And abouyn alle maydyns weel shalt thow be.'

And not only the bedel, but eek the men
And women als[o], wyche stode bysyde,
Whan they thus seyin hyre blod owt ren,
Wepyng ful sore thus on hyre they cryde: 345
'Margarete, for the we sorwe this tyde!
Olibrius in hys ire the hastyth to spille.
Beleue hym, we counsele, and so lyue stylle!'

Whan Margarete amonge the sharp shours
Off tormentrye these wurdys dede here,
Quod shee, 'O ye wykkyd counsellours,   350

325 pleynly] vttyrly Ar   326 nothyng] nowyse Ar   327 Wiche] That Ar
328 thys herde] herd this Ar   329 bad] comaundyd Ar   eyr ful] eyr Ar   330 be]
to be Ar   battys] yerdys Ar   whan] whan that Ar   331 heuene] heueneward Ar
332 Deuouhthly] Deuouuhthly Ab   334 be confoundyd] confoundyd be Ar   vttyrly]
endelesly Ar   335 was in] in Ab   341 abouyn] past Ar   342 the¹] this Ar
343 also] alse Ab   348 and so] and Ar   stylle] yet stylle Ar   349 the] hyr Ar

Men and wummen, what do ye here?
Goth to youre werkys! for wythowtyn pere
That lord wych syttyth in trone ful hy
355   Ys myn helpere-this wyl knowe I.

Also, moreouyr, I wyl ye knowe,
And in youre mynde [doth] yt aduertyse,
That whan Gabriel hys horn doth blowe
In the day of the gret and last assyse,
360   And alle men in body and soule vpryse,
Than shall my soule be thys torment
Be sauyd from that hard iugement.

Wherefore, yf ye wyl sauyd be
Thylk tyme, I counsele yow feythfully,
365   Alle fals goddys forsakyth ye,
And leuyth in my God, wych ys myhty
In vertu, and heryth alle men gladly
Wh[i]che to hym preye, puryd from vyhs,
And opnyth hem the gatis of paradys.

370   Alle fals goddys doth ye forsake
Hastely therfore, be counsel of me,
Whiche byn not ellys, I vndyrtake,
But gold or syluyr, stonys or tre,
That neyther moun spekyn, gon, here, ne see
375   Formyd by man; and if my sentence
Ye not byleue, makyth experience, |

f. 131ᵛᵃ   And ye shul moun perceyuyn sensibyly
That thei han feet and mown not gon,
Erys not herynge, and eye also sothly
380   Not seynge, for in hem ys non
Spiryt of lyf, ner fleshhe ne boon
On hyre badyis; to swych godhede
No [wyhs] man [owyth] to takyn hede.

354 That] The Ar   wych] that Ar   356 knowe] troste Ar   357 doth] wee
Ab   360 And alle] Whan Ar   368 Whiche] Whche Ab   374 neyther moun
spekyn gon here ne see] goon ne mown speke here ne see Ar   377 moun perceyuyn]
weel prouyn Ar   379 also] om. Ar   383 wyhs] wylys Ab   owyth] swych Ab

Wherfore, my counsel yf ye wyl do,
My soule for yowrs, ye sauyd shul be.   385
But thow, o tiraunt, wyche wylt not s[o],
And Sathanas werkys euere dost,' quod she,
'Thy fadyr, and ageyn the hy maieste
Of oo god berkyst as a dogge shameles,
In helle thy peyne shal byn endeles.'   390

Olibrius, thys herynge, fel in a rage,
Euene as a man owt of hys mynde,
And bad hys tormentours in that owtrage
Hyre tendir flesshe to race and rende,
So hopynge of hyre to makyn an ende.   395
And in thys menewyle she vp hyr eye
To heuene lyftyd, and thus dede seye:

'Bysegyd I am wyth wyckyd counsel,
And manye doggys han enuyrond me,
Wych ageyns me fers ben and cruel.   400
Wherfore me counforte, lord, I prey the,
And sende doun from heuene, my helpe to be,
A culuyr whyht, of thy specyal grace,
Er than I do deye, here in thys place.

And, lord, also, yf yt [plese] the,   405
I yt wold besheche with al myn herte,
That I onys myn aduersarye myht see
Wych wyth me fytyth and me wolde peruerte,
And I hym shuld make ful sore to smerte,
And yiuyn exau[m]ple be my victory   410
Alle virgyns to trusten in thy mercy.'

In the menetyme of hyre preyre,
They rentyn hyre flesshe on euery syde
So dispitously, that than a ryuer
Hyre blood to grounde swyftere dede glyde,   415

385 sauyd shul] shul saf Ar   386 so] se Ab   397 lyftyd] dede lyfte Ar   dede]
gan Ar   400 ageyns me fers ben] ben ageyn me fers Ar   403 of thy specyal]
lord of thy grace Ar   404 I do] I Ar   405 lord also] also lord Ar   plese] plesed
Ab   406 I yt] I Ar   407 onys myn aduersarye myht] myht onys myn aduersarye
Ar   410 exaumple] exaunple Ab

That the v[n]pitous prefect hys eyne dede hyde
[Wyth] hys mantel, and myht not soffere to see
Blood rennynge owt so gret plente.

And whan he saw hyre han swich stedfastnesse
420   In suffraunce, 'Margarete!' he lowde dede crye,
'Consente to me, and wyth hertly mekenesse
Wurshype my goddys, ne hap thou euyl deye.'
'Thy counsel,' quod she, 'I fully denye;
For yf I of my flesshe shulde han mercy,
425   My soule shulde perysshe, as shal thyn sothly.'

Whan he herd thys, to takyn hyre doun
Hys tormentours from that hy iebet
He bad, and into a ryht therk presoun
He comaundyd anoon hyre to be shet.
430   And euene as the clok had seuene smet,
She entryd into that place lothly,
Hyre b[ly]ssyng, and thus she preyid mekely: |

f. 131vb   'Byhold me, lord, wych am the oonly
Douhtyr of my fadir, and he h[a]th me
435   For the forsakyn, and so hym haue I.
Hens aftir wyl thou my fadir be!
And graunte that I may myn enmy see,
Wych wyth me f[yhty]th, face to face,
Geyns whom I not what I trespace.

440   Of al thynge, lord, thou art the iuge.
Twyn hym and me deme rethfully.
And for thou art only my refuge,
On hym I pleyne that wrangyd am y
And woundyd also ful greuously.
445   Yet yif thou, lord, be not wroth with me,
I sette ryht not by al hys enmyte.'

---

416 vnpitous] vpitous Ab   417 Wyth] Which Ab   419 saw] sey Ar
425 shulde perysshe] perysh shuld Ar   426 herd] sey Ar   429 hyre to] she
shuld Ar   shet] set Ar   430 had seuene] seuene had Ar   432 blyssyng] bassyng
Ab   preyid] seyd Ar   434 hath] hith Ab   438 fyhtyth] feth Ab   440 art
the] art Ar   443 wrangyd] hurt Ar

And whyl that she thus ocupyid was
Ful deuouhtly in here preyere,
An huge dragoun, glastrynge as glas,
Sodenly from a corner dede appere   450
Of the prisoun, wyth an horrible chere.
Hys erys were gylt, hys berd was long,
Hys teeth of yrin were myhty & strong;

Owt hys nosethyrls foul smoke he blew,
Hys eyne twynkyd as sterris by nyght,   455
Hys tunge vpon hys heed he threw,
In hys hand a swerd bornysshd bryht.
And anon the prisoun wex ful of lyht,
Of the fiyr whiche that owt de[de] renne
From hys mouth, whiche faste dede brenne.   460

Whan Margarete hym sey, ful pale of chere
She wex, and for very feyr treuly,
She had foryetyn that God hyre preyere
Had hard, in wych she thus dede crye:
'Shewe me, lord, onys myn enmy   465
Or than I deye', and aftyr seyde she,
'Lete not thys dragoun, lord, hurtyn me.'

Thys horrible beste vpon hyre heed
Put hys mouth, whyl she thus seyd,
And eek hys tunge, wych was ryht reed   470
Vndyr hyre hele anoon he leyd,
And swelwyd hyre in euene at a breyd.
And whan here cros in hys mouth dede encres,
He brast on two, and she skapyd harmles.

And whan she thus had the victory   475
Of hym, thorgh grace of God entere,
On the lefth syde euene [faste] therby
Anothyr deuyl sodenly bygan appere,

455 twynkyd] glastryd Ar   456 vpon] ouyr Ar   heed] crowne Ar   457 hand]
clawys Ar   459 whiche that] whiche Ar   dede] de Ab   460 whiche] & Ar   dede]
gan Ar   462 wex] was Ar   466 aftyr] aftyr thus Ar   467 hurtyn] noyen Ar
470 ryht] fer Ar   477 faste] fastyd Ab   therby] hyrby Ar   478 bygan] ther gan
Ar

Wych on hyre lokyd wyth a lothly chere.
480   And at the laste he thus owt abrayid
With a sneuelynge voys, and thus he seyid:

'Ryht now myn owyn dere brothir Ruffyn,
In a dragonys lyknesse to the I sent.
And whan he the hol had sweluyd in,
485   Vnwarly, er he wyste what yt ment,
Wyth thy wycchecrafth hys lyf was spent;
For wyth a cros thou dedyst hym breke;
Whos deth I now am comyn to wreke.' |

f. 132ra   As sone these wurdys as he had seyd,
490   By hys longe heres she gan hym kecche
And vndyr hyre ryht foot she hym leyid,
And thus dede seyin: 'O thou woful wrecche,
Lete be thy cursyd and froward tecche
My maydynhood to tempte, f[or] myn helpe sothly
495   Ys Crist, whos name duryth endelysly.'

Treue at thys wurd, a ful gret lytht
Illumynyd sodeynly that derk presoun,
And a cros apperyd in heuene ful bryth,
On wich a whyht dowe lyth adoun,
500   And seyde, 'Margarete!' with a sweet soun,
'Alle seyntys in heuene the abyde,
And the gatis of paradhys ben opnyd wyde.'

Thanne Margarete, to God aftyr dev thankynge,
To the fend hyre turnyd and thus dede seye:
505   'Tel me of whens thow art, foul thyng.'
'Seruaunt of Crist', quod he, 'I prey[e]
Fro my nekke thy foot remeue aweye,
And al werkyng I wyl the telle,
Doon bothyn in erthe and eek in helle.'

479 lokyd] dede loke Ar   481 thus he] to hyr Ar   482 myn owyn] myn
Ar   484 whan he] whanne Ar   the hol had] had the hool Ar   486 spent] shent
Ar   487 a cros] tokne of a cros Ar   492 dede seyin] seyde Ar   493 thy]
this Ar   494 for] fro Ab   499 a whyht] a Ar   lyth] descendyd Ar   501 the]
do the Ar   503 to God aftyr] aftyr to God Ar   506 I] I the Ar   preye] preys Ab
508 werkyng] my werkys Ar

Afftyr thys anoon, of here ientylnesse,   510
Out of hys nekke hyre foot to remeue
Sofftely she began, and of hys dysstresse
Whan he hyre felte hym so releue,
'Gramercy,' he seyde, 'and, by yowre lyue,
Now wyl I, lady, onto youre damaunde   515
Answere brefly, as ye me comaunde.

My surname, lady, ys clepyd Belchys.
Sathanas oure reulere ys and oure kyng.
And in the bookys pleynly wrytyn ys
Of Iamnes and Mambras, oure ospryng,   520
Oure gouernaunce, and al oure werkyng.
But to yowre purpos: yf ye yt lyste to here,
I wyl yow declaryn how we comyn here.

Salomon, of the childeryn of Israel
The wisest kyng that euere was,   525
Shet onys of vs, as storyis doo tel,
Many thousentis in a vessel of bras;
And whan Babilonyes comyn into that plaas,
And wendyn gret tresore to haue founde,
The vesseles they brokyn, and vs v[n]bounde.   530

And thus, whan we vnboundyn were,
Al erthe inviroun we dede fille,
Serchyng whom we myht noye and dere,
For thys propyrte longyth euere tille.'
'Thys gouernaunce,' quod she, 'forsothe ys ylle.   535
Wherfore goo, deuyl, hom to thy kyn!'
And with that wurd, the erthe swellwyd [hym in].

The next day aftyr, fers Olibrius
Hyre comaundyd be brouht to hys presence;
To whom ful goodly he seyde euene thus: 540
'Consente, I counsele, to my sentence,

511 foot to] foot Ar   517 lady] treuly Ar   523 yow] shortly Ar   526 Shet
onys of vs] Of vs dede shette Ar   527 in] onys in Ar   530 and vs] and Ab
vnbounde] vnnbounde Ab   532 fille] fulfylle Ar   536 deuyl] Sathanas Ar
537 hym in] yn Ab   540 goodly] softly Ar

And to oure goddys offre frankencence,
Deuouhtly knelyng vpon thy kne,
And past alle wummen I wele loue the.' |

f. 132ʳᵇ

'Laboure', quod she, 'no more in veyn,
546   But take thys answere for final:
Thy goddys neuere wurshipyn shal I, certeyn,
Nyr by thy loue y set ryht not at al;
For not longe hereaftyr deyin thow shal,
550   And whan thou deed art buryid in helle,
Wherfore with the me ne lyste to melle.'

Thys herd, Olibrius bygan to crye,
'Tormentours! tourmentours!' as he wood were,
'With glowynge fiyrbrondys faste you hye,
555   This wycchys sydys to brenne and sere,
As longe as ony flesshe ye fynde there!
And whan she weel warmyd ys in thys wyse,
In fayr cold watir hyre doth baptyse.'

As he comaundyd, doon was anoon,
560   That wery pyte yt was to beholde
How on bothe sydys, euene to the bon,
Hyre flesshe was brent with brondys manyfolde,
And aftir, boundyn, how into watyr colde
The[y] hyre kest, that this chaung sodeyne
565   From hete to cold shuld encrecyn hyre peyne.

But God, hys seruauntys wyche forsake
Neuere wyl, ner sufferyn hem to myscheue,
Sodeynly maad the erthe to quake,
And queynt the fiyr wich hyre dede greue,
570   And so in the watir dede hyre releue,
That vnboundyn and harmles she cam owte,
Wich marual was to hem that stod abowte.

---

546 for] euene for Ar   550 whan thou deed art] aftyr thy deth be Ar   552 Thys
herd Olibrius] Whan Olibrius herd this he Ar   556 ony flesshe ye] ye ony flesh Ar
558 hyre doth] doth hyre Ar   560 yt was] was it Ar   564 They] The Ab
566–7 forsake | Neuere] neuere | forsake Ar   569 wich] that Ar   570 dede
hyre] hyr dede Ar   572 marual] wundyr Ar

For wich miracle fyue thousent anoon
Were there conuertyd and martyrid also;
And whan Olibrius saw the mattir thus goon,   575
Bethynkyng what best was for to do,
And dredyng more puple wold turnyn hyre to
Yf she lengere dede lyue, withowtyn let
Sentencyd hyre heed of to be smet.

Of wych sentence ful glad she was,   580
Hauyng ful trust in Goddys goodnesse.
And whan she was brouth into the plaas
Where she shuld reseyuyn hyre iuwesse,
Ful replenysshd wyth charitablnesse,
Malcus she preyid, with humble chere,   585
Of leycer to makyn a short preyere.

And whan Malcus hyre had grauntyd space,
She set hyre doun on hyre eythyr kne,
And, vpward to heuene lyftynge hyre face,
Thus gan for to prye: 590
'In eternyte O lord euere regnyng, haue mercy on me.
And for thy gret pyte, O blissyd Ihe[su],
There trespasse foryiue whiche me pursu.

Moreouyr, lord, louly I the byseche
For them specyally that myn passyoun   595
Eythir write or rede, or other do teche,
Or cherche or chapel make yf thei moun,
Or lyth or launpe fynde of deuocioun
To me-ward: lord, of thy grete grace,
Hem repentaunce graunte er they hens pace. | 600

Also yf wummen in trauaylyng be   f. 132va
Oppressyd wyth peyne and greuaunce,
And for helpe deuouhtly prye to me,
Graunt hem, lord, good delyueraunce.

575 saw] sey Ar   578 dede lyue] lyuyd Ar   let] more let Ar   584 Ful]
Fully Ar   587 Malcus] he Ar   588 on hyre] on Ar   592 Ihesu] Iheseu
Ab   593 whiche] that Ar   596 write or rede] rede or wryte Ar   599 of]
for Ar   603 prye] do preye Ar   604 lord] sone Ar

605   And generally, lord, in ony malechaunce,
        Yf to me for socour men calle and crye,
        Graunt hem sone counfort and remedye.'

        Whan she thus endyd had hyre preyere,
        Sodeynly from heuene this woys cam doun,
610   So lowde that alle men myht yt here:
        'Herd ys, Margarete, thyn orisoun,
        And grauntyd, that who with deuocyoun
        In ony dyshese doth preye to the,
        For thy sake sothly he herd shal be.'

615   And wyth thys wourd hyre face to Malchus
        She turnyd, and seyde with ryth glad chere:
        'Brothyr, that the bad doon Olibrius,
        Now to performe do thy deuyr,
        For I not what lengere I shulde doon her.'
620   And Malchus anoon, withowte let,
        Euene at oo strook hyre heed of smet.

        But vnnethe hyre body sonere to grunde
        Fel, than here soule was in heuene blys.
        Now, glorious lady, lete thy pyte habounde,
625   Oure soulys to brynge where thy soule ys,
        For thanne of ioye shul we neuere mys,
        Wedyr vs mote brynge the holy trinite.
        Sey yche man 'amen', for cheryte.

    Here endyth the ly[f] of Seynt Margarete

    The translacyoun of Seynt Margarete from Antioche
        From the tyme of the incarnacyoun
630   Of Ihesu Crist nyne hundryd yer
        And eyghte, be trewe computacyoun,
        Whan Sergius was vniuersyl clauyculer
        Of the cherche, and in Ytayle themper

---

616 ryth] ful Ar   617 bad doon] do bad Ar   619 what lengere] lengere what Ar
I shulde] to Ar   620 let] more let Ar   628 for] pur Ar   628.1 *Serjeantson*
lines 869–938 not in Ab   rubric: lyf] ly Ab   633 the] holy Ar   in Ytayle th] the sool
Ar

Had Baryngarie, the caas byfelle
Whiche I now shal rathere touche than telle.   635

Thys secunde yer of thys forseyd pope,
Sergius, and the twelfte indiccyoun,
As by cronyclers I vndyrgrope,
Byfyl a greuous dyssencyoun
Twyx the patriarc of Antioche toun,   640
Eusebye, and [hym that was be] tyrannye
That tyme was prince of here polycye.

Andranicus hyht that prynce sothelye,
Wych, whyl that Eusebye absent was,
As I seyde byforn, thorgh tirannye   645
Vsurpyd the pryncehood of that plas;
Wereof byfel a ful heuy caas;
For thorgh there tweynys debat and stryf
Ful many a man dede lesyn hys lyf. |

The pro[ce]sse to declare were to long,   f. 132ᵛᵇ
And askyth ful many a circumstaunce   651
To telle clerly how gret wrong
Thys prince dede, and to what myschaunce
The cyte he brough thorgh mysgouernaunce,
And by what simulacoun his sone in lawe,   655
Synward, by nyht he brouht on dawe.

Y wyl not tellyn here what accacyoun
He feynyd the patriaarc to [pursu],
Nyr how by hys simulat faccoun,
Myche puple to hys fauour he dreu.   660
Wherfore, al prolyxyte to eschow,
I wel lete pass[e] al maner dygressioun,
And shortly gon on to the conclusyoun.

634 the] this Ar   635 now] her Ar   rathere touche] touche rathere Ar
636 Thys] The Ar   thys] the Ar   637 and the] and Ar   639 Byfyl] Fel
Ar   a] a ful Ar   641 hym that was be] em wych by Ab   645 thorgh] be
Ar   647 byfel] fel Ar   650 processe] prosse Ab   651 And] And it Ar
655 simulacoun] treytourye Ar   658 pursu] presoun Ab   659 Nyr] And Ar
how by hys] & be what Ar   661 al prolyxyte] prolyxyte Ar   662 passe] passent
Ab

Whan ner distroyid by hys surquydrye,
665   Of Antioche was the gret cyte
With fiyr and swerd ful cruellye,
Many a fayr cherche ther brent he,
That reuthe and pyte yt was to see;
Amo[n]ge wyche of Seynt Margarete was oon,
670   Wherof lefth neythir stykke ne ston.

In thys seyd sherche was an abbeye,
A solemne of munkys whyl that yt stood,
Whereof the abot was, as cronycles sey[e],
That tyme a religious man and good,
675   Austyn by name, and of nobyl blood,
Born in the cuntre of Lumbardye,
In an old cyte wyche ys clepyd Pauye.

Whan thys abbot sey the gret myschyf,
Bothe of the cyte and ee[k] of hys abbeye,
680   And the impossibylyte yt to releff,
Hys spirit from hym went ner aweye;
Hym thouhte h[e] yaf no fors to deye.
And whan he thus longe had stonde confuse,
At the laste in hymself he thus dede muse:

685   'I am but a foreyn in thys cuntre,
And haue here no frend me to counsayle.
Wherfore me thinkyth yt best for me
Hoom to returnyn into Ytayle,
Wherof good frenschepe I may not fayle,
690   For ther ys the issu of myn genealogye,
And specyaly in the cyte of Pauye.'

And whan in this purpos he fyxyd was,
Hys own cuntre to gon hoom to,

664 ner distroyid by] of Antyoche thorg Ar   665 Of Antioche] Ner destroyd
Ar   gret] fayr Ar   669 Amonge] Amoge Ab   670 lefth] he left Ar
673 Whereof] Of wych Ar   seye] seyde Ab   676 the] a Ar   of] clepyd Ar
677 In] And of Ar   an old] an Ar   wyche ys clepyd] callyd Ar   678 abbot] Austyn
Ar   679 and eek] and eel Ab; and Ar   680 impossibylyte] impossybylnesse Ar
681 from hym went ner] ner went from hym Ar   682 he] ha Ab   684 At the] At
Ar   686 counsayle] auayle Ar   688 Hoom] Ageyn Ar   691 Pauye] Papye
Ar

He cest hym to caryin of that plaas
The bodyis of holy virgyns two,   695
Of Margarete and of Euprepye also,
To profyhth of the cherche, and eek honoure
In Payue of Cirus the confessour.

For lernyd he hadde ful secretlye
Off a prest in hys last confessyoun,   700
Vbald by name, whan he shuld dye,
Wych was a man of gret deuocyoun,
How of Seynt Margarete he fynde shuld moun
The body, and where that yt dede reste,
Of gold and syluyr in a lytyl cheste. | 705

And for he mygh not alone do   f. 133ra
Hys dyser, of hys seruauntis tweyne
Preuyly oo tyme he clepyd hym to,
Wyche Robert and Lucas clepyd were, certeyne,
And feythfully of hem he gan to freyne   710
Yf they to hym woldyn trewe be,
And goon hom with hym to hys cuntre.

And yf thei so wolde, he hem hyht
Of gold and syluir gret habundaunce,
And that he shulde doon al hys myht   715
Wyth sporis gylt hem bothe to avaunce,
And that they shulde ryde with spere and launce;
And they hym assuryd with writtynge and seel,
That they cloos shuld kepyn al hys counsel.

'Felaas', quoth he, 'myn entent   720
Ys meuyd of pure deuocyoun,
Out of thys place wyche ys brent,

694 hym to] to Ar   of] owt of Ar   696 Of] Seynt Ar   of] seynt Ar
698 Cirus] seynt Sire Ar   705 lytyl] fayr Ar   707 Hys dyser] That he desyryd
Ar   seruauntis] men Ar   709 Robert and Lucas] Lucas & Robert Ar   clepyd were]
were clepyd Ar   711 trewe] trewe men Ar   712 goon hom with hym] wyth hym
goon hom Ar   713 so wolde] wold so Ar   hem] them there Ar   714 syluir]
tresore Ar   718 writtynge] scrypture Ar   719 That they cloos shuld] Euere
cloos to Ar   720 myn] treuly myn Ar   721 Ys meuyd] Meuyd is euene Ar
722 brent] her brent Ar

And brouht to myschef and desolacioun,
Of summe reliquys to make translacioun,
725   And specyally of that holy virgine pure
Seynt Margarete, and in Pauye here shryne.'

Whan thei had herd hys entent pure,
They to hym sworn trewe for to be
And, bothe wyth seel and eek scripture,
730   The[y] maad hym sufficyent suyrte
Hys counsel to kepe cloos and secre;
'For plenly', they seyde, 'be Goddys grace,
To that good dede he inspiryd was.'

And sone aftyr thys they come alle thre,
735   Preyuely by nyht onto the place
Where Austyn had lernyd the relykes [hyd] be,
Of Seynt Margarete, by Goddys grace,
And anoon so depe they dede race,
Tyl at the laste a cheste they founde,
740   With iryn and bras myghtyly bounde.

And wythowtyn was wrytyn this scripture,
Euene abouyn vpon the cheste:
'Here wythinne, of the virgine pure
Seynt Margarete, the body doth reste.'
745   And wythowte taryinge they yt al tobreste,
And in a wessel of seluyr, wyth gymmys fresshly
Araiyd, thei founde that blyssyd body.

Wyche whan thei seyn they were ful glad,
And anoon tokyn yt vp ful reuerently,
750   And to a mannys hous they yt lad,
Crisper by name, wyche dwellyd by,

    723 to myschef and] as ye see to gret Ar   724 make] make a Ar   725 holy
virgine pure] blyssyd & holy virgyne Ar   726 here] hem do Ar   727–33 Ar
reads: Whan they thys herde, wyth ryht glad cher | Fully they approuyd al his entent, | And
seyden, whan-euere in this mater | He wolde procede, they shuld assent | 'For here,' quod
they, 'it arn but shent. | Wherfore to performyn this holy decre | We trowe that god hath
inspyryd the.'   730 They] The Ab   736 hyd] bed Ab   738 race] in race
Ar   741 And] And euene Ar   was wrytyn] wrytyn Ar   742 Euene] Wrytyn Ar
745 taryinge] let Ar   746 wessel of seluyr] syluerene vessel Ar   747 that] this
Ar   750 they] preuyly Ar   751 by] ther ny Ar

And Austyn the abbott louyd enterly;
But what they broughte they nold hym telle,
And foure dayis aftir thei there dede dwelle.

In whyche menetyme hem redy,   755
Mad for to takyn forth here iourne;
But the syluyrene arc they broke, sothly,
And trussyd the body in a lokyr of tre,
That of richesse shuld no suspicyoun be.
And, anoon, leue takyn, to shyp they went,   760
A graceous tyme God to hem sent. |

For whithowtyn eythir peryl or feer,   f. 133rb
To Brunduse port they dede applye,
And whan they had refresshd hem ther,
Thre hor[s] anoon they dede bye,   765
And to Rome faste they dede hem hye,
Where with a ful deuouht courage
The[y] wentyn aboutyn here pilgrimage

And whan ful nyr dayis fyhftene
Thus in holy placys visitacioun   770
They had ben excercisyd, and mad hem clene,
Euene as they wentyn in the stacioun,
A sodeyn flyx thereu Austyn doun,
Whiche hym so sore dede oppresse,
That to deyin he wende of that seknesse.   775

Wherfore, as goodly as he myht,
Seynge no lyklynesse to ben amendyd,

752 And] Wych Ar; *lines 751–2 reversed in Ar*   754 thei there] thei Ar
755 menetyme] tyme they maad menetyme   756 Mad for] In hasty wyse Ar
759 richesse] tresore Ar   760 anoon] aftyr Ar   761 A] And a Ab   graceous
tyme God to hem] god of his grace hem fayr speed Ar   762 For] For anoon Ar
763 Brunduse port] the port of Brundusye Ar   764 had] weel had Ar   765 Thre
hors anoon] Anoon thre hors Ar   dede] dede hem Ar   766 And] And forth Ar
faste they dede hem hye] they hem faste dede hye Ar   767 with a ful deuouht
courage] dylygently and wyth deuocyoun Ar   768 They] The Ab   wentyn aboutyn
here pilgrimage] labouryd to purchasyn holy pardoun   769 whan] whan they Ar
770 Thus in holy placys visitacioun] Hemself wyth a deuouth carage Ar   771 They
had ben] Had Ar   hem] ful Ar   772–4 Ar *reads:* And goon to many an holy stage | Of
the reed flyx the gret owtrage | Sodeynly dede Austyn so sore oppresse   775 wende]
trowyd Ar   776 myht] cowde or myht Ar

Of hys ost leue he took at nyht,
And payid for al that he had dyspendyd.
780 And at morne, whan he hym had comendyd
To Petyr and Paule, hys hors he nam,
And vnnethe that day to Sowteris he cam.

And whith gret laboure the nexte day
He cam to the cherche of blyssyd Victory
785 The virgine, wyche stant, as men se may,
In the hy weye, Venus halle by,
Where reseyuyd he was ful honestly,
Swych tyme as the solemnyzacyoun
Shuld ben of here cherchis fyrst dedycacyoun,

790 Wych on the seuente day dede falle
Of octobir, as yt there wrytyn ys,
Where Austyn offryd vp in a palle
Thre of Seynt Margaretes rebbys;
And whan the peple there sey thys,
795 They hem reseyuyd with ful glad cher,
And in honoure of hyre dedyn halwyn an autir.

And aftyrward, wythin dayis to,
That they from this cherche dede pace,
Of Seynt Petyr they come to
800 In the vale Palentes, a religious place
Of munkys, whos abbot hyght Boniface,
Where he was receyuyd wurshpfully,
And in hys syknesse tretid [cherytabylly].

---

778 leue he took at] he took his leue that Ar   780 And at morne] On morwe Ar
782 day] nyht Ar   he cam] cam Ar   783 And whith] whith Ar   laboure] labour
they come Ar   784 He cam to] Onto Ar   787 reseyuyd he was] they hym rece-
uyd Ar   788 Swych] Wych Ar   as] as shuld Ar   789 Shuld ben] ben Ar
here cherchis] that cherche the Ar   791 as yt] euene as Ar   793 Thre] Oon Ar
794 there] ther dwellyng Ar   795 hem] it Ar   796 honoure of hyre] hyr honour
Ar   797 And aftyrward] Fro whens Ar   798 That they from this cherche] Wyth
gret syknesse whan they Ar   799 they come to] a relygyous place Ar   800 a religious place] they come to Ar   801 whos abbot hyght] blake and Ar   802 Where
he was receyuyd] The Abot hyht, wher Ar   803 And in hys syknesse tretid] Austyn
was receyuyd & Ar   cherytabylly] cherchabylly Ab

And whan Austyn sey that hys seknesse
Yche day encrecyd more and more,   805
And cowde see no wye of lyklynesse
To askapyn, wepynge ful sore,
The abbot Boniface he sent fore,
To whom, in presence of hys couent,
He thus declaryd ys entent: 810

'Allas!', quoth he, 'that as a straungere
And as a man vnknowyn in thys cuntre,
Ineuitably I muste deyin here,
For euere encrecyth myn infirmyte.
Nertheles, vertu of necessyte   815
I wyl make, werfore euene now,
My spyryt I comende to God and yow. |

Moreouyr also, I wyl that ye wete   f. 133ᵛᵃ
T[w]o precyous relikys I here haue with me;
That ys to seyne, of Seynt Margarete   820
The body, and of the virgine fre,
Eupepye, the heed, in a cophyn of tre,
Whiche from Antioche I hedyr haue brought,
And to Pauye thoo bern yt was my thouht.

But syth I see deeth me faste neyhe to,   825
And I of lyuynge may haue no lengere spas,
Wyl my wyttys ben fresche and my mynde also,
These reliquis I yiue to thys holy place,
Bysychyng yow of yowre specyal grace,
That ye for me wyln preyin enterly,   830
And myn obite day kepyn from hens yerly.'

804 Austyn] he Ar   807 wepynge ful sore] anoon he sent fore Ar   808 he
sent fore] & wepyng ful sore Ar   809 whom] hym Ar   couent] hool couent Ar
810 thus] pleynly Ar   declaryd] declaryd thus Ar   811 that] euene Ar   812 as
a man] as Ar   in] also in Ar   814 euere] alwey Ar   816 werfore euene] and
therfore Ar   817 My spyryt] To god my soule Ar   comende to God] comende Ar
818 wyl that] wyl Ar   819 Two] Thoo Ab   823 I hedyr] I Ar   824 thoo
bern] them led Ar   826 of lyuynge] to lyue Ar   829 Bysychyng yow of yowre
specyal] You therfore askynge this oonly Ar   830 enterly] specyally Ar   831 And
myn obite day kepyn from hens] And therto my annyuersarye kepyn Ar

Whan the[y] herd thys, God principally
And hym the[y] thankyd, with herte entere,
And that he desyryd so deuouhthly
835 They hym grauntyd, with ful glad chere,
And anoon alle the munkys in fere
'*Te deum laudamus*' ful meryly sunge,
And alle here bellys solemnely runge.

Than the abbot reuestyd, and his munkys alle,
840 With torchis and taprys brynnynge ful cler,
These precyous relikys, curyd with a palle,
Born and settyd vp on the hye autir;
And eyght dayis aftir, wyth ful glad cher,
They mad gret feste and solemnyte,
845 And manye folke thedyr come them to se.

In wyche menetyme thys blyssyd man,
Austyn, whiche yaf to that holy place
These relikys, whan that he had tan
Alle hys rythtys, to Goddys grace
850 Comendyd hys soule, and hens dede passe,
The sexteynde kalende, as writyng doth preue,
Of Nouembre, whan fallyth Seynt Lukys eue.

And whan they hys dyrige in goodly maner
Had don, to cherche ful religiously
855 Hys body they bore, and bysydyn an autyr
Of Seynt Blase yt buryid ful wurshypfully.
And aftir they hem bysyid riht diligently,
To performen vp the solemnizacyoun
Of these blyssyd relikys translacyoun.

832 they] the Ab   833 And hym the] They Ar   thankyd] thankyd and hym Ar
837 ful meryly] deuouthly Ar   838 solemnely] ful solemnely Ar   839 Than]
And Ar   reuestyd] copyd Ar   and] with Ar   845 manye folk] meche peple Ar   come
them] it cam Ar   847 whiche] whiche that Ar   to] onto Ar   holy place] place Ar
848 relikys] holy relikys Ar   that he] he Ar   850 Comendyd] He commendyd Ar
851 kalende] kalendys Ar   852 whan fallyth] euene on Ar   854 don] seyde Ar
to] to here Ar   857 aftir they] aftyrward Ar   859 blyssyd] holy seyd Ar

And thogh Calyxtys day, martyr & pope,   860
Whiche fallyth of Octobyr the thretende day,
As by old wrytynge I vndyrgrope,
The fyrst day was of this solemne aray,
Which reuelacyoun or translacioun clepid be may,
Of Margaretes body, yet eyghte dayis more   865
They solemnely kept, as ys seyid before.
And at thys tyme God for hyre wrought

Manye myraclis, wiche I writynge haue see
Albeyt for hast I reherce hem nouht,
For to othere thyngys I wyl spedyn me,   870
And also for to eschewe prolyxyte,
S`t´epdam of fauour, aftyr the sentence
In a vers of Mathu Vindocinence. |

The secunde translacyoun   f. 133vb
But for as meche as nothyng perpetuel
Ys in thys word, ner stable of a staat,   875
For the gret werrys that sone aftyr fel
In thylk cuntre, thorugh stryff and debat
Of sundry cytes, thys place desolat
In short tyme was leyfth, and stood alone,
Whoos dwellers for feer dede flyn ychoone.   880

Aftir this sone, whan yt was knowe
That thys abbeye was in swych desolacyon,
And by the trumpet of fame abowte was blowe,
The Ruuyllyans madyn a congregacyoun,
And of here clerkys g[a]dryd a processyoun   885
Off oure ladyis cherche, and wyth gret reuerens,
Seynt Margaretys body they dede fecche thens.

860 And] For Ar   martyr &] martyr Ab   863 was] were Ar   865 Margaretes]
seynt Margretys Ar   866 ys seyid] seyd is Ar   867 And at thys tyme] In wych
eyghte dayis ther Ar   for hyre wrought] wrought Ar   868 myraclis] grete miraclys
Ar   wiche I writynge] as I wrytyn Ar   869 hast] hast that Ar   870 For] Or for
Ar   wyl] wold Ar   871 for to] to Ar   875 of a] in oo Ar   879 In short
tyme was leyfth] Wyth-inne fewe yerys was Ar   880 for] thens for Ar   881 Aftir
this sone] Sone aftyr this Ar   883 abowte was] aboute Ar   885 of here] alle the
Ar   gadryd] gradryd Ab   a] in Ar   887 dede fecche] fecchyd Ar

And whan they had this body brought
Into oure ladyis cherche with solempnyte,
890   In tablys of marbyl, coryously wrouht,
They yt shrynyd with Seynt Felycite,
Whoos feste fallyth, as writyn fynde we,
Wyth Seynt Clement, wych, as I reme[m]bre,
Ys euene the nynte kalende of Decembre.

895   Where, whanne these virgins shrynyd in sam,
An hundryd yer or more had leyin,
Swych mysche[f] to the Ruuyllyans cam
That doun yt was bete and mad pleyn;
And so longe yt enduryd so, certeyn,
900   And with trees & busshys so wylde grew,
That were yt was vnnethe ony knew.

The thrydde translacyoun

But whan yt plesyd the souereyn goodnesse
Of God, wych syt in heuene aboue,
To deleueryn owt of that wyldyrnesse
905   These two virgyns wych he dede loue,
To counfort of myche folk and byhoue,
He chees a persone of a straunge cuntre,
Of ther translac[i]oun ministyr to be.

Whan the yer of grace on the nou[m]bre ran
910   Of a thousent and hundryd and therto fyue,
The fyrste yer of the secunde Vrban,
Pope of Rome, as croniclers dryue,
And Herry the thrydde was alyue,
And had the sool reule of al the empere,
915   Thys reuelacyoun was mad as ye shul here.

---

892 writyn fynde we] men may se Ar   893 wych] and Ar   remembre] remen-
bre Ab   894 Ys euene] It is Ar   895 these] these two Ar   shrynyd in] in Ar
896 had] had shrynyd Ar   897 myschef] mysechep Ab   the Ruuyllyans] Ruyllyan
Ar   899 enduryd so] so abood Ar   907 of a] of Ar   908 translacioun]
translacoun Ab   909 noumbre] nounbre Ar   910 and'] foure Ab   and therto]
and Ar   912 Pope] The pope Ar   croniclers] cronycles Ar   914 of al] of Ar
915 was mad] maad was Ar   as] that Ar

Twyn Naplys, that tyme, and Teranice,
In a wode of the markys of that cuntre,
Two heremytys dwellyd, whom God illumyne
Vouchydsaf wyth grace in that degre
To lyuyn, and hys seruauntys to be.   920
Ioon hyht the toon, to whoom dede appere
Seynt Margarete, seying on thys manere:

'Ioon, Goddys seruaunte, as faste as thow kan,
On myn erand Mount Flassk go to,
Onto the preour of Seynt Flauyan,   925
Wich there ys clepyd Burgundio,
And sey hym that he his deuer doo,
That I and also Seynt Fylycite
In solitarye place no lengere lefth be.' |

'Whoo art thou that to me spekyst', quoth he,   f. 134ʳᵃ
And byddyst me don that I ne kan?'   931
'I am Goddys handmaydyn', quoth she,
'Margarete in Antioche that martyrdam dede tan
Vndyr fers Olibrius, wiche pre[fect] was than.
But whan the cyte was ner nouht,   935
On Austyn to Tuskayne me priuyly brouht.'

'Lady', quoth Ioon, 'y knowe not that place,
Ner where and in what plage of the word yt ys.'
'Kare nat', quoth she, 'for wyl that grace
Ys thy lode guyde, thou mayst not mys;   940
For, were so thou goo, yt shal the wys,
And al that longyth to thy necessyte
Shal be prouydyd by God and by me.'

---

925 Onto] And vnto Ar   926 there ys] is ther Ar   927 that] god wil that
Ar   928 I and also] neythyr I ner Ar   929 place no] place Ar   930 thou]
thou quod Ion Ar   to me spekyst] spekyst to me Ar   932 am] am Margrete Ar
933 Margarete] That Ar   martyrdam dede tan] dede martyrdam tan Ar   934 prefect]
present Ar   935 the] that Ar   was] wyth scysme was Ar   936 me priuyly] fro
thens me Ar   937 knowe not] not knowe Ar   938 where and in what plage of
the word] in what maner cuntre Ar   940 Ys thy lode guyde] Of god the guydyth Ar
941 so] euere Ar   943 by me] me Ar

Whan Ioon herd this, withowte taryinge,
945   He took hys felaue and gan hym forth hye
Vpon hys iourne, fully trostyng
That the grace of God shuld hym ryht gye.
And so yt dede, for in short tyme, sothlye,
To Mount Flask they cam, were she ageyn
950   To Ioon apperid, and thys dede seyin:

'Sey the priour that he sende hastely
To Ruuyllyan, whiche ys now wyldyrnesse,
Onto the place where of Seynt Mary
The cherche was; and there, with bysynesse
955   Of deluyng, men shul fyndyn expresse,
In tabls of marbyl, wyth a scripture,
My body and Felicites, the virgine pure.'

And anoon Ioon to the preour went,
And gan hym to tellyn, euene by and by,
960   Of whom and why he thedyr was sent,
And chargyd hym to doon yt hastyly;
For, were yt don, he hym hom wolde hy.
But no credence was youyn to hys tellyng;
Wherfore Ioon awey wente sore wepynge.

965   He was ful heuy that he had lost
So meche laboure, as hym thouht, in veyn.
And as he homward wente onto hys ost,
In the opyn strete Seynt Margarete ageyn
Apperyd to hym, and thus dede seyin:
970   'Be not sory, Ioon, but ageyn hym to
Goo, and efthsonys thyn erand doo.'

'Iwys, lady', quoth Ioon, 'he nyl credens
In no wyse my wourdys yiue to.'

944 herd this] this herd Ar   taryinge] lettyng Ar   948 in short tyme] ryht sone Ar
949 they] he Ar   950 Ioon] hym Ar   951 Sey] Go sey Ar   952 ys now]
now is Ar   953 Onto] And to Ar   955 men] they Ar   957 the virgine pure]
I hem ensure Ar   961 chargyd] preyd Ar   doon] performyn Ar   963 no] he no
Ar   was youyn] yaf Ar   tellyng] talkyng Ar   964 awey wente sore] went awey Ar
965 heuy] sory Ar   966 as hym] hym Ar   967 homward wente] went homward
Ar   onto] to Ar   970 Be not sory Ioon] Ion, be not heuy Ar

'Yit goo!' quoth she, 'and, er thou come thens,
He shal happyly enspiryd byn so   975
With grace that he shal assentyn to do
Lych as thou seyist, and holde the trewe;
Or elles forsothe he shal yt rewe.'

'Lady', quoth Ioon, 'in thys meuyd matere
Me thynkyth best were, saf yowre reuerence,   980
That ye youreself to hym dede appere,
And shewyd hym pleynly youre sentence;
For thanne muste he nedys yiuyn credence.'
'Nay, Ioon', quoth she, 'God wyl not so.
But by the he wyl thys erand be do.' | 985

Whan Ioon herd thys, and othere also   f. 134ʳᵇ
Whiche stodyn bysyde, ful many oon,
Herdyn al this talkyng b[e]twyx hem to,
They seyde that they wold with hym goon
Onto the preour, at that anon,   990
And of alle these wurdys, bothe more and lesse,
Pleynly they wolde hym bern witnesse.

Whan thys was doon, the priour dede leue
Ionys wurdys, and, withowte lettynge,
The treuthe herof that he myght preue,   995
Men thedyr he sent to make serchynge;
And they there labouryd in deluynge
In the cherche pauiment, fro morne tyl eue,
But they founde nouht, wyche dede hem greue.

Aftyr thys in angyr they hom ageyn   1000
Turnyd, and seydyn euene thus to Ioon:
'Thou hast vs maad to labouryn in veyn,
For of oure labour fruht ys come noon.'

975 happyly] wyth grace Ar   976 With grace] Happyly Ar   979 Ioon] he Ar
meuyd matere] matere Ar   983 muste he nedys] he nedys must Ar   984 God]
Nay God Ar   985 he wyl] he wyl he wyl Ab   erand] massage Ar   988 al this] this
Ar   betwyx] botwyx Ab   989 that they] they Ar   990 at] and Ar   993 thys
was] thys Ab   998 morne] morwe Ar   999 wyche] that Ar   1000 Aftyr
thys in] And anoon for Ar   1003] oure labour] oure Ab

'Seris,' quoth he, 'yif ye wyl goon
1005   Ageyn with me, by Goddys grace
I shal yow bryngyn onto the place.'

They folwyd hys wyl and turnyd ageyn,
And, albeyt he neuere cam there byforn,
'Here ys the place', quoth he, 'certeyn,
1010   Where brymblys greuyn and many a thorn.
Here shal y hope no laboure by lorn.'
Where the[y] dede delue, and anoon they founde,
More thanne they sowtyn in that stounde.

For afftir the bodyis of the virgins twoo,
1015   Bothe Felycite and eek Margarete,
Thre rybbys th[er] they foundyn also
Of Cosme and Damyan, smellyng ful swete;
And an epitaphye wych in marbyl was wrete
On thys wyse: 'Lo! here in this cheste
1020   Of Margarete and Felicite the bodyis do reste.'

Whan thei thys seyin, with gret gladnesse
To Mount Flask hoom they word sent.
And anoon the preour with gret bysynesse
Maad a processioun and thedir went,
1025   And them hoom to brynge was diligent.
And al the puple folwyd bysyly,
Syngyng and preinge deuouhtly.

And whyl thus ocupiyd in syngynge they were,
Sodeynly nyht hem dede take,
1030   And anoon they wente and wist not where,
And eueremore greu moo cloudys blake,
And they for feer gunne tremelyn and quake,

1004 yif ye] ye Ab   wyl] lyst to Ar   1006 onto] euene Ar   1008 byforn]
toforn Ar   1010 brymblys greuyn] growe brymblys Ar   1012 they] Ar; the Ab
anoon they founde] wythinne a stounde Ar   1013 in that stounde] ther they founde
Ar   1014 afftir] wyth Ar   1015 Bothe Felycite] Felycite Ar   eek] eek Seynt Ar
1016 ther] Ar; thre Ab   1018 wych in] of Ar   1020 Of Margarete and Felicite
the bodyis] Margretys body & felicites Ar   1022 hoom] anoon Ar   1023 anoon]
thanne Ar   1024 Maad] Gadryd Ar   1026 bysyly] ful bysyly Ar   1028 they
were] were Ar   1030 and²] they Ar   1032 gunne tremelyn and quake] tremelyng
gunne quake Ar

And with oo woys they lowde dede cry,
'Seynt Margarete, on vs haue mercy!'

And anoon, as the[i] thus preyid had,   1035
A gret bryhtnesse ouyr hem dede sprede,
As though heuene openyd ben had;
Wich to Mount Flask ryght dede hem lede.
And euere as thei dede forth procede,
The lyht went euene ouyr hem sothly,   1040
Tyl they comyn vp into the toun on hy. |

And whan they come byforn the hous   f. 134va
Of oon whoom Beucase men dede calle,
These relikys so heuy and so ponderous
De[de] growe anoon, that vndyr he[m] alle   1045
Myht them not bern past the stalle;
Wherfore men supposyd that they leste
In that place stille to abydyn and reste.

Vpon whiche they alle in fere
To Beucase seydyn: 'Syth God wyl   1050
That a cherche shulde byn mad here
For these relikys, thyn hous ther tyl
Yif vp, we counsele, with a good wyl.
And yf thou wylt not so, we wyln yt bye,
Or a bettyr therfore th[e] yiuyn, treulye.'   1055

Beucace seyde nay, yt shuld not be.
And sodeynly bygan swych a tempeste
Of thundyr and leuene, that dayis thre
Yt contunyd stylle, and neuere dede reste.
Whan Beucase thys saw, hym thouht yt best   1060
To takyn anothir hous and hys relece;
And so he dede, and the tempest gan sece.

1034 vs] vs now Ar   1035 thei] the Ab   1037 openyd] euene opyn Ar
1039 dede forth] forth dede Ar   1040 ouyr] wyth Ar   1041 vp into] vp Ar
1043 whoom] that Ar   1045 Dede] de Ab   hem] heym Ab   1046 the] his Ar
1047 supposyd] conceyuyd Ar   1048 stille to] stille Ar   1053 with a] with Ar
1054 wylt] wyt Ar   1055 a bettyr therfore the yiuyn] yeue the a bettyr therfore Ar
the] they Ab   1061 anothir hous] anothir Ar   hys] hys hous Ar

Aftir thys, in a ful solemne wyse,
Into that hous the relikys they bere;
1065   And as goodly as they cowde deuyse,
Anoon a cherche they dede make there.
In wyche yet restyn, as I dede lere,
The bodyis of the two virgins swete,
Seynt Filicite and Seynt Margarete.

1070   Many a miracle there s[hew]yd was,
In the tyme of thys translacyoun,
And oftyn hath byn syth, in that holy place,
Whiche to wrytyn were to gret ocupacyoun;
For truly, afftir myn estimacyoun,
1075   Yf they were wretyn, yt ocupyin more
Wolde than al the remnaunt byfore.

Thys thridde translacyoun of this virgine swete
Treuly, as I me now remembre,
I mene thys blyssyd martyr Margarete,
1080   The seuentende day was of Nouembre,
And the fyftende kalende of Decembre,
Wych day intytlyd ys in the honour
Of glorious Hugo, bysshop and confessoure.

Now, blyssyd virgine, whiche at Mount Flaske
1085   Schrynyd lyist in a ryht fayr autere,
Graunte me the bone whiche I now aske:
Fyrst, that I may pardone han her
Of al myn synnys, and aftir, partener
Of the ioye and blysse ben where thow dost dwelle,
1090   Whiche how gret byn no tunge may telle.

Here endyn the thre translacyouns of Seynt Margarete. |

1063 in a] in Ar   1069 and] and eek Ar   1070 shewyd] Ar sweuyd Ab
1072 hath byn syth] sythyn hath ben Ar   1073 to] *om.* Ar   1074 truly] sekyrly Ar
1075 ocupyin] contune Ar   1077 thridde] secunde Ar   this] the Ar   1078 now]
now kan Ar   1079 thys] the Ar   1082 in] into Ar   1085 Schrynyd lyist]
Lyist shrynyd Ar   ryht] ful Ar   1086 whiche] that Ar   1087 pardone han]
purchase pardone Ar   1089 ioye and blysse] ioye Ar   1090 byn] is Ar   may]
kan Ar

[116. ALEXIS]

The tyme of Archadons and Honoricus the emperours there was in Rome   f. 134vb
a man clepyd Eufemianus, a gret lord and aftir the emperours the grettest
wythin here paleys, the whiche hadde waytyng vpon hym for to seruyn
hym thre thousent, whiche weryd goldene gardyls and sylkene garnementys. Thes wurthy man Eufemianus was a wundyr mercyful and elmesful   5
man, for he euerey day in ys hous had thre tablys spred for pouere men
and pilgrimis, fadyrles chyldryn and wydwys, whoom he wold seen seruyd
hymself. Wych doon, he went to mete with othyre religious and deuouht
men vndyr the dreed of God.

Hys wyf, whos name was Aglaes, was acordyd to hym bothe of berthe   10
and of grace. And whan they had longe be togedyr wythowte chyld, at the
last God grauntyd hym a sone whom they clepyd Alexius. Aftir whiche
tyme they, with on assent, madyn a comenaunt to lyuyn contynent and
neuere aftir to han flesshly knowleche neythyr of odyr. Whoos yunge sone
Alexius set to scole so profyhtyd and encrecyd that in alle libral sciencis   15
he had a souereyn excellence. And whan he cam to age for to be mariyd,
a gret lordys doutyr owt of the emperours hous w[a]s chosyn and mariyd
onto hym.

And whan the day of the mariage was doon and the nyht cam in wych
he and she were togedyr in here priuy cha[m]byr, anoon thys holy yung   20
man bygan to exsortyn and steryn hys wyf to the loue of chastite and clennesse, and to loue God and to drede. And whan he had weel instruct here
and enformyd and set here in the affeccyoun of perfeccyoun, he took hyre
hy[s] g[ol]d ryng and the bokyl of hys bauderyk wych he was gyrt wyth,
and seyde to hyre on thys wyse: 'Haue, wyf', quoth he, 'and kepe these   25
tokknys tyl yt plese God that we mete ageyn togedyr, and God mote be
bytwyxyn vs.' Wych don, anoon he tok a certeyn quantite of hys good wyth
hym and wente priuyly, no man wetynge, to the see and from thens ouyr
to a cyte clepyd Laedicye, and fro thens to a cyte of Syrye clepyd Edissa,
where in a cherche of oure lady was an im[a]ge of oure lord Ihesu Crist,   30
mad withoute mannys werk.

Whedyr whan he was comyn, al that euere he brouht wyth hym he
delt aboutyn and yaf onto pouere men and, puttyng on pouere mennys
clothynge, he set hem doun amo[n]g othere pouere men in the porch of
oure ladyis cherche. And of the elmesse whiche was youyn hym that was   35

17 was] whoos   20 chambyr] chaunbyr   24 hys] hy   gold] glod
30 image] imge   34 among] amog

nessessarie to hys quotidian lyuynge he reseruyd and kept, and the residue therof he delt forthwyth onto the pouere puple. But whan the fadyr
of Aley, Eufemyan, herd of hys sonys sodeyn and vnwar goynge awey, he
was wundyr sory and heuy, and anoon he sente aboutyn massageris into
40 euery cuntre rounde abowtyn Rome for to sekyn hym and for to enquerin
of hym. Amonge whiche summe comyn to cyte of Edissa and, not knowyng hym but wyl knowyn of hym, they deltyn hym elmesse among othire
pouere men. The which whan he took, he yaf thankyng to God and seyde:
'Lord God, gramercy, which hast suffryd me to takyn elmesse of myn owyn
45 seruauntys!' And whan these massagers had goon al the cuntrees whiche
they were sent to, they comyn hom ageyn and browtyn tydyngys that he
myht nowher be founden. The modyr of hym, from tyme that he was
goon, maad hyre couche of sak cloth in hyre chaumbyr and, sorwynge and
f. 135ra l[a]mentabylly | wepyng, seyd on thys whise: 'Here wyl I cont[inu]ely aby-
50 dyn in sorwe and in heuynesse tyl I may han tydyngis ageyn of myn sone.'
To whoom hys yung wyf cam and seyde [t]o on this wyse: 'Iwys, modyr,
tyl I may heryn of my swete spouse, as a solitarye turtyl here chastly I shal
abydyn with the.'
　And whanne this blyssyd man Alex had contunyd seuyntene yer in God-
55 dys seruyse in the forseyd porch of oure ladyis cherche, the ymage of oure
lady weche was the[r] seyde to the wardeyn or the kepere of the scherche:
'Make the man of God to comyn in, for he ys wurthy! The kyngdam of
heuene and the spiryt of God restyth vpon hym, for hys preyere lych as
incens steyith vp and ascendyth in the syht of God.' And whan the kepere,
60 dowtyng of whom this was seyd, had haskyd, the ymage answerde ageyn
and seyde: 'The man whiche sittyth withowtyn in the porch, he yt ys.'
Wich seyde, anoon the kepere went owt and brouht hym in by the hand
into the cherche. And whan this reuelacyoun was puplysshid and knowyn,
and yche man bygan to don to Alex wurship and reuerence and he not
65 wylyng han yt, anoon he went thens ageyn to Laodicye. From wens he
took a shyp and, purposyng to goon into a cyte of Cilicye clepid Tarsus, by
Goddys prouydence the shyp was dryuyn into Rome port at Ostye. And
whan Alex sau thys he thouht in hys herte on this wise: 'Syth I am now
here, I shal moun dwellyn in myn fadrys hous vnknowyn and byn onerous
70 ner chargaunt to noon othyr.' Whervpon he met vpon a day with ys fadyr
comyng from the pales onuyrond with gret multitude of peple, and bygan
to cryin onto hym vpon this wyse and seyde: 'Seruaunt of God, comaunde
me, a pilgrym, to be reseyuyd into thyn hous and to be kept and fed wyth

49 lamentabylly] lementabylly　continuely] contunely　51 to] do　56 ther]
the　65 anoon he] anoon

the crommys wyche fallyn from thyn table, that God therthorgh wyl the
rathere han mercy on thy pylgrym.' Wych request whan Eufemian herde, 75
for loue of hys sone he comaundyd hym to be brouht in and assingnyd hym
a place and a seruaunt, and chargid that he shuld be seruyd with mete of
his owe[n] table. Whiche doon, he anoon perseuerauntly yaf hym to medy-
tacyoun and preere and maad hys body lene with abstinence and fasting.
And for he was in al hys demenyng symple and meke, lowly and pacy- 80
ent, the seruauntys of the place mokkyd hym and skornyd hym and dedyn
hym manye iniuryis and wrongis, and ful offtyn tymys poryd the watyr of
here vesselys wasshynge vpon hys heed. But he pacyently withowtyn grucchyng suffryd alle these thingys. And thus othir seuyntene yer he dwellyd
in hys own fadrys hous, vnknowyn to hym and to alle hys, an holy lyf and 85
a perfyth.

Afftyr whiche tyme, he, seyng in spirit the t[e]rme of hys labour faste to
drawyn to an ende, askyd penne and enke and parchemyn and wrot al the
ordre of hys lyf. Whiche doon, on the next sunday folwyng was herd a voys
in the sanctewarye seying on this wyse: '*Venite ad me omnes qui laboratis &* 90
cetera: Comyth to me ye alle wych labouryn and trauaylyn and ben chargyd
with gret byrdens and I shal reffressyn yow.' And all the peple for very feer
of this voys fel doun plat vpon here face. And anoon ther com anothir voys
doun from heuene and seyde: 'Sekyth the seruaunt of God that he may
pre[y] for the cyte of Rome.' And whan they had seyht and foundyn hym 95
not, the thridde tyme the voys bad hem sekyn in Eufemyans hous. Whom
whan they askyd afftyr Goddys seruaunt he seyde he knew noon swych
in hys hous. | And whanne the emperours Honorius and Archadius were f. 135rb
comyn with the pope Innocent and innumerable peple to Eufemyan hous,
the ministir of Alex cam to hys lord and seyde: 'Syre, y may wyl leuyn that 100
yt be youre pilgrym whoom ye kepyn. For I knowe wyl that he ys a man
of greth holy lyf and of maruelous pacience.' Eufemyan heryng this ran
anoon to the place wher he dwellyd and he foynd hym and hys face and his
cher as bryht shynynge as yt had ben of an aungel. And whan he sau the
chartre in his hand he wolde han takyn yt owt but he myht not. Wherfore 105
anoon he went owt and told the pope and the Emperours the caas, and they
forthwith wentyn wher he lay and seydyn on this wyse: 'Albeyt that we be
sennerys, yet we han here the gouernaunce of regalye and the vniuerseel
cure of temperal and spiritual gouernaunce. And therfore we desire to see
the wrytyng wych thow holdyst in thy hand, wherby we moun haue the 110
more cleer notys and knowyng what thou art.' And these wurdys seyde,
the pope wente to the body and tok the chartre in his hand and he lete

78 owen] owe   87 terme] torme   95 prey] preun

yt of anoon and maad yt to be red byforn al the multitude and hys fadir.
And whan Eufemian herd the processe red, for verry feer he was abasshd
115 and astoynyd and fel in a traunce as thogh he had be ded. And whan afftir a
while he cam ageyn to hyms[el]ff, he rent hys clothis and plukkyd the herys
of hys heed and of hys berd and gretly to troublyn hym. And at the laste
he fel doun vpon hys sonys body and began to cryin on this wyse: 'Wo, my
sone, and allas! Why hast thow thus troblyd and so many yeris put me in
120 sorwe and in heuynesse? Allas, me wrecche, that y see the wardeyn and the
kepere of myn age lying on a cowche and not spekyng to me! Allas, allas!
What counfort hensforward shal I mowe haue?' The modyr of Alex heryng
this, as a lyoness brekyth the net, so rent hyre clothis and discheuele cam
rennynge. And whan for the multitude of peple sche mygh not [reche the
125 body], to the cros she bygan to cryin and seyn: 'Serys, I [ask ye], yiuyth
me space and leysir that I may see my [consolacion] of myn soule wych
soukyd my brestis.' And whan [she came to] the body she began to cryin
and seyin: 'Allas, my sone, allas! Why woldyst thou thus doon to vs? Why
hast thow, the lyht of my eyne, thus cruelly don to vs? Sey not thow thy
130 fadyr and me, wrecche, thy modyr, wepyng and sorwyng for the? And,
that notwithstondynge, that to vs thow woldyst not disclosin thys[el]f and
sheuyn vs the. Allas, whi suffryddyst thow thy seruaunts thus to reuylyn,
rebukyn and wrongin the?'

Wiche wurdys and othir lych seyid, s[h]e efthsonys fel doun ageyn vpon
135 the body and now spred hyre armys vpon hys armys, and hyre body [on hys
body], and kessyd hys aungelly che[re], and seyde: 'Allas, sone, allas! Who
shal yiuyn to myn eyne a welle of terys that I may nyght and day bewaylyn
and compleyn the sorwe and the heuynesse of my s[ou]le?' And nat oonly
thus the fadyr and the modyr compleynyd and weylyd the deth of here
140 sone, but at the laste cam forth hys wyf, rynny[n]ge, wepynge and seyinge:
'Wo me, allas, for thys day y am desolat and maad a wydwe. Now haue I not
to whom I may haue recours to in tyme of my nede. Now ys myn myrour
brokyn and al myn hope ys perysshd. Wherfore, hen[s]forward begynne
ony sorwe wiche shall han noon ende.' The pepil stondyng aboutyn and
f. 135va heryng the lamentable tragedyes of fadyr and | modyr and wyf, bygunnyn
146 to wepyn with hem s[orowful]ly. Aftyr thys, anoon the pope and the emperours leid this holy body vpon a fayr fertre and brou into the myddys of

116 hymselff] hymsleff   124–7 *Some text is missing owing to the removal of an initial
and a surrounding border. Text restored by comparison with LgA.*   131 thyself] thy-
slef   134 she] see   135–6 on hys body] on hys body on hys body   136 chere]
the last two letters are missing owing to the removal of the initial   138 soule] solue
140 rynnynge] rynnyge   143 hensforward] henforward   146 sorowfully] sero-
wufly

the cyte. And anoon as yt was denouncyd to the peple that the seruaunat
of God was foundyn whom al the cyte sey[k]e, they comyn alle owt lych
swarmys of been in an hoot somerys day to metyn with this blyssyd body; 150
forthwith th[e]y were curyd and maad hool whatsoeuere here syknysse
were. The emperours and the pope seyng these grete meruales bygunnyn
to bern hemself this blyssyd tresoure, that they myhtyn also ben halwyd by
touch of this holy body. And thanne the emperours, seying the importu-
nyte of the pepyl pees, they comaundyd gold and syluyr to be throwyn and 155
frowyd in the strete that the peple myht ben ocupyid with gadryng of the
monye, and so sufferyd the holy body to be brou to the place of hys sepulture. But the peple, al the affeccyoun of monye set asyde, precyd euere
importunely to touche this holy relyk, thys blyssyd body. And so with gret
difficulte and labour they brouht thys holy tresore onto the temple of Seynt 160
Boniface the martir, and there seuene dayis solempny singe in the seruyse
of God and of hys holy confessour Alex, they dede makyn a fertre arayid
with gold and syluyr, and with precious stonys, and leyid this blyssyd body
therin with gret reuerence and wurshyp the seuyntende day of Iuyl. Of
wych fertre whan this holy body was leyid cam owt a flauour of swetnesse 165
that passyd the sauour of ony apotecaryis shop. Thys blyssyd Alex, this
holy man, passyd owt of thys werd the sextende kalende of August aboute
the yers of oure lord thre hundryd nynty and eyghte.

[117. MARY MAGDALEN]

The prologe of Marie Maudelyns lyf
    [O]f a Marie to writyn I wyl bygynne
    The lyf, as God me wyl yiuyn grace.
    I mene not Marie withowtyn synne,
    Whiche of al mankynde bar the solace,
    But hyre I mene wyche of hyre trespace,   5
    In Simondys hous whan she cam in,
    Pardone thurgh penaunce dede purchace,
    Et clepid ys Mary Maudelyn.

    And wurthyly thys name Marye
    To hyr pertenyth, as yt semyth me,   10
    For as *Legenda Aurea* doth specyfye,

148 yt was] yt   149 seyke] seyde   151 they] thy   168 oure lord]
oure   1 Of] f. *The initial has been removed*   2 me] we Ar   wyl yiuyn] yeuyn wyl
Ar   8 Et] And Ar *over an erasure*

Maria hath these interpretaciouns thre:
Fyrst yt bytoknyth 'a byttyr see',
'An illumynere', or ellys 'maad lyth';
15   And these thre thyngis in excellent degre
This blyssyd Marie Maudelyn had ful ryght.

And by these thre thyngis we vndirstonde moun
The thre beste thyngis whiche thys Mari chees,
As owtward penaunce and inward contemplac[i]oun,
20   And vpward blysse wyche neuere shal sees;
Of whiche God s[ey]de, withowte les,
That the beste part to hyre chees Marie,
Wyche euere shal enduryn and neuere discres,
But with hyre abydyn eternally. |

f. 135vb   The fyrst part whiche that hyght penytence
26   Bycause of the [s]yn, wich ys getyng of blys,
Shal hyre be byrefth by no violence;
Ner the secunde, of contemplacyoun, for that ys
Contunyd with heuenely ioy wich neuere shal mys,
30   Wherfore yt may nat fayle in no degre;
Ner the thridde, of heuene, may sece, ywys,
For the mesure therof ys eternyte.

For as meche thanne as thys Mary
The beste part chees of penaunce doyng,
35   'A byttyr see' be clepyd ryght conuenyently
She may, me semyth, for in that thyng
Gret bytyrnesse she felt whan repentyng
Byhynde Crist she stod shamefastly,
And wyth the terys shed in hyre wepynge
40   Hys feet shee wesshe ful deuouhtly.

In that also of inward contemplacyoun
The beste part she chees in thys lyf here,
To hyre longyth the secunde interpretacyoun,
Whiche ys to seyne 'an illumynere',
45   Or 'a yiuere of lyht', in wurdys more clere;

19 contemplacioun] contemplacoun Ab   21 seyde] syde Ab   26 syn] fyn Ab
synne Ar   29 ioy wich] wich Ar Ab   41 also] also that Ar

For [in] hyre contemplacyoun she took swych lyht
With wich many on, as ye afftyr shul here,
In gostly goodnesse she mad shyne bryht.

In that the best part of heuenely blys
Thys Marie chees in here affeccyoun,   50
Wurthyly 'illumynyd' she clepyd ys.
For now abouyn in the celestial regioun
Illumynyd she ys, with cler cognicyoun
In hyre soule, and aftir shal finally,
Whan compleet ys the general resurreccioun,   55
Illumynyd ben in hyre glorious body.

Thys Marye ys also clepyd Maudelyn
Conuenyenly, afftyr Ianuencys degre,
For thys w[u]rd Magdalena, in latyn,
By the interpretacyoun bytoknyth thyngis thre,   60
As 'gylty', 'streynghthyd' and 'wurthy of degre';
Whiche thre thyngis by deu applic[ac]ioun
Moun clerly shewyn what was she,
Byforn and in and afftyr hyre con[u]ercyoun.

Byforn hyre conuercyoun she was gylty   65
Off sinful lyuyng by the abhominacyoun,
Dysseueryd from God and heuenely cumpany,
Defamyd also in the werdys opynioun
In Ierusalem and in al that regioun;
And bysydyn alle these mischeuys her,   70
Sche bounde was by an obligacioun
With the deuyl to dwellyn in endlees feer.

But afftyr thys, in here conuercyoun,
Whan she forsook al hyre fyrst foly,
And hyre repentyd of hyre transgressioun,   75
And with penaunce purchacyd hyre mercy,
Than was she strenghthyd and mad myhty,
For as many delytys in sundry wysys

46 in] and Ab   59 wurd] ward Ab   in] wych is Ar   62 applicacioun] appli-
cioun Ab   64 conuercyoun] conercyoun Ab   66 Off] Be of Ar   78 in] as
in Ar

Off synnys shee hadde in hyre body,
80   So manye of hyres[el]f she mad sacryficys. |

Aftyr hyre conuercyoun eek in gostly grace
How stronge she wex and how myhty,
Whooso lyst to knowe, he hens not pace
Tyl completly red be thys story,
85   Wych bothe of the gospel, that kan not ly,
And of hyre legende togedyr ys bounde,
And he shal fynd that, where wrecchydly
Synne regnyd, grace dooth superhabounde.

Now, gracyous lady, Marie maudelyn,
90   Wyche grace afftyr synne copiously founde,
Lete not Sathanas wyth hys subtyl gyn
Of hem that the seruyn the soulys confounde.
And generally, lady, lete the grace redounde
To alle them whiche yt lyst to pursu;
95   Counforte hem, and kepe hem heyl and sounde,
And alle temptacyoun them helpe to eschou.

And specyally, lady, to the humble entent
Of hym vouchesaf for to entende,
Whiche aftyr hys simple entendement
100   To translate hym bysyid thy legende;
Purchace hym grace his lyf to amende
Er than he passe from thys owtlaury,
And helpe hym finally vp to ascende,
Aftyr hys fatal cours, to blysse heuenely.

Here endyth the prologe & folwyth the lyf.
105   Thys blyssed Marye Maudelyn,
To spekyn afftyr werdly dingnyte,
Born was of the most wurthy kyn

80 hyreself] hyreslef Ab   83 Whooso] Whoo Ar   to knowe] knowe Ar   hens not] not hens Ar   93 generally] specyaly Ar   the] þi Ar   94 alle them whiche yt lyst to pursu] dame Isabel, þe countesse of Hu Ar   95 hem¹] hyr Ar   hem²] hyr both Ar   96 temptacyoun] temptacyouns Ar   them helpe] help hyr Ar   97 And specyally] Also Ar   99 aftyr hys simple entendement] at þe seyd ladyis comaundement Ar   103 hym finally] hem both Ar   104 hys] hyr Ar   heuenely] heuenely. Amen Ar   104.1 Here endyth the prologe & folwyth the lyf] Her begynnys the lyf of Marye Maudelyn

Whiche that tyme was in that cuntre,
For of the royal blood descendyd she,
Whos fadyr hyht Cirus, a man wurthy,   110
And hyre modyr clepyd was Euchary.

A brothir she had wych vsyd was
In hys f[er]st dayis to ben a soudyour,
Lazarus by name, whom thrugh hys grace
Froom deth to lyf reysyd oure saueour   115
At request of hyre and hys herbergour
Marthe, hyre sustir, as doth testifie
Ioon in hys gospel, wych wyl not lye.

And these thre, as seyth story,
Twyn hem diuydyd the possessyoun   120
Of here genyteurs, Cirus and Euchary,
So that a castel clepyd Magdalum
To Mary fel in ther departisoun,
Wherof she namyd was Magdalyne,
As Ianuencys legende doth determyne.   125

And nat only this Marie by successyoun
Thus of fortune surmountyd in dygnyte,
But also thorghowt al that regioun,
She of naturys yiftys had the souereynte
Passyd alle wummen in souereyn beute,   130
For, as yt semyt to ych mannys syht,
Fayrere than she no wumman be myght. |

Thus thanne in hyre were these thre   f. 136rb
Togedyr ioynyd in gret excellence,
Youth, habundaunce, and eek bewte,   135
Whiche oftyn for lak [of] dw dyligence
Mynistris ben vnto insolence,
And of alle vycys the bryngers in,
And so they were in Mary Maudelyn.

113 ferst] frest Ab   119 story] the story Ar   122 clepyd] callyd Ar
130 Passyd] And passyd Ar   wummen in] wummen Ar   souereyn] excellent Ar
136 of] and Ab

140 For al here youthe in discillauynesse
Of hyre body so vnshamefastly
She dyspendyd, and in sinfulnesse
So comoun she was, that ful pitusly
Hyre name she lost, for of foly
145 So in the syte was sprunge hyre fame,
That 'Mary the synnere' there dede hyre name.

Thus longe tyme in hyre wrecchydnesse
She contunyd and hyre lustys dede pursu,
Tyl at the laste, thorghe the mercyfulnesse
150 Compunct she was of oure lord Ihesu,
Wiche that tyme lyuyd and tawt vertu,
Through whoos doctrine she was in [entent]
Of hyre [f]orelyf to make amendement.

Vpon whiche sone aftyr, as she wyl knew,
155 Whanne to mete was bodyn oure saueour
Wyth oon Symon leprous, a pharisu,
A precyous oynement sweet of odour
She went and broht, and in the same our
The box with the oynement in hire hand she nam,
160 And vnbodyn to Simundys feste she cam.

And whan she was comyn into the place
Where Ihesu was, for shamefastnesse
Of hyre foul lyf, byforn hys face
She nolde appere, but dede hyre dresse
165 Byhyndyn hys bak, and wyth gret byttyrnesse
And sorwe of herte she gan to wepe,
And fel down and toward hys feet dede crepe.

Where whan she cam, with herte contryht
Teerys owt she shedde so plenteuously
170 That hys feet therwith wasshyn she myght,
And so she dede ful deuouhtly,
And with hyre herys hem wypte diligently,

146 there] thei Ar   151 that tyme] that Ar   152 entent] euentent Ab
153 forelyf] sorelyf Ab   158 the] that Ar   159 with the] with Ar   161 was]
w Ar

And aftyr hem kissyd and with deuouhte entent
Hem she anoy[nt]yd with the sweet oynement.

And thogh wyth hyre mouth owtwardly 175
To hym no word she dede expresse,
In al thys tyme in wych so bysyly
Shee shewid thys meke obsequyousnesse,
Yet, of hyre wepyng by the gretnesse,
Of hyre hert she shewyd the corage, 180
As thog[h] she had vsyd this language:

'O most meke lord, whiche knowyst al thing,
And art of hertys the inward serchere,
Whiche, as yt semyth by thy techyng,
Desiryst not the deeth of a synnere 185
But that he be conuertyd and lyue lengere,
Thou knowyst weel, lord, as I doo wene,
What my wepyng, my sighyng and my sorwe doth mene. |

Y am a synnere, and of euery cryme f. 136ᵛᵃ
With spottys defoulyd ful horrybyly, 190
And so haue I contunyd ful long tyme
Syth wyt and dyscrecioun fyrst had I;
Reforme me now, lord, for thy mercy,
And in thys gret nede be my socour,
Wiche oonly consideryst sorwe and laboure.' 195

Whan Symon thys w[u]mman at Cristis fete
Thus ocupiyd saw, he thouhte thys:
'Yf he thys were a wery prophete,
He shuld weel knowyn, withowte mys,
Wyche and what manyr wumman thys ys; 200
For a synnere she ys, and of badde fame
Thorughowt thys cyte labouryd hyre name.'

173 hem kissyd and] þat Ar   with] with a Ar   174 Hem she] Hem Ar   anoyntyd]
anoytyd Ab   177 in] om. Ar   181 thogh] thoght Ab   183 serchere] knoware
Ar   196 wumman] wimman Ab   197 saw] sey Ar   200 wumman thys] this
wumman Ar   202 labouryd] labouryth Ar

But Crist, wiche that knewyth al thyng,
Both wurd and werk and thought pryuy,
205 Wylyng yiuyn Symon a re[b]ukyng
Of hys temerarye doom, ful benyngnely
To hym hys cher turnyd and seyde goodly:
'Symon, sumwhat I haue to seyn to the.'
'Maistir, what thou wylt, sey anoon!' quod he.

210 'Two dettours', quod Cristis, 'to oon feneratour
Where whylom, Simon, in a cuntre.
Fyue hundryd pens awt the toon de[t]tour,
The tothyr but fyfty; and for pouerte
Hem bothe distreynyd, bothyn pardonyd he.
215 Than ask I the, Simon, wych of these two
[Det]tours the creditour was most holdyn to?'

'Iwys', quoth Simon, 'as yt semyth to me,
Aftyr the iudicyal of very resoun,
To louyn the creditour most holdyn was he
220 Whiche of hys dette had most pardoun.
Thys ys pleynly, maystir, myn op[y]nyoun.'
'Thou answeryst', quod Crist, 'ful ryhtfully,
Simon, but now lyst what sey shal I.

Simon, I entryd into thyn hous,
225 And to my feet watyr thou youe noon me;
Thys wumma[n] thou demyst vycious,
Syth that she entryd, as alle men may see,
With teerys of hyre eyne shed in plente
My feet shee hath wasshe ful deuouhtly,
230 And with hyre herys them wept dilygently.

Kys profryddyst me noon, but she my feet
Hath kessyd ful ofte; ner myn heed to
Oyle pu[t]tyst thow no[on], but wyth onyment sweet
Anoyntyd she hath myn feet bothe two.

205 rebukyng] rewukyng Ar   212 dettour] dectour Ab   215 Than] Than I
Ab   216 Dettours] Doctours Ab   219 the] hys Ar   221 opynyoun] opny-
oun Ab   223 lyst] herkyn Ar   226 wumman] wummam Ab   thou] whom thou
Ar   233 puttyst] pustyst Ab   noon] now Ab   but wyth] but Ab

And for she hath thys dede doo,   235
And so many loue toknys shewyd to me,
Many[e] synnys to hyre foryowyn now be.'

And whan she thus onto the pharisewe
Excusyd was by Crist ful curteysly,
Alle thyngys lefth, she dede swe   240
Where euere he wente ful deuouhtly.
And for she ryche was, habundantly
She mynistryd hym and hys in there nede,
As in Lukys gospel pleynly men may rede. |

And thus aftyr by processe successyffly   f. 136vb
Wyth Crist she grew in swych famylyaryte,   246
That hyre he cherschyd ryht singulerly,
And with hyre sustyr oftyn herberwyd was he,
Wiche for hym and hys kepte hospitalyte,
I mene Marthe, of the flyx he dede cure   250
Wiche twelue yer toforn on here dede dure.

Thys was [in] Bethanye, where togedere dede dwelle
Marthe and Marye and here brothir Lazarus,
Whedyr ful oftyn, as the gospelles cun telle,
To hys herberwe returnyd oure lord Ihesus,   255
For in the cyte of Ierusalem he was odyous,
Where ful seldum he ony cowde fynde
Whiche hym to herberwyn wold be so kynde.

O how blyssyd and happy was that hous
In wiche to takyn hys hospitalyte   260
Vouchydsaf that lord most gracious!
Ful blyssyd also were thoo thre
Whiche chosyn wern hys oostys to be,
And hym to fedyn [in] hys bodyly nede
Wiche aungels fedyth with hys godhede.   265

235 she] she thus Ar   237 Manye] Manys Ab   240 dede] dede hym Ar
241 Where] Where so Ar   250 of] from Ar   he] whom he Ar   251 toforn]
togedyr Ar   252 in] and Ab   262 thoo] thei al Ar   263 to] for to Ar
264 in] and Ab

Lo, thus may we seen how euere mercyful
God ys, and synners ful bysy to saue,
By thys womman in specyal, wiche synful
Fyrst was, and afftyr dede mercy craue,
270 Thorgh wyche not oonly she dede haue
Of hyre gret synnys a remyssyoun,
But also she atteynyd to hy perfeccyoun.

And not only she atteynyd to perfeccyoun
Of h[oo]ly lyf, but also singulerly
275 To Crist she extendyd hyre affeccyoun,
That where-euere he was, she drow hym ny
And lystnyd hys wurdys ful deuouhtly;
Wherfore whan ony wyht hyre dede acuse,
Euere redy was Crist hyre to excuce.

280 Exaunple vs shewyth in hys gospel
Seynt Luc, seyinge that oure lord gracyous
Ihesus whylom entred into a castel,
And Martha hym reseyuyd into hyre hous.
But Marye hyre sustir was so desirous
285 Hys wurdys to here, that for deuocyon
Euene at hys feet shee hyre set doun.

Wherfore whanne Marthe, wyche dede bysynesse
Crist to seruyn, hyre sittynge sey so,
She bygan to acusyn hyre of ydylnesse
290 And seyde, 'O lord, chargist thou not, loo,
How me my sustir suffryth alone to do
Al thynge? I prey the bydde hyre vp ryse
And helpe me to doon to the ceruyse.'

But Crist, wyche iuge was interpellat,
295 As seyth Seynt Austyn in a sermoun,
Anoon bycam Maryis aduocat,
Ageyns hyre susteris accusacyoun
He fond a resonable excusacyoun;

And anoon to Marthe in hyr bysynesse
Hys entent thyse wyse he gan to expresse: | 300

'Martha, Martha,' quod he, 'thou art bysy,   f. 137ʳᵃ
And abowte manye thingys troublyd sore;
But oo thyng, Marthe, sykyr, ys necessarye,
Wych Marie hath chosyn: to lystnyn my lore,
Wych neuere shal fayle; wyte wyl therfore   305
That bettyr part sothly chosyn hath she,
Wych takyn from hyre shal neuere be.'

By thys processe we seen that the ocupacyoun
Of actyf lyf in thys mortalyte,
To the lyf of inward contemplacyoun   310
May in no wyse paryficat be;
Wyche two lyuys fyguryd fynde we
In these two sustrys, Marthe and Marie,
As vpon Ioon Seynt Austyn doth testifie.

Marthys lyf wyth gret byttyrnesse   315
Medlyd ys, but the lyf of Marye
Ys enbawmyd al wyth swetnesse;
Yit bothyn ben good, as doth dyscrye
The example byforn, wherfore enuye
Betwyx thoo t[w]eyne owyth no more to be   320
Than ys betwyx a posatyf and comparatyf degre.

Moreouyr, to shewen the singulerte
Of loue wych haddyn ryht specyally
Of God past othere these personys thre,
Seynt Ioon in hys gospel seyth thus pleynly: 325
'God louyd Marthe and hyre sustyr Marye,
And Lazar the brothir of them bothe tweyne.'
No wytnesse of [loue] may be more pleyne.

But yet in loue amonge these thre,
To spekyn aftyr degrees of comparisoun,   330

299 bysynesse] bysy Ab   300 thyse wyse] thyse Ab   302 sore] ful sore Ar
303 Marthe sykyr] sykyr Marthe Ar   306 That] That the Ar   320 thoo] them
Ar   tweyne] theyne Ab   321 and] and a Ar   326 Marthe] Marthe quod he Ar
328 loue] lord Ab

Marye stood in the superlatyf degre,
As by processes foluynge we shul see moun,
Bothe byforn and aftyr the resureccyoun;
Byforn, by the miracle whan Crist from helle
335   Lazar dede clepyn, as Ioon doth telle.

Whan Lazarus, languryd in Bethanye,
Lay seek, and Crist thanne was absent
Byyounde Iordan, owt of Iewerye,
Marye and Marthe a massager sent
340   Thedyr to hym wyth here entent,
Vndyr thys forme and by these wurdys:
'Loo, he whom thou louyst, lord, seek ys.'

And in thys mene tyme Lazar dede dye,
And than thus Crist seyde to hys dysciplys:
345   'Lazarus oure frend ys aslepe, sothlye.
Lete vs goon wakyn hym'; thanne they seyde this:
'Yf he be aslepe he saf ynow ys.
What shuld we doon there? Hast thou forgete
How the to be slayn the Iewys doon threte?'

350   Than Crist hem told euene opynly
That Lazarus deed was, in wurdys pleyn;
Wherfore returnyd into Iewery
He wolde, hym for to clepyn ageyn
From deth to lyf, thys ys certeyn.
355   And anoon forthwyth he dede hym hye
Euene the ryht weye to Bethanye. |

f. 137rb   But for to drawyn to the conclusyoun
Of oure entent [& to leuyn] many a circumstaunce,
Marthe fyrst met hym wythowte the toun,
360   And had wyth hym a longe dalyaunce,
But Mary was at hom in hyre carful traunce
Tyl of Cristis comyng she warnyd was,
And thanne to hym she wente a ful gret pas.

334 by] in Ar   336 languryd] langwyryng Ar   344 thus Crist] Crist thus Ar
345 ys aslepe] slepyth Ar   346 they] the Ar   352 returnyd into] returnyn onto
Ar   356 the] in the Ar   358 & to leuyn] lefth Ab

Whan she hym saw, ful sore wepyng
She seyid thus: 'Lord, yf thou haddyst her be,   365
My br[o]thyr, as pleynly ys my trowynge,
Had not be deed as now ys he.'
And whanne Crist hyre sey wepyng, for very pyte
He wepte also, and to hyre thus seyd:
'Were ys the place wyche ye hym in leyd?'   370

Whedyr whan he was come they dede seye,
Stondynge euene by the grauys brynke,
'Syre, foure dayis past byn seyth he dede deye,
Wherfore we trowe the body doth stynke;
And so but weyn were, as we doo thynke,   375
Ony more to don.' 'Yet,' quod he anon,
'From the graue remeuyth [th]e ston.'

Whan the ston was of, he gan to pleyne
And to be troublyd in spirit ful meruelously,
And vp to heueneward lyftyng hys eyne,   380
Wyth a gret voys he thus dede sey:
'Lazar, come owt!' and anoon hastely
He owt cam bounde, and hys dyscyplys to
Crist hym delyueryd hys bondys to vndo.

A ful woundyr syth yt was to see   385
That he foure dayis wyche ded had leyin,
And sempte, as ys seyd, stynkyng to haue be,
Shuld thus to lyf be reysyd ageyn;
But in thys matyr ys no more to seyin
But that swyche maruayls loue kan do: 390
Quia fortis vt mors est dileccio.

And sone afftyr thys, at a souper
In Symoundys hous whan Ihesu was,
And oon of the suppers was seyid Lazer,
And Marthe dede ministryn in that plaas,   395

366 brothyr] brethyr Ab   372 euene] ful euene Ar   373 past byn] ben past
Ar   375 doo] now Ar   377 From] From of Ar   graue] grae Ab   the] se
Ab   378 Whan] And whan Ar   381 sey] crye Ar   387 to haue] haue Ar
394 suppers] sytters Ar

Marye, enflau[mm]yd wyth gostly gras,
Anoon wyth a ful precyous oynement
Cristys feet to anoytyn deuouhtly went.

And whan she hys feet anoytyd had wyl,
400   And he therwylys dede syttyn ful stylle,
Vpon hys heed she poryd the tothyr dyl,
Whoos odour al the hous dede fylle.
Quod Iudas, 'Thys oynement why do ye spylle,
For thre hundryd pens wych myht sold be
405   And de[l]t to pore men in thes cyte?'

And anon Crist, Marye to saue
F[ro]m blame, vsyng hys aduocacye,
Seyde thus: 'Pore men ye alwey shul haue
Wyth yow, syrs, but not me, sothlye;
410   Wherfore thys woumman wych deuouhtlye
Me to anoynte dede hyre bysy cure,
A misterye hath shewyd of myn sepulture. |

f. 137ᵛᵃ   Wherfore I wyl that ye weel knowe,
Hereafftyr whan the gospel shal be
415   Thorghtowt the werd by prechours sowe,
Than shal yt be seyd in many a cuntre
That thys she dede in wurshyp of me.'
Lo, thus that Iudas seyde hyre to confounde,
Crist to [hyr] laude yt made to redounde.

420   See now thanne how thys perfyht creature
Conioynyd was onto hy[r] creatour,
Of trewe loue thorgh affeccyoun pure,
And eek he to hyre in synguler [a]mour;
For ner of hys lyf in the last our,
425   Euene but a lytyl byforn hys passyoun,
Of hyre he mad thys specyal commendacioun.

396 enflaummyd] enflaunmyd Ab   405 delt] dett Ab   406 to] for to Ar
407 From] Form Ab   419 hyr] oure Ab   made to] made Ar   421 hyr] hys
Ab   423 amour] onour Ab

Moreouyr afftyr thys, whan Crist was take
And cruelly naylyd vpon a tre,
And alle hys dyscyplys had hym forsake,
So feruent to hym was hyre cheryte   430
That for no feer she fro hym wold fle,
But euere on hym she was waytyng,
Tyl he buryid was in euenyng.

And whan he was buryid, wyth gret mornyng
She wente swete oynement for to bye;   435
And afftyr the sabat the next morwenyng
Onto the sepulcre she gan hyre hye,
And wyth hyre wente anothyr Marye;
And of hyre thedyr-goynge thys was the entent,
Cristys body to anoytyn wyth hyre oynement.   440

But whan they come ther and he was goon,
As an aungel hym told the same tyde,
And alle othere wentyn awey anon,
She al only there dede abyde,
And in the graue ful oftyn on euery syde   445
She lokyd bysyly wyth a wepyng ihe,
Yf onywher here loue she myht aspye.

And forasmyche as she so perseueraunt was
In abydyng whan othere wentyn awey,
Therfore she hadde that specyal gras   450
That fyrst of alle oure lord she sey,
Apperyng, as hym had lyst to play,
In the lyknesse of a gardener;
But whan he seyde 'Marye', she knew hys cheer.

And whan she hym knew, onto hys feet   455
Wyth ful glad herte she doun dede falle,
And wold hym han kyssyd but he hyre nold lete,
But thus seyde, 'Marye, the not appalle;
And goo sey Petyr and my dysciplys alle

433 was] was euyn Ar   in] in the Ar   442 the] that Ar   447 onywher here
loue] hyr loue onywhere Ar   448 she so] so Ab   457 hym] hem Ar   hyre nold]
nold hyr Ar

460　　　That I am vprysyn, as thou doost see,
　　　　And shal byforn h[e]m goon into Galylee.'

　　　　Lo, thus and many outhyr wyse,
　　　　As in the gospel men moun aspye,
　　　　And myche betyr than I now kan deuyse,
465　　　Preuylegyd was thys blyssyd Marie
　　　　Wyth singuler chershyng of hyre loue, Mess[y]e,
　　　　Bothe in hys lyuyng and in hys passyoun,
　　　　And fro deth to lyue in hys resurreccyoun. |

f. 137vb　　Nowe haue I sheuyd, aftyr the gospel,
470　　　Of thys Marys lyf a gret partye;
　　　　Of the remnaunt forth now wyl I telle,
　　　　Lych as Ianuence yt doth discrye,
　　　　Yf grace my wyt and my penne do gye,
　　　　And God also my fare so longe
475　　　Tyl yt be doon vouchesaf to prolonge.

　　　　But er than y ferthere in thys matere,
　　　　Wyche I haue promysyd, do procede,
　　　　I the byseche, Marie, wyth hert entere,
　　　　Purchace me grace bettyr lyf to lede
480　　　Than I do yeet, and euere me spede
　　　　In alle my werkys and gete me blys
　　　　Whan I hens pace wyche neuere shal mys.

　　　　The fourtende yer by trewe computacyon
　　　　Aftyr Crist was risyn from deth to lyue,
485　　　Whan Steuene wyth stonys had throwyn doun
　　　　The Iewys, as Ianuence doth dyscryue,
　　　　And owt of Iewerye Cristys dysciplys dede dryue,
　　　　Ful many a cuntre they dede seche,
　　　　Godys wurdys therin to sowe and teche.

461 hem] hym Ab　　　462 outhyr] anoþir Ar　　　463 gospel] gospelys Ar
466 Messye] Messe Ab　　468 in] aftyr Ar　　474 fare] state Ar　　480 euere
me] that lady Ar　　481 my] hyr Ar　me] hyr Ar　　482 Whan I hens pace wyche
neuere shal mys] Wych of this wrytyng cause princypal ysse Ar　　488 they] the Ar

And in the tyme of thys persecucyoun, lo,   490
Lych as seyid Ianuence doth telle,
Oon of the seuenety dysciplys and two
In Ierusalem wyth the apostlys dede dwelle,
To whom by Petyr, as yt byfylle,
Commyttyd was Marie Maudelyn;   495
And thys dysciplys name was Maximyn.

And wyth these two were, the soth to telle,
Togedyr assocyid in oo cumpanye,
Lazar and Martha and ek Macelle,
Hyre handmaydyn, and blyssyd Cedonye,   500
Wyche as the gospel doth dyscrye
Blynd was from hys natyuyte,
And Crist meruelously hym maad to see.

These alle togedyr, and many anothir
Of cristene men, by the cruel decre   505
Of Iewys, wythowtyn sterne or oothyr,
In a shyp were set vpon the see,
To that entent they drynklyd shuld be;
But as Goddys prouidence hem dede gye
Alle saf to Marsilye they dede applye.   510

Whethir whan they come, with humble entent
They thankyd God of there passage,
And euene forthwyth to londe they went;
But them wold no man grauntyn [h]ostage.
Wherfore they tokyn here herbergage   515
In a porch, tyl that bettyr myht be,
Of a temple of the folk of that cuntre.

And whan that blyssyd Maudelyn dede see
Meche folk thedyr comyn to sacrifice
To the ydols, ryht anoon she   520
Wyth a plesaunt cher vp dede ryse,
And wyth a fayr face in desert wyse

She hem reuokyd from hyre ydolatrie,
And prechyd hem Crist most stedfastlye. |

　　　　　Alle that hyre herdyn awundryd were,
526　　　What for hyre bewte on that oo party,
　　　　　And for the facundye wych she vsyd there,
　　　　　And for the swetnesse eek of hyre eloquency,
　　　　　Wych from hyre mouth cam so plesauntly
530　　　That they haddyn a we[r]y delectacyoun
　　　　　Stylle to stondyn and to heryn hyre predicacyoun.

　　　　　And no wundyr thoght that mouth sothly
　　　　　Wyche so fayre kyssys and so swete
　　　　　So oftyn had prentyd and so deuouhtly
535　　　Vpon Crist oure saluatours feete,
　　　　　Diuers tymys whan she hym dede mete,
　　　　　Past othere swych grace had and fauour
　　　　　Of Goddys wurd to shewe the sauour.

　　　　　Sone aftyr thys, onto that phane
540　　　The prince and hys wyf of that cuntre
　　　　　Comyn to sacrificyn to Dyane,
　　　　　That a chyld hem sende vouchesaf she;
　　　　　And whan Marie Maudelyn thys dede see,
　　　　　Of Crist she hem made a long sermoun,
545　　　And counselyd h[e]m to lyuyn here supersticyoun.

　　　　　But al that tyme, the sooth to seyin,
　　　　　Maryis wurdys auaylyd no thyng,
　　　　　For as they cam they hom ageyn Wentyn,
　　　　　obstinat in here errour stondyng.
550　　　And nat longe aftyr, whyl slepynge
　　　　　Was thys lady, to hyre appere
　　　　　Dede Maudelyn, seying on thys manere:

　　　　　'Why ys yt that thou and thyn husbonde here
　　　　　In rychesse haboundyn thus pleynteuosly,

　　530 wery] wey Ab　　　531 to] om. Ar　　　534 prentyd] bredyd Ar　　　537 and]
in Ar　　　542 sende] sende wold Ar　　　545 hem] hym Ab　　　546 al] at Ar
553 ys yt] ys Ar　　thou and thyn husbonde] thine husbonde & thow Ar

And in hunger and cold Goddys seyntys dere 555
Ye suffern to perysshyn myscheuously?'
And hyre dede thretyn that she treuly
Shuld hyre repente, but she wold meue
Hyre housbonde there myschyff to releue.

But she ne wold for no thyng 560
To hyre husbonde tellyn hyre visioun;
Wherfore, on the nexte nyht folwyng,
Whan the lady slepte as she was woun,
In alle vysys to hyre lych apparycyoun
Mary Maudeleyn maad and in conform degre, 565
But yet to hyre housbonde yt tellyn nold shee.

And for she ne wolde hyre byddyng doo,
The thridde nyht Marie dede appere,
Whyl they dede slepe, to them bothe two,
Angryly and with a brennyng chere 570
As al the hous had byn [o]nfeere;
And on hem lokyng with a ferful eye,
To hem bothe togedyr thus dede seye:

'Art thow aslepe, o tyraunt cruel,
And a me[m]bre of thy fadyr Sathanas, 575
Wyth thys serpent thy wyf wych nolde telle
To the my wurd as she bodyn was,
For she the nolde heuyin with the caas?
Wherfore, syth she myn eran[d] nold do,
Y now appere togedyr to yow bothe two. | 580

What resoun ys thys, thou cursyd enimy f. 138rb
Of Cristys cros, that thou fed shalt be
Wyth diuers metys thus dylycatly,
And aftyrward thus esyly to restyn the,
And Goddys seruauntys thou doost see 585
Wyth hungyr and myschef byforn thyn yhe
Perysshyn? Wherfore thou shalt abye.

563 the lady slepte] she dede slepe Ar   566 yt tellyn] tellyn Ar   571 onfeere]
vnfeere Ab; afere Ar   575 membre] menbre Ab   579 erand] erant Ab

Thou lyist here in a staatly paleys,
Bywrappyd in clothys of sylk and gold,
590   And they lyin in a ful sympyle hurdeys,
And lykly for to be deed for cold.
And thou ne lyst yt onys it to byhold,
Ner of hem to haue reuthe ner pyte,
Albeyt ych day yt ys told to the.

595   Wenyst thou for to askapyn fre
And pen[yl]es for thys gret trespaas?
Nay, pleynly, tyraunt, I warne the
Thow stondyst in a ful per[yl]ous caas,
And art lykly to criin eueremore "Allas",
600   Lesse to my wurdys that thou intende
And of thy mysreule the sone amende.'

Whan blyssyd Marie thys wyse had seyd,
She went hyre wey, and the matrone
Sodeynly owt of hyre sleep abreyid,
605   And sore bygan to sythyn and grone.
And to hyre husbonde, wych eek maad mone
For the same cause, wythowte lettyng
Euene thus she seyde, for dred quakyng:

'What cheer wyth you, syre? Dede ye owt see
610   The syht that I had in my vysyoun?'
'Ya, ya, wyf! And that causyth me
To be now in gret tribulacioun.
I ne wot what we best mow doon:
Whether to be reulyd afftyr hyre byddyng,
615   Or elles stylle to kepyn oure old lyuyng.'

'Iwys, syre,' quod she, 'myn opinyoun
Ys thys, that bettyr ys to obeye
[T]han to fallyn into the indignacyoun
Of hyre God, and myscheuously to deye.'
620   'Be yt so thanne,' he anoon dede seye.

590 in a] in Ar   592 yt] lyst Ar   596 penyles] peynlees Ar   598 perylous]
perlyous Ab   600 that] at Ar   intende] attende Ar   610 The] Thys
613 we best] best we Ar   mow doon] do moun Ar   617 ys] yt ys Ar   618 Than]
Whan   619 to deye] deye Ar

And afftyr to here hous they dede lede,
And minystryd hym al that they had nede.

Whan Marye sone aftyr vpon a day
Prechyd, the prince hyre askyd opynly:
'Throwyst that thou defende may   625
The feyth wych thou techest s[o] besyly?'
'Ya, that I may,' quod Marie pleynly,
'Be dayly miraclis and by wytnesse, iwys,
Of oure mastyr Petyr, wych at Rome ys.'

Than thus quoth the prince and hys wyf also: 630
'We be redy, lo, in al thyng to [o]beye
Whateuere thou comaunde vs to do,
Vpon a condycioun that we the seye.
That ys to seyne, yf thou wylt preye
Thy God to vs that a [c]hyld be bore   635
To byn oure eyr; we aske no more.' |

'Iwys', quod Marie, 'and in thys matere   f. 138ᵛᵃ
As for thys thyng shal no lettyng be.'
And anoon she gan wyth herte entere
For hem to prein, and herd was shee;   640
And wythinne short whyle, as men myht see,
This lady conceyuyd and with chylde was,
Wheche to them bothe was gret solaas.

Whan thys prince wyth chyld hy[s] wyf seye,
He hym fully dysposyd for to byleue,   645
And to Petyr [he] purposyd to take the weye,
Maryis doctrine that he myht preue.
Vpon wyche purpos to takyn hys leue
To hys wyf he went wyth deuouht chere;
And she hym answerde on thys manere: 650

'A, good sere, what woldyst thou doo?
Woldyst thou now thus forsakyn me

621 dede] hem dede Ar   626 so] se Ab   631 We be redy lo] Lo we be redy
Ar   obeye] abeye Ab   634 yf] yt Ar   635 chyld] shyld Ab   644 hys] hy
Ab   645 hym fully] hym Ar   dysposyd] dysposyd fully Ar   646 he] hem Ab
652 now thus] thus now Ar

In the plyht that I now am comyn to?
Nay, nay, certeyn, yt may not be,
For dowteles I wyl goon forth wyth the
And partener byn of thyn euenture,
As longe as the lyf in my body wyl dure.'

'Nay sykyr, wyf, so may yt not be',
Quod the prince, 'in the plyht ye arn in now;
For many grete perylys arn in the see,
And many a waue therin rysyth [r]ow.
Wherfore beth at hom and restyth yow,
And I shal goon for vs bothe two
Thys holy pylgrymage for to doo.'

But not forthan, as yt ys the guyse
Of wummen, she nolde hyre purpos lete;
Wherfore ful oftyn in most humble wyse
Sore wepynge she fel doun to hys feete,
And neuere wolde sece tyl he hyre dede hete
Wyth hym to goon, and thanne ful myry
She was, and anoon hyre maad redy.

And as sone aftyr than as was redy
Here sheep and al that longyd therto,
In the gouernaunce of blyssyd Mary
Al that they haddyn they dede doo;
And she the shuldrys of them bothe two
Of Cristys cros wyth a tokene dede syngne,
That the deuyl geyns hem shuld not maligne.

And whan they seylyd hadde but oo day,
And in here seyl [the] wynd ful blew,
Er they were war a sodeyn afray
And a gret tempest vpon hem grew,
So that alle men noon othyr knew
But that they must nedys perysshe and deye,
And for very feer they lowde dede crye.

653 now am] am now Ar   660 arn] ben Ar   661 row] now Ab   663 And I]
And Ab   671 hyre] she hyre Ar   678 geyns hem] hem ageyns Ar   680 the]
they Ab   682 And a] And Ab

And whyl they wern in thys dystresse
And wyth tempest passyd to and fro,
So gret angwysshe cam to the princesse
That chyld she hadde in that gret woo.
And therwyth the prince to hyre dede go;   690
And whan he cam, he here dede foond,
And the chyld lyinge vndyr hyre ryht honde. |

And anoon the chyld bygan to crye,   f. 138vb
Dysiryng to han had sum solas
Of hys modrys brestis, but thoo were drye,   695
For wythowte dowte she deed was.
And whan the prince sey thys pitous caas,
He sorwyd and wepte ful byttyrly,
And therwyth thus cryid ful pitously:

'Allas, allas wrecche! What shal I do?   700
A chyld I dysyrid, but infortuna[t]ly
For chyld and modyr lost arn bothe two.
Allas, also, allas! why [dye] not I?'
And therwyth the shepmen gunne to cry,
'Throw owt thys body into the see,   705
Or ellys by lyklynesse alle peryssh shul we!

For this for to certeyn we alle weel knowe,
Wyl yt ys here-inne the tempest nyl sece.'
And as they yt hent owt for to throwe,
The prince amonge hem anoon dede prece,   710
And seyde, 'Seris, I beseche yow of sum relece;
And thogh ye ne haue mercy on hyre ner me,
Yit of the yunge infaunt hath sum pyte.

Suffryth, syrs, a whyle for Goddys sake,
Ne hap the wumman in ony kothe be,   715
And may returne and ageyn lyf take.'
And whyl he thus seyde, he dede see
Not fer on hyl, and thanne thouht he,

695 brestis] pappys Ar   699 ful] ryht Ar   701 infortunatly] infortunaly Ab
703 dye] dede Ab   707 this for to] this Ar   708 ys here-inne] herein ys Ar

'Bettyr ys yt yundyr hem bothe to graue,
720   Than fysshys to here pray them shuld haue.'

And natwythstondynge that wyth watri ihe
The shypman he preyid and yaf hem yiftys also,
Vnnethe they wold to hys entent hem pley;
And whan he that hyl was comyn vnto,
725   He labouryd sore yt for to vndo,
Them to han buryd aftir hys entent,
But entryn ther myht noon instr[u]ment.

And whan he saw that yt wold nat be,
Hys wyuys ded body he dede doun leye
730   Wrappyd in hyre mantyl, vndyr a tre,
And on hyre brest the chyld wyth wepyng eye;
And er he thens dede takyn hys weye,
As deuouhtly as he best cowde deuyse,
He knelyd doun and preyid on this wyse:

735   'O Marye Maudelyn, to my perdycioun
And to the encres of my wrecchydnesse
To Marsile cuntre why dedyst thou com,
Me for to puttyn in swych dystresse?
Askyddyst thou of thy Goddys goodnesse
740   For thys skyl a chyld onto my wyf,
That thus they bothe shulde lese here lyf?

Y wot neuere; but thys woot I weel,
That she deed ys as I now see
And so shal the [c]hyld in ful short seel,
745   For he nouht hath wyth fostryd to be.
Nertheles, syth I hym had by the,
Lych as I haue don al myn othyr thyng,
I commytte hym to thyn and thy Goddys kepyng. |

f. 139ra   And yf he be myhty, as thow doost teche,
750   The modrys soule he haue in hys memorye;

719 ys yt] it is Ar   725 labouryd sore] ful sore laboryd Ar   727 instrument]
instriment Ab   731 wyth] wyth a Ar   733 best cowde] coude best Ar
734 on] euene Ar   736 to the] to Ar   744 chyld] shyld Ab   748 hym]
hem Ar

And thorght thy preyrs I louly byseche,
That the chyld not perysh, shew he mercy.'
And wyth the mantel he hem bothe dede wry;
And nowt oo wurd more myht he seyn
For sorwe, but went to the shyp ageyn.   755

And aftyr whan he to londe dede come,
On hys iourne he faste forth went
Seynt Petyr for to sekyn in Rome.
And whan Petyr hym sey, he hys entent
Of hym aske dede, and what yt ment,   760
Hys marke, and whens he come and why;
And he Petyr tolde al euenne by and by.

Whan Petyr had herd al thys processe,
'Pees be to the', quod he, 'wyth pacience.
Thou art wolcome, for in sothfastnesse   765
To holsum counsel thou hast youyn credence.
And be not heuy of thy wyuys absence,
Thogh she and hyre child a whyle do slepe;
For God ys strong inow hem bothe to kepe.'

And aftyr thys, to confermyn hys holy entent   770
And to stablysshyn hym in hys newe grace,
To Ierusalem wyth hym Seynt Petyr went;
And there, to encres of hys goostly solace,
He hym led and shewyd hym euery place
Where Crist prechyd and sufferyd and roos ageyn,   775
And where of hys dysciplis he was last seyin.

And whan he in pilgrimage and in preyer,
And in lernynge of the feyth diligently,
Out of hys cuntre had byn ful to yer,
He homward ageyn ful deuouhtly   780
Hys iourne took; and casually
To the hyl he neyhyd where he dede lye
Hys wyf, wyche owtward pitously dede deye.

753 he hem bothe] hem both he Ar   760 aske dede] dede aske Ar   yt] that Ar
762 Petyr tolde] told Petyr Ar   763 thys] thi Ar   764 quod he] he seyd Ar
766 youyn] þoue Ar

And he the shy[p]men preyid hertyly,
785   And yaf hem large yiftys also,
To rydyn on ankyr a whyle therby,
Whyl he the seyid hyl myht go to,
To see wat was wyth hys wyf do
And wyth hys [c]hyld, and they folwyd hys wyl,
790   And in a bot hym launchyd onto the hyl.

And as toward the hyl he dede goo,
A lyty[l] chyld al nakyd rennyng
On a clyf he perceyuyd to and fro,
On chyldyrns wyse bysyly pleying,
795   And smale stonys into the see castyng;
And as myry he sempte and as glad
As thoght he many moo felaas had had.

And thys same chyld was certeynly
His sone, whom by specyal grace
800   Blyssyd Mary Maudelyn meruelously
Had thoo two yer fostryd in that place.
And whan the chyld perceyuyd hys fadrys face,
As he wych byforn neuere seeyn men
For fer awhey he faste dede ren. |

f. 139rb   And streyt thedyr where hys modyr dede lye,
806   As he was wone to doon he went,
And wyth hyr mantel he dede hym wrye,
And in hys mouth anoon hyre pappe he hent
And bygan to soukyn wyth bysy entent.
810   And thys prince, sore amaruayld of the caas,
Ful faste hym hyid tyl he ther was.

And anoon as he thedyr cam
And fond the chyld lyin and soukyn,
In bothyn hys armys he yt nam,
815   And oon hys knees he dede doun knelyn,

784 shypmen] shymen Ab   785 yaf hem] hem yaf Ar   large] greth Ar
787 seyid hyl] hyl seyd Ar   789 chyld] shyld   791 as] as he Ar   hyl he]
hyl Ar   792 lytyl] lytyt Ar   796 sempte] semyd to be Ar   797 he
many] he Ar   803 wych] that Ar   byforn] beforn had Ar   809 wyth] in Ar
810 thys] the Ar   sore amaruayld] ameruaylde sore Ar   the] þis Ar   814 yt] it up
Ar

And wyth al hys herte to Mary Maudelyn,
And as deuouhtly as he cowd best deuyse,
He yaf hyre thankyng on thys wyse:

'O thou blyssyd Marye Maudelyn,
Honour, laude and wurshyp to the,   820
Whyche thys two yer thys tendyr chyld myn
Hast oonly of thy gret benyngnyte
Kept and fostryd in thys wundyr degre!
Weel hast thou shewyd, blyssyd lady, her
That grace fer passyth naturs pouer.   825

Moreouyr, blyssyd lady, in no manere
Myht I haue, me thynkyth, more felicyte
Than that my wyf wych deed lyith here
From deth to lyf myht reuyguryd be,
And wyth me returne to my cuntre,   830
Wych the to moun I haue ful confidence
Of my chyldys kepyng by experyence.'

And as he hys preyere thus dede make,
Hys wyf anoon bygan vp for to ryse,
Lych as from sleep she had don wake;   835
And as deuouhtly as she cowd dyuyse
To Mary Maudelyn she seyd thys wyse:
'Gret ys thy meryht in Goddys syht,
O blyssyd lady, and so ys thy myht.

Gramercy, lady, wyche me helpyng   840
Were, thorgh thy grace and throgh thy chyrite,
In alle the pressurys of my chyldyng,
And my mydwyf eek vouchyddystsaf to be;
And moreouyr thorgh thy benyngnyte
In yche nede to me were as redy   845
A[s] euere was handmayde to hyre lady.'

817 as he] as Ar   819 O thou] O Ar   822 thy gret] thy Ar   834 for to]
to Ar   839 ys] ys eke Ar   841 grace] greth grace Ar   and throgh thy] and Ar
846 As] And Ab

And whan the prince these wurdys dede here,
Gretly abasshyd he maad thys crye:
'Art thou [al]yue, myn ownyn wyff dere?'

850 'Ya, sere, that I am,' quoth she, 'sothly,
And now f[ir]st ageyn hedyr am comyn I
And haue maad an ende of the viage
Wyche thou hast doon, and the same pylgrimage.

For lych as Seynt Petyr led the
855 To Ierusalem, and shewyd the euery place
Where that Crist prechyd in oure freelte,
Where he deyid and ros and hens dede pace;
So blyssyd Maudelyn of hyre good grace
Wyth you me led and shewyd ych del,
860 Wych in my mynde I pren[d]yd haue w[e]l.' |

And anon to reherschyn she bygan
Hyre husbondys iourne euene by and by,
And what they seyde or were and whan,
And faylyd on no poynt substancially.
865 And thanne aftyr thank[in]ge to g[o]d hertely
To shyp they went, and withinne schorte while
They myryly applyit oonto Marsile.

And anoon as they nere come to londe
And gunne to ent[r]yn into here cyte,
870 With hyre dyssyples Mary they fond
Prechynge the peple, as wone was she,
And the pryn[ce] and hys wyf with gre[t] humylyte
Sore wepynge to hyre fete doun fel,
And tyl al here iourne hyre opynly dede tel.

875 And aftyr thys anoon they baptysyd were
O[f] blyssyd Maximyn ful deuouhtly,
And alle ydols templys wyche were there

847 And whan] whan Ar   849 alyue] olyue Ab   851 first] frist Ab   am
comyn] comyn am Ar   856 Where that] Where Ar   860 prendyd] prenyd Ab
wel] wyl Ab   863 they] the Ar   or] & Ar   864 on] in Ar   865 And] An Ar
thankinge] thankge Ab   god] good Ab   868 nere] wer Ar   869 entryn] enteyn
Ab   872 prynce] prynod Ab   gret] greth Ar; gre Ab   873 hyre fete] hyre Ar
874 And tyl] And Ar   876 Of] O Ab

They dystroyid forthwith, diligently
The[y] maydyn vp cherchys euene by and by,
And with oon assent they chese to be   880
Blyssyd Lazaar bisshop of that cyte.

Whan thys was doon they went th[en]s,
Blyssyd Maudelyn and hyre cumpany,
And come to a cyte clepyd A[q]uens,
Wyche, with miraclis shewyd plenteuously,   885
To Crist was conuertyd ryht redyly,
And Maximyn bysshop of that cyte maad;
Wyche doon, blyssyd Maudelyn was glaad;

For [from] thensforward hyre her[t]e was set
To yiuyn hyre oonly to contemplacioun,   890
And al thyng forsakyn that myht hyre let;
For wiche entent, by an euynly inspiracioun,
In a wyldyrnesse she took hyre habytacyoun
Ordeynyd by aungels in a bareyn plaas,
Where she thrytty wyntyr vnknowyn was.   895

In wyche place was growyng no tre,
Ner herby, ner watyr, ner no solace
To hyre bodely counfort in no degre;
And thys was oonly to shewyn that grace
Of oure saueour so hyre dede enbrace,   900
That he hyre wolde in euery nede
Withe heuenely foode alone do fede.

For euery day in that desolat plaas
Seuene sythe into the eyr ful hye
Withe aungels handys she vp leftyd was,   905
And with hyre bodely eerys heuenely armonye
There she herde, with wiche melodye
In body and soule she fed was so weel
That of bodely foode she nedyd no deel.

878 forthwith] forthwith & Ar   879 They] The Ab   882 thens] thus Ab
884 Aquens] Aguens   889 from] fer Ab   thensforward] hensforward Ar   herte]
here Ab   895 Where she] Where Ar   wyntyr] wyntyr she Ar

910 And in thys menetyme yt so byfylle
That a pryst, dysyringe to lyuyn solitaryly,
But twelue forlong hym [maad] a celle
From that place where dwellyd Mary,
And there hym ocupyid ful holyly
915 In studye of deuouht contemplacyon,
Whom God there shewyd thys reuelacyoun: |

f. 139vb Hym thouhte he saw with hys bodyly ihe
Aungels comyn doun in gret bryghtnesse,
And bern vp a body abouyn the skye,
920 Of melodyous song with gret swetnesse;
And whan an our or more, as he dede gesse,
They had ther byn meryly syngynge,
To the seyd place they yt doun dede brynge.

And whan the pryst had seyn thys syht,
925 Dysyringe to knowyn ful feruently
What thyng yt was, yf yt be myht,
Purposyd hym to goo the place more ny;
But fyrst he preyid God ful mekely
That in hys iourne he hym wolde spede,
930 And to that place the ryht weye hym lede.

But whan he thus forward was goon,
And to the place bygan to comyn as ny
As a man myht haue cast a stoon,
Hys leggys to faltryn gunne sodeynly,
935 That he no ferthere goon myht sothly,
But for to returnyn hoomward ageyn
Hys leggys were myhty ynow certeyn.

And whan aseyid had thus to and fro
Dyuers sythys, and yt wold not be,
940 Hym thouhte yt was nat for to do,
Thedyrward to precyn as in that degre,
For yt to knowyn not wurthy was he

912 hym] he Ar   maad] maid Ab   914 hym] he hym Ar   921 And] An Ar
922 had ther] ther had Ar   928 ful mekely] deuouthly Ar   929 That] Tht Ar
938 whan] whan he Ar   to and fro] fro & to Ar   942 not wurthy] vnworthy Ar

As hym semyd, wherfore ful hye
In the name of oure sauiour he thus dede crye:

'I coniure the by the vertu pure   945
Of God, thou that art dwellynge
In that caue, yf a resonable creature
Thou be, lete me haue knowlechyng
What thou art, withowte feynyng!'
And thys thryis seyid, Marie ageyn   950
To hym thus answerde in wurdys pleyn:

'Come hydyr more ner, and of euery thyng
Whiche thy soule desiryth enuereyd to be,
Thou shal[t] han sufficyent certyfying,
As meche as nedyth to byn knowyn of the.'   955
And anoon ful ferfully forth went he;
But vnnethe he goon had half the weye,
That thus to hym Marye [efthsonys] dede saye:

'Hast thou ony mynde in the gospel
Of oon Marye, most famous synere,   960
Whiche as [Lu]c pleynly doth tel,
Cristys feet wessh wyt many a tere,
And aftyr hem wyptyn with hyre heere,
And so of hyre synnys by Goddys grace
Plener indulgence she dede purchace.'   965

'Yis,' quoth the prest, 'I haue good mynde,
And thrytty wy[n]tyr byn past and moo,
As in holy cherche we wrytyn fynde,
Syth she mennys cumpany departyd fro.'
'I am the same wumman,' quoth Mary thoo,   970
'And in thys place here solitarily
Al thys tyme vnknowyn dwellyd haue y. |

And lych as thow were sufferyd to see   f. 140ra
Yistyrday, ryht so quotydyanly

954 shalt] shald Ab   955 as] as it Ar   knowyn] kowyn Ar   958 efthsonys] of
thys onys Ab   961 Luc] hic Ab   963 hyre] hyre owyn Ar   966 Yis] þis Ar
967 wyntyr] wyatyr Ab   970 the] that Ar   same wumman] same Ar   974 ryht
so] ryht Ar

975 Aungelys lyftyn seuene syths vp me,
And han doon syth fyrst hydyr cam I.
And for now yt plesyth oure lordys mercy
Me vp to takyn into continuel blys,
To blyssyd Maximyn go telle al thys.

980 And moreouyr I wyl thou hym seye also
That on esterne day nex folwyng,
Whan he vp resyth, as he ys wone,
To matynys in the grey morwenyng,
To hys oratorye he goo withowte lettyng,
985 Where by holy aungels mynistery
He me fynde shal brouht ful redy.'

And whan the pryst thys voys herd had,
Lych the voys of an aungel cler,
Thogh he nowt sey yit ful glad
990 He was to ben the massager
Of so holy and of so blyssyd mater,
And to Maximyn he wente redyly
And dede hys erand euene by and by.

Whan blyssyd Maximyn herd had al thys
995 Of the preyst, onto oure saueour
Wyth al the entent of hys herte, iwys,
He yaf thankyng, laude and honour;
And the day assyngnyd and eek the our,
In hys oratorye Mary he fond stondyng
1000 [A]mong aungels ha[ndys] wyche hyre thedyr dede brynge.

And oon this wise was hyre stondyng,
From the erthe fully two cubytys space
Aungels handys hyre vp holdynge;
And so gret bryhnesse was in hyre face,
1005 That esyere yt was the sunnys compace

978 into] to Ar   blys] bys Ar   982 wone] wone to do Ar   986 fynde shal
brouht] brouht shal fyndyn Ar   994 Whan blyssyd] Whan Ar   995 saueour]
saluatour Ar   1000 Among] Mong Ab   handys] had Ab

In the most cler day to byholdyn and see
Than the gret bryhnesse of hyre bewte.

Maximyn thys seyng abasshyd was
To byholdyn the bryhtnesse of hyre cher,
And anoon to hym she turnyd hyre faas   1010
And seyde, 'Fadyr, beth ye not in dwer;
But boldly, fadyr, comyth to me ner.
I am youre douhtyr; why do ye fle?
Wherfore, fadyr, dredles comyth to me.'

And whan gadryd was al the clergye,   1015
And the seid prest present was ther,
Of the bysshop she reseyuyd Cristys body,
Out shedyng ful many a wepyng teer.
And euene forthwith, withowtyn feer,
Byforn the awtyr she hyre doun dede lye,   1020
And withowte ony peyne ther dede deye.

And whan forth passyd the soule was
Of thys blyssyd wumman and most holy,
A ful redolent odour in the same plaas
Euene forthwyth greu sodeynly,   1025
Whiche seuene dayis afftyr lastyd continely,
Wherby many oon of her syknesse
Where curyd, thorgh meryt of hyr goodnesse. |

And aftyr thys blyssyd Maximiyn   f. 140rb
The body there buryid deuouhtly   1030
Of the apostelesse Mary Maudelyn,
With oynement anoyntyd, smellyng sweetly.
And whan he shuld deyin, euene hyre by
He chargyd hys body buryid to be;
And so yt was with gret solemnyte.   1035

But long tyme aftyr, whan the [ye]r of grace
On seuene hundryd ran and fourt[y] and nyne,

1006 most cler] clerest Ar   1007 Than the] the Ab   the gret] the Ar
1011 beth ye] beth Ar   1021 peyne] peyne she Ar   1026 afftyr lastyd] afftyr Ab
1032 anoyntyd] anoyntyng Ar   1036 yer] ye yer Ab   1037 fourty] fourtyn Ab

Translatyd was from thys seyd place
Thys holy apostelesse, Mary Maudelyne,
1040   To Vicelac, and there leyid in shryne
By oon clepyd Girardus, a lord in Burgundye,
Where as men wenyn she yit doth lye.

Now, glorious apostelesse, whiche aboue the skye
Crownyd art in blysse and the heuenely regyoun,
1045   Thy seruauntys in erthe gouerne and gye,
And euere hem kepe vndyr thy proteccyoun,
And of here synnys hem purchace remissioun;
And whan here mortal fate hens hem doth sende,
To t[h]e ioye hem brynge which neu[er]e shal ende.

Here endyth the lyf of blissyd Marie Maudelyn.

[118. APOLLINARIS]

The lyf of Seynt Appolinare

[A]ppolinaris was an holy bysshop ordeynyd & sacryd by Seynt Petyr
at Rome and sent from thens to the cyte of Rauenne for to conuerte that
peple onto Cristys feyth. Whedyr whan he cam the tribune of the cyte had
5   a seek wyf whoom he curyd and maad hool. For whiche cause bothe hyre
husbonde and she were conuertyd and baptisyd with al here houshold. And
whan thys was told oonto the iuge of the cyte, anoon he chargyd hym to be
takyn and to be led to the temple of Iupiter for to sacrificyn. Whedyr he
cam, he seyde to the prestys of the temple: 'Thys gold and the syluyr wiche
10   ys hangyn vp here abowtyn these ydols were bettyr to be dysperbyld and
youyn oonto pore men, than for to be hangyn vp and offryd oon to deuyls.'
Whiche wurd seyd, anoon he was takyn and betyn with battys tyl that he
was lefth half ded. Whom hys dysciplys leddyn priuyly into a wydwys hous,
where he was kept sexe monyths tyl he was ful recuryd ageyn.
15   Aftyr wych tyme he went to a cyte clepyd Classence for to curyn there
a wurthy man wyche was doum and myht not spekyn. And as sone as he
entryd into hys hous a damysyl, wych had an vnclene spirit, bygan to cryin
owt vpon hym and seyin: 'Goo hens, thou seruaunt of God, or I shal make
the to be boundyn and to be drawyn owt of the cyte by the feet!' And whan

1044 and] in Ar   1046 euere] eueremore Ar   1048 hens hem doth] doth hem
hens Ar   1049 the] te Ab   neuere] neue Ab   shal] shal haue Ar   2 Appolinaris]
initial A has been cut out

Appolinaris herd thys, he rebukyd the vnclene spirit, and conpellyd hym 20
to goon owt of the damysel. And whan he had maad hys preyere vpon the
doum man, anoon he spak and byleuyd, and moo than fyue hundryd men
with hem. This seying the remnaunt paynyms of the cyte, they betyn hym
with battis, | chargynge hym that he shuld not namy[n] Ihesu. But not   f. 140ᵛᵃ
forthan, as he lay vpon the grund he [euer] cryid and seyde: 'Ihesu', quoth 25
he, 'ys very God.' Wherfore they madyn hym to stoondyn barefoot vpon
hoot brynnyng colys. And whan they ceyn that therfore he wold not se[c]yn
to knowleche stedfastly Ihesu Crist to ben very God, they wyth gret rebuk
and despyht dryuyn hym owt of the cyte.

   Aboute that same tyme the duc of Rauenne, clepyd Rufus Patricius, had 30
a seek dowtyr. And anoon he sent for Appolinare for to comyn and curyn
hyre. But, as sone as seyid Appolinare entryd the dukys dore, hys dowtyr
deyid. For wych cause, with gret sorwe and heuynesse, Rufus cam to Appolinare and seyde to hym on thys wyse: 'Allas that euere thou entryddyst
within myn hous. Fore oure gret goddys ben w[ro]th therfore and wyl not 35
curyn my dowtyr. What mayst thou now don in thys caas?' 'Dreed not',
quoth Appolinar, 'but only make me an oth that, yf thy douhtyr reuyue
and turne ageyn to lyf, thou shalt nat lettyn hyre to f[o]lwyn hyre saueour
yf she wyl.' And anoon as Rufus had maad hys ooth, Appolinaris a short
preyere, the maydyn roos vp quyk and heyl, knowlechyng the name and the 40
myht of oure lord Ihesu Crist. And forthwyth hyre modyr and she with a
gret multitude moo were baptisyd, and the douthtyr abood a mayden stylle.

   But whan the emperour was informyd of al thys matyr, anoon he wroot
to the prefect of the pretorye that or he shuld compellyn Appollinarie to
sacrifi[s]yn, or ellys that he shulde exilyn hym owt of the cuntre. But whan 45
the prefect myht not makyn hym to sacrifysyn, fyrst he comaundyd hym to
be betyn with battys and aftyrward to be spred ab[rode on] a iebet. Where
whan he stedfastly knowlychyd [Cryste], boylyng watyr to be poryd in hys
woundys, [and] with gret whyhte of iyryn, to be ban[y]shyd the cyte and
exilyd. And whan the cristene puple saw thys gret cruelte and vnpitous- 50
nesse, they in a brunt rune vpon the paynyms and slown of hem abowte
two hundryd men or mo. Thys seying, the prefect he wente and hym hyd,
but fryst he shet the bysshop Apolinar in a streyt prisoun. And on the next
morwyn hee put hym in a shyp, myhtyly boundyn with thre clerkys whiche
that folwyd hym, and sent hym into exyl. In whiche iourne, aftyr a gret 55

24 namyn] namyd   25 euer] euery   27 secyn] seyn   35 wroth] worth
38 folwyn] felwyn   45 sacrifisyn] sacrifiyn   46–7 to be] to   47 to be] to
47–9 abrode . . . and] *Text is missing owing to the removal of an initial. The missing text has been
restored by comparison with LgA.*   49 banyshyd] banshyd

tempest, he askapyd the peryl of the see wyth two clerkys oonly and wyth
to sowdyours, the whiche two he baptysyd at the same tyde. But aftyr thys
he com ageyn to Rauenne and there he was takyn anoon of the paynyms
and led to the temple of Apollo to don sacrifice. In whiche temple, as sone
60 as he saw the simulacre he cursyd yt and sodenly yt fel doun abrast. And
whan the bysshops of the templys sey thys, anoon they presentyd hym to
the iuge of the cyte clepyd Taurus. The whiche iuge hadde a sone blynd,
whoom blyssyd Appollinar mad to seen. Wherfore the seyd iuge was conuertyd and maad the blyssyd bysshop to dwellyn in a maner of hys foure
65 yer. In thys menetyme the bysshops of the templys maad relacioun herof to
the emperour Vaspasianus, acusyng hym of gret iniurye don to hyre goddys. The whiche emperoure sent wurd agayn that whoosoeuere dede ony
f. 140ᵛᵇ iniurye to the goddys, that or he shulde makyn a seeth and amendys, | or
ellys that he shulde be pryuyd of hys cyte: 'For yt ys not', quoth he, 'ryhtful
70 that we shulde vengyn goddys. But they hemself, yf they be wroth', quoth
he, 'shuld moun vengyn hem of here enmyis whan they wyln.'
　　Aftyr wiche tyme oon clepyd Demonestes Patricius chargyd the bysshop that he shuld doo sacrifise. And whan he saw that he in no wyse wolde
sacrifysyn, he deliueryd hym onto a centuryoun whiche thanne neuly was
75 maad a cristene man. At whoos preyer and gret instaunce the blyssyd bysshop went into the strete of the lyprys to hydyn hym there a whyle fro the
gret furyous woodnesse of the paynyms. But they folwyd hym thedyr and
betyn hym euene to the deeth. Where seuene dayis aftyr he lyuyd, and aftyr
many an holy exhortacyoun youyn onto hys dyscypls, he yald vp hys spirit
80 into Goddys handys. Whoos body cristene men buryid wurshupfully in
the same place, abowte the yeris of oure lord seuynty, vndyr the emperour
Vaspasian.
　　Of thys blyssyd martyr thus writyth Seynt Ambrose in a pr[e]face: 'The
ryth wurthy bysshop Appollinaris wos sent of Seynt Petyr to Rome to
85 shewe there the name of Ihesu to the mysbyleuyng puple. The whiche bisshop, wyl he shewyd many wundre werkys of vertu to hem that byleuyd
in Crist of the mysbelyinge men, he was cruelly schorgyd and betyn and
hys body rent with many dyuers tormentriys. But that the feythful puple
shulde not feryn and byn abassyd in hys vexacyoun, the tyme of tormen-
90 trye he shewyd in the name of oure lord Ihesu Crist many apostlys tooknys.
For he reysyd a maydyn fro deth to lyf, he yold blynde men here syht and to
a doum man he restoryd speche. He deliueryd a damysele from the deuyls
possesyoun, he curyd lyprys and threw doun a temple with a simulacre.
O most wurthy bysshop to han the maruelous laude and preconye of prey-

74 onto a] onto　　　　83 preface] proface

syng, the wych wyth pontifical dignite deseruyd apostls pouer and autorite! 95
O mythty cheuyntyn of Crist, the wiche in old yeris constantly prechyd
among peynys Ihesu Crist, the redemptour of the werd!' *Hec Ambrose.*
    Here endyth the lyf of Seynt Appolinare

[119. CHRISTINA]

Here bygynnyth the lyf of Seynt Cristine
    Whylom byside the lake of Wulsyne
    Stood a cyte wych Tire clepyd was,
    As olde storyis determyne,
    Weelful and ful of werdly solaas.
    Y[t]t wantyd not ellys but Goddys grace;   5
    For Cristis feyth yt wolde no wyse tan,
    Wych fersly dede pursu in euery plaas
    The cruel emperour that tyme Dioclicyan.

    Of thys seyd cyte was a wurthy man,
    To spekyn as of werdly dyngnyte   10
    Prefect, whoos name was clepyd Vrban,
    And maystyr of knythys also was he.
    A wyf he had acordyng to hys degre,
    Wyche yssuyd out of the blood emperial
    But hethene they were bothe two, parde,   15
    And of the sect wych paynyms men cal. |

    But lych as oftyn of a ful sharp thron   f. 141ra
    Flours spryngyn fayr and delycious,
    And of foul erthe growyth fayr corn,
    Goold eek and syluyr and stonys precious,   20
    So of these hethene folk and vicyous,
    Wiche in ydolatrye here lyfe dede fyne,
    A mayde bothe fayre and eek gracyous
    Was born, whos name they clepyd Cristine.

    And whan Cristine twelue yere was of age,   25
    Not oonly she had gret bodyly beute,

---

1 lake of] lake Ar   3 determyne] do termyne Ar   4 Weelful] Weldful Ar
5 Ytt] Itt Ar Yit Ab   19 fayr] good Ar

But also wyhs she was, prudent and sage
Past all the wummen of that cyte;
And to loue and serue only purposyd she
Of heuene and erthe the lord omnipotent,
And for a menetyme she kept secre
From fadyr and modyr hyre holy entent.

Vrban, consideryng the fressh colour
Of Cristine hys douhtyr, and the gret bewte,
Dede makyn an hy and a solempne tour,
In wych wyth twelue maydyns put was she;
For he wold not opynly she seyn shuld be,
Dredyng the peryls that myht befalle;
And goldene goddys hyre ordeynyd he
Whiche she shuld wurshype and for helpe to calle.

Wowers thedyr comyn ful many oon,
Dysyringe to han hyre in mariage,
But hyre fadyr them auoydyd euerychon,
Alleggyng the tendyrnesse of hyre age.
And moreouyr he seyde that hyre corage,
As he weel knew, was Goddys to serue,
From whos seruyse she nolde owtrage
For no man thogh she shulde sterue.

And no dowte thys blyssyd Cristine
Dysposyd was al anothyr wyse
Than hyre fadyr wende or cowde dyuyne,
For holy hyre herte to Goddys seruyse
Appliyd was, wherfore sacrifyse
To hyre fadrys ydols doon she ne wold
As he bodyn had, but hertely dede despyse
Alle hys goddys forgyd of syluyr and gold.

Wherfore the gumys and the frankencens
Whiche he [h]ad ordeynyd offryd to be
Of hyre to the honour and to the reuerens
Of hys goddys, in a wyndow set she

27 wyhs she was] sche was wys Ar   35 a] a ful Ar   41 thedyr] there Ar
50 al] al on Ar   54 To hyre fadrys] to Ar   55 he] hir fadyr Ar   58 had]
bad Ab

Whiche estward stood, where she myht see
Bothe sunne and mone and many sterrys clere
Coursly forth passyn, ych in hys degre,
Whereof she maruayld seying thys manere:

'Gret is that God, and magnyfyid to be   65
Most wurthy, wych thorgh hys grace
Only and for noon othyr necessyte
Alle these hath ordeynyd for mannys solace.
But my fadrys goddys wyth hyre goldene face
Kun not don so, aftyr myn entent,   70
Wherfore hys name be gloryfyid in euery place,
Whoos dwellyng ys aboue the firmament. |

Hym Y oonly wyl seruyn and noon othyr   f. 141rb
Whyl that I lyue, thogh I shuld deye;
For shal I neuere for fadyr ner modyr,   75
Ner for no creature, turne othyr weye.
In thys me stablysshe, lord, I the preye,
And suffre me neuere to go the fro;
For thogh I the not see wyth my bodyly eye,
Yit in the lord only I truste, and in no mo.'   80

Thus thys Cristine ful dayis seuene
Forth went and wold not sacrifise
To othyr doon, but to God of heuene.
And thanne the twelue maydyns to hyre seruyse
Whiche hyre fadyr specyally dede dyuyse   85
Byforn hyre knelyng with gret reuerence,
All togedyr in ful humbyl wyse
Thus to hyre expressed here sentence:

'O lady, whos face ys emperyal
And ouyr alle to regnin most wurthy,   90
To whom may neythyr gret ner smal
In bewte comparyd ben egally,
We gretly marualyn the cause whi,

64 seying] & seyd on Ar   manere] degre Ar   66 grace] good grace Ar
74 that] at Ar   thogh] thogh that Ar   78 the fro] therefro Ar   80 lord
only I truste] I trust oonly lorde Ar   84 the] tho Ar   90 alle to] to Ar

And yet vs looth were the to greue
95   That, as vs semyth, vnresonabylly
Thou erryst from thy fadrys byleue.

Thou wurshypyst a god wich we not knowe,
Ner noon of oure auncetris vs beforn;
And yf thys fame to thy fadyr be blowe,
100   Thys ys doutlees: we be but lorn.
But vs were bettyr neuere to haue be b[or]n;
For he wyl seyin that by oure suggestioun,
And anoon othyr byleue, throgh we yt had sworn,
Brouht thou were into that opynyoun.

105   And yf algatys yt come therto,
That he yt vs bere on hande styfly,
Whedyr shul we fle? What shul we do?
Allas, we confoundyd byn vttyrly!
Haue on thynself, we byseche, mercy
110   Fryst and formeste, and aftyr on vs,
And suffere not for a lytyl foly
Bothe vs and the to perysshe thus.'

Whanne these maydyns [o]on thys manere
Had maad hyre compleynt thus pitously
115   Wepyng, Cristine with a sad chere
To h[e]m answerde thus benygnely:
'Why sey ye thus, maydyns? Wold ye that
YShulde to these ydols for socour craue,
Whiche as I weel knowe [sensibylly]
120   Moun me ner othere hurte ner saue?

Not so, damysels, but thys hold I best,
Hym to wurshypyn and seruyn wych wyl and may
Bothe body and soule makyn to rest
Here, and in ioye wyche lestyth ay,
125   Where neuere ys nyth but euere ys day
A thowsend fold bryhtere than ony ys here.

94 to] for to Ar   101 to haue] haue Ar   born] bron Ab   104 into] in Ar
105 yt] that yt Ar   113 oon] son Ab   116 hem] hym Ab   119 sensibylly]
seyn sibylly Ab   124 wyche] that Ar   125 euere ys] euere Ar

Hym wyl I wurshypyn, thys ys no nay,
Euere wyl I lyue wyth herte entere.' |

And wyl they thus were in here talkyng,   f. 141va
Here fadyr cam into byholdyn and see   130
Yf hys douhtyr maad deuly hyre offrynge
To hys goddys as comaundyd had he.
But she nolde to h[y]m attendyn in no degre,
But, opnyng hyre wyndone, with a wepynge eye
Vpward to heuene deuo[u]thly lokyd shee,   135
And in hyre herte dede wurshype and preye.

And whan Vrban of Cristine sey this cher,
He hyre clepyd to hym in goodly wyse
And seyde, 'Dere douhtyr, why comyst no nyr
Onto my goddys and dost hem sacrifice,   140
Lych as of me thou hast lernyd the guyse
From thylk tyme thou were fyrst bore?
Wherfore, come forth, as I the deuyse,
And do now as thou hast doon here byfore.

Knowyst thou no weel wyth what laboure   145
And wepyng, douthtyr, and with what heuynesse,
Wyth how gret reuerence and eek honour,
Y the purchacyd of my goddys goodnesse?
Ne hap thanne for thyn vnkyndenesse
They in here wretthe on the take wreche,   150
Come forth [anoon], and with al lowlynesse
Do to hem sacrifise, I the byseche.'

Thys blyssyd Cristine, inspirid wyth grace,
To hyr fadyr thus seyde ful demurely:
'Thynkyst thow, fadyr, that I trespace   155
For I wurshype God in heuene on hy?'
'Nay, douhtyr,' quoth he, 'but thys I holde foly,

129 thus were] were thus Ar   133 she nolde] she Ar   hym] hem Ab   in] wold in Ar   135 deuouthly] deuothly Ab   136 And] And God Ar   138 hyre clepyd] clepyd hir Ar   wyse] voyse Ar   141 of me thou] thou off me Ar   142 thou] that thou Ar   were fyrst] fyrst was Ar   146 and with] and Ar   149 for] that for Ar   151 anoon] anoon anoon Ab   154 To hyr fadyr thus seyde] Thus seyde to hir fadyr Ar   155 fadyr] juge Ar

That thou in thyn herte doost supprise
And tendryst oo God so affecteuously,
160   That for hym alle othere thou doost despise.'

'Heldest thou my seruyse thanne spent and loost,
Sey treuly, Y the byseche' quoth she,
'Wythe wych fadyr, sone and holy gost
Y doo wurshype?' 'Nay, but thanne,' quoth he,
165   Syth not oonly oon thou wurshypst, but thre,
As thou doost knowlechen here opynly,
Why wylt thou not in lyche degre
Othyr goddys wyth hym seruyn comounely?'

'Now perceyue Y ryht weel,' quoth Cristine,
170   'That thow wantyst wyt and vndyrstondynge,
And lakkyst the influence of grace diuine
To knowyn the hy misterye of thys thynge,
How thre personys han but oo be[y]nge
In substance, and woldyst so crafftyly
175   To that fals conclusyoun me brynge
That mo goddys than on wurshypyn shold Y.

Yt wyl not ben. Y knowe thy wyle,
And how bysy thou art to deceyuyn me;
But yit shalt thou me not so bygyle,
180   Vndyr the nou[m]byr of aternyte.
Laboure no more, for yt shal not be;
For but oo God neuere wurshype shal I.
And yet I knowleche that there byn personys thre,
So dist[inc]t that non ys othyr treuly. |

f. 141ᵛᵇ   Hym wyl I loue, hym wyl I serue,
186   Wyth wery and hertly su[b]ieccyoun,
Wych from al euyl me may preserue,
And in ych nede by my proteccyoun,
And not thy goddys wyche neythir moun
190   Here, ner seen, ner vndyrstonde,

161 spent] veyn Ar   162 treuly] treuth Ar   163 Wythe wych] wych Ar
173 beynge] Ar benynge Ab   179 me not] not me Ar   180 noumbyr] noun-
byr Ab   183 byn] ern Ar   184 distinct] distunt Ab   186 subieccyoun] Ar
suieccyoun Ab   187 me may] may me Ar

Ner from here place meuyn neythyr vp ne doun,
W[ith]owt helpe of mannys hand.

Wherfore me ordeyne newe frankencens,
Whiche with al clennesse of herte I may
Offryn vp to hys souereyn reuerence,   195
Whiche regnyth in heuene and hath ay.
Also me ordeyne newe and clene aray,
In wyche, dyspoylyd of myn old clothyng,
I may hym of f[or]yifnesse pray
Of tho defautys whiche I dede ying.'   200

And anoon hire fadyr, aftyr hyre entent,
As hastyly as he yt cowde deuyse,
Ordeynyd hyre a newe garnement
And newe encens eek for sacrifice.
And when yt come was, she hyre dede disgyse   205
And went vp to hyre wyndow abowe,
And maad hyre offryng in ful humbly wyse,
Thus seyinge to hyre lord, hir loue:

'O lord, whiche dwellyst in heuene aboue,
O saueour, wyche of thy fadyr were sent   210
Onto thys w[orl]d for mannys loue,
And for hym suffryddyst ful hard iugement;
O blysful Ihesu, accepte the entent
Of thyn handmayde and me strong make
That I neuere, for swych tor[m]ent   215
As me ys ordeynyd, do the forsake,'

Whan she thus had preyid, byforn hy[r] face
An aungel stood, bothe bryht and cler,
And seyde: 'O Cristine, fulfyld with grace,
Oure lord hath herd thy preyer.   220
Be strong in hym and make good cheer,
For of thre iugys thou examynyd shalt be;

191 neythyr vp] vp Ar   192 Withowt] Ar; Whiche owt Ab   196 hath] hath
doon Ar   197 me ordeyne] ordeyn me Ar   199 foryifnesse] Ar; froyifnesse
Ab   211 world] Ar; wrod Ab   212 for hym suffrydyst] suffriddyst for hym Ar
213 blysful] blyssyd Ar   215 torment] Ar; tornement Ab   217 hyr] hys Ab

But God the forsake wyl in no maner,
That hys vertu glorifyid may ben in the.'

225 'Now, lord God,' quoth Cristine, 'myn helpere be,
That no man of me haue the victorye.'
'Thy dysir ys grauntyd, Cristine,' quoth he;
And wyth that a loof she perceyuyd hyre by,
As whyht as snow, and thanne hony
230 Swettere, wyche whan she dede take
And yt had tastyd ful deuouhtly,
To God thus thankynge she dede make:

'Gramercy, lord, ful of goodnesse,
Whiche me a loof of immortalyte
235 Hast sent in tokene of foryifnesse
Of my synnys thorgh thy pyte.
Gramercy, lord, of thy cheryte
Wych hast me kept that I am not deed;
For thorgh my fadrys gret cruelte
240 These twelue dayis er saw I no breed.' |

f. 142ʳᵃ And at euyn hyre fadrys goddys ychon
Of gold and syluyr, stondyng by a wal,
Cristine brak on pecys many on,
And by a wyndowe let hem doun fal
245 Into the strete, and pore men dede cal,
And maad of hem a dystribucyon
To alle that come, bothe gret and smal,
Not dredyng hyre fadrys persecucyoun.

The nexte morwe whan Vrban anoon
250 Cam vp hys douhtyr for to see,
And fonde hys goddys dysperbyld and goon,
In hys irous p[a]ssyoun, ful of cruelte,
Hys douhtris maydyns to hym clepyd he,
And thus to h[e]m seyde ful sturdyly:
255 'Where arn, in hasty wyse tellyth me,
My gloryous goddys and vndeedly?'

224 glorifyid may] may glorifyde Ar   231 yt had] had yt Ar   240 twelue
dayis] dayis tuelue Ar   252 passyoun] possyoun Ab   254 hem] hym Ab

At thys wurd these maydyns fel doun,
So aferd they wern of hys cruel chere,
And seydyn: 'Syre, of vs thou hast domynacyoun
And ma[y]st with vs doon what thou wylt here;   260
We may the not fleen in no manere:
Wherfore ple[y]nly we wyl thou knowe,
That at thys wyndowe thy douhtyr dere
Thy goldene goddys dede alle owt throwe.'

Whan Vrban these maydyns wurdys dede here,   265
Hys douhtir he smot ful boystously
Vpon the cheke, and seyde on this manere:
'Tellyth me where ben myn goddys redyly,
Ere I the assayle with more tormentry.'
'Yf they byn goddys lete hem speke,' quoth she,   270
'For hemself beforn vs here opynly,
And so shewyn and prouyn here godly dygnyte.'

As she thus had seyd, in hyre presence
He sentencyd the maydyns hefded to be;
And anoon executyd was hys sentence.   275
Quod Cristine, 'O tiraunt withowte pyte,
Why sleest these innocentys in thys degre
Wythowte cause? I the warne sothly,
Thys blood shal wurthyly dampnyn the,
And Goddys veniauns shal the folwyn hastyly.'   280

Whan Vrban thys herde, ful furyously
With yerdys hyre comaundyd betyn to be.
And anoon she shorgyd was so cruelly
That very pyte yt was to byholde and see.
Yet wern hyre tortours werse greuyd than she,   285
For so wery they were that they doun dede falle.
Vrban thys seying ner wod was he,
And thretyd hem, and cowardys hem dede calle.

---

259 of vs thou hast] þou hast of us Ar   260 mayst] Ar; mast Ab   with vs doon]
doon wyth us Ar   262 pleynly] plenly Ab   271 beforn vs here] here all Ar
272 shewyn and prouyn] prouyn Ar   285 tortours] turmentours Ar

But wyl blyssyd Cristine thus turmentyd was,
290   She neythir chaungyd colour ne chere,
For fulfillyd she was with heuenely solas;
And to hyre fadyr she seyde on this manere:
'O thou hateful to God and to man in fere,
What may thy peynys and thy thretys doo?
295   Seest thou not thy seruauntys ouyrcomyn here,
And th[y] fadyr the deuyl and thyn owyn wyt also?' |

f. 142rb   Thanne comaundyd thys Vrban, withowte let,
Of strong iryn a coler ful vnpitously
Aboute hyre nekke faste to be shet,
300   And abowtyn handys and feet chenys myhty,
And so into presoun to be put cruelly.
Wych doon, he hom wente to hys plaas,
And fel doun platlyngys, sorwynge heuyly
That he of hys douhtyr so dyspysyd was.

305   Whan Cristines modyr pleynly had herd
How she of hyre fadyr swych tormentry
Had sufferyd, as a mad wumman she ferd,
Rendyng hyre clothys, euene by and by,
And dust she threwe on hyre heed on hy,
310   And to the presoun thus arayid she went,
Where, fallyng doun and wepyng pytously,
To hyre douhtyr she told thus here entent:

'O douhtyr Cristine, haue mercy on me
Thy wrecchyd modyr, for the al oonly
315   I haue and no mo, wich awtyst to be
The lyth of myn eye: thynke, douhtyr, that
I Ten monythys the bar in my body,
And wyth gret peyne into this wer[l]d the brouht.
Ys thys wurshyp, dowtyr, thus singulerly
320   To wurshypy[n] a god wich we knowe nouht?'

290 neythir chaungyd] chaungid neythir Ar   colour ne chere] hir colour ne hir chere
Ar   293 and to] and Ar   296 thy] Ar; they Ab   301 into] in Ar   cruelly]
ful cruelly Ar   302 to] onto Ar   304 he of hys douhtyr] of her doughtyr he Ar
307 mad] wood Ar   309 dust] asshes Ar   threwe] strowed Ar   312 told] expressyd Ar   318 werld] Ar; werd Ab   320 wurshypyn] Ar; wurshypyng Ab   wich]
at Ar

But she whom grace dede illumine,
To hyr modyr thus answerde anoon ageyn:
'Ys ther ony of thy kyn clepyd Cristine?'
'Noon that I knowe,' quoth hyre modyr, 'certeyn'.
'But thou thanne trauaylyst' [quod she] 'in veyn   325
To clepe me douhtyr, and lesyst [thy] laboure;
For thys I wyl thou knowe in wurdys pleyne:
My name I haue of Crist my creatour.

He ys my fadyr, he ys my modyr also,
Whiche me hath clepyd to heuenely ch[iualr]y.   330
Hym wyl I seruyn, hym wyl I wurshype doo,
Whiche me assuryd hath to han victory
Of alle tho that, blyndyd by ydolatrye,
Not wurshypyn the God that omnipotent ys,
And alle tho mawmetys fully to dyffye,   335
In whos seruyse ye excercisyn yow amys.

Wherfore goo hens, and laboure nomore.
Clepe me not douhtyr; here I the forsake.'
And she hom wente withoutyn more,
And al this processe tolde to hyre make.   340
And he for angyr gan tremelyn and quake,
And by hys goddys swor that the nexte day,
Yf he lyuyd, he veniauns shude take
Of hys douhtrys wurdys withowte delay.

The nexte morwe he Cristine dede bryngge   345
To the pretorie opynly, and whan wummen seye
Thus cruelly tre[t]yd this fayir maydyn yinge,
Among hem was many a wepyng eye,
And with a grete vois they thus dede preye:
'O God of thys mayde, hir helpe, preye we,   350
And thus shame[fu]lly ne suffre hir for too deye,
Wyche in tendyr age doth to the flee.' |

325 quod she] thou Ab   326 thy] thyl Ab   329 my] *om.* Ar   330 chi-
ualry] chawarly Ab   336 excercisyn yow] you excercysyn Ar   341 he for] for Ab
347 tretyd] tredyd Ab   351 shamefully] shameally Ab

f. 142va   Whan Vrban here sey, syttyng in hys see,
                 'Cristine,' quoth he, 'what ys the cause why,
355   Aftyr the custum vsid in thys cuntre,
                 To oure goddys thou sacrifisyst not reuerently,
                 Whiche mow the helpyn in this errour sothly,
                 Wherein throgh rekkelesheed thou arte falle?
                 And yf thou nylt, I shal with tormentry
360   The assaylyn, and neuere more douhtyr calle.'

                 'Iwys, cruel tirant,' quoth thanne Cristine,
                 'Thou dost me gret grace, yf thou wylt so,
                 Neuere aftyr to clepe me douhtir thyn.
                 I not hou for me thou myht more doo.'
365   And aftyr that wurd he hyre comaundyd, lo,
                 On a iebet to byn hangyn euene there present;
                 And the tormentours anoon hyre come to,
                 And with instrumentis of iryn hyre sydys they rent.

                 And whil these tormentours so cruelly dede wape
370   Cristines sydys and hyre flessh dede race,
                 A gobet therof, as she had lyst to iape,
                 Sche threu, thus seyinge, into hyre fadrys face:
                 'O old shrewe of yet ylle dayis that pace,
                 Syth thou desiryst flessh for to ete,
375   Seeke no ferthere in noon othir place.
                 Haue of thyn owyn and faste gynne to frete.'

                 Whan Vrban, of pacience hauyng no deel,
                 These wurdys herde, he hys douhtyr dere,
                 From the iebet doun takyn, on an iyrnene weel
380   To be set hyre bad, and to make vndyr gret fere;
                 And that no pyte in hym shuld appere,
                 Oyle castyn therin he bad cruelly.
                 In whiche tyme to heuene-ward hyre chere
                 She lyftyd vp, and preyid thus deuouhtly:

385   'O God in heuene whiche hast thy dwellyng place,
                 Fadyr of Crist Ihesu wyche euere blyssyd be,

357 sothly] treuly Ar   369 And whil] whil Ar   wape] schrape Ar   373 of
yet] of Ar   375 in] ner in Ar   377 Whan] And whan Ar   378 These] The
Ar

Thyn handmaydyn here, of thy specyal grace,
And in this gret conflict, forsake not me.
Shewe on this feer thy mygh[t] and thy pouste,
Whiche here ys ordeynyd to my torment,   390
That they mowe knowyn wych knowe not the,
That thou alone art lord omnipotent.'

And whan Cristine had on thys manere
Endyd hyre preyere and yt fully doo,
Sodeynly sprang abowtyn the feer,   395
And brent a thousend and fyue hundryd also
Of hem whiche sacrifice the ydols dede to.
And anoon Vrban to hym dede calle
Cristine, and seyde, 'telle me faste who
This wycchecrafth the tawt, foule hym byfalle!'   400

The[se] wurdys Cristine answerd thus to:
'O cruel tiraunt, ful of vnpyte,
What nede ys to aske the demaunde who
This wycchecraft me tawt, syth I told the
That Crist my fadyr ys, and non but he,   405
Whiche pacience me yiuyth to suffre moun.
He ys lyth of the blynde that mow not see,
And ioye of hem that suffryn tribulacoun. |

He ys myn mastyr, he al oonly tawt me   f. 142vb
The dreed of hym and eek al ryh[t]wysnesse.   410
So perfyht of hym a maystyr ys nowher as he,
Thorgh whos doctrine al thy frowardnesse
I haue ouyrcomyn, and alle the cruelnesse
Of swyche tormentys as thow canst deuyse.
Wherfore thy power, bothe more and lesse,   415
Wyth Sathanas thy fadyr Y despise.'

Wyth the[se] wur[d]is, Vrban, sore agreuyd
And troublyd in hymself tempesteuously,
Thynkyng heuy thus to be repreuyd,

389 myght] Ar; mygh Ab   401 These] The Ab   409 he] & he Ar
410 ryhtwysnesse] ryhwysnesse   413 the] thi Ar   417 these] Ar; the Ab
wurdis] Ar; wurthis Ab

420 Bythouhte what wyse he myht vttyrly
Here lesyn; and shettyn he hyre dede hastyly
Into a derk presoun wythowte solace,
Into whiche she entrid ryht gladly,
Singynge and thankyng God in that place.

425 And as sone as Cristine thus entrid was
Into that horryble and lothful lake,
Th[re] aungels apperid byforn hyre face,
Bryngyng hyre breed as whyht as lake,
Wyth othyr mete, and anoon dede take
430 Hyre woundys cure; and she, vp lokynge
To heuene-ward, bygan hyre preyere make
Wyth deuo[u]th courage, this wyse seyinge:

'O lord Ihesu Crist, thankyd thou be,
Whiche of thy grace and of thy goodnesse
435 Vouchyddystsaf not to forgete me
Thyn handmayde in my dystresse,
But hast me sent of thy ientylnesse,
By thyn holy aungls heuenely mete,
Swych as ryht weel Y dar expresse
440 In al erthe shulde men noon gete.'

And that same nyht thys cursyd man
Fyue seriauntys onto the presoun bad goon,
Y mene the vnpitous and cruel Vrban,
And byndyn he hem bad an heuy stoon
445 To Cristyns nekke, and forthwith anoon
Hyre caryin and castyn into the see.
And as he comaundyd, they went ychon
And performyd hys cursyd and cruel de[c]re.

And whanne in the see they had throwe
450 Cristine, thus boundyn to a ston heuy,
The men hom faste ageyn dede rowe;
And anoon of aungels a gret cumpany

420 Bythouhte] He þought Ar   422 Into] In Ar   427 Thre] There Ab
432 deuouth] Ar; deuoth Ab   441 same] self Ar   448 decre] degre Ab
451 The] These Ar

Dedyn hyre vplyfte, with whyche on hy
On the watyr she went, in no manere
Hurt ner apeyryd; and thanne hertly   455
To God she maad thus hyre preyere:

'O lord, wyth Moyses thy seruaunte entere
Whiche wentyst, and Pharao, wiche dede pursu
Thy puple, drynklyddyst in the salt mere,
And guydyst Petyr whan the tempest greu,   460
Thyn handmayde now sawe by the same vertu,
And the lauatorye me graunte of immortalyte
Here in this watyr, o blyssyd lord Ihesu,
And with lyht of grace illumyne now me.' |

And w[hy]l blyssyd Cristine thus dede preye,   f. 143ra
Goddys maieste to hyre she saw comyng,   466
And on hys heed seet a goldene crow[n]e she seye;
Of pure purpyl a stole was hys clothyng;
And with odours of rychels ful swete smellyng,
Byforn passyd aungels ful many oon,   470
And with ympnys and psalmys weel tunyng,
Thousendys of aungels aftyr hym dede goon.

Whan Cristine thys glorious syht dede see,
Doun plat she fel vpon the watyr cler,
For wyth gret feer astoynyd was she.   475
And anoon the good lord, comyng hyre ner,
Lyftyd hyre vp, and seyde, 'Be of good cheer,
Cristine, dere douhtyr! Y am thy saueour
Whom thou louyst and seruyst wyth herte entere.
Y come to delyuere the from ydols errour.   480

I am Ihesu, lord of the heuenyly oost,
Lyht, grauntere of grace to hem, in humble wyse,
Whiche my fadyr clepyn and me and the holy gost,
And alle fals mawmetys hertly despyse.'

453 whyche] whom Ar   454 in] on Ar   458 wiche] þad Ar   464 with]
with the Ar   465 whyl] wyhl Ab   467 crowne] Ar; crowe Ab   468 pure
purpyl] purpyl pure Ar   470 Byforn] Byforn hym Ar   ful many] many Ar
473 Whan] And whan Ar   477 Lyftyd hyre vp] Hyr up lyft Ar   483 Whiche]
That Ar   clepyn and me and] & me clepyn Ar

485   And with that wurd he hyre dede baptise
       With his own handys in the salt see,
       And from the watyr whan she de[de] vpryse,
       In the myddys he hyre set of the cyte.

       Thanne Cristine, knelyng on eythir kne,
490   Thankyd enterly God of hys gret grace;
       And vpward with that hyre eyne lyftyd she,
       And saw heuene opynyn and Ihesu in pace;
       And therwith she fel doun on hyre face,
       Dew reuerence doynge to Crist, God almyht.
495   And aftyr she entryd into here fadrys place,
       In preye[r] contunynge tyl yt greu daylyht.

       And whan the day sprongyn and fled was the nyht,
       And Vrban in hys pretorie Cristine fond preying,
       He gretly amaruaylyd was of that syht,
500   And th[r]etyd hys seriauntys that they had wenyng
       Hym illudyd; and, withowte lettyng,
       To presoun he hyre chargid to be sent.
       And the nexte day, euene in the morwenyng,
       He comaundyd byforn hym here to be present.

505   'Cristine,' quoth he, 'what enchauntement
       Vsyst thou, that drynk[l]yn the may not the see?'
       'Marryd in thy resoun and in thi wittis blent,
       Withowtyn vndyrstondyng thou art,' quoth she,
       'And ellys weel knowyn thou shuldyst that me
510   This nyht my god Ihesu dede baptise;
       Wherfore thy fadyr the deuyl and eek the,
       With alle thy mawmattis, dreedles Y dyspyse.'

       These wurdys Vrban so sore dede agrise,
       That anoon to prisoun he hyre sent ageyn,
515   Purposyng the next day, in most cruel wyse,
       Wythowte more dalay, hyre to slee, certeyn.

487 dede] de Ab   489 Thanne] And thanne Ar   490 hys gret] hys Ar
496 preyer] Ar; preye Ab   499 amaruaylyd] ameruel Ar   500 thretyd] Ar; the-
retyd Ab   502 to] anoon to Ar   503 And] On Ar   505 he] he than Ar
506 drynklyn] Ar; drynkkyn Ab   the may] may the Ar   512 mawmattis] fals goddys
Ar   dreedles Y] Y dreedles Ar

[W]hat dost thou, Vrban? Thou labouryst in veyn,
For victorye of two moo she muste han with the,
As to hyre by reuelacion told was wurdys pleyn.
For wiche conclusyoun she preyid in this degre: | 520

'O lord Ihesu Crist, whiche doun to me   f. 143rb
Thys nyth from heuene come for my solace,
And me dedist baptise in the salt see
Wyth thyn own handys, of thy special grace,
Byhold how thyn handmayde Vrban doth manace   525
Tomorwe to sleen throgh hys cruel wreche;
Lord, aftir hys merytis lete hym hens pace,
And frustrat hym of hys wyl, Y the, lord, byseche.'

Thys preyer endyd, as doth the story teche,
Entryng the presoun, she God dede magnifie.   530
And that same nyht fel on hym the wreche
That she preyid for; wth swych tormentrye
The deuyl hym vexid that he lowde gan crie,
For alle hys entrayls for very peyne gun swelle;
And in the same owr horrybilly dede dye,   535
And aftyr his desert streyt wente to helle.

And whanne men to Cristine [t]his thyng dede telle,
Knelyng, deuouhtly she thus maad hyre preyere:
'Lord God, gramercy, of al goodnesse the welle,
That thou on Vrban hast shewyd thy powere,   540
Whiche from thy promyssys was foreyn and strangere.
The semyth, lord, honour and preysyng of alle m[e]n,
Whiche with thyn only sone and the holy gost in fere
Lyuyst and regnyst, oo God, now and euere, Amen.'

Not longe aftyr that, whan the ryhtwysnesse   545
Of God on Vrban had thus weniaunce take,
And Cristine delyuerid owt of distresse,
A newe prefect the emperour dede make,

517 What] That Ab   519 wurdys] ful Ar   528 the lord] the Ar
531 wreche] wrehe Ar   534 gun] dyde Ar   535 owr] owr he Ar   536 desert
streyt] desert Ar   to] to the deuyl of Ar   537 this] his Ab   538 Knelyng] Sche
knelyd Ar   she thus] thus Ar   542 men] meen Ab   545 aftyr that] aftyr Ar

Whiche gret lust hadde for to doo wrake
550   On cristene puple in euery plaas
Where euere he ony cowde kecche or take;
And Zyon thys prefectis name was.

And anoon was presentyd hym al the caas
Of Cristine, by the officers of the cyte;
555   And whan he yt redde, with a pale faas,
He astoynyd was of that straunge nouelte.
And anoon he askyd where she myht be,
And they ful redyly hym dede telle
That neythir hid ner fled was she,
560   But in that cyte she stille dede dwelle.

And moreouyr thus in his herte
He thoughte: 'To here goddys to sacrifice
Yf swych tormentys hyre ne myht conuerte,
How shal Y doo, and in what wyse
565   Shal Y moun hyre feryn and agrise,
To myn conclusyoun that she assente?'
And anoon, by vertu of his offise,
He chargyd men forth hyre to presente.

And whan she brough[t] was hym byforn,
570   Thus with fayr speche he hyre gan assayle,
And seyde, 'O damysel, wurthyly born,
And to oftyn, me semyth, dystressyd in gayle,
Y wolde wete what yt the may auayle
To forsakyn the goddys whiche lyuyn ay
575   And of hyre godhede makyn a [m]ayle
And wurshipyn on wyche the helpe ne may. |

f. 143ᵛᵃ   Not so, douhtyr, but aftyr my counsel
Come forth, and to oure goddys sacrifice,
And I thy dignite to the emperour shal tel,
580   And thy byrthe, and in ful hasty wyse

550 puple] men Ar   551 Where euere] Where Ar   ony cowde] coude eny Ar
553 was] was hit Ar   556 straunge nouelte] nouelte Ar   563 Yf swych] swyth Ar
565 moun hyre] hir moun Ar   569 brought] brough Ab   573 the may] may þe
Ar   575 mayle] Ar; ionffayle Ab   576 wyche] that Ar   579 emperour]
comperour Ar   580 And] Off Ar

Thow maryid shal ben aftir oure guyse
To sum c[uri]el of rygh[t] gret dignite.
And so to grete wurshype thou shalt ryse,
As pertenyth to thy berthe and to thy bewte.'

'Cese, iuge, these wurdys,' quoth Cristine, 'to me,   585
For sekyr in veyn ys al thy laboure;
For pleynly Y wyl thou knowe,' quoth she,
'That neythir thou ner thyn emperour
Shal do me forsakyn my creatour,
Crist Ihesu, of heuene the kyng,   590
And doon these ydols godly honoure,
Whiche by mannys hand haue here beyng.'

'Damesel,' quoth he, 'thou art to blame,
Thus at the bygynny[n]g me to rehete,
But Y the shal techyn a newe game,   595
Whiche shal the makyn blood for to swete.'
And with yerdys anoon he hyre bad be bete
Of hys tormentours ful vnpitously,
But not forthan she ne wolde lete
Hym to rebuke thus stedfastly: 600

'O cruel tiraunt, ful of malincoly,
Art thou nat asshamyd with so lytyl peyne
Me to assayle? wenyst thou not that I
Thys and mo assayid haue, yis certeyne?
Thy brothyr Vrban me ne myth constreyne   605
These ydols to wurshype ner to serue.
Tak thys for answere in wurdys pl[e]yne:
Ner thou ne shalt, thogh Y shuld sterue.'

Zyon, agreuyd with this answere,
A vessel of bras, ful hoot brynnynge,   610
Ful of pych, rosyn, oyle and smere,
Withoute let he thedyr dede brynge,
And bad castyn therin this maydyn yinge,

582 curiel] cruel Ab   ryght] rygh Ab   584 pertenyth to] askyth Ar   and to] and
Ar   592 haue here] here Ab   594 bygynnyng] bygynnyg Ab   595 the shal]
shal the Ar   603 that] at Ar   607 pleyne] plyne Ab   608 Y shuld] thou
doo me Ar   611 pych] pyhe Ar

And assyngnyd foure men with stauys myhty
615 Of iryn therin hyre to tourne and swynge,
That she myht deye the more hastely.

Whan Cristyne saw thys vessel stondyng,
To heuene with teris she kyst hyre eye,
And seyde, 'O God, lord of al thyng,
620 Wyth lowly herte to the Y preye,
To thre childryn whiche quengyddyst the leye
Of the flawmyd furneys, be now present
To thyn handmayde, and lete me not deye
Wyth this horrible and cruel torment.'

625 And whan she thus had offryd hyre hertys entent
To God, er the tormentours comyn hyre ner,
To the seyd vessel she frely went,
And leyd hire therin wyth a glad cher;
And in no wyse hurt hyre the feer;
630 For with heuenly dew she enbawmyd was,
So as she had in a ful fressh herber
Among flours leyin and amang grene gras. |

f. 143vb   'Cristine,' quoth Zyon, 'as Y now weel see,
This fer hath the touchyd yet no thyng.
635 Wherfore, aftir the counsel of me,
To oure [im]mortal goddys yiue thankyng,
And with frankencence come make offeryng
To hem, lych as thou knowist the guyse,
Thourgh whoos vertu and specyal werkyng
640 Thou art preseruyd now in this wyse.'

'Syre iuge,' quoth Cristine, 'what hys thy name?'
'My name,' quoth he, 'yf thou lyst to knowe,
Ys Zyon, wych by the trumpet of fame
In many a countre ful wyde ys bloue.'
645 'Thys name,' quoth she, 'ryhtfully I trowe
To the pertenyth, for of blynde ydolys,

Doum and crokyd, whiche to ourethrowe
Yit ys no maystir, a name thys ys.'

Zyon, thys herynge, comaundyd and bad
That anoon hyre heed shuld shauyn be,   650
And br[enny]nge colys thervpon [h]e sprad.
And whan wummen thys seyin of that cyte,
They cryid, and seyde, 'O iuge, thin de[c]re
Ys wrong and wrouht ful vnryhtfully,
For in thys maydyn as myche as ys in the   655
Alle women thou confoundyst vttyrly.'

Whan this was doun, anoon hastyly
To presoun agayn he hyre sent thens;
And on the next morwyn folwyng erly
He hyre chargyd be brouht to hys presens;   660
And thus he expressyd hyre hys sentens:
'Cristine, lete vs now to the temple goo,
And wurshype ther Appollos hy reuerens,
That he the deleuere wyl fro this woo.'

And anoon forthwith thys blyssyd Cristine,   665
Hyre hool trust in God fully puttynge,
And by influence inspiryd of grace dyuine
Wyth the iuge and al the puple folwynge,
Entryd the temple and in the myddys stondynge,
To the hethene puple seyde on this wyse: 670
'Seeth now the treuthe of Goddys werkyng,
And byhold how Y now shal sacrifice.'

And whyl they abydyn to seen the yssu
Of hyre entent, she preyid on this manere:
'O my lyht, Crist! O myn hope, Ihesu!   675
O, of God the only bygotyn entere!
O my blyssyd lord! Here the preyere
Of thyn handmayde, and this ydol lothly

648 maystir] maystry Ar   651 brennynge] brynge Ab   he] be Ab   652 that]
this Ar   653 decre] degre Ab   655 in thys] in Ar   as ys] as Ar   664 That
he] That Ar   669 Entryd] Entryng Ar

Distroye and breke al to poudyr here,
680   By wich manye erryn dampnabylly!'

And whan hyre preyere thus endyd had she,
The ydol fel doun owt of hys place
Al into poudyr, as yche man myght see;
And for feer the iuge eek fel on hys face.
685   And whan he had so leyin a long space,
He roos vp and seyde wyth gret wundryng:
'Cristine, thou hast don gret trespace.
Thy wycchecraftys passyn al oure kunnyng.' |

f. 144ʳᵃ   Whan Cristine herde thus Zyon seyin,
690   She bygan to sy[hi]n ful heuyly,
And with a lowde voys she seyde ageyn:
'O cursyd tiraunt, and the very enemy
Of God in heuene and of alle holy,
Thou seyist that Appollo shuld a god be,
695   By whom manye soulys erryn greuosly.
And yet by mannys hand mad was he.

Swich a god is nouht, as thynkyth me.'
And thanne she lokyd on the puple abowte
And seyde, 'Syrs, byholdyth here and see
700   Youre god to whom ye were wone to lowte.
Lo where he lytth; hys eye ys owte.
But to reysyn hym ye you now dresse;
And yf ye ne moun, withowte dowte,
Knowith that swych godheed ys fonnydnesse.'

705   At the[se] wurdys bothe sage and wyse,
Ful many a paynym conuertyd was,
And bygunne to cryin vpon this wyse:
'O God and lord ouyr euery plaas,
And of Cristine thy seruaunt, graunte vs gras
710   Thyn holy name bothe to loue and drede.

682 owt of] euyn from Ar   684 iuge eek] iuge Ar   690 syhin] syihn Ab
691 And with] And Ar   lowde] grete Ar   692 and the] and Ar   702 hym] hym
up Ar   705 these] the Ab   707 vpon] on Ar

And forgyue vs, lord, this gret trespas
That we to ydols han takyn swych hede.

We were deceyuyd for lak of doctrine,
And so in ydolatrie oure errour was longe,
But now, th[u]rgh helpe of thys blyssyd virgine,   715
The trewe byleue we doon vndyrfonge,
Wych for to kepyn, lord, make vs strong,
And neuere to forsakyn, thogh we shuld deye,
And with goostly ioye and with heuenely song
Thyne holy name euere to glorifie.'   720

And at that tyme conuertyd were ther
Thre thousend paynyms by trewe computacioun.
And whan Zyon this sey, for very feer,
What for Apollo hys goddys desolacyoun,
And what for the puplys sodeyn transmutacyoun,   725
He fel doun and deyid euene sodeynly.
And whanne to Cristine was maad relacyoun,
She thankyd God, seyinge thus deuouhtly:

'Gramercy, lord, wyche art eu[yr] redy
To hem that trustyn in thy goodnesse,   730
Whiche also sheuyst oftyn how myhty
Thow art here enemyis to represse.'
And whanne she this thankyng had maad expresse,
On that was the iugis assessour
To presoun hyre sent of hys cruelnesse,   735
Tyl a newe iuge come from the emperoure.

Whan Cristine was entryd that loth[l]y tour,
She, knelynge, seyde thus: 'O eternally
Regnyng in blysse, fadyr, creatour,
Wyth Ihesu Crist thi sone bygotyn oonly,   740
Wyth whom the holy goost eek egally
Lyuyth and regnyth, and yet ye alle thre,

715 thurgh] thrgh Ab   718 to] it to Ar   729 euyr] euene Ab   733 this]
that Ar   had maad expresse] expresse Ar   737 Whan] And whan Ar   lothly] lothtly
Ab   738 knelynge seyde] knelyd seying Ar   740 thi sone] sone Ab   742 and
yet] yet Ar

In personys distinct substancyally,
Arn but oo god in trinyte. |

Gramercy, lord, wich of thy benygnyte
746   Vouchystsaf thy promys to aco[m]plise,
Wyche thou, lord, madyst onys to me
By an holy aungel in gracyous wyse,
My fadrys counsel whan Y dede despyse,
750   That thre iugis shulde, ful cruelly,
With tormentys assayin me to agrise;
And of alle thou me grauntyddyst the victory.

Gramercy, lord, for now weel troste
Y That the gracyous tyme aprochyth ner,
755   Wych thou wylt me takyn to thy mercy
And brynge me abouyn the sterris cler.
For to iugis ben forth passyd hyr
Within short tyme, as knowyn alle men.
Now, lord, shewe me thy goodly chyr,
760   In blysse eterne where thow regnyst, amen.'

Anoon aftyr that Zyon was forth went
Where Goddys ryhtwysnesse hym wold han,
From the emperour anoon was sent
A newe iuge to Tyre, clepyd Iulian,
765   A paynym eek and a ful cruel man,
Whoos ioye and lust [was] euere newe,
Aftyr the wil of hys fadyr Sathan,
Crist and cristene for to pursue.

Vpon wiche he was ful inquisityf
770   Of iugys actys whiche were hym byfore,
And anoon presentyd was hym the lyf
O[f] blyssyd Cristine and of al hyre lore,
And how thogh two iugis haddyn yt sw[o]re,

---

746 acomplise] aconplise Ab   747 lord madyst] madyst lord Ar   751 tormen-
tys] torment Ar   754 the gracyous] the Ar   tyme] tyme lord Ar   aprochyth]
aprochyde Ar   756 brynge me] brynge Ar   761 was forth] furth was
Ar   762 han] haue Ar   766 was] om. Ab   768 cristene] Cristyne Ar
771 presentyd was] was presentyd Ar   772 Of] O Ab   773 swore] swere Ab

She ne myht be brouht from hyre entent.
And anoon Iulian, withowtyn more,   775
For hyre to presoun hys officers sent.

And whanne to hys presence she was brouht:
'By thy wycchecraffth many wundrys,' quoth he,
'Thou hast don; but yet dowte yt nowt
Thou shalt in no wyse ouyrcomyn me.   780
Wherfore do sacrifice, Y counsele the,
To oure [im]mortal goddys, or Y shal applie
To the swych peynys wych ferful shuld be
To thy Ihesu, Iosephs sone and Marye.'

'Hold thy pees,' ful lowde Cristine gan crye,   785
'O tiraunt, cruel wythowte discrecyoun,
And lych a man fallyn into frenesye!
This iniurye no wyhs [myn] eerys here moun,
That thou, as a dogge withowte resoun
Berkyng, blaspheme that name holy,   790
In whoos honour euery kne bowith doun
Of heuene and erthe and of helle lothly.'

Whan Iulian thys herd he wex angry,
And in angyr anoon comaundyd he
In an ouene thre dayis cont[inu]ely,   795
Wich fersly brent, hyre shet to be.
But Cristine, trustynge in the trinyte,
With tokene of the cros hyre forheed markynge,
Entryd the fornes, where whan was [she],
God she dede preyse deuouhtly syngynge. | 800

And whan the soudyours withowte stondynge   f. 144ᵛᵃ
Herdyn hyre withinne thus God magnyfye,
To Iulyan they runne, euene thus seynge:
'We the byseche, sire, ful humbyllye,
Wratthe the not with vs, for whan we aspye   805

774 myht be] myght Ar   777 to hys presence she was] she was to hys presens Ar
782 immortal] mortal Ab   783 swych] wych Ar   784 Iosephs sone] born of
Ioseph Ar   787 into] into a Ar   788 myn] mennys Ab   792 and erthe] &
of erth Ar   794 in] in his Ar   795 continuely] contunely Ar   798 of the]
of Ar   799 she] here Ab

Dede Cristine, in the fornys, whom shet had we,
Gret God of heuene preysyn and glorifie,
Ful faste for feer wee away dede flee.'

Iulyan, astoynyd of this newe caas,
810 Comaundyd the ouene vndo to be.
Wherin Cristine, as shynyng was
As ys the sunne in hys degre;
And anoon al harmles owt cam she,
Preseruyd by the grace of Goddys vertu,
815 And with ympnys and songys ful of melode
She extollyd and preysyd hyre lord Ihesu.

And with that Iulyan hyre dede comaunde
Toforn hys bench to be maad present,
And of hyre he askyst this demaunde:
820 'Why preuaylyst thou? And by what enchauntement
Ys yt that thou art not al tobrent?
Sey me anoon, or ellys pleynly
Thy tendyr body shal ben al torent
With sundry peynys and dyuers tormentry.'

825 Yet efthsonys quoth Cristine, 'Hold thy pees,
O vnhappy tirant, voyd of al goodnesse.
To aske swyche demaundys sumtyme cees,
Wich [thou] owyst to knowe for thy cursydnesse.
But by thy thretys and thy malicyousnesse
830 Y set not, for as feythfully as Y kan
In Ihesu Y truste and in hys mercyfulnesse,
And drede not to me what do ony man.'

Wyth this answere wood was Iulyan,
And clepyd to hym on whiche had kunnynge
835 Serpentys to charme, and as he wold han
Hys lordshype hym chargyd withowte lettynge
To hornyd serpentys forth for to brynge,
And to snakys withal, and whan they com were:

'Y trowe,' quoth he, 'that al thyn enchauntynge
Shal not letten these serpentys the for to dere.'   840

'Thow art euere alyche newe for to lere,'
Quoth Cristine, 'O fonne, as in thys degre.
Wenyst thou my God lych thy goddys were
Of nounpouwer? Nay, pleynly,' quoth she,
'For he that in alle my tornementys ha[th] be   845
My helpere, and me neuere dede forsake,
May, yf he wyl, now defendyn me,
And of alle thyn serpentys me victryhs make.'

And with that wurd, to doon hyre wrake,
Vpon hyre heed the serpentys two   850
He dede doo caste and eythir snake,
Wenyng that they hyre harm shuld do;
But as sone as the serpentys comyn hyre to,
They claspyd hyre helys and the dust dede lykke
Therfro, and on hyre pappys they heng also   855
Lyk smale infauntys wych kun no wykke. |

Thys syhte with sorwe the herte dede prykke   f. 144ᵛᵇ
Of Iulyan, and anoon onto the incantatour:
'Thy crafth,' quoth he, 'ys not worth a flykke!
Y trowe thou art [turnyd] to thys wicchis errour.'   860
And with that the ma[n] dede al his laboure
To stiryn hem with wurdys of wycchecraft
To haue stungyn hyre, but that same our
They hyre lefthe and hym hys lyf byrafth.

And whan the puple whiche ther present was   865
Sey the inca[n]tatour deed on thys manere,
They were so aferd of the veniable caas
That aftyr that our for no mystere
Durst noon of hem comyn Cristine nere,
Ner touche neythir serpent ner snake.   870

840 for to] to Ar   845 hath] haht Ab   847 yf] and Ar   855 on
hyre pappys they heng] heng upon hir pappys Ar   859 quoth he] he seyde Ar
860 turnyd] turmentyd Ab   861 man] mars Ab Ar   866 incantatour] incatatour
Ab   867 the]þis Ar   869 noon] oon Ar

Cristine, this seyng, to heuene hyr cher
Kest vp, and thus hyre preyere dede make:

'O lord God, whiche in heuene doost dwelle,
And sentyst thy sone oure kynde to tan,
875 And clepedyst Lazer ageyn from helle,
Here me, thyn handmayde, wich as Y can
The lowly byseche for thys deed maan.
Quyke hym, Lord, ageyn, throgh thy mercy,
That alle men yt seyng that resoun han
880 May glorifie thy name endlesly.'

Whan she thus had endyd hyre prayere,
Thys voys from heuene cam doun opynly:
'O blyssyd Cristine, my douhtyr dere,
Truste in me, goode douhtyr stedefastly,
885 And do forth as thou hast perseuerauntly.
For this Y wyl to alle men knowe be,
With the Y am in alle thy werkys sothly,
And what thou askyst ys grantyd to the.'

And sodeynly the erthe maad a roryng,
890 And blyssyd Cristine, bothe sage and wyhs,
Crouchyd the body, thus loude crying:
'In the name of Ihesu Crist, man, ryhs!'
And anoon he ros, and in ful humbyl wyse
Byforn Cristine he fel, and thus gan seyn:
895 'Euere thankyng to God, most of pryhs,
Whiche from deeth to lyf me hath reysed ageyn.'

Iulyan thys seyng was sory, certeyn,
And to hyre thus seyde, with cher gyr[n]yng:
'Now alle thy wycchecraftys syth here pleyn
900 Thou shewyd hast, to oure goddys withowte lettyng
Returne Y counsele, hem louly thankyng

877 thys] thi Ar   878 Lord ageyn] ageyne lord Ar   879 men yt] men Ar
that] wych Ar   880 glorifie thy name] thy name glorify now & Ar   881 Whan]
And whan Ar   888 what thou] what Ab   895 God] thi God Ar   896 from]
me from Ar   lyf me] lyf Ar   898 gyrnyng] gyryng Ar   899 syth] syth thou Ar
900 Thou shewyd hast] Hast shewyd Ar   901 Y counsele] ageyn Ar

That they so longe and benyngnely
Han the suffryd,' to wyche talkynge
Cristine thus answerde ful redyly:

'O wytles man and withowtyn dreed, treuly,   905
Of God, and ee[k] withowtyn vndyrstondyng,
In thy soule blyndyd ful dolorously,
Sey not thyn eyne here brod lokyng
My Goddys werkys, the heuenely kyng,
And of hys blyssyd sone, Crist Ihesu,   910
Whiche he hath wrouht, alle men seyng,
Thorgh the myht and the grace of ys vertu?'

Aftyr þis Iulyan in his malyncoly
Commaundyd hir brystis of to kyt be,
And anoon it was doon ful cruelly,   915
Wythowtyn eþir mercy or pyte.
'O straungere from treuth, Iulyan,' quod she,
'Syth þou my pappys aweye doost rase,
In tokyn of clennes of uirginite,
Lo, mylk for blood þereout doth pase.'   920

And lokyng to heuene-ward she seyd þus:
'Wyth al myne hert, lord, gramercy to þe,
Kyng of al werdys, Cryst Ihesus,
þat þou vouchysdsafe euery lettyng from me
Of my body awey kut for to be.   925
Now knou I well, þrogh þi proteccyoun,
That I redye am to end my mortalyte,
And þe crown to take of incorrupcyoun.'

Whan she had endyd þus hir vrysoun,
Iulyane wyth angyr & malyncoly blent,   930
Comaundyde wythoutyn ony delacyoun
Eftsonys to presoun hir to be sent;
Where she, knelyng wyth ane holy entent,
Al þat nyht aftyr, ful deuoutly

935 Magnifyid our Lord God omnipotent,
Hys holy name blyssyng contynuelly.

And on þe next morou he bad eerly
Hir to be broght onto his presence.
And whan she com was, he hir askyd why
940 She nold assentyn to her pryncys sentence.
'Com furth,' quod he, '& now offre encence
To our goddys, or ellys wythout deley
I shal þe sleen; lat hym mak defence,
Thy god whom þou seruyst, yf þat he may.'

945 'Knowst þou not, wreche,' quod Cristyne,
'þat goddys pacience þe to penytence
Abydyth lenger & gladly wold inclyne?
But þou þrough þi frowerd negligence
Alwey mysvsyst his blyssyd pacience.
950 Of cursyd custum plounchyd in þe myre,
And makying of purpose wylful resystence
Tresoryst þe veniaunce into þe day of yre.'

Iulyan, angryd wyth þat Cristine seyde,
Commaundyd hir tong out kut to be;
955 But Cristyne þus fyrst deuoutly preyde:
'Lord Ihesu Cryst, wych from my natiuite
Hast me kept & neuer forsoke me,
Kepe me now, & þin handmayd here,
And grant me my batayl to endyn in þe,
960 For of my reste þe tyme drauyht nere.'

And anoon in þe eyr men dyde here
A voys þus seying: 'For þou hast for me
Suffryd mych peyn, my doughtir dere,
And euer bene pacient in al aduersite,
965 Therfoor þe gatys of heuyn to þe
Bene now wyd opynnyd; come in meryly,
Ant rest in pese & tranquillyte,
And resseyue þe croun of blys endlesly!'

But notwythstondyng þis voys heuenly,
Iulyan bad hem doon his commaundement,   970
And anoon hir tong þei rent out cruelly.
And whyl sche was in þis torment,
Of hir tong a pese wyth a mychty entent
She spyt in his face, & hys oon eye
So sore it smet þat þe sycht was blent,   975
And wyth þat to hym she þus dyde seye:

'Iulyan, wrecche, þi desyre was vnkouth
To etyn ane instrument of my body,
Wherfor my tounge out of my mouth
Thow hast do drawe dyspytuosly,   980
Wych euyr was wone to prey[s]e besely
Goddys hye name, whyl þat it myht.
Yet haue I spe[c]he, & þou wurthyly
Off þine oon eye hast lost þe sycht.'

Iulyan þis heryng, his hunters dyde charge   985
Cristyne to sleyn & þat hastyly.
And anoon on hir syde wyth wondys large
They hir dide smyte ful vnpetously.
Than Cristyn þus preyid: 'þrough þi mercy,
Lord, tak my spyrith onto þi grace.'   990
And wyth þat word, out of hir body
To heuyn blys hir soul dede pace,

And anoon aungelys in þat same plase
Gunne Iulyane tormentyn, in sundry degre,
Wyth so grete peynys þat he cryed, 'Allase!   995
What shal I doo now? Se I wel,' quod he,
'That for Crystyne þis commyth to me,
Whom I haue sleyn ful vnpetously.'
And whan he þus long tormentyd had be,
He sterf & went to endles torment[r]y.   1000

And whan Iulyane was þus passyd & goon,
Oon wych was of Cristyns kynrede,

þat heryng, þiddyr came anoon,
Wych God dide bothyn loue & drede;
1005   And for he hopyd to haue heuene to mede,
In Appolloos temple he made a memory,
Whedyr Crystynys relikys he dyde lede
And þere hem beryid ful solem[n]ely.

Examynyd was þis blyssyd Cristyne,
1010   The tyme of þe emperour Dyoclecyan,
Under thre iugys, lych as determyne
The legend off hir ful wel can.
Fyrst by hir own fadyr, clepyd Vrban,
Aftyr be Zyon, a cruel tormentour,
1015   But last & werst was þis Iulyan,
Vndyr whom she endyd al hir labour.

Thus fourtene yere was hir martyrdame
Contunyd vnder þeis iugys thre,
Wych wyth hir constaunce she ouyrcame,
1020   In Tyre, þat tyme a grete cyte,
Where fynally also martyrd was she,
As in hir lyfe who wyl redyn may,
þe nynt kalend of august, as fynd we,
Wych þat tyme fel on a thursday.

1025   Now I the besech, O blyssyd Cristyne,
Wych regnyst wyth Cryst in his heuenly tour,
As it is wele worthi, mercyful inclyne
Thy petous erys onto the translatour
Wych þi legend compylyd, not wythout labour,
1030   In Englyssh tunge; and help, lady, þat he
Of his mortale lyf in þe last our
Of his goos[t]ly enmyse may victour be.

Graunt also, lady, al þo þat þe
Worshypyn & seruyn of syngulere affeccioun,
1035   Ere þan þai deyin repentaunth to be,
And of al here synnys to make confessyoun

1008 solemnely] solemmly Ar   1029 Wych] Wyth Ar   1032 goostly] goosly
Ar

Wyth ful purpose of deu satisfaccioun,
Ere þei depart from þis outlaurye,
And aftyr wyth þe in þe heuenly relygyoun
Eternally god to preyse & magnyfye.   1040
Amen. mercy Ihesu & gramercy. |

[120. NAZARIUS]

Here bygynnyth the prologe of Seynt Nazaryius lyf   f. 145ra

Nazarius ys as meche in si[g]nificac[i]oun as Nazarenus, the whiche
wurd Nazarenus hath fyue sundry interpretacions, as 'haluyd', 'clene',
'desseueryd', 'florysshyng' or 'kepyng'. In a man ben foundyn fyue thyngis to wyche moun ben appliyd these fyue interpretaciounys, as though,   5
affeccioun, entent, werkyng and spekynge. Mannys though shulde ben
hooly, the affeccioun pure and c[l]ene, the entent rygh and nat wrong, the
werkyng ryghful and the speche moderat and modest. 'Alle the[se]', quod
Ianuence, 'were foundyn in blyssid Nazarie, wherfore conueniently he may
be clepyd Nazarenus.'   10

Celsus ys as meche to seyne as 'hy' or 'leftyd vp', and that conueniently
for he lifftid hymselff hye abouyn hymself whan, with the [h]y vertu of
hys soule, he ouercam the youthe of his body. These twynys lyf and passioun, as yt ys seyd, fond Seynt Ambrose in the libelle of Seynt Geruasye
and Seynt Prothasie. But in summe bokys yt ys foundyn that a philosophir 15
deuouht to Seynt Nazarie wrot hys lyf, the whyche Ceracius that buryid
the seyntis bodyis leyde in here graue at here heed. *Hec Ianuencys.*

The lyf of Nazarie & a child clepyd Celsus.

Nazarius was the sone of a rygh wurthi man whos name was Affricanus,
a iew of sect, but hys mothir hyght Perpetua, oon of the most wurthi wum-   20
men of the Romanys and therwith a perfyht cristene wumman, baptisyd of
Seynt Petyr the apostil. T[his Naza]rius, seying the gret variaunce that was
betwyx hy[m] and his modyr in obseruaunce of religioun, for his modyr
kept the laue of baptem and his fadyr the lawe of the sabat, he stood in
maner of a dowte to whethiris maner of lyuyng he myht drawyn, and spe-   25
cially for as meche as ych of hem was bysy to stiryn to here opinyoun. But
at the laste he was determynyd, by the stiring of Goddys grace, to folwyn

---

2 significacioun] singnificacoun   7 clene] chene   8 these] the   12 hy]
by   22 This Nazarius] *text missing owing to a removed initial on the verso of the leaf*
23 hym] *text missing owing to a removed initial on the verso of the leaf*   27 he was] he

hys modrys steppis. Wherfore he took the holy baptem of blyssyd Line,
Seynt Petris disiple, whiche aftyrward was pope. And whan his fadyr saw

30 this, he bysiyd hym to peruertyn hym from his holy purpos, shewyng hym
and declaryng onto hym alle maner of peynys with whiche Cristene men
were turmentyd and brouht adawe; but yt auaylyd not. For constantly and
stedfastly he knowlechid and prechyd Crist. Wherfore hys fadyr and his
modyr, dredyng that yf he were aspyud he shulde be slayn, preyid hym

35 that he wolde goon owt of Rome. At whos request and preyere he wente
owt of Rome and took with hym of hys fadrys tresour seuene somers ladyn,
the whiche he delt abowtyn to pore men by the cytes of Ytayle as he wente.

The tente yer of hys gooyng owt fro Rome he cam to Plesaunce and fro
thens he wente to Melan. And there he fond in prisoun the blyssyd and

40 holy men Geruasye and Prothasie, whoom he visityd and counfortyd and

f. 145rb with his holy admonicyouns exhortyd | to pacyens and to perseueraunce.
Whan this was aspiyd, anoon he was takyn and brouht byfore the meyr
and, for he constauntly confessyd Crist, was betyn with battys and aftyr
dryuyn owt of the cyte. And as he wandryd abowtyn fro place to place,

45 his modyr, whiche was deed, apperid onto hym and confortyd hym and
amonestyd hym for to goon into Fraunce. Whedyr whan he cam he turnyd
into a cyte clepyd Gemellus, where, whanne he had gadryd meche peple to
Cristis feyth, a wurthy wumman of the cyte offryd onto hym here sone, a
comely chyld whoos name was Cel[s]us, preying hym that he wolde bapti-

50 syn hym and ledyn hym forth with hym. And whan the prefect of Fraunce
herd thys, he took Nazarye and dede byndyn hys handys byhyndyn hym
and put a gret cheyne aboutyn his nekke and shet hym in a deep derk prisoun, and Celsion ther chyld with hym, purposyng in the nexte morwe to
assaylyn hem alle with newe tormentys and with more cruel. This percey-

55 wyng, hys wif seynt hym word that the doom was [un]rihful wich decernyd
to turmentyn innocentys and also presumpteuous that chargyd to vengyn
the wrongys of goddys, the wyche byn myghty inow to wengyn here own
wrongys. At whiche amenicyoun the prefect meuyd delyueryd Nazarie and
his chyld owt of prisoun and yaf hem liberte to goo whethir they woldyn,

60 be so they prechyd no more there. For that he algatys amonestyd hem and
vntyrly interdytid hem that they shulde not don yt.

And so fro thens they wentyn to the cyte of Treuers, where Nazarius
prechid and conuertyd meche peple to Cristis feyth and byldyd there a
cherche. And whanne Cornelius the viker of that cuntre herd this, anoon

65 he sent to the Emperour Nero tydyngis therof, and sente an hundryd sowdyours for to bryngyn hem to hym, the which foundyn hem bysyde the

49 Celsus] Cellus   53 with hym] with   55 unrihful] wrihful

oretorye whiche Nazarius had maad. Whoos handys anoon they boundyn
byhyndyn hym and seydyn that Nero had sent hem for hym. 'Wyche as
youre kyng ys', quoth he, 'swych ys hys meene. Why ne had ye comyn
honestly to me and seyd "the Emperour Nero sendyth for the", and at the 70
ferst wurd I shuld haue comyn?' But not forthan they leddyn hem forth
with hem boundyn, and Celsum hys chyld, wepyng for his maister, they
betyn and dryuyn hym forth afftyr hym.

And whan Nero saw hem he chargyd hem to be shet in prisoun tyl he
had bethough hym with what maner of torment he myht makyn an ende 75
of hem. In this menewhile Nero sent hys huntys to huntyn aftyr wylde
bestis, and sodeynly a gret multitude of hem brast into Neroes gardyn, the
whiche rentyn and slouyn manye of hys men in so meche that Nero hymself was affesyd and fleed. And in hys flyht he hurt hys foot so that vnnethis
with gret difficulte he mygh comyn into hys paleys. And manye dayis aftyr 80
he languryd on the wounde of hys foot. But at the laste, whan he remembryd hym Nazarie and his child, he trowyd verily that hys goddys hadde be
wroth with hym for he let hym lyuyn so longe. Wherfore he sent anoon hys
sowdyourys and bad hem that they shulde weel betyn bothe Nazarie and
the chyld, and aftyr that bryngyn hym to hys presence. And whan Nero 85
sau the face of Nazarie | shynyng and brygh as the sunne, wenyng to haue f. 145ᵛᵃ
byn ylludyd with fantastical deceyt, he seyde to hym on this wyse: 'Put
away, Nazarie, al this wicchecrafth and do sacrifyce onto owre goddys, yf
thou wilt lyuyn!' And forthwith he chargid hem to be led onto the temple,
where whan they comyn Nazarius preyid alle men to gon out of the temple. 90
Whiche don, aftyr a short preyere of Nazarie, alle the ydols fel dooun, and
the temple eek, and wern al tobrost. And whan Nero herd this, he chargyd
that Nazarius and his chyld shulde byn throwyn doun heedlyngis into the
see. And yf they achapid, that they shuld byn brent whoosoeuere myght
kicchyn hym. 95

And anoon aftir the degre thei were leyd fer vp in tho the see and throwyn owt heedly[n]gis. The whiche as sone as was doon, a gret and greuous
tempest grew abowte the ship that led hem. But where that Nazarie and his
child wern yt was fayr and peseble watyr, and nothyng troblous wedyr. And
whan the shypman seyin this, and dredyng for to perisshyn, they were sory 100
and repentyd hem of the iniurye and wrong don onto the seynt. Wherevpon whan they seyin Nazarie with hys chyld goyng vpon the see pesible
and queyt comyng onto the shyp, and throug hys preyere the troublous
tempest sey[c]in, they byleuyd and were baptisid, and aftir that broughtyn
hem onto the cyte of Gene. 105

97 heedlyngis] heedlygis   104 seycin] seyin

W[h]ere whan they had longe prechid, at the laste they returnyd to the cyte of Melan where the[y] had lefth the Seynt Geruasie and Prothasie. But whan Anelinus the prefat herd this, the child Celsus abydyun in a wurshipfyl matronys hous, he exilid and banysshid Nazarie, the whiche
110 returnyd ageyn to Rome and fonde there hys fadyr, an hold man, conuertyd to Crist. Whoom whan he had askyd by what mene or occacyoun he was conuertyd, he answerde ageyn and seyde that Seynt Petir apperid onto hym and amonestyd hym that he shuld foluyn hys wyf and hys sone whiche were goon forth byforn hym.

115 And aftyr this Nazarie was conpellyd through gret wrong and iniurye by the bysshopys of the templys to returnyn to Melan, fro whens they were banysshid. Whedir he cam he was presentyd with Celsus his child to the meyr of the cyte, at whoos comaundement and dom they were led owt at the gate wiche ys clepyd Romana and there hefdeed. Whiche on the
120 nexte nyght foluynge apperyddyn to a cristene man clepyd Cerianus, and bodyn hym that he shuld takyn here bodyis and buryin hem in a deep pyt in here hous for dred of Nero. Whom seyd Cireanus preyid louly that they wolde curyn and makyn hool hys douhtyr whiche lay bedlawre; and so they dedyn. Whiche doon, he dyligently buryid here bodyis lych as they bodyn,
125 the whiche bodyis long tyme aftyr Seynt Ambrose fond by reuelacioun. Of whom Nazarie he fond lying hool and incorupt, with heer and breed and alle othir thyngis as thow he had hem buryid the same day, and therwith he saueryd with the redolens of ma[r]uelous swetnesse. Whoom he translatyd thens and buryid solempnely in the apostelys cherche, but Celsum he let
130 stylle ther [he] lay byforn. The passioun of these martirs was aboute the yers of oure lord fyfty and seuene. *Deo gracias.* |

[121. FELIX POPE]

f. 145vb The lyf of Felys pope

Whanne Constancius, the sone of gret Constantyn, was emperour and was infect with Arri[a]ns hereseye, oon clepyd Liberius was pope of Rome. Whom, for he wold not consentyin to the sey[d] Arrians hereseie, the
5 emperour banysshid and exilyd owt of Rome, where he abood thre yer. In whiche menewhyle al the charge of Rome chees concordly oon clepyd Felix to ben pope in stede of Liberye. The whiche blyssyd pope gadryd a counsel, and in presence of eyghte and fourty b[i]sshopys he dampnyd

| 106 where] were | 107 they] the | 128 maruelous] mauelous | 130 he] yd |
| 3 Arrians] Arrins | 4 seyd] seynt | 8 bisshopys] bosshopys | |

the emperour [Constancius] an Arryan and an heretyk, with two prestis
whiche wern the emperouris fautours and counselouris in the seyd here-   10
sie. For whiche cause the emperour Constancius hauyng indignacioun kest
owt Felix from hys dignite and reuokyd and callyd ageyn Liberie, whom he
had banysschyd byforn, promittyng hym that he shulde ben restorid ageyn
to the papal dignite vpon a condicioun that he wolde comoun with hym
and with swyche othere as Felix had condempnyd. Liberius, heryng this   15
promissid of the emperour, and atteidiat and wer[y] of his exil, acceptyd
the condicioun and consentyd to the Arryans herysie. By the occacioun
whereof greu a gret persecucioun of the clergie, in so myche that manye
prestis and clerkys, the pope not defendyng hem, wern slayn withinne holy
cherche. And not longe aftyr blyssyd Felix, whiche was deposyd from the   20
papal dignite and dwellyd in a maner of his withowte Rome, was brouht
thens and hefded in Rome, aboute ye yers of oure lord thre hundryd and
fourty & cetera.

[122. SIMPLICIUS AND FAUSTINUS]

Simplicij, Faustini et Beatricius

[T]he tyme of Dioclicyan and Maximian the emperours, two wurshipful brethryn, Simplicius and Faustinus, in the cyte of Rome, aftir gret and
gracious turmentys, wern hefdyd and here bodys throwyn into Tyber ouyr
the brygge clepyd *Pons Lapidius*. Whoos sustyr aftyrward by reuelacioun,   5
Biatrice by name, with helpe of two holy prestis, Crispus & Iohannes,
gadrid hem vp and buryid hem in a place clepyd *Sextum Philippi* in the
weye Portuence, the fourte kalende of August.

Aftyr whiche tyme, wyl the seyd Beatrix with blyssyd Lucyne was in
hyre preyere, oon clepid Lucrecius, the prefectis wykyr, desirynge to han   10
here possessioun, mad hyre to be takyn and to be brough onto a temple and
chargyd to don sacrifice. And for she wolde not she was put in prisoun, and
there priuyly by [n]ygh stranglyd of Lucrecys seruantys, whoom blyssyd
Lucina buryid bisydyn tho holy martyrs, here brethyrn. Whan Lucrecius
thus had mordryd thys holy madyn, he anoon entrid into hyre place and   15
took possessioun therof and maad a gret feste therin onto hys frendys.
And as they setyn in mete etynge and drynkynge, meryly and blasphe-
mynge cristene feyth and byleu[e] and scorny[n]ge holy martyrs, a soukyng
chyld lying wrappy[d] in a wummannys lappe whiche sat there wyth hem

9 Constancius] Constancicius   16 wery] weru   2 The] he   13 nygh]
mygh   18 byleue] byleuyd   scornynge] scornyge   19 wrappyd] wrappyng

20   at the table, sodeynly bygan to c[r]yin wit[h] a loude [vo]ys and seyde on
f. 146ʳᵃ this wyse: 'Lucres, lystene what I seye! Thou | hast slayn and thou hast
     entryd wrongfully. Wherfore thou art youyn by iugement and doom into
     the handys of thyn en[e]my'. Wyche w[ur]d, Lucrecius anoon, tremelyng
     and quakynge, was arrept and takyn with a deuyle and vexid [with] hym
25   ful thre owris, miserabyly and wrecchydly deyid in the same feste. And
     whanne they wyche were there present sey thys, anoon they were conuer-
     tyd to Cristis feyth and to oldyn forth to alle wyche wolde heryn yt how
     blyssyd Beatricis deth was vengyd in the feste. The passioun of this blys-
     syd Beatrice and hyre brethryn was doon abowte the yeris of oure lord two
30   hundryd eyghte and seuene & cetera. *Deo Gracias.*

[123. MARTHA]

The lyf of Seynt Martha Cristys hostesse.

     Martha, the nobyl and wurthy ostesse of Crist, linyally descendynge of
     the blood royal, was douthtyr of Cirus and Euchary, and sustir to Marie
     Maudelyn and Lazar, whoom foure dayis deed Crist callid ageyn to lyff
5   owt of hys grace. Hyre fadyr Cyrus was duc of manye of the marchis of
     Syree and of the see cost, aftyr woos deth Martha and hyre sustyr posse-
     did by hyre modrys ryht the enheritaunce of thre grete lordshypys, as the
     castel clepyd Magdalun, eythir Bethanye, and a part of the cyte of Ierusa-
     lem. This Martha had neuer noon husbond, as ferforth as we kun redyn,
10   but beynge stylle a maydyn was oftyn Cristis ostesse and herberour, and
     diligently and deuouhtly mynistrid onto hym and seruyd hym, and wolde
     that hyre sustir Marie shulde haue doon the same. For, as hyre semyd, to
     seruyn so wurthy a gest al the word suffesyd not.
         Aftyr the ascencyoun of Crist, whan dispercyoun was maad of hys dys-
15   siplys into diuers plagis of the wor[l]d, this Martha, with hyre sustir and
     hyre brothir and blyssyd Maximian and many othere, were put in takylles
     and a stereles shyp for to han byn perysshd. But through the myghty hand
     of God they come saf and sure to Marcile, and fro thens to the terrytorye
     of Aquence, where, aftyr that hyre sustyr Marye was goon to wyldyrnesse,
20   she abood stylle and conuertyd to the feyth myche peple by hyre doctrine
     and techynge. For she was ful facunde and ful eloquent in spekynge and
     prechynge, and ful exempler in al hyre conuersacioun and lyuyng, and

ful myghty in wundris and miraclis werkynge, amonge whiche manye this
was oon.

Ther was that tyme vpon the flood clepyd Rodanus, in a wode bytwix 25
Relaces and Auenyoun, a dragoun, ha[lf] beste and half fysshe, grettere
thanne an ox and lengere than an hors, whoos teeth wern sharp as a swerd.
This dragoun was comyn doun from Galicia in Asia, gendryd of a watyr
serpent clepyd Leuiathan, and of a beste cruel gendryd in that cuntre clepyd Onachus. This forseyd dragoun throwyth owt hys tunge byhyndyn at 30
hem that chasyn hym as far space as a plowe may eryn on a day, and that
comyth as myhtyly owt as a darte, and al that yt touchyth yt brynyth as
eny feir. Tho this monstruous dragoun, at the request and preyere of the
peple, wente this blissyd maydyn Martha, and fond hym in a wode fedynge
hym on a deed man. And | whan she cam at hym, she kyst vpon hym holy f. 146ʳᵇ
water and shewyd hym a tokne of the cros, and anoon he stood as stylle as a 36
sheep whyl she bond hym with hyre own gyrdyl. And forthwith the peple
fyl vpon hym and with stonys and speris madyn an ende of hym. This dragoun was clepid of the peple of that lond Terrascinus. In remembraunce
whereof that place ys now clepyd Terrascinus, wiche byforn clepyd was 40
Nerluc, that ys to seyne the blak place, in as miche as there were woodys,
the whiche with the thyknesse of here braunchis and bowys madyn swych
vmbris and shaduys that the seyl semyd blak.

In wyche place blyssyd Martha, by licence of hyre maister Maximian,
fro thensforward abood a[nd] dwellyd and tendyd fully to deuocioun and 45
preyd. Wherfore aftyrward she gadryd to hyre a gret co[n]uent of susterys
and a gret cherche maad in wurshipe of oure lady. She leuyd a ful sharp and
streyt lyf, for fysshe, eryn and shese, and al maner fatnesse eschewynge;
she was content with oo meel on the day. And hundryd sythis on the day,
and as many syths on the nyght, she knelyd to God in preyere.   50

Vpon a tyme whan blyssyd Martha prechyd bytwix the flood Rodanus
and the cyte of Auynyoun, a yong man was on the tothir syde of the flood
whiche desiry[n] to heryn hyre prechyng. And for as meche as he wantyd
feriage he put of hys clothis for to han swummyn ouer, and sodeynly the
[m]yght of the strem turnyd hym vpsodoun and chekyd hym. Whoos body 55
vnnethe foundyn the secunde day was brough and presentyd byforn hyre
feet for that entent that she shulde rysyn hym vp agayn from deth to lyff.
And she, hauyng conpassioun on hym, fyl doun plat vpon the ground in
the forme of a cros and maad hyre preyere on this wyse: 'Adonay Lord
Ihesu Crist, my derwurthy ost, whiche onys reysyddyst from deth to lyf 60

26 half] hafl   45 and] a   46 conuent] couent   53 desiryn] desiryng
55 myght] nyght

my wylbelouyd brothir Lazar whan he had leyin foure dayis ded in hys
gra[u]e! Byhold the feyth of the peple stondynge here aboute and ryse vp
thy yung man ageyn, as thou dedyst hym!' Wiche seyid, she ros and pullyd
hym vp by the hand and he roos vp quyk and byleuyd in Crist and was
65 baptizid.

Eusebius, in the fyfte book *De Ecclesiastica Historia*, tellyth that the
wumman whiche was delyueryd from the blody emerowdys maad in hyre
cowrt in an herbyr an image lych to Crist, wy[t]he the garnement and the
hem lych as she had seyin yt and f[eel]d yt, and dede therto gret reuerence
70 and wurshepe, and a[non] the herbys whiche grewyn vndyr the image and
whern byforn of no valu ner of no vertu, as sone as thoo towchyd the hem
of this images garnementys, they tok swych vertu therby that alle maner
syknesses were curyd and maad hool therwith. Seynt Ambrose seyth that
this wumman was Martha. Seynt Ierom also tellyth, and yt ys put in *Histo-*
75 *ria Tripartita*, that Iulianus Apostata took awey that image and set there hys
statue, the wheche sone aftyr with a thundyr clap was smet al to powdir.

Thys nobyl hostesse of God, whiche oftyn tyme had herberwyd hym
hyre in erth[e], hadde knowelache by reuelacioun whanne she shulde ben
herberwyd with hym in heuene, and al the hol yer byforn she labouryd
f. 146va in the feuers. And eyghte dayis byforn hyre own | passage she herde the
81 armonyous concent of aungels leding vp hyre susteris soule onto the blysse
of heuene. And anoon she clepyd togedyr al the co[n]uent and bretheryn
and susteryn and seyde to hem on thys wyse: 'O ye my owyn f[e]las, sustryn
and brethyrn, I beseche yow hertely beth glad and mery with me! For now
85 I here how gladly and how myryly aungels ledyn myn sustrys soule abouyn
for the sterryd firmament into the ioyis of celestial paradis. O most fayr
and myn wylbelouyd sustyr, farwyl! For thou shalt euere lyuyn with my
maystir and myn oost in the ioye whiche ys perpetual and intermynable'.

And forthwith, knowynge in spirit that hyre obit day was also ny, she
90 amonestyd hyre felashepe that they shuldyn wycchyn abowtyn hyre with
candel-lyht tyl the tyme of hyre passage were complet and performyd.
But the nyght byforn hyre passage aboute mydnyht, alle hyre keperys beyinge aslepe, sodeynly ther cam a gret wynde and blew owt and quenchyd
alle the candelys. Wherfore she, dredyng that there was gret multitude of
95 wykkyd spiritis, bygan anoon to preyin on thys wyse: 'My lord God and
my derewurthy oost, loo how myn enmys byn gadryd togedyr hyre ageyns
me, shewynge wrytyn alle the euyl dedys whiche I haue doon in al myn
lyf! Wherfore, good lord, I besheche the, be not thou fer me but intende,

mercyful lord, for to helpyn me!' Whiche preyere entendyd, she saw hyre
sustyr comyn with a brond of fer in hyre hand, wherwith she lyht ageyn the 100
candelys whiche wern blowyn owt. And forthwith, whil yich of hem gret
othir by here propyr name, sodeynly cam [Cri]st hymself seyinge thus:
'Come, my weel-belouyd hostesse, for where I am thou shalt be with me.
Thou were wone whanne I dwellyd in erthe to reseyue me gladly in thyn
herberwe. And therfore, now I dwelle in heuene, I wele as gladly reseyuyn 105
the to myn dwellynge place.'

And sone aftyr, whan the our of hyre passage cam, she maad hyre to byn
brou owt into the opyn eyr that she myght seen heuene. Wherfore whan
[she was brought] she had hem leyn hyre doun vpon the erthe and the
dust and the signe of the cros to byn holdyn byforn hyre. Wiche doon, she 110
preyid oon this wyse: 'My nobyl and blyssyd oost, kepe me now thy pore
seruaunt! And lych as thou vouchystdyst sumtyme to byn herberwyd with
me, so vouchesaf that from hensforward I may be loggyd with the.' And,
this seyd, she bad that the passioun of Luc shal byn red byforn hyre. And
whan he cam to these wurdys: *Pater, in manus tuas & cetera*: 'Fadyr, into 115
thyn handys I comende my spirit', she yald vp into the handys of God hyre
spirit.

Vpon the nexte day folwynge, whiche was sunday, wyl the funeral office
was seyid abowtyn hyre body, whyl Seynt Fronto, bysshop of Petrogori-
cas, was at messe abowte the our of tierce and, syttyng in hys chayir afftir 120
the epistil, was aslepe, oure lord Ihesu app[e]rid onto hym, seying on this
wyse: 'My wylbelouyd Fronto, yf thou wylt performy[n] and fulffylly[n]
that thou sumtyme byhyhtyst myn oostesse, ryse vp lyhtly and folwe me.'
And so hym thoughte he dede, and anoon sodeynly they comyn to Terrascon and performyd syngyng and alle othere answerynge al the funeral 125
seruyse, and with here owyn handys leyid the body in the | graue. But f. 146vb
whanne at Pictagoricas the grayel and othir thyngis were seyd and sunge
as yt awte, and the dekne whiche shulde redyn the gospel comyng to the
bysshop to askyn hys be[n]ysoun wook hym, he vnnethe wakyn answere[d]
on this wyse: 'O brothyryn, why haue ye wakyd me? Oure lord Ihesu Crist 130
led me to the body of hys ostesse Marthe and we han put hyre in hyre graue.
Wherfore I prey yow sendyth anoon massagerys thedyr glad to brynge me
my rynge and myn glouys of grey, whiche I deleueryd to the sexteyn whan
I dysposyd me to buryin the body of Cristis holy herbeiour Marthe, and
forgat hem there for haste whan ye wook me and clepid me vp.' Anoon 135

102 Crist] cast   109 she was brought] she was brough she was brought
113 may be] may   115 *tuas*] tutuas   121 apperid] apparid   122 performyn]
performyd   fulffyllyn] fulffyllynge   129 benysoun] be wysoun   answered] answere

masengerys wer[n] sent forth to Terrascon and foundyn yt soth that the
b[i]sshop had seyd. And they broutyn hym hom hys gold ryng and oon of
hys glouys oonly, for the tothir the sexteyn kept ther stylle into testimonye
and wytnesse of that gret miracle. And this blyssyd bysshop Fronto, tel-
140 lynge the peple this processe, addyd this more thertoo: 'What tyme', quoth
he, 'oure lord Ihesu Crist and I haue buryid his holy hostesse and wentyn
forth, out of the cherche a br[o]thir of the place folwyd aftyr vs and askyd
our lord what was hys name. To whom oure lord answerd no word, but he
shewyd hym a lytyl book wherin was rygh not ellys wrytyn but this ver-
145 sicle: "*In memoria eterna erit iusta hospita mea ab audicione mala non timebit
in die nouissimo*: In euerelastynge mynde shal ben my ryghtful houeste, ner
she shal not byn aferd of euyl-heryng in the laste day".'.

Amonge manye grete miraclis dayly shewynge at this blyssyd wummannys toumbe, this was oon. Clodoueus, the Frensshe kynge, aftyr that he
150 was conuertyd and baptizid of Seynt Rymygye, had a gret and a greuous
peyne in hys [reines], whereof ne leche cowde don hym no remedy. And
whan he herde of the grete miraclis at the seyid place, deuouthly he went
thedyr on pylgrimage, and er thanne he was thens he was perfyhly helyd
and neuere felt more of that syknesse aftyr. Wherfore he richely endewyd
155 that place and alle the townys, castelys and lordshypys thre myle abowte on
bothe sydys of Rodanus flood, he yaf therto and mad yt fre from al maner
chargis and grauntyd yt the preuylege of perpetuel liberte.

Marcella, Marthys handmaydyn, whiche seyde to oure lord, as yt ys
wrytyn in the gospel of Luc, these wurdys: 'Blyssyd be the wumbe that
160 bar the and the brestys eek which youe the souken', wroot the lyf of hyre
maisteresse. The whiche Marcelle, aftyr hyre maisteresse deth, went into
a cuntre or a cyte clepyd Salauonia and prechyd there Cristys gospell, and
ten yer afftyr hyre maistresse she deyid and went hoom to hyre in the blysse
of heuene, & cetera.

[124. ABDON AND SENNEN]

The liuys of Abdon & Sennen

Whan Decius, Emperour of Rome, had conqueryd and subiugat Babilonye and othere prouincys ther abowtyn to hys empere, he fond there
certeyn cristene men whoom he led with hym to the cyte of Corduba
f. 147ra and there he mad an ende of hem with certeyn peynys and | turmentys.
6 Whos bodyis two lytyl kyngys, Abdon and Sennen, for they wern Cris-

136 wern] wernt　　　137 bisshop] bosshop　　　142 brothir] brthir　　　151 reines]
om.　　　158 yt ys] yt

tis seruauntis, buryd preuyly by nyght. Wherfore they wern acusid and
brought byforn the Emperour Decius, to whom he seyde on this wyse: 'Be
ye now maad so greet folys that ye remembre not how ye for? Because that
ye wurshipe not goddys arn bytrayid in the Romayns handys and ours.'   10
To whoom blyssyd Abdon answerd on this wyse: 'In caas, by the fauour of
oure lord Ihesu Crist, we be rathere victours and ouyrcomers than ouyrcomyn. For we servyn hym whiche, not for a tyme as yowre goddys, but
endlesly, lyuyn and regnyth to God in the blysse of heuene.' At whiche answere Decius the emperour wex wroth and anoon he shargid hem bothyn   15
myghtyly to be boundyn with chenys and to be shet vp in a streyt prisoun.
And they with a glad cher entrid the prisoun, seydyn on this wyse: 'Loo,
thys ys the ioye whiche we han alwey hopyd and trustyd of oure lord God.
For this owith to be the fylycite of a cristene man: to sufferyn dyspyht and
reprof, torment and peyne for Cristys sake.'   20

And whan they thus had [ben] prisound foure monyths, Decius wente
to Rome and led with hym Abdon and Sennen boundyn with chenys. Whedyr whan he was comyn he maad a gret gadryng of the senatours, chargyng
hem alle to assemblyn in a comoun place wiche was clepyd Telludis, with
Valerian the prefect, the fefte kalende of August. And whan they wern alle   25
comyn togedyr, Decius comaundyd Abdon and Sennen to be brouth forth
boundyn byforn hem alle, seyinge to the senat on this wyse: 'Loo serys,
oure goddys and oure [godesses] han diliueryd into oure handys these two,
here fers and cruel aduersaryis. Loo, here the enmys of the comoun profyth
and of al the Romayn empere!' And whan they were brouht in the clothis   30
of gold and arayid with precious stonys, al the senat was armaruaylyd in
the byholdynge of hem. But not forthan, whan the[y] were put to questioun of hyre byleue, they, nothyng aferd, boldly and constauntly byforn
hem alle knoweleched Crist to be God alone, and [n]oon othir but he in
heuene and in erthe, and in helle othere goddys of folk to be deuyls. Wher-   35
fore Decius, wroth, delyueryd hem to the prefect Valeryan, chargynge hym
that, yf they wolde not wurshipyn the simulacre of hys god the su[nn]e, he
shuld makyn hem to byn deuouryd by wilde bestys. Whoom Valerianus
anoon, despoylyd of here clothis, ledde to the su[nn]ys similacre bysyde
the comown place clepyd Amphiteatrum, and they, as sone as they seyin   40
yt, spittyn thervpon and despisid yt. Wherfore the prefect dede hem be
betyn with whippys of leed and aftyr that to be led in Amphitaitrum and
two leons to be letyn loos to hem. The whiche leons, as sone as they seyin
Cristis seruauntis, they begunne to makyn a gret rorynge and forthwith

45 they wentyn and leydyn hem doun at here feet, shewyng in that that they
weryn rathere comyn to kepyn hem than to hurtyn hem. And whan the
prefect saw this, he sent in swerd man to sleen hem, chargyng that whan
they were deed he[re] feet shuld be boundyn togedyr and here bodyis drawyn owt and throwyn byforn the similacre of the sunne, were they leyin
50 thre dayis.

f. 147rb   Aftyr wiche tyme a sodekene clepyd Quirinus, | whiche dwellynge
bysyde the Amphiteatre, gadrid here bodyis by nyht and wond hem in
an arc of leed and buryid hem in hys hous, where they leyin to the tyme
of gret Constantyn, whan they shewyd hemself and were translatyd from
55 thens onto a cimitorie clepid *Cimitorium Ponciam*. The passioun of hem
was abowte the yers of oure lord two hundryd and fyfty & cetera.

[125. GERMANUS]

The lyf of Seynt German

Germanus, of the nobillest and of the wurthyest blood b[or]n of the cyte
clepyd Altissidorence in Fraunce, in hys yunge dayis sufficiently instruct
in alle the seuene liberal sciens, went afftyrward to Rome for to lere cyuyl,
5 wherein he so profityd there in short tyme that the senat of Rome puttyn hym to that wurshipe and dignyte that they sentyn hym ageyn into
Fraunce and youyn hym the sool reule and the gouernaunce of the duchye
of Norma[n]dye. And amonge othir cytes he had in singuler cherce the
cyte of his byrthe, Altissidorence, and most was vsid to dwelle therin. In
10 the myddys of whiche cete he had stondynge a fayre pinote-tre, vpon the
braunches wherof he was wone to hangge the hedys of the wylde bestys
whiche he had takyn by huntynge. Whom the holy bisshop of the cyte, clepyd Amator, vndyrnam of that vanite, and monestyd hym that he shulde
do smytyn doun the tre that therby noon euyl occasioun myht growyn to
15 cristene men, but hem in no wyse wolde assentyn therto. Wherfore, oo
tyme whan Germanus was absent, the seyid bisshop dede fellyn doun the
tre and brent yt. The whiche dede as sone as Germanus wiste, he, hauynge
forgetyn cristene condicoun, cam with strong armyd hand and thretyd to
fleen the bysshop. But he, informyd by reuelacioun that Germanus shulde
20 byn hys successour, yaf place to his ire and fleed to a cyte clepid *Augustu
Domini*. And not longe aftyr this blissyd bysshope cam ageyn to the cyte
Altissidorence and fon Germanus in the cherche and shet hym therin and
sacryd hym, prophecying that he shulde succedyn afftyr hym. And so yt

48 here] he   2 born] bron   8 Normandye] Normadye   22 in the] the

was, for within fewe dayis aftyr this blyssyd bysshop Amator dayid and
anoon al the peple ches German to byn hys successour. By wiche eleccioun 25
Germanus anoon was chaungyd into anothir man, and al hys substance
youyn into the vse of pore men, and hys wyf chaungyd into hys sustyr.

Thretty wyntyr aftyr, so he chastysyd hys flesshe that he neuere eet
bred maad of wete, ne neuere drank wyn, ne neuere tastyd oyle, ner eysyl,
ner potage and ner neuere took salt for to saueryn with hys mete. At hys 30
myl he fyrst tastyd asshs and aftyr barly bred. Twyis oonly in the yeer, as
at Cristemesse and at Estryn, he took wyn, but not forthan he thoo dayis
quenchyd the mygh of the wyn with watir. And notwithstondynge that
he euery day fastyng, yit not forthan he neuere dissoluyd hys fast tyl euesong tyme. Somyr ner wentyr he vsyd no clothis moo than on heyre and 35
a cote and a couele, and yet this was not chaungyd tyl yt was asshs, hayre
and saccloth, and noon pylue vndyr hys heed. Seyntys reliquis he bar alway
abowtyn hys nekke. Euere mornyng | he was lyst wepyn, slepyng was alwey f. 147ᵛᵃ
clad, selde dede he of hys hosyn and hys shoys, and more seldom vndede
he hys gerdyl. Al that he dede was abouyn the nature of man. Swych was 40
hys lyf that yf he had wantyd myraclis yt had byn incredible. And so pleyn-
teuous wern hys miraclis that, yf meritys of good lyf had not goon byforn,
yt myght haue be trewyd to haue ben fantesies or illusiouns.

He onys was herberwyd in a place where aftyr that they had supposid
hys ost gan make redy mete for a newe soper, whereof he, gretly amaruay- 45
lyd, askyd hym for whoom he dytht that mete. 'Sekyr, syre', quoth the ost,
'for the goode wummen which arn wone to goon be nyhte and preyin for vs
and aftyr comyn hedyr to hyre sopyr whyl we ben in oure beddys.' Whan
Germanus the holy byshop herd this, he wecchyd that nyght to seen and
knowyn what thys nyht-goyinge myht me[n]yn. And anoon he saw a gret 50
multitude of deuyls in the lyknesse of men and wummen syttyn doun at the
table, whom he, in spirit knowynge and what they wern, chargyd hem to
sittyn stylle and not to goon awey. Whiche don, he clepyd vp hys oost and
al the houshold and askyd hem yf they kn[e]we owt that peple, and they
answerden and seydyn 'ya', they wern here ny neyhbors. 'That this may be 55
knowyn veryly', quoth this holy man, 'anoon sendyth to hyre housys and
enqueryth whethyr they ben here or there.' As he comaundyd they dedyn,
and foundyn hem alle at hom in hyre beddys. Whereof the answere youyn,
he co[n]iuryd the spirytys and they knowelechyd that they wern deuyls,
which in swyche similitudys and lyknessys wentyn aboutyn on nyhtys by 60
housys for to illudyn men.

38 lyst wepyn] lyst; *semper gemens LgA*   41 that yf] that   50 menyn] mewyn
54 knewe] knwe   59 coniuryd] coiuryd

This tyme also the bysshop of the cyte of Tracocens, whos name was
Lupus, floresshd a[n]d flouryd in fame and name of holy leuyng. For, as
yt ys wrytyn, whan Kyng Attilas onys bysegyd the cyte of Tracocens, this
65 seyid Lupus the bysshop cryid owt ouyr the gate and askyd what he was
that cam thus to troublyn and vexyn the cyte. 'I am', quoth the Kynge
Attilas, 'the scorge of God.' 'Forsoth', quo[th] he ageyn, 'and I am Lupus,
the wastour and the distroyere of Goddys folk, whiche am ryght wil wurthy for to ben shorgyd; and therfore the scorge of God hys wolcome.' And
70 anoon he dede settyn opyn the g[a]te and letyn hem in and they entrid
and wentyn through the cyte fro gate to gate, no man seyinge, ner no man
hurtynge. And so, confusyd in hemself, brokyn vp here sege and wentyn
here weye.

What tyme Pelagris herysie bygan to spredyn abrod in Brytaynie, blys-
75 syd Germanus, takynge with hym the forseyd bysshop Trococence, Lupus,
cam thedyr for prechyn therageyns. And wyl they wern in the see, ther
grew so gret a tempest sodeynly that they alle dreddyn to han per[i]schid.
And anoon, at the priere of Seynt German, the tempest secyd and the [see]
f. 147vb   as pesible and as calm as though there | had no tempest ben many a day
80 byforn. And soo they come to londe safly and were reseyuyd there of the
peple wurshupfully, byforn whos comynge into Ynglond deuyls whiche
ocupyid diueres mennys bodyis toldyn byforn of here comynge, whoom
German at hys comynge drof owt of the seyd bodyis and delyueryd hem
from the deuyls malicyous vexacioun. And whan they had doon that they
85 come fore, that ys to seyne whan they had confoundyd the heretykys, they
returnyd hom ageyn.

Yt happyd hym onys to leyin seek in a place the whiche sodeynly fel on
a feir. Wherfore men preyin hym that he wold be forn owt that he myghte
askapyn the hurt of the feir, but he wolde not. And notwithstondynge that
90 the [flamme] consumyd and wastyd alle the howsys runde abowte, yeet the
hous wiche he lay in yt touchyd rygh not.

The secunde tyme that he went into Britayne ageyns the Pylagyans, oon
of hys dycyplys wolde haue goon with hym and therfore he folwyd aftyr
hym. And whan he cam to a place clepid Cormacorum he syknyd there and
95 deid. Blyssyd Germanus, in returnyng hom ageyn, cam to the same place
and dede ben opnyd hys dyscipls graue and clepyd hym by hys name, and
askyd hym what he dede and whethir he wolde turnyn ageyn to lyf and
dwellyn lengere with hym. To whoom he, lyftynge vp hys heed, answerde
and seyde that he was ryght weel at ese and had al thynge at hys plesaunce,

63 and] ad   67 quoth] quoht   70 gate] grate   77 perischid] perschid
78 see] seex   90 flamme] famme

ner to comyn agayn into the werd he nothynge desiryd, whiche seyid, at the 100
comaundeme[n]t of hys mastir, and leyid doun ageyn hys heed and restyd
in oure lord.

Whan thys blyssyd man oo tyme prechyd in Bretayne ageyns the
heretyk, the kynge of the cuntre denyid hym and hys herberue and wolde
not receyuyn hem to hospitalite. And as the kyngis netherde cam from the 105
kyngis place wythe hys vitayls and wente homward to hys own tugurrye, yt
happyd hym to seen blyssyd German with hys felachepe oppressyd [with]
hungyr and malese. And anoon he had conpassyoun and pyte vpon hem,
and led hem with hym into hys pouere herberue and slow a calf whiche
he had and no moo, and seruyd hem with al and maad hem as good cheer 110
as he cowde. And whan they had suppyd, Germanus comaunded alle the
bonys of the calf to ben gaderyd togedere and to be leyid vpon the skyn.
And, afftyr a short preyere, the calf roos vp ageyn, hol and heyl as yt was
byforn that yt was slayn. On the nexte morwyn Seynt German met with
the kyng and askyd hym boldly and opynly why he denyid hym and hyse 115
herbewe. At which questyoun the kyng, gretly astoynyd, cowde answeryn
no wurd. And anoon the bysshop Germanus lad the kyng goon hys weye
owt and yiuyn place to hys bettyr. Whiche wurdys seyid, at the wyl of
God he clepyd in the netherde and hys wyf and, alle men present there
wundrynge, he mad hym kyng and hyre quen. And fro that tyme forward 120
the Britoun kyngis | comyn owt of netherdys blood.   f. 148ra

Whan the Saxonis foutyn ageyns the Britons and that in conparisoun
of hem they were but fewe. Whan the seyinge Synt German and hys [fela-
shype] come forby hem, they clepyd hem to hem and herdyn hem prechyn.
At whos amonicyons they were conuertyd and dysposyd hem to ben bap- 125
tisyd, and vpon Estryn day nexte folwyng, through gret ferueur of feyth,
they kestyn awey here armour and purposyd hem not that day for to fyhtyn. And whan here enimys herdyn this, they boldly comyn vpon hem whyl
they wern vnarmyd. Seynt German, perceyuynge this, counselyd hem and
bad that [whan] they herde hym cryin 'Alleluya!', they alle with oo mouth 130
shuld cryin the same. And so they dedyn. At whiche cry swych a terour
and feer fel vpon here enmyis that they threwyn awey here armour and
fleddyn, wenynge that not only the hyllys, but that also heuene shulde han
fallyn doun vpon hem.

Vpon the tyme as thys blyssyd man wente in the cyte of Augustudine he 135
cam by the tombe of Seynt Cassian, and anon he askyd hym how he ferde.
And he forthwith, alle men herynge, answerde and seyde that he was in

101 comaundement] comaundemet   107 with] with with   110 and maad]
and   123–4 felashype] falasphype   130 whan] whan whan   they herde] they

good quiet and rest and abood the comynge of oure redemptour. 'Reste stylle', quoth he ageyn, 'longe in Crist, and preye for vs tendyrly that we
140 movn deservyn the ioyis of that holy resurreccyoun.'

Onys whan thys bysshop cam to the cyte of Rauenne he was wurshipfully reseyuyd there of the quen, Placida by name, and here sone Valentynian. To whoom the quen at sopetyme sent a syluyr dysshe, ful of rygh delicat metys. The whiche present he reseyuyd benignely and yaf the mete
145 onto hys seruantis, and reseryud the dysshe to make therof distribucyoun to pore men. And in stede of this present he sente hyre ageyn a troone dysshe ful of barly bred. The whiche she reseyuyd rygh gladly, and had that vessel in swych cherte that aftyrward she dede yt byn curyd with syluyr.

Yt happyd also that oo tyme the seyd quen preyid hym to mete and he
150 grauntyd hyre to comyn. But, for as meche as he was so brokyn with abstinence and whithe [gret] labours that he myght not goon from hys into hyre paleys on hys feet, he rood vpoon hys asse, the whiche, whil they wern at mete, sodeynly deyid in the stable. And whan the quen herd this, she curtesly sent hym hyre own palfrey: a buxum hors and a softe berynge. And
155 whan he saw this fayr palfrey he refusyd yt and wolde not rydyn theron, but 'brynge me', quoth he, 'myn asse! For he that brought me hedyr muste nedys bern me hoom ageyn.' And whan the deed careyn was brough to hys presence, 'Ryhs vp', quoth he, 'and lete vs goon hoom ageyn to oure in.' And anoon the asse ros vp and shok hym as thogh he had noon arm, and
160 bar hys maystyr hoom ageyn.

But er this holy bysshop went owt of Rauene he tolde the quen and othere pleynly that he shulde not longe abydyn in this word. And anoon
f. 148rb aftyr there | too[k] hym an accesse, and the seuente day aftyr he wente to oure lord, whoos body was karyid hoom into Fraunce, lyche as he had
165 preyid the quen byforn. The date of this holy bisshop deth was the yer of grace foure hundryd and on and twenty.

But, for as meche as blissid Germanus in hys goyinge owtward maad a promisse to [that] holy man Eusebye, the bisshop Vercellence, that in hys retorn homward he shuld haluyn hys cherche, and he had tydyngis
170 that Seynt German was passid to God, he dysposyd hym to halwyn the cherche hymself. For wyche cause he comaundyd tapyrs to ben lyght, but as faste as they were lyght they were quenchyd and put out ageyn. Wherby the blyssyd bisshop Eusebye supposyd veryly that [o]r the dedicacyoun therof was reseruyd to anothir tyme, or to anothir bisshop. And
175 nat longe aftyr thys, the body of Seynt German was brought to Vercellence and set in the cherche. And as sone as the body was set doun, sodeynly

151 gret] and gret   163 took] tool   168 that] han   173 or] er

alle the candels of the cherche wern lyght withowtyn ony helpe of mannys hand. Whiche doun, the blyssyd bysshop Eusebie, remembrynge of
Seynt Germans byhest, supposyd veryly that the promys whiche he mad
to hym lyuynge, he performyd aftyr hys deth. But here yt ys to byn markyd 180
and vndyrstondyn that this Eusebye was not he wyche was clepyd Eusebius Magnus, the grete doctour, for he deyid the tyme that Valens was
emperoure, more thanne fyfty vyntyr byforn that Seynt German deyid &
cetera.

[126. EUSEBIUS]

The lyf of Seynt Eusebye

Eusebius, the gret doctour and myghty wal of holy cherche, took baptem and name of Pope Eusebie. In whiche baptem aung[e]ls handys wern
seen lyftynge hym vp from the fountston. This Eusebie was alwey a maydyn and therwith rygh excellent in bodyly bewte, for whiche a matrone 5
onys, enameryd vpon hym, wold priuyly han goon to hys bed, but by
aungelys she was lettyd that she myght not comyn at hym. Wherfore, on
the nexte morwyn, she wente onto hym and fel doun on hyre knees and
lamentabylly askyd hym foryifnesse.

This blyssyd Eusebie, whan he was maad a pryst, enduyd was with 10
so gret holynesse that oftyn tyme at hys messe aungels were seen lyftyn
vp the sacrement bytwyx hys handys. Aftyr thys, whan the eresye of the
Arrians had ner infect al Ytayle, the emperour Constaunce fauouryng the
same herasye, Iulius pope sacryd Eusebie bisshop Vercellence, the whiche
that tyme was the souereyn see of al. And whanne the heretykys seyin that 15
Eusebie was maad this wyse a bisshop, they anoon shettyn alle the dory[s]
of the cherche, that he shuld not comyn in. But Eusebie, as sone as he cam
into the cyte and sey the dorys of the cherche shet ageyns hym, he knelyd
doun vpon hys knees and preyid a short preyere byforn the dore of the
heed cherche, the whiche ys of oure lady. And anoon frely the dore opnyd 20
and he entryd in.

And anon Auxencium, corupt with the Arrians heresie, the bisshop of
Melan he kest owt of hys benifyce and | ordaynyd in hys stede a good feyth- f. 148ᵛᵃ
fyl man clepyd Denyhs. And thus thys blyssid Eusebie purifiyd and purgyd
the cherche of the occydent or the west from the Arrians herysie, lych as 25
Attanasye purgyd the cherche of the orient or the Est. The auctour of thys
herysie was oon clepyd Arrius, a pryst of the cherche of Alixaundyr, the
which hele that Crist was but a pure creature and that he was maad that

3 aungels] aungls   16 dorys] dorych   22 Arrians heresie] Arrians

God shuld makyn vs by hym as by an instrument. And for this opynyoun
30 Constancius the emperour maad a counsel to be clepyd in the cyte clepid
Nicea, the wheche counsel ys clepyd by the cherche *Concilium Niceum*. In
whiche counsel Arrius was dampnyd for on heretyk and hys opynioun for
an heresie. This Arrius deyid aftyr on an horible deth for alle hys bowayls
and alle hys intrayle and hys lyf therwith passid from hym be the funde-
35 ment as he sat on a sege. The emperour also Constancius, Constantynis
sone, was eek infectid with this seyid heresie, for whiche cause he sore
pursuyid Eusebie. And fryst he gadryd togedyr a gret counsel of bissho-
pis amonge whiche he clepid Denyhs, whoom Eusebie had maad bishop of
Melan, and to Eusebie also he sent diuers and sundry epistls. But Eusebie,
40 supposynge malice to preuaylyn through multitude, he wolde nat comyn
there but he excusid hym by age. Ageyns whiche excusacioun the emperour set the counsel at Melan, the whiche was not fer from hym. Whiche
councel gadry[d], whan the emperour saw that Eusebie cam not, he comaundyd the Arrians to writyn here feyth and mad De[nyh]s the bisshop
45 of the same cyte, with nyne and twenty othere bisshops to subscribyn. And
whan Eusebie herd this, he took hys iourne to Melan-ward, tellynge hem
whiche he went fro that myche tribulacioun and persecucyoun he knewe
weel was to hym-ward. And whan he cam to a flood, ouyr whiche he muste
nedys passyn, and the sory boot, and withoute more yt cam ouyr to hym
50 and led hym and hys ouyr withoutyn ony shypman or gouernour saf the
grace of God. Wherfore the bysshop of Melan, Denyhs, [louly] prostrat
fel doun and askyd hym foryifnesse of that he had doun.

And whan he cam to Melan the emperour, neythir with thretis ner with
byhestys, cowd not meuyn hym to subscribyn, and hys resoun was this: 'Ye
55 seyin', quoth he, 'that the sone ys lesse than fadyr, and Goddys sone seyith that [t]he disciple ys not abouyn hys maister. Whi thanne haue ye maad
myn sone more than me and preferrid my dyscip[l]e byforn me, whiche by
weye of resoun owt rathere to folwyn me?' At whiche resoun they were
sumwhat meuyd and broughtyn forth the i[n]strument in whiche Dyonys
60 prescribyd and alle othere had subscribyd and shewyd yt hym. And whan
he saw yt, 'Sekyr', quoth he, 'I wyl neuere whiche am souereyn vndyrwri-
tyn hym whiche ys my sone and my subiect. Wherfore, yf ye wylle that I
wryte, brennyth this instrumen[t] and ordayneth anothyr in wyche I may
f. 148ᵛᵇ prescribe my sone and | my dysciple.' And so, by the wyl of God and the
65 prudence of Eusebie, that instrument was brent anon in whiche Denys

38 Denyhs] Deuyls   43 gadryd] gadryl   44 Denyhs] deuyls   51 Denyhs
louly] Denyhs and louly   56 the] he   57 dysciple] dyscipe   59 instrument]
instrumen   63 instrument] instument

with nyne a[nd] twen[ty] othere busshops had subscribyd. Wych don, the
Arrians wretyn a neue inst[r]ument, the whiche they presentyd to Eusebie and to alle the othere bisshops for to subscribyn. But alle the bisshops,
hertyd and confortyd by Eusebie, fully resistyd and woldyn anoon of hem
alle subscribyn, but rathere were glaad that the instrument wherto con- 70
streynyd they had subscribyd byforn was brent and dystroyid. For wiche
cause the emperour Constancius was so angry that he delyueryd Eusebie to the Arrians and yaf hem leue to don with hym what they wolde.
And they anoon tokyn hym vp from ama[n]ge alle the bisshops and fryst
myghtyly they schorgyd hym and aftyr that they drowyn hym by the feet 75
dooun from the hyest grece of the paleys on to the lowest, and efthsonys
from the lowest ageyn vp to the heyeste. And whan he had sore bled of
the gret brosure of hys heed and wolde yet in no wyse consentyn to subscribyn, they boundyn hys handys byhyndyn hys bak and puttyn a roppe
aboutyn hys nekke and so drowyn hym abowtyn hedyr and thedyr. But he 80
yaf thankynge to God, seyinge allewey that for the confessioun of Cristys
feyth he was redy no[t] oonly to sufferyn but also to deyin. This seyin,
the emperour bannysshyd and exilyd Pope Liberie, Denyhs, Paulin and
alle the othere bisshops, whiche through here exemple and confort wolde
not consentyn to subscribyn. But Eusebie the Arrians leddyn to a cyte in 85
a Palestine clepyd Sicepolus, and there they shet hym in so streyt a place
that the lenghthe therof was shortere and the brede narwere than he, so
that he myght neythyr puttyn owt hys feet ner turnyn hym fro the to syde
to the tothir, his hede hangynge doun so loue so that he mygh no more
meuyn of al hys body but hys elbowys and hys shuldrys. 90

But sone aftyr this, whan Constancius was deed and Iulianus succee-
dyd aftyr hym, he, desirynge to plesyn alle men, comaundyd alle the exilid
bisshops to be clepyd hom ageyn and the templys of goddys to byn opnyd,
and ych man to leuyn pesiblely vndyr what lawe he wolde. And by this
occasioun Eusebie was also delyueryd and cam to Attanasie, and told hym 95
how and what he had sufferyd for Cristis feyth. But aftyr that Iulyan and
Iouinian were deed, by whoom the Arrians where gretly sopyt and slakyd,
Eusebie returnyd hom ageyn to Vercellence and was ther reseyuyd of al the
peple with gret ioye and gladnesse. Not forthan anon aftyr, whan Valens
held the emperere, the Arrians bygunne to spryngyn vp ageyn and waxyn 100
bold and myhty where through they | besegyd Eusebies place and drawyn f. 149ra
hym owt therof and slown hym with stonys. Whos body ys buryid in the
cherche whiche he mad hymself. Yt ys seyd that through hys preyere he

66 and twenty] atwen   67 instrument] instument   74 amange] amage
82 not] nos

gat this grace of God to hys cyte Vercellence: that noon Arrian may lyuyn
105 therin. Aftyr the cro[ni]cles he lyuyd at the leste foure score yer. And he
flouryd aboute the yers of oure lord thre hundryd and fyfty & cetera. *Deo
gracias.*

[127. MACHABEES]

The passioun of the seuene Machabeis

As seyth Ianuence, the oryental cherche, whiche ys clepyd *Ecclesiastica
Grecoy*, vsyth comounly to holdyn the festys of the holy fadrys of the Old
Testement with the seyntis of the Newe Testament, swyche tymys as they
5 fallyn in the kalendyr; but the occidental cherche, that ys to seyne *Ecclesiastica Latinorum*, doth not so. For of the olde fadrys, in as myche as they
wentyn to helle, oure cherche solemnyzyth on the festys, saf the Innocentis
and the Macabeis.

And why we specyally haluyn the feste of the Machabeis more than
10 othere, notwithstonde that they wentyn to helle as wyl as othere, Ianuence
assignyth foure causis. The fyrste cause, quoth he, for the prerogatyf of
martyrdam; werfore they ben priuilegyd byforn al [and here] feste haluyd
past alle othere. And this [seith] *Histori[a] Scolastica*.

Thre othere reson[s] [ben offred by] Belet in hys *Summ[a] de officiis*,
15 where oon ys for representacioun. For there were seuene in noumbre, and
the noumbre of seuene betokenyth vniuersite or al. And so in these seuene
byn signifyid alle the fadrys of the Old Testement whiche as be wourthi to
byn alwyd.

The secunde resoun aftyr Ioon Belet ys for exau[m]ple of suffraunce.
20 For syth these seuene sufferyd so meche for the laue of Moyses, myche
more owte we to suffryn for the laue of Crist y[n] the gospel.

And the thridde resoun ys coincident wyth this, whiche ys the cause of
here passioun. And this cause ys nouht ellys but zeel of Goddys lawe and
kepynge of here paternal tradicions, the whiche for they wold not breke
25 they suffryd gladly al maner peynys whiche the cruel tira[un]th Antiochius
cowde applyin onto hem, as yt ys wrytyn in the secunde bok of the Maca-
beys in the sexte and the seuynte chapitres. Where yt ys seyid that, aftyr
the tyme that the blyssyd pryst Eleazarus was cruelly slayn for he wolde
not agenys here laue etyn swynys flesshe, yt happyd seuene brethryn to

105 cronicles] crouncles   12 *Missing text is owing to a removed initial on the verso
of this leaf. Text has been supplied by comparison with LgA.*   13 *Historia*] Historijs
14 resons] reson   19 exaumple] exaunple   21 yn] ys   25 tiraunth] tiranith
26 yt ys] yt

byn takyn with here modyr and to be conpellyd to that wich was defendyd 30
by here laue, that ys to seyne to etyn swynys flesshe. Of whiche seuene
brethryn, oon armyd in zeel of here lawe seyde to the tiraunt on thys wyse:
'What sekyst thou', quoth he, 'and what desirist thou to lerne of vs? I wyl
that thou knowe this sykyrly, that we be redy to deyin rathere than to breke
the lawe of God and of oure fadrys.' With thys answere the kynge angryd, 35
comaundyd anoon gret frying pannys and gret pottis of bras to be mad
brynny[n]ge hoot. Whiche doon, he bad that the tunge of hym wych fryst
spak shuld be kut owt of hys heed and | the skyn of hys heed to be pluk- f. 149ʳᵇ
kyd of and hys feet to byn kut of, alle hys brethren stondynge bysydyn and
byholdynge. And whan al this was don, he chargyd hym to byn throwyn 40
in the fryinge panne and therin to byn turnyd to and fro, vp and doun,
and fryid.

And whil this was in doynge, the tothere sexte brethyrn with here
modyr exortyd yche of hem othere to constaunce and stedefastnesse and
myhtyly to deyin, seyinge on this wyse: 'Oure lord whiche beholdyth the 45
treuthe of oure cause shal be counfortyd in vs, as Moyses testifyith in hys
canticle where he seyth thus: & in seruis suis consolabit Deus: "God shal be
counfortyd," quoth he, "in hys seruauntis".' And whan this fryst brothir
was thus slayn, they toke the secunde and pullyd the skyn of hys heed,
and askyd hym yf he wolde etyn or alle the membris of hys body wern 50
rent asundyr as hys brothrys w[er]n. To whom he answerde in hys modrys
tunge and seyde 'Nay', he wolde nouht. Wherfore they anoon seruyd hym
lych as they had seruyd hys brothir in al degreis. The whiche whanne he
cam to ende of hys lyf, he seyde to the tiraunt on thys wyse: 'Thou, most
cursyd tiraunt, fleest vs here in this present lyf, but the kynge of al the 55
wor[l]d shal reysyn vs vp ageyn in the resurreccioun of euerelestynge lyf.'

Aftyr this the thredde was drawyn forth and illudyd and, as sone as hys
tunge was askyd, he put yt owt and shof forth hys armys and with gret constaunce seyde thus: 'From heuene I had these membris and now, for the
loue of the lord of heuene, I set hem at nouth and despice hem, fully trus- 60
tynge at conuenient tyme to reseyuyn hem ageyn of hym.' And whanne
the kynge herd this wurdys, bothe hymself and alle that wern with hym
maruayld gretly the constaunce and the stedfastnesse of the yunge mannys herte. And whan this brothir was deed, they took forth the fourte and
on lych wyse tormentyd hym. And whan he shulde deyin he seyde thus to 65
the kynge: 'Ful hope ys youyn to hym that on thys wyse byn put to deth of
men for God, that at the laste they shul be reysyd ageyn by God endlesly

37 brynnynge] brynnyge   51 wern] wren   56 world] word

to lyuyn with God. But thou, cruel tirant, shalt rysyn ageyn not to endles
lyf in God, but to en[d]les dampnacyoun by the ryghtfull dom of God.'

70   The fyfte brothir also, whan he was seruyd lych as hys brethryn had
ben and cam to hys laste ende, he lokyt vpon the kynge, seyinge on this
wyse: 'Thou coruptible criature, hauynge pouer among men, doost now
here what thou wylt. But not forthan wyl thou not trowyn oure kynrede
and oure nacyoun to be so forsakyn of oure lord God, but that yf thou abyde
75 a while thou shalt seen yt han pouer of God to turmentyn and to punys-
shyn bothe the and thyne.' Afftyr thys the sexte, tormentyd and drawyn
to hys ende, seyde thus: 'Take heed, tiraunt, what I seye! That we suffere
now ys for oure self, for we han synnyd in oure lord. And therfore wurthyly
we suffere thus. But wyl thou not hopyn awey vnpunysshid that thow so
80 malepertly to fytyn ageyns God and wylt thou or nygh thy lord.'

In al this mene tyme the modyr of hem, wurthy the remembraunce of
good men, stondyge and seyinge thus perysshyn hyre sonys alle vpon oo
day, bar yt not only esely and with a glad herte, but also she exhortyd with
f. 149va hyre own voys hem alle and eche | of hem to t[o]lleraunce and pacyent
85 sufferaunce of alle maner of tornementis and of deth, seyinge to hem thus:
'Sonys, I wot not how ye apperyddyn in myn wombe for I yaf yow neythir
spirit, soule, ner lyf, ner I formyd not the lin[e]amentis of yowre membrys.
Seyth yt ys so thanne that the creature of the wer[l]d, the whiche formyd
mannys and fond the bygynnynge of hem natiuite, haue youyn yow lyf and
90 membrys and ye despisyn them and al yowre sel[f] for hys lauys, he shal
restoryn yow through hys mercy, lyf[e] and membrys meche betyr than
they be now in conuenyence tyme.' Whan Antiochius saw hy[m] thus despysyd of the sexe brethryn whiche wern dede, and the seuente and the
yungest of alle yet lyuyd and was not assaylyd yet with no peyne, he dede
95 that he cowde with ammonycions and plesaunt suasions, conformynge hys
wurdys with an ooth by hys goddys for to deceyuyn hym and peruertyn
[hym], that yf he wolde doon afftyr hys counsel and forsakyn hys lawe and
turne to hys laue, he wolde sittyn hym in gret wele and prosperite and tretyn hym as his special and trusty frend, and neuere to fayle hym wyl he
100 lyuydde. And whan he sau that the yunge mannys herte, as yt sempte, was
nat inclinid to hys entent as he wolde, anoon he clepid hys modyr and mad
hyre suasions that she shulde stiryn and ex[ci]tyn hym to his helthe.

And whanne he hadde longe callyd vpon the yunge mannys modyr,
at the laste she byhest hym that she wolde makyn suasioun to hyre sone.

---

69 endles] enles   84 tolleraunce] telleraunce   87 lineamentis] linieamentis
88 werld] werd   90 self] selp   91 lyfe] lyft   92 hym] hys   97 hym]
thyn   102 excityn] exatyn

Whiche seyid, she turnyd hyre to hym-ward and, illudynge and scornynge 105
the cruel tirant, sche seyde to hyre sone, in hyre owyn language, on this
wyse: 'Sone, haue mercy and pyte on me, whiche bar the in my wombe
nyne monythis and norshyd the and fosteryd with myn mylke thre yer, and
haue brough the vp into [t]hys age. Sone, I beseche the, beholde heuene
and erthe, and al that ys conteynyd withinne bothe, and vndirstonde wyl 110
that God made alle these thyngis of nouht and mankende also. Wherfore
drede not thys kynge, this manquellere, but, egal and wurthi to thy brethyrin, take boldly deth, that I may fynde the with thy brethyrn in the mercy
of God.'

And whil hys modyr seyde these wurdys, the yunge man bygan to cryin 115
to the tormentours on thys wyse: 'What abyde ye? Whoom susteyne y[e]?
Pleynly I wyl ye wetyn that I wyl abyde in no wyse to the precept of the
kyng, but to the comaundement of the laue. And thou tiraunt', quoth he to
the kyng, 'whiche art inuentour and fyndere of al this malyce ageyn[e]s the
Hebreus, shalt not ascapyn the hand of God. That we suffery[n] here ys 120
for oure synnys and, thogh oure lord for oure vndyrnymyng be a litil wroth
with vs, yet he shal be reconcilid ageyn to hys seruauntys. But thou, o most
cursyd and most cruel tiraunt, be not to veynly extollyd in that thou hast
byn inflaumyd ageyns myn br[o]thir. For wete yt weel, thou art nat ascapyd
from the hand and the dom of God almyhty, whiche al thynge clerly seeth 125
and byholdyth. | For now my brethyrn, by tolleraunce and sufferynge of f. 149[vb]
a lityl tormynt arn vndyr the testement of euerelestynge lyf, but thou, by
the ryghtful doom of God, shalt bere the peyne that longith to thi pride.
But I, lych as my brethyrn han doon, offere my soule and myn lyf for myn
fadrys lawys, besechyng enterly God of heuene to be propicious onto oure 130
nacyon and that he vouchesaf with tormyntis and scorgynge to make the
to knowlechyn that he ys God alone and [n]on but he, and that hys ire and
wrathe, whiche he hath ryghfully had to be my nacyoun, may endyn and
secyn in me and in myn brethyrn.' This herynge, the kynge wex wood and
most cruelly of alle hys brethyrn he exercisid hys tirannye in hym, hauynge 135
dysdeyn and skorn so gretly to be despisid of hym. And whan thus were
slayn alle these seuene brethyrn, last of alle, with cruel examynacyoun, he
maad a[n] ende of here modyr. *Hec 2⁰ Mac 7. Deo gracias.*

---

109 thys] hys   116 ye] y   119 ageynes] ageynges   120 sufferyn]
sufferyng   124 brothir] brethir   132 non] anon.   138 an] and

[128. PETER IN CHAINS]

The feste of Seynt Petir clepyd ad Vincula

[T]he feste of Seynt Petyr clepid 'ad vincula' was ordeynyd for foure causis: fryst in remembraunce and mynde of the delyuerance of Seynt Petyr fro prisoun, for deliueraunce also of Seynt Alexandyr the pope, for
5 destruccyoun of a ryte of paynymrye and for getynge of absolucioun of goostyly bondys.

The fyrste cause, as I seyde, of this festys institucyoun was for remembraunce and mynde of Seynt Peterys delyueraunce fro prisoun. As yt ys seyd in *Ecclesiastic[a] histori[a]*, Herodes Agrippa cam to Rome where he
10 was wundyr familiar with Gaius, the neve of Tiberius the emperour. And vpon a tyme as they two setyn togedyr in a char, Herodes lyftyd vp hys handys to heuene-ward and seyde on this wyse: 'O wolde God', quoth he, 'that I onys mygh seen the deth of this old Tiberye and the lord alone of al the word.' Whiche wyssh the chariettyr herynge wente and told *y*t anoon
15 to the emperour Tiberie. For wich cause hauynge indignacioun, Tyberye the emperoure with Heroud, he sent hym to prisoun. Wher, vpon a day, as he sat lenynge vpon a tre in the braunchys whereof sat an owle and on whiche also was with hym in prisoun and, cunnynge in augurye, seyde to hym on thys wyse: 'Be not aferd! For in short tyme thou shalt be delyueryd
20 and so hyly enhaunsyd and lyftyd vp to wurshipe that th[y] frendys shul be styryd to enuye the and in that prosperite thou shalt deyin. And whan that thou seest this foul ouyr the, wete thou weel that thou shalt nat lyuyn abouyn the fefte day aftyr.'

Not longe aftyr this Tiberius deyid and Gaius succedyd into the
25 empere, and not only took Hero[u]d owt of prisoun, but also he dede hym thys excellent wurshipe: that he mad hym a kyng and sent hym into Iewerie. Whithir, anoon as he was comyn, he dede hys bysynesse to
f. 150ʳᵃ wexyn and trobyllyn summe of Cristys cherche. And whan | he had slayn Iamys, Ionys brothyr, seyinge weel that yt was plesaunt to the Iewys that
30 he dede, he byseyde hym also for to takyn Petyr. And soo he dede and put hym in prisoun, purposynge aftyr Estryn to bryngyn hym forth onto the peple. But by ministerye of an aungel by nyghte he was vnbundyn and led owt of the prisoun and restoryd to hys liberte, to goon whedyr he wolde and prechyn. But this malicious werkynge of Heroud the kyng
35 abood not longe vnvengyd. For the nexte day aftyr that Petyr was goon

2 The] *initial T has been removed*   4 also of] also   9 *Ecclesiastica historia*] ecclesiasticus historijs   20 thy] they   25 Heroud] Heround   31 hym in] hym

he sente afftyr hys keperys, purposynge hym for to chastysyn hem with greuous for the flyht of Petyr. Nertheles God wolde not sufferen hym to performyn hys cruel entent that Petrys solucyoun from presoun shuld not byn of othere mennys harm the occasioun. For forthwith he wente into Cesarye and there was he slayn by an aungel. 40

And as Iosepheus tellyth, *19° Antiquitatum*, whan he was comyn to Cesarye, and al the cuntre hool was gadryd onto hym, he, arayid in a bryghte shynyng [g]arnement coryously and mervelously wrouht of g[ol]d and siluyr, erly on a morwyn cam forth to the teatre. Where whan hys glo- ryous garnement had onys reseyuyd the bryght bemys of the sunne, the 45 bryhtnesse of the metal yaf double lyht and swych terrour causyd in hem that byhyldyn yt that they wende that abouyn the comoune nature of man there had be sum godly thynge within hym. And anoon the voys of the fla- terynge peple began to crin to hym and seyin: 'Hedyrtoward, syre, we han reseyuyd the as pure man and dred the, but now we knowleche veryly that 50 thou art abouyn the comoun nature of man. And so hensforward we wyl heldyn the God and wurshipyn the.' And whil he stood stylle, delitynge hym in the veyn preysynge and laude of the p[e]p[l]e, and neythir in word ne dede wolde refusyn the godly wurships falsly offeryd onto hym, vnwarly as he lokyd vpward he saw his aungel stayng on a lyne abouyn hys heed, 55 that ys to seyne an owle, the fatal massager of hys ny deth. Wiche whan he saw, he lokyd vpon the peple and seyde to hem on this wyse: 'Allas', quoth he, 'lo Y, yowre god, deye.' For he knewe weel by the diuynacyon of augurye told hym whan he was in prisoun that he myth not lyuyn past fyue dayis. And anoon the aungel of God smet hym so greuously in hys 60 entrayls that the foure dayis aftyr wermys etyn hem asundyr, and a stank so abhomynabylly that no man, for h[o]rrour of the sauyr, wolde ne durste comyn ner hym. And the fyfte day miseryeusly he deyid and wente hom thedyr he had deseruyd. *Hec Iosephus.*

In memorie, therfore, and rememberaunce of the gracyous deli- 65 ueraunce owt of prisoun of the prince of the apostlys, Petyr, and of the sodeyn veniaunce wich folwyd anon aftyr vpon the cruel tiraunt Heroude, holy cherche solemnyzyth this feste and clepyth yt the feste of Seynt Petyr ad vincula. And thefore ys red in the messe of this day the p[i]stel of the apostlys Actys, the whiche special[ly] spekyth of this seyd deliueraunce. 70

The secunde cause of the institucyoun of this feste was for remem- braunce of the deliueraunce of Pope Alexandyr owt of prisoun, the whiche Alexandyr was the sexte pope | aftyr Petyr, and conuertyd to the feyth the f. 150rb

43 garnement] arnement   gold] glod   52 the God and] the   53 peple] pope
62 horrour] herrour   69 pistel] postel   70 specially] specialyally

prefect of Rome Hermete. These two bothe, Alexis and Hermete, wern
75 in hold and prisonyd for Cristis feyth of a tribune clepyd Quirinus, but in
sundry prisounys. And vpon a day the tribune cam to Hermete the pre-
fecte and seyde to hym on this wyse: 'I maruayle gretly that thou, whiche
art holdyn a prudent man, w[i]lt thus fonnydly losyn the dignite and the
honour of prefecture and dremyn anothyr lyf than this present lyf.' 'Iwys
80 tribune', quoth Hermes, 'not longe byforn these dayis I skornyd hem also
whiche byleuyd swyche thyngis, and trowyd only that ther had byn noon
othir lyf than this.' 'Hermes', quoth Quirinus, 'make me to prouyn that
ther ys anothir lyf than this and anoon thou shalt han me a disciple of
thy feyth.' To whom Hermes answerde ageyn and seyde: 'Sykyr', quoth
85 he, 'the holy preyst and pope Alisaundyr can myche bettyr teche the this
thynge than I.'

Quoth Quirinus: 'I preyid the that thou shuldyst makyn me to prouyn
that I desyryd and now thou sendyst me to Alexandyr, whom for hys synne
and hys myslyuynge I kepe in prisoun faste boundyn. Nertheles I shal
90 dowblyn yowre bondys, bothe of Alisaundyr and of yow, and yf I in the
morwe fynde the with hym or hym with the, I shal yiuyn credence to yowre
wourdys.'

And anon he dede as he seyde, and told Alexaundre what and why
he de[de]. And anoon aftyr that Quirinus was goon, Alixandir bygan to
95 preye. And forthwith God sente an aungel whiche ledde hym onto Hermete, where he was in prisoun. And whan Quirinus cam and fond hem
togedyr he was gretly amaruaylyd. And whan blyssyd Hermete had told to
Quirine how Alixaundir had reysyd hys sone fro deth to lyf, Quirinus seyde
to Alixander on this wyse: 'I haue a douhtyr clepid Balbina, the whiche
100 ys guttous. Make here heyle therof and I byhete the that I wyl reseyuyn
thy feyth.' Quoth Alixandre ageyn: 'Go faste and brynge to me [hyre] to
my prisoun'. Syth thou art now her, how shuld I', quoth Quirinus, 'fynde
the in thy prisoun?' 'Go thy way anon', quoth Alixander ageyn, 'for he that
brought me hedyr shal brynge me ageyn thedyr weel inow.'
105   The tribune Quirinus wente and fet hys douhtir and led here to Alix-
anderis prisoun. And whan he fonde hym there, he fel doun at hys feet and
preyid for hys dowtyr. And she also bygan to blyssyn Alixandrys cheynes,
preyinge hym for to han helthe. 'Lete be, douhtyr', quoth Alixander, 'kesse
not my chenys but seke vp Seynt Petyris cheynys and kesse thoo and thou
110 shalt byn hool and heyl.' This herynge, Quirinus diligently dede sekyn vp
in the prisoun where Petir was the cheynes whiche he was boundyn with,
the whiche as sone as his douhtyr hadde kyssyd she was hool perfyhtly.

Whan Quirinus saw thys, he askyd Alixandir foryifnesse and deliueryd
hym owt of prisoun and, with hys houshold and manye othere, reseyuyd
the feyth and was cristenyd. Wich doon, Alixandyr ordeynyd thys feste to   115
byn holdyn in the kalendys of August and maad a cherche and put in the
chenys of Seynt Petyr, and clepyd yt the cherche of Seynt | Petyr ad vin-   f. 150ᵛᵃ
cula. To whiche cherche myche peple comyth on thys day for to kessyn the
seyid cheynys.

The thrydde cause of the institucioun of thys feste ys this, aftyr the sen-   120
tence of Bede. Octauianus and Antonius conceyuyd togedyr by a funte, for
Antonius had to wyfis Octauians sustyr, by acord diuidyd the empere of
the word betwyx hem so that Octauian han in the west Ytayle, Fraunce and
Spayne and Antonie in the est had Asye and Affric. But, for as myche as
Antonie was disslauy and leccherous and forsook hys wyf, Octauians sus-   125
tyr, and weddyd Cleopatre, the quen of Egipt, Octauian, hauynge indignacioun therof, wente estward into Asia ageyns hym and in alle thyngis ouyrcam hym. Antonye and Cleopatre, ouyrcomyn of Octauyan, fleddyn awey
and slowyn hemself for sorwe.

Aftyr this Octauyan dest[ro]yid the kyngdam of Egipt and mad yt a   130
prouince of Rome. Fro thens he went to Alisaundyr and spoylyd yt of alle
here rychesse and bar hem to Rome, wherby he encrecyd so the comoun
profytht of the cyte that a man myghte aftyrward byin in the cyte for a peny
that sumtyme was sold for foure. And for as myche as by cyuyl batayles the
cyte of Rome was gretly byforn wastyd and apeyrid, he soo reparyd yt and   135
renewyd yt, that he mygh wyl seyin therof hymself: 'I fonde Rome a cyte
of tyil, but I haue left yt a cyte of marbyl.' And for as meche as so gretly
augmentyd and encrecyd the comoun profyht of the cyte he was the fyrste
emperour that was clepid Augustus, of whom alle othere emperours aftyr
hym were clepid Augusti, lych as of Iulius Cesar they were clepid Cesares.   140
Moreouyr the monyth wyche byforn was clepyd Sextilis, for yt was the
sexte monyth fro March, the peple ascryuyd to hym and clepid yt August,
in remembraunce of a vi[c]torie wiche he had the fryst day of the sey[d]
monyth.

The whiche day the Romayns solemnizyd fro thensforward in wurshipe   145
of hym onto the tyme of Theodosie, whos rengne bygan aboute the yers
of oure lord foure hundyrd and fyue and twenty. Whos douthtyr Eudosia,
the wyf of Valentinian, wente to Ierusalem on pylgrimage, to whom a Iew
for a singuler and gret yiffte yaf two chenys with which Petyr was boundyn in Heroudys prisoun. And whan she cam hom ageyn to Rome and   150

130 destroyid] destrwyid   135 yt and] yt   143 victorie] vitorie   seyd] seyth
148 wente to] to   149 yiffte yaf] yiffte

sey how alle the peple solemnizyd and halwyd the fryste day of August
in wurship of an hethene man, she was verily sory that so gret reuerence
and solemnite was doon for a dampnyd man. And considerynge weel that
yt was not esy to drawyn the peple fro so longe rotyd consuetude, sche
155 bethout hyre in hyreself that she wold asayin to han that day halwyd and
wurshipid of Seynt Petyr, and han yt clepid 'ad vincula'. Wherevpon she
had a communi[ca]cyoun with the pope, that tyme clepyd Pelagie, and he
rygh gladly acceptyd and aprouyd hyre holy entent. And he and she togedyr, with plesaunte suasiouns exhortyd and inductyd the peple, that the
f. 150vb memorye | of the dampnyd prince of paynyms myht ben foryetyn, and
161 solemne memorie of the prince of the apostlys mygh ben had the same
day. And whan they seyin that alle the peple yaf assent to here suasiouns
and, fully condiscendynge to here purpos, the quein brought forth anoon
the sheynys whiche sche had at Ierusalem and seruyd hem to al the peple.
165 And the pope brough forth the sheyne with wiche Seynt Peter was boundyn in prisoun by Nero. The whiche ioynyd to the othyr twoo, anoon
they by miracle were turnyd into on, as thouht yt hade byn mad so at
the bygynnynge. The whiche chene the pope and quen offeryd vp in a
cherche of Seynt Petyr and namyd yt 'ad vincula'. The whiche cherche the
170 pope enduyd with manye grete priuilegis and ordeynyd that al holy cherche
shulde obseruyn and kepyn the seyd feste vniuerselly and in euery place.
Hec Beda.

But what vertu and grace this seyd shene hadde yt was weel prouyd
and shewyd the yer of grace nyne hundryd and fourty, vpon an erl, the
175 ny kynnysma[n] of Otto the emperour, whoom opynly, in the syht of alle
men, the deuyl wexyd so cruelly that he al torent hymself with hys own
teeth. The whiche erl anoon, at the emperours comaundement, was led to
Rome to the pope Ioon, that Seynt Petrys cheyne myht be leyd aboutyn
hys nekke, hopynge that therby he shulde be releuyd. Abowten whos
180 nekke ferst was put anothir cheyne, wherby he was nothynge amendyd.
But, as sone aftyr that as the very cheyne was put aboutyn hys nekke, the
deuyl myht not suffryn the gret myhty vertu therof, but lowde rorynge
and cryinge he wente hys wey. Thys seynge oon Theodorius, *Methensis
episcopus*, took the chene in hys hand and seyde pleynly that he wolde
185 not leuyn but hys hand were kut awey therfro. Wherfore betwyx the
pope and the clerge and the seyd byshop greu anoon a gret stryf and
contencyoun. The whiche perceyuynge, the emperour, whiche that tyme
was there present, brak the stryf betwyx hem and for to satisfyin the
bysshops he gat grace of the pope that he shulde youyn the bysshop

157 communicacyoun] communicyoun   175 kynnysman] kynnysmam

an amulet of the same cheyne. Whiche doon he was content and al   190
contencioun secyd.

Miletus tellith in his cronicle, and the same ys foundyn in *Historia tri-*
partita, that in tho dayis at a cyte clepid Epirum, ther apperid an huge gret
dragoun, in whoos mouth a bisshop clepid Donatus, a man of gret and
singuler vertu, spit a tokene of a cros fryst mad in hys own forheed, and   195
anoon the dragoun strof. Whoos carien that the eyre shuld not byn infec-
tyd therwith, vnnethe eyghte 30k of oxyn myht drawyn to the place where
yt shulde be brent.

In the same cronicle, and in the same story, yt ys also foundyn that the
deuyl, transfigurynge hymself into the lyknesse of Moyses, gadyrid toge-   200
dyr alle the Iewys, the whiche wern al abowtyn in that cuntre, vpon to an
hy tumlynge crag stondyng on the see brynge, counselynge hem to folwyn
hym and he shulde ledyn hem drye foot throgh the see on the lond | of   f. 151ᵣₐ
by[h]est, where he manye deludyd with a weyn hope and slow. Summe
throwyn veryly that deuyl dede this for to vengyn hym vpon hem, for as   205
myche as by occasyoun of a Iew the wurshipe of Octauyan was distroiyd
and secyd. Wherfore manye of the Iewes wheche ascapyd fl[e]d to feyth
and wern baptizyd. *Hec in historia Tripartita.*

The fourte cause of inst[itu]cioun of thys feste may ben assignyd on this
wyse, and that morally, for as meche as oure lord Ihesu meruelously dyli-   210
ueryd Petyr from hys bondys and yaf hym powyr to byndyn and vnbyndyn
in erthe. We, whiche byn boundyn with the bondys of synne, nedyn to byn
vnboundyn. Therfore we, in this solemnyte whiche ys clepid 'ad vincula',
besechyn hym that, lych as he was vnboundyn of hys bondys bodyly, so he
vouchesaf aftyr the power whiche he hath takyn of God to vnbyndyn vs   215
gostly from the intollerable bondys of synne.

And that this laste cause of this festis in[sti]tucyoun be resonablely assignyd may redely be knowyn and perceyuyd of hem that takyn heed that the
epestil of this day remembryth the vnbyndynge of Petyr from bodyly prisoun, the pouer eek whiche the gospel towc[h]yth comyttyd onto hem, and   220
how the orisoun also of the day that we myghte ben assoylyd of hym makyth
a special supplicacoun onto hym.

And that Seynt Petyr, by the keyes of the cherche committyd onto hym,
oftyn tyme assoylyth and vnbyndyth hem which ellys shulde be dampnyd,
yt ys clerly shewyd by a processe told in the book of miraclis of oure lady,   225
where yt ys seyid thus: In the cyte of Coleyne, in the m[o]nastorie of Seynt

204 byhest] bynhest   and slow] slow and deludyd   207 fled] fleld
209 institucioun] instancioun   210 meche as] meche   217 institucyoun]
infatucyoun   220 towchyth] towcyth   226 monastorie] manastorie

Petyr, was a munk lyth of gouernaunce, dislauy and lecherous. Yt happyd this munk to be preuent with sodeyn deth, whoom anoon environd a
gret multitude of deuyls, myghtyly acusynge hym. Of whiche oon seyde
230 thus: 'I am Coueytyse, whom oftyn ageyns the comaundement of God
thou hast desiryd.' 'I am Veynglorye', quoth anothir, 'through whiche thou
hast oftyn amonge folke the veynly reioyisshd.' 'I am Lesyng', quoth the
thridde, 'throgh whiche thou hast ful oftyn hem whiche thou hast at alle
tyme disslauyly the delytyd.' And so forth ych synne aftyr other myghtyly
235 hym acusyd. Ageyns whoom hys good werkes whiche he had don bysyly
hym excusyd, whereof oon seyde thus: 'I am Obedyence, by whiche thou
submyttyst the to the souereyns.' 'I am', quoth anothir, 'the psalmodye,
wherin by syngyng thou hast myche ben excercisid and also by redynge.'
In wych menetyme Seynt Petyr, patron of the monastorie, wente vp to the
240 iuge to preyin for his mon[k]. To whom oure lord answerde and seyde:
'Petyr, knowyst not thou how the prophete by inspiracioun of me seyde:
"Lord, whoo shal dwellyn in thi tabernacle, or whoo shal restyn in thyn
holy hyl"? And he answerde ageyn and seythe: "he that werkyth ryhtwysnesse entryth in withowtyn spot." How may thanne this munk be sauyd,
245 whiche neythir entrid in withoute spot, ner hath noth wrouht rythwys-
f. 151rb nesse?' But Petyr, instantly preyinge for | thys munke and also oure lady,
at the laste oure lord yaf the sentence that his soule shulde turnyn ageyn
onto the body and so don penaunce, yf he wolde. Whiche sentence youyn,
anoon Petyr, with the keye whiche he held in hys hand, maad the deuyl
250 aferd and drof hym awhey, and the soule of the deed munk he delyueryd
into the handys of oon whiche was felawe onto the seyd munk and bad
hym ledyn yt ageyn into the body. The whiche persone, whan he brouht
ageyn the soule to the body, for ys part he asskyd this salary: that euery
day, as longe as he shulde abydyn in the body aftyr that, he shulde seyin
255 the penitencyal psalme '*Miserere mei deus*' and that oftyn he shulde makyn
clene hys graue with bysinys. This munk thanne, reuyguryd and turnyd
ageyn to lyf, tolde alle men whiche woldyn heryn al that he had seyn and
diligently performyd the thyngis whiche he was enioynyd & cetera.

[129. STEPHEN POPE]

The lyf of Seynt Steuene pope & martir.
Whan the gret per[secu]cioun of Cristis feyth was excercysyd in Rome

240 monk] monuk   243–4 ryhtwysnesse entryth] ryhtwysnesse and he andswe-
ryth ageyn and seyth he that werkyth ryhtwysnesse and entryth   246 munke] muke
2 persecucioun] perfeccioun

vndyr Valeryan and Galien ocupiynge the empere, the blyssyd man Seynt
Steuene, beynge pope, gadryd togedyr al hys clergie and exhortid hem that
they for Cristis sake shulde gladly and [constauntly] reseyuyn and takyn 5
the coroun or the palme of martirdam. This blyssyd man ordeynyd thre
prestis, seuene dekenys and sextene clerkys, whiche dayly he ta[l]kyd and
spak of the kyngdam of heuene. And many honest and wurthi folk, sterid
by the grace of God, comyn to hym and were baptizid of hym. Amonge
whiche was baptizid of hym oon clepid Nemesius, a tribun, with al his 10
houshold and his douhtyr Lucilla, the whiche was blynd and maad to seen
ageyn by the seyid blyssid Pope Steuene. Anothir tribun also was baptizid
of hym, clepyd Olimpius, with his wiff Exuperia and hys sone Theodolus,
and as manye as byleuyd in the houshold of Olimpius. The whiche alle
aftyrward, thorgh a glorius confession, tokyn the palme of martirdam and 15
wentyn to blysse of heuene.

And, for as meche as the persecucyoun was gret and sharp, this blyssid
Steuene seyde messis and kept hys consultacyouns, and tawt and baptisyd meche peple in dyueres placis priuyly, as in martyris criptis and cauys
and cimitorijs. For whiche cause the emperours deden here bysynesse to 20
takyn hym or eny of hys clerkys, and with cruel examinacioun to puttyn
hem to deth. And at the laste, whan they haddyn aspiyd where he was,
they sentyn gret multitude of knyhtys to takyn hym and hys clerkys and
to brynkyn to here presence. And whan they weren takyn and brouht to
the paleys, Pope Steuene entryd alone onto Valerians tribunal bench. To 25
whoom Valerian seyde on this wyse: 'Art thou Steuene, wiche with thi
crafth byfryst the to turnyn vp-so-doun the comoun profyht, and with thy
suasions and exhortacyons labouryst to make the peple to goon from the
seruyse and the wurshipe of oure goddys?' | 'As for the comoun profy[t]h', f. 151va
quoth Steuene ageyn, 'I wil thou wete that I turne [it] not vp-so-doun but 30
for the weelfare therof. And for the saluacioun of the peple, I counsele and
exhorte hem for to forsakyn deuyls wyche byn wurshipid in ydols dede,
and to turnyn ageyn to very quek God in heuene, and to knowe Ihesu Crist
to byn the sone of God, whiche with the fadyr and with the holy gost ys
consubstancial and co[e]terne. Withoute wiche may no man be sauyd but 35
must nedys perisshyn with the deuyl into euerelestynge deth.'

At whiche answer[e] Valerian wood yaf anoon this sentence: that he
shulde be led to Martys temple and, yf he wolde not wurshipen Mar-
tis abhominabele similacre, that euene there hys heed shulde be smet of.
And anon as this blissid man was led owt at the gate clepid *Porta Appia* of 40

5 constauntly] constauntly if ne were   7 talkyd] takkyd   29 profyth] profygh
30 it] I   35 coeterne] cocterne   37 answere] answerde

Valerians knythtys, and he saw afor Martys temple whedyr he was chargyd
to be led, he lyftyd vp hys hyne to heuene and seyde on this vyse: 'Lord
God and fadyr of oure lord Ihesu Crist, the whiche distroydist the tour
of confusioun of Babylonye, distroye now this place, wherin the pep[li]s
45 soulys perisshin by wurshipenge of ydols by the deuyls s[t]uperfacioun.'
And anoon as this was seyid ther gru swych a tempest of gret thundryn,
and swych a cr[ie] and feyr of lyhtnynge, that the most part of the temple
tumpled doun, and the knyhtis whiche ledde Steuene, for dred and feyr,
leftyn hym and fleddyn awey. Thys seyng, blyssyd Steuene, with alle the
50 cristene men, wente to Seynt Lucyes cimiterie, and, aftyr a gret exhorta-
cioun and an holy, the pope offryd for hem a sacrifice to oure lord God
almyghty.

But as sone as Valerian herde what was don, he sente moo knyhtis than
there were byforn to don execucioun of the sentence whiche he had youyn
55 vpon the Pope Steuene. The whiche comyn and foundyn hym makyng to
God a sacrifice and stedfastly, and withowtyn ony dred, performyng that
he had bygunnyn, and they presumptouously percyd in and smettyn of hys
heed, in hys see the secunde day of August. Whoos body with his heed was
buryid in the same place where hys blood was shed, the whiche place was
60 and his clepid into this day *Cimitorium Kalixti & cetera.*

[130. FINDING OF STEPHEN]

The Inuencion of Seynt Steuene

The Inuencioun or the fyndynge of the body of Seynt Steuene, the
fryste martyr for Cristis sake aftyr that Crist was rysyn from deth to lyf, was
in the seuente yer of the Empere of Honorye, the yer of grace foure hundy-
5 rid and seuentene. And here yt ys to byn notyd er we procede ony ferthere
in oure processe that thre festis ben foundyn of Seynt Steuene bysydyn
hys passioun: as the inuencyoun, the translacioun and the vnyoun. The
passioun of Seynt Steuene ys solemnisyd the nexte day aftyr Cristemesse
day and whi yt shal be told anon hereaftyr. The inuencyoun of this blissid
10 martirs body was maad on thys maner wyse.

f. 151vb   Ther was in the teritorie | of Ierusalem dwellynge a prest, whoos name
was Lucianus, whoom Gennadius reknyht amonge the nobyl and wurthi
men in hys book *De Viris illustribus.* This prest, as he lay in hys bed vpon
a fryday nyht and was, as yt semyd hym, ner wakynge, had this maner of
15 visioun. Hym thoughte that a semly staturyd old man and fayr, facyd with

44 peplis] pephs   45 stuperfacioun] superfacioun   47 crie] criour

a longe berd, clad in a whiht stole in whiche were wouyn gemmys of gold
and goldene crossis, hys hosyn and shoon beynge gylt in the ouyr-part
therof, apperid onto hym seyinge on this maner, touchynge hym with a
yerde of g[ol]d whiche he bar in hys hand: 'Diligently do thy deuyr and thi
bysinesse to fyndyn vp oure grauys, for we ben hyd in an vnwurthi place   20
and in an vncomely. Wherfore goo thou to Ioon, the bysshop of Ierusalem,
and sey hym that he take vs vp and burye vs in a more conuenyent place
and a more wurthi. For syth that gret drouthte and tribulacioun hath put
the word in gret trouble and heuynesse, yt ys Goddys wyl, by meryt of
oure suffragiys and oure preyers, to be to the word propicious and to she-   25
wyn hys mercyfulnesse.' Quoth Lucianus the prest ageyn to hym: 'Good
syre, who art thou whiche on this [maner wyse] apperyst now here onto
me?' 'I am', quoth he ageyn to Lucyan, '[G]amaliel, wiche norysshd vp
Poule the postille and at my feet tawt hym the lawe. He that lyith with me
ys Stephanus, whom the Iewys slowyn with stonys and throwyn hys body   30
withowte the cyte for to han byn deuouryd with whylde bestis and with
foulys, but that wolde not he sufferyn to whoom this blyssyd martir kept
hys feyth vndefoulyd. Wherfore I wyth gret reuerence gadryd vp hys body
and buryid yt in myn own newe graue.

Anothir whiche also lyth with me ys Nicodemus, my newu, the whiche   35
aftyr the gospel cam to speke with Ihesu by nyht, whiche also of Petyr and
Ioon was baptizid. Wherfore the princys of the prestys shuldyn han slayn
hym, had they not lefth for reuerence of vs, and that he was ny to vs of
kenrede. Not forthan for al vs they despoylyd al hys substaunce, depryuyd
hym of hys princehood and al towundyd they leftyn hym, half quyk and   40
half deed. Whom I also took to me into myn hous and fewe dayis aftyr,
whan he was ded, I maad hym to byn buryid at blissid Steuenys feet.

The thredde also whiche ly[t]h with me ys Abibas, my sone, the whiche
in hys twenty wyntyr of age took the baptem with me and, beynge stylle a
maydyn, with Poule my disciple lernyd the lawe of me. But my wyf Ethua   45
and my sone Selemias, the whiche woldyn not reseyuyn Cristis feyth,
w[e]re not wurthy to byn buryid with vs, whom thou shalt fyndyn buryid in
anothir place, but here grauys ydyl thou shalt fyndyn and empty.' Whiche
processe told, blyssid Gamaliel passid away from Lucyans syht and whan
he wook he preyid God that, yf this visioun were trewe, yt myht apperyn   50
agayn onto hym the secunde tyme and the thrydde. The nexte fryday folwynge he apperyd ageyn onto hym, lych in alle wyses as he dede byfore,
and askyd hym why he was negligent to don swyche thyngis as he |

19 gold] glod   27 maner wyse] wyse on this maner wyse   28 Gamaliel]
samaliel   43 lyth] lych   47 were] where   53 *Ends defective.*

[131. DOMINIC]

f. 152ra . . . ingys and they aftyr good deliberacyoun to yiue sentence whethir
shulde ben holdyn. And amonge manye libellys maad of diuers feythful,
the libelle of Dominic was singulerly chosyn to be presentyd to the iugis
examinacioun. And, aftyr longe discrepaunce bytwyx the iugis, at the laste
5 the comoun degre of hem was thys: that bothe libellys shuldyn be cast in
a gret feyr maad for the same cause, and whiche of hem that brent not
they iugyd fully that libelle tor conteyne t[he] very trewe feyth. Whiche
doon, the heretykis libel, as sone as yt touchyd the fyir, brente and was
consumpt anoon. But blyssyd Dominic libel not only brent not but also,
10 as sone as yt touchyth the feyr, yt styrt owt ageyn a fer weye from the feyr,
withowtyn blemyssh or hurt in ony wyse. The whiche, the secunde and the
thryde tyme throwyn into the fyir, ageyn st[yr]t owt fe[r]ther fro, lych as
yt dede fyrst.

Aftyr whiche tyme, whan alle men wentyn hoom ageyn, yche man into
15 hys owyn cuntre, and the bysshop Exonience was ded, Seynt Dominic only,
with a fewe drawynge onto hym, abood there stylle and constauntly and
persyuerantly prechid and tawt the trewe doctrine of the feyth ageyns the
heretykis. Whoom the aduersariys of treuthe dayly mokkyd and skornyd,
spittyd vpon hym and throwyng at hym dung and al maner fylthe and
20 vnclennesse, and knyttyn at hys bak for sko[r]n burrys and wyspys and
swyche othir thyngis. And not only that but also threttyd hym for to slen
hym. To whom he answerde ageyn withowtyn ony feer and seyde: 'I am
not', quoth he, 'wurthi the glory of martyrdam, ner I haue not deseruyd
that maner deeth.' Wherfore swyche placys as was seyid that wayt was maad
25 for hym, not ony vnaferd but also singynge and myry he went the same weye.
Whereof they gretly amaruaylyd seydyn to hym on this wyse: 'Haast thou,
Dominic, noon h[o]rroure of deth? What woldyst thou han don yf we haddyn takyn the in swyche a place?' 'Sekyr', quoth he ageyn, 'I wolde han
bysowt yow that ye wolde not han slayn me ouyr hastyly, but by processe
30 and successyfly han mutilat and but awey alle myn membrys and shewyd
hem me byforn myn eyne, and aftyr that to han put owt myn eyne and so,
half deed, to han lefth my body lyin and walwyn in myn ow[y]n blood. Or
ellys at the leste to han slayn me with what deeth you [h]ad best likyd.'

Yt happyd oo tyme that on of the feythful for penurye and myschef drow
35 to the felashepe of the heretykis. And whanne blyssyd Dominic knew yt,

---

1 *Starts defective at top of f. 152ra*.   7 the] to   12 styrt] stryt   ferther] fether
20 skorn] skon   27 horroure] herrour   32 owyn] ownyn   33 had] bad

hauynge co[m]passioun and pyte vpon the man, fully determynyd within
hymself that he wolde han sold hymself, that with the pryhs of hymself he
myht han releuyd the man of hys bodyly penurye and nede and redemyd
hym from the errow[r]e that he was drawyn to, co[m]pellyd by miserye and
nede. And so he shulde han doon, ne had the mercy of God prouydyd for   40
the mannys delyueraunce anothir | weye of remedye.   f. 152rb

Anothir tyme a w[u]mman lamentabylle compleynyd onto hym that
hyre brothir was in captiu[i]te and thraldam amonge Sa[r]asyns and she
had no werwith for to quytyn hys raunsum. And he anoon, meuyd with
co[m]passioun and pyte, offryd hymself to be sold for to quyten hym ther- 45
with. But God whiche knewe hym there [t]he more necessarye for manye
folk gostly redempcyoun wolde not sufferyn hym.

Thys seyid blyssid man was onys herberwyd in the partis of Tholose
w[ith] certeyn matronys, the whiche where deceyuyd with heretykys vndyr
an ostentacyoun of religioun. And whan he perseyuyd how yt was, he   50
abood stylle with hem a lentone for to wynnyn hem ageyn to the trewe
feyth. The whiche tyme he fastyd euery day breed and watyr and wecched
the most part of the nyht. And whanne the necessite of nature askyd to
restyn hys wery membrys, he lenyd doun vpon a bare bench and so slepte
a lytyl wyle. And thus by good exau[m]ple of lyuynge and holy doctrine of   55
techynge, he w[a]n ageyn these matronys to the trewe feyth and byleue.

Aftyr thys blyssyd man inwardly bygan to thynkyn hym to makyn an
ordre whos office shulde byn to goon abowte the word and to prechyn and
to strengthyn the feyth of holy cherche ageyn heretykis. And whan he had
dwellyd in the partys of Tholose ten yer afftyr the deth of bisshop Exo-   60
nience tyl the tyme that the counsel Latarenence shulde byn holdyn at
Rome, he wente thedyr to that general counsel with oon clepyd Fulco,
the bisshop of Tholowse, where he askyd of the Pope Innocent to han hys
ordre confermyd in the name of prechouris to hym and to hys successou-
ris. To whos peticyoun whan the seyd pope sumwhat yaf hymself straunge,   65
vpon a nyth slepynge hym thowte the cherche Latranence sodeynly sempte
that yt shulde han ben ouyrthrowyn. And as he stood ferfully and byhild
yt, Dominic hym thowthe cam anoon and put therageyns hyse shuldrys
and myhtyly bar yt vp, that yt myht not fally[n]. And whan he wook, he,
weel vndyrsto[n]denge the visioun, gladly grauntyd to Dominic the peti-   70
cioun that he askyd, amonestyng hym that he shulde turnyn agey[n] to his

36 compassioun] conpassioun   39 errowre] errowe   compellyd] con-
pelled   42 wumman] wuumman   43 captiuite] captiuute   Sarasyns]
Satasyns   45 compassioun] conpassioun   46 the] he   49 with] whiche
55 exaumple] exauumple   56 wan] whan   58 word] world   67 han ben]
han   69 fallyn] fally   70 vndyrstondenge] vndyrstodenge   71 ageyn]
ageyns

brethyrn, and that he and they shuldyn chesyn hem sum approuyd rewle
to lyuyn vndyr. And thanne whanne he come ageyn he shulde han the
confirmacyoun of hys ordre, lyche as he desiryd. And whan he cam ageyn
75 to his brethryn, aboute the no[m]bre of sextene, and told hem the popys
answere, anoon fryst the holy gost clepyd to, they chesyn alle concordly
and with oon assent the reule of the nobyl and wurthy prechour Seynt
Austyn, addynge therto certeyn obseruaunces of streytere lyuyn by maner
of constitucyons, the whiche they oblysshyd hemself to kepyn. In which
80 menetyme Pope Innocence deed, of his successour Honorie Dominic askyd
and gat the confirmacyoun of hys ordre, the yer of grace a thousent two
hundryd and sextene.

f. 152 va   Aftyr whiche tyme, wyl he in the cherche | of Seynt Petyr preyid en-
terly for the encres and the dilatacyoun of hys ordre, hym thoughte he
85 saw Petyr and Poule comynge onto hym. Of whiche the fyrste, that ys to
seyne Seynt Petyr, as hym semyd, took hym a staf and Seynt Poule a book,
seying to hym on this wyse: 'Goo forth and preche! For to this ministerye and office thou art chosyn of God.' And forthwith hym thoughte he
saw hys brethryn disperbild al abowten the word, goynge t[w]o and two
90 [to]gedyr and p[r]echyn the word of God. Wherfore whanne he cam ageyn
to Tholose he disperbild his brethryn, sendynge summe to Spayne, summe
to Paryhs and summe to Bononye, but hymself aftyr that returnyd ageyn
to Rome.

A lityl byforn the institucyoun of thys ordre of prechourys, a certeyn
95 munk, rauassh[i]d in spirit, saw oure lady knelynge and ioynynge hyre handys, bysyly preyinge hyre sone to han mercy vpon mankynde. And whanne
oure lord Ihesu had dyuers tymys and oftyn youyn hym[se]lf da[un]gerous
and straunge onto hys pytous modrys preyre, at the laste he seyide onto
here this wyse: 'Modyr, what owey or may I doon more for mank[ende]
100 than I haue doo? I haue sent onto hym patriarkis and prophetis and lytyl
they amenden hem. I cam to hem mys[elf] and aftyr I sente onto hem myn
apostlys and bothe me and hem they cruelly slowyn. Aftyrward I sente onto
hem my martyrs, my confessours and myn doctours, and lytyl heed or non
they took to hem. But nertheles, modyr, syth yt ys not leeffull to me to deny
105 in the thyn askynge, I graunte the that I shal sendyn hem myn prechours,
by whoom they shal moun byn illumynyd, or I shal comyn ageyns hem.'

A lych visioun anothir saw that tyme that the twelue abbottys of the
Cystrews ordre were sent to Tholose ageyns the heretykis, where yt ys

75 nombre] nounbre	89 two] to	90 togedyr] gedyr	prechyn]
prchyn	95 rauasshid] rauasshd	97 hymself] hymslef	daungerous]
damgerous	99 mankende] makyngende	101 myself] myslef	106 or I] I

seyid that whanne oure lady had preyid hyre sone, lych as ys seyid byforn, and had concludyd hyre preyere on this wyse: 'Good sone, thou owyst not to don to mankynde aftyr here maleys but aftyr thi mercy', he, ouyrcomen with here preyere, answerdyn: 'At thy wyl, modyr, I shal now doo with hem myn mercy. For I shal sendyn to hym myn prechouris for to techen hem and for to monestyn hem, whom yf they wyl not heryn and amendyn hem, I shal no lengere sparyn hem.'

Yt ys red in the gestys of the Erl Mountfort that w[h]an Seynt Domi-nic oonys had prechyd ageyns heretykis, the auctorites which he allegyd he put in wrytynge and delyueryd yt to oon of the heretikis to takyn delibe-racioun and auysement how he wolde answere therto. And the same nyht, whanne alle the heretykis were gadyrid togydyr by the fyir, he, the whiche had reseyuyd the cedule of Seynt Dominic, brouht yt forth among hem. To whom hys felaas bodyn that he shulde throwyn yt in the feyir and, yf yt brente not, they wolde prechyn the feyth of the cherche of Rome for trewe. The whiche cedule throwyn into the fyir, whan yt had byn therin a while, styrt owt ageyn vnbrent and vnhurt. And so yt was don twyis or thryis, and euere | yt stryt owt saf and hol. And whanne the heretykys seyin this, obdurat in here maleyes, they confedryd hem togedyr with on ooth that non of hem shule disclosyn ner pupplysshe this mater. Not forthan the[r] was a k[ny]ht amonge hem the whiche was sumwat inclinyd to oure feyth-ward and he, as God wolde, pupplisshyd yt aftyrward. And this thynge was don in a place the whiche ys clepyd Mons Victorialis.

A certeyn frere menour, the whiche longe tyme had ben Seynt Fraunces felawe, tolde this story [to] diuers frere prechourys: 'The tyme', quoth he, 'that Seynt Dominic labouryd at Rome to the pope for the confirmacyoun of hys ordre, vpon a nyht as he was in hys preyere, he saw in spirit Crist abouyn hym in the eyr, hauynge thre sperys in his hand and shakynge hem dounward ageyns the word. To whom anoon hym thouhte cam rennynge hys modyr and askyd hym what he wolde don. "Modyr", quoth he ageyn, "the word ys ful of these synnys: pride, lecherye and couetyse. And ther-fore I purpose me to sleen mankynde with these thre sperys." "A, dere sone", quod she ageyn, "I biseche yow enterly, tempryth sumwhat youre cruelnesse and abydyth yit a while of youre veniaunce, and letyth yowre ryhtwyhsnesse be medlyd with mercy." "Modyr", quoth he, "see ye not what iniuryis and wrongis byn dayly don to me?" "Yit, sone, I beseche yow beth pacient and abydyth a while. I haue here a feythful seruaunt and a myghty champyoun, the whiche shal reynyn ouyr al abowte, and with the

110

115

120

125

f. 152vb

130

135

140

145

---

116 whan] wan   128 ther] the   129 knyht] kynht   133 to] whiche shal telle to

swerd of the word shal ouyrcomyn the word and makyn yt subiet onto the.
To whom I shal conioynyn anothir seru[aunt] whiche I haue, and he shal
don the same." "Certeyn, modyr", quoth Crist ageyn, "and I, quemyd,
150 accepte the bone. But yet I wolde seen these two whom thou purposist to
sende to performyn this holy office." And anoon oure lady presentyd to
hyre swete sone Seynt Dominic, whoom he benyngnely and gladly acceptyd and comendyd hym and ablyd hym to the seyd office. Whiche don the
blissid lady offryd onto here sone in lych wyse Seynt Fraunceys, whoom
155 Crist also gladly admyttyd to the same occupacyoun. Seynt Dominic in this
visioun diligently byholdynge hys felawe thus by Crist and his modyr assocyid onto hym, notwithstondenge that he neuere had seyn hym byforn. Yet
on the nexte day, whan he fond hym in the cherche he knewe hym withowte
tellynge or techynge of ony man. And anoon he wente onto hym and hal-
160 syd hym and kyssyd hym, and seyde to hym on this wyse: "Thou art my
felaue. Thou shalt renne with me. Lete vs stondyn togedyr myhtyly and
there schal not aduersarie preuaylen ageyn vs." And anoon he declaryd
onto hym by ordre the processe of his reualacyoun. And so from that tyme
forth they were knyt togydyr in herte and soule, and chargyd hyre brethryn
165 euere aftyr for to ben vsid and knyt togedyr in affeccyoun euere aftyr.'

Whanne blyssyd Dominic had onys reseyuyd onto hys ordre a nouyce,
oon born of Naplys cuntre, the felaas of hym byforn his conuercyoun had |
f. 153ʳᵃ so peruertyd hym that fully he desiryd to turnyn ageyn to the word, and for
that entent he instauntly askyd ageyn his secular clothis. The whiche caas
170 whanne Seynt Dominic knew, he anoon bygan to preyin. And whanne they
had dispoylyd this yunge man his religious clothis and put vpon his seculer sh[yr]t, he bygan with gret voys to cryin on this wyse: 'Allas! I waxe
ouyr hoot, I brenne, I consume! Pullyth of, pullyth of this cursyd shyrt,
the whiche thus intollerabylly brynnyth and distroyith me.' Ner he myth
175 neuere restyn tyl he was dispoylyd therof and was clad ageyn in religious
clothis and turnyd ageyn to the cloystir.

Oo tyme whanne Seynt Dominic was at Bononye and hys brethryn were
gon to slepyn, a certeyn brothir, a conuers, anoon was vexyd with a spirit.
And hys mayster, oon clepyd Frater Rainerius, forthwith wente and told
180 yt to Seynt Dominic, and he anoon bad hym be brouth into the cherche
byforn the auter. And whanne vnnethe ten brethyrn myhtyn brynkyn hym
thedir and he was comyn, Seynt Dominic seyde on this wyse: 'I coniure
the, o wrecchyd spiryt, and charge the that thou telle me whi thou vexyst
thus this creature of God!' To whom the spirit answerd thus: 'I vexe hym
185 ryhtfully for he hath deseruyd yt. Yistirday he drank in the cyte withowte

148 seruaunt] seruanaunt   172 shyrt] shryt

leue. And whanne he draunke he maad no tokene of the cros, ner blyssyd
not the drynke. Wherfore, whyl he drank, I entryd in hym in the lyknesse
of a popyn and, for to seyin more treuly, he drowe me in with the wyn.'
And that he so drank was foundyn trewe. In this menetyme the fyrste peel
was runge to matyns, whiche whan the foul spirit herde, anoon he creyid   190
and seyde: 'Here may I no lengere abyden, for the hedyd felaas bygynnyn
to ryse.' And thus at the preyere of Seynt Dominic he went owt of the man
and wexyd hym no more.

Whanne this blyssyd man onnys in the partys of Tholose wente ouyr
a flood, casuelly and vnwarly hys bokys fellyn into the watyr. And the   195
thrydde day aftyr yt happyd a fysshere to castyn in hys hook on the same
place where the bokys fyllyn and, wenynge to han had a gret fyssh, he
pullyd vp the bookys as clene and as drye as they had be kept in an almarie.

Thys blyssyd man cam onys to a monasterye and fond al his brethyrn at
reste. And for he wold not vnqueytyn hem he bygan to makyn a preyere and   200
anoon, the gatys beynge shet, bothe he and hys felawe entrid in withowte
ony mannys helpe. And in lych wyse, in the tyme of conflyct with the
heretykys, whanne he and a conuers of the Cistrens comyn to a cherche and
foundyn yt shet, at the preyere of Dominic they foundyn hemself withinne
and al the nyght aftyr they wecchyd and preyid.   205

Aftyr gret laboure in iournyinge the holy man had in custome to swagyn
hys trust at sum welle that, whanne he come to hys herberwe, he shulde
not be notyd of excesse in drynkyn.

A scolyr whiche was libidi[n]ous and myche youyn to lust of hys flesshe
cam onys to the place of frerys for to heryn messe, and yt happyd Seynt   210
Dominic to byn at messe the same tyme. And whan | tyme of offerynge   f. 153rb
cam, thys scoler cam, as yt was the guyse, and kessyd hys hand with a gret
deuocyoun. Of wyche kysse hym thoute he felte comyn owt of his hand so
gret a flauour of swetnesse as he neuere had felt byforn. And fro that tyme
forth the inordinel hete of flesshly lust was so colyd and quenchid in hym   215
that he neuere was ouyrcome therwith aftyr that tyme.

A serteyn prest, seyinge oftyn tyme blyssyd Dominic and hys brethyrn
feruently and dylygently ocupyin hem in prechynge, he purposyd hym
fully to drawyn to here felashepe and to ben assocyat onto hem, be so
that he myght han the newe testament, necessarie as hym thoughte to a   220
prechour of Goddys word. And anoon as this pryst had this in hys thouhte,
a yonge man stood euene by hym, berynge vndyr his lappe the whiche
newe testament ven[dable] and for to selle, the whiche the pryst with gret
ioye and gladnesse bowt of hem anoon. But yet thys prest, stondynge in

225 dowte what he myghte don, anoon aftyr a short preyere for grace he mad
a tokene of the cros vpon the book withowtyn and opnydd yt. And anoon
the fyrste capityl that cam to hys syht was that whiche was seyid to Petyr
in the Actys of the apostlys, where yt ys seyid thus: 'Ryhs vp and go doun
and goo with hem, nothyng dowtynge, for I haue sent hem.' With these
230 wurdys the prest, weel hertyd and comfortyd, wente forthwith and drow
hym to here felashepe.

Whylom in the cyte of Tholose was a master of diuynyte, famous and
notable of kunnynge. Thys mayster beynge regent, vpon a morwe, as he
sat byforn day preuydynge hys lessoun whiche he shulde redyn, sodeynly
235 oppressyd with sleep he lenyd hys heed doun on hys chayer. And anoon
hym thouthte were presentyd onto hym seuene fayre brygh sterrys. And
whyl he gretly maruaylyd of the n[o]uelte of that present, sodeynly thoo
seuene sterris grewyn so gret, bothen in quantite and also in lyth, that they
illumynyd and mad bryht al the word. And whan thys mayster wook, and
240 what this visioun myghte menyn set gretly ameruaylynge, euene forthwith
cam into the scole blyssyd Dominic, and with hym sexe brethryn of hys
own ordre, and mekely seyde to the mayster that yt was here purpos for to
hauntyn hys scole and to heryn hys lessouns. Wherby anoon the seyd mayster conseyuyd and dempte that the seuene sterris whiche wern presentyd
245 onto hym sygnifyid the seuene personys, Dominic and hys brethryn.

Onys wyl Seynt Dominic was at Rome ther cam thedyr with the bisshop
of Orlyons oon clepyd Reynold, the deen of Seynt Amian in Orlyons, the
whiche deen had ben regent at Paryhs in lawe canoun fyue yer togedyr.
This seyid wurthi man had longe ben in purpos to han lefth alle othere
250 thyngis and to han ocupyid hym in prechynge, but he cowde not fynde the
menys to performyn hys entent. And whanne he had communyd with a
cardynal and told hym hys entent and he ageyn-ward had enformyd hym
of the instytucioun of the newe ordre of prechourys, anoon Dominic was
f. 153ᵛᵃ sent | fore and herde also hys entent. Aftyr whiche tyme, withowte more,
255 this wurthy man, with inward deliberacioun purposyd to entrin into this
newe prechours ordre. And anon aftyr he fel into a greuous accesse, the
whiche wexyd hym so sore that men vtturly despeyryddyn hys helthe. This
herynge Seynt Dominic, anoon he ran to hys quotidian and customable
armure preyere and specially he besoute oure lady, to whos tuicyoun he
260 had commyttyd the singuler cure and charge of hys newe religioun, that
at the laste, by medyacioun of hyre, oure lord wolde grauntyn hym this
mannys lyf for a mene tyme. At whiche preyere oure blyssyd lady cam be-
twyxyn two maydyns of passynge gret bewte and visibilly apperyd to seyid

237 nouelte] neuelte

Reynold as he lay wakynge and abydynge deth, and with a pleasaunt chere
seyde to hym on this wyse: 'Reynold, aske of me what thou wylt and I shal   265
grauntyn yt the.' And as he lay, takynge within hymself auesement and
deliberacyoun what he myght askyn, oon of the forseyd maydenys counselyd hym that he shulde nothynge askyn but that he fully shulde commyttyn
hys wyl and his peticyoun to the wyl of the quen of mercy. And whanne he
had don as this maydyn counselyd hym, anon the quen of mercy put forth   270
hyre maydenly hand and with an helful oynement whiche she brough with
hyre she anoy[n]tyd hys eyne, his erys, his mouth, hys nosetherlys, hys
handys, hys feet and his reynis, seyinge at ych of hem the propyr f[o]rme
of wurdys ordeynyd therfore, saf at the reynys she seyde thus: 'Thy reynys
mote be gyrt streyte with the gerdyl of continence and chastyte.' But at the   275
feet she vsid this maner of seyinge: 'I anoy[n]te thy feet to byn maad redy to
gon aboutyn to prechyn the gospel of pes.' Whiche seyid, she addyd therto
this clause: 'The thrydde day aftyr this I shal sende onto the a vyol of resty-
tucyoun of perfyth helthe.' And aftyr this she schewyd hym the prechours
habyte and seyde: 'Loo! Thys ys the habyte of thyn ordre.' And this same   280
visioun in alle degreys saw Seynt Dominic as he lay in his preyere.

And the nexte morwe whan he cam to the seyid Reynol[d] and fond
hym heyl and hool and had herd of hym al the processe of his visioun, he
took the abyte which oure lady had shewyd hym. For byforn he and hys
frerys weryn and vsyd for here habyte surplyihs. The thred day oure lady   285
cam ageyn onto hym lych as she had promysyd hym, and so anoy[n]tyd al
hys body that, not only she quenchyd in hym the brynnynge hete of the
feuyrs, but also al the ardour of concupiscence in hys flesshly membrys,
and so meche that, as he afftyrward knowlechyd hymself, he neuere aftyr
[felt] therin the tirannye of the fryste meuyngis. This same visioun efth-   290
sonys shewynge ageyn a religious man of the ordre of the hospitulers saw
Seynt Dominic beynge present, and was gretly astoynyd therwith. Also
Seynt Dominic hymself puplysshyd and shewyd the same visioun to manye
frerys and specialy aftyr hys deth. Thes seyid Reynold, this wyse mad a |
frere, was fyrst sente to Bononye, where instauntly he prechyd and gretly   f. 153vb
encrecyd the nou[m]bre of fryris. Fro thens he sent to Parys, nat manye   296
yers aftyr he slepte in oure lord.

A younge man whiche was the newe of Steuene the cardinal de *Noua
Fossa* rekleesly syttynge vpon an hors, fel vnwarly heedlyngys into a deep
dyche and was pullyd vp deed. Whoom his frendys presentyd to Seynt   300
Dominic and, as sone as had preyid for hym, he roos vp ageyn heyl and

272 anoyntyd] anoytid   273 forme] ferme   276 anoynte] anoyte
282 Reynold]Reynol   286 anoyntyd]anoytyd   290 felt]he felt   296 noumbre]
nouunbre

quyk. In the cherche of Seynt Cristofere a werkman, hyrid for to refres-
shyn and to amendyn the ruine therof, the whiche a sodeyn fallynge therof
was brou doun to grunde, and the mater whyche lay vpon hym maad an
305 ende of hym and slou hym. Whoos body, whan yt was drawyn from vndyr
the materye, Seynt Dominic bad be brouht onto hym and anon, through
hys preyeres, the man recuryd bothe lyf and helthe.

Onys was brouht onto hym a man, the whiche was vexyd with manye
deuyls. And blyssyd Dominic anoon took a stole and fyrst he keste yt
310 aboutyn hys owyn nekke and afftyr he g[yr]t yt aboutyn the vexyd mannys nekke, chargynge the deuyls that they no more shulde vexyn the man.
Whiche doon, they anon bygunne to be tormentyd and peynyd in the mannys body. Wherfore they cryid and seydyn on this wyse: 'Dominic, suffere
vs for to gon owt of thys man. Whi tormentyst vs thus in hys body?' 'Sykyr',
315 quoth he, 'I wyl not lete yow goon hens, but ye fynde me borwys that
ye shul no more comyn here ageyn to weryn thys man.' 'What borwys',
quoth they ageyn, 'asky[st] thou of vs for suerte?' 'I aske', quoth he, 'the
holy seynty[s] whos bodyis restyn here in this cherche.' 'Sykyr', quoth
they, 'we mowe not, for oure merytys han deseruyd yt.' 'Forsothe', quoth
320 he, 'ye muste nedys getyn hem, or ellys I wyl not dylyueryn you owt of
yowre peyne here.' 'We wyl thanne', quoth they, 'doon oure bysynesse to
getyn hem.' And sone aftyr they seydyn: 'Lo, sere, w[e] han get hem, albeyt
that we be not wurthy that holy martyrs shuldyn byn oure borwis.' 'What
tokene shal I han', quoth he, 'that ye han get hem lych as ye seyin?' 'Goo',
325 quoth they, 'to the capse wherein these holy martyrs heedys ben kepte, and
ye shul fynden yt turnyd in.' And lych as they seydyn yt was foundyn.

Whanne this blyssyd man prechyd onys, certeyn matronys, illudyd
and deseyuyd by heretikis, comyn to hym aftyr hys sermoun and seyde:
'Seruaunte of God, yf thoo thyngis be trewe whiche thou this day hast
330 prechyd, oure soulys han longe with the spirit of errour ben excecat
and blyndyd.' Thanne this [h]oly man seyde ageyn to hem on this wyse:
'Dowthtris, beth constaunt and stedefast and abydyth a wyle, and ye shul
seen anoon what lord ye han drawyn to.' And forthwith they seyin come
forth amonge hem a foul beste, hauynge the lyknesse of a gret cat, with
335 gret blak eyne glastrynge and brynnynge, whoos tonge was longe and
brood and blody and hyng dou[n] to the nouylle. The tayle was crokyd,
stondynge ryht vp byhynde, shewynge here foul taylende wheresoeuere
f. 154ra yt turnyd, fro whens cam owt an intollerable | stynk. And whan thys
beste had runne a lytyl while to and fro amonge these matronys, at the

310 gyrt] gryt   317 askyst] askyd   318 seyntys] seyntyns   322 we] whe
331 holy] oly   334 a gret] gret   336 doun] douun

laste by the belle roop yt ran vp into the stepyl and was no more seyin 340
thereaftyr. This seyinge, the seyid matronys youyn thankynge to God and
were conuertyd ageyn to the trewe feyth of holy cherche.

Whanne this holy man o tyme had conuyct certeyn heretykys and they
were condempnyd to be brent, as he lokyd amonge hem he saw oon whoos
name was Raymundus. And anoon he seyde to hys ministris: 'Kepyth hym 345
thus, and in no wyse brennyth hym with hys felaas!' And for[th]with he
turnyd hym to the seyde Raymundus cherly: 'Sone, I wee[t] that, thow yt
be longe, yet at the laste thow shalt ben a good man and holy.' So this Ray-
mund, delyueryd that tyme fro deth, twenty wyntyr aftyr contunyd stylle
in hys herisie. Aftyr wich tyme he was conuertyd and mad a frere prechour, 350
and lyuyd in that ordre an holy lyf and maad a blyssyd ende. This holy man
was meruelously enduyd with the spirit of prophecye, as yt semyth wyl
bothe by this forseyd process and by many othere whiche foluyn heraf-
tyr. Whereof oon ys that onys whyl he was in the cyte of Rome at Seynt
Syxtys with his brethyrn, sodenly the spirit of prophecye stirynge hym, he 355
clepyd alle hys brethyrn onto chapitre and tolde hem opynly that within
short tyme foure of hem shuld deyin, tweyne in body and tweyne in soule.
And longe aftyr two freris deyid and two forsokyn the ordre.

Anothir tyme also whan he was at Bononye ther was a maistir clepid
Conrad, a Ducheman, whoom hys brethyrn desiryd sore to han in to here 360
ordre. And as yt happyd vpon the vigilye of oure ladyis day the assumpcioun, Dominic had communicacyoun and ta[l]kyng with the priour of the
monastorie clepyd *Casa Marie* of the ordre of the Cisteence. And aftyr the
exigence of the mater and of a singuler famuliar trust, Seynt Dominic seyid
thus to the priour: 'I knowleche to the, priour, that I ne neuere er dede 365
to non and that I will thou neuere bywreye wyl I lyve, that I neuere yet
askyd thyng of God in al myn lyf, but that I haue had myn askyng aftyr my
desyre.' To whom whan priour seyde that he trowyd verely of prophecye
answered ageyn and seyde that the priour shulde lyuyn longe aftyr hym;
and so he dede. 'Seth yt ys so thanne', quoth the priour ageyn, 'that thou 370
hast that grace in Goddys sytht, fadyr, aske of hym that he wyl yiue the
maystyr Conrade to hy[s] ordre, for thi brethyrn gretly desiryn yt.' 'Good
brothir', quoth Dominic, 'thou askyst an hard thynge.' And the same nyth,
whan complyn was don, alle hys brethyrn goynge to here reste, Dominic
alone abod stylle in the cherche and al nyht wecchyd in preyere, as he was 375
acustomyd to don. And anon on the morwyn, whan alle the frerys were
gadryd togedere in the quer for to seyin prime, and the chauntour bygan

346 forthwith] forwith   347 weet] weel   362 talkyng] takkyng   372 hys]
hym

'*Iam lucys & cetera*', Mayster Conr[a]d, whiche was to ben a newe sterre in
short tyme, vnwarly cam in and fel don at Seynt Domynycs feet, meekely
f. 154rb and instauntly askynge | the habyte of hys ordre, and deuoutly took yt and
381 perseuerauntly kept yt.

This holy fadyr, this blyssyd man Seynt Dominic, was a man of gret
constaunce and stedfastnesse, of gret dyscrecyoun and sadnesse, and in al
hys demenynge ful of prudence and cheritabylnesse. For on daylyht with
385 hys brethyrn, saf alwey the tenour of honeste, no man was more comoun
than he. In the nyth hourys in vigilis, in preyers and in contemplacyoun,
no man was more prompit, ner more diligent than he. So that the day he
departyd to hys neyhbors and the nyght to God, to whoom of hys eyne he
mad a welle of [t]eeris. Ful oftyn tyme whan Cristys body was leftyd vp at
390 messe he was rauasshd into an excesse or aliuacyoun of mende, as though
he had seyin Crist incarnat present to hys bodyly eye. For whiche cause a
longe tyme he herd not messe with hys othere brethren. Hys custum was
ryht oftyn to takyn hys nyht-reste in cherche where vnnethe or seldum he
had ony certeyn restynge place. For wheresoeuere the nessecyte of reste or
395 sleep constreynyd hym there, where yt byforn an awter or bouynge doun
hys hed and lenynge ageyns a ston, he satysfyid naturis nede with a lytyl
sleep. Moreouyr euery nyht for the most part he receyuyd thre discyplynys
of hys own handys with a cheyne of yryn, that ys to seyne oon for hymself,
anothir for the synners whiche leuyn in the word, and the thridde for hem
400 whiche lyin in the peynys of purgatorye.

Yt happyd hym onys to be chosyn byshop Cotoranence but he wolde
not receyuy[n] yt, for pleynly he afermyd that he rathere wolde forsaken
lond for euere thanne to assentyn to ony eleccyoun maad of hym to ony
maner dy[g]nyte. He was onys askyd why he had leuere dwellyn in Carca-
405 sone and in the dyocyse therof than in Tholose and in the dyocyse therof.
To whiche demaunde he answerde and seyde thus: 'For in Tholose', quoth
he, 'and in the dyocyse therof, I fynde many men that wurshipe and preysyn me, but in Carcesone and the dyocyse therof alle men inpugnyn and
ageyn-seyin me.' Anothyr tyme askyd in what book he stoodyid moste, 'In
410 the book of cheryte', quoth he.

Vpon a nyght, as he wecchyd at Bononye in the cherche, the deuyl apperyd onto hym in lyknesse of a frere. Whoom whan he wende had byn a
frere he made hym a sygne that he shulde goon to restyn hym with othere
freris. Whoom the deuyl mokkynge and scornynge answerde ageyn with
415 the same toknys. Wherfore this holy man, dysirynge to wetyn who yt was

378 Conrad] Conrid   389 teeris] sterris   402 receyuyn] receyuynge
404 dygnyte] dyngnyte   408 inpugnyn] inpugnyn and

that thus contempnyd hys comaundement, lytht a candele at the lampe. And as sone as he saw hys face he knew weel whoo he was. Whom, aftyr that he had weel rebukyd and vndyrnomyn hym, he chargyd hym to ans- weren hym of certeyn constitucyouns. And frest he askyd hym wherof he temp[t]yd hys frerys in the quer. Quoth he ageyn: 'To comyn late in and hastily to goon owt ageyn.' Fro thens he led hym to the dormytorye and askyd whereof he temptyd hem ther. 'To slepe sore', quoth the deuyl, 'and to reyse sl[o]wly and so to absenten hem from Goddys seruyse.' From | thens to the refectorie or the [frey]tour they wentyn, where he askyd hym wherin he temptyd hem there. 'Summe', quoth he, 'to etyn to myche that so the[y] moun offendyn in glotonye, and summe to etyn to lytyl, where- through they mowe be to feble and to weyke to seruyn God and to obseruyn and kepyn the obseruaunce of here religioun.' In the collocutorye or the parlour askyd whereof the deuyl temptyd frers, anon he walwyd hys tounge al aboutyn hys mouth and maad an vnsauery confuhs noyse. And whan Seynt Dominyc askyd hym what he mente therby, he answerde ageyn and seyde thus: 'Thys place ys al-togedyr myn. For whan they comyn here toge- dyr to spekyn, I styre hym to spekyn confuhsly and anon to abydyn othrys answere, to ocupyin the tyme with ydyl and veyn wurdys, with obloquye and detraccyoun and with wurdys of rybaudrye, of chydynge and of con- tencyoun.' Aftyr thys, whan they come to the chapityrhous dore, the deuyl wold entryn for nothynge but turnyd awey his face and seyde: 'Here wyl I neuere entryn ne comyn withinne. For this hous ys acursyd. Here lese I al that I wynne in othir placys. For whanne I haue maad ony frere to offendyn by neglygence in ony othyr place, yf he come into hys hous and proclame hymself, anoon in this cursyd place he hys purgyd and mad clene. And so al my forme laboure ys but lost.' Wyche wurdys seyid, sodeynly he vanysshyd awey.

 These and many moo vundyrfu[l] thyngis byn writtyn in the book of thys holy and blyssyd mannys lyf, the whiche for here innumerable multi- tude I passe ouyr at thys tyme. And at the laste, whan the ende of hys temperal pilgrymage bygan to neyhyn, the whiche God of hys eternal prouidence dysposyd to byn at Bononye, he bygan anon to languryn with a greuous bodyly syknesse. To whom the dyssoluynge of hys body and the departicyoun of hys soule therfro was shewyd in a visioun on this wyse. Hym thouth that he saw a passynge fayr younge man clepyd hym, seyinge on this wyse: 'Come my loue, come to ioye! Come!' Aftyr whiche clepynge of God he callyd onto twelue frerys of the couent of Bononye and, that he

420 temptyd] temperyd 423 slowly] slawly 424 freytour] streynour
426 they] the 442 but lost] but 444 vundyrful] vundyrfully

shulde not lyuyn hem dyshertyd and as fadyrles childryn, he mad byforn
455 hem hys testement on this wyse: 'These be the thyngis whiche I bequethe
and leue to you as to my chyldryn and to myn sones, to haue possessioun
of by ryght of enherytaunce withoutyn ende. Hath cheryte, loueth humylyte and takyth into yowre possessioun gladly wylful pouerte.' And this
as streytly as he cowde and myghte he defendyd, that neuere ne man into
460 hys ordre shulde inducyn ner bryngyn temperal possessiounys, terrybylly
bysechynge and preyinge the curs of God and hys to falle to hym, the
whiche presumyd to spottyn or to defoulyn the prechours ordre with the
venym of erdly ryches. And whanne he sey his brethren sorwyn withoutyn
consolacyoun for his departynge from hem, he seyde ful fadyrly and with
f. 154vb swete wurdys: 'My dere sonys, letyth not my bodyly departysoun | in no
466 vise troblyn yow, ner discounforty[n] yow, nothyng doutynge but that ye
shul haue me more profitable on to yow deed than quyk.' Whiche seyid and
hys last our of temperal lyf comyn, he restid in oure lord the yer of grace
a thousent two hundryd and on and twenty. Whos passage was shewyd by
470 reuelacioun the same day and the same our to ʻaʼ fryre clepyd Guale, that
tyme beynge of the frerys prechourys of Bricia and aftyrward bysshop of
the same cyte, on this wyse:
　　This seyid priour casually that tyme beynge in the frerys stepyl, yt happyd hym as he lenyd to a wal to fallyn aslepe, and anoon hym thoughte that
475 he saw heuene opnyn and two leddres to be letyn doun to the erthe, [whos]
ouyr endys Crist and his modyr heldyn in here handys, and aungels mery
syngynge wentyn doun by the same leddrys. And at the nether ende of
these leddrys, euene bytwyx bothen fastnynge onto hem was set a chayer
and oon sat theron with hys face curyd. And anoon forthwith Ihesu and his
480 modyr pullyddyn vp the leddere by the stauys therof, tyl the chayer and
the syttere wern entrid into heuene. Whiche doon, yt closyd vp ageyn.
And the priour wook and forthwith went to Bononye and fond that Seynt
Dominic was passyd to God the same tyme that he had the visioun.
　　Anothir frere also, whos name was Roo, dwellynge at Tybur, the same
485 day and our that blyssyd Dominic passyd, mad hym redy to gon to messe.
And for as meche as he had herd seyid that his holy fadyr Dominik languryd, whan he cam to that place of the c[a]noun where yt ys vsid to preyin
for the quyk and wold han preyid for ys maister, sodeynly he was rauasshd and sey the seruaunt of God, Dominic, laureat with a lorrer croune
490 maruelously shynynge, gon with two rygh reuerent and wurshipful, to hys
semyng, withoutyn Bononye in the gret comoun hyweye. And, notyng the

464 he seyde] he　　　466 discounfortyn] discounfortyd　　　475 whos] whos whos
487 canoun] conoun

day and the our of this reuelacyoun, he fond and prouyd that the same day
and the same our this holy man passid owt of this word.

What tyme the body of this blyssyd man had longe leyin in the erthe
and hys holynesse mygh not ben hyd, dayly gronynge and encrecynge gret   495
multytude of myraclis, yt plesyd to the deuocioun of feythful peple to
translatyn yt to han hyere and a more wurshipful place. For whiche cause,
what tyme the graue was ondon and the ston abouyn remeuyd, so gret a
sauoure of sweet odour cam owt therof that yt semyth rathere a potika-
ryis shoppe to han ben opnyd than a graue. And not only so, but yt passyd   500
excellently the odour of alle maner sweet and delycious o[yn]ementis, ner
yt myght be lyknyd to the flauour of noon natural thyng ner artificial. And
not only this swet sauour was in the bonys and in the poudyr of this holy
body, ner in the capse whiche this holy body lay in, but also yt was in al the
erthe round aboute the body wyche was cast vp with the body, in so myche   505
[that | whan the seyid erthe] was karyid thens far and into diuers cuntres,   f. 155ra
yt kept the sweetnesse of the odour many a day aftyr. The handys also of
the freris whiche ony thynge towchynge of these holy relyquys, notwithstondynge eyther rubbynge or wassynge a long while aftyr, in testimonye
of hys holynesse keptyn stylle the sauour of that redolent swetnesse.   510

In the prouince of Vngarye a man of gret wourthynesse, for singuler
deuocyoun whiche he had to Seynt Dominic, wente with his wyf and hys
yunge sone to a cyte clepyd Ferulu to wurshipyn the reliquys whiche were
had there of the seyd seynt, where hys sone wex so seek that euene there he
deyid. Whoos body the fadyr leyid byforn the auter whithe a lamentabyl   515
voys, seying on this wyse: 'Blyssyd and holy fadyr, Dominic, I am hedyr
to the whithe my sone glad and mery, and now I goo awey fro the withoute
sone orbat and heuy. Yet, gode fadyr, yiue me ageyn myn sone! Restore
me the gladnesse of myn herte, that I may gon as glad and as myry hens as
I was in myn comynge hedyr.' And at mydnyth foluynge the cheld ros vp   520
ageyn, heyl and sound, and wente aboute the cherche. And on the nexte
morwyn returnyd homward ageyn with hys fadyr and his modyr withoutyn
ony syknesse.

A younge man wich was bothe the bondman of a gret lady and hyre
seruaunt, vpon a tyme as he wente on fysshynge, vnwarly fel in the watyr   525
and was drynklyd. For whoos vpreysynge ageyn to lyf hys lady preyid spe-
cialy to Seynt Dominic, makynge a vou that, yf he myght lyuyn ageyn,
she shulde goon on pylgrymage to hys reliquys on hyre bare feet and also
makyn hym fre of seruage and yeldynge hym to hys lyberte. Whiche seyin

501 oynementis] onymentis   506 that whan the seyid erthe] that whan the seyid
erthe that whan the seyid erthe

530 anoon, the younge man roos vp heyl and sounde and the lady performyd
that she byhygh.

A pore man, whiche tweynty wentyr had languryd bedrede and was
blynd, had a gret fe[r]uent desyr to visityn the relikys of Seynt Dominic.
Where vpon oo tyme he bygan to assayin to rysyn owt of hys bed alone.
535 And so he dede. And whan he was vpon his feet hee bygan to assayin yf
he myght goon alone. And anoon hym thoughte that he felt hymself sumwat stronge to goon and his syht sumwat began to cleryn. And so dayly,
as he wente forth on hys pylgrymage, bothe hys myth of goynge and eek
hys seyht encrecyd euere more and more so that, by the tyme he cam to
540 the place where the relikys were, he felte hymself fully hool boothe in hys
lymys and also in his syht.

In Sycile also, in a cyte clepyd Augusta, a maydyn labouryd and wexyd
with a ston coude no remedye han by no leche but that nedys she muste byn
coruyn. For whiche cause the modyr of the maydyn gretly abasshyd, dre-
545 dynge the perel of keruynge, commendyd hyre to the tuicyoun and reule
of Seynt Dominic, to whom she hadde a singuler deuocyoun and a specyal afeccyoun. And on the nexte nygh foluynge Seynt Dominic cam to
f. 155ʳᵇ the maydyn whyl sche was aslepe and put the ston whiche | greuyd hyre
in hyre hand and wente in hys weye. And whan the maydyn awook and
550 fond the stoon in hyre hand and hyreself delyueryd of hyre peyne, she
roos anoon and told here modyr hyre visioun and sheuyd hyre the stoon.
Whereof the modyr ioyful and glad, on the nexte morwyn wente with hyre
douthtyr onto the freris and there, in testimonye and wytnesse of so gret a
miracle, offeryd vp the ston to ben hangyn vp byforn the ymage of Seynt
555 Dominic.

Anothyr woman in the seyd cuntre of Sicile, at a toun clepyd Placca,
had a sone the whiche intollerable was turmentyd with a syknesse of scro-
phelys or kernelys, swych as chyldryn arn wone to han in here nekkys,
whereof no leche cowde doon hym remydyis. Hys modyr seyng that, mad
560 a wou to God and to Seynt Dominic that, yf he myghte be delyueryd of
his peyne, that he shulde frely labouryn and withowtyn hyre in the werk of
freris cherche wich that tyme was in makyng. And on the nexte nyht aftyr,
oon in a frerys habyte apperyd onto hyre slepynge and seyde: 'Wo[mman],
knowyst thou verigres, pych and the burredokke?' And whan she seyde
565 'Ya', 'Wel', quoth he, 'thanne take these thyngis and stampe hem togedyr
and incorperat he[m] togedyr with the iows of poret and sprede yt vpon
herdys, and wynde yt aboutyn hys nekke and he shal ben hol.' And whanne

she wooke, she dede as she was bodyn and he was hool anoon, and aftyr
diligently performyd hys modrys byhest.

At Tripoline also, in a monastorie clepyd Maddalean, a nunne b[or]n of 570
nobyl blood, whoos name was Maria, labouringe in manye diuers syknesse
hadde an hurt on hyre leg, the anguyssh wherof was so gret and so greuous
that euery our they l[o]kyd whan she shulde han deyid. This seyid nunne,
thus anguysshd and turmentyd, preyid on this wyse: 'My Lord God in
heuene, I am not wurthy of myself to preyin to the, ner to ben herd of the. 575
But I bys[eche] my special lord, Seynt Dominic, that he vouchesaf to byn
medyatour for me to the, that through meryt of hys goodnesse I may han
that I haue not deseruyd through my wrecchydnesse.' And whan she longe
had preyid thus, with gret habundaunce of teerys she fel in a trawns. And
as hire thoughte she saw Seynt Dominic and too frerys with hym comyn 580
at the corteyn whiche henge byforn hyre bed, and seyinge to hyre on this
wyse: 'Why desiryst thou so sore to byn mad hol?' 'Syre', quoth she, 'that
I myghte seruyn God more deuoutly thanne I haue don.' Whiche seyd,
he took from vndyr hys cope a[n] onyment of gret redolent and maruelous
swetnesse and anoyntyd therwith hyre leg, and anon yt was maad hool. And 585
thanne seyde thus to hyre doughtyr: 'This onyment ys ful precious, swet
and hard to kepyn.' Whereof whan she askyd hym the cause, he answerde
hyre ageyn on this wyse: 'Thes onyment', quoth he, 'ys precyous for yt ys
the sygne of loue, the whiche ys so precyous that yt may be bouht with
nothynge and for amonge the yiftys of God ther ys non bytyr ner grettere 590
sweet than | yt ys, for than charite may nothynge byn swettere. Hard yt ys f. 155va
to kepyn, for [withowte] good bysynesse yt ys sone lost.'

Whiche wurdys seyid, anoon forthwith he wente to hyre sustyr slepynge
in the dortour and tolde here that he had helyd hyre sustyr. At wiche wourd
she wook and wente to hyre sustyr and fond yt treuthe that was seyid onto 595
hyre. And whan she saw that hyre leg was anoy[n]tyd with a sensible oynement, whereof sum fletyd on hyre leg stylle, she took rausylke and wypte
hyre leg therwith, and so gaderyd vp the onyment. The whiche sheuyd to
the abbesse and the confessoure had so redolent and so swet an odur that
they where euene astoynyd. And whan she had also told hem hyre visioun, 600
they thankyd God and Seynd Dominic and keptyn the onyment with gret
reuerence.

Whan Dominics deuoutht matronys, in a cyte clepyd Augusta, had ben
at the solemnyte of whiche translacyon of Seynt Dominic at the freres
and comyn hom ageyn and foundyn a woman syttynge in the strete and 605

570 born] bron   573 lokyd] lekyd   576 byseche] bysheche   584 an] and
591 sweet than] sweet   592 withowte] owte   596 anoyntyd] anoytyd

spynnynge, they cheritably blamyd hyre, forasmeche as she absteynyd not
that day from seruyl werk at the reuerense of that blyssyd and holy fadyr
Seynt Dominic. To whom she skornfully answerde ageyn on this wyse: 'Ye
that arne the byʒotys, that ys to seyne the emperours of the freris, halwyth
610 this holy mannys feste. As who seyth I am non of thoo, and therfore I wele
not haluyn.' And as sone as [s]he had seyid that word hyre eyne bygunne
to bolnyn and to yechyn, and wurmys bygunnyn to spryngyn owt of hem so
plenteuously that a neyhboure of here in a short tyme pykyd owt eyghtene.
Anoon this woman comp[unc]t was led to the freris. Whereaftyr that she
615 had confessyd hire defaute and mad a vow that she neuere shulde detrac-
tyn Seynt Dominic more, and that she shulde trewely halwyn hys feste,
she was restoryd ageyn to helthe anoon, or thanne that she wente thens.

    How acceptable and plesaunt the place ys to God where this holy
blyssyd mannys body restyth, manye grete and meruelous myraclis she-
620 wyd there euydently declarynge. Whereof on told here at this tyme mote
suff[ic]yn. Mayster Alexander, bysshop Vindomence, tellyth in hys pos-
tills vpon this word of the sautyr *Misericordia et veritas obuiauerunt &*
cetera, that ther was a scolyr in Bononye al youyn to the vanit[e]s of the
word and to lust and to lykynge of the flesshe, the whiche had onys swych
625 a visioun. Hym thoughte that he was in a gret feld and sodeynly there
grew so gret tempest that he was fayn to fleen to house. And the fyrste
hous that he cam to, he fond yt faste shet. Where whan he knokkyd faste,
preyinge to be letyn in, the ostesse fro withinne answerde on this wyse: 'I,
Ryghwyssnesse, dwelle here and this hys myn hous. And, for as meche as
630 thou art vnryhtful and not ryghtful, thou shalt nat entryn here.' At whiche
he, heuy and sory, wente hys weye. And seyinge anothir hous he went
f. 155vb therto, knokkyng and preyinge to be | latyn in. To whom fro withinne
the ostesse answerde thus: 'I am Truthe and this ys myn hous. But hedyr
shalt thou not entryn. For treuthe wyl not receyuyn hem that hatyn.
635 Wherfore seke ferthere, here comyst thou not.' This seyid he fledde to
the thrydde hous, stondynge a lytyl thens, desirynge to han ben reseyuyd
there. But fro withinne this was his answere: 'This ys the dwellynge place
of Pees, whedyr moun entryn noone but men of good wyl. For pes ys
not grauntyd to vnpitous and wykkyd men. Nertheles, for as meche as I
640 thynke thouthtis of pees and not of afflicyoun, I wyl yeue the helful and
profitable counsel. A lytyl hens dwellyth a sustyr of myn, the whiche ys
alwey wone to reseyuyn wrecchys and myscheuyd peple swyche as thou
art. Thedyr goo, aftyr my counsel, and yt may be for thyn auayle.' Whedyr

606–7 not that] not   611 she] he   614 compunct] compount   621 suffi-
cyn] sufferyn   623 vanites] vanitates

whan he cam, this was hys answere fro withinne. 'I am Mercy whiche
dwelle here. Wherfore, yf thou desire to be sauyd from the perel of this   645
tempest, go into the place of the frere prechourys in Bononye. For there
thou shalt fynde the stabyl of doctryne, the crebbe of scripture, the asse of
sempylnesse with the ox of dyscrecyoun, Marie the illumynynge and Ihesu
child the sauynge.' Whanne this scolyr awook and wyl remembryd hym
of hys visioun, anoon he wente to the frere prechouris and, rehercynge   650
hem hys visioun by ordre, mekely he askyd here abyte and deuouthly
receyuyd yt.

Anothir scolyr was there whos name was Nicholas, the whiche was
vexyd with a greuous peyne in hys bak and in hys knes, so that he mygh not
rysyn owt of hys bed. And moreouyr hys lefth hepe was so dryid vp and   655
vaxyn seer, that al hys hope of recure was ful goon. And oo tyme as he lay
and bythough hym he maad hys vou anoon to God and to Seynt Dominic,
purposynge to offeryn there a candele as long as hymself. For whiche entent he dede hym be met with the thredde that the candele shulde be mad
of. And whan the lengthe of hym was motyn owt, he mad the thredde to be   660
gyrt aboutyn hys nekke and his brest and hys kne, at euery gyrdynge clepynge the name of Ihesu and Seynt Dominic. Whiche don, anon he felte
hys peyne alleggyd and relesyd and bygan to cryin and seyin: 'Wurshipe
b[e] to God and Seynt Dominic, I am deleueryd!' And anoon, wepynge for
ioye, he roos vp withowtyn ony helpe and wente on hys feet withowtyn ony   665
thyng to leuyn vpon to the freris, and parformyd his byhest. These miraclis
and many moo, ner withoute nombre, God ha[th] wrouht by hys seruaunt
Dominic. To whom be laude and preysynge withoutyn ende. Amen.

[132. SIXTUS]

The lyf of Sixti, Felicissimi & Agapiti

Sixtus, born of Athenas, a philosophir fryst and aftyr Cristis dysciple, a
Pope of Rome, with his tweyne deknys was presentyd to the reuleris | of the   f. 156ra
empere Decius & Valerianus. Whoom wan Decius cowde by no suasyons
inclinyn to ydolatrye, he mad hym to be led to the temple of Mart, there to   5
do sacrifice or ellys to be shet vp in Mamortys warde. But whan he wolde
not sacrificyn and was led forth-ward to Mamortys warde, anothir dekne
of hys clepyd Laurence cryid aftyr hym and seyde: 'Whedyr goste thou,
fadyr, withoute thi sone? And whethir goost thow, holy prest, withoute
a ministre, withoute whom thou neuere were wone to don sacrifise? What   10

664 be] by   667 hath] haht

thyng ys yt in me that hath dysplesyd thy fadyrhood? Hast thou owt prouyd
me vntreue? Good fadyr, late experience teche you whethir ye han chosyn
an able ministre or nouht, to whom ye han commyttyd the dyspensacyoun of Cristys body and of hys blood.' To whoom blyssyd Sixtus answerde
15 ageyn on this wyse: 'Sone, I neythyr leue the ner forsake. But this I wyl
thou knowe, that grettere and sharpere bataylys ben ordeynyd to the for
Cristys feyth. For we as aldernemen han reseyuyd the cours of more esy
confli[c]t, but the abydyth of the tiraunt more glorious triumphe and victorye. For, aftyr th[r]e dayis, thou, dekne, shal folwyn me, prest. But in
20 this menetyme take the tresoure of the cherche and dyspose yt there as
thy discrecyoun thynkyth best.' And anoon at this comaundement blyssyd
Laurence, within thoo thre dayis, disposyd and dystrebutyd onto pouere
men al the tresoure of the cherche. Vpon the thrydde day the pr[e]fecte
yaf this decre: that Sixtus the pope with his two deknys, of whiche oon
25 was clepyd Felicissimus the tothir Agapitus, shulde be led to the temple of
Mart to doon sacrifise. And yf they wolde not sacrificyn to ben hefdyd. And
as they were led forth to here iewesse-ward, Laurence folwyd, criynge on
this wyse: 'Forsake me not now, holy fadyr, but le[t]e me goon with the!
For sekyrly I haue spent the tresoure the whiche thou comaundyst me.'
30 This herynge, the sowdyourys of the prefect heldyn Laurence with hem
and hefdyd Sixtum with hys two deknys in the same place, the sexte day
of August.

Vpon whiche same day ys holdyn the feste of the transfiguracyoun of
oure lord. And in summe cherchys the sacrement of Cristys blood ys mad
35 the selue of newe wyn, yf yt mowe be get, or ellys at the leste of summe
ryp grape wroungyn into the chalys. On thys day also byn blyssyd clus-
trys of grapys, and the pope comunyth of the same. And the cause why
this ys don ys for as myche as oure lord seyde to hys discipulys in hys laste
sopyr, whanne he ordeynyd the sacrement on this wyse: *Non bibam amodo*
40 *& cetera*: 'I shal nat drynkyn hensforward of this kynde of wyn tyl I drynke
yt newe in myn fadrys kyngdam.' The transfiguracioun of oure lord, and
that he clepyd newe wyn, representyth to vs th[e innouacyon] glorious,
the whiche Crist had afftyr hys resureccioun. And therfore this day of
hys transfiguracioun, the whiche representyth Crystys resurreccioun, ys |
f. 156rb   seyht newe wyn. Not that this day Crist was transfiguryd, but that this day
46 Cristys transfiguracioun by his apostelys was manifestat and shewyd. *Hec
in libro Mitrali & cetera*.

18 conflict] conflijt   19 thre] the   23 prefecte] prfecte   28 lete] lede
35 the leste] the   42 the innouacyon] them oniouacyoun

[133. DONATUS]

The lyf of Seynt Donat

[S]eynt Donatus was educat and brough forth in hys yonge with Iulian, wiche was fryst a munk and promyttyd to the ordre of a subdekne, but af[t]irward, apostata bothe from hys ordre and also from Cristis feyth, aspiryd to the empere. And anoon as he had optenyd hys entent and was mad 5 emperoure, he greu of cristene men a cruel persecutor, and fyrst of alle he slou the fadyr and the mothyr of blysse[d] Donat. For whiche cause he fledde to a cyte clepyd Arecium, wherfore he dwellyd with an holy munk clepyd Hyllaryan and wrouth there many wundyrful thyngis. Of this seyd cyte the meyre, or the prefect, had a sone, the whiche was wexyd with an 10 euyl spiryt. And whanne the fadyr of this child had brough hym to the presen[c]e of Donat, the vnclene spirit bygan to cryin and seyin: 'O Donate, whi constreynyst thou me to gon owt with tormentys? In the name of oure lord Ihesu Crist I require the that thou be not heuy to me, ner conpelle me not to gon hens owt of myn hous.' But that notwithstondenge, at the 15 preyere of blyssyd Donat the chyld was maad hool and deliueryd from the euyl spiritis vexacyoun.

Ther was also a man in the cyte whoos name was Eustaas, gaderer of the emperys monye in Tuskayne. At a certeyn tyme this Eustas wente fer owte and lefte the comoun monye in hys wyuys kepynge. In whiche mene- 20 tyme i[t] happyd that prouince to ben troubylyd with enmyis. Wherfore Eufrosina, so was Eustas wyuys name, hyd this monye and preuent with sorwe and feer she deyid. Whanne hyre husbonde cam hom and cowde not fyndyn the monye, wetynge weel that he and alle his chyldryn shulde ben bonden and distroyid therfore, he mad a lamentable mornynge and sorwe 25 and wente to blyssed Donat and told hym the caas, preyinge hym of helpe and remedye. Donat, hauynge pyte and conpassioun vpon hym, wente with hym to hys wyuys graue and, aftyr that he had mad a short preyere, stondynge vp, with a cler woys, he seyde thus: 'Eufrosina, I adiure the, by the vertu of the holy gost, that thou telle vs the treuthe wher thou hast don the 30 emperial mony, for the princys of the court purposyd hem to vexe thyn husbonde therfore.' And anoon cam a voys owt of the graue and seyde: 'In the entre of the chaumbre, vndyr the threshwold, for dred of enmyis I bedalf yt.' And there, lych as the woys seyde, they foundyn yt.

Not longe aftyr this the bysshop of that cyte, Satirus, deyid, and al 35

2 Seynt] *initial cut out*   4 aftirward] affirward   7 blyssed] blysse
11–12 presence] presente   19 certeyn tyme] certeyn   21 it] I   35 of that] of

the clerge concordly chees Donat to succedyn aftyr hym. And so yt happyd that, aftyr the bysshop had seyid messe vpon a festful day, and al the
pepyl was comunyd with Cristis body of hys hand, and the dekne brouhte
the chalys with Cristis blood to comunyn hem therwith, with a sodeyn
40 irrup[c]youn of paynyms, the chalys vnwarly fel owt of the deknes hand |
f. 156ᵛᵃ and brast ageyns the erthe on manye pecys. Wherfore, whanne bothe the
bysshop and the pope were sory and heuy, anoon he gadryd togedyr the
pecys and preyid. And forthwith yt was reformyd ageyn into the fyrste
shap, al saf oo pece the whiche the deuyl hydde. And that pece ys yet kepet
45 in the same cherche into te[stimonye] of the miracle.

There was in that cuntre a w[elle] with venym that whoosoeuere drank
thereof dyed therwith anoon. And so y[t] happyd, as bysshop Donat cam
rygh that wey vpon hys asse for to makyn a preyere for helynge of the welle,
a gret dragoun sodeynly cam owt of the welle and with his tayl in[u]oluyd
50 the asses feet, and with hys body and hys heed he leftyd vpon hymself
ageyns the bysshop. Whoom as sone as blyssyd Donat had smet with a
whippe whiche he bar in hys hand, or ellys as summe seyin as sone as he
had spyt in hys mouth, he deyyd withoutyn ony more. And afftyr, anoon
as he had maad hys preyre, the welle was hool and hoolsum.

55 Anothyr tyme, as he and hys felachepe goynge by the weye had gret
thrust, he made short preyere and anoon ther sprang vp a velle, were as
was neuere noon byforn, to recreacyoun and refresshynge of hym and hyse,
and to alle that euere draunke therof.

Afftyr whan the douthtyr of Theodosye the emperour was wexyd with
60 a wykkyd spyrit and was brough to Donat for helpe, anoon he seyde to the
spirit on this wyse: 'Goo owt, thou vnclene spirit, and dwelle no lengere in
this fayr creature of God!' 'Syth I muste owt', thanne quoth the deuyl, 'yiue
me weye wherby, and place whedyr I shal goon.' Quoth Donat ageyn: 'Fro
whens come thou hydyr sykyr?' Quoth the spirit ageyn: 'Fro wyldyrnesse.'
65 'Fro thens thou come turne ageyn thanne', quoth the bysshop. 'Sykyr',
quoth he ageyn, 'I se in the the tokne of a cros, owt of whiche comyth a
gret fyr, the whiche makyth me so aferd that I ne wot not whedyr I may
goon. Wherfore y prey the, graunte me a place of passage and I shall goon
awey anoon.' 'Weel', quoth the bisshop, 'I yi[u]e the lycence of passage.
70 Go [thy] wey faste onto thyn own place!' Whiche seyid, the deuyl shook al
the hous and wente hys weye.

---

40 irrupcyoun] irrupticyoun   45 testimonye] te, *owing to removal of the initial on
recto*   46 welle] *om. owing to removal of the initial on recto*   47 dyed therwith]
with, *owing to removal of the initial on recto* yt] y   49 inuoluyd] inoluyd   66 the]
the] the   69 yiue] yinge   70 thy] they

Oon tyme also, as a deed man was brou to hys buryinge, ther cam oon
with a selyd chartyr or an obligacioun and seyde that the deed man aute
hym two hundyryd shylyng, wherfore he seyde pleynly that the c[or]s shuld
not be buryid tyl the dette where payid. Whanne the sely wydue wyche was 75
the deed mannys wyff herd this, sore wepynge she wente to the bysshop
and told hym the cas and the processe therof, feythfully affermynge at the
laste ende of hyre tale that he was trewely payd byforn of the summe of
mony whiche he wrongfully chalangyd. Thys herynge, the bisshop ros vp
and with the wydwe wente forth thedyr where the deed body lay, and took 80
hym be the hand and seyde: 'Man, take heed and here!' 'Sere, so I do',
quoth he. 'Rys!' quoth the bysshop ageyn, 'and syt and make reknynge
with this man wiche lettyth the and wyl nat sufferyn the to be buryid.'
And anoon the deed man sat vp and con[ui]ctyd the todyr aforn alle men,
shewyng | how and whanne he had payid hym the monye the whiche he f. 156ᵛᵇ
wrongfully askyd of hym. And forthwith he took the chartyr owt of the fals 86
chalengers hand and brak yt with hys own hand. Whiche doon [he] turnyd
hym to the bysshop, seyinge on this wyse: 'Good fadyr, comaunde me to
gon ageyn to slepyn.' 'Sone', quoth he, 'in Godys name now goo to thy
reste!' And forthwith he leyid hym doun and hys frendys buryid hym.   90

Afftyrward, whan ner thre yer togedyr yt hadde not reynyd in that
cuntre, and of that gret droute greu gret bareynnesse, the mysbyleuyng
peple wente to Theodosye the emperour, preynge that he wolde delyueryn
hem the bysshop Donat. For pleynly they seydyn that he with hys wycchecrafth had causyd al this myschef. And whanne the emperour herd this, he 95
preyd the bysshop to preye to God for reyn; and so he dede. And forthwith
God sent so copyous plente of watyr that the emperour and al the peple
were through wet. But the bysshop went hom no drope sene vpon hys
clothis.

That tyme that the Go[th]ys wastyd and dystroyid Itayle, myche 100
peple wentyn away from the feyth and becomyn hethene. And for as
meche as Donat the bysshop and Hillarianus the munk vndyrnomyn
[E]uadracianum the prefect of hys apostasie, he, hauynge dysdeyn,
chargy[d] hem to don sacrifice to Iupiter. And for they wolde not, he mad
Hillarian to be spoylyd and betyn tyl he yald vp the gost. Donat also, fyrst 105
enprisound, aftyr he mad to byn hefdyd.

74 cors] cros   84 conuictyd] comictyd   87 he] the   100 Gothys] Gos-
tys   wastyd and] wastyd   103 Euadracianum] Quadracianum   104 chargyd]
chargynge

[134. CYRIACUS]

Vita sanctorum Ciriaci Largi & Saiaragdi

Ciriacus was an holy dekne, ordeynyd and maad by the pope Marcelle.
And aftyrward, takyn and led to the emperoure Maximian, he was sent
with othyr felas for to diggyn grauyl and herthe and to bern yt vpon hys
5   shuldryn in the place clepyd Term Dyoclyciane, where was also dampnyd the oly old man Saturninus, whoom Ciriacus and Sisinius holpyn to
bern hys taske werk and his dayly iournees. Not longe aftyr, Ciriacus was
put in prisoun and by the prefect of the cyte sente aftyr to hys answere.
And whyl Apronianus Camentarientis brouht forth Ciriacum, sodeynly
10   a voys with lyght cam fro heuene, seyinge on this wyse: '*Wen*[i]*te, bene-
dicti patris mei & cetera*: Comyth, ye blyssyd chylderyn of my fadyr, takyth
the kyngdam that ys ordeynyd for yow from the bygynnynge of the word!'
Thys herynge, Apronianus anon byleuyd and was conuertyd and, comynge
byforn the prefect, knowlechyd Crist. To whom the prefect seyde on this
15   wyse: 'Apronyan, art thou now bycomyn a cristene man?' 'Whoo wurth
me', quoth Apronyan ageyn, 'for I haue lost my dayis.' 'Trewely Apronyan', quoth the prefect ageyn, 'thou shalt lese thy dayis.' And anoon he
comaundyd hym to byn hefdyd; Saturninus and Sisinius, for they wolde
not sacrificyn, wern aftyr dyuers tormentriys hefdyd.
20   Di[o]clycianus dowtyr Archemia was vexyd with a deuyl and he cryid
by the maydyns mouth and seyde: 'I shal nat goon owt but yf Ciriacus the
dekne come hedyr!' And whan Ciriacus was comyn and comaundyd the
f. 157ʳᵃ   spirit to gon | owt, he answerde and seyde: 'Yf thou wylt, Ciriac, that I
go owt, yiue me sum vessel that I may entryn in.' Quoth Ciriacus ageyn:
25   'Lo here my body! Entre in yf thoo mayst.' 'I may not', quoth he, 'entren
into thy body, for yt ys shet and selyd [ouy]ral on yche syde. Wherfore
be auysyd, for yf thou kast me owt now here, I shal make the to gon into
Babilonye.' But whan this spirit was compellyd to goon owt ageyns hys
wyl, Archemia seyde pleynly that she saw werely the god whom Siria[c]us
30   prechyd. And whanne Ciriacus had baptysyd hyre and dwellyd in the hous
wiche Dioclician and Sorena his wyf had youyn hym, there cam a massager
to Dioclicyan fro the kyng of Pers, preynge hym that he wolde sende thedyr Ciriacum, for hys douthtyr was vexid with a deuyl. And anoon Ciriacus
with othir twoo deknes, Largus and Smaragdus, were s[ent] in a shyp to
35   Babilonye. And whan he cam to the maydens presence, the deuyl cryid by

10 *Wenite*] Wente   18 hym to] to   20 Dioclycianus] Diclycianus
26 ouyral] ouyuyr   29 Siriacus] Siriaus   34 sent] spen

hyre mouth and seyde: 'Art thou not wery, Ciriac?' 'Nay, forsothe', quoth
Ciriac, 'I am not wery but ouyral gouernyd by Goddys helpe I am strong.'
'Yet at the laste', quoth the deuyl, 'I haue brough the thedyr I wolde.'
'Iwys', quoth Ciriacus, 'and shal putte the fro thens thou woldyst ben,
oure lord Ihesu Crist mote bydde the goon owt.' At wyche word the deuyl 40
wente owt anoon, criynge and seyinge: 'O how ferful ys this name the wich
conpellyth me for to gon owt.' And thus whanne Ciriacus had maad heyl
the maydyn, he baptysyd hyre and here fadir and hyre modyr with meche
othir peple. To whoom the kynge offryd manye grete yiftys but he wolde
noon reseyuyn therof. But whanne he hadde fastyd there fourty dayis on 45
breed and watyr, he with his felaas returnyd ageyn to Rome.

Dioclicyan deyid and Maximian his sone succedyd. The whiche, for
angyr of hys sustyr whom Ciriacus had baptisyd, he mad hym nakyd to
be drawyn byforn hys [c]har boundyn with shenys. Aftyr whiche tyme he
delyueryd hym with hys felas to a vykyr clepyd Carpasius, chargyng hym 50
that he compellyd hem to don sacrifice or ellys to sleen hem with diuers
tormentis. And whanne he hadde dystreynyd hem vpon iebettis and poryd
hoot moltyn pych vpon here hedys, he maad here hedys to be smet of;
and so sent here soulys to the blysse of heuene. Aftyr whiche tyme Carpasius gat of the emperour Ciriacus hous, and, in the despyht of cristene 55
men, bathyd hymself in the same place where Ciriacus was wone to bapti-
sin in. And, wyl he with nynetene felaas eet and drank and held ryot and
reuel, sodeynly they alle fel doun deed. Wherfore, fro that tyme forward
the bath was shet vp, and paynyms and hethene men begunne to dredyn
and wurshipyn cristene men. *Deo gracias.*   60

[135. ROMANUS]

The lyf of Seynt Roman

Romanus was oon of the seuene knyhtys principal with the emperour
Decius. And oo tyme as he saw blyssyd Laurence stedfastly sufferyd and
pacyently tormentys put onto hym, and feythfully exortynge | hem that f. 157ʳᵇ
stondyn aboutyn hym to the feyth of Ihesu Crist, anon in hys herte he 5
bygan to leuyn. And as he stod and byhyld attentyfly, he sau an aungyl
stondyng byforn Laurence gladly, and wepynge hys wou[n]dys diligently
with a towayle, and makyn hem hoo[l] veryly. And, marualynge of this
syghte, he seyde to Seynt Laurence on this wyse: 'Seruaunt of God, I see
byforn the stondynge a ful fayre yunge man with a towayle in hys hand 10

45 on breed] breed   49 char] shar   7 woundys] wouundys   8 hool]
hook

and wepynge thi wou[n]dys. Wherfore I require the by Cri[s]t, whom thou
knolechyst, that thou tarye nat to baptyse me that I may atteyne to the
croune of blysse with the.' And forthwith the seyd knyth Romanus wente
and fet a vessel with watyr, waytynge an oportune tyme whanne he mygh
15 be baptysyd. Whan Laurence saw this, he gladly blyssyd the water and
baptysyd hym, and sacrid hym a knyth of heuenly cheualrye. And whanne
Decius herd seyn this, he, meuyd with gret woodnesse, seyde: 'Allas, we
byn ouercomyn with wicchecraft!' And anon he chargyd Romanum to be
brough to his presence. Whiche don, or than ony questyoun or wourd was
20 meuye to hym, he with a lowd voys bygan to cryin and seyin: 'I am a cristene man and the emperoure, and thi goddys I dysspyse for Cristis sake.'
At wiche wurd the emperour, in his woodnesse, wythowte more, chargyd
that the same our hys heed shulde be smet of. And forthwith he was led
withoute wallys *Porta Salaria*, and there hefdyd the fyffte ide of August.
25 Whoos body Iustinus buryid in *Agro Verano* in a caue, where Crist hath
shevyd manye miraclis for hys knyghtis sake. *Deo gracias.*

[136. LAURENCE]

The martirdam of Seynt Laurence

Laurencius is as meche as 'holdynge lauream'. Laurea ys a coroune mad
of braunchis and leuys of laurer, with whiche maner of crou[n]e in old tyme
victouris in bataylys and conquerou[r]s were wone for synguler wurshyp
5 to be crounyd. The laurer tre ys priuylegyd in foure thyngis. For yt ys
a shewere of victory with continuel grennesse, glad and mery, plesaunt
in smellyng and verteuous in werkynge. Conuenyently thanne for these
foure thyngis Laurencius ys seyid of Laurius. Fryst for in hys passyoun he
opteynyd and gat victory. For as yt seyid in hys legende, Decius, seyinge
10 hys gret constaunce and stedfastnesse of herte in the peynys applyid onto
hym, confuhs in hymself, seyde thus: 'I trowe veryly that we ben ouyrcomyn.' Laurencius had also the verdure and the grenesse of the laure by
clennesse and purite of soule. And therfore he seyde '*Mea nox & cetera.*
My nyht hath no thyrknesse 'but' alle my thyngis shynyn in bryhnesse.'
15 He hath now the plesaunt odour of the laurer by perpetuyte and euerles-
tyngenesse of hys memorye and mynde. And therfore yt ys appliyd to hym
that Dauid seyth in the sautyr book: '*Dispersit dedit.* He disperbyld and
yaf aboutyn to pouere men. Wherfore hys ryghtwysse dwellyth withowtyn ende.' And anothyr place: '*In memoria eterna & cetera.* In the endeles

---

11 woundys] wouundys   Crist] Cristis   3 croune] crouune   4 conquerours]
conquerous

memorie shal be the ryhtfull and he shal nat feryn of euyl herynge', *psal-* 20
mus. Effect of verteuous wherkynge had blyssyd Laurence | by hys holy   f. 157ᵛᵃ
and deuouht prechynge by wiche he conuertyd to the feyth of Crist Lucille,
Ipolyt and Roman. The medicynal werkynge of the laurer tre ys that yt
brekith the stoon, yt helpyth defnesse and yt dredith no lyhtynge. In lyk-
wyse Seynt Laurence brekyth hard stony hertis, yeldyth gostly herynge 25
and defendyth from the thundyr clap of reprof euerelastynge.

The martirdam of Seynt Laurence

As seyith Ioon Belet, whan Sixtus bysshop of the syte of Rome wente
oo tyme into Spayne, he fond ther two yunge men, Laurence and Vincent
his cosyn, adornyd with honeste of maneris and clerly shynyng in alle here 30
werkes, and brough hem with hem to Rome. Of whiche the ton, that ys
to seyne Vincent, returnyd ageyn to Spayne and there endyd hys lyf by a
glorious triumphe, as yt ys seyd byforn in the fyrste part of this werk and
in the monyth of Ianuarie. The tothir, that ys to seyne Laurence, abood
stylle at Rome with seyid pope Sixtus, whoom he made his herchedekne. 35
In this popys tyme Philyp the emperour and Philip his sone reseyuyd the
feyth of Crist and fully entendyd to wursh[i]ppyn and enbel[i]sshyn Cristis cherche. This Philyp was the fryste emperour whiche reseyuyd Cristis
feyth in Rome, whoom Origenes as summe seyin co[n]uertyd, albeyt that
summe othere seyin that blyssyd Poncius sh[u]ld haue conuertyd hym. 40
This emperoure regnyd in the thousent yer from the fyrste fundacyoun
of the cyte of Rome and conuenyent yt was the thousend yer shuld rathere
ben dedicat and haluyd to Crist than to ydols, for this yer, that ys to seyne
the thousend yer, was halwyd of the Romayns with gret apparayle of pleyis
and of spe[ct]aclis. 45

This emperour Philip had a knyht with hym, a hole man and an hardy
and ryght famous in harmys and in batayles, whoos name was Decius. Yt
happyd so in this menewhile that Fraunce rebellyd ageyns the Romayn
empere, for whiche cause the emperour sent this seyid Decius as an expert
man and victor[i]us to subiugatyn ageyn them to the emperour. The 50
whiche Decius had a prosperous iourny and, al thynge performyd and
don aftyr his entent, with triumpha[n]t victorie he returnyd ageyn-ward
to Rome. And whan the emperour Philyp herd how fortunat expedycioun
he had in his iourne, welynge doun to hym the more singuler and special
wurship, he cam ageyns hym fro Rome to Verone and there met with 55

37 wurshippyn] wurshppyn   enbelisshyn] enbelsshyn   39 conuertyd] couertyd   40 shuld] shald   45 spectaclis] spectakaclis   50 victorius] victorus
52 triumphant] triumphat

hym. But, for as meche as the propyrte and the dysposicioun of shrewys
ys that the more they be wurshypd and en[h]aunssid the more proud they
byn, anoon he bygan to coueytyn and to byn ambicyous of the empere,
and bygan to conspiryn the deth of his lord the emperour. For wych cause
60 he cam priuyly into the emperours tente or pauileoun and, as he lay and
slepte vnwarly, he s[m]et of hys heed and wente hys weye. And anoon
f. 157vb forthwith wyth preyere, yiftys and with promissys, he drow onto | hym
the ost wyche cam with the emperour. Wych don, with a sad and sobyr
pas, he took hys weye forth toward Rome. The emperouris sone, yunge
65 Philyp, heryng of hys fadris deth, wex sore aferd. Wherefore anon al hys
fadrys tresoure and hys own also he deleueryd into the handys of blyssyd
Sixtus and of Laurence for this skyl: that in cas that Decius slou hym
they shulde dysposyn the seyid good onto the cherche and onto poure
men. And this doon Philip fledde and hid hym fro the face of Decius,
70 whoom the senat of Rome met with and reseyuyd gladly and conformyd
hym into the empere. And that it shuld not be trowyd or supposyd that
he had slayn hys lord tretourly but only for [z]eel of ydolatrye, anoon he
bygan most cruelly to pursuyn cristene men, comaundyd and chargynge
hem withowte ony mercy to be slayn wheresoeuere they mygh be foun-
75 dyn. In whiche persecucyoun, amonge many othere, Philip hys lordys
sone was slayn and martird. Aftyr whiche tyme Decius bygan to makyn
inquisycioun and see[k]yn of hys lordys tresoure. And anoon was blyssyd
Sixtus presentyd onto hym as for a cristene man and for hym whiche had
the emperours tresourys, whoom Decius chargyd to be put in prisoun
80 into the tyme that he wolde forsakyn Crist and telle where the emperours
tresoure was. And as he wente to prisoun-ward, blyssyd Laurence foluyd
aftyr, cryinge on this wyse: 'Whedyr goost thou, fadyr, withowte thy sone,
and whedyr walkyst thou, holy prest, withoute a seruaunt or a ministir?
Thou were neuere wone to do sacrifice withoutyn a dekne. What ys that
85 in me that hath displesyd thy fadirhood? Hast thou owt, fadyr, prouyd
me vnkynde? Good fadyr, take experience certeynly wethir thou hast
chosyn an able ministre or nouht, to whoom thou hast committyd the
dyspensacyoun of oure lordys blood.' To whoom blyssyd Sixtus answerde
ageyn on this wyse: 'Sone, sykyrly I neythir leue the ner forsake the, but
90 grettere conflictys and bataylys for Cristys feyth byn aftyrward comynge
to the. We, as agyd folk and feble, haue reseyuyd the cours of lythtere and
more esy fyht, but the, as younge, strong and myghty, abydyth a more
glorious triumphe of the tiraunt and a more famous victorie. For aftyr the

57 enhaunssid] enchaunssid   61 smet] semet   71 that it] that   72 zeel]
yeel   77 seekyn] seegyn

thrydde day thou, dekne, shalt foluyn me, prest.' Whiche wurdys seyid,
he committyd onto hym the tresouris of the cherche, chargynge hym to 95
dysposyn hem to cherchis and to pore men. And anoon blyssyd Laurence
seyte bothe day and nyght dylygently cristene men, and ministryd to yche
of hem as he perceyuyd here [n]ede. In whiche vicitacyoun tyme he cam
into a wydwys hous, the whiche had manye cristene men hyd wythin
hyre. The whiche wydwe longe had languryd with a greuous syknesse in 100
the heed, whom, by puttynge to of hys handys, he curyd and mad heyl
perfythly, and, alle the pore mennys feet wasshyn, he yaf hem elmesse
and went his wey. The same nyth alle he cam into a cristene mannys hous,
where here he fond a blynd man whom, a tokne of the cros mad with his
hand vpon hys eyne, he illumynyd | and mad to sen. f. 158ra

Aftyr thys, whan blyssyd Sextus, for he wold nat obeyin to Decius ner 106
don sacrifice to deuyls, was led forth for to ben hefdyd, blyssyd Laurence
ran aftyr hym seying on this wyse: 'Wyl thou not, fadyr, forsake me now ner
leue me behynde, for I haue spent al the tresoure whiche thou delyueryst
onto me!' Thys heringe the soudyours, anoon they tokyn blyssid Laurence 110
and committyd hym to Par[t]he[ni]e tribuno, and he presentyd hy[m] to
Decius. And he askyd Laurence on this wyse: 'Where', quoth he, 'ben
the tresouris of the sherche, the whiche as we knowe wyl were commityd
to th[y] gouerna[un]ce and kepynge?' To whiche questyon, for as meche
as blyssyd Laurence wolde yeu[e] non answere, Decius deliueryd hym to 115
Valerian the prefect, chargynge hym that, yf he wolde not tellyn hym where
wern the tresouris of the cherche and offeryn onto ydolys, that he shuld
bryngyn hym to deth with diuers tormentys and peynis. This Valerianus
the prefect comittyd to a viker clepyd Ipolitus, and he shet hym vp in prisoun with manye othere. In whiche prisoun amonge alle was a payny[m] 120
clepid Lucillus, the whiche with longe wepynge had lost hys sygh and was
blynde. To whoom whan Laurence had hygh that he shuld restoryn ageyn
his sygh yf he wold byleuyn on oure lord Ihesu Crist and take baptem,
anon he instauntly askyd to be baptisid. And anoon Laurence took watyr
in hys hand and seyde to hym thus: 'Alle thynges ben wasshyn and mad 125
clene in confessioun.' And whan he dylygently had askyd hym of the arti-
clis of the feyth and he had knowelechyd hymself to beleuyn hem alle,
anoon he poryd the water vpon his heed and baptisyd hym in the name of
Criste. Wiche doon, i[m]mediatly he the whiche was blynd reseyuyd syht
and mygh seen. For wiche cause many blynde men comyn to Laurence in 130

98 nede] rede   111 hym¹ to] hym   Parthenie] Parchemie   hym²] hys
114 thy] the   gouernaunce] gouernauunce   115 yeue] yeui   120 paynym]
paynin   129 immediatly] inmediatly

prisoun and were mad to seen. This considerynge, Ipolitus seyde to Laurence o[n] this wyse: 'Sheue me the tresoure of the cherche!' 'Iwys Ipolite',
quoth Laurence ageyn, 'yf thou wilt byleuyn into oure lord Ihesu Crist,
bothe I shal sheue the tresore and also y byhete the euerelestynge lyf.' To
135 whoom Ipolitus thus seyde ageyn: 'Yf thou performe in dede that thou
byhetyst in word, I shal don that thou amonestyst.' And in that same oure
Ipolitus byleuyd and was baptisid with al hys houshold.

Aftyr this Valerian sente to Ipolit that he shulde pleyntyn onto hym
Laurence. 'O Ipolyte', quoth Laurence, 'go we togedyr, for bothe to the
140 and to me ys maad redy euerelestynge ioye.' And whanne they come bothe
toforn Valereanus tribunal bench, anoon questyon was maad to Laurence
of the cherches tresours. Wherof Laurence askyth thre dayis respyth, the
wheche vndyr the suyrte of Ipolit Valereanus grauntyd hym. In wiche thre
dayis blyssyd Laurence gadryd togeder a gret multitude of crokyd pore
145 men, lame and blynde, and presentyd hem to Decius in the paleys clepyd
Palatium Salustianum, seyinge on this wyse: 'Lo these ben the tresours
euerlastynge, the whiche neuere menusyn ner lessen but euere encresyn
f. 158rb and growyn, whiche ben dysperbyld and sprenklyth abrood in | euerych
singulerly and in alle foundyn hool v[ni]uerselly. The handys of these
150 men han brou vp the tresoure of the cherche into the blysse of heuene.'
To whom Valerianus in the presence of Decius seyde thus ageyn: 'Whi
art thou thus chaungable and turnyst abowte by many thyngis? And put
awey thy wycchecrafth and do sacrifice to oure goddys!' Quoth Laurence
sadly ageyn: 'Valerian, sey me now whoo owith rathere to be wurshipd,
155 the makere or ellys that ys maad?' Decius, wroth with this answere,
coma[un]dyd hym myhtyly to be betyn with scorpions and, that don, al
maner kynde of scorpiouns to be brough byforn hym and thus thanne
seyde onto hym: 'Do sacrifice to oure goddys, that thou mowe askapyn
these maner of tormentys!' 'O thou vnhappy', quoth Laurence ageyn,
160 'these byn the dedicat metys the whiche I aluey haue desyrid.' 'Yf these
ben so dedicat metys, Laurence, as thou seyist', quoth Decius, 'telle vs
where we mo[un] fynde swych mad felaas lyk to the that we mowe byddyn
hem to mete with the.' 'Nay, nay', quoth Laurence, 'they haue youyn vp
here namys to heuene and thou art not wurthi to seen hem.' Whan Decius
165 herd thys, anoon he comaundyd hym to be spoylyd of his clothis and
nakyd to byn betyn with battys and aftyr that hoot brennynge platys to
byn applyid to hys sydys. In whiche tyme blyssid Laurence preyid on this
wyse: 'Lord Ihesu Crist, God of God, haue mercy on me thy servaunt.

132 on] oun   149 vniuerselly] vniuuerselly   155 wroth with] wroth
156 comaundyd] comauundyd   162 moun] mouun

Whan I was acusyd I denyid not thin holy name, and whanne I was askyd I
confessyd the to be my God.' To whom Decius seyde ageyn on this wyse: 170
'I woot wel that by whichecraft thou deludyst these tormentis, but not
forthan with alle the whichecraftys thou kanst thou shalt not deludyn me.
For I testifie my goddys and myn goddessis, but y[f] thou sacrifice I shal
make the to steruyn with diuers tormentys. Whiche seyid, he maad hym
to byn betyn with ledene whippys. Whiche doon, Laurence preyid and 175
seyde: 'Lord Ihesu Crist, take my spirit to the.' And forthwith, herynge
the emperour, a voys cam to Laurence from heuene seyinge on this wyse:
'Abyde Laurence, for manye conflictys and bataylys ben yet to be don
onto the!'And whanne Decius herd this, he wex ner wood and in his
madnesse thus cryid: 'O ye Romaynys, herd ye not how deuyls co[un]selyd 180
this cursyd man, the whiche neythyr wourshippyth goddys, ner dredith
tormentis, ner non angry pryncis?' Whiche seyid, he comaundyd hym to
be betyn ageyn with scorpyons.

And whil this was in doyinge, Laurence smelyd and thankyd God and
preyid for hem whiche stodyn aboutyn hym. In that same our a knyth ston- 185
dynge bysidyn, whos name was Romanus, byleuyd to Crist and seyde thus
to blissyd Laurence: 'I see stondynge beforn the a ryht fayr yunglynge,
and with a fayr lynene cloth wepynge thy membris. Wherfore I adiure the,
by the lord on whom thou leuyst, fo[rs]ake me not, but haste that I were
baptysid.' Quoth Decius to Valerianus: 'I trowe verely that by whichecraft 190
we byn ouyrcomyn.' And anoon he comaundyd Laurence to be led ageyn
to prisoun, whedyr Romanus bouht a vessel ful of watyr and fel doun at
Laurences feet and preyid hym to be baptysyd. And so he was, as yt ys
seyid byforn in seyid | Romaunus lyf.   f. 158va

The same nyght aftyr that Romanus was deed, Laurence was brough 195
ageyn to Decius presence, whedyr also were brough alle maner kyndys of
tormentys. And anoon Decius seyde to blyssyd Laurence: 'Doo sacrifice
to goddys, or ellys alle this nygh shal be spent in the with tormentys.' To
whom seyde thus Seynt Laurence ageyn: 'My nyht hath ne thyrknesse,
but alle myn thyngis ben in lygh and bryhnesse.' Whan Decius saw this, 200
'Bryngith forth', quoth he, 'a bed of yryn, that rebell Laurence may reste
therein.' And anoon was brouth forth a gret rostyng yryn, with thre rybbys, and a ston of whyht marbyl was leyid aboue theron, thirlyd thorgh with
holys in dyueris placis, vpon whiche the ministris spred Laurence abrood,
hoote brynnynge coolys throwyn vndyr and myghtyly blowyn. And with 205
irene forkys they pressyd hym to [th]e ston, the flaume comynge vp and

173 yf] yt   178 to be don] don   180 counselyd] couunselyd   189 forsake]
fors sake   206 the] be

in by the holys the whiche wern on the ston. And whil this was in doynge,
Decius counselyd hym to do sacrifice to goddys. 'I', quoth Laurence ageyn,
'haue offerid myself a sacrifice to God in heuene into an odour of swet-
210 nesse. For a contriht spirit ys a sacrifice to God.' And turnynge hys speche
to Valerian, he seyde to hym on this wyse: 'Lerne, thou wrecche Valerian,
how gret ys the vertu of myn lord God. For these colys yif to me refresshynge, and to the they shul yeuyn euerelestynge torment. For my lord
in heuene knowith that I, acusyd, denyid not, askyd, I knowlechid my lord
215 Ihesu Crist, and now, roost, I yiue my lord thankynge. O how gret ys youre
madnesse, ye vnhappy men, the whiche wyl not knowyn how gret refresshynge these colys doon to me, and no maner hurt ner brynnynge.' And
alle men whiche stood bysydyn maruayld that Decius ha[d] coma[un]dyd
hym to be rost quyk, but Laurence with a fayr and rygh glad cher seyde:
220 'Thankynge be to the lord Ihesu Crist, wiche haste vouchydsaf to con-
fortyn me.' And, liftynge vp hys heyne to Decius-ward, he seyde to hym
thus: 'See, wrecche, see! Now thou hast rost the to syde, turne and ete
wyl the tothyr syde refressh.' Wych seyid, he yaf thankynge to God, seyinge on this wyse: 'Lord Ihesu Crist, gramercy that I haye deseruyd to
225 entryn within thyn gatys.' Whithe wich wurdys he yald vp the spirit and
deyid. This seyng, Decius with Valerian, the body leftyth vpon the gry-
dyl, wentyn confuhs in hemself into the paleys of Tiberie. And erly on
the next morwyn Ipolitus ful the body and with helpe of a prest clepyd
Iustinus buryid yt, anoyntyd with swet smellyng onymentys, in a feld cle-
230 pyd *Ager Veranus*, aboute the yers of oure lord twoo hundryd and sixti &
cetera.
      Seynt Gregori tellyth in his Dialogis that in Sabina was a nunne, the
whiche in hyre flessh was chast but in hyre tounge she was nice and dislauy. This nunne deyid and was buryid in a cherche of Seynt Laurence
235 byfor hys autyr, and the nygh foluynge she was by deuyls takyn vp and
departyd asundyr; the to part was left hol and not hurt, the tothir was
skorkyl and brent visibly to yche mannys syht. Gregorius Turonensis tellyth that there was a prest whiche bysyid hym to reparyn a cherche of Seynt
f. 158vb Laurence. And so yt happyd that oon of the bemys by neclygence | was
240 kut to short. This perceyuyd of the prest, anon he preyid Seynt Laurence
that he whiche oftyn in his lef had faueryd and fosteryd pouere men, wold
now relewyn hys penurye for he was not of powyr to byin a newe. And anon
sodeynly the bem gru owt so long that whan yt was vpon the werk a gret
part superhabundyd. The whiche part by lytyl and by sundry whilys kut
245 of and curyd theriwth manye dyuers syknessis. Seynt Gregori tellith also

218 had] hat   comaundyd] comauundyd   242 was not] was

in his Dialogis that oon clepyd Sanctulus, welynge repary[n] a cherche of
Seynt Laurence wiche was brent of Longobardys, hyrid hym many werkemen. And as yt happyd vpon a day he lakkyd bred to settyn byforn hem.
Wherfore Sanctulus, rygh sory and heuy, preyid Seynt Laurence of helpe.
Aftyr whiche tyme, as he lokyd into his ouene he perceyuyd therin a pas-   250
synge fayre whyht loof, the whiche hem sempte vnnethe sufficient for thre
mennys fode at oo mel. But Seynt Laurence, not welynge that hys werkemen shuldyn faylyn breed, so multipliyd this loof that yt sufferyd to alle
his werkemen the space of ten dayis. In a cherche also of Seynt Laurence
at Malan was a chalys of cristal, a passynge fayr vessel. The whiche, as yt   255
was brouth to the awter-ward vpon a festeful day, fel owt of the deknys
hand and brast on manye pecis. The dekne, gretly abasshd and sory of the
caas, with gret heuynesse gaderid vp alle the fragmentis and leyid hem
vpon the autyr. And aftyr a preyere mad to Laurence he fond the shalys
as hool and as sund as euere yt was byfore. Yt ys red also in a book of   260
oure ladyis miraclis that sum tyme in Rome was a iuge, Steuene by name,
whiche gladly wolde takyn yifftys and peruertyn ryghful domys. This iuge
took awey violently thre housis of Seynt Laurence and a gardyn of Seynt
Anneys, and kept hem vnrythfully. Yt happyd this man to deyin and to be
brouth to the dom of God, whom whan Seynt Laurence saw comynge, with   265
gret indignacioun he neyhyd onto hym and thrijs greuously uo[r]p hym
by the arm and greuyd hym with gret peyne. Seynt Anneys, also persey-
uynge hym with othir vi[rgin]s, turnyd awey hyre face and wolde not lokyn
on hym. And anoon the iuge yaf ys sentence and seyde: 'For as meche as
he this hath wrongfully takyn awey othir mennys good, and takynge yifftys   270
sold treuthe, therfore lete hym be delyueryd hens and put in Iudas my trai-
tours place.' And anoon Sanctus Proiectus, to whom seyid Steuene had a
synguler affeccioun in his lyf, cam to Seynt Laurence and to Seynt Anneys
and preyid for hym. At whos instance alle they with oure lady wentyn to
the iuge and preyid for hym. At whos request the iuge grauntyd hym the   275
space of thritty dayis to gon ageyn to his body and so to doo pena[un]ce
yf he wolde. And whanne he shulde goon oure lady yaf singulerly in comaundement that he shulde seyin this psalme: *Beati i[mm]aculati,* euery
day aftyr as longe as he leuyd. And whanne he was comyn ageyn to his
body, hys arm was as swart and as blak brent as thogh he had sufferyd yt   280
in body. The whiche signe abood with hym durynge the tyme of thrytty
dayis, aftyr whiche the iuge had grantyd hym of lyf. In whiche dayis he

246 reparyn] reparynge   266 uorp] uoop   268 virgins] vinrgis
276 penaunce] penauunce   278 *immaculati] inmaculati*

f. 158ra maad | restitucioun of al that he had mystakyn and dede penaunce for hys
synnys, and the threttydde day deyid & wente to blysse.

285 We reddyn in the lyf of Seynt Herry, the emperour, that he and his wyf
Kaugnegundys lyuyn togedyr maydenys a longe tyme. And at the laste, by
the deuyls stirynge, he fel in a suspecioun bytwyx his wyf and a k[ny]ht of
his, for purgacioun wherof he mad here to gon ouyr brennynge sharis fyftene paas bare foot. And whan she bygan to goon she seyde on this wyse:
290 'Crist Ihesu, as thou knowyst me vntouchyd and vndefoulyd bothyn of
Herry and of alle othere, so be thou myn helpe at this tyme!' And anon cam
a voys from heuene and seyde: 'Mayde Marie shal deliueryn the, mayde
Kanegund!' Whiche seyde, alle men seyynge, she went ouyr alle the sharis
withoute wem or hurt. Not longe aftyr, whan the seyid Herry the empe-
295 rour shuld dyin, a gret+multitude of deuyls with grete dene went forby
the celle of an holy hermyte, the whiche opnyd his wyndowe and askyd
hym that cam last of hem what they were. 'We byn', quoth he, 'a legioun
of deuyls whiche goon to the emperours deyinge, to wete yf we fynde ony
thyng propyr of oure in hym.' 'I charge the', quoth the hermyte, 'that thou
300 come ageyn by me and telle me how ye han sped.' And whan he cam ageyn,
he seyde that they had rygh not profytynge in here iourne. For whanne
bothe his good dedys and his euyl were leyid in the balauncys, brent Laurence cam with a goldene pot in his hand of a gret whyte. And whan we
wende to han had the victory, he sodeynly threu the pot in the balaunce,
305 and anoon yt pullyd vp oure balaunce as nouth had byn therin. 'Wherfore', quoth he, 'I in myn malyncoly rent of the toon ere of the pot.' This
pot he clepid a chalys, whiche the seyid emperour yaf to a cherche of Seynt
Laurence. And for yt was so gret of quantyte and so heuy, he dede makyn
theron tweyne eris to beryn yt with. And aftyrward, whan the emperour
310 deyid, the toon ere of the chalys was foundyn rent awey lych as the deuyl
told the holy hermyte.

And here yt ys to be notyd that the passioun of Seynt Laurence exce-
dit and supercellyth alle othere martiris passiouns in foure thyngis, as yt
may gadryn of Seynt Austyns and Se[y]nt Maximus wurdys: fryst in bit-
315 tyrnesse [of] passioun, the secunde in effect and profygh, the thridde in
constaunce or strenghthe, the fourte in marualous sygh and the manyr of
vi[c]torie. O the fryste, that ys to seyne of bittyrnesse, thus seyith blyssyd
Maximus, or as sum men opinyn Seynt Ambrose: 'Seynt Laurence', quoth
he, 'was not oonly slayn with a short and simple passioun, for he that ys
320 hefdyd deyid onys and anoon, he that ys drynklyd ys in a brunt delyueryd

287 knyht] kynht   314 Seynt] Sent   315 of] of of   317 victorie] vitorie

hens, and so ys he that ys [th]rist in the fyir and brent. But this blyssyd
martyr Laurence was turmentyd with longe and manyfold peyne, soo that
deth faylyd hym not to turmentyn but yt faylith to endyn his tormentis.
We redyn', quoth he, 'that the thre holy childrys wentyn aboutyn in the
flaume of here peynis and trodyn vndyr here feet the grete globis of fyre. 325
Not forthan Seynt Laurence ys [to be] preferrid with more ioye, for they
wentyn in the flaume of herre peynis but he lay doun therin. They bore
doun the flame with her steppys, but he | suffryd yt brynnynge his sydys. f. 158ʳᵇ
They, stondynge in here peyne, pr[e]yid God here handys vp lyftynge, but
he with al hys body bysoute God do[un] in the fyir lyinge.' Hec ille. 330

And here also yt ys to be markyd that Seynt Laurence aftyr Seynt
Steuene hath amonge alle othere martyrs the primacye, not for that he
sufferyd more peyne thanne othere, for many suffryd as gret peyne and
summe more than he, but thys primacye hath he for sexe causis. Fryst for
the place whiche he sufferyd in as Rome, the whiche ys the heed cyte 335
of the word and the sete souereyn of the holy apostoyle. The secunde
cause ys for the office of prechynge, the whiche he excellently exercisid
and fulfillyd. The thridde cause ys for the prudent and discret distribucyoun of the tresours committyd onto hym. These thre causis assignyth
Willelmus Altissidorencis. The fourte cause ys auctentyk and approuyd 340
martirdam passynge many othere, as manye gret doctours han auctorisid
and approuyd with here manyfold sermouns. The fifte cause ys for the
dyngnyte of his degre, for he was erchedekne of the apostelsee. Aftyr
whoom, as manye sayin, was neuere in the Romayn cherche see non othir
archedekne. The sexte cause was for the greuousnesse of the tormentys 345
whiche he sufferyd, for he was rostyd on an yirnene gredyle. Whereof seyith Seynt Austyn on this wyse: 'Yt was comaundyd that his rent lendys and
al todiuidyd and kut with many diuers peyne to be rost in the fyr, that by
the irene gredyl, the whiche by his continuel feruour and hete had myghte
the more to tormentyn, his peyne shuld be the grettere and the lengere 350
durynge.' Hec Augustinus.

The secunde thynge wherin the passioun of Seynt Laurence superex-
cellyth ther martyris passioun ys effect and profyht. For, aftyr the sentence of Seynt Austyn and Maximum, the byttyrnesse of hys peyne mad
hym [hy] in glor[i]ficacioun, n[o]table in fame and opynioun, laudable in 355
deuocioun, and gret and noble in mutacyoun. Fryst of his heuynesse in
glorificacioun, seyth Seynt Austyn in a sermoun by maner of apostropha-
cioun, spekynge to Decius on this wyse: 'O thou persecutor Decius, thou

wex wood ageyns Cristis martir, but, the more thou were wood ageyns
360 hym, the more thou encrecyddyst the palme of uyctorye to hym, and as
faste as thou aggreggiddyst hys peyne, thou moriddyst hys croune. And
so thy male engyn, by wiche thou labouryddyst to don hym shame and
shenshype, turnyd to hys gret glorie, whanne the instrumentis of tormentrye ordeynyd to distroyin hym where bryngeris into hym of triumphat
365 victori and eternal wurshipe.' *Hec Augustinus in summa.*

Also Maximus, or as summe seyn Ambrosius, seyth thus: 'Alle yt',
quoth he, 'that in blyssid Laurence the tendyr membris were rent, brokyn and dyssoluyd, not forthan the most and the strengthe of [f]eyith
in hym was ful hool, neythir rent, brokyn ner dissoluyd. And so whil he
370 suffred damage and hurt in his body, he purchasid and gat hym lucre of
helthe in his soule.' 'Verily blyssid was this man Seynt Laurence', quoth
Austyn in a sermown, 'whoom neythir cruel fyir ner othir torment myght
chaunge from Cristys feyth. Wherfore holy relegioun crownyd hym in
euerelestynge reste.' *Hec Augustinus.*

375 Also the byttyrnesse of Laurences peyne, as yt ys seyid biforn, mad hym
notable in fame and opinyoun, and to this alludyth Maximus or Ambro-
f. 158va sius, seyinge | on this wyse: 'Conuenyently', quoth he, 'now we conparyn
and lyknyn blyssyd Laurence to the g[r]eyn of mustard seed, for he, brosyd with diuers passiouns, sent owt through the word the fauour and the
380 sauour of his gracious misterie. This Laurence of nature', quoth he, 'in
his body was meke, lityl and vnknowyn. But, aftyr that he was wexid rent
and brent, he poryd owt the odour of his nobylnesse to alle the cherchis
throughowt the werd.' Also the same Maximus in anothir sermoun seyth
thus: 'Yt ys an holy and a plesaunt thyng to God that we shulde wurshi-
385 pyn the spiritual byrthe of Seynt Laurence, that ys to seyne hys passion,
with a singuler and special deuocyoun. For through his brygh glemynge
flaumys Cristis victorious cherche this day shynyth in al the word. And his
passyoun illumynyth al the word.' *Hec ille.*

The bittyrnesse also of Seynt Laurence peyne mad hym laudable and
390 wurthi preysyng in opynyoun. And this shewith Seynt Austyn in a sermoun by threfold resoun, seyinge on this wyse: 'We owyn to reseyuyn and
to wurshipyn Seynt Laurence with alle maner swetnesse and deuocyoun.
Frist for he yaf hys pre[cyous] blood for oure lord. Also for he gat vs no lityl
but gret prerogatyf, anempst hym shewynge what owith to byn the feyth
395 of a cristene man of whos felachepe and cumpany ma[r]tris dyseruyn to
ben parteners. The thridde skyl ys for he was so holy a man of so good

368 feyith] seytth   378 greyn] geyn   393 precyous] preyours   395 martris]
matris   396 for he] for

conuersacioun that he deseruyd to fynde the crowne of martyrdam in the
tyme of pees.' *Hec Augustinus.*

The fourte wyse the byttyrnesse of Seynt Laurences passioun mad hym
gret and nobyl is in imitacyoun. For as seyith Seynt Austyn: 'The gret   400
cause and principal of his passioun was that by exaunple of hym othere
shulde be stirid to foluyn hym.' And that in thre thyngis ys, seyith Ianuence. Fryst in myhty sufferaunce of aduersites. And this ys the sentence of
Seynt Austyn in a sermoun, seyinge on thi wyse: 'To enformyn and techyn
the peple of God ys no forme of leuyn more profitable than the forme of   405
martirs. Eloquencye', quo[th] he, 'ys esy to make peroracioun and resoun
effectual to make suasyoun. But not forthan exaunplis ben more myhty
than w[o]rdys and bettyr yt ys to teche with werk than with voys. In this
most excellent kynde of doctrine the blyssyd martyr Laurence had a singuler dingnite, whiche with so maruelous strengthe of soule was enduyd   410
that, not only in tyme of persecucyoun he went not bak, but also with
the exaunple of his tolleraunce he hertyd and maad stronge othere to doo
the same.' *Hec Augustinus.*

The secunde that maad Seynt Laurence nobyl and gret in imitacyoun
ys gretnesse of feyth and feruour, whereof Maximus, or as othere seyin   415
Ambrosius, in a sermoun seyith thus: 'Whil blyssyd Laurence throgh his
feruent feyth ouercam the flaumys of the fyr, of feyth ouyrcomyn the intollerable flaumys of the fyir of helle.' The thridde thynge makyth Seynt
Laurence imitable was brynnynge loue. For as seyid Maximus, or Ambrosius seyith: 'The same lygh that he was brent with he illuminyd pleynly   420
al the word, and with the flaumys that he sufferid | he mad hoot alle cris-   f. 158ᵛᵇ
tene mennys hertys.' And, concludyd alle these thre thyngis in on, he seyth
thus: 'By the exaunple of blyssed Laurence we byn prouokyd to martirdam
for the fryste, inflaumyd to feyth for the seconde, and maad hoot to loue
and deuocyoun for the thrydde.'   425

The thrydde thyng in whiche blyssyd Laurence passioun was most
excellent was constaunce or strengthe. For, as seyth Seynt Austyn: 'Blyssyd Laurence abood with Crist not only to temptacyoun, but also to the
tirauntis interrogac[i]oun, to the most byttyr examinacioun and furious
concremacyoun, and finally to perempcyoun. In whiche longe deth, for he   430
had weel etyn and weel drinkyn, as though he had be maad fat with that
mete and drynke with that chalys, he felt not his tormentis ner he went not
abak cowardly, but succedyd and entrid into the kyngdam of heuene myghtyly.' *Hec ille.* And so constaunt and so stronge he was that not oonly he

---

400 is in] is   406 quoth] quoht   408 wordys] wardys   429 interrogacioun]
interrogacoun

435 wente not vndyr ner faylyd not in hys tormentis, but also, as seyith Maxi-
     mus, by the tormentis he was maad more myghty perfyht in dreed, more
     feruent in loue, and more mercy and iocund in feruour of deuocyoun. 'As
     towchinge the fryste', quoth Maximus, 'Laurence was spred abrod vpon a
     gridyrin and on the gret globys of flaumynge fyir and oftyn turnyd from
440 syde to syde. But not forthan, the more peyne that he sufferyd the more he
     dredde Crist his lord. As towchynge the secunde', seyith the seyid Maxi-
     mus or Ambrosus, 'lych as the greyn of mustard, the more yt ys grunden
     and brokyn the myhtyere yt ys, so blyssyd Laurence, the more he suffe-
     ryd of peyne and torment the more he was en[f]laumyd with the loue of
445 God. And as towchynge the thridde, the herte of hym', quoth Maximus,
     'in so gret magnanimyte of Cristys feyth wex hoot within hym that alle the
     tormentis of his body dysposid and set at nouth, and alle tormentys and
     peynis ouercomyn. Iocund, he scornyd his cruel turmentour.' *Hec ibi.*
         The fourte excellent of blyssyd Laurencys passioun was the merue-
450 lous feyth and the maner of his victorie. For blyssyd Laurence, as yt may
     be gadryd of wurdys of Seynt Austyn and of Maximus, had fyue owt-
     ward fyirys, the whiche he myghtyly ouercam and quenchyd. The fyrste
     fyir was the feyr of helle, the secunde of materyal flaume, the thrydde of
     flesshly concupiscence, the fourte of ardent auarice and the fyfte of furious
455 woodnesse.
         Of the quenchyng of the fryste fyr, that ys the fyir of helle, Maxi-
     mus seyith thus: 'Trowyst thou', quoth he, 'that Laurence myghte yeue
     place or goon abak for a momentanye brenynge of his body, to whom feyth
     had quenchid the euerelestynge ardour of the fyir of helle.' And the same
460 Maximus seyith thus in anothir place: 'Laurence passith', quoth he, 'by
     momentanye and erdly fyir, but he aschapid the flaume of the euereles-
     tynge brynnynge fyir of helle.' [Of] the quenchyng of the secunde fyir,
     that ys [m]ateryal, the seyid Maximus or Ambrosus seyth thus: 'Laurence
     labouryd in bodyly brynynge, but the loue of God consumyd and quen-
465 chid the material ardour.' And in anothir the same Maximus seyith thus:
f. 159ʳᵃ 'Albeyt that the inportune turmentour put vndyr | stykkys and encrecyd
     the flaume, yet not forthan blyssyd Laurence through the gret hete of feyth
     felt not tho owtward flaumys.' Seynt Austyn acordynge herto seyth that the
     cherite of cristen Laurence mygh not byn ouyrcomyn with the ow[tw]ard
470 flaume, for [s]lauere was the fyir that brent owthforth than was the fyir
     that bren withinne.
         Of the quenchynge of the thrydde fyir, that ys the fyir of carnel con-

---

444 enflaumyd] enfaumyd   452 whiche he] whiche   462 Of] O
463 materyal] nateryal   469 owtward] owtard   470 slauere] flauere

cupiscence, thus seyth Maximus: 'See', quoth he, 'how blyssyd Laurence
passith by the material fyir and was not brent, but illumynyd and shon
more brygh. He brent that he shuld not brynnyn, that ys to seyne he brent 475
owtward with mater[i]al fyir that he shud not brennyn with the fyir of fleshly lykynge & cetera.' Of the quenchynge of the fourte fyir, that is auarous
couetyse, and how yt vanysshd awey in th[e] man whiche dysyrith the tresoure of the cherche, seyth Seynt Austyn on this wyse: 'Decius, coueytous
of monye and enuye of treuthe, was armyd with doubyll brond of fyir: with 480
auaryce to gete with gold, and with cruelte to takyn auey Crist. But, iwys,
thou getyst not, ner thou profytist nat, O thou mannys creuelnesse. F[o]r
neythir thou getest gold ner profyth with thi malys. For whil Laurence
goth vp to Crist in heuene, thou faylyst and vanysshist with thy flaumys
in erthe.' *Hec Augustinus.*   485
O[f] the quenchynge of the fyfte fyir, that ys to seyne of creuel
woodnesse, thus seyth Maxi[m]us: 'The ministris of flaumys ouercomyn
by Laurence, by constaunce and stedfastnesse he quente al hoote fyir
of mannys malice and wykkydnesse. And to this poynt oonly procedyd
and profytyd the deuyls entent, that the tru[e] feythfull Laurence shuld 490
goon glorious to God and the cruelnesse of his persecutours, confus[e] in
the[m]self, with his fyrys shuld secyn, vanysshyn and perysshyn.' And that
the woodnesse of the persecutours was a fyir shewyd the same Maxi[m]us,
seying on this wyse: 'The paynymys woodnesse, inflaumyd with the fyir
of malyhs, maad redy a brynnynge gredyle for to vengyn the flaumys of 495
inward indignac[i]oun with the flaumys of owtward fyir.'
And no woundyr though blyssyd Laurence ouyrcam these fyue owtward
fyris, for, as yt may be gadryd of the same Maximus wurdys, he had within
hym thre refresshyngis, and bar thre fyris in hys herte, by the whiche he
ouyrcam al owtward fyir. The fyrste refrygerie was feruent desyre of the 500
blysse of heuene, the secunde was medyac[i]oun and thyngkyng of Goddys laue, and the thrydde was puryte and clennesse of conscience. Of the
fyrste refrygerye spekyth Maximus or Ambro[s]us on this wyse: 'Blyssyd
Laurence mygh not felyn the torment of fyir in his bowaylys, the whiche
had the refrigerye of feruent desire of paradys in hys wyttys. For, th[o]ugh 505
his flysh brent lay byforn the tyrauntis feet and hys body soulelees and
dred, yet suffere [he] non detriment ner hurt in herthe, whoos soule dwellynge with God in heuene.' Of the secunde refresshynge, thus seyth the

476 material] maternal   478 the] tho   482 For] Fer   486 Of]
O   487 Maximus] Maxius   490 true] truthe   491 confuse] confush
492 themself] theself   493 Maximus] Maxius   496 indignacioun] indignacoun
501 medyacioun] mediacoun   503 Ambrosus] Ambrous   505 though] through
507 he] he he

f. 159rb same Maxi[m]us: 'Whil Laurence | though[t] and remembryd the tyme
510 of his passyoun, Cristis preceptys and hys comaundementys, alle that he
felte owtward was cold to hys semynge. And of the thridde refresshynge
he seyth on thys wyse: 'The moste myhty martyr Laurence ys inflaumyd
and brent in alle hys bowayls. But not forthan, remembrynge the kyngdam
of heuene in his soule, as gloryous victour he ioyith and his glad throgh
515 refrygirye of the clernesse of hys conscience.'
    Moreouyr, aftyr the seyid Maximus, this blyssyd martyr had also thre
inward fyrys, by the gret flaumys wherof he ouyrcam al maner owtward
fyirys. The fyrste fyir was gretnesse of feyth, the secunde ardent loue and
the thrydde was wery trewe knoweleche of God. Of the fryste fyir Maxi-
520 mus seyith thus: 'As meche as in Laurence the f[er]uour of feyth wex hoot,
so myche the flaume of torment wex cold. And that the fer[u]our of feyth',
quoth he, 'ys the saluatoris fyir, hymself wittnessith in the gospel, seyinge on this wyse *Ignem veny mittere & cetera*: "I am come to throuyn fyir
into the erthe." With wyche fyir blyssyd Laurence inflaumyd felt not the
525 brynnynge of material fyir.' Of the secunde seyith the efte seyid Maximus or Ambro[s]us: 'Martyr Laurence brent owtward in body with the
hoot flaumys of the wood tormentour, but a grettere fyir of the flaume
of Cristys loue warmyd hym soo inward that he yaf no fors of the lessere
fyir owtward.' And of the thridde fyir thus seyith also the same doctour:
530 'The most cruel flaume of the persecutor mygh not ouyrcomyn the most
myghty martyr Laurence. For the hote glem of treue knowelage of God
had so inflaumyd hys mynde and his soule that al maner peyne and torment
applyid onto hym owtward, or he felt not or he ouyrcam yt.' *Hec Maximus
vel Ambro[s]us.*
535   Blissid Laurence also hath abouyn other martirs thre singuler preuile-
gys as touchyng hys office in holy cherche. The fyrste ys in a vigoure, the
whiche he hath alone amonge othere martirs. And here yt ys to be notyd
that, as seyth Iohannes Belet, the vigilyis of seyntys byn turnyd into fastys,
for manye surfetys and mysgouernaunce wiche were sumtyme vsyd in vigi-
540 lys. For in old tyme yt was an vse and a custom that on the euyn of diuers
seyntys festys men [and] here wyuys and here chyldryn and here seruauntys wentyn to cherche, and there with fyir and lygh wycchyd al nygh. And
for as meche as manye aduenters and othere enorme and grete synnys were
exercisid and vsid vndyr the occasioun therof, the cherche turnyd the vigi-
545 lyis into fastyngis. And so remaynyth yet in the cherche the name of the

509 Maximus] Maxius   thought] though   520 feruour] fauour   521 feruour]
ferour   523 am come] am   526 Ambrosus] Ambrous   534 Ambrosus]
Ambrous   537 ys to] ys   541 and] in

vigile in remembraunce oonly of the old custum. The secunde priuilege
of Seynt Laurence ys that he alone with Seynt Steuene amonge alle martirs hath an octaue, as Martyn hath amonge the confessours. The thridde
priuilege of Seynt Laurance ys in returnyng of hys antiphonys with vers,
the whiche he alone hath with Seynt Poule for excellence of doctrine and   550
predicac[i]oun and he for excellence of peyneful passioun |

Osbertus de Clara, a munke of Westemenstyr and priour of the place the   f. 159ᵛᵃ
tyme of the translac[i]oun of Seynt Edward kyng and confessour, in a pistyl
whiche he wrot a nunne and hys nyfte, tellyth a notable and a confortable
miracle of Seynt Laurence, and as I remembre me weel, the fryste tyme   555
that I was at Rome in Pope Martyns tyme, I saw the same myracle writyn on
a table hangynge on the north syde of his tumbe. And the miracle ys this.
Ther was whilom in Seynt Laurens cherche in Rome in *Agro Verano* where
his body restyd a cler[k], a good man and a deuouth, the whiche yche nyth
lay in the cherche, whos offyce was heche nyth at mydnyth to rysyn and   560
ryngyn and to clepyn vpon the munkis to matynys. And whanne this clerk
ad longe and many yers contunyd in hys office withowte defaute, yt happyd
hym vpon a wedenys nygh a lytyl to ouyrslepyn his tyme. And whanne he
wook, as he lay lokynge forth and doutynge whethir his tyme was past or
for to comyn, sodeynly, or he was war, [ther] cam at the est gabyl wyn-   565
downe a passynge gret lygh and brythnesse and ther in a rygh comely man
arayid lych a dekne on the most ryal and glorious wyse, and with hym a sex
or seuene rygh fayre childryn alle clad in whiht. And forthwith he cam to
the clerkys beddys syde and with a lityl whiht yerde whiche he bar in his
hand he, towchynge hym softly, seyde: 'For as meche as thou hast longe de-   570
fautelees kept thyn office and now a lytyl hast ouerslept thy tyme, that thou
shuldyst not fallyn in blame I am comyn to yiue the warnynge.' To whom
this clerk, gretly abasshid, seyde ageyn on this wyse: 'A good glorious syre,
whoo be ye, the wyche vouchesaf thus benyngly and thus gracyously to me
and to yiue me warnynge for to avoydyn my blame?' 'I am', quoth he ageyn,   575
'the patroun of the place, Laurence, to whoom thou longe hast doon good
and plesaunte seruyce, wherfor thou shalt not lesyn thy mede.' 'O gracious syre', quoth the clerk thanne, 'what byn these fayre yunglynges the
whiche ye bryngyn here with yow?' 'These', quoth Laurence, 'ben soulys
whiche I haue this nyght delyueryd owt of purgatorye. For this singuler   580
priuilege God of his mercyful grace hath grauntyd me: that euery wednys
nyth I goo doun into purgatorye and as manye of hem whiche haddyn ony
synguler affecc[i]oun or deuocyoun to me in here lyf moun touche myche

---

551 predicacioun] predicacoun   553 translacioun] translacoun   559 clerk]
cler   565 ther] ther ther   583 affeccioun] affecoun

myn tonycle gon with me and I presente hem to the blysse of heuene. And
585 therfore ryhs vp anon and excite vp myn ser[ua]untis, and telle hem this
reualacyoun. And concele hem to be perseueraunt in myn seruyse, that in
tyme comynge I may seruyn hem on the same wyse.' 'Iwys sere', quoth
this clerk ageyn, 'I drede me sore that withoute sum specyal tokne they
shal yiuyn to myn tellynge but lytyl or non credence. But rathere they
590 wyl seyin that I haue feynyd this visioun of myn own heed too escusyn
with the neclygence of my late resyng.' 'Sey hem thanne', quoth Laurence
f. 159vb ageyn, 'that the | thretty day aftyr this thou thiself shalt deyin as I haue
youe the warnynge. And yf thou doo not, hem yeue no credence to thy
seyinge. Wherfore in this menetyme make the redy and the nexte wednys
595 nygh foluynge aftyr thi passage, for the meryt of the good seruyse that thou
hast don to me, I shal lede the with me lych as I do now these sowlys onto
the blysse of heuene.' Whiche wurdys seyid, he turnyd hym and with the
soulys and the lygh went owt ageyn at the wyndone where he cam in at.
And in here goyng owt the soulys syngyn thys antiphone of Seynt Lau-
600 rence: *In craticula te deum non negaui*, on the most melodyous wyse that
euere this clerk, as he reportyth, had herd the dayis of his lyf byfore. This
doon, anoon this man was vp and clepyd the munkys to matynys. And on
the nexte morwyn, with many a ter of byttyr compunccyoun, he told hem
lych as he was comaundyd the forseyd reuelac[iou]n. And the thrittyd day
605 aftyr deyid, lych as blyssyd Laurence had youyn hym warnynge and pre-
monicyoun, the wiche was of that he seyde an euident confirmacioun. In
remembraunce of wiche reuelac[i]oun men moun seyn in many a cherche
in Rome Seynt Laurance peyntyd on wallys and on tablys stondynge in
the myddys of a fyir lych a dekne, and smale chyldryn hangynge vpon his
610 lappis. This reuelacyoun telle I here for that entent that they, the whiche
in wurship of Seynt Ioon Baptist on the wednysday don ony othir special
deuocyon, for that entent that through medyacyoun his preyere they shul
not deyin withoute shryffte an[d] comunyca[ci]on shuldyn also han with al
remembraunce of Seynt Laurence, that by mene of hys helpe they mowe
615 the sonere be deleueryd owt of the peynys of purgatorye and to comyn to
endles saluacyoun. Amen.

585 seruauntis] seruauauntis   604 reuelacioun] reuelacouun   607 reuelacioun]
reuelacoun   613 and] an   comunycacion] comunycaon

[137. HIPPOLYTUS]

The lyf of Seynt Ipolit

Aftyr the tyme that Ipolytus, throgh helpe of a prest clepyd Iustinus, had buryid the body of Seynt Laurance, as yt ys towchid byforn in his lyf, he wente hoom into his hous and, pees youyn to al hys houshold and fredam, they alle wore comunyd with the sacrement of the autyr, the whiche 5 Iustinus the prest brough thedyr. Whiche don and the table set for to gon to mete, or than they eet ony mussel come soudyours and tokyn Ipolyt and leddyn hym to the emperoure. Whoom whan Decius the emperour sav smyllynge he seyde to hym on this wyse: 'Art thou, Ipolit, now bycomyn a wycche whiche, as yt ys seyid, hast stolyn Laurences body?' 'For sothe', 10 quoth Ipolit to hym ageyn, 'I sey not nay but that I tok blyssyd Laurences body and buryid yt not as wycche but as a trewe cristene man.' At wych answere Decius wex wood and comaundyd hym anon to be spoylyd of his cristene habyte and to be betyn on the mouth with stonys, seyinge to hym on | thys wyse: 'Now yet at the leste doo sacrifice that thou mow lyvyn f. 160ra and not perisshyn with Laurence.' 'Oure lord graunte', quoth Ipolit, 'that 16 I mowe be wurthy the exaumble of blyssyd Laurence whoom thou with thi defoulyd mouth were bold to nemene and rehersyn his name.'

Aftyr whiche wurd Decius comaundyd hym to be betyn with battys and his flesh to byn rent with iyryn combys. And whil they thus turmentyd 20 hym, he euere with a lowde woys knouelechyd hymself to byn a cristene man. And whan Decius sau that he scornyd hym and set at nouth al these tormentys, anoon he mad hym to be clad ageyn in knyhthly clethis the whiche he was wone to vsyn, exortynge hym to kepyn stylle his frenchepe and his chiualrye. But Ipolitus seyid that he pleynly wold kepyn Cristys 25 chiualrye. But Ipolitus seyid that he pleynly wold kepyn Cristys chiualrye and now othir. Wherfore Decius in hys woodnesse dyliueryd hym to Valerian the prefect and yaf hym alle his godys, for that entent that he shulde bryngen hym to a shamefull ende. And anoon, inquisicioun maad, al his houshold was foundyn cristene, wherfore alle they were presentyd 30 toforn Valerianus bench and chargyd for to sacrify[n]. And anoon an old matrone Concordia, the norys of Ipolit, took the answere for hem alle and s[e]yde: 'We han leuere clenly and chastly deyin with oure lord Ipolit than to leuyn vnclenly and vnchastly withowtyn hym.' 'The kynde of bonde men and bond women', quoth Valerian, 'wyl neuere byn amendyd 35 withoute torment.' And anoon he comaundyd hyre, Ipolit beynge present

31 sacrificyn] sacrificyd   33 seyde] syde

and gladly yt seyinge, to be betyn with whippys of leed tyl [s]he yaf vp hire
spirit into Cristis handys. Wyche doon, Ipolit yaf thankynge to God that his
norice was sent byforn to blysse of heuene in the presence of hym and of alle
40 his mene. Whiche don Valerianus maad Ipolit to be led with alle his houshold owt at the gate wich ys clepid *Porta Tiburtina*. And as they wentyn
thedyr-ward Ipolit counfortyd hem, seyinge on this wyse: 'For nothyng,
brethyrn, look ye ben aferd. For ye and I han oo God and oo Lord.' And
whanne they wern withoute the gate, Valerian comaundyd hem alle to ben
45 hefdyd in Ipolitys presence, and thanne the feet of hym to ben boundyn to
the nekkys of wylde hors and to be drawyn amonge brymblys and brerys,
craggys and stonys tyl he were ded. Whos body with the bodyis of alle hys
felashipe, Iustinus, a pryst, stal priuyly by nygh and buryid hem bysyde the
body of Seynt Laurence, saf the body of Ipolitys norys he cowde not fyndyn
50 for yt was cast into a gret gonge. The whiche was aftyrward foundyn on
this wyse. A soudyour whos name was Porphirus, wenynge that Concordia
had g[ol]d or gemmys or summe othere precyous stonys hid in hyre garnementys, wente to a gonge fermere whoos name was Hyrenus, the wiche
was preuyly a cristene man, and seyde to hym on this wyse: 'Kyp counsel
55 that I shal telle the and yit shal byn a gret auayle to thy crafth. Threttene
dayis past Valeryan comaundyd amonge Ipolitys mene a creditarye of his
to be slayn with wyppis of led and aftyr to be throuyn in a gonge. Drawe
f. 160ʳᵇ hyre | vp, for I trowe veryly that she hath gold and precyous stonys hyd
in hyre clothis.' 'Shewe me the place', quoth Hireneus, 'where the bod[y]
60 lyth and I shal kepe counsel and takyn yt vp and what I fynde thou shalt
han part.' And whan the body was takyn vp and nothinge foundyn in hyre
clothis, the soudyoure went his wey and let the body with Hyrenee. And
he clepith to hym anothir cristene man clepyd Habundius, and they two
brou the body to Iustin and he, glad and thanky[s] youyn to God, buryid yt
65 byside the body of Ipolit and his felaas, the seuynte kalende of septembre.
And whan Valerian herd seyin this, he mad Hyrene and Habundium to be
cast quyk into the same gonge. Whoos bodyis Iustinus stal and buryid hem
bysydyn al the othere of Ipolitus mene the numbre of nynetene. Aftyr this
oo tyme whan Decius, sittynge in a goldene char and Valerianus the prefect
70 with hym, wentyn to comoun place clepit Amphiteatrum for to tormentyn
there cristene men, sodeynly Decius vexyd began to crin and seyn: 'O Ipolite, whi ledyst thou me boundyn with shenys?' Valerianus also vexid with
anothir deuyle cryid also and seyde: 'O Laurence, whether ledyst thou me
also boundyn with brynnynge chenys?' And the same our Valerian wre-

37 she] he   52 gold] glod   59 body] bodyis   64 thankys] thankyd

chidly deyid. But Decius was led hom ageyn to his hous and thre dayis 75
contunely vexid with a deuyl he cryid and seyde: 'O Laurence, I adiure
the that thou sece sumwat of thi turmentys.' And thus he deyid and went
thedyr that God wolde.

And whanne hys wyf Triphonia herd this, alle thyngis lefth, with hyre
doutyr Cirilla went to Iustyn the holy prest and was baptizid and, had mad 80
hyre preyere, she deyid and wente to heuene. Whoos body Iustinus buryid
bysyde the body of blyssyd Ipolit. And whanne seuene and fourty knythtys
or soudyours of Decius herdyn seyn that the qwen and hyre doutyr where
cristenyd, they comyn with here wyuys to Iustin for the same entent. And
Deonisius, whiche was nex pope aftyr Sixtus, baptizid hem alle. Whom 85
alle for they wolde not sacrificy[n] Claudius, the nexte emperour aftyr
Decius, mad for to byn hefdyd. Whoos bodyis wern also buryid aboute
Seynt Laurence in *Agro Verano.*

A certeyn rual, Petrius by name, onys vpon Marie Maudelyns feste put
his oxyn in the plow and wente and eryd his lond. And for his bestys drow 90
not to his plesaunce he cursyd hem horibily. And sodeynly ther cam a lyhtnynge from heuene and brent vp plou and bestes and turmentyd hym with
an intollerable peyne. For the fyir of the leuene fastnyd on his leg so sore
that flessh and seneuys consumpt and wastyd, the bonys of his they apperyd bare and the leg fel euene auey from the body. And anoon he fledde 95
as he myght to a cherche and with terys and preyeris bysoute oure lady to
releuyn hym of his peyne. And sone aftyr vpon a nygh oure lady with Seynt
Ipolit cam onto hym whil he was aslepe a[nd] bad Ipolit that he shulde
restoryn Petir ageyn his leg. And anoon Ipolit wente and took Petris leg
out of the hole where he had hyd yt and sete yt ageyn to his they, as yt | 100
had byn a gryffe into a stook of a tre. In whiche greffynge or settynge in f. 160ᵛᵃ
ageyn Petyr sufferyd swych a peyne that with his cry he wook al the mene
of the houshold. And they anoon rysyn vp and tokyn lyth and comyn to
Petyr where he lay and foundyn hym han leggis to theyis and to feet. And,
wenynge they had be deleueryd, efthsonys oon aftyr anothir the[y] gro- 105
pyd hym and foundyn werely that yt was soth and no delusioun. And with
gret pullynge and callyng whan they had wakyd hym they askyd hym how
this cam aboutyn. But he awakyd, wenyng that they had iapyd hym, twyis
or tryis touchid hymself and feld that yt was so and he was therof gretly
amaruaylyd. Nertheles the newe whyrlebon in the hepe was more softe 110
than the olde and not sufficyently myghty to b[e]ryn vp and susteyne with
the body. Wherfore, that the miracle myht the more be pupplysshid and

86 sacrificyn] sacrificyd   90 his] his his   98 and] a   105 they] the
111 beryn] bryn

opynly shewyd, twelue monythis aftyr Petyr haltyd. Aftyr wiche tyme oure
lady with Ipolit apperid ageyn onto hym and bad Ipolit that he shulde sup-
115 plyin and performyn that was to lytyl byforn to Petris perfiht curyd. And
that oure lady comaundyd don, Petyr awook and, felynge his self perfyhly
hool, anoon alle the word forsookyn he becam a reclus, where he sufferyd
manye greuous temptaciounys of the deuyl. For offtyn tyme he apperyd
onto hym in the lyknesse of a nakyd wumman, and the more bysy he was
120 to resistyn the more importune she was to preycyn vpon hym and temptyn
hym. And whan he longe had be[n] temptyd on this wyse, at the laste he
took a prestys stole about his nekke. Wich don the deuyl fled awey and lefte
there a foul styngkynge careyn. Whereof greu so gret a stynk that no man
wiche sau yt trowyn othir but that yt was the careyn of sum deed woum-
125 man, the whiche the deuyl had takyn vp to illudyn with this holy man *&*
cetera.

[138. SIMPLICIANUS]

The lyf of Seynt Simplician Bysshop of Melan

The blyssyd confessour of Crist Symplicianus, fryst dwellynge at Rome
conuertynge to feyth the gret oratour and reth[o]rian Victorius, aftyrward
al the caduc werd despysyd he fled to desert clad in an abyte of blak,
5 hauynge the forme and the shap of a cros gyrt abouyn, with a thong of ledyr
withowtyn ony barre. The colour of the habyte brynggyn to his remembraunce that he was a synnere mad hym sory. The forme of the abyte, the
whiche was in the maner of a cros, remembryd hym the mene of foryifnesse
of his synne, that [his] Cristis passioun, and that mad hym mery. And the
10 gyrdyl of ledyr, wherwith his habite was streynyd onto hym, syngnifyid
that by mortificac[i]oun of his fleysh he was crucyfyid to the werd and the
werd to hym.

f. 160vb   Thus this blyssyd man Simplycian maad lyuyd longe | solitarye bysyde
the cyte of Melane and was in gret reputacyoun bothe of the bysshop, that
15 tyme Seynt Ambrose, and of alle the peple. And no woundyr for from
his yowthe he was an exemplarye of gret holynesse, of mansuetude and
of buxumnesse, as witnessith Seynt Austyn *octauo Confessiones* by a longe
processe. And therfore, whanne he was conuertyd by Seynt Ambrose, oure
lord sente a stirynge into his soule, as in the seyid place of his confes-
20 syou[n]s, to gon to Simplician, the whiche semyd to hym a good seruaunt
of God. And veryly yt was so, for the grace of God shoon in hym. To

---

121 ben] be   3 rethorian] rethrorian   9 his] his his   11 mortificacioun]
mortificacoun   19–20 confessyouns] confessyours

whom whan he cam and had told hym the gret circuyt of his longe errourys, Simplician anoon exhortyd hym to the mekenesse of Crist.

And amonge manye othere examplis he told hym how whilom he had conuertyd the gra[t]e rethorian Victorian at Rome. The whiche Victorian, for the gret excellence he had in kunnynge bothe in philosophie, rethoric and eloquencye and in alle the liberal science, deseruyd to han that the men of the werd holdyn for an excellent wurshipe, a statue or an ymage in the opyn markyt of Rome. 'And notwithstondynge alle these thyngis', quoth Simplician, 'the seyid Victorin was not ashamyd aftyrward to be Cristys child, and to puttyn his nekke vndyr the yook of Cristis mekenesse.' And than he told Austyn how that [t]he seyid Victorin, whan he had diligently enserchid Cristene letterys and the helful doctrine of holy cherche, seyid oftyn tyme to hym not opynly but preuyly on this wyse: 'Knowe now weel, Simplician, that I am a cristene man.' And how that he seyde ageyn to hym: 'I shal not leuy[n] yt but I see the in the cherche.' And how that Victorin smylynge wold thus concludy[n] ageyn: '*E*[*r*]*go*, the cherche wallys makyn a cristene man.'

'Nertheles', quoth Simplycian, 'whan Victorin had fully lernyd the trewe doctrine of the gospelle, dredynge to be deuydyd of God byforn his aungelys in heuene yf he were aferd to knowelechin Crist byforn men here in herthe, sodeynly he seyde to me "Symplician, go we into cherche, for sykyr I wyl becomyn a cristene man". Where whanne we comyn', quoth Symplician, 'and alle thyngis performyd that shulde be don, and the tyme cam that they whiche shuldyn reseyuyn the baptem shulde makyn here professioun, the wiche was set in a forme vndyr certeyn wurdys, there was brough hym a book for to han don yt priualy, in as meche as he was shamefast. But he wolde not so, but opynly byforn alle the p[e]ple he pronunced his feyth with an hy and cler voys. Al Rome maruaylyd and Cristys cherche singulerly ioyinge.' And whanne that Austyn had herd this processe and story of Victorin, anoon he ardently desiryd to folwyn yt, and for that entent Simplician told yt.

Gret grace and merit had this blyssyd fadyr Simplician anempst God in conuercyoun of these two most excellent oratours and doctours, Austyn and Victorin, who[o] from the most foule membrys of Sathanas | he turnyd into most fayr sonys of the Trinite. And not oonly he had this in Austyns conuers[ioun], but also aftyrward with the seyid Austyn in conuersacioun. For aftyr the tyme that he was baptizid of Seynt Ambrose he

---

25 grate] grace   32 the] he   36 leuyn] leuyt   37 concludyn] concludyd   *Ergo*] Ego   48 peple] pleple   52 for that] for   55 whoo] whos 57 conuersioun] conuersacioun

gaderyd herymytys and mad a collegie of hem, amonge whoom blyssyd
60 Simplician yaf an exampler reule and forme of good conuersacyoun, as he
tellith in his sermounys *Ad fratres suos in heremo*. The seyid nobil fadyr
Simplician, whanne Seynt Ambrose was passid forth to his fadris by the
comoun passage of bodyly deth, succedyd and was bysshop of Melan aftyr
hym. But not forthan, thogh he throgh the wyl of God and his grace where
65 thus exaltyd and set vp in pontyfical wurship and dignyte, he was neuere
the more lyftyd vp and enhaunsyd in his herte by pride, but, fully and per-
fihtly groundyd in the vertu of humylyte, gouernyd the peple committyd
to his cure, vert[u]ously in the simpylnesse of spirit vndyr the yerde of
the dreed of God, pasturid his sheep with the dilicat fode of doctrine to
70 techyn, goynge beforn hem and shewynge hem the rygh weye to heuene-
ward by the sad conuersacioun of his holy lyuynge. And so at the laste,
whan his dayis of his leuynge where ful complet and fulfyllyd, in a good
age he restyd in pees at the clepynge of oure lord Ihesu Crist. To whoom
[b]e honoure, laude and glorie now and endelessly, Amen.

[139. CLARE]

The lyf of Seynt Clare.
    Whilom in the cyte of Assise dwellyd a wurshipfull man whoos wyf, cle-
pyd Ertolana, brouth f[or]th onys in this gardyn of hyre wombe a braunche
of gret vertu and of singuler grace. This seyid Ortalana oo tyme whan she
5 neyhid faste, th[at] this braunche shuld florysshyn and procedyn forth,
she knelyd byforn the crucifix in the cherche and preyid Crist crucifiyd
enterly to preseruyn hyre in hyre chyldynge from hurt and fro perel. And
as she lay oftyn and manye sythis makynge the same preere, she herd a
voys from heuene seyinge to here on this wyse: 'Woman, dred not ner be
10 not aferd. For thou shalt brynge forth a cler lyth, the wyche shal clerly
illumyny[n] and makyn brygh the word.' For whiche cause, whanne hyre
chyld was born and brough to the baptem, she mad yt to clepyn Clara, fully
trostynge that the reuelacyoun, the wyse was sheuyd onto hyre, shulde in
tyme comynge be fulfullyd in hyre chyld.
15   This yunge chyld Clara, anoon as she bygan to growyn in yers, she
greu also in the disposicioun of good maneris and vertuous werkys. And
amonge alle othere vertuhs, the whiche she plenteuous habundyd in pyte
and compassioun of hem that wern in miserie or in nede, greu with hyre

68 vertuously] vertuuously   74 be] he   2 whoos wyf] whoos   3 forth]
froth   5 that] the   11 illumynyn] illumynyd

from hyre youthe, for hyre hond was euere opyn and redy. And that hyre
sacrifice mygh be the more plesaunt and acceptable to God, she wythdrow 20
delicacyis and deyntyf metys from hyre propyr and by priuy massageris
sent hem to refresse the nedy and the seke.

The | s[o]licitude and the studye of holy preyere was to hyre homly f. 161rb
and frendeful and quotydyanly famuliar. In wyche she was ofte tyme so
towchid with the swetnesse of Ihesu Crist and so drawyn vp to the deli- 25
cys of deuouhte contemplacyoun that she myghte verely seyin with Seynt
Poule: 'In heuene ys myn conuersacyoun.' Vndyr hyre softe and dilicat
clothis owtwart she vsyd a sharp hayre nexte hyre flesshe inward, and so,
lyche Seynt Cicile, florisshyng into the werd-ward by outeward apparince,
al flesshly and bodyly mariage fully in wyl and purpos forsakyn and abdicat, 30
to Goddys kepynge she comendyd hyre continence. But lych [a] potecaris
shoppe ful of delicious odoramentys, swete gummys and precyous, with
hyre dylectabyl [s]auour refresshyth and confortyd alle thoo that dwelly[n]
ny therby and also hem wyche passyn, rygh so this blyssyd virgine Clara,
refert and fulfyllyd with the swet odoure of manyfold vertuhs, trewe fame 35
berynge forth the flauour therof, was knowyn and diuulgy[d], hyre not
wotynge ner desirynge, amonge the peple and magnifiyd and preysyd of
hem as the merit of vertu askith. Swyche wern the tastys of hyre vertu
the fryste f[r]outys of the spirit and preludyis or for pleyis of holynesse of
[t]his blyssyd maydyn Clare at hoom in hyre fadrys hous in the tyme of 40
hyre tendyr youthe.

Aftyr this, whan the notable fame of blyssyd Francesse, the whiche as
a newe man was sent of God to renewyn ageyn the old foryetyn weye of
perfeccyoun of crucyfyid Crist, folwynge his steppys cam to the ere of this
nobyl virgine Clara, the fadir of spiritis inspirynge here with grace as sone 45
as she myghte han ony opertunyte of tyme and place to spekyn with hym,
she dysclosyd and opnyd onto hym hyre hool entent and al the preuy desire
of hyre herte. Whiche herd and knowyn, anoon Fraunceys as an heuenely
wower yaf hyre suasioun and consel to contempnyn and forsakyn the werd
and al flesshly matrimonye and oonly to be mariyd to the louere of purite 50
and clennesse, Crist Ihesu, and so in the scole of pure virginite to folue
the lamb of God wheresoeuere hee goo. To whoos holsum counsel Clare,
enflaumyd with the ardoure of heuenely fyir, taryid not longe to grauntyn assent, but fully and hertely she offeryd hyre therto and committyd
hyre and submittyd hyre to his reule and gouernaunce. And anoon Cris- 55
tys seruaunt Frauncesse counselyd hyre and chargid hyre that on the nexte

23 solicitude] salicitude   31 a] as   33 sauour] fauour   dwellyn] dwellynge
36 diuulgyd] diuulgyl   39 froutys] foutys   40 this] his

sunday aftyr, the whiche shulde be Palme Sunday, she shulde procedy[n]
forth opynly amonge othere folke to bern hyre palme as rially arayid as she
was wond to ben. And at euyn, al werdly pompe and vanite forsakyn and
60 lefte byhyndyn, she shulde gon owt of the castel with Crist and dysposyn hyre to bern upperite of the cros and to foluyn the steppys of Cristis
passioun.

And she, neythir slow ner rekeles to fulfellyn and to performyn this
helfull counselle, the tyme assignyd she forsook fadyr and modyr kyn and
65 wyn, hous and hom and wente to a place clepyd Sancta Maria de Porti-
uncula orde aungel, where Fraunceys with his brethiren, obseruynge the
whiche, and the excubyis of holy religioun, reseyuyd this prudent may-
f. 161ᵛᵃ dyn, | comyng with a lygh lampe in hyre handys; that ys to seyne with
exempler bryghnesse of gode werkys onto hyre spouse Crist Ihesu. And
70 fryst byforn the autyr of oure lady they clepyn of hyre heer and [clad] hyre
in the habyt of holy religioun. Thus the holy relygioun of pouere minores-
ses took the bygynnynge of Seynt Fraunces, that in the cherche of hyre the
whiche ys quen of alle maydenys and chef gemme of virginite, oure lady
Seynt Marie.

75 The r[u]mour of this dede anoon fley al aboute the cyte, wherfore his
cosyns and hyre ny kynnysmen comyn anoon rynnynge thedyr, and summe
with glosynge and summe with thretynge and violence byseyd hem to
puttyn the blyssyd maydenys purpos. But she, stedfastly rotyd in God,
neythir for byhestys nor for thretys wolde goon with hym, but ran to the
80 autyr and held hyre by the clothis therof and sweuyd hyre pollyd heed and
seyde pleynly that she wolde not turnyn ageyn to the vomyt. Wherfore
they wentyn away confuhs in hemself. Aftyr this, by the counsel and the
ordinaunce of Seynt Fraunces, she went to takyn hyre abydynge and dwellynge place in the cherche of Seynt Damian. In whiche, whill Fraunceys
85 onys lay in his preyere, he herd a voys fro the cros seyinge to hym on this
wyse: 'Fraunceys, repare myn hous! The whiche, as thou seest, ys ner al
dystroyid.'

This nobyl virgine had a younge tendyr sustyr clepid Anneys, whom
she louyd singulerly weel, for whoos conuercyoun from the werdys conuer-
90 sacioun she preyid God enterly. And she opteynyd and gat wat she desyrid.
For sextene day aftyr that Clare was conuertyd, God conuertyd hyre sustyr Anneys and maad hyre to renne awey from hyre fadyr and modyr and
to gon to hyre sustyr Clare, whom she reseyuyd with gret ioye and thankyd deuouhly of his grace. But whanne hyre cosins and hyre othir kenrede

---

57 procedyn] procedyd   70 clad] cladly   75 rumour] ruumour   90 gat
wat] gat

herde this, ful of care and heuynesse they wente to hyre and fryst with   95
glosyng wurdys and fayre byhestys they l[a]boured for to han hyre thens.
And whanne they seyn that yt wolde not byn that they desiryd, they violently leydyn handys vpon hyre and summe shouyd and summe pullyd
and summe drowyn hyre be hyre heer. Anneys lowde bygan to cryin and
preyid hyre sustyr to preyin God for hyre that the wykkyd wiolence of   100
these, hyre kynnysmen, mygh be compescyd and ouyrcomyn. And so yt
was, for whan they had brough hyre to a lytyl reuyr bysydyn the place,
vndyr hem alle mygh noon karyin hyre ouyr, notwithstondynge that myche
other folk ran for to helpyn hym. And whan they seyin that in no wyse they
mygh preuaylen, they turnyd the miracle into a iape, seyinge on this wyse: 105
'This maydyn hath al this nygh', quoth they, 'etyn leed and therfore she ys
waxyn thus heuy.' And thus, confuhs in hemself and frustrat of hyre entent, wentyn hyre wey and lyftyn hyre there, whoom hyre sustyr Clare fet
in ageyn with a glad cher. And Seynt Fraunceys cleppyd of hyre | heer and   f. 161vb
sacryd hy[r]e and sheuyd hyre the weye of perfecc[i]oun with hyre sustyr.   110

   And aftyr this the fame of Clare fer springynge and clerly shynyng,
manye wurthi mennys douhterys and nobyl maydenys forsokyn the word
and foluyd hyre steppys. And thus bygan the oly ordere of thoo closyd
ladyis the whiche men clepyn menuressys. The modyr also of Clare, Orto-
lana, aftyr the tyme she had visityd the holy lond on pilgrimage and cam   115
hom ageyn, she wente to here douhterys and holyly and deuouhtly lyuyd
with hem. And whanne blyssyd Clare had maad hyre preyere and professioun and byhygh obedyence to Se[y]nt Fraunces, the thride yer aftyr hyre
conuercyoun he constreynyd hyre, alle be that she was loth therto, to han
the cure and the gouernaunce of hyre sustris vndyr hy[re] and maad hyre   120
here abbesse. But as hyre wurshipe greu, so gru hyre vertu. For in hyre
habite she wex more abiect in obsequie and seruice of hyre sustris, more
prompt and redy in wurd, more m[o]dest, in abstinesse more schars and
preyere more feruent, in exaumple more war and in alle manere vertu more
perfihte.   125

   Moreouyr this louere of holy pouerte stodyid alway that, lych as in
the begynnynge of hyre conuercyoun she had distract al that she had and
youyn yt to pore men, aftyr the exaumple of Seynt Fraunces, rygh nouht
to reseruyn to hyreself, holdyn in hyre estimacyoun alle temperal thyng to
byn as dung o[r] fylthe. Wherfore whan Pope Gregory the [ninth] wold han   130
prouidyd suffyciently for hyre monasterie he myhte in no wyse inducyn

96 laboured] lauboured   97 And whanne] And   110 hyre] hyure
perfeccioun] perfeccoun   118 Seynt] Sent   120 hyre] hym   123 modest]
medest   130 or] of   ninth] thredde

blyssyd Clare to assentyn therto. Moreouyr, whanne she was set in the
laste ende of hyre lyf and fully was enflawmyd with the loue of mendicite,
she purchacyd of Pope Innocent the fourte a priuilege of pouerte to hyre
135 monasterye and of beggerye. And in so myche she was affect therto that
whan elmesse faylyd, purchacyd by beggerye, she was very glad to etyn of
the brokyn pecys of bred and sempte very sory to seen hool louys.

   And so yt happyd oo tyme whanne breed beggyd faylyd, by mene of
hyre preyere an half loff was multyplyid into fyfty sufficyently precyous.
140 In [l]ykwyse anothir tyme whan oyle lakkyth, a wessel wyche she wasshyn was foundyn euene ful. What shuld I seyn of hyre penaunce and the
mortyficacyoun of hyre flesshe, but that a kyrtyl and an vnthryfty mentyl
was euene curyng of hyre body owtward, the bare ground or to-cuttyng of
wynys at the moste was hyre matras, a blokkis ende hyre pilwe. Inward to
145 hyr body smale cordys steynyd a sharpe heyre and sumtyme [she hadde]
nex hyre bar skyn the skyn of a swyn, the hery syde clyppyd and turnyd
to the flesshe-ward. And su[m]tyme whanne she was syk, febele in body,
the flesshe syde was turnyd inward and leyid vndyr hyre a pilue of chaf.
f. 162ᵗᵃ As longe as she | was heyl she fastyd in breed and watyr tw[e]i lentons,
150 the toon byforn Estryn and the tothir byforn Cristemesse. In whiche tyme,
only on the sunday she drank a lytyl wyn. Thre dayis in the wouuke she
eet mete and the residue hyre abstinence passid for the mesure of mannys
estimacioun so that to hyre susteris she sempte more lyk to be woundryd
than to be foluyd. And al this notwit[h]stondynge she was alwey sound of
155 cher and weel colouryd.

   In Goddys seruice she euere p[re]uentyd the our and was the fryste
aluey that cam therto. She range the belle, she lygh the lampys and not
only hire bed, but eek the paument, she wattrid and mad moyste with hyre
terys. Vpon the nygh the aungyl of thirknesse apperyd onto hyre in the lyk-
160 nesse of a blak chi[l]d and seyde: 'Clare, wepe not so meche! For yf thou
doo, thou shalt be blynd.' To whoom she answerde ageyn and seyde: 'Ther
shall neuere body be blynd that seeth God.' At wyche answere the wykkyd
spirit vanysshd. And not only this blyssyd woman Clare had gret and singuler exercise in preyinge, but also therwith she had prompt and redy effect
165 in getynge of swych thynges that she preyid fore, as the processis shewyn
whiche foluyn hyre aftyr.

   Whan in Frederykys tyme the tiraunt an oost cam ageyns Assise, yt
happyd certeyn arblastis of the Sarasuns to brekyn into the cloystyr of the

140 lykwyse] kykwyse   145 she hadde] she hadde she had   146 bar skyn]
bar   147 sumtyme] suumtyme   149 twei] twel   152 and] and and
154 notwithstondynge] notwitstondynge   156 preuentyd] puentyd   160 child]
chid

ladyis. And whanne blyssyd Clare herd this, albeyt that she was rygh seek in body, yet with a constaunt herte she comaundyd that she shuld be set euene byforn the dore and the pyx with the sacrement of Cristys body bysydyn hyre. Wych don she, with a lamentable voys and cher, preyid to God and seyde: 'Lord God, I beseche the w[i]th al myn herte, kepe these thy seruauntys and thi handmaydyns, the whiche I may not kepyn, lord, withoute thy special helpe.' To whom ageyn, as yt had byn the voys of a younge infaunt, answerde and seyde: 'I wylle and shal kepyn hem alwey.' 'Ya, also lord', quoth she, 'kepe and defende this cyte, the whiche for thi sake and for thi loue susteynyth vs and fedyth weel.' 'Clare', quoth the woys ageyn, 'for thy sake, thogh this cyte suffere dyuers vexacyouns and trublys, yet yt shal be delyueryd.' At whyche wurd the vnfeythful peplys woodnesse was represshid and confoundyd. For lych as they comyn in by the wallys arrogaunt and presumptuous, so, non hurt don, they wentyn owt ageyn be the same ferful and timourous. And as sone as th[y]s doon, she chargyd alle hyre susteris that, whil she lyuyd, they shulde telle no man of the voys whiche they had here. And so by mene of hyre preyeris this cyte and the cloystyr were deleueryd from hyre enmyis.

Anothir tyme whanne oon clepid Vitalis, a proud man and a capteyn of Frederykkys ost, inpungnyd Assi[s]e and dystroyid and wastyd al the cuntre theraboute, blyssyd Clare threw dust on hyre heed and on hyre susteris and preyid deuouhtly to God for remedye. And anoon God herd hyre preyere withowtyn ony delay, | for on the nexte day the cruel tiraunt took his host and wente awey thens and, not longe aftyr, was hefdyd for hys cruelte. And not only the cruelte thus of men, but also of deuyls, this blyssid maydyn C[l]are ouyrcam by the effectual werkynge of hyre preyere, as yt semyth by that foluyth.

For a womann of the diosie cam oo tyme to hyre monasterye, yiuy[n]g God thanky[s] that he, by the merytys of Clare, had delyueryd hyre from fyue deuyls, the whiche knowlechyd opynly that the preyeris of Clare brentyn hem and dryuyn hem owt of here herberwe and here dwellynge place. Thes gracyous lady Clare, as a syngulyr wurshipe of the cros, many folk she deleueryd from many perelys be the tokene of the cros. For a frere clepid Steuene, vexyd with a furye or a woodnesse, whom Seynt Fraunces seynt onto here, she markyd with a tokene of a cros and leyid hym to slepyn in the place where she was wone to preyin. And whan he wook he was al heyl and hool. A child also of Spelece clepid Machiolus, the which of wauntonnesse and chyldhood had sheuyn a ston by hys nosethryl into hys heed,

173 with] wth   183 thys] theys   188 Assise] Assie   194 Clare] Chare
196 yiuyng] yiuyg   197 thankys] thankyth

she, with the syngne of a cros maad on his nose, deliueryd hym anoon and
mad hym hool. A child also of Peruse, the which had a spot in his yhe,
blyssyd of Clare was dylyueryd therof and maad hool. Foure susteris also,
210 whereof on clepyd Beneuenita from a fystula, anothir clepyd Amata from
the feuerys, the cowhe, a stych vndyr the syde and the dropisie. And the
thridde sustyr of Peruse, whiche two yer had be specheles, and the fourte
sustyr clepyd Christian, longe deef, with a tokene of the cros she curyd and
maad heyl. This blyssyd wo[u]man also, onys as she cam into the susteris
215 infirmarye, wyth fyue tokenys of the cros curyd and maad hool fyue seeke
langurynge susteris. These and manye woundyrfull thyngis wrough this
blyssyd lady Clare, bothe in hyre lyf and aftyr hyre deth, the whiche, yf
alle were wrytyn, woldyn ocupyin a gret book alone, and therfore I passe
hem ouyr at this tyme.

220   Whanne this blyssyd and holy ladyis resolucyoun and the terme of hyre
mortall passage cam ner, Pope Innocent the thridde, with alle his hool
court cam to Assise. And anoon aftyr hys comynge he wente to vicytyn
Clare and comunyd hyre and assoylyd hyre. All hyre susteris were sory
that she shulde departyn from hem. Amonge whiche alle, hyre owyn sus-
225 tyr Anneys with wepynge terys bysowt hyre entirly that she shuld not
goon awey and leuyn hyre byhynde. To whoom she answerde ageyn and
seyde: 'Sustyr, yt plesith God that I shall passyn now. Wherfore leue thy
wepynge. For with fewe dayis aftyr thou shalt also comyn to God. But yet,
er than thou come, thou shalt reseyuyn a gret and synguler counfort.' And
230 whanne this blyssyd lady Clare had leyin seuenetene dayis and no mete
receyuyd, and through vertu performyd in hyre syknesse she had counfortyd alle hyre susterys in oure lord, anon cam Crist with a gret ost of
aung[e]ls, oure lady syk with a bryghnesse that with a fayr cumpanye of
f. 162ᵛᵃ virginis, of whoos coroun cam | owt swych a bryghnesse that within Cla-
235 rys hous yt chacyd awey al the nyghtys thyrknesse. And anoon oure lady
wente to Clarys beed and louyngly bowyd doun and ha[l]syd hyre sonys
seruaunt. Wiche don, forthwith the tothire virgins broutyn forth a mantel of maruelously swet odour and wrappyd therin Claris body, wyth wich
odour she, visibylly counfortyd, yeld vp hyre spirit into Cristys handys.
240 And not manye dayis aftyr Anneys, hyre sustyr, lych as she had promysyd,
was callyd a[w]ey from this vale of miserye and wrechydnesse onto the
hye hyl of heuene, therwhithe hyre sustyr to lyuyn euere in perpetuall
ioye and gladnesse, whethir alle Seynt Clarys seruauntis oure lord God

214 wouman] wouuman   230 dayis and] and   233 aungels] aungls
236 halsyd] haslyd   241 awey] alle wey

finally mote brynge for hys gracious mercyfulnesse. Amen, mercy Ihesu
and gr[a]mercy.   245

[140. TIBURTIUS PREFECT OF ROME]

The lyf of Tiburce the prefectis sone of Rome.

Tiburcyus, the sone of Cromacius the prefect of Rome, whoom blyssyd
Sebastian and Tra[n]quillyn instruct in the feyth and Sanctus Policarpus
the prest baptysyd and his mene a thousend and foure hundryd, whan his
fadyr at the counsel of Gaius the pope for gret fere of persecucyoun fledde 5
with gret multitude of peple into Chaumpanye, as yt seyth byforn in Seynt
Sebastians lyf, enflaumyd with the loue and the desier of martyrdam abood
stylle in Rome and ocupyid hym with the pope Gaius in fastyngis and
preyeris and othere good dedys. In which menetyme yt happyd hym to
come forby a man the whiche was fallyn fro an hy lyfte and so brosyd and 10
brokyn bothe heed and alle hys othere membrs that, as alle folke thougtyn,
ther was non othir remedye but faste to prouydyn for his sepulture. Whom
whan Tiburcius saw he wente onto hym and bygan deuouhtly to seyin ouyr
hys wundys hys Paternoster and hys Crede. And anoon forthwith this man
was as hool and as heyl as he neuere had had fal ner hurt. Whiche don, 15
anoon he callyd aseyde fro the multytude of peple hys fadyr and modyr
and his othyr frendys, and bygan to tellyn hem the vertu of Cristis name.
And whanne he saw here hertys affeccyoun fixid in the dred of God, he
led hem to the pope Gaium and he baptizid bothyn hem and here sone,
yiuynge laude and preysynge to God for his helthe.   20

And whill this gret tempest of persecucioun gru dayly and encresid,
oon cam to pope Gaius and offeryd hym to hym wyth simulat feyth, pretendyng to byn a cristene man but in treuthe he was apostata fraudelent and deseyuable in word and sly and wyly in hys werk. And for as
meche as Tiburcius oftyn vndyrnam hym for his tonsure, the whiche he 25
wolde han forgyd on hys forheed by barbouris crafth, for he drank ofte,
for he absteynyd hym from fastyngis and preyers and yaf hym to sleep
and sluggynesse whil othyr kept the nygh [watch]e in ympnys and prey-
syngis of God. These and swyche othir vndyrnymyngis of | Tiburs he f. 162ᵛᵇ
feynyd hym to sufferen pacyently and vndyr that he labouryd crafftely that 30
paynyms shuldyn takyn preyinge bothe Tiburs and hym togedyr, and so
to be led to the iugis secretarye. Whedyr whan they wern brough, the iuge

---

245 gramercy] gromercy   3 Tranquillyn] Traquillyn   5 fere of] of
12–13 Whom whan] Whom   28 watche] whiche

Fabyan seyde thus to hym, wych by sotilte and crafth had bytrayid himself: 'Felawe, what ys thy name?' 'Syre', quoth he ageyn, 'Torquatus.' 'What

35 ys thi sect and thy professioun?' quoth Fabianus ageyn to hym. 'Forsothe', quoth he, 'Sire, I professe cristene feyth and am a cristene man.' 'Knowyst not thou weel', quoth Fabianus, 'that oure inuincible princys han comaun- dyd that whooso wylle not doon sacrifice to oure immortal goddys shulde be distroyid with diuers tormentys?' Quoth Torquatus ageyn to Fabyan:

40 'Syre, this ys my maystyr', sheuynge Tiburs, 'and he hath alwey tawt me. Wherfore ryghtful yt ys and sky[l]ful that whatsoeuere I see hym doo, I doo the same.'

Aftyr wyche wurd Fabian couertyd hym to Tiburs, seyinge this wyse: 'Hast thou not herd what Torquatus seyith hyre?' 'Yis, syre iuge, yis. But

45 longe yt ys gon syth Torquatus hath ly[e]d hymself to byn a cristene man. But the vertu of this holy name beryth yt full heuyly and ful greuously the name to byn vsurpyd of maneris and condicyouns contrarye to the name. For sykyrly this cristene name ys oonly of and syngulerly propyr of the foluerys of Cristys vertu, and of thoo veryly philosophyrs the whiche

50 myghty and constauntly fyhtyn ageyns synne and labouryn to depres- syn and to brosyn the lustys of the flesshe. Ner trowe neuere hym, rygh wurshipful syre, to byn a cristene man, the whiche in leccherous blaunkys- synge and of hymself louyth to han hys heer craftyly leyd on hys forheed and the barboure oftyn to kembyn his heed the whiche also sothly beryth

55 his shulderis, the whiche gladly talkyth wyth men and more gladly byhyl- dyth woummen. Swych corupt and pestelent men God neuere wouchesaf to han to his se[r]uauntys. Nertheles [this] Torquatus seyith that as he seeyth me don, so wyl he doon. Here in thy sygh this day thou shalt prouyn hym to ben a lyere. For swyche as he hath alway ben, now he shal apperyn.'

60 To whom Fabian seyde ageyn on this wyse: 'Thou shalt don more wyhsly for thyn helthe yf thou wylt be reulyd by my counsel. The whiche ys that thou despice not the princys decres and comaundementys, and doo reue- rence and wourshipe to oure goddys.' 'Treuly', quoth Tiburcius ageyn, 'I can no bettyr counsell yeuyn to myn helthe than for to despice goddys and

65 goddessis and to knowleche deuouhtly oo God and oo lord Ihesu Crist, very God and very Goddys sone in heuene.' At this [wurd] Torquatus tur- nyd hym to Fabian the iuge and seyde to hym on this wyse: 'Lo syre, this Tiburce ys not only a cruel cristene man in hymself, but also he dysey- uyth manye men and techyth alle oure goddys to be deuyls. For he with

70 his felaas day and nygh ys exercysid in wychecraftys |

[141. ASSUMPTION OF OUR LADY]

. . . neuere dedly mannys tunge atteyne to tellyn yt. Thre maydens there   f. 164ra
were there whiche whan they had pa[r]t of oure ladyis robe for to wasshyn
hyre body, the bryghnesse therof was so gret that yt myghte be towchyd but
not seyn. And so longe this lygh enduryd tyl the maydyns had wasshe the
body and maad yt redy to the bere. Whiche don the apostelys whithe gret   5
reuerence leyd yt thervpon and Ioon forthwith seyde to Petyr: 'O fadyr
Petyr, thou shalt bern this palme byforn the bere. For God hath preferryd
the byforn vs alle and ordeynyd the to byn princie and federe of his shep.'
'Nay brothir', quoth Petyr ageyn, 'thow owyst rathere to b[er]n yt than I,
for thou art a maydyn [chosyn] of God. And therfore yt ys wurthi thou   10
bere the maydyns palme. Thou also by a singulyr priuylege of virginete
lenyst at the laste soper on oure lordys brest and where there inebriat with
the flood of cunnynge and of helful wysdam. And ryghtful yt semyth that
thou wyche hast reseyuyd of the sone most of yifte do to the modyr most
wurshipe. Thou therfore shalt b[er]n the palme and I wyl bern the body,   15
and oure othir brethiryn shal gon aboutyn and yiuen laude and thankynge
to God.' 'For sothe, brothir Petyr', quoth Poule thanne, 'and I wyche am
leest of alle the postelys wyl b[er]n the body with the.' And whanne they
two leftyd vp the bere Petyr bygan to seyin: *In exitu Israel de Egipto, Alleluya.* And the remnaunt of the apostelis seyde forth the tothir deel. And   20
anoon oure lord so curyd with a skye the bere and the apostelys that, though
here voys were herd, yet were they not seen. Aung[e]ls also were there present and sungyn with the apostelys and fulfyld al that lond with the sownd
of hyre melydyous swetnesse.

And whanne this gret swet me[lo]dye was herd aboute in the cyte, yche   25
man swyftly went owt of his hous for to enqueryn what this mygh menyn.
And anoon on seyde that the dysciplys of Ihesu born Marie, hys modyr,
deed to the buryinge. At whiche word alle men runne to armen hem and
yche man exortynge othir and seyde: 'Go we faste, go we, and lete vs
alle his dysciplis and aftyr brennyn the bodye of hyre, the wyche bar that   30
deceyuere.' And whanne the prince of the prestys cam forth and saw al this
gret sole[m]nyte, he was bothe astoynyd and wroth, and in hys gret angyr
he seyde: 'See here the tabernacle of hym whiche hath troblyd alle oure
kynrede, how myche wurchipe and glorie yt hath now!' And this seyid, he

---

1 *Begins defective owing to lost leaf.*   2 part] pat   ladyis robe] ladyis   9 bern]
bren   10 chosyn] closyd (*LgA electus*)   15 bern] bren   18 bern]
bren   22 Aungels] Aungls   25 melodye] medolye   26 his hous] his
32 solemnyte] solennyte

35 ran and put his handys onto the bere for to han throwyn yt doun. And
sodeynly bothe his handys wexyd seer and heng fast vpon the bere and
myghte noth therfro. And therwith he suffryd an intollerable peyne in his
harmys, which mad hym to cryin and to roryn horribly. The remnaunt of
the peple that cam with hym by the aungels in the cloudys where smet with
40 a blyndnesse, that they mygh not seen.

f. 164rb   The prince thanne, | vexyd with thys intollerable peyne, seyde on this
wyse: 'Holy Petyr, dyspise me not in this tribulac[i]oun but preye for me
to oure lord, Y entierly byseche the. Haue mynde how I onys stood by the
whanne the handmayde acusid the and excusid the.' 'We be now bysy in the
45 exequiys of oure lady, wherfore we mow not yet ententyn to thy cure. Nertheles, yf thou woldyst byleuyn into oure lorde Ihesu Crist and into this his
modyr wyche bar hym, I trowe verily thou shuldyst han ful helthe anon.'
'I beleue', quod he ageyn, 'Ihesu Crist to byn very Goddys sone and this
hyre to byn hys most holy modyr.' Whiche wurdys seyd, anoon his handys
50 were loos from the bere and bothe the seernesse and the sornesse of hys
armys was sodeynly reformyd and relessid. And whanne Petyr saw this, he
bad hym comyn and kyssyn the bere and seyin thus: 'I beleue into oure
lord Ihesu Crist, whoom this wo[mm]an bar in hyre wombe and aftyr his
berthe abood a mayde.' Whiche don, he [w]as hool as euere he was and
55 yaf thankynge to God. To whoom Petyr seyde efthsonys ageyn: 'Take this
palme of Ioon myn brothris hand and touche with al the see[k] peple, and
whoo that wyl byleuyn shal seen ageyn. And whoso wylle not byleuyn shal
be blynd stylle euere aftyr.

This don the[y] bar forth oure ladyis body and puttyn yt in the newe
60 graue and abydyn there stylle hyre maystris ageyn-comynge. And on the
thridde day foluynge Ihesu Crist cam with gret multitude of aung[e]ls and
salutyd hem thus, seying: 'Pees be to yow myn brethrin.' 'Wurshipe and
ioye', quoth they ageyn, 'to God whiche werkyst grete maruaylys alone.'
'What honoure and wurshipe', quoth he to hem 'semyth you now that I
65 awte to doon onto myn modyr?' 'Yt semyth to vs, lord, thy seruauntys',
quoth they, 'that lych as thou hast ouyrcomyn deth and regnyst eternally
sittynge onto the rygh hand of thy fadyr, so thou owyst to reysyn ageyn the
body of the modyr and glorifyin hyre on thy rygh hand endlesly.'

Whiche seyid, Michael th`e´ archaungyl anon cam forth and brough
70 oure ladyis soule with hym and presentyd onto oure lord Ihesu hyre sone.
And he anon seyde on this wyse: 'Ryhs vp my loue, my neyboure, my dowe,
the wessel of lyf, the temple, the reclinatorie of al the trynite, ryhs vp! For

42 tribulacioun] tribulacoun   53 womman] wouuman   54 was] as
56 seek] seel   59 they] the   61 aungels] aungls

lych as thou neuere in body ner soule feltyst ony spot of synne, so I wylle
that thy body fele no resolucyoun ageyn into erthe, ner no lengere be taryid
from glorific[ac]ioun in blysse.' And forthwith the soule entryd into the   75
body and ros gloriously from the graue, and was led vp with Crist and alle
the heuenely cumpanye into the blysse of heuene.

Al this ys in the book of no sykyr auctoryte, whereof Seynt Ierom
makyth mencyoun in hys sermoun of the assumpcioun of oure lady *ad
Paulam* and *Eustochyum*. Nertheles serteyn thyngis byn in the seyid book   80
wyche byn wurthy credence and arn approuyd of holy fadrys and be nyne
in | numbre, as that to oure lady was byhyght and yowyn alle manyr coun-   f. 164 va
forth, the gaderyng togeder of alle the apostelys, hyre passage withoute
sorwe, the makynge redy of hyre sepulture in the vale of Iosaphath, the
deuocyoun of hyre exequiys, the metyng with hyre of Crist and of the   85
court of heuene, the persecusioun of the Iewys, the shewynge of miraclis
on hem that towchid hyre, in takynge vp in the body and soule, and that
hyre clothis abydyn in hyre graue to the counforth of feythful peple, as yt
was sheuyd by miracle of oon of hyre clothis in Normandye, and was this:
Whanne onys the duek of Normandye had bysegyd the cyte of Carnotence,   90
the bysshop of the same cyte took a cote of oure lady wiche was kept in the
same cherche and heng yt vpon a shafte instede of a banyr, and with that
b[or]n byforn hem and his peple wentyn boldly and sekyrly ageyn here
en[im]ys. At whoos comynge alle contrarye of stod stylle astoynyd, smet
with a sodeyn blyndnesse and tremelynge for feer. And whanne they of   95
the cyte perceyuyd that they addyd to doun of God here cruelnesse and
fellyn vpon hem and sloun and hurt manye of hem. The whiche veniaunce
semyd gretly to haue dysplesid oure lady, in as meche as the cote of hyre
sodeynly vanysshid awey and the contrarye peple was also restorid ageyn
to seyth.   100

Here yt ys also to be notyd that oure blyssid lady Seynt Marie roos
vp hool or integrally, myrely, wurshipfully and excellently. That she was
assumpt and takyn vp integrally not only ys reuerently byleuyd of holy
cherche, but also summe doctouris of the cherche labouryn with euident
resouns to prouyn yt. Seynt Barnard makyth this resoun: Syth yt ys so that   105
God hath mad so wurshipfull the precious bodyis of Petyr and Poule, and
so uirifiyd hem that they han singuler placis deputyd to the wurshipe of
hem, and that alle peplis in this plac[e] shulde wurshepe hem. Yf yt be so
thanne that Maryis body be in herthe and in no special place seyith ner
singulerly wurshipe, it semyth that God hath bettyr haue louyd Petyr and   110

75 glorificacioun] glorificioun   90 cyte of] cyte   93 born] bron
94 enimys] enmys   101 to be] to   108 place] placis   110 it semyth]
semyth

Poule thanne his modyr, in as meche as he sufferid rathere here bodyis to byn wurshipd than hyrs.

Seynt Ierom also seyith that the eyghtende kalende of septembre oure lady stey vp to heuene. And though that of the bodyly assumpcioun he
115 seyde in the bygynnyng that yt ys more sure holy cherche pitously to dow-tyn thanne temeraryly to diffynin, yet aftyrward, in the same sermoun, he semyth to determynyn the treuthe of hyre bodyly assumpcioun, seyinge on this wyse: 'And yf yt be so', quoth he, 'that summe seyin the resurreccioun to byn ful complet in body and soule of hem whiche rysyn vp with Crist
120 in his resurreccioun, and also that summe leuyn the kepere of the mayden Ioon to ioyen with Crist in his glor'i' fiyd flessh, why not rathere shulde this be leuyd of the modyr, as whoo seyith myche rathere?' And prouyd his
f. 164vb resoun he concludyd thus: 'He that seyith', quoth he, '"Wourshipe | thy fadyr and thy mothir in [on] place" and in the gospel seyde "I cam not to
125 breke the laue but to fulfyllyn yt", sykyrly he wurshipid his modyr abouyn alle othir.' Hic Ieromus.

Seynt Austyn also not only aff[e]rmyth this sentence but conformyth yt eek by thre resonis. Wherof the fryste ys groundyd vpon the vnyte and the oonheed of Cristys flesshe and his modyrs, of wyche he seyith thus:
130 'Rootenesse and gendrynge of wyrmys hys the opprobrie and the dyspiht of mannys nature, causith of syne from wicche opprobrie Crist was fre and except. Syth thanne hys flesshe and his modrys w[er]n oon, for of hyre he took his fleyssh, wherefore she reioysyth conuenyently the same priuyleg and liberte.' The secunde resounys ys takyn of the dygnyte and
135 wurthinesse of hyre body. 'Yt ys congruent and conuenyent', quoth he, 'the throne of God, the cha[um]byr of God, in tabernacle of Crist to be kept in heuene thanne in erthe. Thes was the body of Cristis modyr, wher-fore ther he ys muste nedys byn hys tabernacle.' The thridde resoun ys groundyd on the most perfyth integrite of the maydyns fleyssh. And for
140 this resoun he seyith thus: 'Be glad, lady, with a ioye inumerable, bothyn in body and soule in thi soule and by thi sone. For noon corupcioun of body may folue there where aftyr thi sonys byrthe foluyd noo corupcyoun of virginite.' And aftyr he concludyd in seyi[ng]: 'Mote euere that lady be incorupte in body, whom so grace profundyd bothe in soule and body.
145 Mote she euere be lyuynge, whiche gendryd in hyre body and brough forth the perfyth lyf of euery thyng. Mote she euere be with hym whom she bar in hyre wombe, fodmyd and norisshyd owt of hyre wombe. I mene Marie,

124 on] no   127 affermyth] afformyth   132 wern] wren   136 chaumbyr]
chauunber   143 seying] seyith

Goddys modyr, Goddys ministyr and Goddys seruitour. Of whom, for I dar non othir, felyn othir to seyin I ne wele presumyn.' *Hec Augustinus.*

And her to acordyn wyl these nobyl versiours vers: [*Scandit*] *ad ethera* 150 *virgo puerpera, virgula Iesse. Non sine corpore, sed sine tempore tendit adesse.* The secunde wyse this blyssid lady, as ys seyid byforn, was assumpt and takyn vp gladly and meryly. This testat [Seynt] Gerardus in his omyl[ys] seyinge thus: 'Thes day heuynes takyn vp mayde Marye gladyd aungelis ioyinge, archaung[e]ls iubilyng, troun lawinge, dominaciones seyinge, 155 principatus armonizinge, prelates harpynge, cherubyn and saraphyn ympnizing or ympnis singynge, and leddyn hyre vp with swych solemnyte to the tribunal bench of Goddys mageste.' *Hec ille.*

The thridde wyse oure lady was this day takyn vp wurshipfully, for Ihesu hymself and alle the feleshepe of the heuenely [host], as yt ys 160 seyid byforn, cam owt of heuene to metyn with hyre. And Seynt Ierom, approuynge the same, seyith on this wyse: 'Whoo may', quoth he, 'suffisyn to thynkyn how glorious the quen of this word p[a]ssid forth today and with how affect of | deuosion alle the multitude of the heuynly legions f. 165ra cam to metyn with hyre, and with how many songis she was brouth byforn 165 the throne of God, and whithe how plesaunt a cher with a brygh, and wythe how godly halsynges and kyssyngis she was reseywid of hyre sone and enhaunsyd abouyn euery creature.'

And, in anothir place, thus seyith the same Ierom: 'This day yt ys to be l[e]uyd the sheualry of heuene to han goon owt to metyn with the modyr of 170 God of heuene, and to han en[u]yrond hyre with a gret lygh and to han led hyre to the trone of God with songis of gret ioye and gladnesse. Yt ys to by leuyd also the chiualrie of heuenely Ierusalem to han gon owt this day to metyn with hyre and to han ioiyd with ioye wich may non byn spokyn. For this feste wiche ys to vs annuel ys to hym dayly continuel. Yt ys to by leuyd 175 also', quoth he, 'that our saluatour Crist Ihesu cam owt solempnely ageyns hyre and, with gret ioye and gladnesse, receyuyd hyre and set hyre by in a trone of euerelestynge blysse. Or ellys she shulde not han fulfyld that he comau[n]dyd: "Wurship[e] thi fadyr and thy modyr".' *Hec Ieromus.*

The fourte wyse whiche she was assumpt and takyn vp excellently 180 whanne she, as seyiht the same Ierom, beynge a pure and vndefoulyd mayde atteynyd to the heythe of the heuenely throne and was gloriously crounyd and set as quen of heuene on Cristys rygh syde. *Hec Ieromus.* Gerardus also in his omelyis explityth this same processis by mannye

---

150 *Scandit*] Transith   153 Seynt] feyth   omylys] omylyous   155 archaungels]
archaungls   160 host] of   163 passid] possid   170 leuyd] louyd
171 enuyrond] enmyrond   179 comaundyd] comauundyd   Wurshipe] Wurships
180 fourte wyse] fourte

185 diuers and coriously endytyd circumstauncys, the whiche for yt ys diffuhs
and prolix I passe ouyr at this tyme.

Thus thanne on the foure wysis this blyssid lady, this glorious quen,
thes modyr of mercy, assumpt and enhaunsid syt on the trone of blysse as
a trewe and a feythful aduocat and mediatrice for mankynde, hyre beynge
190 in the vale of miserie and of wrecchidnesse. Wherefore no synnere owyth to
despeyrin or dowtyn of foryiffnesse, yf he clepe to hyre with contriht herte
and with louly mekenesse. Of this blyssid aduocat thus seyith Seynt Bernard in a sermoun: 'Wylt thou man han an aduocat to Crist? Renne to oure
lady, for the sone shal heryn the modyr. Moreouyr', quoth he, 'whatso-
195 euere yt be that thou wylt offryn to Crist, haue mynde to comendyn yt
to Marie yf thou wylt not be refusyd, for she ys the leddere of synneris
and here most singuler trost. And pleynly', quoth he, 'she faylith neythir
mygh ner wyl. For she ys quen of heuene bothe mercyful and also modyr
of mercy.' *Hec Bernardus.*

200 O[f] whos mercyful grace shewyd to man in sundry wyse, myn auctour
Ianuensis reherseth certeyn miraclis, of wyche compendyously summe I
shall towchyn and summe leuyn and remittyn to Ianuesse in the same fest.
Ther was whilom a clerk, deuouth onto oure lady, the whiche was wone
ageyns the sorue she had of Cristis woundys fyue to seyin onto here yche
205 day these fyue gaudes: *Gaude, dei genitrix, virgo immaculata. Gaude, que*
f. 165rb *gaudium | ab angelo suscepisti. Gaude, que genuisti eterni luminis claritatem.*
Gaude, mater, gaude, sancta dei genitrix virgo. Tu sola innupta, te laudat om-
nis factura. Domini pro nobis interpella. Amen. And whanne this clerk take
with passynge gret syknesse was euene brough to the laste ende of hys lyf
210 and bygan gretly to byn abasshid, oure lady apperid onto hym and seyde:
'Whi, sone, tremelyst thou [for] feer whiche so oftyn hast counseld me to
ioyin? Now also ioye thou! And that thou mowe ioyin endlesly come with
me!' And with that he yald vp the spirit and went forth with oure lady.
Ther was also a serteyn munke, sliper in flessh but deuouth to oure lady.
215 This munke, v[po]n a nygh as wente to performyn hys fleysshly wrecchidnesse as he was to do, as he wente forby an autyr of oure lady he salutyd
hyre lowly. Wens as he shulde han gon ouyr a watyr to the place of his
hauntynge foly, rekelesly he fel into the watyr and was drynklyd.

Whoos soule whanne the deuyls had rauysshid and aungels comyn for
220 to han deliueryd yt, the deuyls seydyn: 'Wherfore arn ye comyn hydyr?
Weel ye wetyn that in the soule ye haue no part.' Wiche seyid, forthwith
cam oure lady and blamyd hem that they presumyd to takyn hyre seruauntis soule. 'Sykyr', quoth they ageyn, 'for wee foundyn hym endyn his lyf in

185 yt ys] yt   200 Of] O   211 for] so   215 vpon] vn

oure werkys.' 'Yt ys not truthe', quoth she, 'that ye seyin. For I wote wyl
that whedyr so euere he wente he salutyd me or than he wente. Nertheles, 225
yf ye seyin that I doo you wrong or violence, late vs putten yt in the dom of
oure souereyn iuge.' And whanne they had pletyd this mater byforn hym,
yt plesyd hym to yeue a decre that the soule shulde turnyn ageyn into the
body and do penaunce yf he wolde. In this m[e]netyme his br[e]thirin, seyinge the tyme of matyns rynggynge past, for he was sexteyn they went and 230
seycyn hym and foundyn they had drawyn vp and stodyn maruelynge of
the caas. Sodeynly he returnyd to lyf and opynly knowlechyd his defaute
and lefth hys syn[ne] and lyuyd longe aftyr and amendyd his lyff.

Ther was a knyth in a cuntre, a wurthi man and a ryche, the whiche
with an vndiscret liberalite that he vsith was brouht to so gret necessite 235
that he wich wone to yiuyn grete, nede[d] smale. This knygh had a wyf,
a passynge fayr womman in nature but myche more in grace, and specially to oure lady she was singulerly deuouth. And whan a serteyn day of
sole[m]nyte neyhid, in whiche this knygh was wone to yiuyn monye grete
and large yifftys and had not werwith to performyn yt at that tyme, gretly 240
confoundyd in hymself and asshamyd, he went from hom and kept hym in
a lange place and solitarie tyl the tyme were past, where he myghte lamentyn and sorwyn his miserious fortune and eschewyn shame. Where wil
he was, sodeynly cam to hym a terrible and a ferful hors, but a more te-
rible and a more ferful sittere thervpon. The whiche seyde to hym on this 245
wyse: | 'Sey me, thou manly knyht, what ys the cause whi thou darkyst f. 165ᵛᵃ
thus here and mor[n]ist so heuyly?' To whom whan this knyth had told al
his male auenture and his sinistre fortune, he seyde ageyn to hym thus:
'Yf thou conforme the to my wyl and obeye me in no lytyl thyng, I shal
make the more to haboundyn in richesse, in welthe and in wourshepe than 250
euere thou dedist byforn.' And anoon this knyhte promysyd the pri[n]ce of
therk[n]esse to don whatsoeuere he comaundyd, be so that he performyd
his byhest. 'Goo hom', quoth he, 'into thyn hous, knyht, and in swyche a
place thou shalt fynde gret whyte of g[ol]d and syluyr and gret noumbre
of precyous stonys. For whiche al I aske no more but that swych a day thou 255
brynge hydyr thi wyf to me, to doo with hyre what I wyl.'

This condycioun grauntyd, the knygh returnyd hom ageyn and fond
alle thoo thyngis whiche the prince of dyrknesse had promysid hym. Wher-
witht anoon he boute statly paleys, quyt owt his londys set to morgage, yaf
large yifftys and ordeynyd hym hors and harneys on the fresshest wyse, 260

---

229 menetyme] manetyme   brethirin] brthirin   233 synne] syneyd
236 neded] nede   239 solemnyte] solennyte   247 mornist] morwist
251 prince] price   252 therknesse] therkilesse   254 gold] glod

and seruauntys and mene in rygh gret nou[m]bre. And whan the tyme
cam ner whanne he muste performyn also ageyn to the seyid prince of
thirknesse his byhest, anon he cam to hys wyf and bad hyre makyn hyre
redy to horsbak for nedys the[y] muste reydyn togidyr a lityl iourne. And
265 she, not presumynge ner beynge wil to geynseyin his comaundement, with
gret fer mad hyre redy and wente forth with hym, comendynge hyreself
deuouhtly to oure ladyis tuycyoun. And whan they had rydin a good weye
and come casuelly forby a cherche, by hyre housbondys leue she lyth doun
and wente into cherche and knelyd doun byforn an ymage of oure lady,
270 hyre housbonde the knygh abydynge stylle withoute. And as she lay in
hyre preyere, comaundyng hyre to the gouernaunce of oure lady, sodeynly
she fyl aslepe. And anon oure lady cam doun fro the autyr and in abite and
lyknes of the knythtys wyf went owt and tok the hors and rod forth with
hym, his wyf abydynge aslepe in the cherche. And whanne they come ny
275 to the place limityd and assignyd, anoon the prince of thirknesse with gret
noyse and dene cam thedyr. But as sone as he cam ner he bygan to qua-
ken and to tremelyn and d[ur]st not neyhyn, saf at the laste he spak to the
knygh and seyde: 'O thou most vntrewe man of alle men, why hast thou
skornyd me and illudyd me thus, and for so manye beneficys which I haue
280 shewyd and don to the hast this wyse mokkyd me? For I seyde to the that
thou shuldyst han brough me thy wyf and thou hast brough with the my
lordys modyr, Marye, my most en[i]mye. Y desire thi wyf for to haue ben
vengyd on hyre of the manye grete iniuryis which she hath don to me, and
thou hast brough me hydir hyre whiche may tormente me and at hyre wyl
f. 165vb   castyn doun me into the pit of helle.' This talkyng herynge, | the knygh
286 wex gretly astoynyd and so sore abasshid that he cowde speke no worud.
And anoon oure lady turnyd hyre to the deuyl-ward and seyde on this wyse:
'By that malepertnesse presumyddyst thou, o wykkyd spirit, to haue noyid
my deuouth seruau[n]t? Knowe yt wyll that thou shalt not skapyn awey
290 vnpunysshid, for this sentence I iuge vpon the: that thou descende euene
doun to helle and [n]euere aftyr this tyme presume to neye or hurtyn ony
persone whiche hath deuocioun to me.' This sentense youyn, the deuyl
sore rorynge and cryinge wente his weye. And the knygh forthwith lygh
doun of his hors and fel doun byforn oure ladyis feet and askyd hyre grace
295 and mercy. Whoom whan oure lady had blamyd and rebukyd, she led hym
ageyn to his wyf, where she lay in the cherche and slepte, and chargyd
hym to cher[i]shyn hyre and throwyn awey alle the rychesse the deuyl had
youyn hym for hire. And whanne he cam ageyn to the cherche where she

261 noumbre] nouunbre   264 they] the   277 durst] drust   282 enimye]
enmye   289 seruaunt] seruauunt   291 neuere] euere   297 cherishyn]
chershyn

lay and slepte and he had awakyd hyre and told hyre al the processe as
yt was fallyn, they wentyn hom togedyr and, as oure lady coma[un]dyd 300
kestyn away the deuyls rychesses, they lyuyddyn togedyr in the laude and
seruise of oure lady onto hyre lyuys ende, haboundynge bothyn in bodyly
and goostly rychesses throgh helpe of oure lady, to whoom be laude and
preysyng endelessly.

A synful wrecche onys oppreshid with the intollerable byrdene of synne 305
was rauasshid in sp[i]rit to the doom of God. And anoon Sathanas cam
forth and seyde: 'In this caytyf soule, sire iuge, ye haue no rygh. For yt
longht al to myn lordchepe whereof Y haue a comoun instrument.' 'Where
ys thyn instrument?' quoth the iuge, 'shewe yt!' 'I haue', quoth he, 'an
instrument endityd by thyn owyn mouth in the pretorie of paradys and 310
decernyd to enduryn perpetuelly and ys this: Thou seydyst with good deliberacioun: "In what oure ye shul etyn of this tre, signifyinge the tre of
knowynge of good and euyl, ye shul deyin." Syth thanne he th[u]s by lyneal
descent comyth of the same progenye that this was seyid to, by the rygh of
the seyd instrument he muste deye with me.' Quoth the iuge thanne: 'Man, 315
I grauntte the grace to spekyn for thiself.' And whanne he held his pees
and spak not, the deuyl seyde ageyn: 'This soule ys myn also', quoth he,
'by prescripcioun. For I haue had possessioun therof thritty wentyr. And
al this tyme he hath obeyid me as my propyr seruaunt.' And for as meche
as the man held his pees and spak not, the deuyl seyde ageyn the thridde 320
tyme: 'Yet I chalange hym for myn for this sky[l]: Albeyt that per[a]uenture
he hath do summe good dedys, not forthan his euyl dedys incomperabilly
passyn hem.'

And whanne the iuge saw that he coude not answere for hymself, he
wold not sodeynly | yiuyn the sentence but yaf hym eyghte dayis respite, f. 166ra
and that the eyghte day shulde apperyn byforn hym and swern to these 326
accusacions. Whan this pore caytyf was passid owt of the iugis presence al
mornynge and eyuy[n], on met with hym and freynyd of hym the cause whi
he was so sory. To whom whan he had told al the processe, 'Fere the not',
quoth he ageyn, 'for I shal helpe the as for the friste poynt weel inow, for 330
my name ys Treuthe.' Eftsonys he met with anothir, the whiche promysid
hym helpe as for the secunde poynt, whos name was Ryhtwyssnesse.

And whan the eyghte day was comyn, anon Sathanas was redy to pursuyn his matyr and purposyd ageyn his friste conclucioun. 'As to this
poynt', quoth Truthe anon, 'I sey thus: that ther byn tweyne dethis for 335

---

300 oure lady] oure   comaundyd] comauundyd   306 spirit] sprit   313 thus]
this   316 whanne he] whanne   321 skyl] skyk   perauenture] peruenture
328 eyuyn] eyuy

synne, as deth of the body and deth of helle. And this instrument which
thou, deuyl, allegyst spekyth of the friste deth and not of the secunde. The
whiche I proue thus: alle men byn pertiners of bodyly deth, but not alle
men gon to helle.' And whanne the deuyl saw that he faylyd of his fryste
340 conclusioun, anoon he purposid the secunde. To the whiche Ryghwisnesse
answerde on this wyse: 'Th[o]gh thou, deuyl, hast had this mannys seruyse
as thou seyist this thritty wyntyr, yit mayist thou not allegge prescripcioun.
For yt hath offtyn ben int[er]rupt by remormour of reson and repentaunce
and confessioun and penaunce, whanne his conscience grucchid to seruyn
345 so c[r]uel a lord.' And this seyd Sathanas purposid the thridde conclusioun. And, for as meche as the man faylith an aduocat to answere for hym,
the iuge chargid anoon a balaunce to be brouth forth and alle his dedys to
byn wh[ein], gode and badde. In whiche menetyme, Treuthe and Ryht-
wisnesse counselyd the sely penaunt to han recours in his mynde and in
350 his herte to the quen of mercy, whiche sat on the iugis rygh hand and to
preyin hyre to byn his hope at this nede. And whanne he had so doon,
anoon she ros vp and put hyre hand to the balaunce, wherein wern his
fewe gode dedys. And the deuyl drow sore ageyns hyre, but she preuaylid
and delyueryd the synnere. Whiche, whanne he cam ageyn to himself, he
355 chaungyd hys maners and lyuyd bettyr aftyr thanne he had don byforn.

The yer of oure lord fyue hundryd and seuene and twenty, in the cite
of Butyrid, while cristene men wern houseld, a Iewes child cam into the
cherche with cristene mennys childryn and took the comunyoun with hem.
And whanne he came hom and, examynyd of his fadyr had told hym as yt
360 was, his fadyr in his woodnesse thru hym into an hoot brynnynge forneys,
the whiche was ther byforn hym. And anoon oure lady, in the lyknesse of
an ymage the whiche the [c]hild saw in the cherche stondynge vpon the
f. 166rb autyr, [cam] into the forneys to hym and kept hym that ther mygh | no
fyir hurtyn hym. The modyr also of the child with hyre criynge gadryd
365 thedir meche peple, bothe Iewys and cristene folk. Whiche whanne they
seyin the child in the myddys of the flaume and not brynnyn, they pullyd
hym owt of the fyir and askyd hym how he was so kept harmles from the
fyir. 'Forsothe', quoth the child ageyn, 'the wourshepeful lady wiche stant
vpon the awtyr in the cherche curyd me and kept me, that noo fyir myht
370 touche me.' Wherfore the cristene peple vndyrstondy[n] that yt was the
image of oure lady and forthwith they kest the fadyr of the child in the

341 Thogh] Throgh   343 interrupt] intrupt   345 cruel] couel
348 whein] whom   362 child] shild   363 cam] and cam   370 vndyrstondyn]
vndyrstondyng

same furneys, and in a moment he was consumpt byforn here face, and
the child aftyr was cristnyd and bycam oure ladyis seruaunt.

Certeyn munkys vpon a morwyn sumwat beforn day, stondynge by a
riu[i]rsyde and ocupiyd hem with veyn fables and ydil wurdys. And euene 375
sodeynly they herdyn a gret noyse of rewers comynge doun with cours
in the ryuir, whom the munkys askyd who they were. And they answerde
that they wern deuyls and they leddyn to helle the soule of on Ebronie
whiche was stiward of the kyngis hous of Fraunce, for he was apostata
of the monesterie of Seynt Galle. This herynge, these munkys wex sore 380
aferd and loude bygunne to cryin and seyn: 'Seynt Marie, preye for vs!'
'In a good tyme for yow', quoth the deuyls ageyn, 'preyd ye Marye to be
youre helpe, for ellys we shulle al to han rent yow and drynk[l]yd you, in
as myche as we founde yow stondyn thus ydilly ocupyin and in on tyme.
But she who[m] ye callyd to l[e]ttyd vs.' This seyid they wentyn forth to 385
helle and the munkys to here monestorye.

Ther was whilom also a woman whom a deuyl in a mannys lyknesse
oftyn illudyd and dede hyre meche trouble, the whiche had assayid manye
remedyis, as fastynge, preyinge, confessioun and holy watyr sprynglyng,
but not forthan secyd not. And at the laste a good man yaf hyre counsel 390
that, as sone as euere sche sey comyn, she shulde lyftyn vp hyre handys
and crie loude and seyin thus: 'Seynte Marie, helpe me!' Whiche whanne
she dede he ran abak as though he had byn hyt in the forheed with a ston,
seyinge on this wyse: 'An eyuyl deuyl mote entryn into his mouth that
tawt the this lesson.' And anoon he vanysshid awey and neuere wexid hyre 395
aftyr. Blyssyd mote be that swete lady, now and euere. Amen.

[142. BERNARD]

The lyf of Seynt Barnard the hooly Abot.

Seynt Bernard was b[or]n in Burgundye at the castel of Fontans of a
noble fad[y]r and modyr and religious. His fadris name was Tetelinus, a
wurthi | knygh to the wur[d]ward and not lesse wurthi of conuersacyoun f. 166ᵛᵃ
to God-ward. Aelet was his modrys name, acordynge to hyre husbonde 5
bothyn in byrthe and in condiciouns. This blyssyd woman brouth forth
seuene chyldryn: sexe sonys, a douthtyr, the whiche alle wern religious:
the sonys munkys, and the douthtyr a nunne whiche also, as sone as they
wern born, she offeryd vp to God with hire own handys, fostrid hem and

372–3 and the] and   375 riuirsyde] riursyde   383 drynklyd] drynk-
kyd   385 whom] whon   lettyd] lottyd   2 born] bron   3 fadyr] fadryst
4 wurdward] wurward

10 norshid hem with here owune brestis, infoundy[d] by a manyr the nature
of hyre goodnesse with the fode of hyre own mylke. And whanne they grewyn, as longe as they wern vndyr hyre handys she fedde hem with most
groos and most comoun metys, rathere norysshynge hem, as yt sempte, to
cloystyr than to court.

15 But whanne she was with hyre thridde sone, the whiche was Barnard,
and bar hym in hyre wombe, vpon a nyght she thouthte that she had within
hyre a fayre whighte whelp, on the bak sumwhat rody, and this whelp to
hyre semynge dede berkyn in hyre wombe. The whiche vision whan she
had told to a good holy man he, with a prophetical woys, answerde ageyn
20 and seyde: 'Thou shalt be the modyr of a nobyl, the whiche in tyme to
come shal ben a kepere of Goddys hous, and gretly shal berkyn ageyns the
enmyis therof. He shal byn an excellent prechour and with the grace of his
medycinable tunge he shal curyn myche folk.'

Oo tyme, whil Barnard was a child and greuously vexyd with heed-
25 ache, ther cam to hym a woman forto han charmyd [hym]. And whanne
he perceyuyd what she mente, with gret indignacyon he put hyre away
from hym and bygan to cryin and wolde in no wyse suffryn hyre to doon
hire crafth. For euene forthwith, as he ros to flen the womman, he felte
hym fully deliueryd and al hool. Also oo tyme, on the moste holy nyght of
30 Cristys natyuite, whan child Barnard aboot in the cherche the seruise of
matyns and desirid to knowyn what our of the nygh Crist Ihesu was born,
sodeynly he apperid byforn his eyne, as he that tyme had be newe born of
oure lady his modyr. Wherfore, as longe as he lyuyd, he trowyd veryly that
that same was the our of Cristis byrthe. Fro that our thanne forward, in
35 alle thoo thyngis that longyn to the sacrement of Cristys natyuite, his wit
and his felynge was the profoundere and his speche and his langage the
copioushere. A[s] yt semyth by the notable werk wyche he mad aftyr into
laude and preysynge of oure lady, in whiche he coriously [explytid] this
lessoun of Luc: *Missus est.*

40 And whanne the old enmy of mankynde sey the helthefull entent of this
nobil child Barnard, he had enuye with his holy purpos of chastite and set
byforn hym manye and diuers snars of temptacioun for to makyn to brekyn
yt. Yt fyl so that oo tyme he set his eye fyx longe on a woman by stirynge
f. 166ᵛᵇ of the deuyl. But anoon he wex ashamyd | and for to chastice this defaute
45 he was to hymself a rigerous iuge. And forthwith he wente in to a pond of
cold watyr and as longe aboud therin that he was ner bloodles. But this cam
therof by helpe of Goddys gracyous influence: that fro that tyme forth was

10 infoundyd] infoundyn   19 had told] had   25 hym] y   37 As] At
38 explytid] he explytid

quenchid in hym al the brennynge hete of flesshly concupiscence. Sone
aftyr this same tyme a yung damysel, by the deuyls suggestyoun, went to
Barnard into his beed nakyd. Whom whanne he felte, kepyng pees and syl-   50
ence, he yaf hyre place and turnyd hym from hyre-ward onto the tothir syde
and lay stylle and slepte. This wrecchid daunsel perceyuyd this, lay stylle
a whyle sufferynge and bydynge whanne he wolde han turnyd hym ageyn
to here-ward. And whanne he felte that he dede not, she vnshamefastly
bygan to styrin hym and to pokyn hym. And aftyr that more vnchame-   55
fastly she touchyd hym and handlyd hym. But not forthan he lay stylle,
withowte mewynge and withowte tityllacyoun of flesshly sterynge. Wyche
perceywyd, she wex ashamyd and roos vp and fledde awey.

Anothir tyme whan he was herberwyd in a weduys hous she, considerynge his youthe and the comelynesse of persone and gladsumnesse of   60
cheer, was gretly enflaumyd with an vnleful con[c]upiscence of hym. For
whiche cause she mad hym a seperat bed by hymself alone, not fer from
hyre chambyr. And whanne alle folk were to bedde [wente] to hym, whom
as sone as he felte hem bygan lowde to criyn and seyin: 'Theuys, theuys.'
At whiche voyis the woman fledde, the mene ros and lygh a candele and   65
seyth the theuys but they founde noon. Wherfore alle wenten ageyn to
bedde and restyd, saf oonly this w[r]ecchid womman cowde no rest han.
But efthsonys she wente ageyn, and he cryid: 'Theus, theuys' ageyn. She
fled, the seruauntis rysyn, the theuys were southt and nat foundyn, for he
wych oonly knew yt wolde no puplysshyn yt. Thus this wrecchid woman,   70
vnneth ouyrcomyn with feer and with despeyr, cesyd and wente no more.
And on the nexte day, as they wentyn forth in here iourne, his felas blamyd
hym and askyd hym what he drempte that he so ofte cryid 'theuys.' 'Felas',
quoth he ageyn, 'werely this nyght was hy wythe a thef, for oure hostesse
wolde this nyght han robbyd me of myn most precyous i[e]wel: chastite.'   75
Considerynge thanne Barnard that yt ys not sikyr to dwellyn ny the serpent, he termynyd in hymself that he wolde fleen and sone aftyr to entryn
into the Cistrencys ordre. The whiche entent whanne his brethyrn kne-
wyn, they labourid with alle menys and weyis they cowdyn for to chaungyn
hym from his purpos. But sykyr, swych grace God grauntyd hym, that not   80
oonly they myghte not remeuen hym therfro, but he to the same ordre
brouhte alle hys bretheryn and manye moo therto. Nertheles Gerard, hys
brothyr, a wurthi knyth, held fryste | alle his wurdys veyn and set lytyl   f. 167ra
or not by alle his holy counselys and exhortaciouns. Not forthan Barnard,
feruent in feyth and flamyd with the zeel of brothirly cherite, seyde to hym   85

on this wyse: 'I wot weel, brothir, I woot wel that [vexa]cyoun alone shal yiuin vndyrstondynge to thyn herynge.' And with that he pokyd his brothir with his fyngyr vndyr the syde and seyde: 'Ther shal comyn a day, brothir, and that shal sone comyn, whanne a spere shal percyn this syde and makyn
90 a wey to thyn herte to letyn y[n] that counsel whiche thou now throwist awey and dispisyst.' And, not manye dayis aftyr, Gerard was takyn of hys eni[m]yis and a spere shouyn into hys side where his brothir [put his] fyngyr. And aftyr he was put in prisoun. Whom Bernard wente to wysityn there he was in prisoun. And whanne he myghte not be sufferid to spekyn
95 wyth hym, he cryid onto hym and seyde: 'Gerard brothir, wete weel that the tyme ys ny whanne we shul goon togedyr to entryn into a mo[n]asterie!' And the same nygh foluynge his fetrys feel from his feet and the prisoun dore wyde opyn. And he feld owt meryly and told his brothir that he had chaungyd purpos and wolde byn a munk. The yer thanne of oure lord a
100 thousend an hundryd and twelue Bernard, the seruaunte of God, beyinge two and twenty wentyr of age, with moo than thritty felaas entrid the Cistrencis ordre, the fiftend yer aftyr the instytucioun of the same ordre. And whanne Barnard with his bretherin wente owt of here fadris hous toward the monasterie, Guido, the eldest brothir, seyinge [Niu]ard, here yungest
105 brethere, pleyin in the strete with othere chyldryn, seyde to hym thus: 'Be mery, br[o]thir [Niu]ard, be mery!' quoth he, 'for al the lond of oure possessioun longith now alone to the.' To whoom chyld [Niu]ard but nat childly answerd ageyn and seyde: 'A brothir, shuld ye han heuene and leue to me oonly erthe? Sykyr, brothir, yn this diuysoun or departisoun ys not
110 euenly mad.' And whanne he a lytyl while abydynge stylle at hom with his fadyr, not longe aftyr he foluyd his bretheryn. Thus this blyssid man Barnard entrid the Cistrencis ordre to seruyn God, was anoon so absort hool into spirit and soo holly kynt and mancipat to God that he sempte to han lost the vse of alle his bodyly wyttys. For whanne he hadde a yer byn in
115 the celle of the nouycis he wyste not wethir the hous were voutyd or nat. And as oftyn as he entryd the cherche that yer, he knew nat how manye wyndouys wern in the est heed therof. For ther that wern thre he wende ther had beyn but on.

Whanne the abot of Cistriencis sent serteyn munkys to byldyn an hous
f. 167rb in Claravalle, | he made Barnard abbot to hem, where long tyme they lyuyd
121 in gret pouerte and madyn here potage ful oftyn of the leuys of a vaylde tre clepyd Fagus, and breed of barly, myle and fecchys. This blyssid seruaunt

86 vexacyon] saxocyon   90 yn] yt   92 enimyis] eninyis   put his] his put his
96 monasterie] menasterie   104 Niuard] Vnard   106 brothir] brthir   Niuard]
Vnard   107 Niuard] Vnard

of God vsyd to wecchyn past the possibilite of mannys nature. For ful oftyn
he conpleynyd and seyde that he lost neuere so meche tyme as whanne he
slepte. And therfore he seyde that yt was a couenyent similitude and lyk- 125
nesse bytwyxe sleep and deth. And whanne he herde ony man snoryn in his
sleep or sey hym lyin inordinatly and slepyn, vnnethe he myghte suffryn
yt pacyently.

Seldum or euere drow hym appetit or lust to mete, and that he eet was
oonly for dred of defaute. Wherfore he wente euere to mete as he shulde 130
han goon to torment. And aftyr mete he wolde rekenyn with hym how
meche he had etyn and, yf he fond that ony tyme he had excedyd mesure
in etynge, he wold not letyn yt passyn vnpunysshyd. And in so meche he
had ouyrcomyn the lust of glotonye that he lost a gret part of dicernynge the
sauours and the tastys of mete and drynk. For oo tyme he dranke oyle reke- 135
lesly ministrid hym and hem and he wyste yt not tyl aftyrward he wundryd
that his lyppys wern so anoyntyd. Also [certeyn] dayis he eet raw blood
instede of buttyr and discernyd not what y[t] was. Oonly in watyr he had
sum sauour, for in goynge in yt refresshid weel, he seyid, his chekys and
hys throte. Whatsoeuere he coude of scripture he lernyd yt, as he seyde, 140
in wodys and feldys, by preyers and meditacyons. And as he was wone to
seyn amonge his frendys, he had neuere othere maystris thanne ookys and
fagys. In hys clothyng pouerte plesid hym euere, filthe and vnclennesse
neuere. For clothis, he seyde, arn the iugis or the shewers of a negligent
soule or of a ve[i]nglorious soule. This blyssyd man neuere low so but that 145
his lauhynge nedyd rathere a spore than brydyl.

Thre maner kyndys of pacience he was wone to seyne ben nedful to a
man: oon in iniurye of wordys and nothynge ageyns harm or damage of
goodys, the thridde ageyns hurt of body or membris. And alle these thre
kyndys of pacyence he sheuyd hymself to han exemplerly by experience. 150
As for the fryste we redyn that, onys whan he frendly had wrytyn a pistil to
a b[i]sshop, amonestyng hym helthefully, he, gretly angryd threwith, wrot
ageyn to hym rygh byttyrly bygynnynge his pistil on this wyse: 'Salutem
and not the spirit of blasphemye.' To whom Barnard, vndyr the sheld of
pacyence, wrot ageyn on this wyse: 'Sere, sothly I trowe that I haue not the 155
spirit of blasphemye and we[r]ely woot that neythyr I wolde seyin euyl to
ony man, ner cursyn no man, and specially not to the prince of myn peple.'

See here pacyence in wurdys as towchynge the secunde kynde of
pacyence, that ys ageyns harm | and damage of goodys. We fynden that f. 167ᵛᵃ
a certeyn abbot sent hym sex hundryd marc of syluyr to bylden with a 160

137 certeyn] he certeyn   138 yt] ys   145 veinglorious] venglorious
152 bisshop] bosshop   156 werely] weely

monastorie, the whiche summe was takyn awey by the weye of brigauntys.
And whan tydynges ther were brough to Barnard he, armyd with pacience,
seyde not ellys but thus: 'Blyssyd be God whiche hath sparid me of gret
charge.'

165   'And also', quoth he, 'for to skylle yt ys whi yt shulde the esilyere be
brou and sparyd to hem that takyn yt', [quoth] he. 'For the Romayn coueytyse brybid yt, singnifiynge that yt wern Romayn the whiche tokyn yt
awey, for Romayns comounly ben coueytous. Anothir s[k]yl ys', quoth he,
'for a gret monye yiuyth a gret occasioun and so dede this m[o]nye hem.'

170   And as for the thridde kynde of pacyence, yt ys seyid that onys a reguler
chanoun cam to hym and preyid hym instauntly that he wolde reseyuyn
hym a munk. And whanne he wolde not assentyn to hym, but rathere
monestid hym to turnyn ageyn to his cherche, the chanon seyde ageyn to
hym: 'Why ys yt thanne that thou in thy bookys hast comendyd so meche

175   perfeccyoun of lyuynge, syth thou wilt not grauntyn yt to hem wyche
desiry[n] yt? Wolde God I had hyre thoo bookys in myn hand and sykyr
I shulde rendyn hem or brynnyn hem.' 'Treuly', quoth Bernard ageyn,
'thou shalt fynde in noon of hem but that thou myghtyst be perfyht in
thy cloystyr. For in alle tho bokys I haue aluey comendyd amendynge of

180   manerys, not change of pla[ce].' Whith wyche answere the chanoun angri
stric vpon hym inpetuously, and so greuously smet hym on the chec[k]e
that fryst yt was reed and aftyr b[o]lene. And whanne they whiche stod
by seyin this, they woldyn han runnyn vpon hym. But Barnard preuent
hym, criyinge and adiurynge hem by the name of Crist that no man shulde

185   towchyn hym, ner don hym ony bodyly harm.

This blyssyd fadyr was wone to seyin to hym that comyn to entrin his
ordre on this wyse: 'Sonys, yf ye wyl comyn in here, leuyth there withoute
youre bodyis, the whiche ye han brouth with you from the word. Oonly
yowre spiri[t]s motyn entryn in here, for the flessh profityd rygh nough.'

190   The fadyr of blyssyd Barnard, lefth alone in his hous, forsook the word
and wente intho the monasterye and, aftyr a lytyl tyme abydynge there,
he deyid in a good age. The sustyr also of hym, weddyd in the word and
perysshynge in delytis, wente oo tyme to the monasterie for to vicytyn
hyre brethirin. And whan she cam with a gret feleshepe and in proud aray,

195   he abhorryd hyre as the deuyls net spred abrod to takyn with soulys, and
wold not onys assentyn for to seen hyre. And whanne she saw that noon
of hyre brethiryn wolde comyn owt for to metyn with hire, and herd on of

166 quoth] fyir quoth   168 skyl] slyl   169 monye] manye   176 desiryn]
desirynge   180 place] plauc   181 checke] cheche   182 bolene] belene
189 spirits] spiris

the porters lyknyn hyre to foul doung inuoluyd and curyd in fayir | clo- f. 167vb
thys, anoon she brast on wepynge and seyde: 'For sothe, sers, although I
haue be a synnere, Crist deyid for swyche! And for I knowe me to ben a   200
synnere, therefore I come to sekyn the communicacyoun and the counsel of good men. And though my brothir dispice my flesshe, lete not the
seruaunte of Crist dispicyn my soule. But lete hym comyn and comaun-
dyn and, whatsoeuere he comaunde, I shall fulfillyn.' And whan this was
told to Barnard he com owt hyre with ys brethyrin, and herd hyre seyin 205
hyre entent. Wherevpon, for as meche as she myghte not be diuorcyd from
hyre husbonde, fryst of alle he interdytyd hyre al the ioye and pompe of
the word, and councelyd hyre to foluyn the forme of here modyr, and sent
hyre hoom ageyn. Whiche whanne she cam hoom ageyn was so sodeynly
chaungid that she sempte to ledyn an hermytys lyf and to ben alynyd from 210
al the word. And at the laste, by many [oportune] preyers, she ouyrcam
hyre housbonde and gat leue to entryn into a monasterye, there to seruyn
God euere whil she lyuyth aftyr.

Oo tyme whan this blyssyd seruaunt of God was seek and brough, as yt
sempte, to the laste bre[th] of his spirit, he was comaundyd, as hym thoute, 215
to comyn and apperyn byforn the bench of the hy iuge, where Sathanas
anoon was redy ageyns hym with manye and dyuers acusacions. Whiche
whanne he had vttryd on the most cruel wyse, the seruaunte of God, nothynge aferd ner abasshid, answerd ageyn therto thus seyinge: 'I am rygh
wyl aknowe that I am not wurthi, ner by my propyr merytys I may not 220
chalangyn the kyngdam of [heuene]. Not forthan, I wot weel that my lord
Ihesu Crist opteynyth yt and hath by double rygh: by en[h]eritaunce of his
fadris possessioun and also by merit of his passioun. My lord ys content
wyth the ton and the todyr he hath youyn me. Of whos yifte and not of
myn merytys I am bold and not aferd to chalangyn yt.' By swyche answere 225
Sathan confoundyd went his weye and Barnard returnyd ageyn to lyf.

Anothyr tyme whan this blyssid man was so seek that yche man wende
that he shulde haue deyid, his brethiryn entyrly and hertely preyid for hym
and anoon he f[elt]e hymself amendynge. Wherfore, anoon his brethyrin gadryd togedyr, he seyde to hym on this wyse: 'O myn wilbelouyd 230
brethryn, why holde ye me, wrecche, here stylle? Iwys, brethyr, ye byn
strengere than I [and] preuaylyd. Hensforward, gode brethern, sparith me,
sparith me and letyth me goon hens!' With so gret abstinence, laboure and
vigilijs this holy abot oppressyd and bar doun his flesshe, that he languryd
with so gret syknesse that vnnethe he mygh foluyn the couent.   235

Of manye cytyes this man was chosyn to byn a b[i]sshop but specialy |
f. 168ʳᵃ of Ianueye and of Malan. To whom he euere manerly excusid hym, neythyr dynynge hyre desyre ner graunty[nge], but euere excusynge hym and
seyynge that he was nat hys own, but finally he was ordeynyd to seruyn
240 othere. And therfore hys brethyrin, by hys own counsel, had so prouydid
that by the popis auctorite was grauntyd hem that ageyns here wyll no man
shulde takyn hyre ioye from hem. Vpon a tyme whanne this blyssid fadyr
had visityd a couent of the Chartyrhous and they were gretly counfortyd
in alle thynges by his holy exortaciouns, oo [thyng] ther was that sumwhat
245 meuyd the priour of the same place, that ys to seyne that Barnardys sadyl
was to good and pretendyd to lytyl pouerte. And whanne the priour had
seyid this to oon of hyse and he had told yt hym, he not lesse wundrynge
than the priour askyd what manyr sadyl yt was. For notwithstondyng that
he had rydyn therin fro C[l]areual thedyr, yit wyst he nat what was the
250 aray of hys sadyl. Anothyr tyme yt happyd hym to rydyn al a day besydyn
the lake Lausanence, and yit he saw yt not. And at euyn whanne he cam
to hys loggynge, they that rydyn with hym talkynge of the seyid lake, he
askyd hem where that lake was. Wherof they alle wern gretly amaruaylyd,
stondyng that they redyn therby al day.

255   Gret and excellent mekenesse was in this man, for the mekenesse of hys
herte superexcellyd and ouyrcam the hynesse of hys name. For of alle men
he was holdyn in reputacyoun hyest, and he helde hymself of alle men the
febylest. And whom alle men preferryd byforn hem, he hymself preferryd
to no man. And as he oftyn knowlechyd hymself, whanne he was amonge
260 the hye wurships and most fauour of men, hym thoughte hymself chaungyd into anothyr man and that he was absent, venynge that al that was
seyid had byn but a drem. But whanne he was amonge more sympyl brethryn, where he mygh vsyn hys wyl-bylouyd frend mekenesse, there hym
thoughte he was turnyd ageyn into his propyr persone, and fond gret mater
265 of gladnesse. Moreouyr, as touchynge his ocupacioun, sykyr he was euere
foundyn or preynge or redynge, or writynge or thynkyng, or hys brethryn
and othere with holy exhortacyoun edyfyinge.

Vpon a tyme also whanne he prechid to the p[e]ple, and they dylygently
and deuothly reseyuyd alle hys wurdys, this maner st[yr]t into his mynde.
270 'Trewely now prechyd thou wyl and art gladly herd of alle men, and of
yche man holdyn a whys man.' At whiche temptacyoun he stood a lytyl
while stylle and bythough whedyr he shulde procedyn forth or makyn an
ende. And anoon, confortyd with G[o]dys helpe, priuyly he answerde the

236 bisshop] bosshop   238 grauntynge] grauntyd   244 thyng] thyng thyng
249 Clareual] Careual   268 peple] pleple   269 styrt] stryt   273 Godys]
Goodys

temptacyoun and seyde: 'Neythyr I began ner I wil not endyn in the.' And
aftyr that he procedyd forth | in hys sermoun tyl he cam to the ende.   f. 168rb

Onys in his monasteri[y] he had a mu[n]k with hym, a ribaude and a   276
pleyere and a mysreulyd man, the whiche styrid with [an] euyl spirit wolde
algatys turnyn ageyn onto the word. Whoom whanne Barnard myghte in
no wyse makyn to abydyn, he askyd hym what craftht he wolde leuyn by
in the word. 'Syre', quoth he, 'I kan weel pleyin at the dyis and therby I   280
purpose for to lyuyn.' 'Yf I yeue the thanne', quoth Bernard, 'a stook or
an heed to pleyin whithe, wylt thou thanne euery yeer comyn ageyn to me
and departyn with me thy wynnyngys?' And thanne he was ryght glad and
mery and sykyrly byhyght hym that he so wolde. Whoom on this condi-
cyoun Bernard dylyueryd fyue and twenty shylyngys and he wente forth   285
his wey; and this dede this holy fadyr forto clepyn hym ageyn therby. And
so yt byfyl aftyrward. This felaue withinne fewe dayis aftyr loste al th[at]
Seynt Barnard had takyn hym and, for he nought hadde to lyue by, he
turnyd ageyn to the monastorie gate. And whanne he herd this he gladly
went owt to hym and held abrood hys lappe for to reseyuyn hys part of the   290
lucre. 'Forsothe fadyr', quoth he, 'I haue ryght not wunnyn, and therto
I haue lost yowre stook. Wherfore, yf ye wyll reseyuyn me, here I am.'
'Treuly', quoth Bernard ageyn, 'syth yt ys so, bettyr yt ys that I reseyue
the thanne to lesyn bothyn.' Anothyr tyme as Bernard rood were he had
for to don, he met with an vplondysh man to whom amonge here comuni-   295
cacyoun he compleynyd of the vnstabylnesse of his mynde. Thes heryng,
the man dyspisid hym and seyde that he had euere stabyl mynde ynow in
his preyere. Whoom Bernard welynge conuictyn and shewyn hym hys own
presoumcyoun, he seyde to hym thus: 'Stonde a lytyl from vs and se[y]e
thy Pater noster withowte waueryng of thy mynde, and thou shalt han the   300
hors that I sytte vpon, be so vpon thy feyth thou sey me treuthe.' Glad was
thys man, hopynge to wynne Barnardys hors. And anon he gaderyd hymself within hymself with as wyl he cowde and began. And vnnethe he was
in the myddys that he thoughte whedyr he shulde han the sadyl with the
hors or not. Wherfore he yald hym to Barnard and askyd hym foryifnesse   305
of hys contempt and corectyd hys presumpcyon.

A yung munke clepid Robert, ny of kyn to Barnard and sumtyme hys
clerc, deceyuyd in his youthe by the suasioun of othre, went awey fro hym
to Ouerne. And whanne this blyssyd fadyr had dissim[u]lyd his goynge for
a tyme, he purposid to reuoukyn hym by an epistyl. This wyche whanne   310

276 monasteriy] monasteriys   munk] muk   277 an] and   286 his wey] wey
287 that] the   299 seye] seyde   307 clepid Robert] clepid   309 dissimulyd]
dissimlyd

he endytid vndyr a pentys and anothir munke wroot yt, ther cam a sodeyn reyn and he that wrot wold han secyd. But blyssyd Barnard bad hym not byn aferd to waytyn the werk of God. And he wrot forth at his comaunde-ment, vpon whom fel no drope of watyr notwitstondynge that yt reynyd

f. 168va euene | rounde aboute.

316   Oo tyme whanne he was sent from the pope to Melan to reconcilyn the citezeyns with the cherche and, his cause sped, was returnyd ageyn to Pauye, a man of the same [cyte], hauynge a wyff a demonyac and vexyd with a deuyl, brough hyre to his presence. And anon the deuyl, by the mouth

320 of the woman, brast owt into contumely of Barnard and seyde: 'He this, whiche etyth poret, caule and rau herbys, shall nat dryuyn me owt of myn old wom[a]n!' At whiche wurd Goddys seruaunt sent hem to Seynt Cir[u]s cherche but he, wylynge deferre and doo wurchip to his gest, wold no cure shewyn vpon hyre. And so she was brough ageyn to the abot Barnard and

325 anoon the deuyl bygan to chateryn by the wommannys mouth, and seyde: 'Neythir Cir[us] ne Barnardus shall dryuyn me owt of myn hous!' 'Iwys, deuyl', quoth Barnard, 'that ys soth! For neythir ne Cirus ne Barnardus, but oure lord Ihesus shall dryuyn the owt of thyn hous.' And anon as he had mad a shert preyere, the deuyl cryd by the womannys mouth and

330 seyde: 'Allas, allas, I wolde fayn goon owt of this old woman for I sore brent in hyre. Ful gladly I wolde goon but I may not, for the gret lord wyl not.' 'And whoo ys the gret lord that lettyth?' 'Ihesus of Nazareth', quod he. 'Seyst thou hym euere', quoth Barnard, 'Ya, sykyr', quoth the deuyl. 'Where?' quoth Barnard. 'In blysse', quoth the deuyl. 'Whi were

335 thou sumtyme in blysse?' quoth Barnard. 'Ya', quoth he, 'but with Lucy-fyr I fyl owt, as manye moo dedyn.' Alle these thyngis told the deuyl by the womannys mouth with a mornynge voyis, alle men herynge. 'Woldyst thou not thanne', quoth Barnard, 'turny[n] ageyn into the same blysse?' To whiche questioun the deuyl, mowyng and skornynge, answerde ageyn

340 and seyde: 'Yt ys to late, yt ys to late.' This seyid, aftyr a short preyere of Barnard the deuyl wente owt of the woman anoon. But as sone as Barnard was passid thens, the deuyl bygan to assaylyn the woman ageyn. Whereof whanne Barnard was certefyid by hyre husbonde, he sente hyre a scrowe to hangyn aboute hyre nekke wich seyde thus: 'In the name of oure lord Ihesu

345 Crist I bydde the deuyl that thou no more be bold to towchyn this woman.' Wyche scrowe hangyn aboute here nekke, the deuyl durst no more comyn ny hyre.

   In Aquitanye whilom a woman was illudyd and vexyd sexe yeer togedyr

318 cyte] of the cyte   322 woman] women   Cirus] Cires   326 Cirus] Cirulus
328 as he] as   334–5 were thou] were   338 turnyn] turnyd   342 the deuyl]
the

with swych a spirit as ys clepid *spiritus incubus*. The whiche, whan Barnard
cam to the countre, wente to the woman and with grete thretis warnyd 350
hyre that she shuld not comyn at Goddys seruaunt. For yf she dede, he
that was byforn hyre louere shul aftyrward been hyre enmye and hyre pur-
suere. But not forthan this womman wente to blyssyd Barnard, with gret
lamentacyoun and sorue she told hym al hyre heuynesse. 'Take with the,
woman', quoth he, 'my staf, and ley it in | thy bed and late hym doon f. 168ᵛᵇ
what he may.' And whanne she had doon as he bad hyre, anon he cam but 356
neythir he d[ur]ste presumyn to don as he was wone to doon, ner onys to
touchen the bed. But not forthan he thretyd hyre that, whanne Barnard
was goon, he shulde be vengid vpon here. And whanne she tolde this to
Barnard, he anoon gadrid alle the puple togedyr and chargid yche man 360
to han a candel in his hand lygh. Whiche doon he, with alle ther present,
accursid the deuyl and enterdytyd hym communicacyoun and touchynge
of this woman euere aftyr. And thus was delyuyrid and sauyd this woman
from the deuyls illucyoun.

Anothir tyme whanne this holy man was sent of the pope into the same 365
cuntre with a legacye for to reconcilyn the duc of Gyayn to the cherche,
and the seyid duc refusid and forsook alle the weyis and menys of recon-
ciliacyoun, vpon a day he wente to messe, the duc whom he had acursid
stondynge withowte the dore and abydynge. And whanne '*Pax domini*' was
seyid, he leyde Cristis body on the patene and took yt with hym, and with 370
a fyrry face and flaumyd he wente owt. And with these wurdys terribily he
spak to the duc: 'We han oftyn preyid this, alwey hast thou dispicyd vs. Lo,
here comyth to the the maydyns sone, the whiche ys lord of the cherche
that thou pursuist. Loo, here ys thy iuge, in whoos handys standyth thy
soule and the helthe therof, where thou wylt despicyn hym as thou hast 375
doon his seruauntys.' At whiche wurdys the duc sodeynly wex astoynyd
and, febblyd in hys membris, fel doun at ys feet. Whoom the holy fadyr
spornyd with his feet and bad hym rysyn vp and heryn the sentence of
God. And he anoon, ful of dred and feer, roos vp and offeryd hym lowly
to fulfyllyn whatsoeuere he wolde comaunden hym. 380

Whanne the seruaunt anothyr tyme entryd the kyngdam of Germanye
for to settyn at reste a gret dyscord, an erchibysshop sente onto hym a
wurshipful clerc of hys for to wolcomyn hym. To whom whanne this clerc
seyd that his lord had sent hym to hym to conueyin hym, he answerde ageyn
and seyde that anothir lord sent hym. Wherof he, gretly amaruaylyd, affer- 385
myd certeynly that he was sent of noon othir lord than of the erchebishop.

'Thou art deceyuyd, sone', quoth he, 'thou art deceyuyd. A grettere lord
than the erchebishop sent, for Ihesu Crist sent the to me.' Wich wurd
the clerc vndyrstondynge seyde ageyn: 'Whi, fadyr, wenyst I wolde ben
390 a munk? God forbede yt, fadyr, for I though yt not, ner yt cam neuere
in mynde.' What shal[l] be seyid more? In that same iourne this same clerc
forsook the word and was mad a munk.

    A wurthi knyth and notable of byrthe the word forsookyn, was mad a
munk. Oo tyme as he foluyd this blyssyd fadyr, he wex greuously vexyd
f. 169ra with temtacyoun. Whoom oon of the brethryn seyng heuy askyd hym | the
396 cause of hys heuynesse. 'Sykyr', quoth he ageyn, 'whateuere the cause be
of my heuynesse, this woot I weel, that I shall neuere be merye in this lyf.'
Which answere whanne the seyid brothir told here fadyr, anoon he preyid
for hym to God deuouthly. Whiche doon, anoon the seyid mu[n]k whiche
400 was temptyd and was sory aftyrward apperyd and sempte more iocund
and more mery thanne he sempte toforn sory and heuy. The cause wherof
whan his othir brothir had askyd the cause, his answere was reuer[s] of hys
othir answere. 'For though I seyde byforn that I shulde neuere be mery,
now I seye that aftyr this I shall neuere be sory.'

405   Whan blyssyd Malachye, a bisshop of Yrlond, whoos lyff the holy fadyr
Barnard had descryid byforn full of vertuhs, passid owt of this word to
Cristys mercy and the seruaunt offeryd the holy ost for hym, by the reuelacioun of God he knewe hym in blysse. By the same lordys inspiracyoun,
aftyr the comunyoun he chaungyd the forme of preyere in hys postcomoun
410 and with a glad voys he seyde on this wyse: 'Lord God, whiche this day
hast blyssyd Malachie egal to the merytys of thy seyntys, graunte, we beseche, that we wyche haluy[n] the feste of his precious deth mote folue the
example of his holy lyf.' And whanne the chauntour mad hym a tokene that
he erryd, he answerde ageyn and seyde 'Nay, sykyr, I erre not, but I woot
415 right wyll what I seye.'

    And forthwith he wente to the cros and blyssyd his holy feet. At the
laste, whanne this holy fadrys passage owt of this word cam ner, he seyde
to hys brethryn on this wyse: 'Brethyrn, thre thyngis I comende onto you
and leue hem to kepyn the whiche, wylle I haue runne in the furlong of
420 this present, I remembre me to han kept with alle my strengthes: First I
wolde neuere make slaundre to no man. And yf I ony tyme fel therin, I
secid yt as I myghte. The secunde ys that I trustyd euere betir to anothir
mannys wi[ll] than to myn own. The thrydde ys that, though ony man hurt

me or w[ro]ngyd me, I askyd neuere veniaunce vpon hym. Seeth thanne
how I leue you cherite, mekenesse and pacyence.' And so, aftyr werkynge 425
of manye grete miraclis and the byldyn of an hundryd and sexty monasteries, and sexty wyntyr and thre of his ly[f] comple[y]t, the yeer of grace
a thousent an hundryd and thre and fyfty, thys blyssyd and holy fadyr,
amonge hys dyssyplis handys, slepte of oure lord. And aftyr his deth he
shewyd his ioye to manye diuers personys. Of whiche alle oon I wyl reher- 430
syn in special. The day of his d[e]th he apperid to a certeyn abbot and
bad hym foluy[n] hym. To whoom, foluynge hym as he bad, he seyde on
this wyse: 'Lo', quoth he, 'now we be comyn to the mount Liban thou
shalt abydyn here and I shal goon vp.' And whan the abbot had askyd hym
why he wolde goon vp, 'Lerny[n], sykyr, I wele', | quoth he, whom we f. 169rb
wenyn no man to be lyk in the word, lernynge as in cunnynge. 'In this word 436
here', quoth he ageyn, 'is no kunnynge ner no verrey knoweleche of truthe.
Abouyn ys the plenitude and fulnesse of kunnynge and the very perfyth
knowleche of [treuth].' And with this wurd he vanysshd, whiche day the
abbot markyd; Barnard deyid. Manye othere and inummerable miraclis 440
owre lord hath wrouth by this holy man, whiche were to longe to tellyn.
Wherfore the byforn seyid shul suffisyn for this tyme & cetera.

[143. BARTHOLOMEW]

The lyf of Seynt Bartilmeu th'appos't'le.

Bartylmeu the apostyl of oure lord Ihesu Crist comynge into Ynde,
whiche ys in the est ende of the word, wente into a temple wherein was
an ydol clepyd Asteroth and there abood as a pylgrym. In this ydol was
dwellynge a deuyl whiche seyde hymself that he curyd and mad hool seek 5
folk. But that was nat, quoth Ianuence, in helthe-yiuynge, but by with-
drauynge of harm and hurt. And, for as meche that the temple was ful
of langurynge and seek foolk and they of the ydol mygh han noon answere, they wentyn to anothyr cyte where was wurchepyd anothyr ydol
whos name was Beryt, whom they askyd whi Astrot, here ydol, yaf hem 10
non answere now as he was wone to don. 'Iwys', quoth Beryt, 'for youre
god ys so boundyn in the throte and in the nekke with fyir brynynge shenys that vnnethe he may breth[y]n, and spekyn may he not. And thus hath
he ben fro the our that the apostyl of God, Bartylmeu, entryd into hys

424 wrongyd] worngyd   426-7 monasteries and sexty wyntyr] wyntyr
427 lyf] ly   compleyt] compleynt   431 deth] dyth   431-2 and bad]
and   432 foluyn] foluynge   435 Lernyn] Lernynge   439 treuth] reut he
4 ydol was] ydol   13 brethyn] brethryn

15 temple.' 'And woo ys this Bartylmeu', quoth they, 'whiche thus hath boundyn oure lord God Asterot.' 'Sykyr', quoth Beryt, 'he ys the frend of God
almyghty, the whiche ys comyn into this prouince for to voydyn owt therof
alle othere goddys.' 'Telle [v]s thanne', quoth they, 'a tokne how we may
knowyn hym.' 'Hys heer', quoth Beryt, 'ys blak and crisp, hys flesshe wyte,
20 gret eyne, his nosethyrlys euene and ryht, hys b[er]d longe hauynge a feue
whyte herys, a cote whyth barryd with purpyl and thervpon a white mantyl,
hauynge in yche cornyr purpyl gemmys. These sexe and tweynty wyntyr
past wex neuere his clothis ner hys sandals old ner foul. An hundryd sythis
on the day, and as manye sythis on the neght, he preyith knelynge. Aun-
25 gels also of God goon aluey with hym, the whiche neuere suffryn hym to
be wery, ner to hungryn, ne to threstyn. He ys alwey of oo cheer and euere
glad and mery. He forseeth alle thyngis and of alle nacyouns he vndyr-
stondyth the languagys and kan spekyn the tungys. And also he knowyth
now how and what I speke with you. And whanne ye sekyn hym, happyly,
30 yf he wyl, ye shul fyndyn hym. And yf he wyl not, ye shul not. Wherfore I
f. 169ᵛᵃ beseche | yow, yf ye happe to fynde, preyith hym that he come not hedyr
ne happe that ys aungls doo no to me here as they han don to my felawe
Asteroth there.'

And whanne they comyn hom and two dayis diligently had seyht and
35 not fowndyn, the thridde day a demoniac criyd this wyse and seyde: 'O
apostel of God, Bartilmeu, th[y] pryers brynne me.' To whom Bartylmeu
seyde ageyn: 'Hoold thy pees, deuyl, and goo ow[t] of this man.' And anoon
he was delyueryd. And whanne the kynge of that regioun, Polemius by
name, whiche had a douthtyr that was lunatyk, herd how thys demoniac
40 was delyueryd, he sente to the apostyll, preyinge hym that he wolde comyn
and makyn hool hys dowtyr. To whoom whanne he cam and saw hys douthtyr lyin boundyn with cheynys, for as she wolde bytyn alle thoo whiche
come ny hyre and foule ferde with hem, he bad anon that she shulde byn
vnbounden. And whanne the ministris d[ur]st not comyn ny here, he seyde
45 to hem: 'I haue boundyn the deuyl whiche was with here and ye byn aferd
to vnbyndyn hyre.' And as sone as she was vnboundyn she was hool and the
apostyl goon. This seynge, the kyng anoon dede chargyn camayls with gold
and syluyr and precyous stonys and maad the apostyl to be seyht, but he
myght not byn foundyn. But on the nexte morwe the apostyl apperyd with
50 the kyng in hys bedchaumbyr and seyde to hym thus: 'Wherfore seytist
thou me yistyrday al day with gold and syluyr and precyous stonys? These
yifftys byn nessessarie to hem whiche louyn erdly thyngis, but pleynly, sire,

18 vs] ys   20 berd] bred   34 two dayis] two   36 thy] they   37 owt]
owut   44 durst] drust

I neythir desire erdly thyng nor flesshly.' And anoon he bygan to teche the
kyng of the manyr of oure redempcyoun, shewynge hym how Crist ouyrcam the deuyl by maruelous congruensse, by power, by rythwyssnesse and   55
by wysdam. 'Fryst congruent yt was', quoth he, 'and conuenyent that, lych
as the deuyl ouyrcam the sone of a mayde, that ys to seyne Adam mad of
the erthe, wyl yt was a mayde shulde byn ouyrcomyn of a mayde, that ys
to seyne of Ihesu Crist the sone of Marye the mayde. Myhtyly he ouyrcam
hym whan myhtyly he kest hym owt of his lordship, whiche he vsurpyd   60
by the victory had and the castynge owt of the fryste man. And lych as he
ouyrcomyth a tiraunt sendyth oueral the lond his officers to excellyn his
tityl and to throwe dou[n] the tirantis signys, ryght so Crist, victour of the
deuyl, sendyth aboutyn ouyral hys massagers to auoydyn the deuyls wurchipe and to magnyfyin and excellyn hys wurshipe. Ryhtfully also Crist   65
wroughte, for rygh yt was that he whiche ouyrcomynge man etyng held
man ouyrcomyn, of a man fastynge shulde no lengere holdyn man. Wyhsly
also he ouyrcam hym whanne the deuyls fals crafft he illudyd by hys hy
wysdam. The craft of the deuyl was by sotyl awayt to han takyn | Crist in   f. 169vb
desert, lych as the sperhauke takyth a berd. The deuyls sotyl awayt on Crist   70
in desert was this: yf this man hungyr not as man, withowtyn ony doute
he ys God. Yf hungyr, as I ouyrcam Adam by mete so shal I don hym.
But God wyshly ouyrcam hym, whanne he myghte not be knowyn for he
hungryd, ner he myghte not be ouyrcomyn for as meche as consentyd not
to the deuyls temptacyoun but resistyt yt.'   75
    And whanne the blyssyd apostil Bartylmeu had longe prechid to the
kyng the sacramentys of the feyth, he seyde onto hym that, yf he wolde
beleuyn and be baptyzid, he shulde shewyn hym hys god boundyn. And on
the nexte day whanne the bysshop[s] of the temple dedyn sacrifice bysyde
the kyngis palays onto here god, he bygan loude to criyin and to seyin: 80
'Cecith, wrecchys, secyth to do sacrifice to me ne hap that ye suffere wers
thyngis than I. For I am boundyn with fiyr brynnynge chenys of the aungels
of Ihesu Crist whoom the Iewys crucyfiyd, wenynge whanne they flowyn
hym that deth mygh han holdyn hym. But he put deth, whiche ys owre
quen, in captyuite and thraldam, and bond oure prince in the fyir bryn-   85
nynge bondys of deth.' At whiche word alle that wern there took ropys and
keste hem ouyr the ydol for to han pullyd yt doun, but they myghte not.
And an[on] the apostyl comaundyd the deuyl to gon owt of the ydol and
brekyn yt hymself. Whoos comaundement he fulfillyd anon. And not only
he brak hys w[e]yn ydol, but also alle the ydols of the temple. Whiche don   90

55 the deuyl] the   63 doun] douun   79 bysshops] bysshop   88 anon]
anam   90 weyn] wyn

the apostyl curyd and maad hool alle the seek men in the temple whiche
longe had veynly abydyn Astrotys helpe. Aftyr this the apostil dedicat and
halwyd the temple and bad the deuyl gon hys wey into a desert place. And
thanne anoon an aungyl of God apperyd there visibly, and fley aboute the
95 temple and enpryntyd with his fyngyr a syngne of the cros in the foure cor-
ners therof, seyinge thus: 'This seyith oure lord: "lych as I haue curyd yow
whiche wern seek from youre bodyly syknesse, ryght so this temple shal
be maad clene from al manyr fylthe of ydols. And aftyr that I shal shewe
yow the dwellen therof, byforn whoom the apostyl hath bodyn goon into
100 desert." Whoom whan ye seen, beth not aferd but swych a marke as ye han
seen me mad in the stonys, prendyth ye with youre thoumbe in youre for-
hedys.' Whiche wurdys seyid, anoon he shewyd hem an Ethiop blakkere
than soot, with a sharp face and a longe berd, hys here hangynge doun
to hys feet, hys eyne flaumynge, sendyng owt sparkys as hoot brynnynge
105 iryn, brethyng owt flaumys of brent brenston bothe at hys mouth and at hys
nosethyrlys, hys handys boundyn at hys bak wyth fyir brynnygne cheynys.
To whoom the aungyl thus seyde: 'For as meche as thou herdyst the pre-
f. 170ra cept of the apostyl and hast brokyn alle the | ydolys in the temple, I shall
vnbyndyn the. And loke thou goo into swych a place where no man dwel-
110 lyth, and there I charge the to abydyn tyl the day of doom.' And whanne
he thus was vnboundyn of the aungyl, with a gret rorynge and lamentable
whoulynge he went hys weye, God wot wydyr. But the aungyl of God, alle
men seyinge, fley vp ageyn onto the blysse of heuene.

Al this seyinge the kynge, he, with hys wyf and his childryn and alle
115 hys peple, was baptizid. But the kyng forsook hys kyngdam and bycam
the apostlys dyscyple and foluyd hym aboute. Whanne the bysshops of the
temple sey this they were wroth and, alle gadryd togedyr, they wentyn to
Astriages, Polemyus brothir, and madyn a greuous compleynt of the lesyng
of here goddys, of the subuercyon of here temple and deceyt of here kyng
120 by wycchecraft, and al thys doon by the apostil. Astriages, hauyng of this
martyr gret indygnacyoun, sente a thousent for to takyn the apostil. To
whom, brough byforn hym, he seyde on this wyse: 'Art thou he that hast
peruertyd myn brothir?' 'I haue not', quoth the apostil ageyn, '[peruertyd],
but conuertyd thi brothir.' 'Weel', quoth Astriages, 'sikyr, lych as thou hast
125 mad my brothir to forsakyn hys god and to don sacrifice to thy god, so shal
I do the forsakyn and to doon sacrifice to myn god.' 'I haue', quoth the
apostil, 'boundyn the god whom thi brothir wurshipd and shewyd hym
boundyn, and maad hym to brekyn hys simulacre. Yf thou now thus seruyn

123 peruertyd] not peruertyd

my God thou mayst sone prouoke to the sacrifice of thy god. And yf thou
mow not I shal breke thy god and thanne byleue thou on my God.'   130

This wurd seyde, anon cam a massager and brough Astriages tidyn-
gys that hys god Baldic was tumblyd do[un] and brokyn al to nouht. And
whanne Kyng Astriages herd this, he rente hys purpyl that he had on and
comaundyd the apostyl to byn bete with battys, and aftir that to byn flayn
al quyk and sithyn, as yt ys seyd in summe legendys, to byn hefdyd. Whoos   135
body cristene stolyn and buryid yt wurshipfully. The Kyng Astriages and
the bysshops of the temple, euene forthwith stranglyd with deuyls, deyid
and wente hom with hem to helle. Kyng Polemye maad a bysshope, twenty
wentyr ocupiyd that office laudabylly and aftyr, ful of vertuous merytys,
restid in oure lord.   140

Of the kynde of hys passioun there byn dyuers opinyouns. For Seynt
Dorotheus seyith that he was crucyfiyd, whoos wurdys byn these: 'Bartylmeu prechid to the men of Ynde, the whiche yaf hem fryst the gospel
aftyr Mathu in here tunge. He deyid in Albano, a cyte of Armenie, the[r]
crucyfiyd and hauynge hys heed dounward.' *Hec ille*. Sanctus Theodorius   145
seyith that he was flayn. In manye othere bokys ys oonly red that he was
hefdyd. | But thys contrariousnesse may byn assoylyd on this wyse. Yt   f. 170rb
may be seyid that he was fryst crucyfiyd of the peple. Aftyr on the same
place, er thanne he deyid, that he was [f]layn and at the laste hefdyd.

The yer of oure lord thre hundryd and oon and thritty, Sarecenys   150
comyng to Cicile wastyd and dystroyd the yle clepyd Liparis, where the
body of Seynt Bartilmeu restid, and brokyn his graue and dysperbyld his
bonys. But for as meche as yt myghte be doutyd how hys bonys come to
that yle so feer fro there he was martyrid, here yt ys to be notyd that the
peple where he was fryst buryid, seying dayly at hys graue so gret miraclis   155
wrough and therby his body gretly wurshiphd, they haddyn indignacyoun
therof. Wherfore they puttyn yt in a web of led and threwyn yt into the
see. And so, by the werkyng of Goddys singuler and special grace, yt cam
to the forseyid yle and there yt was buriyd ageyn, and lay there tyl the
Sarasinys comyn at this tyme and disperbyld hem, as yt ys seyid byforn.   160
And whanne they were goon, the blyssid apostyl apperid to a munk and
seyde: 'Rys vp and goo gadyr togedyr my bonys, for they ben disperbyld
and cast abrood.' 'By what resoun', quoth the munk ageyn, 'shulde we
gadryn thy bonys or doo the ony wurshipe, syth thou suffryddyst vs to be
dystroyid and woldyst not helpyn vs?' 'Sykyr', quoth he, 'God hath sparyd   165
the peple of this yle longe tyme for my myritis and my preyeris. But the

132 doun] douun   144 ther] the   149 flayn] slayn   166 for my] for

peplis synnys continuely growynge and cryinge veniauns to heneue, I
myghte now no grace getyn for hem.' 'How shal I thanne knowe yowre
bonys', quoth the munk, 'amonge so manye othere as be dysperblyd?'
170 'Goo by nyght', quoth he, 'and tho thou seest shynyn as fiyr gadyr for to
ben myne.' As he comaundyd the munk dede, and karye[d] hem ouyr the
see to the heed cyte of Apulie clepyd Beneuentum.

    The holy abot and doctour Theodorus, among othere, thus seyith of
this blyssid apostil: 'The apostil of God, Bartilmeu, prechyd fryst in Ly-
175 coonye, aftyrward in Inde, at the laste in Albano, a cyte of Armenye the
more, where he was slayn, hefdyd and buryid. This Bartilmeu, as I opine',
quoth he, 'whanne he was fyrst sent to prechyn, herd oure lord seyin to
hym thus: "Goo, my disciple, to prechyn. Goo to batayle and be partener of perilis. I haue performyd my fadrys wyl and endyd hys werk, maad
180 hys fyrste wytnesse. Folue thy maistyr and thy lord. Put flesshe for flesshe
and blood for blood and, whatsoeuere I haue sufferyd, suffere thou. Thyn
armowre mote be benyngnyte and buxumnesse amonge euyldoers, pacience amonges hem whiche that perysshyn." The apostil seyde not "nay",
but as a fey[th]ful seruaunt obeyinge his lordys comaundementis wente
185 forth gladly as the leyht of the word to illumynyn thirknesse, as the salt
f. 170ᵛᵃ of the erthe to sauour with vnsauery | [peple], and as a good plowman to
performyn gostely tilthe.'

    And aftyr a long processe of hys lyf and of his fyrste translac[i]oun in
to the yle clepid Lyparis, he concludyd on this wyse: 'Now farewyl blys-
190 syd of blyssyd, o thryis blyssid Bartilmeu, whiche art the br[i]thnesse of
Goddys lyght, the fysshere of holy cherche, the swete fruht of the quyk
palme, and woundere of the deuyl whiche woundyd the word with hys
theffte and robberye. Ioye and be glad, o sunne of the word illumynynge alle
thyngis, mouth of God, tunge of fyir sheuynge wysdam, welle cont[i]nuely
195 bolynge vp helthe, whiche halwysdyst the see with thy woundyrful pathis
and depoyntyddyst the erthe purpil with thy reed blood, and aftyr that
wentyst euene vp to heuene. Where in the mydys of Goddys ost thou shy-
nyst with the bry[ght]nesse of blysse that may not wykkyn, and ioyist wythe
the gladnesse whiche neuere shal secyn.' *Hec Theodorus.* Whydyr, throuh
200 the merytys of blyssed Bartilmeu, finally vs brynge Crist Ihesu, amen.

171 karyed] karye   184 feythful] feythtful   186 peple] pleple   188 trans-
lacioun] translacoun   190 brithnesse] brothnesse   194 continuely] contunely
198 bryghtnesse] bryngnesse

[144. AUGUSTINE]

The prologe into Seynt Austyns lyf

This name Augustinus was congruently youyn to Seynt Austyn for thre causis: as for excellence of dignite, for feruour of loue and cherite, and for interpretacyoun of the name. As for excellence fyrst of dyngnite yt longyth to hym conuenyently. For lych as August[u]s the emperour superexcellyd 5 alle kyngys, as Austyn surmountyd alle doctourys, as seyith Remigius. For whiche cause, whanne alle othere doctours byn lyknyd to sterrys, scripture seyinge Daniel 12°: 'They that techyn othere men to ryghtwyssnesse shul shynyn as sterrys perpetually.' Austyn alone ys comparyd to the sunne, as yt ys reed in the epistil of hys feste, where yt ys seyd that as a brygh sunne 10 he shoon in the temple of God. The secunde congruense bytwyx Austyn and his name ys for feruour of loue and charite. For lych as the monyth of August ys more feruent in hete than othere monyths, so Austyn passith in parfyth loue and charite manye othere doctours. Of wych hete and feruour he hymself spekyth in hys Confessiouns in dyuers placys. 15

The thride congruence bytwyx Austyn and his name ys for the interpretacyoun therof. For Augustinus ys diriuyid of *Augio es*, whiche signifyith to encrecyn, and *Austin* whiche singnifyith a cyte. And *ana* whiche singnifiyth vpward or abouyn. And so Augustinus ys as meche to seyne as increcynge the cyte vpward, that ys to seyne the blysse of heuene. Wher- 20 fore yt ys seyid in his epistil th[at] he preuaylyd to amplyfye or to make large the cyte. Or ellys, as yt ys seyid in the glosarie, Augustinus ys as myche to seyne as gret werkynge, brygh shynynge | and hap- f. 170ᵛᵇ pyly regnynge. Gret werkynge was Austyn in hys lyue, bryght shynynge in hys famous doctrine, and happyly regnynge afftyr hys deth in the blysse 25 of heuene.

The lyf of thys blyssyd man Austyn wrot Possidonius Calamensis Episcopus, sumtyme hys dyssyple, as seyth Cassiodorus in his book clepyd *De Viris Illustribus et cetera*.

The lyf of Seynt Austyn the Doctour. 30

The holy and glorious doctour Seynt Austin was b[or]n in Affrica in a cyte clepyd Tagatence of a nobyl and w[o]rthy linage, whos fadyr hyht Patricius, a hethene man tyl the yer byforn that he deyid. Hys modrys name was Monica, a cristene woman and an holy. This Austyn, in hys nownage

5 Augustus] Augustius   21 that] the   31 born] bron   32 worthy] warthy

35 vertuously educat and brouth at hoom, lernyd suffyciently hys bookis in
the cyte Maudarence and in bryff tyme, so that aboute the sextente yer of
hys age he thaute retheric in Cartage, the whiche he had fyrst tauht in hys
own cyte Tagatence.

This seyid Austyn, oo tyme why[l] he was ying, was gretly and gre-
40 uously vexid in hys stomook. Wherfore his modyr, dredynge hys deth,
counseld hym for to byn cristenyd, but his fadyr, which that tyme was
hethene, wolde not sufferyn yt. And so for a tyme his baptem was delayid.
In which menetyme, by helpe of grace, hys peyne secyd and he was
hool. And per[a]uenture hys puryficacyoun by baptem was deferrid, for
45 as meche as yf he lyuyd he shulde nedys be defoulyd more yet, and his
offence shulde be the more greuous yf he synnyd aftyr his baptem. The
letters of Gru whiche he was tauht he hatyd, but Latyn letteris he loued
wyl inow. Soo gret was his wyt and his entendement so sotil, that alle the
liberal science he vndyrstod by hymself whanne he red hem, withowtyn
50 ony techyn[g] of man. As he seyith hymself in hys Confessiouns, where he
concludyth thus: 'Whatsoeuere I rede of crafft of spekynge, of dysputynge,
of fyguris, of musikys, and of wit, I vndyrstood withowtyn ony difficulte,
no man outward techynge me. Lord God', quoth he, 'thou knowyst that
redinesse of vndyrstondynge and the sharpnesse of lernynge ys thy yifte,
55 but yit, Lord, dede I noo sacrifice therof.' *Hic ibi.*

But, for as meche as kunnynge withowte cherite edyfiy[th] not, but
blowyth and bolnyth into pride, God sufferid hym to fallyn into the
Man[i]ches heresie, the whiche affyrmyn that Crist took a fantastical
and not a very body, and denyn also the laste resurreccioun, with manye
60 othir lowid opynyouns. And this was whanne he was nynetene yer old,
and he contunyd therin nyne yer ful. And so fer he was brough into here
f. 171ra fonnydnesse | that he wende that a fygge tre had wept whanne a fygge or
a lef ys plukkyd therfro, as he seyth in hys Confessions.

Moreouyr, also whan he was nyntene yer old and redde a book of Tullius
65 wiche ys clepyd Hortencius, wherein ys tawt how the vanyte of the word
shuld be dyspisid, for so myche yt plesith hym weel. But, for as meche as
the name of Crist, the whiche he had imbibid, that ys to seyne drunkyn
yt in from hys modrys brest, was not there, yt rauasshid hym not al. In
the tyme thanne that he was thus merykyd in the Manichees herese, his
70 modyr wepte for hym many a byttyr teer. And on a tyme as blyssid womman was bysy to preyin for hyre sone, here thoute she stood in a reule of
tre, sory and heuy, and a yunge man cam to hyre smylynge and askyd hyre

---

35 hys bookis] hys   39 whyl] why   44 perauenture] peruenture
50 techyng] techyn   56 edyfiyth] ediyfyd   58 Maniches] Manuches

the cause of here heuynesse. And whanne she had answerd hym and seyde
that she lamentyd and mornyd the perdiciown of hyre sone Austyn, he
seyde ageyn to here meryly: 'Be of good cheer, woman, for ther thou art,   75
ther ys he.' And anoon forthwith she saw hym stondyn[g] bysydyn hyre
in the same reule. Which visioun whanne she told hyre sone, he cauthe-
lously answerd ageyn and seyde: 'Modyr, thou art deceyuyd. For yt was
not seyd to the "Where thou art, ther ys he", but rathere "Where he ys,
ther art thou".' 'Nay sykyr, nay, sone', quoth she ageyn, 'not so. But thus   80
yt was seyid to me: "Where thou art, there ys he".' Aftyrward this bysy
modyr preyid a certeyn byshop that he wolde spekyn with hyre sone and
refellyn hys errours. Aftyr longe inportune instaunce of hyre preyinge, he
to hyre seyde ageyn, euene wery of hyre inportunite: 'Goo froo me', quoth
he, 'by so thou lyue. For yt ys inpossible that the sone of these so many   85
terrys shulde perysshyn.' The whiche answere Monica as gladly took as yt
had sowndynge from heuene.

And whanne that Austyn had in Cartage t[aut] reth[or]ic manye yers,
hys modyr not w[e]teng, wente to Rome, and there togydir manye dysciplis, and tawt the same faculte there. I[n] whiche menewhile they of Malan   90
sentyn to the prefect of Rome, whiche that tyme was clepid Simacus, preyinge hym to sendyn hem a doctoure in Rethoric. And at here gret instaunce
and request Austyn was sent thedyr, where that tyme was bysshop the
weel-belouyd seruaunt of God and famously knowyn to al the word, blyssyd Ambrose. And whanne blyssyd Monica herd of hyre sonys pilgrimage,   95
she cowde han no reste tyl she seye hym. And so with gret difficulte, bothe
on lond and watyr, she cam to Malan to hym. Whidyr whan she cam and
fond hym wauerynge and titubamich, that ys to seyne neythir manichee
ner cristene man, she was glad that he was delyueryd of falsheed, albeyt
that he not yet had get the truthe. | And Seynt Ambrose she louyd as   f. 171rb
an aungel of God, knowynge weel that by hym hyre sone was brough to   101
that vacillaunt indeference, and fully trostynge that he shulde by hym be
brouth of cristene feyth to the perfyth credence. Ambrose was lovyd by the
peple, and was a man of gret and singuler elequence. Austyn drow myche
to hym and was rygh glad to heryn hym, nerthe[l]es he aluey rygh sus-   105
pens and wakyrly lystenynge, ne hap that ony thyng shulde be seyid eythir
for the manichees errour er ther ageyns. And as yt happyd, or for to seyin
more truly as yt was dysposid and ordeynyd by the eternal prouidence of
God, blyssyd Ambrose vpon a day disputyd longe ageyns that erroure, and

76 stondyng] stondyn   88 taut] twaut   rethoric] rethroic   89 weteng wente]
wenteng   90 In] I   99 he was] he   103 Ambrose was lovyd by the] the
105 nertheles] nerthees

110 vttyrly bothe with auctorites and resons disprouyd yt, in so meche that fro
that tyme forth the openioun was fully put awey from Austyns herte. And
what fel to hym aftyr this he tellyth in hys Confessiouns, seyinge on this
wyse: 'Lord God, whan I fyrst knewe the, thou beet ageeyn the infirmyte
and the febylnesse of myn syth, shynynge in me maruelously; and I treme-
115 lyd in mynself with loue and errour. And I fond myself to byn fer fro the
in the regioun of vnlyknesse, as thow I had herd thy woys from hy abouyn
seyinge to me on this wise: "I am the mete of grete men growe and thou
shall etyn me, but yet thou shalt not chaunge me into the, as thow doost
the mete of thy flesshe, but thou shalt be chaungyd into me".'
120 And whanne, as yt seyid forth there, the weye of God plesyth hym but
yet yt yrkyth hym to gon therby, God sent into his soule a styrynge of wyl
to gon to Simplicyan the ermyte, in whom shoon the grace of God, to tellyn
hym hys inward meuynge and stiryngys and to heryin ageyn of hym whiche
were an able maner of lyuynge to goon in the weye of God, wherein, aftyr
125 his felynge, on wente oo wyse, anothyr anothyr wyse. Whatsoeuere he dede
in the word dysplesid hym, for the swetnesse of God and the bewte of his
hous, the whiche he louydde. Simplicyan anoon bygan to exhortyn hym
to the mekenesse of Crist. And among manye othir thyngis he told hym
of the gret philosophir and retherrian of Rome, the whiche for hys gret
130 excellence in kunnynge deseruyd and had a statue set in the opyn market
in Rome, that the cyteseyns of this word holdyn a gret wurthyneese; how
that aftyr this gret werdly pompe was not ashamyd to byn Cristis chyld.
'This Victorinus', quoth Simplycian, 'whom I knew familiarly at Rome,
whom I exhortyd to the mekenesse of Crist as I now do yow. And he offtyn
135 answerde me and seyde: "Knowe wyll now that I am a Cristene man." To
whoom also whanne I seyde "I wylle not leuyn yt but yf I see the in the
f. 171va cherche", he myryly concludyd ageyn on this wyse: "Than | semyth yt",
quoth he, "that the cherche wallys makyn cristene men." At the laste he
seyde feythfully to me and sadly: "Goo we, Simplicyan, into the cherche;
140 for sekyr I wele ben a cristene man." And whan we comyn into the cherche
and the our cam whanne he shulde makyn a professioun of Cristene feyth,
as alle men dedyn wyche comyn therto, the whiche profe[ss]ioun was mad
vndyr a certeyn forme of wordys, for as [meche as] he was sumtyme shamefast ther was takyn hym a book therof for to haue yt priuyly, but he wold
145 not. But opynly he stood vp in the cherche and with an hy voyis he declaryd hys feyth, al men there present yt herynge; Rome maruaylyng and the
cherche ioyinge.'

142 professioun] profeffessioun   143 meche as] meche as meche as

And thanne cam oon from Affrica, a fr[e]nd of Austyn c[l]epyd Poncianus, and rehersyd th[e]re the lyf and the miraclis of gret Antonye, the
which examplys Austyn, gretly meuyd and enflaumyd, feruently desiryd 150
for to foluyn hem. In so myche that he, basshyd bothe in herte and in
cher, seyde to Alipie hys felaue on this wyse: 'What ys that we sufferyn
and what ys that we heryn, o Alipie? Simple vntawt men rysyn vp, and we
with ow[r]e doctrinis slydryin into helle.' Wyche wurdys seyde, he wente
into a gardyn bysydyn the hous and kest doun hymself there vndyr a fygge 155
tre and, most bittyrli wepynge, he brast owt with this lamentable voys and
seyde: 'How longe, lord, how longe? Tomorwe, tomorwe! Whi not now?
A lord, suffere now, suffere a litil. Allas, now hath no maner and a litil
ys goon into longe tyme.' And many anothir dolorus compleynt he made,
condempnynge hys slauthe and preyinge God mekely of helpe, as whooso 160
wyl sekyn yt shall fyndyn in his Confessiouns. And aftyr this longe byttyr
wepynge and his lamentable conpleynt, sodeynly he herd a voys seyin thus:
'Take and rede, take and rede.' A[t] which wurd he lokyd vp and saw a
book of Seynt Poulys epistyls lyinge vpon a pleying tabler and he opnyd
anon. And the fyrste thyng that cam to hys eye was this: *Induimini domi-* 165
num Ihesum Christum et carnis curam ne feceritis in desiderijs, that is to seyne:
'Clothe yow, or doth on, oure lord Ihesu and beth not bysy to performyn
the flesshely desiris!' And as sone as he had red this processe, withoute
more anoon, as thouh a lyht of sykyrnesse had be infoundyd in his soule,
alle the therk clowdys of doute vanysshid awey from hym. 170
   In thys menetyme sodeynly he was tormentyd with so huge a peyne of
his tooth that, as he seyth in Confessiouns, he was ner brough to the open-
youn of phylosophir clepid Cornelius, the whiche held that the souereyn
goodnesse of mannys soule ys wysdam. And so gret and so greuous was
the peyne that yt beryth hym hys speche. Wherfore he wrot in tabls | of f. 171ᵛᵇ
wex, preyinge hem that wern abowtyn hym for to preyin for hym. And 176
anon alle they knelyd doun to preyin, and he hymself wyth hem, that God
wolde swagyn hys peyne. And euene sodeynly the peyne wente awey and
he was hool.
   Aftyr this h[e] wrot to Seynt Ambrose how he was dysposid, preyinge 180
hym of counsel what book of holy scripture he shuld redyn, wherby he
mygh byn the more able and the more redy to receyuyn the grace of cristene feyth. And he counselyd hym to takyn Isaye the profete, for as meche
as yt sempt to hym that he was the most opyn tellere of the gospel and of
the clepynge of the folk to the feyth. But Austyn, not vndyrstondyng the 185

148 frend] frond   clepyd] chepyd   149 there] thre   154 owre] owte
163 At] And   172 his tooth] his   180 he] his

bygynnynge and wenynge that yt were also hard, he wolde no more rede
ther tyl he were more exercysid in redynge of holy scripture. And whan
the feste of Estryn cam, in the thre and thrytty yer of hys age, he reseyuyd of Seynt Ambrose the holy sacrement of baptem wyth his sone clepyd
190 Deodatus, a wytty chyld whom he begat whan he was hethene, and a philosophir and anothir frend of hys clepyd Alipius. In whyche baptem, as
seyth Dacyus in his cronicle, Ambrose bygan and seyde: *Te Deum Laudamus*, and Austyn answerde *Te dominum confitemur.* And so they two, oon
aftyr anothir, madyn that ympne togydyr.

195 Aftyr whiche tyme Austyn, maruaylously and perfyhtly confermyd in
the feyth, forsook al the ope and trust whiche he had in the word and
renouncyd the scolys which he gouernyd, and fully purposyd hym to
seruyn God alone. And with what swetnesse of Goddys loue he was touchyd aftyr this he tellyth in hys Confessiouns, seyinge on this wyse: 'Lord
200 God, thou settyst myn herte with thy cherite and I bar this wurdys fyxid
in myn bowayls as shar[p] aruys.' And so forth manye thyngis he seyth
of gret and hy contemplacions, the which I leue to the reders solicitude
to sekyn.

Aftyr this he took with hym hys modyr, hys sone, Nebrye and Euodye
205 and othir dyuers hermytis whiche blyssid Simplician had grauntyd hym,
and turnyd ageyn to Afric-ward. But whanne he cam to Ostye, hys blyssyd modyr deyid and was buryid there. Aftyr whoos deth he wente forth
hom to hys own passiouns where, with hem that wenten with hym and with
othere frendys that drow to hym, in fastyng and preyeris wrot bookys and
210 ta[w]th hem whiche wern vnkunnynge. Whoos fame sp[re]d aboutyn ouer
al, for in his bokys and in alle hys werkys he was maruaylous. And euere he
eschewid to gon to ony cyte wiche wantyd a b[i]sshop, that he in no wyse
shulde be lettyd from his entent. In which menewhile a riche man in the
cite of Ipon sent to Austyn that, yf he myghte onys heryn the word of God
f. 172ra by his mouth, that he wold forsakyn | the word. And [w]hanne Austyn
216 herde this he wente thedyr anon, and whanne Valerie the bysshop of the
same cyte herd this he sente for hym. And, allebeyt that he wolde not, he
maad hym a prest in his cherche. For whanne he was mad he wepte ful
sore. And yit summe interpretynge his teris ascryuyd hem to pride, and be
220 manere of confortynge sedyn onto hym: 'Alle yt be that ye be more wurthi
thanne the degre of presthood, yeet b[e]the of good chere. For sekyr the
place of preysthood ys ny to the dyngnite of a bysshop.' And whanne Austyn thus was mad a preyst, anon he maad a monastorie of clerkys within the

| 201 sharp] shard | 210 tawth] twath | spred] sperd | 212 bisshop] bosshop |
| 215 whanne] thanne | 220 yt be] yt | 221 bethe] bothe | |

cherche and bygan to lyuyn with hem aftyr the reule ordeynyd by the holy apostlys; of whoos monasterye were ner ten chosyn to be bysshops. And, 225 for as myche as the forseyd bysshop was a grec and not or lytil instruct in latyn tunge, he yaf Austin licence ageyns the maner of the oriental cherche to preychin byforn hym in his cherche. And whanne manye othere bysshops put defaute in hym therfore, he yaf no fors whyl that yt was doun by hym that he neythir myghte ner cowde doon hi[m]self.   230

In this same tyme of hys preysthood vndyr Valerye he ouercam and drof awey fro thens Fortunat, a prest of the Manichees, whiche with his cautelous do[c]trine deceyuyd meche peple and othere heritykys, and pryncipally them wern twyis baptyzid, as the Donatistys, and purgyd weel that cyte of hem. Valerie, considerynge the good lyuynge, the excellent kun- 235 nynge and the famowus report of his preyst, Austyn, bygan to vaxyn aferd that he shulde byn askyd awey from hem of sum othir cyte for to byn here bysshop, for diuers tymys byforn he had so byn but that he hyd hym in swych a priuy place that he myghte not be foundyn. Wherfore he maad gret instaunce to the erchebysshop of Cartage that he myghte secyn and 240 Austyn byn ordeynyd in his stede, and he gat yt. Werto whanne Austyn wolde not consentyn, by the erchebisshop he was conpellyd and took the cure of the bysshopryche, the whiche to doon in hym, that ys to seyne to byn ordeynyd, his bysshop lyuynge. Whanne he aftyr his consecracioun had lernyd the general counsels prohibicyoun, he disprouyd yt bothe in 245 w[ur]d and wrytynge to the pope. And that he sorwyd and was heuy to haue be don in hym, he wold not shulde be doun in otthere. Wherfore he labouryd and bysiyd hym that in the ordenaunce of bysshops alle the statutys of the fadrys shuld be declaryd onto hem or thanne they were ordeynyd of hem that shuldyn sacryn hem. And as for hymself he wold seyin ful off- 250 tyn this wurd: 'In nothyng sothly I fele, myn lord God', quoth he, 'so wroth wyth me as in that whanne I was not wurthi to be put | at an oore, I was f. 172ʳᵇ put at the helm, in the heed of gouernaunce of a cherche.'

Hys clothynge, hys hosyn and hys shoon, and his othere ornementys were neythyr to shynynge ner to abyect, but of moderat and conpetent 255 habite. For wee redyn that he seyde oftyn thus: 'I knoweleche treuely', quoth he, 'that of a precious garnement I am ashamyd. Wherfore whanne ony ys youe me I selle yt, that for the cloth may not be comyn, the prehs shall be comoun.' Hys table was moderat and skars and bytwyx wurtys and pese or bene potage; sumtyme for gestys and for see[k] men he had 260 fleysshe. And yet in his table he louyd byttyr redynge or dysputynge thanne

230 himself] hiself   233 doctrine] dotrine   246 wurd] wrud   260 seek]
seel

mete or drynk. And ageyns the pestelence of detraccyoun he had these two wers wretyn abouyn his table: *Quisquis amat dictis absentum r[o]dere uitam.* *Hanc mensam indignam nouerit esse sibi*: 'Whoso loue of folk absent the lyff
265 to gnawyn with male-entent, this table to hym vnwurthy lete hym knowe to be.' Sothly wherfore sumtyme whanne othere byss[o]ps most famuliar with hym slakyd here tungis at hys table to detraccioun, [sharply] he wolde vndyrnymyn hem, that he seyde that he wolde puttyn awey the vers or ellys hymself goon fro the table. Oo tyme also whanne he had bodyn certeyn
270 citeseyns to mete, whiche he was familiar with and they with hym, oon of hem more corious thanne othere wente heuily into the kechyn to seen how they shulde faryn. Where whanne he fond a thynge cold he wente to Austyn and askyd hym what mete he had ordeynyd for his gestis that day. To whoom he, nothyng coryous of swyche maner metys, answerde ageyn
275 and seyde: 'For sothe', quoth he, 'and I wot no more than ye.' Wyn he had aluey at his table, but he vsid yt sobyrly aftyr the counsel of Poule to Timo-thee. The vessel wyche he was seruyd with at the table was glas or erthe or marbyl, not for penurye but of purpos and wyl. His sponys only wern of syluyr.
280 Th[re] thyngis also he was woone to seyin that he lernyd of Seynt Ambrose. The fyrste was that he shulde procuryn no wyf to no man, ne hap that yf they acordyd not they shulde cursyn hem bothe. The secunde lessoun was that he shulde counselyn no man ner preyse no man that wolde byn a soudyour, ne hap that yf he iniuryid ony man they wolde arrettyn the
285 defaute to the counselour or the counfortour. The thridde ys that, though he were bodyn to a feste, that he shulde not come ther, ne hap that he passyd the mesure of temperaunce and fel into the foul dych of edacite or glotonye.

Of so gret purite of conscience and of mekenesse was this blyssyd Aus-
290 tyn that he shryuyth hym and mekely acusith hymself to God in the book of hys Confessiouns of tho synnys whiche we holdyn lityl or non. For there he
f. 172va shryuyth | hym of that whanne he was a shyld he pleyid at the bal whanne he shulde han goon to scole. Also of that he wolde not redyn ne lernyn but he were constreynyd therto by his fadyr, or his modyr, or his maystir. Also
295 of that he wolde gladly and delectabylly redyn poetys fablys, and wepte whanne he redde that D[ido] deyid for loue. Also of that he stal sumtyme breed owt of his fadrys celer, for to yeuyn othere chylderyn wyche pleyid with hym. Also of that in chyldryns pley he vsyd offtyn sleythe and gyle and was fraudelent and deceytful victorious. Also of that he stal applis owt

of a mannys yerd nex his vineyerd whanne he was sextene yer old. Also, in 300
the same book of Confessiouns, he shryuyth hym of that lityl delectacyoun that he felte sumtyme in etynge and in drynkynge. In wyche matyr he
seyth thus: 'Lord God, thou tawtyst me that I shulde neyhyn to take mete
and drynk as I shulde takyn medycyn. But whyl I passe', quoth he, 'from
the heuynesse of indigence or nede to the reste of fulnesse, in that passage 305
ys priuyly hyd the snare of concupiscence. Thys passage that I goo by ys
volupteuous delectacyoun, and yet ys ther non weye to go by for to comyn
thedyr whedyr necessite constreynyth to goon. And whanne helthe of body
shulde be cause of etyng and drynkynge, peryllous necessite ioynyth hyre
to goon byforn that yt myghte be don by cause of hyre that I seye me don, 310
or wolde me don, bycause of helthe. Drunkeship, lord, ys fer fro me. Haue
mercy on me, lord, that y[t] come not ny me. I[mmo]derat and noyous
voracite or glotousnesse yet neuere, lord, creep into thy seruant. Shewe
thy mercy, lord, that yt neuere touche me. And whoo ys he, lord, which
ys neuere rau[i]sshyd owt of the boundys of necessite? Whoosoeuere he 315
be, sykyr, lord, he hys gret with the. Lete hym magnifiyn thyn name, lord!
Mercy, I am not that man for I am [a] synful man.' *Hec Augustinus.*

And thus he makyth his confessioun of alle hys fyue wyttys. Heretikys also this blyssyd piler of holy cherche most myghtyly counfoundyd. To
whoom therfore he was so odious that they prechyd opynly that yt was non 320
synne to sleen hym, no more thanne y[t] was to slen a wulf. And moreouyr
they affermyd that, whoo-so slow hym, hys synnys wern foryouyn of God.
Wherfore, ful oftyn whanne he wente owtward, he was waytyd for the same
entent, but the eternal prouidence of God wold not suffryn yt.

Of pore men also he aluey had mynde and liberal yaf hem part of swych 325
as he hadde. And also oftyn he mad holy cherche vessels to be brokyn and
to byn coynyd to redemyn with pore caytyuys. Hous ner lond he wolde
neuere noon byin, and manye heritagis leffth hym by testamentys he for-
sok and seyde that thoo awt rathere be leffth to the dedys chyldryn or to
here ny kyn. | Of swyche thyngis as he hadde he was inplyid ner ocupiyd f. 172ᵛᵇ
with loue ner solicitude therof, but euere nyght and day his meditacyoun 331
and hys mynde was in holy scripture. Of newe byldyng of hous he was
neuere stodyous. Nertheles he wolde not defendyn othere men to makyn
hem, lesse thanne the wern ouer-sumpteuous.

He preysyd also meche hem the whiche haddyn a desi[y]r to deyin and 335
thervpon he oftyn rehersyd exaumplys of thre bysshopis. 'Ambrose', quoth
he, 'my fadyr in Cristys sacrementis, whanne he was in hys laste poynt of

---

312 yt] ys   Immoderat] inmederat   315 rauisshyd] rausshyd   317 a] as
319 also this] also   321 yt] ys   335 desiyr] desiryr

lyuynge and was bysouth of hys citeseyns to prolongyn hys lyf with preyers, answerde ageyn and seyde: "I haue not so lyuyd that me yrkyth to lyuyn
340 amonge yow, ner I drede not to deyin, seyth we han a good lord".' The
wyche answere Austyn gretly extollyd and preysid. He told also of anothir
bysshop, to whom yt was seyd whanne he lay in deyinge that, for he was
yet necessarye, he shulde preyin God that he wolde delyueryn hym. He
answerde ageyn and seyde: 'Yf neuere weel, or yf ony tyme weel, why not
345 now?' 'The thrydde example ys of a bysshop', quoth he, 'of whom Ciprian
seyith that, oo tyme whanne he labouryd in a greuous syknesse and preyid
God yet to ben heyl ageyn, there apperyd to hym a comely yunge man and
grucchid ageyns hym and seyde "Ye drede to sufferyn, ye wyl not goon
hens. What shal y doo to yow?"'
350   Wumman wolde he noon suffryn to dwellyn with hym, neythyr sustyr
ner cosyn, ner hys brotherys douthtrys, the wyche seruyd God togydyr.
For thogh of hys sustyr and nyftys mygh non euyl suspecioun be gendryd,
yit, for as meche personys mow not byn wyth[o]wtyn othere, and also
manye othir muste oftyn comyn to hem, 'Therof', quoth he, 'myghte they
355 wyche arn feble and not rygh stronge eythir mygh be stiryd with tempacy-
ouns of frelnesse, or ellys byn aperyd by mennys euyl suspicyons.' Nor he
wolde neuere spekyn with no woman alone, but yt were in confessioun.
    To his kennysmen he dede so that neythyr they shuldyn han richesse,
ner they shuld nat myche nedyn. Seldum wolde he preyin for ony man,
360 eythir by w[ry]tynge or be wurd. For oftyn the gret or myghty man that
askyth, brosith. Nertheles, whanne he wrot for ony man he tempryd so his
style that he shulde not byn onerous, but rathere deseruyn to byn herd for
curteyse of his entent. Also he wolde rathere aluey here causis bytwyxe
hem that he knewe not, thanne bytwyxyn hys frendys; for bytwyx hem he
365 mygh frely knowyn the truthe. And also, for on of hem he shuld makyn hys
frend: hym, that ys [t]o seyne, for whom by mene of ryghnesse he shulde
yiue the sentence. But of hys frendys he shulde lesyn oon: hym ageyns
whom he shulde yiuyn the sentence.
f. 173ʳᵃ   Of | manye cherchis he was preyid to comyn and prechyn there the
370 wurde of God, and manye men he co[n]uertyd from here errour. And
oftyn tyme he was wone to makyn a digressioun from his purpos in his
sermoun, and thanne he wolde seyin that God had ordeynyd that for the
helthe of sum man there present. As yt happyd onys in a marchaunt of
the monachees, the wyche byn a digressioun of Austin in his sermoun, in

353 wythowtyn] wytheowtyn   360 wrytynge] werytynge   366 to] so
370 conuertyd] couertyd

whiche digressioun he disputyd sore ageyns the manichees heresies, was 375
conuertid.

The tyme that Goti took Rome, and the ydolatres gretly scornyd and
trubylyd the feythful peple, Austin mad the book *de Ciuitate Dei*, in wyche
he sheuyth how that good men own in thys word to be brosyd dou[n] and
shrewis to florisshin, where he spekyth of two cites and here kyngis. 'Of 380
wiche cites', quot[h] he, 'the belderis byn twoo louys. The loue of a mannys self growynge vp to the contempt of God makyth the cyte of the deuyl,
the whiche ys Babilonye. And the loue of God growith to the contempte
of mannys self makyth the cyte of God, the whiche ys Ierusalem.'

In the dayis also of Seynt Austyn the yer of oure lord foure hundryd 385
and fourty, the Wandals and the Alanys, with othir medlyd peple, ocupyid al the prouince of Afric, wastyng and dystroyi[ng] al thynge, neythir
sparynge condic[ioun] of nature, ordyr, ner age ne dingnite. And aftyr
this they come to the cyte of Ipon and bysegyd yt with a stronge hand.
Vndyr whiche tribulac[i]oun blyssid Austyn led a ful bittyr and a lamen- 390
table lyf, to whom his terrys wern his breed bothe nyghte and day, whanne
he saw summe slayn, summe dryuyn awey, cherchis viduat of here spousis,
cytes wastyd and dystroyd with here dwelleris. Whiche mischeuys dayly
grouynge, he clepid togydir his brethiryn and seyde to hem on this wyse:
'I haue preyid my lord God oon of three bonys: that or he deleuere vs from 395
these perilis, or he send vs pacience, or ellys that he weel take me f[ro] this
lyf, that I be not conpellyd to seen so manye mischeuys.

And his thridde peticioun God grauntyd hem, for the thridde monyth
of the sege he syknyd with an accesse and doun therwith in his bed. And,
vndyrstondynge in spirit that the tyme of his bodiys lyf dissoluynge cam 400
faste ner, he dede do writyn the seuene penytencial psalmys and settyn hem
on the wal anempst his beed, and euere lokyd thervpon and red hem plenteuously wepynge. And that he myghte more frely entendyn to God and
hys entent to be lettyd of no man, ten dayis byforn his deth he comau[n]dyd
that no man shulde comyn in but whanne the leche cam, or whanne his 405
refeccioun was brouth to hym. The tyme of syknesse cam to hym anothir
seek man, and instantly preyid hym to puttyn his hand vpon hym, and
he shulde byn hool. 'What ys yt that thou seyist, | sone?', quoth Austyn f. 173rb
ageyn. 'Trowyst thou nat that, yf I myghte ony swych thyng don, I shulde
not don yt to mynself?' But, notwithstondynge this answere of Austyn, 410
the seek man secyd not to preyin lyche as he had preyid byforn, affermynge

379 doun] doum   381 quoth] quot   387 dystroying] dystroyid
388 condicioun] condicidicioun   390 tribulacioun] tribulacoun   396 fro]
fir   404 comaundyd] comauundyd

feythfully that yt was bodyn hym in a visioun that he shulde comyn to hym
and reseyuyn helthe. And thanne, seyinge his feyth, he preyid for hym and
he was hool.

415 In two and tweynty boo[k] of the Cyte of God this blyssid man, Seynt
Austyn, tellyth two miraclys doun of hymself as yt haddyn be don of anothir, seyinge on this wyse: 'I knowe', quoth he, 'that whanne a maydyn in
Ipon hyreself had anoy[n]tyd and a preyst [had] droppid his teris for hyre
in preyere, anoon she was delyueryd of a deuyl.' In the same book also he
420 seyith thus: 'I knowe that a b[i]sshop preyith for a yunge man whoom he
saw not, and forthwith he wantyd the deuyls vexacioun.' No dowte ys that
he seyith these of hymself but, because of mekenesse, he wyl not namyn
hymself. In the same book also of the Cite we redyn that, whanne a see[k]
man by counsel of a leche shulde algatys be kut, and many men doutyd of
425 his lyf i[f] he were kut, with manye terrys the seek man preyid God and
Austyn with hym, and anoon he was hool withoutyn ony kuttyng.

And whan he sau the our of his passage ner comynge, he yaf counsel
for a memorial that non man, where he of neuere so excellent a lyf, shulde
presumyn to passyn owt of this word withowte confessioun and reseyuynge
430 of the sacramentys of Cristys body. And whanne the tyme was comyn, heyl
and hool in alle the membres of his body, with hool syhte and hol he[r]ynge,
the yer of hys age seuenty and sexe and of his bysshopriche fyue and fourty,
alle his brethren stondyng byforn hym and preyinge, he passid hens to here
lord. Testament mad he non, for the pouere man of Crist had not whereof
435 to makyn oon. And he flourid aboute the yers of oure lord four hundyrd.

This blyssid Austyn, sothly the brygh lyghte of wysdam, the buluerk of
treuthe, the meyghty defence of the feyth, the infatigabyl hamyr of heretykis, sourmountyd alle the doctours of the cherche, bothe in with and in
kunnynge, flourynge as weel in exampls of vertuhus and good lyuynge, as
440 in affluence of doctrine and holsoum techenge. And this ys the sentence
of Remigie in a sermoun where, remembrynge Ierom and certeyn othere
doctouris, he concludyd on this wyse: 'Alle these', quoth he, 'Austyn in his
wit and in his kunnynge ouyrcam. For albeyt', quoth he, 'that knowlechyd
hym to han red sexe thousond volumys of Origene, not forthan Austyn
445 wrot so manye thyngis that, thogh a man were ocupyid nyght and day, he
shulde not moun bryngyn aboutyn to writyn hem, and that more ys not for
to redyn hem.' *Hec Remigius.* Volusianus, also Austyn wroot diuers epist-
f. 173va lis, thus bryfly seyth of hym: | 'Sykyrly yt lakkyth to the laue of God,
whatsoeuere yt happith Austyn to foryetyn.' *Hec ille.*

413 he preyid] preyid   415 book] bood   418 anoyntyd] anoytyd   had] had
had   420 bisshop] bosshop   423 seek] seel   425 if] I   431 herynge]
heynge

Seynt Ierom eek in an epistil whiche he wrot to Seynt Austyn hath these 450
wurdys: 'To thi two most witty bookis and shynynge with alle the bryhtnesse of eloquence wiche thou sentyst to me, I myghte not answeren. For
sykyrly, whatsoeuere may be seyid and takyn by wyt, and drauyn owt of
the wellys of holy Scripture, yt ys put of the and disc[re]tly tretid. But yet
I beseche thy reuerence suffere me sumwat to preysyn thy wyt.' And this 455
seyid Ierom, in a book wyche he made of twelue doctours, thus, amonge
othere thyngis, seyth of blyssid Austyn: 'Austyn the bysshop', quoth he,
'flyith as an egle abouyn the hy toppis of hillis and, not consideringe thoo
thyngis whiche ben in rotys of the hillys, pro[no]uncyth and sheuyth with
a brygh and cler fa[u]kun and speche many spacis of heuenys, manye sytys 460
and disposiciouns of londis and the grete c[erkl]ys of watris.' Hic Ieromus.
Seynt Gregorij, also in an epistill, the whiche he wrot to oon clepid
Innocent the prefect of Affric, seyith thus of Austyns bookys: 'That ye
wolde han sent on to you oure exposicioun of holy Iob, wee ioyin and be
glad of yowre studie. Nertheles, yf ye desire to byn fed with delicat fode, 465
redith the werkys of Sent Austyn, youre cuntre man, and in conparisoun
of his depilrid flour ye shul no thinge desiryn of oure bryn.' Hic Gregorius.
Seynt Bernard also clepith seynt Austyn the most myghty hamyr of
heretikys, the whiche seyid Barnard, onys beynge at matyns, slumbrid and
fel aslepe whil the lessons were red of a certeyn tretys of Seyn[t] Austyn. 470
In whiche slep hym thoute he sau a fayr yunge chyld stondynge bysydyn
hym, owt of whos mouth cam so gret a flood of watyr that al the cherche
sempte ful therof, whom Barnard doutyd not to byn Austyn, the whiche
with the welle of his doctrine dewyd and wattryd alle holy cherche.
[A monke] also, in a monasterie clepid Elemosina, onys in the vigile 475
of Seynt Austyn rauasshd in spirit, sau a fayre brygh skye comynge doun
from heuene a[nd] Seynt Austyn sittynge theron in his pontifical habyte.
Whoos eyne as brygh as the sunne bemys illumynyd al the cherche and owt
of hy[m] cam an odour of maruelous redolence. In whiche ys vndyrstonden
bothyn of lyuynge and of doctrine his souereyn excellence. 480
A child, also whilom greuously vexyd with the ston, shul haue be kut
therfore, whos modyr of peryl of deth preyid to Seynt Austyn for hyre
chyld, to whom she had deuocyoun. And as sone as she had endyd hyre
preyere, the ston wente owte with his vryn and so the child was hol.
A myllere onys, which had a singuler deuocioun and affeccioun to Seynt 485
Austyn, with a syknesse clepid the salt flaum was greuyd in his oo lege

454 discretly] discertly   459 pronouncyth] prouncyth   460 faukun] fauknun
461 cerklys] clerkys   468 seynt Austyn] seynt   470 Seynt] Seyn   475 A
monke] Amonge   477 and] a   479 hym] hys

peynfully. And whanne he had oftyn preyid deuouthly to Seynt Austin for
f. 173vb remedye, vpon a nyght whanne he was in his | reste, apperid onto hym as
hym thouthte and touchid his leg with hy[s] hand and maad yt hool. And
490 whanne he wook and fond yt hool he thankyd God and Seynt Austyn.
A certeyn munk, also a singuler louere of Seynt Austyns body [profird]
hym a gret sume of monye for to han oo [f]yngir of his. Which monye
the kepere receyuyd and took hym therfore a fyngyr of anothir deed body,
affyrmynge to hym that yt was Seynt Austins fyngyr, the whiche he resey-
495 uyd deuouthly and reuerently, wurshipt yt and ful oftyn put yt to hys eyne
and streynyd yt to hys brest. Whoos feyth oure lord seyinge, that fyngir
throwyn, meruelously and mercyfully yaf hym oon of Seynt Austyns fyn-
geris. And whanne this munk goon hom into his own cuntre, and many
gret miraclis were wrouthte there by Seynt Austyns fyngyr, the [f]ame
500 ther was brough to Pauye. And whanne the kepere of the body seyde that yt
was anothir deed bodys fyngyr, at the abotys comaundement the graue was
oondon and oon of the fyngris foundyn aweye. And whanne the abot saw
this, he remeuyd [the] kepere from his offyce and chastysid hym sharply
for hys defaute.
505   In Burgundye in a monastarie clepid Fontinellum ther was a munke
clepid Hug[o], the which was righte deuouthte to Seynt Austyn and in his
werkys redynge was feed with a meruelous desir. Thys seyid munk Hugo
preyid oftyn affecteuously and feruently Seynt Austyn that, through his
helpe, he shulde not passyn owt of this word but on his feste. And so, aff-
510 tyr reuolucioun of certeyn yers, the fyftene day byforn Seynt Austy[n]s
feste, a myghty brenynge feuyr took hym, the whiche so consumyd hym
that in the vigilie of Seynt Austyn he was leyid on the bare grounde as
for deed. In whiche menetyme many fayr and comely men, alle clad in
white, come processiounly into the m[o]nasterye, who[o] a wourshipfull
515 fadyr alle arayid in bisshops wede foluyd aftyr. A certeyn munk, beynge
in the cherche and seyinge swyche a solemne processioun comyn in forby
hym, was gretly astoynyd therof and askyd oon of hem what they wern and
whidyr they wern agate. 'Sykyr, brothir', quoth he, 'this ys Seynt Austyn, the grete doctour, the whiche comyth with his bretheryn to visityn
520 his deuouhte seruaunt and to ledyn with hym his soule into the blysse of
heuene.' Whiche seyid, this wurshipfull processioun went streyt into the
infirmarie, where whanne they had byn a lytil while, the soule of the seek
munk departyd from the body and wente vp with this processyoun onto

489 hys] hyd   491 profird] and profird   492 fyngir] syngir   498 this
munk] this   499 fame] same   503 the] to the   506 Hugo] Huge
510 Austyns] Austys   514 monasterye] manasterye   whoo] whoos

the blysse of heuene. We redyn also that, oo tyme whyl Seynt Austyn leuyd
and was bysy in hys stodye, he saw a deuyl come forby hym berynge a gret   525
book [o]n hys nekke. Whoom he chargyd anon by the vertu of God that he
shulde tellyn hym what was wretyn in that gret book. 'In this book', quoth
he, 'be writtyn alle the sennys of men | whiche I kan fynde ouyral where   f. 174ʳᵃ
I goo.' And anon he comau[n]dyd hym that, yf he had ony of his synnys
wretyn in that book, [he sholde rede hem. Whanne the bok was] opnyd   530
ther was nothyng foundyn therin of Austyn but that oo tyme, for bisinesse
in his stodye, he had foryetyn his complyn. Whanne Austyn saw this, he
chargyd hym to abydyn hym there tyl he come ageyn. And anon he wente
into the cherche and seyde that he had o[m]yttyd and lefth. Whiche don he
returnyd and had the deuyl sweuyn hym his book to and fro, and fond the   535
place voyde where Austyn was wretyn. He was wrooth and seyde: 'Thou
hast foule deceyuyd me! Me forthinkyth that I sheuyd the my book. For,
throgh vertu of thy pryeris, thou hast put owt al that I had wretyn.' Wich
seyid he vanysshid.

   Ther was a woman in Ypon, whil Seynt Austyn lyuydde, whiche of cer-   540
teyn malicious men was gretly iniur[y]d. For whiche cause she wente to
hym on a day for to han his counsel and his helpe. And whanne she cam
hom and fond hym stondynge, she salutyd hym reuerently, but he neythir lokyd on here, ner yaf here answere. This woman, supposynge that
for his gret holynesse he wolde not lokyn in a womannys face, she wente   545
more ny to hym on the to syde and told hym hyre mater, but he neythyr
answerde hyre ner took heed of hyre. Wherfore, with gret heuynesse she
turnyd hoom ageyn. Oon the nexte day aftyr, whanne blyssyd Austyn seyde
messe and the same woman was present therat, aftyr the eleuacioun she was
rauasshid in spirit and thouhte that she was brouhte byforn the trone of   550
the blyssid trinite. Where she saw, as hyre thouhte, Austyn stondyn[g] with
his face sumwhat inclinyd dounward and most attentyfly and most subtyly
disputynge of the blyssyd of the Trinite. To whom anon cam a voys, seyinge on this wyse: 'Yistyrday whan thou come to Austyn he was ocupiyd as
thou seest hym ocupiyd now, and therfore he perceyuyd the not there. But   555
now goo ageyn to hym, and thou shalt fyndyn hym beningne and boxsum,
and thou also shalt fyndyn in hym helsum counsel.' And whanne she had
doon as was bodyn hyre, she fond as was promisid hyre.

   An holy man whilom was rauasshid in his contemplecyoun to heuene, as
hym thouhte, where as he saw seyntys in blysse but he cowde not seen there   560

526 on] in   529 comaundyd] comauundyd   530 he sholde rede hem. Whanne
the bok was opnyd] opnyd   534 omyttyd] onyttyd   541 iniuryd] iniurnyd
551 stondyng] stondyn

where that Seynt Austyn was, he askede oon of the seyntis where Austyn was and he answerde hym ageyn and seyde: 'He sittyth al fer abouyn and disputyth of the ioye of the blyssed trinite.'

A prouost of cherche whiche had a singuler affeccioun and deucioun
565 to Seynt Austyn th[re] yer togydir had swych a greuous syknesse that he myghte not risyn owt of his bed. And in the thridde yeer, whanne the solempnyte of Seynt Austins cam and the bellys rungyn to euesong, solempnely anon he bygan to preye to Seynt Austyn with as good deuocy-
f. 174rb oun as he cowde. To whom Seynt Austyn | apperid, al clad in whihte,
570 and clepyd hym by [hys] propyr name and seyde: 'Ryhs vp anon and goo to cherche, and do the seruyse of myn euesong.' And he ros vp hool and sounde and, alle men wundrynge, [he] wente to cherche and deuouthtly performyd that hym was comau[n]dyd.

These miraclis and many mo hath God wrouht for Seynt Austyn whiche
575 were to longe to tellyn, wherefore I passe ouyr for this tyme. But here yt ys to be notyd that thre thyngis ther ben the wheche of wordly men byn meche desiryd, as richesse, welthe and wurshipe. But this blyssyd man Seynt Austyn dyspisid richesse, abhorryd lust and forsook wourshepe, as yt apperith pleynly in the book of his Soliloguyis, where Resoun examynyd
580 hym of alle thre. As touchynge the fyrste, Resoun: 'Desirist thou owt many rychesses?', 'Shulde I now bygynnyn, as whoo seyith? [N]ay!' And anon declarith his wurd: 'For now I am thritty yeer of age, and fourtene yer be past syth I secyd to coueytyn swyche thyngis. For whan I had mete and drynke and cloth I seyht no more in rychesse. For a book whiche
585 [I] bouhte that tyme I redde of Cicero vttyrly set me in the opinyoun that richesse shulde in no wyse be dysiryd.' As for wurshepe, Resoun askyth hym yf he dissire onye, and he answerde in fewe wurdys and sey- ith: 'I knoweleche that sumtyme hyre byforn I haue desirid hem, but now and in these dayis I haue ner forsakyn hem as for volupteuousnesse and
590 lust of the [f]lesshe.' Resoun examynyth in sundry poyntys and fyrst, as towchyng leccherye, he seyth thus: 'What seyist thou of a wyf? Woldyst thou not han oon, yf she were fayre, chast, wel mannerd, and specially yf thou where sykyr that thou shuldyst noon heuynesse ner angyr suffryn of hyre?' And he, answerynge ageyn, seyde: 'Howsoeuere thou wylt poyn-
595 tyn hyre and enhaunsyn hyre with alle maner of goodys, bothe of nature, fortune and grace, I wyl noon.' 'For nothyng I more am determynyd to fleen thanne flesshly communicac[i]oun with women.' 'I aske not', quod

561–2 he askede oon of the seyntis where Austyn was and he] he[2]   565 thre] ther
570 hys] hy hys   572 he] he he   573 comaundyd] comauundyd   581 Nay]
May   585 I] a   590 flesshe] ffleshe   597 communicacioun] communicacoun

Resoun, 'what thou hast determynyd, but I aske the yf thou be not allec-
tyd sumtyme therto, whanne thou seest bewte and youthe with alle othere
thyngis byforn rehersid?' 'Treuly', quoth he, 'I seke, ner desire, rygh not 600
in non of swych thyngis, but rathere whan I thynke theron I haue a detesta-
cyoun and abhominacioun therof.' 'And what', quoth Resoun, 'seyist thou
of mete.' 'Sykyr', quoth he, 'whedyr yt be of mete, or of drynk, or of bathis,
or of ony othyr lust of the body, aske me no more. For pleynly in alle these
I desire no more than that ys vaylaunt and profitable to the helthe of body.' 605
Hic in Soliloquia Augustini.

To makyn an ende thanne of this blyssid and hooly mannys lyff,
Seynt Austyn, I concludyd with Possidonie, the whiche was a dyssiple
of his, longe conuersaunt withe him in hys laste dayis, and aftyr his deth
co[m]pilid his lyf as he saw and knewe. This seyid Possidonie, in ende 610
of hys legende, afftyr that he hath told how | blyssyd Austyn maad noo f. 174va
testament for bodyly pouerte, he concludyth hym to han lefth aftyr hym
myche goostly rychesshe. 'For he leffte', quoth he, 'sufficient of clerge:
monasterijs full stuffyd bothe of men and of women, instructe with
maneris, and arayid whithe bokys, the whiche he had endityd hymself, 615
wherin he lyuyth to vs, thogh that in flesshe he be deed fro vs. I seye
that he leuyth to God and eek to vs. To God he lyuyth, perfytly ioynyd
to hym by perpetuel and inseperable fruycyoun. To vs [he lyuyth] by his
wrytyngis, dayly spekynge to vs after the maner of spekynge of a poete,
the whiche de[de] syttyn these vers vpon hy[s] graue. *Viuere post obitum* 620
vatem vis nosce viator. Quod legis ecce loquor vox tua nempe mea est. 'Swych
a man thanne', quod Possidonie, 'and so wurthi a fadyr, and soo profund a
douctour, mote alle cristene peple wurshipyn, bothe religious and clerkys.
For bothe his doctrine ys instruccyoun of alle feythfull men, and his lyf
forme and reule of alle religious men, and the singuler myrour of oure 625
religioun. Be yt therfore dowtyd to noo man that he ys reseyuyd into the
felaschepe of aungels, where he byholdyth the begynnyng of the vertu of
God in the brythnesse of seyntys, neuere withowte remembraunce and
mynde of his brethyrn, but fully, as I hope and presume, he shall byn a
medyatour to reformyn hem to God.' *Hic Possidonius & cetera.* 630

610 compilid] conpilid   618 he lyuyth] he lyuyth he lyuyth   620 dede] de
hys] hyre